Maryland

MARYLAND

A New Guide to the Old Line State

SECOND EDITION

Earl Arnett
Robert J. Brugger
Edward C. Papenfuse

THE JOHNS HOPKINS UNIVERSITY PRESS
Baltimore & London

Maryland State Archives Studies in Maryland History and Culture, sponsored by the Maryland Hall of Records Commission, the Honorable Parris N. Glendening, Governor, and the Honorable Robert Mack Bell, Chair

First edition 1976
Second edition 1999
Printed in the United States of America on acid-free paper
9 8 7 6 5 4 3 2 1

The Johns Hopkins University Press
2715 North Charles Street
Baltimore, Maryland 21218-4363
www.press.jhu.edu

Library of Congress Cataloging-in-Publication Data will be found at the end of this book.
A catalog record for this book is available from the British Library.

ISBN 0-8018-5979-4
ISBN 0-8018-5980-8 (pbk.)

Contents

TOUR 14 The Lovely Potomac Valley: Montgomery County into Frederick County...441

MacArthur Blvd., Md. 189, Md. 190, Whites Ferry Rd., Md. 28, Park Mills Rd., Mt. Ephraim Rd.

TOUR 15 The Spokes That Made Baltimore a Hub...448

Md. 26, 140, 25, 45, 146, 147, U.S. 1, Md. 150, and U.S. 40 East

TOUR 16 Westminster and Its Byways...491

Part IV WESTERN MARYLAND

The first person to write a travel guide to Maryland was Father Andrew White, a Jesuit priest who came with the first English colonists Lord
Baltimore sent to Maryland in 1633. The expedition arrived in March
1634, landing first on St. Clements Island in the Potomac to avoid the in-
timidating native population assembled on the mainland. In search of a
more favorable place for settlement, the governor purchased an abandoned native village on a tributary of the Potomac. They "gave the name
of St. Mary to the designated city, and in order to prevent any pretext for
injury or occasion for enmity, we bought thirty miles of that land from
the chieftain in exchange for hatchets, axes, hoes and some amount of
cloth." Father White hurriedly completed his first draft in Latin and English by the end of his first month in Maryland, promising more by the
next ship home to England. He kept his promise, revising his account
through three published editions, the last appearing in 1635.

Father White's account generated considerable interest in Maryland
and no doubt inspired many English settlers to come to Maryland. But
the proper guidebook would not develop until the arrival of touring—that
is, traveling for the pleasure of it—and for fully half of Maryland's history,
travel had little to do with recreation or leisure. Indeed, it could be pun-
ishing. A man traveling by stage from Philadelphia to Baltimore in 1795
(ladies traveled rarely, and never alone) might spend his first night on the
road at Elkton in Cecil County after a harrowing 47 miles. The next day he
would rise at 3 a.m. for the 15-mile trip to the Susquehanna, have a quick
breakfast at an inn, ride a crude ferry across the river, and continue for
another 37 miles to Baltimore, arriving about 5 p.m., dirty, tired, and
hardly up to sightseeing. Isaac Weld, who went this way in 1795, wrote
that the road was so bad on the jaunt before breakfast that "the driver frequently had to call the passengers in the stage to lean out of the carriage
first at one side then at the other, to prevent it from oversetting in the
deep ruts with which the road abound[ed]." Travel by water might be
more comfortable, weather permitting, but in most cases took longer
than did horse or stagecoach. From Elkton to Baltimore the ordeal by
stage lasted more than 14 hours; by boat one could make the same journey in 16 hours if winds cooperated.

Private travel by horseback offered no respite. The roads, where they
existed, were not clearly marked, and accommodations often left much
to be desired. The average distance the traveler could cover in a day fell
short of 30 miles. In 1765 William Gregory rode 30 miles from New Castle, Delaware, to Maryland on his way to the Rock Hall Ferry and points
south. By the time he reached his first night's lodging—having once lost
his way for lack of signposts—his horse was exhausted, his "posteriors"

were "ruined," and the side of his head had "swelled up like a pumpkin" thanks to a cold he had caught. The inn was crowded, making matters worse, and a noisy party kept him awake most of the night.

While limited in coverage, the earliest guides to American roads—Christopher Colles's *A Survey of the Roads of the United States of America* (1789) and Moore and Jones's *Traveller's Directory; or, A Pocket Companion* (1802)—gave evidence of the importance of travel, at least of movement, in the American experience. Both volumes contained "trip tickets" that showed the courses of the main road, "with descriptions of the places through which it passes, and intersections of the cross roads." Moore and Jones included "an account of such remarkable objects as are generally interesting to travellers." Most of them, unsurprisingly, were to be found in major cities, between which stops mainly had the purpose of locating food and lodging; the books said little about the surrounding countryside. Moore and Jones described Elkton as being "forty-seven miles and a quarter from Philadelphia, a post and considerable trading town, at the head of navigation on the forks of the two branches of Elk River, about three miles above French Town, where the packets from Baltimore land and embark passengers etc. to and from Philadelphia. Elkton consists of one principal street; it has a courthouse, a jail and an academy."

In the second half of the 19th century, coinciding with expansion of the country's rail system, numerous travelers' guides began to appear. Taintor's *Route and City Guides*—one each for routes from New York to Philadelphia, Baltimore, and Washington—provided brief city tours and said a bit about what the visitor could see at train stations along the way. The entry for Elkton in the 1876 edition of the guide read: "Elkton—Cecil County, Md. 46 m. fr. Phila. fr. Baltimore, 52. This is the county seat of Cecil County and is located a little above the junction of Great and little Elk Creeks. It was settled in 1694 by Swedish fishermen, and was called Head of Elk till 1787, when it received its present name. The prominent buildings, besides the venerable courthouse, are the Elkton Academy, and the Methodist, Episcopal, Presbyterian, and Catholic churches."

The Philadelphia Centennial Exhibition of 1876 helped to usher in the era of true sightseeing. People began to think of traveling great distances purely for amusement. That year J. B. Lippincott published a *Visitors' Guide* to the exhibition, the only one "sold on the exhibition grounds." Over the six-month duration of the exhibition, one in five Americans had the opportunity to purchase this guide in person. By 1893, the year of the Columbian exhibition in Chicago, the leading publisher of European travel guides, the Leipzig firm of Karl Baedeker, decided it was time to produce a comprehensive handbook for travelers in the United States. By then Baedeker guides had become famous in Europe not only for telling the traveler how to get from place to place but also for interpreting, often in great detail, what travelers would see along the way and at their destinations. Prefaces to Baedeker handbooks followed the same formula, regardless of destination: "The chief objects of the Handbook . . . are to supply the traveller with a few remarks on the progress of civilization and art in these interesting countries; to render him as far as possible independent of the embarrassing and expensive services of commissionaires, guides and other of the same Fraternity; to place him in a position to employ his time, his money, and his energy to the best advantage; and thus to enable him to derive the greatest possible amount of pleasure and instruction from his tour." Tellingly, the Baedeker guide to the United States catered more to the British visitor than the traveling American. "The average Englishman," read an observation under the rubric "General Hints," "will probably find the chief physical discomforts in the dirt of the city streets, the roughness of the country roads, the winter overheating of hotels and railway cars (70–75 degrees Fahrenheit by no means unusual) and in many places the habit of spitting on the floor." This guide went through a last revision in 1909.

Afterward, the United States underwent yet another revolution in transportation, this one, of course, featuring the automobile, especially when Henry Ford introduced relatively cheap models like the Model T. Ford enabled average American families to tour the countryside at their leisure, unhindered by train or bus schedules. In 1901 the first automobile Blue Book appeared, and by 1920 it had grown to 13 volumes covering the entire United States and southern Canada. These books were advertised in 1920 as telling one "where to go, and how to get there, giving complete maps of every motor road, running directions at every fork and turn, with mileages, all points of local or historical interest, state motor laws, hotel and garage accommodations, ferry and steamship schedules and rates. A veritable motorist's encyclopedia." In fact, these volumes made little mention of what was to be seen along the way. Historical information was sparse, sandwiched in as footnotes between maps and advertisements. Most of the text was given over to dry-as-dust driving instructions, as in this 56-mile tour from Baltimore to Elkton in a 1922 Maryland version of the Blue Book, written by the Automobile Club of Maryland:

> Baltimore to Philadelphia, Pa. 104.7 M
> Route 20
> Baltimore to Elkton 56.1 M

0.0 From Automobile Club of Maryland Building, Baltimore, east on Mt. Royal ave.
0.1 Left at trolley on Charles st., over R.R. viaduct and across North ave., leaving trolley 0.5.
1.4 Right on E. 33rd st.; into Boulevard.
3.1 Left on Harford road, next right on Erdman ave.
3.9 Half-left with trolley on Belair road; keep left 11.4.
15.9 Left fork at Kingsville.
23.2 Left at Inn, Bel Air, next right 23.3.
28.9 Right fork, Churchville; left at end 30.4.
35.0 Left at stone church beyond R.R.'s, Aberdeen.
39.5 Left on Union ave., Havre de Grace.
39.9 Curve right across long toll bridge, Susquehanna River, thru Perryville 41; Charlestown 47; Northeast 50, into Elkton 56.1.

And so on, for another 48.6 miles.

In 1935 the federal Works Progress Administration (WPA), as part of its efforts to aid unemployed writers, launched the American Guide Series, an ambitious campaign to research and write comprehensive travel guides for each of the 48 states. The principal architect and editor of the series, Katherine Kellock, claimed that she took her inspiration from the

Baedeker guide to Russia, which had kept her from getting hopelessly lost and taught her much on a journey to Tashkent during World War I. The WPA set out to create a Baedeker for the motorist, what one employee called "a sort of public Baedeker, which would point out to the curious traveler the points of real travel value in each state and county." Kellock and the Washington staff supplied comprehensive instructions to each state project on how to go about writing its guide. By December 1935, a staff of 25 people were at work on a guide for Maryland.

It took four years to compile, research, and write. The interpretive essays that filled the first third of the book took enormous staff time to complete. Serious field work on the tours did not begin until January 1938, by which time the Maryland staff had been cut from a record high of 75 people in September 1936 to 62. By the end of 1938 the number had fallen to 47. On February 13 of the following year the Baltimore *Evening Sun* reported that the total cost of the project had reached $165,000 (average pay per worker fluctuated between $78 and $88 per month) and that maintaining the payroll necessary to finish the guide would cost $3,200 a month. The tours remained in a rudimentary state; in the words of two recently hired editors in Baltimore, H. Bowen Smith and Frank J. Reall, the project had placed on their shoulders "the onus of the sorry results of three years of trying to 'muddle through.'" They described the guide as it then stood as "a blend of bad writing and inaccuracies." The Maryland project "suffered under heavy disadvantages," Kellock later recalled; and in 1939, when the national project ended, she herself—with the close cooperation of Smith and Reall—had to "take over preparation for the whole book." With staff equivalent to 40 full-time employees and at an approximate cost of $77,000, the Maryland Writers' Project finally produced *Maryland: A Guide to the Old Line State*, a 543-page tome (348 pages of tours) that the Oxford University Press published in the summer of 1940.

Despite shortcomings that included some inaccuracies, the volume received warm praise and eventually sold some 15,000 copies. Whether or not it was worth the cost is a matter for historians to debate; the project did employ "writers" who might otherwise have gone hungry, and it did, after much pain and travail, produce a volume that reflected well on the whole series.

By 1953, however, the guide was badly outdated. It went out of print in the late 1950s, and the Maryland Hall of Records assumed the task of compiling a new edition. Because of staff shortages, the new book would consist exclusively of tours. A controversy over the terms of the original publishing contract held up work on the revisions until 1957, when, with some fanfare, James H. Bready announced in his Baltimore *Sun* column "Books and Authors" that Lois Green Clark, under the direction of Dr. Morris L. Radoff, state archivist, and with the special assistance of Wilbur Hunter, director of the Peale Museum, had begun work on the new guide. Bready noted that the 40 tours of the original edition directed visitors over "roads that in many stretches have been or soon will be superseded by no-town, no-pause superhighways" and toward old Maryland houses which, in many cases, had been bought by "manorial millionaires" who would be just as happy to have any mention of their homes "deliberately omitted."

Bready estimated that it would take at least two years to complete the revised Maryland guide. As usual, any estimate turned out to be optimistic. Working part time, Ms. Clark—later Lois Green Carr, distinguished student of early Maryland history—found revising, correcting, and editing such a mammoth manuscript to be an enormous task for one person. When in 1964 she departed the Hall of Records, work on it languished until revived in 1973 by the newly hired assistant state archivist, Edward C. Papenfuse. Finally, in October 1975, the staff of the archives delivered an 800-page, 175,000-word typescript containing less than 20 percent of the text of the original guide to the Johns Hopkins University Press. The next month James Bready could at last confidently headline his "Books and Authors" column in the *Sun:* "A New Guide Soon to Arrive." The revised edition, *Maryland: A New Guide to the Old Line State,* appeared in 1976, the combined work of Dr. Carr; the assistant state archivist, Gregory A. Stiverson; Sue Collins, who had gone on the road for two months, covering every mile of every tour (logging more than 6,500 miles) and making corrections wherever necessary; and Dr. Papenfuse, then the new state archivist.

The *New Guide,* with its "glove compartment" trim size and red, white, and black paperback cover, proved highly popular, selling fully as well as the original edition. Although the historical information for which the guidebook was best known remained an invaluable resource as the years passed, travel information once again became increasingly unreliable and the pace of change accelerated. New roads, massive suburban growth, and dramatic changes in Baltimore, Annapolis, and the outskirts of Washington left a guidebook whose final revisions dated from the mid-1970s vulnerable in the details. New historic and recreational sites opened; research in various fields—history, archaeology, marine science—uncovered fresh material. The very definition of "points of interest" shifted with increasing scholarly and public attention to the stories of women and minorities in the Maryland experience. Even so, staff shortages at the state archives made full-scale work on a new edition impossible. The book went into its fourth and last reprinting in 1984. Seven years later, believing it unacceptable to reprint such a dated title, the Johns Hopkins University Press proposed and the archives agreed to a plan whereby the press would provide Earl Arnett, formerly a feature writer for the *Sun* and *Maryland Magazine,* the wherewithal to rewrite the entire *New Guide* while the archives lent him support in kind and gave the draft as thorough a vetting as its resources permitted.

Eventually it became clear that not only the text but the very structure of the volume called for further thought. Thus, we have produced this entirely reframed guidebook. Its structure reflects Maryland's large regions—Southern, Eastern Shore, Central, and Western—and the text proceeds roughly along the historical pattern of settlement while moving the visitor or armchair traveler generally from east to west. A new essay outlines the natural history of the Chesapeake Bay. Discussions of Annapolis, Cambridge, Salisbury, Baltimore, Frederick, Hagerstown, and Cumberland, rather than being relegated to the back of the book, now appear as tours or parts of tours in their regions of the state. In places, interpretive interludes called "close-ups" explore important figures, sites, or issues of interest in greater depth. We have considerably reduced the number of tours.

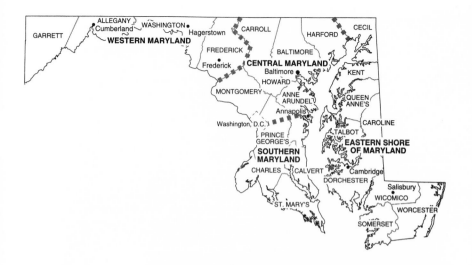

HOW TO USE THIS BOOK

We have combined the tours for the sake of thematic coherence and the traveler's convenience, assuming that many users of the guide will begin their touring in the Washington-Baltimore metropolitan area. Most but not all tours form loops or triangles that return one to (or near) the point of departure. All of them presuppose a willingness to spend a full day on the road, stopping now and then to look at something or to have some refreshment (note, however, that we have avoided mentioning commercial establishments as such), selecting a few if not all of the optional side trips. (Each of the Western Maryland tours will take more than a day to travel.)

Although the endless work of the state highway department renders each guidebook dated not long after its publication, the most interesting way to visit Maryland is to travel the old roads. The latest *New Guide* takes note of superhighways but recommends the slower, more scenic routes. We like to think of this book as useful to a reader before, after, or instead of a drive.

Tour titles and the subjects of close-ups offer a hint of each journey's enticements. We have *centered* the names of places or things that we judge most significant, adding descriptive paragraphs below. Names of other noteworthy places and things appear in **boldface** type within the tours as the traveler would be approaching them. Such places may not call for a stop, but they are worth knowing about. In many cases, the close-ups invite the visitor to get out of the car, walk around a site, and reflect on how the passage of time and large forces have affected the site and the men and women who lived there. They invite thoughts on historical intersections and contingency.

The maps in the latest *New Guide* give the traveler a schematic view of the route a given tour follows, including its highlights, but we presuppose that every car carries a recent official Maryland highway map. We therefore have avoided gratuitous road information (X eventually reaches Y by crossing Z), providing only those directions necessary for touring.

Motorists should remember that it is best if possible to avoid rush hours in metropolitan Washington and Baltimore. We remind walkers who follow the pedestrian tours of Baltimore that, unfortunately, as one may say of most large American cities, not every neighborhood provides the setting for safe, quiet strolling. Readers who carry this book afield should therefore exercise the caution and good judgment appropriate in urban areas and consider driving when walking seems unwise.

Jim Bready's comment that owners of historic houses wish not to be on display probably was accurate when he said it and remains so today. We have erred on the side of inclusion of such homes in this book only out of a belief that Maryland's history belongs to all the people; we nonetheless emphasize that property rights and common civility alike demand that visitors to an area respect the privacy of the sites we have noted are private.

Because the *New Guide* does have its origins in the New Deal and was a work by and for the public and because newspaper and television photojournalism has made current scenes familiar, we have chosen to illustrate the book largely with Works Progress Administration and Farm Security Administration photographs—that is, with images from the period in which the original *Guide* appeared. All of these "retrospectives" are printed in a sepia tone; the legends do not always identify the picture as Depression era. Edwin Remsberg's contemporary views, printed in black ink, vividly illustrate the immensity of the changes the state has undergone since the days before World War II. Some of the Remsberg photos look down the same street or road as one from the late 1930s; in other places, he offers visual commentary on the natural beauty or contemporary attractions of Maryland.

Hoping that this *New Guide* will prove both readable and informative—an introduction to Maryland that will benefit visitor and resident alike and lead to a full appreciation of the state's rich history—we dedicate this work to the late comptroller of Maryland, Louis L. Goldstein. In his nearly 60 years of public service, Louis visited every corner of Maryland and incorporated his unsurpassed knowledge of its past into just about every speech he gave. He understood the blessings that come with being able to place what we see in historical context. He understood why the enthusiasm of Father White proved so contagious; he also asked all of us—even those who are just passing through—to help preserve those historical things that delight us and will inform those who come after.

ACKNOWLEDGMENTS

The authors wish to acknowledge the special and generous assistance of Christopher N. Allan, Emily A. Murphy, Mimi Calver, Kathleen Beard, and Shirley Bodziak of the Maryland State Archives, and Lois Green Carr of the Historic St. Mary's City Commission. Thanks also to staff members at a number of Maryland state agencies who answered queries cheerfully and expeditiously: Ross Kimmel, Patty Manoun, and Donnie Rohrback, Department of Natural Resources; Orlando Ridout V, Mary Louise deSarran, Michael O. Bourne, Ronald L. Andrews, and Barbara Shepherd, Maryland Historical Trust; Claire Richardson, Maryland Geological Survey; Lisa Clem, Maryland Port Administration; Casey Keith,

Maryland Department of Transportation; Dean Kenderdine, Maryland Department of Business and Economic Development; and Estelle S. Seward, Historic St. Mary's City. We also had the benefit of help from John McGrain, Baltimore County Department of Planning and Zoning; Christopher Weeks, Harford County Department of Planning and Zoning; and John E. Terrell Jr., Wicomico County Recreation and Parks Department.

For help in answering questions about Maryland schools, thanks go to (among others) Ken Nichols, Anne Arundel County; Edward F. Centofante, Mervin B. Daughtery, and Brian T. Spiering, Caroline County; Carey Gaddis, Carroll County; Karen Emery, Cecil County; Marita Stup Loose, Frederick County; Lynn H. Bell and Martin R. Green, Garrett County; Phyllis Parker, Howard County; Barbara M. and David A. Kergaard, Kent County; Liz Jenny, Montgomery County; Sherry Unger and John Enkiri, Prince George's County; Cathy Quesenberry, Queen Anne's County; Lana R. Williams, Worcester County; Steve Dugan, Boy's Latin School; Kasha Mutscheller, Bryn Mawr School; Richard K. Jung, Bullis School; Merrill S. Hall, Calvert School; Heidi Blalock, Friends School; Rebecca Waters, Garrison Forest School; Michael Horsey, Georgetown Preparatory School; Patrick Smithwick, Gilman School; Damon F. Bradley, Landon School; Julie Andres Schwait, Park School; and Abby Lattes, Roland Park Country School. On Maryland hospitals, the authors received similar assistance from Russel Kujan, Medical and Chirurgical Faculty of Maryland; Mary Lou Baker, Anne Arundel Medical Center; Kenneth R. Coffey II, Frederick Memorial; Chad Dillard, Good Samaritan; Kellie Peacock, Howard County General; Cindy Merz, Suburban; and Kathy Rogers, Memorial Hospital of Cumberland. Writing brief descriptions of Baltimore points of interest required the help of Teddy Brack, American Visionary Art Museum; Barbara E. Terry, B&O Railroad Museum; Tara Fenlon, Baltimore Museum of Art; Matthew A. White, Baltimore Museum of Industry; Andrea J. Keller, Baltimore Zoo; Elizabeth Sutley, Maryland Historical Society; Linda West, Maryland Science Center; Marla Gregg, National Aquarium in Baltimore; and Ann Wilson, Walters Art Gallery.

Several friends—Joseph L. Arnold, Catonsville; Philip G. Nussear, Hagerstown; and Richard P. Thomsen Jr., Charlottesville, Virginia—supplied critical information on short notice. Earl Arnett wishes to thank his spouse, Ethel Ennis, who often accompanied him on journeys around the state, and his parents, Clyde and Jeanne Arnett, who first encouraged him to read books.

William L. Nelson, who lives and works on the Eastern Shore of Virginia, patiently and skillfully worked on the maps for the book. Special and warm thanks to Anne M. Whitmore, an Annapolis native, friend of Maryland history, and accomplished copyeditor, whose labors exceeded the call of duty, and to Wilma E. Rosenberger of Catonsville and, now, Taneytown, who designed this edition of the *Guide* and made it appear, the authors believe, better than ever.

As do all writers, we must express particular appreciation for the readings others gave discrete parts of the manuscript, commenting on it as it took shape. In this case such helpful persons include George H. Callcott, College Park; Jean B. Russo, Kensington; Ann Jensen, Charlotte Fletcher, and Barbara Moss, Annapolis; Jack Stenger and Davy Henderson McCall, Chestertown; Mrs. John H. Barber, Cambridge; Julia King, Calvert County;

Richard Rivoire, Charles County; Thomas L. Hollowak, Baltimore; John Frye, Hagerstown; and Edward H. Nabb, Cambridge.

We thank them while of course accepting responsibility for our errors. Compiled and rewritten over what turned out to be several years, this book contains much new information. It also, unavoidably, contains errors and dated information. We ask that readers grant the enormity of the task and that they notify us in writing of any mistakes that we can correct in later printings.

In
memory of
Louis L. Goldstein

Maryland

The Maryland Dove, a re-creation of the Dove, one of two ships that carried the original settlers to Maryland, anchored at St. Mary's City

PART I

SOUTHERN MARYLAND

Until about 1960, "Southern Maryland" meant rural, sleepy, to-bacco-growing Maryland—the lower Western Shore between the Potomac and the Chesapeake. The region traditionally included Anne Arundel, Prince George's, Calvert, Charles, and St. Mary's Counties. Since the 1960s, suburban expansion, accompanied by new roads and bridges, has altered the landscape and changed ways of living forever. Anne Arundel County south of Annapolis and Prince George's County south of Andrews Air Force Base retain only traces of the old tobacco culture. Even the three lower counties—Charles, Calvert, and St. Mary's—now demonstrate the effects of tourism, improved transportation, and residential growth. Traditionalists lament the passing of old-fashioned gentility and respect for history; modernists rejoice in the convenience of shopping malls and the loosening of cultural barriers. Weathered tobacco barns in abandoned fields near new housing developments dramatically symbolize these changes.

Events in Southern Maryland gave birth to the colony and the state alike. The first European settlers arrived in St. Mary's City in 1634, there hoping to establish the fourth permanent English "plan-tation" in North America. Only the English villages at Jamestown (1607), Plymouth (1620), and Massachusetts Bay (1630) predated it. Unlike these earlier colonists, the Maryland English arrived under the leadership of a Catholic minority bearing a proprietary charter unique to that time, granted by Charles I to Cecil Calvert, son of his old councillor George Calvert. The Maryland settlers aimed to construct a society reasonably free of the Catholic-Protestant conflict in their native country.

Fevers, poxes, and other contagions took an awful toll in early Maryland. Seven of every ten white adult-male immigrants died be-fore the age of 50; about half their offspring died before the age of 20. Entire Indian villages succumbed to smallpox. Native-born whites developed immunities to common diseases, however, and white settlements gradually expanded up the Patuxent, the Po-tomac, and the Chesapeake Bay. The Calverts issued land grants and collected various fees from the landholders. Virgin forests disap-peared as trees were girdled, then felled (the stumps usually left in the ground to rot) to open corn and tobacco fields.

The first farms tended to be small, owned by planters who grew tobacco, working alongside a few European indentured servants and perhaps one or two African slaves. But within several generations, ownership patterns changed. Small farms continued to dominate the landscape, but tenancy increased, and more land was concentrated in fewer hands. A large population of African slaves contributed to new wealth that supported a gradually rising standard of living for most of the nonslave society.

Africans had arrived in Maryland within five years after the colony's founding. By 1750, nearly 60 percent of the 280,000 African slaves in North America were concentrated in Maryland and Virginia, the two colonies that made up the "Tobacco Coast." The Africans came from many tribes assembled at coastal locations that ranged from the Senegal and Gambia Rivers in the north to the Niger River more than 2,000 miles to the southeast. Slave ships arrived with 10–25 percent or more of the original captives dead from bloody flux, malnutrition, and despair. Ship's captains considered a 10–15 percent attrition rate a cost of business.

George Washington, who arguably knew Maryland better than any other 18th-century non-native, first knew the province by way of its southern counties. As a surveyor and explorer, he visited the mountain reaches of Western Maryland, and as a soldier, man of affairs, and president he traveled at one time or another throughout the state. But he was primarily a prominent figure in the plantation society along the lower Potomac, including the Maryland shore, Charles County in particular. He had friends in Port Tobacco and Upper Marlboro; the dances, theaters, and horse races of Annapolis often drew him to the Maryland capital.

Annapolis supplied the setting for revolutionary events—caustic newspaper exchanges, resolves calling for resistance against British trade restrictions, attacks on merchants who flouted nonimportation, meetings of committees of correspondence and public safety, and then sessions of a revolutionary convention that instructed delegates to a Continental Congress. After further drama and the winning of independence (Congress ratified the Treaty of Paris in the Maryland State House), Annapolis in 1786 provided the site of a convention to discuss interstate problems and the financial woes of Congress; the delegates resolved to hold another meeting in Philadelphia the following year for the purpose of strengthening the ties that bound the united states.

In the 19th century, over succeeding generations, a mellow lower-Potomac culture developed in Southern Maryland. The political and economic center of the state shifted northward and westward. Maryland became more ethnically diverse. Isolated and peaceful, set in its ways, this portion of Maryland continued tobacco cultivation, fished the Chesapeake, and nurtured a southern way of life not much different from that pursued in coastal Georgia or Gulf Coast Mississippi. Many people claimed ancestry among the first families to arrive in Maryland; a deeply ingrained color line kept blacks and whites separate.

The 20th century has added a modern overlay to this slow-moving haven of tradition. The federal government, particularly the navy, has been active along the Potomac since establishment of the Washington Navy Yard on the Anacostia River in 1800; in 1890 it established an ordnance center at Indian Head and continued to expand

in Southern Maryland through the two world wars. As for less official activities, bootleggers found the creeks of the lower Potomac wonderful sanctuaries during Prohibition: and until the legislature passed reform legislation (as some called it) in the 1960s, gambling, especially by way of slot machines, flourished in the region.

With uneven railroad service and poor roads, Southern Maryland traditionally was waterlocked by the Potomac River, the Patuxent River, and Chesapeake Bay. In the mid-20th century this pattern suddenly changed. One bridge went up across the lower Potomac during the New Deal, another over the Patuxent at Benedict in 1950, and a third, in 1977, spanned the lower Patuxent. With the extension of dual highways throughout the region during the 1980s (added to Gov. Albert C. Ritchie's public works of the 1920s), Southern Maryland has become conveniently accessible to commuters between Baltimore and Annapolis and between much of Calvert and Charles Counties and metropolitan Washington.

Population numbers reveal the dramatic effects. Calvert County grew more than 48 percent between 1980 and 1990, the second fastest growth rate in the state. Two hundred years ago, 88,751 people lived in the five tobacco counties. In 1890 the counties had 101,044 residents, a growth rate of about 14 percent. In 1990 the region had 1,385,007 people, an increase of almost 1,300 percent over the past century, most of it during the past 40 years.

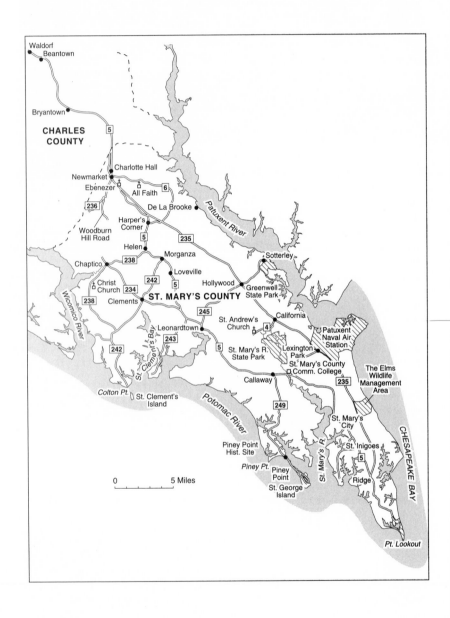

Maryland's Birthplace: St. Mary's County

Md. 5 to St. Mary's City and Return from Point Lookout via Md. 235

Begin this tour at Beantown—reachable from Washington via Md. 5 and from Baltimore and Annapolis via U.S. 301—and follow Md. 5 through three and a half centuries of Maryland history.

Zekiah Swamp Run

About four miles south of Beantown, Md. 5 crosses Zekiah Swamp Run, a marshy stream that runs south for 25 miles before draining into Allens Fresh Run and the Wicomico River. Eons ago, small streams drained the wooded area along the border of Prince George's and Charles Counties now known as the Cedarville State Forest. Beaver ponds slowed the flow through the hardwood forests and created a rich habitat for all kinds of wildlife, which in turn attracted prehistoric hunters. Woodsmen, nature lovers, and some of the descendants of those hunters still come to this swampland, which may derive its name from an American Indian word, *Sacayo,* the name recorded in 1668. European folk usage changed the pronunciation to a colloquial form of the biblical name Hezekiah.

Bordered by farmland, the swamp is seldom more than half a mile wide, but its intricate waterways create a pathless, seemingly timeless band of wilderness through the heart of a county that has increased in population from 47,678 in 1970 to 101,154 in 1990. The Department of the Interior has designated Zekiah Swamp Run a "Wild and Scenic River," and its small related streams are protected under wetlands legislation.

Driving south on Md. 5, one passes through **Bryantown,** a crossroads community in which two brick houses survive from the beginning of the 19th century; next comes Hughesville, and then Md. 5 crosses into **St. Mary's County,** the birthplace of Maryland and the most rural section of Southern Maryland.

Suburban development and military installations have contributed to economic and population growth here since 1940, but the county remains surprisingly true to its 17th-century roots in tobacco and aquaculture. St. Mary's County produces more tobacco than any other Maryland county and frequently leads the state in number of registered watermen. The Roman Catholic Church remains strong here; some residents can trace their family ancestry without a break to the first settlers. Only 14,626 people inhabited the county's 420 square miles in 1940, fewer than in 1790; in 1990 more than 76,000 lived here. Md. 5 travels the length of the county, the southernmost portion of Maryland's Western Shore.

Old White House, the classroom building at Charlotte Hall, during the Depression

Charlotte Hall via Old Md. 5

Just after entering St. Mary's County, turn right onto Old Route 5 toward the historic district of Charlotte Hall, located on the site of a 17th-century sanitarium, where the "Coole Springs of St. Maries" were believed responsible for cures during a 1697–98 pestilence. The Maryland assembly in 1698 appropriated money to buy the springs and build cottages for indigent citizens who became ill.

The community takes its name from the former **Charlotte Hall School,** chartered in 1774 as a free school for Charles, St. Mary's, and Prince George's Counties. As early as 1723 the assembly had called for a free school in each county, but few were actually built. The inhabitants of the southern counties agreed in 1772 to establish a consolidated school named for Charlotte Sophia of Mecklenburg-Strelitz, queen of George III. The word "free" did not apply to tuition or promise admission to the region's substantial African American population; it may have referred to the liberal arts curriculum of classics, languages, and mathematics common to such schools. The trustees met under the charter of 1774, but the school did not open until after the Revolution, in 1797. By 1802 there were 94 students, but enrollment declined. By 1850 it had become a military school. Given the preponderant sympathy in this part of Maryland for the Confederate cause, most of the Charlotte Hall graduates served for the South, but on some battlefields they must have fought against each other. The private school tried to change its orientation in 1975, becoming a coeducational, college prep school. This survival strategy failed, and Charlotte Hall closed the following year; the state acquired the property and converted the facility to the **Charlotte Hall Veterans' Home.** Most of the buildings have been demolished, but the **Old White House,** erected as a classroom building and headmaster's residence in 1803 and restored in 1938, still stands. **St. John's Episcopal Church,** also known as **Dent's Chapel,** is located on the former school grounds. Erected in 1883, this Victorian Gothic structure, now on the National Register of Historic Places, was named in honor of the Rev. Hatch Dent, first principal of the military academy.

The **Ebenezer African Methodist Episcopal Church,** located off Md. 5 just south of the intersection of Routes 5 and 6 at **Newmarket,** signifies the less prosperous but persistent presence of the county's black population. This wooden cabin structure dates to the Civil War era, when Federal troops, aware of Confederate sentiment and military proximity across the Potomac, occupied the county. Long ignored, such sites continue to be identified and preserved in ongoing efforts to document African American history and culture in Southern Maryland.

In this part of St. Mary's County, Md. 5, here coinciding with Md. 235, is lined with commercial development. It bypasses farmlands cultivated by **Amish** families that arrived in the county from Pennsylvania during the 1940s and early 1950s. These traditional farmers, who avoid mechanical and electrical methods as much as possible, have had considerable success in reclaiming worn-out tobacco lands. Their horse-drawn buggies can occasionally be seen on secondary roads south of Md. 5. Rte. 236, known as Thompson Corner Rd., travels south from Charlotte Hall through Amish country, as does Woodburn Hill Rd., which branches south toward the Chaptico Creek valley and dead-ends in the rural countryside. Twice a week at Charlotte Hall, an open-air **farmers' market** features Amish-grown produce and goods.

The traveler may want to continue on Old Route 5, which parallels the main highway to **Harper's Corner.** The old route passes Victorian houses and through the village of **Mechanicsville.** About four miles south of Charlotte Hall at Harper's Corner, Md. 5 branches south as the single-lane Waldorf-Leonardtown Rd.

Side Trip to Chaptico via Md. 238

About three miles farther, Md. 5 veers left toward Morganza. At that junction, a right-hand turn onto Md. 238 (Budds Creek Rd.) and a drive of about four miles takes one to the village of **Chaptico.** It lies on Chaptico Run, which forms a small bay as it empties into the Wicomico River. The name *Chaptico* may be Algonquin for "big-broad-river-it-is" and come from the friendly 17th-century tribe that Gov. Charles Calvert visited in 1663. One of the tribe's leaders even adopted the name Tom Calvert, as a token of respect for the new English regime. The Chopticos and other Maryland tribes did not fare so well when the Catholic Calverts were deposed from 1689 to 1715. John Coode, the leader of rebellious Protestants, made the Chaptico area a muster spot for his soldiers during the bloodless coup of 1689, perhaps a subtle reminder to the tribe that some of the English were not as supportive of peaceful coexistence as the Calverts were. At any rate, the Chopticos had disappeared by the early 18th century, and settlers appropriated their land. Until the Wicomico River silted and turned to marsh later in the 18th century, the town served as a shipping point. It suffered damage from the British as they harassed the lower Potomac in 1813. A few of its prominent, pro-Southern residents were jailed during the Civil War.

Follow Md. 238 south across a wide marshy field to **Christ Church,** set off the road on the east side. Built in 1737, the church has great wooden columns that hold up the arched ceiling of the nave. The existing pews and the woodwork in the chancel date to 1839, the bell tower to 1913. In 1813 British soldiers used the church as a stable and disturbed graves looking for plunder, sacrileges that aroused newspaper condemnation as far away as Boston. The cemetery contains the grave of Gilbert Ireland, high sheriff of St. Mary's County, whose probated will in 1755 requested a "Cheap, black Marble Stone" from Philadelphia. The stone is now gone, but local tradition relates that it contained an explanation for the sheriff's request to be buried upright.

En route to Leonardtown, Md. 5 passes through the crossroads town of **Morganza,** the location of **St. Joseph's Church,** a Catholic church built in 1858 in the Italianate style. The church's cemetery, across the street, dates to the prerevolutionary era. The farms around **Loveville,** located a mile farther southeast, reflect the presence of Amish and Mennonite families.

Side Trip to Colton's Point via Md. 242

From Morganza, the visitor may leave Md. 5 and travel south on Md. 242, known as Colton's Point Rd., which soon leads to **Clements.** Continue farther south on this road through a wide neck formed by St. Clement's Bay and the Wicomico and Potomac Rivers. Much of the land here was patented in 1639 as **St. Clement's Manor** by Dr. Thomas Gerard, one of the wealthiest and most influential early colonists. Robert Cole, an English Catholic immigrant, began a plantation in 1652 on St. Clement's Bay, near an area now known as Mount Pleasant. Other early farms of varying size filled this peninsula. Manorial court records remain from this locale, which was an early center of opposition to the Calverts' proprietorship. From St. Clement's Manor in 1660, Josias Fendall, whom Lord Baltimore had appointed governor in 1657, conspired to set up a Protestant commonwealth under the rule of the assembly.

Md. 239 angles west from Md. 242 to the Wicomico River and **Ocean Hall** (private) at **Bushwood Wharf.** Merchant Robert Slye, who died in 1671, owned this land. He was the first husband of Thomas Gerard's daughter Susannah Gerard, who later married the rebel John Coode. The brick house with its steep gable roof dates from about 1703.

St. Clement's Island

Continue on Md. 242 to **Colton's Point,** a small summer resort from which **St. Clement's Island State Park** is visible across narrow **Dukehart's Channel.** The 61-acre island, accessible only by boat, was the first Maryland land that settlers from the *Ark* and the *Dove* stepped foot upon.

On November 22, 1633, 17 English gentlemen, Catholic younger sons of "good birth and qualitie"; two Jesuit priests and a lay brother; ship's crew and indentured servants—a total of perhaps 200 men, women, and children—left England on two ships. They stopped in the West Indies and then Virginia before sailing up the Chesapeake on March 3, 1634, accompanied by a Virginia pinnace and Henry Fleet, an Indian interpreter and trader. In late April 1634, Father Andrew White wrote a

12-page letter in Latin to his superiors in Rome (in 1998 the Maryland Historical Society purchased this document at a London auction). The letter first went to London, where friends of the Calvert expedition made a copy and translated White's impressions, circulating them under the title "A Brief Relation of the Successefull beginnings of the Lord Baltemore's Plantation in Mary-land." Twenty leagues up the Potomac, Father White recounted, the party reached an island swarming with herons.

> This we called St. Clements, here we first came ashoare; here by the overturning of a shallop we had allmost lost our mades which wee brought along. The linnen they went to wash was much of it lost, which is noe small matter in these partes. The ground is heare, as in very many places, covered with pokiberries, (a little wilde walnut hard of shell, but with a sweet kernell) with ackhornes, black walnut, cedar, saxafras, vines, salladherbes, and such like. It is not above 400 acres, and therefore too little to seat upon for us: therefore they have designed it for a fort to Command the river, meaneing to raise another on the maine land against it, and soe to keep the river from forraigne trade, here being the narrowest of the river.
>
> In this place on our b. Ladies day in lent [March 25, the Feast of the Annunciation], we first offered [the sacrifice of the mass], erected a crosse, and with devotion tooke solemne possession of the Country.

March 25, the date of that ceremony, remains a state holiday, Maryland Day. In 1934, as part of Maryland's tercentenary celebration, the state erected another large cross on the eroding island. About 40 years later, in 1976, St. Mary's County established the **St. Clement's Island–Potomac River Museum** on the mainland across from the island. Modernized in 1984, the museum since 1990 has relied on private funding; it features historical exhibits on the colony's first settlers, the history of the lower Potomac River, and Chesapeake Bay maritime culture.

St. Clement's Island at the time of Maryland's tercentenary, 1934

Newtown Neck via Md. 243

On the northern outskirts of Leonardtown, Md. 243 branches south from Md. 5 to Newtown Neck, a scrawny piece of land jutting into the Potomac between St. Clement's and Breton Bays. **St. Francis Xavier Church,** the oldest Roman Catholic church in Maryland and probably the oldest in the original 13 states, stands at the end of the highway. Fr. James Ashby, who died in 1767, may have built the existing shingled frame church. The brick half-hexagons at each end were added in 1767 and 1816, one for a choir loft and the other for a confessional. A bell inscribed "1791, S.T. Joannes Arden" hangs in the steeple. Between 1685 and 1862 at least some priests of the mission were buried under the church or near it; others may lie in the old cemetery, which sits off the highway. Nearby is a stone monument to the early "Soldiers of Ignatius" who labored here. Resident priests moved to Leonardtown in 1868, reflecting a decline in the congregation. Sunday masses are still said in the old church.

Newtown Manor occupies a site near the church. First known as Manor of Little Brittaine, the unrestored brick house—with its gambrel roof, high ceilings, and priests' "cells"—probably dates to the 1790s. The second story was added in 1816. Tenants rent the property and farm the land for the benefit of the Jesuits. Waterfowl often dot the fields. Surrounded by flat farmland, open sky, and omnipresent water, the location has a dramatic quality befitting the inscription on the church's altar: "Life is journey into the Spirit."

Newtown Neck developed as an early population center for young Maryland. In 1640 the proprietor granted the neck to William Bretton (d. 1672), "gentleman clerk" of the lower house (1637–66), clerk of the council (1637–49) and finally clerk of the Provincial Court (1649–63). At this location Ralph Crouch in 1657 established what may have been the proprietary's first school of humanities. Bretton gave 1½ acres for a Catholic church in 1662 and six years later granted his whole tract "with edifaces and buildings" to the Jesuit order. By 1677 the Jesuits had either taken over the Crouch school or started another, which was held in the existing house or an earlier structure on the site. The Act to Prevent the Growth of Popery (1704) forced the school to close. Thereafter the neck declined in importance, but the Jesuits for many years remained, typically celebrating mass in a small chapel attached to the house.

Leonardtown

Continuing on Md. 5 will take the traveler to the town that has been the St. Mary's County seat since 1708 (50' alt., 1,474 pop.). Laid out on a site known as Shepherd's Old Fields, on high ground above Breton Bay, the town was first named for Col. John Seymour, governor of the province; but the name was changed in 1728 to honor Benedict Leonard Calvert, fourth Lord Baltimore. Benedict Leonard was the second son of Charles Calvert (1637–1715), the third Lord Baltimore and first resident proprietor of Maryland, who lost his power to govern when the colony became a royal province after the English Glorious Revolution of 1688. Charles petitioned the king for restoration of his proprietary but was denied. Much to his father's chagrin, Benedict Leonard renounced his Catholic faith in 1713 in an apparent ploy to regain Maryland. As soon as

Charles died in 1715, the new Lord Baltimore, now a member of Parliament and of the Church of England, petitioned for restoration of his charter. Before the crown could act, however, Benedict Leonard died, at the age of 36, two months after his father. Within a year, King George I returned full proprietary rights to Benedict Leonard's young son Charles, the fifth Lord Baltimore. The Calvert family, now Protestant, would continue as proprietors of Maryland for another generation, until the American Revolution.

The British deemed Leonardtown important enough to raid during the War of 1812, and Union troops occupied it during the Civil War; but with few exceptions, the town has remained a quiet, rural county seat with such familiar American landmarks as a grassy commons, war memorial and flag pole, and surrounding offices and stores. The courthouse, built at the turn of the century and rebuilt in 1957, overlooks Breton Bay, which curves gracefully into the Potomac.

Tudor Hall, an 18th-century frame structure, also overlooks the bay, on a sloping bluff from which more modern houses descend the hillside. This property was acquired in 1744 by Abraham Barnes (ca. 1715–78), a longtime delegate to the Provincial Assembly and in 1774 chairman of the Committee of Observation of St. Mary's County, one of many such local groups which took over government functions just before the Revolution. Either Barnes or his son may have added the one-story brick wings described in a 1798 tax list. Soon after 1815, Francis Scott Key's uncle, Philip Barton Key (d. 1820), bought Tudor Hall, and it remained in his family for several generations. Either he or his son Henry Greenfield Sotheron Key replaced the old frame structure in the center and rebuilt the whole house to two stories of brick. The original kitchen with its huge fireplace and Dutch oven remains intact. The late Mrs. Howard C. Davidson restored Tudor Hall and in 1950 donated it to St. Mary's County Memorial Library Association. The town commissioners now have their offices there.

The **Town Jail,** built around 1876, is located on the courthouse lawn and now houses the museum of the St. Mary's Historical Society. True to the spirit of the age, its three rooms on the second floor were segregated: one for black men, one for white men, and one for women, black and white. The jailor lived on the first floor. During the 1920s, the jail was usually empty, except when revenue officers captured a bootlegger and sentenced him to 30 days or more. Some of the county's most prominent citizens vacationed here during Prohibition. Until the navy came to the county in the 1940s and the increased population necessitated construction of a new jail in the 1950s, the old jail never had much business.

Continuing on Md. 5 out of Leonardtown one passes the county fairgrounds and enters a rural area marked by small streams that empty into the Potomac River to the south and the St. Mary's River to the southeast. Md. 5 passes through the town of Callaway.

Side Trip to St. George Island via Md. 249

From Callaway, Md. 249 takes the traveler farther south into an area of points, coves, and creeks dotted with historic homes. Although suburban waste always poses a problem, the lower Potomac abounds in shellfish, water birds, and other wildlife. The steamboats that once plied these waters have disappeared, replaced in the summertime by legions of recreational boaters.

Just before Md. 249 crosses Md. 244, note **St. George's Episcopal Church,** also known as **Poplar Hill,** on the right in **Valley Lee.** A church has stood among great oaks at or near this location since the mid-17th century, serving one of the oldest Anglican congregations in Maryland. Only two other Anglican congregations existed in the early settlement: one on St. Clement's Manor, where the Catholic leader Thomas Gerard had built a chapel for his Protestant wife and daughters; the other south of St. Mary's City. The Rev. William Wilkinson arrived in 1650 to serve these congregations as the first Anglican rector to make Maryland his permanent home. The tombstone of his successor, Francis Sourton (rector 1663–79), has been uncovered about 25 feet from the present building, along with that of Leigh Massey (d. 1732 or 1733), which reads in part, "educated at Oxford, Rector of this Parish the darling of his Flock and Beloved of all that knew him." Researchers believe that the stones may have been located on the sites of the first three churches built here. Sourton was probably buried in the aisle of the first church and Massey in the chancel of the second. The third church, built of brick about 1760, probably burned around 1799, and the existing brick church was constructed the same year, using the walls of its predecessor. The interior was restored in 1958, and the gravestones now form part of its floor, with Sourton in an aisle and Massey in the chancel. The gravestones of two other rectors also now rest in the church, which appears in the National Register of Historic Places.

Mulberry Fields (private), is located above the Potomac off Md. 244, about four miles west of the church. John Anthony Clarke apparently built the house in 1765. A portico added on the river front about 1830 looks down a steep bluff landscaped into terraces or falls, which descend to the fields, where two rows of giant mulberry trees once supported the planter's small silk industry.

Just south of Valley Lee, Md. 249 intersects Drayden Rd., which turns east and passes **Porto Bello** (private). William Hebb, also a planter, built this estate after 1740 and may have named it in honor of a victory by the British admiral Edward Vernon, who attacked Spanish possessions in the Caribbean during the War of Austrian Succession. Vernon sacked Portobelo, a major Spanish port in Panama, in 1739. (Laurence Washington, George Washington's half brother, also served under Vernon and named Mount Vernon in the admiral's honor.)

West St. Mary's Manor Rd. (off Frog's Marsh Rd. from Drayden) leads to a late-18th-century house of the same name along the river north of Portobello Point. The 2,000-acre manor was granted in 1634 to Capt. Henry Fleet, a Virginia Protestant who acted as Indian guide and interpreter for Leonard Calvert and his Maryland settlers.

Md. 249 continues south beyond Valley Lee to **Piney Point.** A right on Lighthouse Rd. leads to the **Piney Point Lighthouse,** operated by a keeper from 1835 to 1964. This beach location became a popular resort for Washingtonians between 1820 and 1853. President James Monroe stayed here, first in the hotel and later in a cottage that became a summer White House, subsequently destroyed in a 1933 hurricane. John C. Calhoun, Henry Clay, Daniel Webster, and President Franklin Pierce were among the dignitaries who visited Piney Point. During the Civil War, the lighthouse keeper often was threatened by Confederate smugglers who used Piney Point Creek to ferry contraband war supplies across the river to Virginia. Now the creek is occupied by the Steuart Petroleum Company, which operates an oil storage business here. A small county park at the lighthouse, a national historic site, offers limited public access to the area.

Md. 249 passes the **Harry Lundeberg School of Seamanship,** established in 1953 to train men and women for the merchant marine and named for the first president of the Seafarers International Union. The facility moved here in 1968, to the site of a former navy torpedo station.

A steel and concrete bridge carries Md. 249 across a narrow waterway to **St. George Island** at the confluence of the Potomac and St. Mary's Rivers. The island belonged to the Jesuits as part of St. Inigoes Manor until about 1850; it has since become a summer resort area that attracts boaters and supports more than a few seafood restaurants.

Disputes over ownership of the oyster beds around the island (as elsewhere in the Potomac and the Chesapeake Bay) have led to serious conflicts between Maryland and Virginia. In 1785, the two states signed a treaty that allowed watermen from both states to fish in the Potomac, even though Maryland's 1632 charter included Potomac waters to the low-tide mark on the Virginia shore. But as the oyster supply diminished and other fishing declined, Maryland passed conservation measures that Virginians refused to honor. In 1959 the two assemblies set aside the Compact of 1785, and a joint commission now regulates Potomac fisheries. Patrol boats from both states enforce the laws.

Gambling in these waters also has led to interstate tension. For many years in this century, the Maryland side of the Potomac along the riverbanks of Charles and St. Mary's Counties was alive with gambling boats anchored in small coves, often flanked by floating houses of prostitution. Bootleg whiskey came from local distilleries. The lower river became known as the "Las Vegas of the East Coast." Marylanders took advantage of the low-tide-mark state line on the Virginia side by building slot-machine casinos, illegal in Virginia, on piers that extended from the Virginia bank over Maryland waters. Virginia patrons entered these establishments after passing the boundary line, marked clearly on the pier. Then, in a burst of zeal supported by the churches, Maryland outlawed the "river slots," and a phase-out of all slot machines in the state began in 1963. By 1968 they were illegal everywhere.

More recently, Maryland and Virginia have cooperated on a far more important issue than gambling—the protection of the natural environment. The Interstate Commission on the Potomac River Basin, established in 1940 and revised in 1970, attempts to monitor and control water use and pollution in the river's drainage area, which—besides Maryland and Virginia—includes the states of West Virginia and Pennsylvania and the District of Columbia. Improved sewage treatment, particularly at the Blue Plains Plant (along the river inside the District of Columbia just across the Prince George's County line), has reduced but not eliminated river pollution, which poses a continuing problem for the next century.

Cecil's Mill Historic District

East of Md. 249, Md. 5 intersects Md. 471, Indian Bridge Rd., and crosses the St. Mary's River at **Great Mills,** which has developed into a strong tourist attraction. The **Christmas Country Store** is located in **Cecil's Old General Store** (1906), just north of the junction on Md. 471. The Crafts Guild of St. Mary's County operates the facility during warm weather months and the Christmas season. A mill has stood on the site across the road since at least the mid-18th century. The current Old Mill once operated as a sawmill. It now displays a variety of arts and crafts, as well as milling artifacts. The general store and mill were gifts of the Cecil family. The restored mill community has been entered on the National Register of Historic Places.

Beyond the St. Mary's River, the traveler enters one of North America's longest-settled colonial landscapes. The river—narrow when it flows through the state park to the north—begins to widen south of Great Mills and becomes a wide estuary before flowing into the Potomac 10 miles to the southeast. Md. 5 follows the west side of a narrow peninsula formed by the river on the west, the Chesapeake Bay on the east, and the Potomac on the south.

Md. 5 swerves to the south, where it meets Md. 489 and soon passes the **Father Andrew White Memorial,** erected to honor the Jesuit priest who arrived with the *Ark* and the *Dove* in 1634. Father White, at 56 the oldest member of the expedition and leader of the Jesuit contingent, worked as a missionary among the native tribes at Piscataway and Port Tobacco and later wrote an Indian catechism and grammar. He converted and baptized the tayac, or emperor, Kittamaquund, his wife, and infant son. Kittamaquund took his young daughter Mary to St. Mary's City, where she became the special ward of Mistress Margaret Brent (see below).

The **Jesuit Memorial Altar** lies within walking distance on Memorial Rd. It commemorates all the Jesuits who came in the first expedition: Father White; Father John Altham (1589–1640), who worked on Kent Island before his death; and lay brother Thomas Gervase, who died in 1637. The Pilgrims of Maryland Society dedicated the memorial in 1933.

Md. 5 continues past **Pope's Freehold,** a 100-acre tract that Nathaniel Pope, one of George Washington's maternal ancestors, patented in 1641. Thomas Hatton and Philip Calvert, two of the young colony's most influential citizens, lived here after 1649. Hatton, a Protestant supporter of Lord Baltimore and secretary of Maryland, died in the Battle of the Severn in 1655. The youngest son of George Calvert, Philip served as chancellor of the province. He lived here from his arrival in Maryland in 1658 until 1679, when he finished his house at nearby St. Peter's. When Philip died without heirs in late 1682 or early 1683, Pope's Freehold reverted to the proprietor, who retained it as part of his personal holdings, leasing it to tenants. Moses Tabbs (d. 1779), rector of William and Mary Parish, purchased the property in 1763. Archaeological excavations uncovered the site in 1971–72, revealing an early-18th-century house that Tabbs enlarged into a 28' × 32' structure with four rooms on each floor. Tabbs had 10 children, and his income from the parish made him one of the area's wealthiest men. The house was used as a tenement later in the century and abandoned after the middle of the 19th century; excavation revealed many artifacts from this later period.

At this point Md. 5 comes upon the St. Mary's River and the site of Maryland's 17th-century capital. On the left is **Fisherman's Creek** (Chancellor's Creek on earlier maps), which in the 17th century formed the northern boundary for the **St. Mary's Town Lands.**

St. Mary's College of Maryland, also on the left, received a charter in 1839 as St. Mary's Seminary and in 1845 became St. Mary's Female Seminary, one of the oldest such institutions in the United States. Part of the state university system since 1967, it has grown into a widely respected college of liberal arts and sciences.

"St. Mary's Citty"

After visiting St. Clement's Island, young Governor Leonard Calvert led the first Maryland settlers to this small bay at the mouth of the St. George's River. He probably chose it because of its sheltered and convenient location about six miles north of the point where the St. Mary's River joins the Potomac. Contemporary narratives describe a short trek inland and immediate construction of a palisaded fort. As their fears and apprehensions subsided, the colonists dispersed onto manors, freeholds, and missions. In 1636 Lord Baltimore granted 1,200 acres on special terms to the settlers in order to encourage the formation of a town. By 1640 at least ten dwellings, a mill, a forge, and a Catholic chapel had been constructed on these "Town Lands," scattered over 13 separate tracts. The landowners were the colony leaders, and the Town Lands were the colonial capital, but no "town" developed here until the 1660s. By the 1670s a village called "St. Mary's City" had begun to emerge according to what appears to be a baroque plan, perhaps the first of its kind in North America. By the 1680s the settlement consisted of four brick structures—a state house, a mansion named St. Peter's, a Roman Catholic chapel, and a prison—plus several roads along which were scattered various dwellings and public houses.

This development came to an abrupt halt in 1695, when the capital was moved to Annapolis. In the 18th century, when Annapolis became "the Athens of America," St. Mary's City largely reverted to farmland. Trinity Episcopal Church and St. Mary's College were built on a portion of the old town lands in the 19th century. The sites of the first capital remained undisturbed—ignored and almost forgotten. Residents nonetheless kept alive traditions that eventually helped archaeologists locate the state house, chapel, and other structures and fostered local appreciation of the 17th-century effort at religious toleration.

In 1934 Maryland's Tercentenary Commission reconstructed the brick **State House of 1676.** Dr. Henry Chandlee Forman supervised excavations at other sites in the 1930s and stimulated interest in the buried city. In 1966 the state established the St. Mary's City Commission, and a wider public began to realize that Maryland had a true historical treasure on its hands—a relatively undisturbed 17th-century site that could provide scholarly answers to persistent questions. How did the settlers live and work? What were their relationships to the natives? How did generations of families adapt to this new land? What legacies did 17th-century settlers leave to our modern world? The commission has sponsored excavations, developed sites, and conducted festivals, living history exhibits, and seminars in efforts to bring this past alive.

The work has been an ongoing process, as illustrated by the discovery in 1990 of three lead coffins buried in the foundations of the original brick Catholic chapel. The coffins were opened in 1992 with great scientific care and are now believed to contain the remains of Chancellor Philip Calvert (d. 1683) and his wife, Ann Wolseley Calvert, and child. Part of the commission's challenge lies in the difficulty of visualizing a buried settlement from a century so remote from the present. Thanks to costumed interpreters at the archaeological sites and the artifacts uncovered here, the visitor can easily imagine life in the 17th century Maryland capital.

Current plans call for the development of **Historic St. Mary's City,** designated a National Historic Landmark in 1968, into a nationally recognized history park and museum. Several more historic structures are undergoing or eventually will undergo reconstruction; in the meantime, the museum gives the site a three-dimensional reality by means of a recreated street plan and "ghost structures" that indicate where 17th-century buildings once stood. The **Visitor Center** for Historic St. Mary's City contains exhibits as well as maps to guide the traveler through the partially reconstructed city.

Beyond Fisherman's Creek, Fisher Rd. leads to two stabilized archaeological sites on the campus of St. Mary's College of Maryland. The first is **St. John's,** a house built in 1638 by John Lewgar, an Anglican minister who converted to Catholicism and who served as the province's first secretary. Excavations have revealed vestiges of a two-room (hall and parlor) frame house, 1½ stories high. A central brick chimney served both rooms, an arrangement common to southern England farmhouses of the period. The colonists would later use end chimneys, more suited to the heat and humidity of the Chesapeake. Brick foundations and a partial cellar with dressed stone walls give Lewgar's house unusual distinction, since nearly all other 17th-century Maryland houses were of post-in-the-ground construction. Freemen met in this house in 1639 to elect an assembly, and throughout the 1640s, the handful of men who ran the small community of 400–600 used it as a meeting place and courtroom.

Lewgar left Maryland around 1649, and within a few years the house belonged to Simon Overzee, a Dutch merchant who died in 1660. Governor Charles Calvert, who became the third Lord Baltimore in 1676, acquired the old Lewgar house on his arrival in 1661. By 1667, Calvert had moved to Mattapany on the Patuxent, and thereafter St. John's was used for public offices or leased to innkeepers who accommodated visitors during assembly and court sessions. Extensive changes were made to the property over the succeeding decades. The central chimney was removed and the house raised to two stories; other structures were added, as well as an orchard and garden. Occupation continued through part of the first decade after the capital moved to Annapolis.

Just past St. John's—next to Caroline Hall dormitory—lies the **site of the John Hicks House,** excavated in 1969–70. Hicks, a sea captain from Whitehaven in northern England, built this frame, 16' × 40' house with brick end chimneys around 1723. St. Mary's City had disappeared by this time, and Hicks was probably living as a planter and tobacco merchant in a rural area marked by an excellent anchorage. He served a term as sheriff and sat briefly on the Provincial Court. Hicks built a new house nearby in about 1746 and dismantled the old dwelling. When he died in 1753, his estate of £400 marked him as one of the area's richest men. His son William continued the family business of purchasing the crops of neighboring farmers in return for European manufactured goods.

Md. 5 continues beyond Fisher Rd. and crosses **Mill Creek.** College structures surround the pond at the mouth of the creek, near where the *Ark* and *Dove* anchored in March 1634.

Beyond Mill Creek the main road curves to the southeast. The **Freedom of Conscience Monument** sits in the Y formed by the junction of Md. 5 and Md. 584. As part of Maryland's celebration of its Tercentenary, Baltimore sculptor Hans Schuler created this massive limestone figure of a youth emerging from stone. Standing here, one may reflect on the fact that St. Mary's City represented an important, though limited, experiment in religious toleration. George and Cecil Calvert, first and second Lords Baltimore, set out to make Maryland a refuge for Catholics, who in England could not worship in public or hold public office. The Calverts could not, and did not try to, establish a Catholic colony, but they wished to enable Catholics to enjoy religious freedom and the civil rights of other Englishmen.

The monument commemorates passage on April 21, 1649, of An Act Concerning Religion, which provided that "noe person or persons whatsoever in this province . . . professing to believe in Jesus Christ, shall from henceforth bee any waies troubled, Molested or discountenanced for or in respect of his or her religion nor in the free exercise thereof. . . ." Since the bill also provided the death penalty for blaspheming against Christian doctrine, it represented a step backward from the tolerance practiced from the colony's beginning. The legislation did protect Catholics from the Protestants, who had already beheaded Charles I, and announced to other Christian sects that Maryland practiced religious toleration. For 40 years the act provided at least some protection to Catholics and Protestants. Then, in 1689, the experiment ended. Protestant leaders that year overthrew the proprietary government and in 1702 succeeded in establishing the Church of England. In 1705 Maryland law prohibited Catholics from openly practicing their faith and from participating in public life; not until the Revolution did they regain these rights.

Md. 584, the state's shortest highway, makes a small loop with Md. 5 to other portions of the college campus and historic city, angling east at **Calvert Hall,** a partial reconstruction of the first school building, erected in 1844 and destroyed by fire in 1924.

Trinity Episcopal Church, located on **Church Point** beyond Calvert Hall, was built shortly after 1829 with brick salvaged from the old State House, which had served briefly as a courthouse and in 1720, became a chapel for the Anglican William and Mary Parish (the Catholic chapel was demolished); the parish used the chapel for more than a century before tearing it down. Most of the existing Gothic structure of Trinity Church reflects a major overhaul in about 1889. The **Copley Vault** behind the church is believed to hold the remains of Sir Lionel Copley and his wife. Copley (d. 1693) became Maryland's first royal governor after the crown suspended the Calverts' right to rule the province following the Glorious Revolution of 1689.

The **Leonard Calvert Monument** in the churchyard marks the site of a mulberry tree, where the original settlers allegedly met to hear the Calvert charter read soon after their arrival.

Granite markers between the church and the monument indicate the outlines of the original **State House of 1676,** built by Capt. John Quigley for 300,000 pounds of tobacco, worth about £1,250—then a huge sum for public works. Excavations in 1933 revealed walls that largely

conformed to the contract recorded in the assembly journal of 1674. The two-story brick building was cross-shaped with the main section 45 feet long and 30 feet wide. A stair tower and porch tower on either side extended the width of the cross to about 61 feet. Located on the point, the building was the traveler's first view of the city from the water and an impressive sign of Lord Baltimore's power.

Md. 584 turns sharply left at the church and passes on the right some of the Historic St. Mary's City outdoor history exhibits. Admission is by ticket, obtainable at a kiosk in the parking lot here or at the Visitor Center. The Reconstructed State House and Farthing's Ordinary are visible from the road.

A driveway off Md. 584 until recently led to the **Brome-Howard House,** built in 1840 by Dr. John Mackall Brome, a large plantation owner. This restored Greek Revival house has been moved to a site farther down the river, because the town center of 17th-century St. Mary's City lies under and around the site of the house. The structure itself will one day serve as a means of interpreting the 19th-century history of the area.

Md. 584 loops back to Md. 5. As one continues south, the field on the left contains several unexcavated sites, including 17th-century houses, a mill, forges, and possibly the St. Mary's Fort of 1634. Mattapany Rd., which branches left and crosses Mill Creek not far above the mill site, follows an Indian path in existence when the settlers first arrived.

Md. 5 intersects Rosecroft Rd., which runs south down a small neck, with the river on the west and St. Inigoes Creek on the south. The buried foundations of **St. Peter's** lie in a field to the northeast of this junction. In 1658 the family sent Philip Calvert, the first Lord Baltimore's youngest son and half brother of the second Lord Baltimore, to Maryland to set the province's affairs in order after years of confusion and the threat of extinction. He succeeded, and by 1679, on the tract of St. Peter's, he finished a "Great House." This structure may have been the most imposing dwelling of its time in British North America. The brick house was 54 feet square with interior chimneys, equal in size to the Governor's Palace built 25 years later in Williamsburg. The first royal governors, Lionel Copley and Francis Nicholson, lived here. Within a few months after Nicholson moved the provincial capital to Annapolis, a mysterious blast from stored gunpowder demolished St. Peter's. Its bricks and other rubble were still visible in the late 19th century.

Visitor Center

Rosecroft Rd. passes the distinctive blue barns that once belonged to the J. Roland Thomas Dairy Farm. Here the Historic St. Mary's City Commission has established a visitor center that includes a gift shop, information packets, and an exhibit illustrating life in 17th-century Maryland. The Visitor Center is open seven days a week from the first Wednesday in January through the third weekend in December, except for Thanksgiving Day. Here one may purchase the tickets necessary to visit the outdoor exhibits.

Visitors are encouraged to park their vehicles in an adjacent lot and walk to the main attractions: north to nearby **Chapel Land** and **Governor's Field,** that portion of the old St. Mary's Town Lands that became St. Mary's City; or south to the **Godiah Spray Tobacco Plantation.** Those who prefer to drive may return to the parking lot at **Farthing's Ordinary** on Md. 584 or turn right on Rosecroft Rd. to the plantation.

Town Center

North from the Visitor Center, a walking path takes one on a half-mile trip through St. Mary's City. The **Woodland Indian Hamlet Exhibit** includes a **Long House** built with stone-age methods and tools. The first settlers at St. Mary's encountered such dwellings and learned methods of survival from the natives.

The next stop is Chapel Field, **site of the Brick Chapel** that Roman Catholic settlers built in the 1660s. At least one wooden chapel stood here earlier. Excavations in the 1930s exposed the foundations for a 55' × 57' structure in the shape of a great Latin cross. Recent excavations have revealed three lead coffins in what seems to be a Calvert family crypt. The chapel was torn down after 1705, when the assembly outlawed Catholic services except in private homes. Archaeologists have found what seem to be bricks from the church while excavating a probable chapel house built later on St. Inigoes Manor. Plans are in place for a reconstruction of the Brick Chapel at St. Mary's.

Beyond the Brick Chapel, the path passes an 18th-century barn and crosses a field where archaeological surface collections indicate the presence of several 17th- and 18th-century structures. This area offers another possible site for the St. Mary's Fort of 1634, because it is the highest land that fills the documentary description of the fort's location half a mile from the water. A cannon salvaged from the St. Mary's River in 1824 has been placed in the field; a twin of this gun sits on the State House lawn in Annapolis. Both pieces may have been part of the ordnance shipped on the *Ark* with the settlers in 1633–34.

The path continues to the area in which the village chartered as St. Mary's City in 1668 and 1671 first developed. From the earliest days of the colony this location provided a center for provincial activity and authority.

Pope's Fort and the English Civil War

Thomas Hobbes, the great English political philosopher of the 17th century, argued that without the stable authority of a strong monarchy, people knew only "continual fear, and danger of violent death" and, in a famous phrase, that life was "solitary, poor, nasty, brutish and short." Those few Maryland settlers at the time who could read would probably have agreed, especially once the war between king and Parliament reached their shores.

Consider the **site of Leonard Calvert's House,** possibly constructed within the first year or two of settlement. Calvert, Lord Baltimore's brother and Maryland's first governor, later leased the house to Nathaniel Pope, a leading anti-Catholic. In 1645, only 11 years after the settlers arrived, Richard Ingle, an adventurer with previous quarrels in Maryland, arrived with his ship and plundered the colony in the name of Parliament. Many of the settlers, including Leonard Calvert, fled to Virginia. Ingle took revenge on his enemies and seized property. Pope may have offered the house for Ingle's use. In any case, a palisade and moat were constructed around it for defense. When archaeologists found the first signs of the ditch and palisade, they thought they had discovered the original 1634 fort. Now they believe that the site around Calvert's house contains Pope's Fort, the only physical evidence of the English Civil War in America.

Captain Ingle left the province within a year, and Leonard Calvert returned in 1646 with troops hired to reclaim the settlement, which had dwindled to fewer than 100 people. Calvert died suddenly in 1647, and his estate was administered by the remarkable Margaret Brent.

As people tried to resist disease and raise families on their corn and tobacco farms, political turmoil continued. Lord Baltimore needed Protestant support and Protestant settlers. In 1648 he appointed a Protestant governor, William Stone, who purchased Calvert's house and conducted much of his provincial business from here. Stone promptly induced Virginia Puritans to settle in tolerant Maryland. Six years later, taking their cue from Oliver Cromwell in England, these Puritans overthrew the Catholic Calvert regime and moved the center of government across the Patuxent River to Calvert County. Lord Baltimore regained control of the colony in 1657, made a treaty with the Puritans, and appointed another Protestant governor, Josias Fendall, who was supposed to work in concert with Philip Calvert. Fendall, in turn, seems to have conspired to set himself up as governor of an independent commonwealth. Finally, with the restoration of Charles II in England in 1660, Lord Baltimore's proprietary position stabilized. Cecil Calvert replaced Fendall with his brother Philip and then with son and heir, Charles Calvert. The province settled down to nearly 30 years of peaceful growth.

The Inns of St. Mary's

The village that was St. Mary's City grew up around the home of the original governor, the Leonard Calvert House, which in 1662 the province purchased for use as a state house and ordinary or inn (it may have served these dual purposes well before then). From that time forward it was known as the **Country's House.** It is one of the two oldest buildings in Maryland whose history can be followed. As the governor's residence, the house was also a public building, a place for courts, councils, and even assemblies to meet. The house began as a frame structure 50' × 18' with a gabled roof, but around 1641 it was enlarged to 67' × 40', an extraordinary size in 17th-century Maryland. Most of the enlargement consisted of a second structure adjacent to the first, covered by a second gabled roof.

In 1664, an entrepreneur named William Smith took over the ordinary at Country's House, and before his death in 1667 he had nearly completed a second inn, **Smith's Ordinary,** a small frame structure about 100 feet to the south. In 1672 the Dutch innkeeper Garret Van Sweringen acquired it, but it burned in 1678. Work has begun on its reconstruction.

Van Sweringen, with his partner John Quigley or perhaps Smith's successor, Daniel Jenefer, built a third structure some 100 feet east of Smith's Ordinary. At first it housed lawyers' offices, but it may later have been converted into a third ordinary. This house, which was standing in 1672 and referred to in the records as **Two Messages,** awaits excavation. The planter, merchant, and innkeeper Mark Cordea, an immigrant from Normandy, purchased the property in 1673 and sold it to Councillor William Digges in 1686.

Cordea's Hope, another frame house, 21' × 24', has been reconstructed on its original site. It stood 100 feet north of the Two Messages and about as far east of the Country's House, completing a rough square.

Re-created 17th-century house, Historic St. Mary's City, 1997

Mark Cordea had this simplest of the Town Center buildings constructed during or before 1675 and used it as a store, office, and storehouse. Cordea and Van Sweringen were both named aldermen in the two St. Mary's City charters, and both served a term as mayor.

With construction of the State House of 1676, the Country's House continued its functions as an inn. After the capital moved to Annapolis, the wooden building quickly decayed. Bricks now outline its walls and hearths; signs show its conjectured appearance. Interpreters explain all the sites during walking tours scheduled at the Visitor Center in warm weather months.

City Layout

Although no documents refer to it, archaeologists speculate that the regularities of this town square suggest a conscious city plan. Other measurements also hint at a guiding design for St. Mary's. The Brick Chapel of the late 1660s and the brick State House of 1676 are located one-half mile apart; each is 1400 feet from a point at the center of the square. By 1675 all the roads of the town met here. The distance from the landing place at the mouth of Mill Creek to this center point was equal to the distance from the overland entrance to the town, at the mill dam farther up the creek. Thus, two identical triangles share the town square center point. Such regularities probably did not result from chance: by 1660 baroque axial plans had been appearing in European cities for a century. In these plans, principal buildings occupied the points of triangles, and major streets connected the points.

The same pattern can be outlined in St. Mary's City, where principal buildings occupied the points, and the roads roughly followed the sides of similar triangles. Country's House, the first state house, occupied the town square, where the two triangles met. The brick State House of 1676 was located at the northwest corner of the northerly triangle. According to tradition and recent archaeology, the prison was located at the northeast corner. The Brick Chapel occupied the southeast corner of the second triangle, another structure, not yet identified, stood at its northeast corner. If such a plan was deliberate, it was probably envisioned by Lord Baltimore and executed by his surveyor general, Jerome White, who came to Maryland in about 1661 and left late in 1670. White was a Catholic who had lived in Rome and probably had been educated there. Philip Calvert may also have played a part. He had spent five years at the English College in Lisbon, another baroque city.

Future archaeological excavations will uncover more of the village, with findings that may settle the question of an axial plan. If verified, St. Mary's City could claim distinction as the first planned baroque town in North America.

Capital City

In the 1670s and 1680s, St. Mary's City gradually emerged as a small provincial capital. Aldermanbury St. was laid out along the river in 1672, with the survey of six lots that shared the street as their western boundary. The street began at the spot where the State House of 1676 was soon to be built and took a southeasterly direction to the developing town square. Colony leaders took up most of the lots and improved some with inns and offices. In 1675 lots along Middle St. were surveyed, along the route of a path that probably had long led northerly from Leonard Calvert's House (Country's House) to the mouth of Mill Creek. By this time, a road ran east from the town center to a mill on the creek, and another road angled southeast past the Catholic chapel. The large gallow's green was located east of Middle St. near the creek. William Nuthead, prohibited by royal order from printing in Virginia, established his press somewhere in town in 1685, becoming the colony's first printer as well as the first in the American South.

City bylaws in 1685 required all housekeepers to "provide to their Chimneys two ladders, one twenty four foote, and the other twelve foote in length." Most chimneys were not brick and had to be "lathed, filled, dawb'd and plaistered" to hinder fires, which were a constant hazard. The laws also required hogs to be penned and gave the constables the authority to impound any free-roaming swine, which had become a nuisance by killing poultry, invading gardens, and causing quarrels with neighbors.

The landing at St. Mary's was an official port of entry but not a central port. Captains arrived by small boat or horse to clear customs from dozens of anchorages scattered throughout the colony.

Renewed political strife in England finally sealed the fate of St. Mary's, which had quietly prospered despite quarrels with and schemes against the Catholic proprietary. In 1688 Parliament deposed the Catholic King James II and installed in his place the Protestant William III and his wife Mary, daughter of James. This "Glorious Revolution" inspired Protestants to overturn the Catholic government in Maryland. In July 1689, Capt. John Coode organized rebels who claimed that Lord Baltimore's council was plotting to deliver Maryland to the French and Indians. Col. William Digges, a loyal member of the council, led about 80 militiamen to St. Mary's to protect the State House. On July 27, Coode and several hundred armed men arrived in the capital and demanded that Digges surrender. When his men refused to fight, Digges gave up without a shot. A disabled cannon found in the river in 1824 can be seen at the Visitor Center and may have been one of Digges's guns. The rest of the council surrendered at Mattapany four days later.

Charles Calvert, third Lord Baltimore, did not prove as politically adroit in England as his predecessors and found himself powerless to prevent the crown from seizing control of Maryland. Under Francis Nicholson, the second royal governor, the assembly in 1695 moved the provincial capital to Annapolis. By 1708 St. Mary's City had lost its voting population and representation in the assembly. By 1720 the town had virtually disappeared.

Governor's Field Exhibits

On Aldermanbury St., just beyond the Country's House and the town square, the **Margaret Brent Gazebo** honors an early settler whose life shines out of the 17th century with unusual clarity and brilliance. Born around 1600 in Gloucestershire, England, Margaret Brent came to Maryland in 1638 with her sister Mary, two brothers Giles and Fulke, and a number of indentured servants. In 1639 she obtained a 50-acre tract near St. Mary's that she named Sister's Freehold and thereby became the first Maryland woman to own land in her own right. By importing servants, she acquired rights to considerable additional land, and she won the confidence of the Calvert family by demonstrating extraordinary energy and ability in the infant colony. When Leonard Calvert died in 1647, she became the sole executor of his estate, responsible for paying the soldiers he had brought with him from Virginia to reclaim Maryland after Ingle's Rebellion.

The colony was in a shambles, and a severe corn shortage made matters worse. The unfed, unpaid soldiers threatened mutiny. Mistress Brent had herself declared attorney for Lord Baltimore, imported corn from Virginia to feed the soldiers, and sold some of the proprietor's cattle to pay them. The assembly later gave her sole credit for maintaining order and stability until the government could recover.

Brent established a permanent place for herself in feminist history when she appeared before the Maryland assembly on January 21, 1648, and argued for her right to two votes, one for herself and one to discharge her duties as Lord Baltimore's attorney. When the assembly denied her request, she protested its proceedings. Brent may have been the first woman in America to seek the franchise—more than two and a half centuries before Maryland women first voted in 1920.

Mistress Brent's reward for pursuing these responsibilities consisted of an angry complaint from the new Lord Baltimore that she had "meddled" in his affairs. Giles Brent, who had served as acting governor and had engaged in previous quarrels with the proprietor, moved to Virginia in 1650. Margaret and her sister followed. At a time when men outnumbered women about six to one, Mistress Brent never married. Her will, dated December 1663, was probated in Virginia on May 19, 1671.

The bronze relief in the gazebo pictures Margaret Brent's request for the vote. The sculpture is the work of Mary Fraser De Pakh and was presented to the state of Maryland in 1984 by the Margaret Brent Chapter of the Business and Professional Women's Club.

The view from the bluff by the gazebo reveals the entire sweep of the St. Mary's River as it flows southwest to the Potomac. **Chancellor's Point,** in the near distance, was believed by 19th-century local historians to be the site of the first landing.

Follow Aldermanbury St. from the Brent Gazebo. Most of the original Middle St. lots have been appropriated by St. Mary's College construction or destroyed by the development of modern roads.

The **Van Sweringen site** just north of the gazebo marks the location of an office constructed in the 1660s for the provincial secretary and his records, with a chamber for meetings of the council. After construction of the brick state house in 1676, Van Sweringen took over these offices, added a kitchen, and opened a lodging house for the colony leaders. Here legislators and visitors met to talk and drink the colony's best cider. In hot and humid weather, the council was known to adjourn to Van Sweringen's arbor. Van Sweringen also built a coffeehouse here, modeled on the London coffeehouses that were beginning to appear as centers of mercantile sociability.

Beyond Van Sweringen's lies **William Farthing's Ordinary,** a working reconstruction of a 17th-century inn opened in 1984. Its architecture copies that of the Third Haven Meeting House, built in the 1680s in Easton. Farthing was an early-18th-century settler whose name frequently appears in early Maryland legal documents.

From Farthing's, a path down the bluff leads to a wharf at the river, where the *Maryland Dove* has its home berth. (A less steep route follows a road just beyond the reconstructed State House.) Designed by the late William A. Baker and built by James Richardson of Dorchester County, this square-rigged pinnace reproduces as faithfully as possible the vessel that accompanied the *Ark* in 1634. Such supply vessels carried a small crew (the original *Dove* carried seven), required several weeks to cross the Atlantic, and often disappeared at sea. After supplying the settlers and making a trip to New England, the original *Dove* set sail for England from St. Mary's in 1635 and was lost with all hands. The *Maryland Dove* occasionally visits ports along the Chesapeake as part of a nautical training program. A monument to **Mathias de Sousa,** thought to be the first settler of color, stands near the dock. De Sousa arrived on the *Ark* as an indentured servant to the Jesuits and by 1642, as a freeman, sat in the lower house of assembly.

Farther along Aldermanbury St., the **reconstructed State House of 1676,** built in 1934 as part of Maryland's Tercentenary celebration, lies adjacent to the churchyard. To avoid disturbing graves, the reconstruction was not placed on the original site. Architects Herbert Crist, James Edmunds Jr., and Horace Peaslee based their work on archaeological excavation and the original contract for the building. Living-history skits, based on 17th-century records of the courts and assemblies, are offered here between Memorial Day and Labor Day and on weekends during the remaining months that the sites at Historic St. Mary's City are open. Details are posted at the Visitor Center.

The exhibits end here, but Aldermanbury St. once ran farther north to the original State House of 1676.

The reconstructed first state house, St. Mary's City, in 1934

Interior of the state house

Sister's Freehold and Godiah Spray Plantation via Rosecroft Rd.

Beyond the Visitor Center, this route continues south and west down a small neck, with the St. Mary's River on the west and St. Inigoes Creek on the south. The road travels through several of the original St. Mary's Town Land tracts that the Historic St. Mary's City Commission has acquired. They include Margaret Brent's **Sister's Freehold** and about 150 acres owned by Daniel Clocker, a carpenter and servant indentured to Thomas Cornwallis, who arrived in Maryland in 1636. Though poor and illiterate, Clocker by 1660 had acquired 200 acres of land and, at his death in 1675, sat on the Common Council of St. Mary's City. He survived "the seasoning"—an immigrant's first year in the New World, when all sickened and many died—and built a small estate in the expanding tobacco economy. Toward the end of the century, opportunities for such poor men declined and then virtually disappeared as larger plantations supported by slave labor began to dominate the local economy.

Historic St. Mary's City has recreated a **tobacco plantation** on Clocker's property. This living-history exhibit is based on the detailed 10-year account kept for the orphans of Robert Cole. Cole, a Roman Catholic from Heston, near London, brought his family to St. Clement's Manor in 1652. He and his wife died in 1662; the children and servants, overseen by a guardian, lived on the plantation until the oldest son reached age 21 in 1673. The guardian's account of this period, with its detailed account of daily life, may be unique for the 17th-century British colonies. The exhibit includes the planter's house, freedman's cottage, and tobacco houses, in addition to fencing, crops, orchard, and livestock, and is called the **Godiah Spray Tobacco Plantation Exhibit Area.** The name Godiah Spray came from old court records.

St. Inigoes Manor via Villa Rd.

After leaving St. Mary's City, Md. 5 crosses **St. Inigoes Creek** (*Inigo* is a variation of *Ignatius*, after Ignatius Loyola, founder of the Jesuit Order). The creek skirts land that has been cultivated for more than three centuries. At Villa Rd., turn right toward the river. Grayson Rd. cuts north from Villa to **Cross Manor** (private), an 18th-century brick house that stands on a grant made in 1638 to Thomas Cornwallis. "Cornwaleys" (the early spelling) ranked among the most influential settlers who came to Maryland in 1634, and he quickly became one of the colony's leading citizens and landowners. His property suffered severely during Ingle's Rebellion.

Villa Rd. continues past Grayson to the site of the **Naval Air Warfare Center—Aircraft Division,** part of the **Patuxent Naval Air Station.** The navy built Webster Field at this site during World War II and has since used the waterfront site for multiple military purposes. **St. Ignatius Church** on Webster Field Rd. was built in 1788 and restored by navy volunteers in 1953. Both the church and the naval facility are located on the site of **St. Inigoes Manor**—a large tract of land patented in 1641 and 1651 to Cuthbert Fenwick and Ralph Crouch, who held it in trust for the Jesuits.

Father Thomas Copley (1594–1653) came to Maryland in 1636 to serve as superior for the Jesuit mission and moved to St. Inigoes from St. Mary's City in 1644, just before Ingle's Rebellion. Unlike Father White, who concentrated his energies on the native Piscataways, Father Copley bypassed the proprietor and had his Jesuits buy land directly from the tribes, thereby challenging Lord Baltimore's charter rights. Equally dangerous to the proprietor was the Jesuit claim that church property was exempt from secular law, which was the custom in Catholic parts of Europe. When Richard Ingle drove the Catholic government to Virginia in 1645, he arrested the Jesuits and sent Copley back to England in chains along with the aging Father White.

The Jesuits were released on their arrival in England, and the nimble Lord Baltimore delicately protected his interests on two fronts. He knew that he had to avoid charges of developing a Catholic colony or lose his charter. Through his contacts with London merchants who supported Parliament, he negotiated to retain his charter, and he convinced the church in Rome to keep the Jesuits out of his business. By the time Copley returned to Maryland in 1648, the Jesuits had formally renounced their claim to hold land except by grant from the proprietor. Ecclesiastical courts were never instituted in Maryland. Father Copley spent his remaining years trying to recover Jesuit property valued at over £2,000, which Ingle had stolen or destroyed during the "plundering time." The Jesuit order was suppressed in Maryland from 1772 to 1805, but the mission at St. Inigoes remained active into the 19th century.

Returning toward Md. 5, a right turn on Grayson Rd. and another on Beachville Rd. lead to the tip of Kitt Point and a picnic site. Follow either Villa Rd. or Beachville Rd. back to Md. 5, which soon joins Md. 235 at Ridge and continues south to the tip of the peninsula.

Point Lookout State Park and Site of Fort Lincoln

Point Lookout overlooks the confluence of the Potomac River and Chesapeake Bay. In the 1850s a popular summer resort flourished here.

During the Civil War, the Union chose the narrow point for a hospital and prisoner-of-war camp. The camp did not match the horrors of the crowded Andersonville prison for Union soldiers in Georgia (a post-Appomattox War Department report counted 26,436 deaths among the 220,000 Confederates in Union prisons and 22,576 deaths among the 126,950 Union troops held in the South), but conditions were unsanitary and frequently gruesome. Prisoners at Point Lookout caught rats for sport and food. Sidney Lanier, a poet and musician who later taught and performed in Baltimore, spent five months here as a prisoner. More than 3,000 Confederate soldiers perished here, and in 1867 the government moved their remains from land near the prison (now reclaimed by the Chesapeake) to **Point Lookout Confederate Cemetery,** which one may visit upon leaving the park. Two monuments, one erected by the federal government and the other by the state of Maryland, list the names of the known dead.

Fort Lincoln, an earthen structure built late in 1865, protected the point. It has been restored and features a museum as well as living-history exhibits.

The state began to acquire land for a park at Point Lookout in 1962. Now 514 acres offer recreational facilities and magnificent waterscapes that belie the human suffering once endured here.

To return up the Patuxent-Potomac peninsula, follow Md. 5 to the town of Ridge and then take Md. 235 north. This modern highway follows a trail laid out in 1672 from Mattapany Landing near the mouth of the Patuxent River to the northern settlements. It is still known as Three Notch Rd., a name derived from a 1702 law requiring that roads be marked to indicate their destinations. Three equidistant notches on a tree marked the road to a ferry; two notches with another high above meant that the road led to a courthouse; two notches near the ground with a slit pointed to a church.

A right-hand turn on St. James Rd., about five miles from the intersection of Rtes. 5 and 235, leads through the Elms Wildlife Management Area to Elms Beach Park (private).

A ghostly schooner at Point Lookout, grounded at low tide in the late 1920s or early 1930s, as a local photographer captured the event

Lexington Park

Lexington Park (110′ alt., 9,943 pop.), is a residential and commercial cluster around the **Patuxent Naval Air Warfare Center** at Rte. 235's intersection with Md. 246. Fifty years ago, this area was known as Cedar Point; it consisted of a small crossroads named Jarboesville, a village called Pearson's Corner, several estates, a number of farms and the ferry site known as Millstone Landing. After American entry into World War II, the Potomac River Naval Command expanded. The navy in 1943 appropriated more than 6,000 acres here, and this isolated portion of St. Mary's County suddenly filled with naval people from all over the United States. A federal housing project named Lexington Park was built outside the gate, presumably in honor of the original aircraft carrier *Lexington* (lost in the Battle of the Coral Sea), and the name gradually applied to surrounding developments. Lexington Park grew quickly and without much planning. Later suburbs have surrounded the original area, which now shows its age. About 25 percent of the county's population now centers around the naval station, nicknamed "Pax River," which accounts for more than a third of the county's jobs. Today, even with cuts in defense spending, Pax River promises to grow as the country's primary research and testing facility for naval aviation.

The **Patuxent Naval Air Warfare Center Museum,** unique in the country, exhibits the center's activities over the years. Planes, missiles, models, instruments, and other test devices illustrate how the navy's planes have been evaluated since World War II.

Mattapany, a brick house built early in the 19th century, stands on the grounds of the Paxtuxent Naval Air Warfare Center and serves as the official residence of the center's commandant. The house is named for the Indian tribe from whom the Jesuits acquired a village for a mission and storehouse here in the 1630s. Lord Baltimore reclaimed the land in 1641 as part of his resistance to independent church ownership of land, and in 1663, granted Mattapany to Henry Sewall, secretary of the province. In 1666 Jane Sewall, his widow, married Gov. Charles Calvert, later the third Lord Baltimore. By 1668 Calvert had built a "fair House of Brick and Timber" in addition to a fort and magazine there. When in 1689 John Coode's Protestants drove the Catholic councillors from St. Mary's, they took refuge here and surrendered four days after the fall of St. Mary's City. The foundations of an old house, probably Calvert's original dwelling, lie about 250 yards south of Mattapany.

North and east of Lexington Park, Md. 235 passes through the suburban area of **California** (7,626 pop.), apparently so named by navy refugees from the West Coast. At Md. 4, known as St. Andrew's Church Rd., one may turn north toward Annapolis by crossing the **Gov. Thomas Johnson Memorial Bridge,** which commemorates the Calvert County native who served as Maryland's first state governor, in 1777–79.

St. Andrew's Church via Md. 4

One may also turn west on Md. 4 to **St. Andrew's Church,** located slightly more than two miles from the intersection with Md. 235. Built by Samuel Abell Jr. between 1766 and 1768, this brick, gable-roofed structure, apparently unaltered, matches almost exactly the plan submitted to the vestry by designer Richard Boulton. Two towers flank an inset portico; a gallery in the interior fits into the space above the portico and is lit by a Palladian window. A third tower was planned, to complete the resemblance to a medieval church. In 1771 John Friech ("Limner") painted an elaborate altarpiece, with a tablet containing the Lord's Prayer, Ten Commandments, Apostles' Creed, and selections from Exodus. Boulton and Abell also constructed All Faith Church, built at the same time 20 miles to the north. St. Andrew's Parish, erected from All Faith and William and Mary parishes in 1744, included nearby Leonardtown. This church in the woods continued to be the parish church until World War II, when the smaller chapel in Leonardtown, built in 1870, became the parish's center of worship. The chapel was sold in the early 1980s, and the congregation returned to St. Andrew's, restored during that decade.

Just north of California, follow the old road (off to the right) to **Hollywood** and **St. John's Church,** a Catholic frame church built in the Gothic style in 1898. The remains of William H. Barnes, member of the United States Colored Troops who won the Congressional Medal of Honor in 1864 (he died in 1936), lie in an unmarked grave in the churchyard.

Sotterley via Md. 245

At Md. 245, turn east to **Greenwell State Park** and **Sotterley,** the premier Patuxent plantation, which stands above the river with a pastoral and proportional beauty distinctive among Maryland's historic places. James Bowles built the plantation house around 1717 on a 1650 manor originally granted to Thomas Cornwallis. Bowles's widow married George Plater II (1695–1755) in 1729, and the Plater family expanded the property, naming it after an ancient family home in Suffolk, England. George Plater III (1735–92) served on patriotic committees before the Revolution, as a delegate to the Continental Congress, and as president of the Maryland convention that ratified the U.S. Constitution. In 1791–92 he became the sixth elected governor of Maryland, one of the many Southern Maryland gentlemen who dominated the state's postrevolutionary politics.

De La Brooke mansion in the 1930s, its grounds in front suitably landscaped and its rear overlooking the lower Patuxent

The Platers extended the house, adding a drawing room that contains some of the finest woodwork in Maryland. Richard Boulton—designer of All Faith and St. Andrew's churches in the 1760s—created the Chinese Chippendale staircase. The flagstones on the 100-foot portico overlooking the Patuxent were imported from Newcastle. George Washington reportedly admired Sotterley and may have patterned his Mount Vernon mansion after this Maryland model. Certainly the long porticos of the two structures are similar. Sotterley has a less elegant, more informal atmosphere than Mount Vernon. In addition to the famous house, the estate features restored gardens and the original slave quarters. Members of only four families lived here during the 244 years it served as a residence. The Platers lost Sotterley in 1822; it was then occupied by the Briscoe family until 1910, when the Satterlees purchased the property. They restored the mansion and, in 1961, Mabel Satterlee Ingalls deeded Sotterley to a private foundation to open it to the public. In addition to maintaining the property, the Sotterley Mansion Foundation hopes to develop the grounds as a major site and educational museum that will cover three centuries of Southern Maryland culture.

De La Brooke and All Faith Church

Farther up the peninsula on Md. 235 the traveler reaches, on the right, Md. 6, which passes Delabrook Rd. Nearby is **De La Brooke** (private), which owes its origin to a tract surveyed in about 1650 for Robert Brooke, an Oxford University graduate and Inner-Temple barrister who arrived in Maryland with 28 servants, thus qualifying for some 8,000 acres in various land grants. Brooke sided with Puritans Richard Bennett and William Claiborne during the upheavals of 1652–54 and in doing so fell out of favor with Lord Baltimore; but his son, Baker Brooke, who later settled at De La Brooke, married Leonard Calvert's daughter Ann. A handsome house, dating from about 1835, stands on this site. It is visible only from the water.

The **All Faith Church,** built in 1766–68, is located off Md. 6 less than three miles east of the return to Md. 5. This rectangular brick building, built by Samuel Abell Jr. according to a plan by Richard Boulton, serves one of the original parishes of Maryland. The windows have been altered over the years and the interior renovated, but the 18th-century church retains much of its original appearance. The interior resembles that of St. Andrew's Church, 20 miles to the south, built at the same time by the same builder and architect.

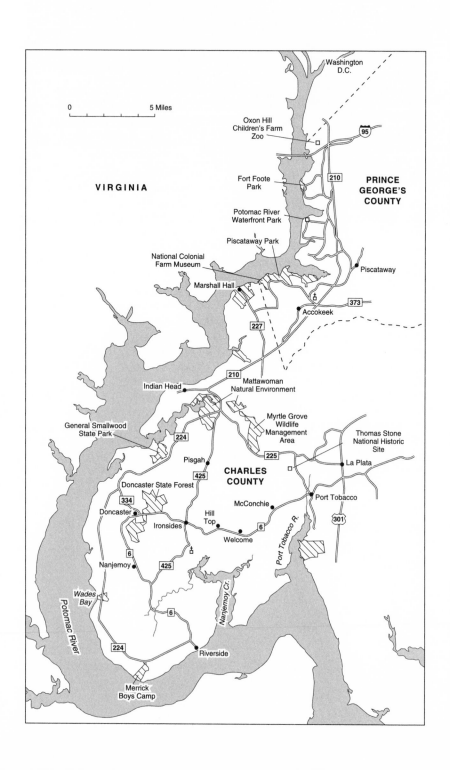

Washington
D.C.

0   5 Miles

Oxon Hill
Children's Farm
Zoo

95

VIRGINIA

210

PRINCE
GEORGE'S
COUNTY

Fort Foote
Park

Potomac River
Waterfront Park

Piscataway Park

National Colonial
Farm Museum

Piscataway

Marshall Hall

373

Accokeek

227

210   Mattawoman
Natural Environment

Indian Head

Myrtle Grove
Wildlife
Management
Area

General Smallwood
State Park

224

Thomas Stone
National Historic
Site

Pisgah

CHARLES
COUNTY

225

La Plata

425

Doncaster State Forest

334

Doncaster

Ironsides

McConchie

Port Tobacco

301

Hill
Top

6

Welcome

Port Tobacco R.

6

Nanjemoy

425

Nanjemoy Cr.

Wades
Bay

Potomac River

6

224

Riverside

Merrick
Boys Camp

Homes of Indians and Revolutionaries: Western Prince George's and Charles Counties

Md. 210, 224, and 6, along the Potomac

South of Washington, the Maryland bank of the Potomac retains elements of traditional Southern Maryland culture amid modern metropolitan expansion. Until the mid-1930s, the portions of Prince George's and Charles Counties adjacent to the Potomac contained worn-out tobacco fields, scrub wood lots, historic plantation houses and churches, waterfront villages, marshy wetlands, and assorted gambling establishments. English, African, and American Indian influences blended here to create discernibly different family patterns and social institutions from those in other parts of the state. Then the Southern Electric Cooperative brought cheap electricity in 1938; water and sewer lines were extended south along the Potomac after World War II, and government installations like the U.S. Naval Ordnance Station at Indian Head brought new residents. Improved roads and suburban growth have since increased the population substantially, created problems of pollution in the river, and reduced farm acreage.

Md. 210 (Indian Head Hwy.) is a multilane, divided highway that links Washington's South Capitol St. with the U.S. Naval Ordnance Center at Indian Head, 22 miles to the south. Primarily a commuter's highway, the road itself offers little interest to the traveler, but secondary roads along its route pass through evocative countryside.

A scene at the Charles County Fair during the Depression. Proud young women display their winning entries in the sewing competition.

Oxon Hill

Oxon Hill Children's Farm Zoo, a federal park dating from 1967,
lies on the Potomac just inside the Capital Beltway and west of Md. 210.
The National Park Service at one time envisioned a national parkway on
the Maryland bank of the Potomac similar to the George Washington
Memorial Parkway, which runs along the Virginia bank from Langley to
Mount Vernon. The vision never materialized, but riverfront land remains
in government hands, including 485 acres that once supported a work
farm for Washington's St. Elizabeth's Hospital. The Oxon Hill Children's
Farm Zoo aims to teach urban children the realities of rural life at the turn
of the century and includes hands-on educational activities.

Oxon Hill Manor via Oxon Hill Rd.

Leave Md. 210 and, just south of the Capital Beltway, take Oxon Hill
Rd., which travels between the river and Md. 210 through an area that
was home to family estates until the 1950s. Councillor John Addison (d.
1709) originally purchased the surrounding land, then known as St. Elizabeth's. His son Thomas (d. 1727) built the original Oxon Hill house,
which stood about half a mile from the road, near the Potomac; the
house burned down in 1895. Thomas's grandson had the lands resurveyed and in 1767 incorporated them into an estate known as **Oxon Hill
Manor,** named presumably for the family's Oxonian connections. John
Hanson, president of the United States under the Articles of Confederation in 1781–82, who earlier owned a farm near Port Tobacco, died at
Oxon Hill on November 15, 1783. Near this site, Sumner Welles (1892–
1960), President Franklin Roosevelt's undersecretary of state from 1937 to
1943, completed a new house in 1928. The U.S. Department of the Interior listed the mansion on the National Register of Historic Places in 1978.

Fort Foote Park via Fort Foote Rd.

Following Oxon Hill Rd., turn right onto Fort Foote Rd. and drive toward the river, where you will encounter **Fort Foote Park,** a small picnic area on the site of a Civil War fort that guarded Washington from
these steep bluffs. While a young man of 24, William H. Seward Jr., son
of Lincoln's secretary of state, supervised the fort's construction. The
stone gun emplacements and the remains of reinforced earthworks, as
well as two unused 25-ton Rodman guns are still visible.

St. John's Church via Livingston Rd.

Fort Foote Rd. circles back to Oxon Hill Rd. After turning right, one
soon comes to Livingston Rd., formerly the main north-south thoroughfare before construction of Md. 210. Livingston Rd. continues south, paralleling Md. 210. It crosses Broad Creek and proceeds to **St. John's Episcopal Church,** on the right, at the edge of the woods on Old St. John's
Way. This brick structure, built in 1766, is a rebuilding of a church constructed in the 1720s. After remodeling the interior in 1820, the congregation replaced the earlier clear panes with stained-glass windows. The
church serves one of Maryland's original parishes, which has changed its
name several times, in a progression that reflects the state's early history:
Piscataway, St. John's, King George's, St. John's.

In the churchyard stands the faded gravestone of Enoch M. Lyles,

St. John's Church, Broad Creek, in the 1930s. It underwent restoration in the early 1970s.

killed in a duel on August 7, 1805. Lyles's father allegedly encouraged the engagement, confident of his son's superior marksmanship. The stone reads in part:

> Yet oh, what hand can paint thy parents' woe,
> God only can punish the hand that gave the blow.

Immediately south of the old church, Livingston Rd. meets Fort Washington Rd. Just before this junction, look for **Harmony Hall** off toward the river. Enoch Magruder may have built this 2½-story brick house, known then as Battersea, in the late 1760s. In 1793–94 two brothers, John and Walter Dulany Addison and their brides rented the house. Their happy cohabitation inspired the new name.

Turn right on Fort Washington Rd. and right again, onto Riverview Rd., for an optional trip to **Potomac River Waterfront Park,** a modest green space that overlooks Broad Creek from the south. Continuing on Riverview Rd. leads one back to Fort Washington Rd.

Fort Washington

Fort Washington Rd. leads to the Potomac River and the first fort erected to defend the federal city of Washington. In 1795 George Washington himself selected the site. The fort rests on high ground above Piscataway Creek, where the Potomac, bending north to the District of Columbia, is visible for miles in both directions. The government purchased the site in 1808 and the following year completed work on the fort, named Fort Warburton after the estate on which it stood. (Warburton Manor, patented in 1661, had been the home of the Digges family, descended from Edward Digges, governor of Virginia from 1652 to 1689.) The fort became a major focus of concern when, in August 1814, a British expeditionary force landed at Benedict and began a march to Washington. Capt. Sam Dyson, commander of the 60-man garrison, had orders, if attacked by land, to blow up the fort and retire. On August 27, three days after the British burned Washington by land attack, a British diversionary and support squadron still advanced slowly up the Potomac. After two hours of bombardment from the relatively small British force on the river, Captain Dyson abandoned the fort and blew up the magazine without firing a shot. The British secured the fort's supplies and sailed six more miles to undefended Alexandria, which meekly surrendered and supplied the invaders with tons of goods as well as 21 prize vessels.

Captain Dyson was court-martialed for this fiasco, and within days after the British retreat, Maj. Pierre Charles L'Enfant began constructing the fort that now stands here. L'Enfant, the temperamental Parisian who designed the basic plan of the District of Columbia, quarreled with the War Department in 1815 and was replaced by Lt. Col. Walker K. Armistead. Work on the fort finally ended in 1824, and it was named for Washington—perhaps in an effort to forget the embarrassments of 10 years earlier. (L'Enfant, who never received adequate compensation for his work, died penniless in 1825 at another Digges family plantation in northern Prince George's County. In 1909, Congress appropriated money for his memorial at Arlington National Cemetery.)

A deep dry moat encircles the entire structure, which is built of granite from nearby Occoquan and trimmed with sandstone from Aquia Creek, both on the Virginia side of the Potomac. A drawbridge leads to a massive Roman arch. The entrance is guarded by a portcullis, flanked by high brick guardhouses built into thick walls which rise 60 feet above the ground. Three levels of gun emplacements, including one at water level, point toward the river. During the Civil War, Fort Foote, upriver, replaced Fort Washington as the capital's principal defense against a river invasion. The garrison at Fort Washington mainly fought boredom and bad weather. In 1939 the Department of the Interior took over the site, only to return it to the army during World War II (it served as the Adjutant General's School and then a prisoner of war camp). Like Oxon Hill Farm and Fort Foote, it has been part of the National Capital Park System since 1946.

Piscataway via Md. 223

Departing Fort Washington, the traveler may take Old Fort Rd., which branches southeast from the fort as an alternative to Md. 210 and Livingston Rd. Follow Old Fort Rd. across Indian Head Hwy. (210) to Livingston Rd., which travels south across Piscataway Creek to an intersection with Md. 223. A sharp turn left on Md. 223 leads to the white settlers' village named **Piscataway,** which owed its name to Maryland's best-known tribe of American Indians.

Piscataway was an important shipping center in the 18th century. A tobacco inspection warehouse was located here, and the town flourished briefly before the Revolution. George Washington advised all foreign ships trading with Mount Vernon to anchor across the Potomac in the fresh waters of Piscataway Creek for a few weeks to destroy the ship-eating teredo worms. For nearby planters Piscataway became a social center, where they imbibed imported madeira and rum with the merchants who supplied them. Philip Fithian, a New Jersey tutor hired by Robert Carter of Virginia, noted in 1774 that a woman with two "bouncing daughters" eager to find a husband among the visiting Scottish traders kept the tavern here.

After the Revolution, deep plowing by local farmers led to heavy silting of local creeks and rivers. Piscataway Creek quickly filled with silt, and by the 1830s more than two miles separated the village from navigable water. Like many isolated areas in Charles and St. Mary's Counties, the locale had a brief 20th-century heyday during Prohibition. "Piscataway corn" reportedly became a favorite beverage in Alexandria speakeasies, and the soldiers at nearby Fort Washington apparently guaranteed that the moonshiners had plenty of sugar for their stills. Now little more than a crossroads, the town and its few buildings hint at an interesting past.

Maryland's Piscataway Indians

Piscataway Creek rises near Andrews Air Force Base and flows gently west to the Potomac, widening for its last two miles into a broad estuary. The Piscataways and earlier tribes lived along this estuary for centuries. When Leonard Calvert and his small group of settlers arrived at the mouth of the Potomac in March 1634, one of their first actions was a courtesy call to the Piscataway tayac, equivalent to an emperor, at his village along the creek. Father Andrew White described the encounter in his account of Maryland's origins:

Here our governour had good advice given him, not to land for good and all, before hee had beene with the Emperour of Paschattoway, and had declared unto him the cause of our comming: which was, first to learne them a divine Doctrine, which would lead their soules to a place of happinesse after this life were ended: and also to enrich them with such ornaments of a civill life, wherewith our Countrey doth abound: and this Emperour being satisfied, none of the inferiour Kings would stirre. In conformity to this advice, hee tooke two Pinnaces, his owne, and another hired at Virginia; and leaving the ship before Saint Clements at Anchor, went up the river, and landing on the south-side, and finding the Indians fled for feare, came to Patomeck Towne, where the king being a child, Archihau his uncle governed both him, and his Countrey for him. Hee gave all the company good wellcome; and one of the company having entred into a little discourse with him touching the errours of their religion, hee seemed well pleased therewith; and at his going away desired him to returne unto him againe, telling him hee should live at his Table, his men should hunt for him, and hee would divide all with him.

From hence they went to Paschattoway. All were heere armed: 500 Bow-men came to the Water-side. The Emperour himself more fearelesse then the rest, came privately aboord, where hee was courteously entertained; and understanding wee came in a peaceable manner, bade us welcome, and gave us leave to sit down in what place of his kingdome wee pleased. While this King was aboard, all the Indians came to the Water-side, fearing treason, whereupon two of the Kings men, that attended him in our shippe were appointed to row on shore to quit them of this feare: but they refusing to goe for feare of the popular fury; the interpretours standing on the deck shewed the King to them that he was in safety, where-with they were satisfied. In this journey the Governour entertained Captaine Henry Fleete and his three barkes; who accepted a proportion in beaver trade to serve us, being skillfull in the tongue, and well beloved of the natives.

Apparently the Piscataways occupied both banks, including the strategic point selected for Fort Washington. Father White established a mission here in the 1630s and wrote a catechism and grammar in the local language. By 1642, however, due to a constant danger from raiding Susquehannocks, the mission had moved south to the Port Tobacco River. The Piscataways looked to the Calvert government for protection from the Susquehannocks and from the aggressive colonists who disturbed their tribal life.

Somewhere along the creek, possibly near Fort Washington, the Susquehannocks built a fort after their defeat by the Iroquois in 1673. Suspected by everyone, they were blamed for raids on both sides of the Potomac which they claimed had been committed by the Seneca. Col. John Washington joined his Virginia militia with a Maryland force led by Thomas Truman to beseige the fort and drive the Susquehannocks away. The Indians held out for seven weeks, until a group of five chiefs came out to negotiate under a flag of truce. The chiefs were murdered, and the frightened survivors crept out of the fort at night and crossed the Potomac into Virginia, where they waged a series of revenge raids. Nathaniel Bacon's expedition against the Indians in 1676 led to the opening shots of Bacon's Rebellion.

Even with the threat of their traditional enemies removed, the Piscataways were unable to resist the settlers' encroachments on their land. In 1697, Tayac Ochotomaquah and a large number from his tribe moved to the mountains of Virginia and refused to come back, despite the urging of their Jesuit defenders. The group remained on the upper Potomac, then drifted north to take refuge in the Long House of the Five Nations. During these migrations, they became known by the Iroquois name of Conoy. In 1735 Lord Baltimore began granting the remaining Piscataway lands to European settlers.

The **site of Moyaone,** the Indian village marked on Capt. John Smith's 1608 map as a "king's house," is located closer to the Potomac than was Piscataway, just below the creek entrance along Bryan Point Rd. This village may have been burned during reprisals following the 1622 massacre of Virginia colonists led by Powhatan's half brother Opechancanough or, according to Alice Ferguson, it was sacked by the "Sinniquos" in 1628. (Whatever the cause, the surviving Piscataways established another village on Piscataway Creek, where they were living when the Maryland settlers arrived.)

Alice L. L. and Henry G. Ferguson, who owned the farm that included the site of Moyaone, began excavations here in 1935 and unearthed extensive ossuaries, in which the Piscataways placed their dead. Since that time, archaeological and anthropological studies at Moyaone have been conducted in cooperation with the Smithsonian Institution. Digs along the creek and nearby have uncovered hundreds of Indian skeletons and artifacts, including thousands of tiny blue, glazed trade beads and thin disks stamped with the rose and thistle. Studies indicate that the site was occupied for hundreds of years by people of varying cultural levels; some cultures may date to the early Christian era. The ancestors of the Piscataways probably came to Southern Maryland between 900 and 1300. None of the excavation sites is clearly marked or accessible to the public, undoubtedly from a desire to protect them from unwanted souvenir hunters. Descendants of the Piscataways are now using provisions of current law to reclaim bones of their ancestors from collections at the Maryland Office of Archaeology and the Smithsonian. (The Potomac tribes honored the bones of their dead and sometimes moved them when the group migrated permanently to another location.)

The Piscataway and related tribes did not completely disappear from Southern Maryland. The Piscataway-Conoy Confederacy, Piscataway Nation, and the Maryland Indian Heritage Society represent small groups that claim tribal remnants in such locations as the village of Piscataway, Port Tobacco, La Plata, Accokeek, and Allens Fresh in Charles County and Brandywine, Clinton, Oxon Hill, Rosaryville, and Upper Marlboro in Prince George's County. These groups estimate that between 5,000 and 7,000 people in Southern Maryland have genetic connections to the Piscataways, although the tribe itself has disappeared. The 1990 Census counted 761 people of American Indian descent in Charles County and 2,339 in Prince George's County. (Montgomery County counted 1,841 and Baltimore City 2,555.)

Piscataway National Park and National Colonial Farm

From Piscataway, return south to Livingston Rd. and follow it south to the junction with Farmington Rd. and turn right. Farmington Rd. leads to **Piscataway National Park.** Occupying adjacent land along the Potomac River and Piscataway Creek, the park preserves Piscataway Indian village sites as well as some of the Maryland shoreline across from George Washington's home, Mount Vernon.

Farmington Rd. bends south and takes one to **Christ Church** (1745). Fire destroyed the original interior of the church in 1856, and it was rebuilt the following year; only the brick walls bespeak its pre-Revolution origins. The first church at this location was a private chapel built in 1698 and officially named a chapel of ease for Piscataway Parish in 1729.

At the intersection of Bryan Point Rd., turn right toward the **National Colonial Farm,** operated by the Accokeek Foundation as a recreation of a mid-18th-century farm. Buildings and fields, including a useful herb garden and orchard, demonstrate the realities of a working farm of the period. During warm weather months, persons dressed in colonial attire portray typical residents and discuss their numerous chores and way of life. Programs also include environmental studies and historical research. Mount Vernon is clearly visible on the wooded Virginia shores almost directly across the Potomac from the farm.

Marshall Hall and Chapman's Landing

From the National Colonial Farm, follow Cactus Hill Rd. and within two miles turn right onto Barry's Hill Rd. and right again on Md. 227 (Cactus Hill becomes Old Marshall Hall Rd. and leads back to Livingston; taking Livingston south brings the traveler to Md. 227).

Md. 227 dead-ends at the remains of **Marshall Hall,** once a popular getaway that featured food, rides, and gambling. Thomas Marshall purchased land here in 1728, and the family farmed it until the 1860s. Postwar economic depression may have forced the Marshalls to sell. Between the 1880s and 1940s, a cluster of "river arks" anchored at nearby Bull Town Cove on the county line. Entrepreneurs on these flat-bottomed boats catered to vessels traveling to and from Washington, offering everything from haircuts, medicine, and general merchandise to whiskey, gambling, and prostitutes. Marshall Hall became famous as a gambling spot between 1949 and 1968, when Charles County offered the only legal slot machines in the United States outside Nevada. The Pot of Gold Casino, once located here, housed hundreds of slot machines and attracted customers from near and afar. Now the site is part of the Piscataway National Park.

Return to Md. 210 via Md. 277 and turn right toward Indian Head. At this point, Md. 210 roughly parallels Chapman's Landing Rd., named for the family that occupied a 19th-century plantation called Mount Aventine. Nearby **Chapman Point** on the river served as a ferry crossing during the colonial period and a fishing ground in the 19th century. A government official in 1876 reported that herring, rockfish, white and yellow perch, sunfish, catfish, bullhead, "Gizzard shad and Mullet sucker" all were caught here. Pomonkey Creek, located just to the north, enjoyed a high reputation for its spring water. The creek took its name from the Pamunkey Indian village that existed near its mouth in the 17th century.

Indian Head

Md. 210 terminates in the town of **Indian Head** (3,531 pop.), which abuts the **U.S. Naval Ordnance Station,** both located on a Potomac peninsula formed by Mattawoman Creek. Early-18th-century charts identified the peninsula as "Pamunkey Indian Lands."

Ensign Robert Brooke Dashiell, whom the navy in 1890 appointed to build a proving ground for naval ordnance here, thought the location the most desolate on the Potomac. He employed local civilians to help build and maintain the facility. A smokeless powder plant was constructed in 1898. The installation expanded and contracted in times of war and peace, adapting its functions as weaponry changed. During World War I, the plant produced torpedoes. In 1921 the torpedo testing was moved downriver to Dahlgren, Virginia, which had a larger range, but by this time the Indian Head complex had turned to more advanced projects. Robert H. Goddard, the rocket pioneer, experimented with propellants here during the 1920s, and scientists still do. During the 1940s, the navy established an **Explosive Ordnance Disposal School** on Stump Neck across the creek; teams from the school deal with emergencies around the world.

Mattawoman Natural Environment Area

Depart Indian Head via Md. 225, which leaves Md. 210 a short distance from the eastern edge of the town and, headed south, crosses the marshlands of the **Mattawoman Natural Environment Area** to a junction with Md. 224. Turn right on Md. 224, which circles the peninsula, crossing the many small streams that wander through pine and scrub woodlands before draining into the Potomac.

Mattawoman Creek rises above Cedarville State Forest in Prince George's County and flows west to the Potomac River, forming the boundary between Prince George's and Charles Counties west of U.S. 301. The creek becomes swampy as it nears the Potomac, creating wetlands that the state has developed into "natural environment areas." As the creek widens into an estuary, the Potomac River flows in a long bend, which begins at Piscataway Creek and curves around to Port Tobacco River. The names encountered on this landscape—Chicamuxen, Nanjemoy, Mattawoman, Pomonkey—remind us of the residents who preceded the English colonists.

General Smallwood State Park

About four miles south on the right a sign marks the entrance to the **General Smallwood State Park,** the site of **Smallwood's Retreat,** once the home of Gen. William Smallwood (1732–92). The state acquired the 629 acres of land for this park in 1954 from the Smallwood Foundation, a private group that had begun reconstructing the house, then in ruins, and later sought state aid. Work on the 1½-story brick dwelling was finally completed in 1958. The first floor is furnished with pieces from the revolutionary period, some from the Smallwood family.

During the Revolution, Smallwood's name and that of his Maryland Battalion were synonymous with rear-guard, last-ditch valor. In July 1776, Smallwood marched from Annapolis with his Maryland troops, uniformed in rich red, to answer George Washington's call for soldiers to defend New York from British invasion. At the Battle of Long Island, the first real test the inexperienced Continental Army faced, most of the American militia fired at and then fled from the attacking British and Hessian troops. Two hundred of Smallwood's Marylanders, under the command of Maj. Mordecai Gist, took part in repeated headlong attacks that held the enemy at bay. Smallwood's battalion lost 37 percent of its men to injury, death, or capture, but his Maryland soldiers became the famed "Old Line," and he was promoted to brigadier.

After Long Island, Smallwood and his men frequently received the most dangerous assignments. Smallwood became a major general in 1780, and some of his soldiers stayed through the war, marching with the French to Yorktown in 1781. The General Assembly elected Smallwood governor of Maryland in 1785. Three years later the lifelong bachelor retired to the little house located here. The Sons of the American Revolution in 1898 erected a five-foot granite monument by the supposed site of his grave, which had been unmarked until that date.

Beyond the park, Md. 224 passes through the village of **Chicamuxen** then runs into Md. 344, which slants southeast to Md. 6 and **Doncaster State Forest.**

Continue the tour by following Md. 224, which turns to the right and becomes Riverside Rd. The road winds around the peninsula, passing bays and old river landings that derive their names from early settlers. **Wades Bay** is named for Zachariah Wade, who owned land here in the 17th century. Bored Civil War soldiers reportedly grew hemp on the nearby waterfront land and sold it for cordage. Dr. Grace G. Purse willed 148 acres east of the bay to the state after 1961; it now awaits development as **Purse State Park.** A right turn at Md. 6 takes one to **Riverside,** an old steamboat landing and river resort.

A few miles north of Riverside on Md. 6 the traveler will cross **Nanjemoy Creek** and farther on pass through the village of the same name, which derives from the Nangemeick Indians. Md. 6 joins Md. 344 at **Doncaster.** Known from this point eastward as the La Plata–Doncaster Rd., Md. 6 next takes one through the **Doncaster State Forest,** more than 1,500 acres of pine woodlands, and on to **Ironsides.**

Araby and Old Durham Church via Md. 425

Less than half a mile north of Ironsides, on Md. 425, one may view the restored mansion of **Araby,** built before 1760. George Washington's diary refers to Araby as the home of the Widow Eilbeck, whose daughter became the wife of George Mason, master of Gunston Hall, across the Potomac, and author of the Virginia Bill of Rights.

Slightly more than a mile south on Md. 425 is the **Old Durham Church.** Erected in about 1732, this plain brick building was altered in the late 18th century and restored in 1932 as a memorial to General Smallwood, who served as a vestryman of that parish. The **Smallwood Memorial Bell Tower** was constructed from bricks salvaged from the ruined house that belonged to the general's sister. The minutes of the Old Durham vestry indicate that the parishioners set the time for Sunday services by a sundial in the churchyard. The vestry book of 1779 provided that "in Case it is cloudy," time would be set by "the majority of Watches which the Owners, on their Honor, think right."

Md. 6 travels farther east, through wooded countryside and the villages of **Hill Top, Welcome,** and **McConchie.** Just before crossing the Port Tobacco River, the road intersects Rose Hill Rd.

Thomas Stone National Historic Site via Rose Hill Rd.

Turn left for a mile up this hilly road to get a view of **Betty's Delight** (private) and **Rose Hill** (private), both of which occupy lofty positions above the river valley. Rose Hill, a handsome five-part mansion, contains many interior details that reflect the first owner's attention to detail. Dr. Gustavus Richard Brown constructed the house after 1783 on land originally part of Betty's Delight. George Washington's friend and physician, Dr. Brown is buried at the bottom of the lower terrace, overlooking the valley.

Slightly more than a mile farther north on Rose Hill Rd. lies **Haber de Venture.** Restored to its 19th-century appearance and open to the public, Haber de Venture has been named the **Thomas Stone National Historic Site.** Thomas Stone (1743–87) was one of four Maryland signers of the Declaration of Independence. He and his wife are buried on the property.

Stone built the main block of this unusual house around 1771. It combines several early Southern Maryland styles. The main section is a 1½-story brick structure with a gambrel roof. A brick passageway leads to the frame wing where, tradition says, Stone once had his office. The present two-story brick and frame wing was built around 1840 on the site of a former kitchen. Haber de Venture remained in the Stone family until 1936, after which the paneling and corner cupboards of the first floor were removed, along with family portraits, to form the Colonial Room at the Baltimore Museum of Art.

Returning to Md. 6 and turning east leads to charming Port Tobacco and U.S. 301. Continuing north to Md. 225 and turning right takes one to La Plata and U.S. 301.

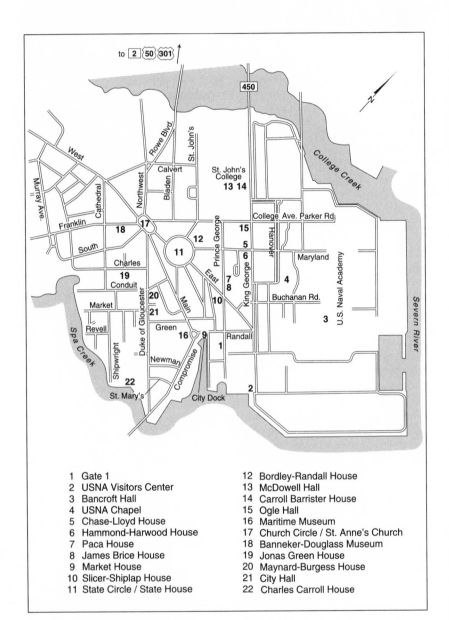

1 Gate 1
2 USNA Visitors Center
3 Bancroft Hall
4 USNA Chapel
5 Chase-Lloyd House
6 Hammond-Harwood House
7 Paca House
8 James Brice House
9 Market House
10 Slicer-Shiplap House
11 State Circle / State House
12 Bordley-Randall House
13 McDowell Hall
14 Carroll Barrister House
15 Ogle Hall
16 Maritime Museum
17 Church Circle / St. Anne's Church
18 Banneker-Douglass Museum
19 Jonas Green House
20 Maynard-Burgess House
21 City Hall
22 Charles Carroll House

Annapolis

Annapolis (20' alt., 33,187 pop.), a gem among America's historic places, combines the intimacies of a small town with the amenities of a city. As capital of Maryland and seat of Anne Arundel County since the 17th century, Annapolis has played a major role in the theater of Chesapeake politics and has made occasional forays onto the national stage. As home of the U.S. Naval Academy and St. John's College, Annapolis enjoys unusual intellectual distinction for a town its size. Politics and education here have felt the tempering effects of southern character—homey hospitality and the enjoyable pursuits of sailing, horse racing, gambling, the theater, fine foods, and after-dinner conversation.

A rich architectural heritage gives Annapolis the quality of a museum, but use and reuse of the buildings for modern purposes gives the town peculiar vitality. When in 1965 the Department of the Interior designated it a National Historic Landmark, Secretary Stewart Udall noted that "Annapolis has the greatest concentration of 18th-century buildings anywhere in the United States." Residents use the buildings in much the same fashion as did their forebears—to live, entertain, make money, craft political deals, and fashion an island of civilization amid the natural beauty of the great Chesapeake Bay. Annapolis encourages walkers, talkers, and sailors—a yeasty combination that for more than 300 years has created a stimulating human environment on the Severn River.

Annapolis originated as a refuge for Virginia dissenters—Puritans—who were fleeing the established Church of England in that colony. Lord Baltimore welcomed these new settlers in 1649. Led by Richard Bennett, the Puritans created a settlement on the river's north bank (now under water) called Providence. Within a year, population in the region had grown so rapidly that the assembly created a new county, named "Annarundell," after the wife of Cecil, second Lord Baltimore.

By 1670 a new settlement, Arundelton, had grown up across the Severn from Providence. In 1684 Robert Proctor, an innkeeper who owned Proctor's Landing on the South River, along with Richard Hill, a merchant and legislator, donated 100 acres for a town, on the small neck between Acton's (now Spa) Creek and Deep (now College) Creek. Surveyor Richard Beard laid out "Anne Arundel Town," which soon thereafter supplanted St. Mary's City as the provincial capital. Attempts had been made as early as 1662 to move Maryland's seat of government to Anne Arundel County. The settlements along the Severn, centrally located, stood at the narrowest part of the bay, thus making travel convenient for those residing on the Eastern Shore. In 1689 the Protestant majority succeeded in bloodlessly overthrowing the Calverts' proprietary regime. The Anglican Church became the official established religion in 1692 (though not legally until 1704), and Catholics were forbidden to worship in public.

William and Mary, the new Protestant monarchs in England, approved of this arrangement and in 1694 appointed Sir Francis Nicholson as the royal governor of Maryland. Nicholson, an experienced administrator, immediately persuaded the assembly to move the seat of government to Anne Arundel Town. After 1695 its new name honored Princess Anne, the future queen of England. For the next 80 years, Annapolis reigned as the center of Maryland colonial life and a thriving exemplar of Anglo-American gentility.

Nicholson adhered to a stern sense of order but demonstrated imagination, both of which influenced the layout of the new capital. He altered the original survey by adding two circles on the knoll above the harbor—one for the State House and one for the Anglican Church—each with radiating streets that followed the main points of the compass. To the north, his plan added house lots in a section called Bloomsbury Square. Such odoriferous trades as tanning and brewing were relegated to the perimeter of town. A "shipcarpenter's lot" appeared along the waterfront, where Nicholson planned tobacco warehouses and a customs office. Two days of the week the governor set aside for markets. In 1696 he persuaded the assembly to charter King William's School, a grammar school that laid the foundation for St. John's College. About the same time Dinah Nuthead moved her late husband's printing press from St. Mary's City to Annapolis. The transfer of power was complete. Catholic Southern Maryland became a backwater.

Nicholson left Maryland in 1698 to become the royal governor of Virginia, where he later designed Williamsburg. Annapolis developed into a provincial capital known throughout the Tidewater for its social events. As the wealth of the colony increased during the 18th century, so did the amenities of its capital city. Annapolis merchants, dependent on tobacco commerce controlled by London factors, had learned the trade's intricacies and were slowly developing their own sources of capital. By the 1740s Chesapeake planters converged on Annapolis, particularly while the assembly was in session, to attend the theater, dance at balls, and wager on races. In contrast to their (increasingly materialistic) Puritan brethren in New England, Maryland planters considered the breeding of fast horses a gentleman's calling; they competed with Virginians in the importation of fine Thoroughbreds. Visitors commented on the elegance of clothing worn by the young ladies at Annapolis assembly balls and remarked on "the playing of cards, dice and backgammon."

During this 18th-century "Golden Age," Annapolis provided a stage upon which doctors, lawyers, merchants, and planters mixed intellectual pursuits with heavy doses of frivolity. A few of these fellows formed the Tuesday Club, preferring the clever sallies of witty conversation and superb dinners—liberally accented with wine, brandy, and punch—to mere philosophical discussion. Meanwhile, lawyers, merchants, and successful tobacco planters built beautifully proportioned Georgian (named for the Hanoverian kings) town houses, many of which still stand.

When in 1771 George Washington lost £8 at the September races, he consoled himself by going to the theater (four times) and attending balls (three). He returned a year later, won £13 on the horses, lost £5 at cards, attended the theater four times, and appeared at one ball. Yet the famed amenities of Annapolis could do little to stem rising resentments against

British mercantile policies. In 1765 Parliament passed the Stamp Act, and Zachariah Hood, formerly a merchant in Annapolis, arrived from England to serve as stamp agent for the crown. Samuel Chase—then a young, ambitious attorney—led a crowd that paraded an effigy of the agent and burned it over a flaming tar barrel. After another mob ransacked the stamp agent's new office, Hood fled to Long Island. Annapolitans also supported the later nonimportation agreements, by which the colonies jointly boycotted all taxed articles, including tea. Anthony Stewart's brig *Peggy Stewart*, named after his daughter, arrived at Annapolis on October 14, 1774. Word spread that Stewart had defied public opinion and paid the tea duty. A mob of radical patriots soon threatened Stewart and his family, and he reluctantly ordered his ship run aground on the far side of Spa Creek. Stewart then set afire both ship and cargo in a spectacle that surpassed the Boston Tea Party.

Most of Maryland's leading revolutionaries lived in Annapolis. William Paca, Samuel Chase, and Charles Carroll of Carrollton—all lawyers and signers of the Declaration of Independence—owned Annapolis houses that still stand. Thomas Stone, the fourth Maryland signer, studied law in Annapolis and lived here later in his career.

Annapolis served as the seat of the state revolutionary government and as a staging area for Maryland soldiers assigned to the front lines. French and American troops stopped in the city en route to Yorktown in 1781. (French officers and local ladies found each other mutually attractive.) In November 1783, following the September Paris peace treaty, Congress convened in the Maryland State House. On December 23, Washington resigned his commission as commander in chief of the Continental Army, in a formal ceremony in the Senate chamber of the State House. Congress formally ratified the Treaty of Paris here the following year and adjourned in June 1784.

Annapolis offered itself as the permanent seat for the new federal government, but political considerations eventually resulted in the creation of a new town, the District of Columbia, on the Potomac. Congress never returned to the Severn, and Annapolis lost its eminence in the Tidewater. Before the town settled down as a state capital, however, it played host in 1786 to delegates of five states, who met to consider the need for a stronger federal government. These delegates called for another convention, which met in Philadelphia in 1787 and drafted the Constitution of the United States. Maryland ratified it in April 1788.

When the first federal census was taken in 1790, Baltimore had a population of 13,503 and was the fastest growing city in the new nation. The population of Annapolis stood at about 2,170 and was stagnant at that time. The capital city's decline from international port and social and commercial center had been quick and dramatic. Visitors who remembered Annapolis before the Revolution were astonished at the change. Even so, the old city successfully resisted various attempts by younger, north county upstarts to move the state capital to Baltimore. As early as the Revolution, Congress had built fortifications at Windmill Point near Annapolis. In 1808 the federal government there erected Fort Severn, which may have dissuaded the British from attacking the state capital during the War of 1812. In the Polk administration the government established a naval school at the fort.

Early in the Civil War, on April 22, 1861, Massachusetts troops under

Benjamin F. Butler bypassed riotous Baltimore and arrived in Annapolis by ferryboat. They soon occupied Annapolis and secured the railroad to Washington. Annapolitans did not resist, although one old gentleman was later said to have walked the 30-mile distance between Baltimore and Annapolis twice a week in order to avoid taking the oath of allegiance required to use the railroad. The military turned the buildings of the temporarily vacant naval school into medical wards and, as necessary, made use of St. John's College. After 1862, thousands of paroled prisoners camped in the area west of town while awaiting exchange, and the area to this day is known as Parole.

After the Civil War, the business of state government and the reestablished naval academy sustained the old town. After 1901, when Theodore Roosevelt, a longtime advocate of a powerful navy, became president, the academy achieved the architectural grandeur that has made it a landmark. Several additional square blocks of the city went behind brick walls, and the navy became a presence, sometimes ominous, in city life. Two world wars intensified this influence. Navy officers began to retire in new houses along the four creeks that empty into the river. Annapolis nearly doubled its area in 1950, when the city annexed Eastport, Wardour, and Parole. The end of legal segregation made visible an African American minority that had played a significant role in the city's history—and the nation's. In 1915, in a landmark Supreme Court case, a black Annapolitan won African Americans the right to vote in municipal elections. In the 1990s Annapolis employment remains tied to state government, the defense department, the tourist trade, and pleasure boating—the building, outfitting, and refitting of boats.

Since World War II, downtown demolition and then suburban development have threatened Annapolis; developers have pressed for more parking lots, new housing, and commercial zoning. In the 1950s and '60s preservationists and civic-minded Annapolitans—St. Clair Wright and other members of Historic Annapolis, Inc., among them—largely turned back the call to raze and renew the old part of the town now known as the historic district. Improved connections with Washington and Baltimore—U.S. 50 and I-97—have only turned up the pressure on land use.

Although menaced by the automobile, Annapolis remains a pleasant place to live and a walker's haven; every street corner supplies continuity with the past. The town requires a pedestrian's pace. During 1783–84, when none of the streets was paved and oxcarts moved up and down Main Street, Thomas Jefferson and James Madison once walked in conversation from their rooming house to the State House, where they observed the town from its magnificent dome. Such graduates of the U.S. Naval Academy as Jimmy Carter and H. Ross Perot escorted their "drags" (dates) on these streets; Perot met his future wife here. The buildings and walkways recall generations of political debates, witty exchanges, financial deals, romantic flirtations, and momentous decisions.

In warm weather and with a light breeze, the simplest and most pleasant way to arrive in Annapolis is by water. The harbor and city dock usually provide adequate anchorage; beware, however, of heavy visitation days like those in October, when the city stages its annual boat show.

By land, the visitor departs U.S. 50 at Rowe Blvd. and drives south. The narrow, tightly controlled streets of Annapolis make automobile parking so difficult in peak season that the best approach may be to leave one's car at the Navy–Marine Corps Stadium (from Rowe Blvd. turn right onto Farragut Rd.); a frequent shuttle operates between the stadium and the historic district. Parking by the day runs to a few dollars, and the shuttle, which makes a loop with several stops downtown, is free on weekends. The lot is open 10:00–8:00 in the summer months, 10:00–6:00 at other times.

On Rowe Blvd. just beyond the stadium, the visitor passes the **J. Millard Tawes State Office Building, District Court Building,** and **Courts of Appeal** on the right and, on the left (parking available) the **Maryland State Archives** (350 Rowe Blvd.). This modern archive facility opened in 1986. It houses the earliest records of the colony and state, a spacious reading room open to researchers Tuesday through Saturday, a gift shop, and permanent exhibits, including "Charting the Chesapeake," an unequaled collection of historical Maryland maps. (To view a list of the extensive holdings of the archives, see its website, at http://www.mdarchives.state.md.us.)

The Annapolis and Anne Arundel County Conference and Visitors Bureau has opened a **Visitors Center** in the first block of West St. To reach it, take the shuttle from the stadium lot or follow Rowe Blvd. across College Creek, bear right onto Northwest St., and turn right into a small parking lot. The center will be straight ahead as one enters the lot. Visitors are encouraged to stop here for information. There are a couple of parking garages nearby. The metered parking farther downtown fills up early in the day.

All of the following tours of Annapolis begin, logically, at **City Dock,** the heart of the town. A **visitor information kiosk** stands next to the Harbormaster Building at about the middle of the dock on its east-

Annapolis's City Dock in the late 1930s

The dock as it appeared a half-century later

ern side. One may there obtain walking maps and other information. In the recent past, as Annapolis has developed into a summertime tourist mecca, a number of professional tours and guidebooks have become available. City Dock also offers food and drink, public restrooms, and telephones.

Standing at the foot of Main St., one can imagine a time when warehouses surrounded this loading point, some of them filled with tobacco headed to Europe, others storing imported goods on behalf of merchant planters. Larger ocean-going vessels can no longer enter these shallow waters, and the dock now serves primarily recreational needs. Fishing boats and pleasure craft tie up here year-round. In the summer months, small sail and motor craft languidly move in and out of the harbor, as much to be seen as to see.

At the entrance to City Dock on Spa Creek, the visitor has a panoramic view from **Susan Campbell Park.** One can see across Spa Creek to Sycamore Point in Eastport as well as down the creek to the confluence of the Severn River and the bay. Annapolis occupies four pieces of land that jut into the Severn River and Chesapeake Bay. The area known as West Annapolis developed on a squatty neck formed by Weems Creek on the north and College Creek on the south. Most of historic Annapolis is located on the neck formed by College Creek and Spa Creek. Eastport occupies the narrower neck formed by Spa Creek and Back Creek, and the Annapolis Golf Club sits on still another short neck formed by Back Creek and Lake Ogleton.

TOUR A: CRUISING THE NAVAL ACADEMY AND RETURNING VIA COLONIAL HOMES AND GARDENS

Gate 1 of the United States Naval Academy (at the eastern end of Randall Street—a few short blocks to the right if one's back is to the water at City Dock) provides the main public entrance to the nation's training ground for naval officers. The academy covers about 300 acres and at any one time—counting firstclassmen (fourth-year students) through fourthclassmen (newcomers or plebes)—trains 4,500 men and women. Inside the gate, look for the academy's **Armel-Leftwich Visitors Center**, just past Halsey Field House on the right. Besides offering a variety of informative material and a gift shop with souvenirs, the center serves as the starting point for a tour-guide service, whose modest fees go to the memorial fund of the Naval Academy Athletic Association. It offers free and indispensible maps for self-guided tours.

Thirteen years after organizing the new federal government, Congress in 1802 passed a measure that established a military academy at West Point, New York. Authorities left the training of naval officers to traditional shipboard experience. The aspirants berthed between the crew—forward—and the officers—aft—and hence became known as midshipmen, which is what all students at the academy are still called. As secretary of the navy in 1845–46, the Boston writer and historian George Bancroft strongly endorsed creation of a naval school, and in October 1845 one was opened on the 10-acre site of Fort Severn (to avoid any congressional opposition, Bancroft quietly had control of the fort shifted to the navy). The school at first consisted of a commander, superintendent, three officers, four civilian professors, and several dozen students housed in a few wooden buildings. At the onset of the Civil War, many midshipmen and some staff from seceding states resigned from the academy (Franklin Buchanan, first superintendent, became the ranking admiral in the Confederate States Navy); as a precaution against any mischief that Southern sympathizers in Annapolis might do, the navy shipped the remaining students to Newport, Rhode Island. In September 1865, when the school returned to Annapolis, the new superintendent, Adm. David Dixon Porter, revised the curriculum, added sports facilities, and rebuilt the physical plant.

Naval victories during the Spanish-American War in 1898 established the United States as a world power with a need for both Atlantic and Pacific fleets. The academy grew accordingly in influence and prestige. Beginning in 1899, as if on cue, the architect Ernest Flagg gave the academy an entirely new and impressive demeanor. His structures surround a commons, called "the Yard"—Bancroft Hall, the chapel, superintendent's house, administration building, and classroom structures. They epitomize the Beaux Arts style and remain one of the most impressive groups of buildings in America.

Today young men and, since 1976, women from every state in the Union compete to enter an environment that emphasizes at every turn the discipline and self-sacrifice the naval service demands from both

Graduating midshipmen not long before the United States entered World War II. Their faces reflected the seriousness of the times

sailors and marines. All candidates must be high school graduates or the equivalent, citizens of the United States, unmarried, of good moral character, and between the ages of 17 and 21. In 1949 Wesley Brown, a Marylander, became the first African American to graduate (James Conyers of South Carolina had been the first African American to enter the academy, in 1872; harassment caused him and two other black midshipmen to withdraw before graduation). Lawrence C. Chambers (class of 1952) became the first African American admiral in 1976.

Each year during Commissioning Week, when the middies graduate, Annapolis fills with visitors and well-wishers for a round of parades, parties, and weddings. Music for such events seldom fails to include "Anchors Aweigh," which Lt. Charles A. Zimmerman, an academy bandmaster, composed in 1907.

Not all areas of the academy are open to the public. One can only imagine the sites described in this paragraph. Not far from the Visitors Center are Lejeune and Ricketts Halls, both athletic facilities. Brownson Rd. passes the most expansive green space at the academy, **Farragut Field,** reclaimed lowland that overlooks the wide water of Spa Creek. The spot bears the name of Tennessee-born Adm. David G. Farragut, who in the Battle of Mobile Bay during the Civil War lashed himself in the rigging and declared, "Damn the torpedoes. Full speed ahead." Beyond the field, at a right angle to Brownson Rd., Santee Rd. passes the **Santee Basin** (named for a ship that for many years after the Civil War served as a gunnery-training vessel and occasional brig, or jail, at the academy). There midshipmen tie up the boats they use in learning the fundamentals of sailing. The boats also provide them weekend recreation. Beyond the basin to the right lies **Dewey Field,** this one filled in on the Severn

River side of the grounds. A Vermont native, Adm. George Dewey (Class of 1858) had served with Farragut at Mobile Bay but won fame for his decisive action against the Spanish at the brief Battle of Manila Bay in 1898—a victory that gained the United States Pacific possessions. **Macdonough Hall** stands on the near side of Santee Rd. The Flagg-designed athletic center honors Capt. Thomas Macdonough, victor in the Battle of Lake Champlain in 1814.

From the Visitors Center one can retrace one's steps toward Gate 1, turning right past Lejeune Hall. On the left stands a row of faculty and administrators' houses, many displaying state and whimsical flags in addition to the Stars and Stripes. One may either turn left and follow Porter Rd. or proceed ahead to massive **Dahlgren Hall,** one of the academy buildings open to the public. (Adm. John A. Dahlgren, an early expert in naval ordinance or gunnery, fought in the Civil War.) An architectural twin to Macdonough Hall, it demonstrates the grandeur Flagg wanted in his design for the academy. Inside, find either basketball courts or ice rink, depending on the season, and a snack and sports bar open to the public. A navy seaplane of the kind battleships and cruisers once carried hangs from the high ceiling. Walking through Dahlgren Hall or along Porter Rd. and turning right at Buchanan Rd. leads one to the superintendent's quarters, **Buchanan House,** a place designed before air conditioning and with extensive entertaining being among its purposes. Farther east (with the chapel dome off to one's left) one soon reaches **the Yard.**

Bancroft Hall looms on the right. Named for George Bancroft, this building (or linked compound of buildings) houses the entire brigade of midshipmen and remains one of the largest domitory complexes in the world. It covers 33 acres and contains five miles of corridors. The rotunda, Memorial Hall, and a model midshipman's room are open to the public.

Inside the courtyard, Tecumseh (or T) Court, notice **Tecumseh,** a bronze copy (made in 1930) of the figurehead of the USS *Delaware.* It faces the entrance to Bancroft Hall. Midshipmen color Tecumseh in full warpaint before football games against Army and toss pennies into his quiver for good luck on exams.

The classroom buildings Michelson and Chauvanet Halls form the eastern side of the Yard. Proceed on Stribling Walk toward the **Mexican Monument,** erected to honor the first naval academy men, four of them, killed in action (during the fighting around Vera Cruz in early 1847). Another set of classroom buildings stands to the north, beyond the monument. At the center the old library, **Mahan Hall** (not open to the public), bears the name of Alfred Thayer Mahan, naval historian, strategic theorist, and late-19th-century president of the Naval War College. Behind Mahan Hall, **Alumni Hall** seats more than 5,700 persons for cultural and athletic events. The academy's new library, **Nimitz Hall,** honors the World War II chief of naval operations, Chester W. Nimitz (Class of 1905), a native Texan.

Turning left on the parallel walkways, one passes between two noteworthy landmarks, a well-maintained **gazebo** on the left, where concerts are performed in the summer, and on the right the **Herndon Monument.** This tall shaft commemorates W. L. Herndon, a naval officer who lost his life while assisting victims of a shipwreck during a storm off Cape Hatteras in 1857. The monument supplies the scene of action when, at the end of each academic year, the plebe class endeavors to climb the monument, which has been slathered with lard by upperclassmen, and to retrieve from its pinnacle a plebe's cap and replace it with an upperclassman's cap. Cheered on by the many spectators, the students are reminded of the necessity for teamwork and determination.

Farther along the walk, one approaches what must be the most beautiful of the academy's structures. The **Naval Academy Chapel,** with a massive 200-foot dome, was dedicated in 1908. Tiffany stained-glass windows in the apse and transepts commemorate the nation's naval heroes, Sampson, Mason, Porter, Farragut among them. The **crypt** beneath the chapel contains the bronze and marble sarcophagus of John Paul Jones (1747–92), the Scottish cabin boy who became an American ship commander in the Revolution and whose defiant words "I have not yet begun to fight" remain a U.S. Navy rallying cry. Jones died in Paris and was buried in an unmarked grave; in 1905 American warships ceremoniously carried his remains back to his adopted country.

Blake Rd. passes in front of the chapel. Facing the chapel, follow the road to the right toward Maryland Ave. There, across the street and to the right, **Preble Hall** (which honors a famed naval commander in President Jefferson's undeclared war with Tripolitan pirates, Commo. Edward Preble) houses 50,000 navy artifacts in the **U.S. Naval Academy Museum.** They include Oliver Hazard Perry's battle flag ("Don't Give Up the Ship"), paintings of naval engagements, one of the world's finest collections of ship models, and other relics that illustrate the navy's rich heritage.

North of Preble on Decatur Rd., find **Leahy Hall** and the office of the dean of admissions. Visitors are encouraged to make inquiries. Decatur Rd., named for War of 1812 hero Stephen Decatur, leads past the academy parade ground, **Worden Field,** named for John L. Worden, commander of the USS Monitor when it battled the ironclad CSS Virginia (former USS Merrimac) in 1862. Decatur Rd. leads across Dorsey Creek to more staff housing, the baseball field, observatory, medical clinic, and cemetery.

From Preble Hall the visitor continues the tour by turning right after exiting the museum, proceeding to Gate 3, and leaving the academy grounds on Maryland Ave.

From here, Maryland Ave. heads southwest to State Circle. In the 18th century, it connected the circle to the Severn and became known as Patriots Walk, because Jefferson and Madison supposedly walked this street on their way to and from congressional meetings at the State House. Maryland Ave. displays a variety of architectural styles. They include Georgian, Greek Revival, Federal, French Second Empire, Italianate, and Victorian—often with borrowings—reflecting the changes every generation makes to its visual environment.

An immediate left at Gate 3, onto Hanover St., takes the visitor to the **Peggy Stewart House** (207, private), a 2¹/₂-story brick dwelling built between 1761 and 1764 by Thomas Rutland, an Anne Arundel County planter. The house was extensively altered in 1894, when the roof was changed from gable to hip form. Anthony Stewart, a local merchant, bought the house in 1772 but fled the country after the Peggy Stewart incident (apparently explaining its name), when an angry mob forced him to burn his own ship and its cargo of tea. Stewart's family joined him in exile at the beginning of the Revolution. Thomas Stone, one of the four Maryland signers of the Declaration of Independence, bought the house in 1779 and lived here until his death, in 1783.

The brick residence at **215–17 Hanover St.** (private), built about 1760, served as the rectory of St. Anne's Parish for 125 years. Its most notable resident was the Rev. Jonathan Boucher, clergyman, teacher, wit, and royalist, whose diaries provide a chronicle of life in prerevolutionary Annapolis. Boucher operated a school here for sons of the Tidewater gentry, including George Washington's stepson, John Parke Custis. Washington often stayed here during his frequent visits to Annapolis before the Revolution.

Returning to Maryland Ave., at 9–11 the visitor may stop to admire the **Lockerman-Tilton House,** which probably dates from about 1740. John Rogers, first chancellor of the state of Maryland, lived here, as did the family of Richard Lockerman, who also lived in the Hammond-Harwood House. A later owner was Josephine Tilton, whose husband, Col. Edward McLane Tilton, accompanied Commo. Matthew Perry on his historic trip to Japan in 1854. Commo. Gordon Ellyson, the Navy's first aviator, had lived in the kitchen wing, converted into a separate house.

At the next intersection the visitor comes to King George St., named after King George I, first Hanoverian king of Great Britain (1714–27). It separates the naval academy from the St. John's campus and other civilians on its way to the harbor. Two landmark houses dominate the corner of Maryland Ave. and King George St.—the Chase-Lloyd House and the Hammond-Harwood House.

Chase-Lloyd House

The **Chase-Lloyd House,** 22 Maryland Ave. (right), is one of the few three-story Georgian colonial town houses south of New England. Samuel Chase (1741–1811), son of a poor Anglican clergyman on the Eastern Shore, began construction of this house in 1769 but soon ran out of money and sold the unfinished building in 1771 to Edward Lloyd IV of Wye House on the Eastern Shore. Lloyd hired the noted architect William Buckland to work two and a half more years on the house, particularly the interior, and may have added the third story to provide an unobstructed view of the harbor.

The brick facade features a dentiled and modillioned cornice, topped by a hip-on-hip roof. A pedimented central pavilion indicates the width of the central hall. A three-story, white-columned portico at one side is one of several later additions, including a rear kitchen wing. The garden facade is organized around a large, graceful Palladian window, which lights the central hall. The simplicity of the massive street facade may reflect the taste of Chase, a self-made lawyer-politician who signed the Declaration of Independence and became an associate justice of the U.S. Supreme Court in 1796. Often embroiled in controversy over alleged conflicts of interest, he was impeached in 1805, during the Jefferson administration, but acquitted by the Senate.

The rich, elegant details of the interior—a perfectly positioned Palladian window-stair-screen combination, an Adam-style coffered ceiling in the parlor, and a mahogany-paneled dining room—reflect Lloyd's aristocratic taste. The scion of a long line of rich planters, Lloyd lived at a much more comfortable and leisurely pace than did Chase. He served in a num-

A Palladian window,
illustrating the elegance
of the Chase House
interior

ber of public offices, managed his large Eastern Shore estate, and fathered Edward Lloyd V, who became governor of Maryland in 1809. Frederick Douglass, born a slave on the Lloyd plantation, recalled Edward Lloyd V as "a gentleman of the olden time, elegant in his apparel, dignified in his deportment, a man of few words and weighty presence." Mary Tayloe Lloyd, the youngest daughter of Edward Lloyd IV, married Francis Scott Key in the front parlor of this house in 1802. The Lloyds kept the house for 73 years, then sold it to Miss Hester Anne Chase. Her niece, Mrs. Samuel Ridout, willed the property in 1875 to a foundation for the care of elderly ladies who "may find a retreat from the vicissitudes of life." The Chase Home, operated under auspices of the Episcopal Church, has occupied the property ever since.

Hammond-Harwood House

On the south side of the street, the Hammond-Harwood House faces the Chase-Lloyd mansion. Number 19 Maryland Ave. has often been described as one of the finest medium-sized houses in the world. It represents the masterpiece of a single architect, William Buckland (1734–74), and is one of the few houses of the period that can be attributed directly to one master craftsman. A Charles Willson Peale portrait of Buckland, now at Yale University, shows the architect working on the plans of this house, which was commissioned by Matthias Hammond, a young patriot active in the early revolutionary movement. Unlike many other dwellings of the period, Buckland's perfectly proportioned Georgian design has been preserved without later additions or "improvements." The symmetrical building consists of a five-bay central section with two-story flankers connected by enclosed passages. The exterior brick, laid in Flem-

An example of William Buckland's attention to detail in the interior of the Hammond-Harwood House

ish bond, has a distinctive salmon color, indicating a base of local Maryland clay. The famous main entrance, often reproduced in photographs and drawings, is framed by slender, engaged Ionic columns and a pediment. Beautifully carved egg-and-dart molding surrounds the door and fanlight; falls of roses ornament the spandrels. Buckland trained in England before coming to the Tidewater in 1755 and achieved mastery over intricate Georgian patterns, so the interior woodwork is more delicately carved than that of the Chase-Lloyd House. The large dining room and ballroom directly above it feature carved trims with beads, acanthus leaves, scrolls, interlaces, and gauge work that colonial craftsmen seldom equalled.

Buckland died before the house was completed in 1776, and Hammond never lived in it. (He retired from political and military affairs in 1776 and spent his remaining years as a bachelor on his family's plantation elsewhere in Anne Arundel County, where he died 10 years later at the age of 46.) Subsequent owners of the house included Ninian Pinkney, brother of the noted lawyer and diplomat William Pinkney, and Jeremiah Townley Chase, cousin of Samuel Chase and chief judge of the Court of Appeals for 25 years. Chase's granddaughter inherited the house and married William Harwood, a grandson of William Buckland. The Harwoods' daughter Hester Ann lived in the house until she died in 1924, when both house and contents were sold at public auction. St. John's College bought the house and operated it as a museum for five years until the lean years of the Depression. Then it stood vacant for a few years until 1940, when the Hammond-Harwood House Association acquired it. This nonprofit corporation continues to maintain and operate the house as a museum.

Paca House

From the Hammond-Harwood House, walk back to Prince George St. and turn left (southeast). The street was named in 1695 after Prince George of Denmark, husband of Anne, who became Queen of Great Britain, and the last Stuart monarch, from 1702 to 1714.

The **Paca House** (86 Prince George St.) has become one of Maryland's chief historic and architectural landmarks. Begun in 1763, just after William Paca married Mary Chew, the large brick house with 37 rooms served as his home from the time it was completed in 1765 until 1780, when he sold it, after the death of his second wife, Ann Harrison. William Paca (1740–99), an attorney from Harford County, served as a member of the Maryland Provincial Assembly from 1767 to 1774, when he became a member of the Committee of Correspondence. He represented Maryland in the Continental Congress from 1774 to 1779 and signed the Declaration of Independence. He was elected governor of Maryland during the Revolution, in 1782, and was governor when the Treaty of Paris was ratified in 1784. He served a third term and was chosen a member of the Maryland Convention that ratified the Constitution of the United States.

Paca sold his house to Thomas Jennings, a fellow attorney, and in the year following Jennings's death in 1796, the house was rented to Henri Stier, a Belgian refugee. Throughout much of the 19th century the house was rental property, although Richard Swann, purveyor to the naval academy, owned it briefly, from 1874 to 1877, using the large garden to grow vegetables for the midshipmen. In 1901, the Security Land Company bought the property and started construction of a hotel, which eventually became a 200-room establishment that extended over the garden, incor-

The William Paca House as it appeared in the early 1930s, before being restored

porating the house as a front lobby. The whole complex was called Carvel Hall after *Richard Carvel* (1899), a best-selling novel about colonial Maryland by an American writer from St. Louis named Winston Churchill who had graduated from the naval academy in 1894. The Carvel Hall Hotel flourished for a few decades as an Annapolis social and political center, then deteriorated and was torn down in 1965. Marcellus Hall, who worked as bellhop and captain at the hotel from 1913 until 1965, personified the institution for many guests. When he died in 1971, a group of newspaper reporters wrote to the *Evening Capital* that "hundreds of Maryland political leaders considered him a personal friend who helped them learn the ways of politics during their first days in Annapolis."

The Historic Annapolis Foundation prevented demolition of the Paca House by buying the house and adjoining terrace and persuading the state of Maryland to buy the long-forgotten, two-acre garden. After a long process of careful restoration, the **Paca Garden** opened to the public in 1973, accompanied by universal critical praise for its authenticity and beauty. The house opened three years later.

The Brice Houses

Across the street from the Paca House, at 195 Prince George St., stands a small, story-and-a-half house with a gambrel roof, sometimes known as the Little Brice House or the **John Brice II House.** John Brice II maintained a store next door and lived here until his death in 1766.

When John Brice II died, he had already begun the preliminary construction of a much larger version of his house at Prince George and East Sts. (42 East St.). His son James completed the work by 1775, creating a four-story, five-part, 33-room structure—the largest Georgian town house in Annapolis. In a detailed account book now among the collections of the Maryland State Archives, he listed expenses for labor and materials totaling more than £4,000—a sum now equivalent to more than $1 million—over a seven-year period.

The **James Brice House** features an interior mahogany staircase, handcarved wood in the ballroom and a barrel-vaulted, second-story corridor which may be unique in 18th-century America. James Brice was a colonel in the Maryland militia during the Revolution and served as mayor of Annapolis in 1782 and 1788. He died in 1801, but his family retained possession of the house until 1876, when it was purchased by another mayor of Annapolis, Thomas E. Martin. St. John's College bought the property in the 1930s; it was used by faculty and students until 1953, when the Wohl family bought the mansion and restored it as a private residence. The International Union of Bricklayers and Allied Craftsmen acquired the house at public auction in 1982.

The **Patrick Creagh House,** 160 Prince George St., built between 1735 and 1747, presents a dramatic contrast to the nearby Brice mansion. Patrick Creagh had many careers in Annapolis: painter, shipbuilder, slave trader, house contractor, brewer, and tobacco merchant. By the time he built this comparatively modest dwelling, he ranked among the richest men in town. Creagh may have indulged in too many ventures, because he was deeply in debt at his death in 1760, and the house was later sold by the sheriff to Absalom Ridgely. Around 1800, the house was occupied by John and Lucy Smith, a free African American couple whose forebears might even have arrived on one of Creagh's ships. Smith operated a livery stable in the rear of the house, and "Aunt Lucy," according to legend, operated a bakeshop here for a number of years.

Below Randall St., the **Sands House,** 130 Prince George St., near the waterfront, is probably the oldest house in Annapolis. This small, clapboard structure with a gambrel roof may date to the late 17th century, the period when Annapolis was first laid out. John Sands, a sailmaker and sailor, bought the house around 1768, and it has remained in the Sands family for succeeding generations.

Randall St. returns to City Dock.

TOUR B: TO STATE CIRCLE AND ST. JOHN'S COLLEGE

Market House, across busy Randall St., stands near the site of a market that first appeared in about 1728 but washed away in a hurricane in 1774—the same storm that blew off the roof of the new State House. Annapolitans reestablished a market here on filled land, and another market house went up in 1858. In 1970 the city restored the long, one-story market house as part of a renewal effort that included making a traffic circle at the intersection of Main and Compromise Sts.

During the colonial period, slave ships often docked in this vicinity. In 1981 Alex Haley (1921–92), the author of *Roots,* participated in a public ceremony directly across from the Market House, where, according to his research, a forebear, Kunte Kinte, arrived on a slave ship in 1770. A plaque on the pavement marks the event.

The **Middleton Tavern** stands on the northeast side of Market Space. Around 1750, Samuel Horatio Middleton bought this tavern property, which was built about 1740, and turned it into a combination inn

The charm of dilapidation: Pinkney St. in about 1938

and store, from which he also ran a ferry and shipbuilding business. John Randall, a mayor of Annapolis and revolutionary veteran, acquired the inn sometime after the proprietor's death in 1770. Members of the Continental Congress stayed here, as did other dignitaries of the colonial period. Long before the Revolution, members of the Tuesday Club—"wits of the first order," as they described themselves—ate, drank, and sang at the tavern. Although greatly altered over the years, this brick landmark still operates as a bar and restaurant where the Tuesday Clubbers would probably feel comfortable.

The 18th-century State House towers above the town, a friendly beacon for generations of sailors. To ascend to it while drinking deeply of the charms of Annapolis, one may walk up Fleet St., turning left on either Cornhill or East St. Even better, perhaps, walk past Middleton Tavern and continue up Pinkney St., a narrow, twisty path that has borne several names over the centuries, including Soapsuds Alley. The **Tobacco Prise Warehouse** at the foot of Pinkney St. may have contained an instrument of the same name, used to press, or "prise," hands (bundles) of tobacco leaf into hogsheads for shipping; more likely the present building dates from the early 19th century and was a store.

The **Slicer-Shiplap House** (18 Pinkney St.), one of the few surviving large houses of the early 18th century (ca. 1720), reflects an English construction style characteristic of the 17th century: steeply pitched roof, gable end, and English bond masonry. The first occupant, sawyer Edward Smith, kept an inn here. Ashbury Sutton, a shipbuilder and ferryman, lived here from 1738 to 1748 and may have been responsible for the unusual shiplap siding. William Slicer, a Scottish cabinetmaker and his descendants occupied the house for the longest time, from about 1800 to 1880. Late in the 19th century, Frank B. Mayer, a well-known local artist, owned the house and from it waged a fight for historic preservation. Two of his large paintings, *Planting the Colony of Maryland* (1893) and *The*

A 1930s-era glimpse of the unpainted Slicer-Shiplap House, where the artist Frank Mayer once lived and worked

Burning of the Peggy Stewart (1898), hang in the State House. Historic Annapolis bought the house in the 1950s, and, except for a few years, has used it as a headquarters ever since. **The Barracks,** at 43 Pinkney St., may have housed troops during the Revolution.

Continue up Pinkney St., lined with small 18th- and 19th-century houses, to East St. Now the site of predominantly 19th-century buildings, East St. originally linked the State House with a mansion Maryland governors lived in until the construction, after the Civil War, of Government House. Turn to the left and climb to State Circle. Just before reaching the circle, note the house at **91 East St.,** built about 1790 as a residence by Capt. James West. In 1868 the Methodist Order of Galilean Fishermen bought the building and, until the 1890s, operated it as a school for African American children. Subsequent uses include apartment building, office space, and barber shop.

State Circle

Following Nicholson's original plan for the capital, streets radiate in all directions from this hilltop. Behind you, East St. now connects to Gate 1 of the naval academy. Clockwise, Cornhill St. links State Circle with Market Space via Fleet St., a charming narrow way. The restored 18th- and 19th-century houses along Cornhill St. provide visual evidence of the craftspeople who once lived in Annapolis and supported more conspicuous lifestyles. Thomas Callahan, a prosperous tailor, lived at 53 Cornhill St.; William Monroe, a moderately successful carpenter, lived at 49. Both built their houses on lots leased from Charles Wallace, a merchant with expansive ideas. In 1769, Wallace purchased a tract of largely undeveloped land that ran from the marshy basin at the foot of Main St. up the hill to State Circle. He then laid out the property into lots along two new streets, Cornhill and Fleet, named after their London counterparts. At the foot of his streets, Wallace envisioned an impressive row of four stores, which would house consumer goods transferred by open, shallow-draft boats from ocean-going ships anchored in the Severn River. Architectural evidence of his vision remains in the brick shell of 26–28 Market Space.

Next comes Francis St., named for Francis Nicholson. Where it joins State Circle, note **1 State Circle,** a two-story frame structure that houses professional offices. It was built ca. 1740, when the population of Annapolis stood at about a thousand persons. In early December 1997, when a five-alarm fire broke out in the adjoining building, firefighters managed to save the landmark by keeping water raining down on the roof.

The **Brooksby-Shaw House,** 21 State Circle, dates to about 1722, when Cornelius Brooksby began building a large, gambrel-roofed house, construction of which was not completed until two years after his death. John Shaw, a cabinetmaker, bought the house in 1784 and may have done work for the Continental Congress and its members that year. Lt. Winfield Scott Schley, who in 1898 commanded the American warships that defeated the Spanish at Santiago, was married here to Anne Franklin. The house eventually passed from the Shaw family, became an Elks lodge for a time, and then was bought by the state of Maryland.

Continuing on, the visitor passes two picturesque alleys, Tate Alley and Chancery Lane, which connect to Main St. The very short School St., named for King William's School, connects State Circle to Church

Circle. The two circles, along with Bloomsbury Square, a residential area planned to the northwest but now filled with state government buildings, formed the major elements in the Nicholson design for Annapolis. **Government House,** commonly known as the Governor's Mansion, stands between the two circles. This Victorian residence was begun in 1868 on the site of two 18th-century mansions. In 1936 the state exchanged its mansard roof and other Victorian features for a neo-Georgian design that included broad gables, chimneys, Palladian windows, and other features of the five-part Georgian model. The remodeling belonged to a widespread official effort at the time (remember that Maryland celebrated its tercentenary anniversary in 1934) to adopt a neocolonial style for all government buildings. Periodically, as new governors occupy the mansion and make personal changes, such as the large Victorian fountain that dates from the 1980s, a public outcry emerges in defense either of tradition or improvisation—all of it reflective of the Annapolitan tension between continuity and change.

Lawyers Mall lies in an open space between Government House and the **Legislative Services Building** (1976), which the state built where the Court of Appeals building once stood. In 1994 the General Assembly appropriated funds for a **statue honoring Justice Thurgood Marshall** (1908–93), a Baltimorean and the first African American to serve on the U.S. Supreme Court (from 1967 to 1991). The Maryland sculptor Toby Mendez crafted the memorial, which stands in a quiet plaza.

Work on the crown jewel of State Circle, Maryland's imposing **State House,** began in March 1772; Robert Eden, the last proprietary governor, helped lay the cornerstone. Two earlier state houses had stood on the same site. The first, completed in 1698, locals called the Stadt House in recognition of King William's Dutch origins. Lightning struck the ediface a year later, igniting a fire that killed a member of the House of Delegates, injured others, and damaged or destroyed many early records. Repaired, the building remained in use until 1704, when fire gutted it completely. The second State House, apparently not an impressive structure, dated from 1707 and soon became the object of ridicule. In 1766 Thomas Jefferson wrote of it derisively; another observer judged it to be "an emblem of public poverty." At last the assembly voted to demolish the structure and build a new one, the majestic building that still stands. In 1774 a hurricane tore off the copper roof and damaged the interior, and the Revolution further slowed construction. But the builder, Charles Wallace, persisted, and in 1779 Maryland lawmakers convened in the new building. Of state capitols, only the Maryland State House has served as the seat of Congress (in 1783–84). The building's intricate wooden dome, designed by Joseph Clark and the largest wooden dome in America, remained unfinished until 1794.

In 1996 roofing workers called attention to the shaky condition of the 800-pound, decorative wood "acorn" atop the dome. Upon close inspection, state officials determined that the acorn had to be replaced; they also discovered that the 28-foot wrought-iron lightning rod that served as a flagpole was original and apparently had been approved by Benjamin Franklin. The acorn and its pedestal came down with the assistance of a helicopter and large crane. Woodworkers from all over the state volunteered their services in crafting a new copper-clad cypress acorn. The rod received a stabilizing steel sleeve. In the spring of 1998 the state under-

The Maryland State House in the 1930s. Its 18th-century exterior as viewed from Francis St.

took a $5 million renovation project on the State House—repainting the white dome, replacing slate roofing, restoring windows, and installing new fire detectors and sprinklers.

Visitors may enter the State House on the North St. side, but the main entrance faces Francis St. and features a one-story, pedimented Corinthian portico with assorted accoutrements, all later additions. The portal opens into a wide, arcaded hall under the central dome, which has arched and oval windows. The delicate plaster ornament in the Adam style is primarily the work of Thomas Dance, an artisan who was killed in a fall from the scaffold as he was finishing the job in 1793.

Inside, to the left, a **Visitors Center** offers information about guided tours.

On the right, the beautiful **Old Senate Chamber** now sits quiet, painstakingly restored to its original appearance. Four of the original desks and three of the chairs remain, the work of noted Annapolis cabinetmaker John Shaw. The other pieces of furniture are reproductions. The Congress of the United States met here from November 26, 1783, to June 3, 1784. In an emotional ceremony in this room on December 23, 1783, George Washington resigned his commission as commander in chief of the Continental Army. In this room on January 14, 1784, Congress formally ratified the Treaty of Paris and in May appointed Thomas Jefferson as minister plenipotentiary to France. Over the fireplace—just where the artist placed it—hangs a portrait by Charles Willson Peale of Washington, with Col. Tench Tilghman, a Marylander who was Washington's aide-de-camp, and the Marquis de Lafayette. Peale had begun his career as a saddler in Annapolis. Several prominent Annapolitans provided the money that enabled him to study at the school of Benjamin West in London. General Lafayette viewed the portrait in 1824 during a revisit to Annapolis for a gala celebration sponsored by the General Assembly. "This city has been the theatre of resolutions most important to the welfare of the United States," Lafayette declared, "and indeed to the general welfare of mankind."

Next to the Old Senate Chamber one will find historic exhibits: a scale model of the State House dome; a facsimile of the contract for the original construction work; and, for most of the year, a full-size reconstruction of the *Federalist,* the small sailboat that Baltimoreans paraded in 1788 to celebrate ratification of the federal Constitution and then sailed to Mount Vernon as a present to George Washington.

To the left of the front door are the **Calvert Room,** with portraits of the Calvert family and Margaret Brent and the **Maryland Silver Room,** with Marylandia that includes the silver service from the USS *Maryland,* ornamented with scenes from throughout the state.

A plaque in the **Rotunda** honors Matthew A. Henson (1866–1955), a native of Charles County in Southern Maryland, who accompanied Adm. Robert E. Peary on seven expeditions to the Arctic and polar regions. (In 1909 Peary claimed credit for being the first man to reach the pole; most scholars now believe that the expedition missed the pole by a few miles.) In 1912 Henson wrote a memoir, *A Black Explorer at the North Pole,* and later in life he received a Congressional Medal and honorary degrees for his service. Additional plaques and exhibits honor the lunar explorers of *Apollo 11* and the crew of the space shuttle *Challenger.*

Today, Maryland lawmakers occupy spaces in the large, west extension of the capitol, completed in 1906 amid controversy over its architectural style. A broad black line on the lobby's marble floor marks the division between the original and later sections. The **Senate Chamber** and **Chamber of the House of Delegates,** both with balconies and skylighted ceilings, are decorated in a modified Italian Renaissance style. Note the marble columns and vaulted arcades. In the 1980s the Senate Chamber underwent extensive restoration.

The sweeping marble steps leading to the second floor in the State House extension of 1906

Inside the Old Treasury Building, State House grounds

On the grounds of the State House one may see several notable monuments. William H. Rinehart's bronze **statue of Roger Brooke Taney** (1777–1864) guards the main entrance. Taney in 1835 succeeded John Marshall as Chief Justice of the U.S. Supreme Court and served until his death in October 1864. Taney studied law in Annapolis (1796–99), was admitted to the bar here, and served in the assembly. To the southwest stands Ephraim Keyser's **statue of Baron de Kalb,** who was killed on August 16, 1780, while leading Maryland and Delaware troops at the Battle of Camden, South Carolina. A **cannon pulled from the St. Mary's River**—it may have been one of the pieces brought from England on the *Ark* in 1634—also sits on the lawn. The **Old Treasury Building,** completed in 1737 as the Office of the Commissioners for Emitting Bills of Credit and later the Office of the Treasurer, joins the State House inside the circle. The brick, cruciform building was restored in 1949.

From State Circle, take North St. away from the capitol and toward the intersection of College Ave. and St. John's St. State office buildings cluster to the left: the **Thomas Hunter Lowe House of Delegates Office Building,** the **William S. James Senate Office Building** (corner of College Ave. and Bladen St.), the **Louis L. Goldstein Treasury Building, State Income Tax Building, Data Processing Building,** and **Old Armory Building.**

On the right one sees the **Bordley-Randall House,** a private residence that may have been built as early as 1716. Thomas Bordley, one of the petitioners for the incorporation of Annapolis, built the original house; his son Stephen (1709–64), a bachelor lawyer known as a connoisseur, developed it to suit his tastes. (Thomas Johnson and William Paca, who both became governors of Maryland after the Revolution, received their legal training in Bordley's office.) Early in its long history, this

2½-story, five-part brick house stood on a four-acre estate. A two-story columned porch on the main unit was replaced in 1860 by a smaller, enclosed porch floored with marble from the State House, which was undergoing repairs at the time.

In the 19th century, the Randall family acquired the house and occupied it for almost a century. Alexander Randall (1803–81) was a representative in the 27th Congress, and his brother Richard (1796–1829) was appointed governor of Liberia, where he died of malignant fever. Reverdy Johnson (1796–1876), a playmate of the young Randalls, was born in this house. Later a U.S. senator, he also served as attorney general in the Zachary Taylor administration. He argued for the proslavery defense in the Dred Scott case before the Supreme Court in 1856 and then served again in the Senate from 1863 until 1868, when he became U.S. minister to Great Britain. Johnson returned to Annapolis in 1869 and died seven years later from injuries sustained in a fall from the front porch of Government House after a state dinner.

Capt. Phillip V. H. Weems, the developer of a celestial navigation system and inventor of widely used navigation instruments, bought the house in 1939. He had instructed Charles Lindbergh in navigation prior to his flight to Paris in 1927 and came out of retirement to brief John Glenn before his space orbital flight in 1962.

St. John's College

Across College Ave. to the right is the **St. John's College** campus, extending from St. John's St. to King George St. and from College Ave. down to College Creek. Like so many Annapolis sites, St. John's has experienced several metamorphoses during its long history. The institution is generally regarded as the successor to King William's School, a grammar school established in 1696 as one of the first public schools in America. Little is known about King William's School; it may not have operated continuously, but it survived in some form until 1785, when some of its funds and books were transferred to St. John's College, chartered in 1784. St. John's was conceived as the center of learning for the Western Shore of Maryland and enjoyed eminent patronage: all of the state's signers of the Declaration of Independence petitioned for its establishment. George Washington sent his nephews, Fairfax and Lawrence Washington, to St. John's in 1794 and his wife's grandson George Washington Parke Custis in 1798. Other early alumni included Francis Scott Key, who graduated in 1796, and Reverdy Johnson.

The act chartering St. John's gave the new school an unfinished structure intended as the governor's residence, as well as state funds and permission to raise money from public subscriptions. But the school had financial difficulties almost from the beginning. As Annapolis waned in the growing shadow of Baltimore after the Revolution, private subscribers reneged on their pledges, and the legislature in 1806 withdrew its annual subsidy. The college closed briefly in 1818, but continued anemically until the Civil War, when Union troops used its campus as a hospital and parole camp. In February 1864, a company of African American soldiers camped here. Their parade through the streets of Annapolis allegedly inspired 120 local African American men and boys to enlist. Meantime, St. John's operated on an irregular basis, in the form of one master and a few students who met in private houses.

After the war, the naval academy attempted to buy the physical plant and did acquire a portion of the campus east of King George St.—a cow pasture that the college had rented to townspeople for grazing stock. St. John's survived as a military academy from 1886 to 1923, when it became a regular liberal arts college with successful football and lacrosse teams. Then the Depression hit Annapolis, and the college lost both enrollment and accreditation.

In 1937 Stringfellow Barr and Scott Buchanan came to the rescue from the University of Chicago and launched the school in an innovative, controversial direction in American higher education. As president and dean, respectively, they dropped intercollegiate athletics and initiated the Great Books Program, founded on the traditional ideas of liberal education. Graduates complete a four-year course of study based on about 130 basic texts ranging from Plato to Einstein. Students discuss these works in small seminars and laboratories conducted by "tutors." This experiment proved its value and continues today. In 1948 the school admitted its first African American student; it became coeducational in 1951. Almost 500 students now reside at the Annapolis campus. In 1964 the school established another one, in Santa Fe, New Mexico, which employs the same curriculum.

The college encourages visitors to stroll through its historic campus. A diagonal pathway leads from the intersection of College Ave. and St. John's St., past the **Old Hall of Records Building.** The Maryland Hall of Records dates to Maryland's Tercentenary Commission, which planned the state's 300th birthday celebration in 1934. St. John's donated the land for this building, built in 1935 for the preservation of Maryland's extensive but incomplete records (some of the documents transferred to Annapolis from St. Mary's City in 1695–96 fell into the Patuxent River; others were destroyed in the disastrous State House fire in 1704). The Hall of Records, renamed the State Archives in 1984, answered a long-recognized need for a centralized archival agency. In 1993 the state sold the Hall of Records Building to St. John's for use as a library. The connection between the college and the State Archives has involved more than space, however. The college's 70,000-volume collection includes "Dr. Bray's Library," more than 400 volumes sent in 1699 by Princess Anne to the don of King William's School. The library made up the largest collection of books in the colonies at the time and formed the nucleus of what some claimed to be the first free library in North America (most required payment for access). The fragile Bray volumes are now stored at the State Archives, where they are accessible to scholars.

Walk east on College Ave. and turn left past a replica of the Liberty Bell to **McDowell Hall,** named for John McDowell, the first president of the college. In 1742, the General Assembly authorized Gov. Thomas Bladen to buy four acres and build "a Dwelling House and other Conveniences for the Residence of the Governor of Maryland for the Time being," the cost not to exceed £4,000. Bladen employed a Scottish architect, Simon Duff, to build the house, but the project exceeded the budgeted costs and was abandoned after two years. Benjamin Mifflin, a Philadelphian visiting Annapolis in 1762, noted: "Viewd Bladens Folly as the Inhabitants Call it, the ruins of a Spacious Building begun by Gov Bladen but carried no further than the Brick Work & Joists 2 Stories High but if Finished would have been a Beautiful Edifice." After 40 years of neglect, the building was given to the college, which completed the work. When Lafayette visited Annapolis in 1824, the hall was the scene of two banquets and a ball in his honor. During the Civil War, the building served as a clearing station for exchanged Union prisoners and as headquarters of the Union Army Medical Corps. Fire gutted the structure in 1909, and it was reconstructed on the undamaged foundation, incorporating remains of the original walls.

Several local 18th-century structures have been moved to the campus, including the house of Charles Carroll the Barrister (see below) and the **Chancellor Johnson House.** The most modern structures, located on the St. John's St. side of the campus, are **Francis Scott Key Auditorium** and **Mellon Hall,** designed by the California firm of Neutra and Alexander and dedicated by President Eisenhower in 1958. The 600-seat auditorium is frequently used for community events.

From McDowell Hall, walk northeast toward King George St., passing the **Liberty Tree,** a tulip poplar roughly 30 feet in circumference which is believed to be over 400 years old. Revolutionary orators exhorted their audiences under its limbs; almost certainly, Joseph Pilmoor preached the first Methodist sermon in Annapolis under its branches on July 11, 1772. Commencement speakers have held forth under its shelter since 1929. Like the college itself, this venerable tree has weathered many challenges. It has become an enduring symbol of survival. In 1840, boys ignited gunpowder in its hollow trunk and set it afire. Zealous citizens extinguished the blaze, and the next spring, the heat of the fire having freed the tree of parasites, it burst forth with exceptional vigor. The Liberty Tree stands on a grassy area in front of **Woodward Hall,** once the library and now the home of computer labs and the Graduate Institute, a program that follows the Great Books curriculum and leads to a Master of Arts degree. The King William Room provides space for special events and senior oral examinations.

Continue east to King George St. The **Charles Carroll the Barrister House** stands immediately to the left. This 2½-story frame building was originally built in 1722–23 for Dr. Charles Carroll on the corner of Main and Conduit Sts. His son—called Charles Carroll the Barrister, to distinguish him from his distant cousin, Charles Carroll of Carrollton—was born in the house in 1724. Like his Catholic cousin, the Anglican barrister became a noted lawyer and patriot; he may have written the Maryland Declaration of Rights, adopted on November 3, 1776, as part of the state's first constitution. To prevent its demolition, preservationists and city officials in 1955 moved the building six blocks to its present site. St. John's now uses the restored house as its admissions office.

From this southeast corner of the campus, the visitor may walk down King George St. to Maryland Ave., turning right to browse in the shops that line both sides of the street as it proceeds to State Circle and perhaps choosing the Francis St.-to-Main St. route back to City Dock; or one may simply follow King George St. to Randall St., there turning right to the dock. In either case, one passes **Ogle Hall** at the corner of King George St. and College Ave. Now home to the U.S. Naval Academy Alumni Association, the 2½-story brick house was built in 1739 for Dr. William Stevenson. Samuel Ogle, a Prince George's County planter and three-time colonial governor of Maryland, occupied the house from 1747 until his death in 1752. The Ogle family, including Benjamin Ogle, who became governor of Maryland in 1798, were associated with this house until after the Civil War. Vice Adm. David Dixon Porter, superintendent of the naval academy during its rebuilding after the Civil War, also lived here. The alumni association acquired the property in 1945 and restored it.

TOUR C: TO CHURCH CIRCLE VIA MAIN ST. AND RETURN ON DUKE OF GLOUCESTER ST. AND SIDE STREETS

Until the 20th century, Main St. was known as Church St., the link between Church Circle and City Dock. With the East St. vista from State Circle now substantially blocked by the naval academy, the sweeping straight-line view from hillside to dockside, conceived in the original Nicholson plan, becomes most visible here. Main St. has become a crowded, busy avenue, lined with restaurants, offices, and shops, where people compete for the parking spaces on either side of the street. The following walk begins at the foot of Main St., although it can easily be reversed.

The junction of Main and Compromise Sts. at City Dock has a long maritime history, represented by the restored 18th-century victualling warehouse at 77 Main St. (the Continental army stored supplies in it). The Historic Annapolis Foundation operates this site as a **Maritime Museum** with exhibits illustrating the town's colonial maritime trades and making available a strong selection of books, crafts, and other keepsake items. The large brick building at the corner of Main and Green Sts. has been a retail shop since 1790.

The ascent up Main St.—with its many shops and diverse architectural styles—lends itself to browsing. The pie-shaped building at 155 Main St. dates from the late Georgian period. Narrow Francis St. branches north to State Circle; Conduit St. intersects Main St. from the southwest. Dr. Charles Carroll's house stood at the latter intersection before it was moved to the St. John's College campus. Farther up the street on the right, Chancery Ln. rises in a series of steps to State Circle.

Henry Price built the brick half of the **Price House** (232–36 Main St.) before 1830. It rests on the site of a saddlery and sign-painting shop that Charles Willson Peale operated between 1763 and 1765. A third-generation Annapolitan and "free man of color," Price was a lay minister in the Annapolis Station Methodist Episcopal Church and later a founder of the Asbury United Methodist Church. He owned this property from 1819 until his death in 1863. Price's grandson, Daniel Hale Williams, lived in this house for a few years while attending Stanton School. In 1897, Dr. Williams, a graduate of the Chicago Medical School, performed the world's first successful operation on the human heart while surgeon-in-chief at Freedmen's Hospital in Washington.

The flat-iron-shaped **Maryland Inn** points toward Church Circle, but look for the front entrance on Main St. just before the circle. Thomas Hyde built this brick building as an inn in the 1770s, on this lot between Main and Duke of Gloucester Sts., originally known as "the Drummer's Lot." (The town drummer was a conspicuous figure in colonial Annapolis, announcing market days and calling the citizens to community events.) Hyde advertised his establishment in the Maryland Gazette as "an elegant brick house adjoining Church Circle in a dry and healthy part of the city, 100 feet front, 3 story high, 22 rooms, 20 fireplaces, 2 kitchens. Rooms mostly large and well furnished, and is one of the first houses in the State for a house of entertainment, for which purpose it was originally intended." More than 200 years later the description still fits. The inn was restored in 1953, and many improvements have since been added to the building, which still serves as hotel, restaurant, and "house of entertainment." The King of France Tavern for many years featured one of the region's most accomplished jazz guitarists, Charlie Byrd.

Church Circle

As at State Circle, a number of streets radiate from Church Circle—in this case eight—each with its own character and landmarks. Clockwise from Main St., Duke of Gloucester St. slants southeast in a straight line to Compromise St. and the bridge over Spa Creek. Next, South St. passes private and government offices and residences. Franklin St., originally known as Doctor St., contains more structures of historical interest. The **Anne Arundel County Courthouse,** built in the Federal style, dates from 1824. The central porch and tower were added in 1892, and the building has been expanded several times since. **Reynolds' Tavern,** across Franklin St., was standing in 1747 and may have been built in the 1730s. The brick building was leased in 1745 to William Reynolds, who used it as a tavern. His son Robert ran the tavern and also worked as a hatter and stocking manufacturer. The building later housed a bank and then, around 1936, the Annapolis Public Library. Now restored to its original function, the two-story tavern has broad end chimneys, a dormered gambrel roof, and an unusual stringcourse that arches over each first floor window, forming a wavy line across the front.

The **Banneker-Douglass Museum of Afro-American Life and History** (84 Franklin St.), dedicated in 1984, is located in a former church about a block down Franklin from Church Circle. The church became an important community symbol during the 1970s and now serves as a center for the study and exhibit of African American history and culture, particularly in Maryland.

The Bethel congregation of the African Methodist Episcopal Church acquired this property in 1874, 10 years after the abolition of slavery in Maryland, and soon thereafter began construction of this brick, Victorian Gothic church. Some members of the congregation had been slaves; most had low incomes and had previously worshiped in simpler, frame buildings in segregated sections of the city far removed from the power and influence represented by nearby St. Anne's. The church traced its beginnings to free African Americans who had established a congregation around 1799, affiliating with the A.M.E. after the latter's formation in Philadelphia in 1816 (see Baltimore: Sharp St.). The church building, with honey oak interior and stained-glass windows, was completed in 1876 at a cost of $7,000 and was used for 98 years by the congregation, which at some point changed its name to "Mount Moriah." When the congregation grew wealthier and more influential, they moved to a larger, more modern building, on Bay Ridge Ave. in Eastport. They sold the downtown property in 1970 to Anne Arundel County, which planned to demolish the building and use the land as a parking lot. The ensuing battle to save Mount Moriah lasted four years. Historic Annapolis, the Maryland Commission on African American History and Culture, and a Citizens Committee for the Preservation of Mount Moriah Church led the battle that eventually resulted in the formation of the present museum, named for Benjamin Banneker and Frederick Douglass.

At Franklin and Cathedral Sts. one finds the sprawling **Anne Arundel Medical Center,** which started in 1902 as the Annapolis Emergency Hospital and between 1949 and 1989 bore the name Anne Arundel General Hospital. Specializing in women's and children's services, orthopedics, oncology, and cardiology, the center since 1989 has been in the process of moving to a new location about two miles north and west at the AAMC Medical Park.

Franklin St. continues southwest past Acton Place, location of a large, two-story brick mansion which may date to around 1745. **Acton,** named for a 17th-century land grant to Richard Acton, may have been built by Philip Hammond, father of Matthias Hammond, builder of the Hammond-Harwood House. At the time of its construction, this country house stood well beyond the town limits of Annapolis.

Continuing the clockwise progression around Church Circle one encounters West St. Because there were no bridges over the Severn River or its various creeks until 1886, West St. for almost two centuries offered the only access to Annapolis by land travel. Called Cowpens Ln. in the 18th century, the street was lined with boardinghouses, taverns, and the homes of storekeepers and craftsmen. It remained unpaved until after the Civil War. The rise of the automobile at the turn of the century and the first street car (1908) slowly changed its appearance and wholly commercialized it. One may walk a few blocks up West St. to see some landmarks.

Philip Syng, noted Maryland silversmith, lived on West St. in the early 18th century as did William Faris, silversmith, watchmaker, and innkeeper. The colonial-period building at 26 West St. forms part of the Annapolis and Anne Arundel County Visitors Bureau. Across the street and near the corner of West and Church Circle, the versatile Faris operated a tavern called the Crown and Dial beginning in the late 1750s. The structure at Number 18 was built soon after the Revolution. Just beyond it, at Numbers 28–30 is the **Ghiselin Boarding House.** Thomas Jefferson lodged at the latter for several months in the winter of 1783–84 during the Annapolis session of the Continental Congress. His diary notes that he paid five shillings a day for a room plus an additional two shillings and sixpence for firewood. He often dined with the widow Ghiselin, even though she had earlier been accused by a local resident of serving oyster shells in her stew. The **Golder House,** 42–50 West St., is named after a man who kept a store here at the Sign of the Waggon and Horse until 1765, when he died from eating poisonous mushrooms. For many years after the Revolution the house was used as a tavern, under such names as the Sign of the Pennsylvania Farmer and Hunter's Tavern.

On the opposite (south) side of West St. are the **sites of Annapolis's second colonial theater, the home of Samuel Chase** in the 1770s, and **William Faris's shop.** The lower end of the triangle formed by Cathedral and West Sts. was developed by Allen Quynn, a prosperous cordwainer (shoemaker), who served as a vestryman of St. Anne's Parish, mayor, and long-time delegate to the General Assembly.

The original town gate was located at the end of the first block of West St. (south side). In 1697 two triangular houses flanked the gate.

The race course that the **Maryland Jockey Club** used lay just beyond the city gate, west of Calvert St. Founded in Annapolis in 1743, the club awarded the Annapolis Subscription Plate, second oldest known racing trophy in America, to Dr. George Steuart's horse *Dungannon* on May 4, 1743. The French and Indian War and the Revolution interrupted meetings of the Maryland Jockey Club, but they formed part of the Annapolis social scene until about 1830, when the races moved to Baltimore.

From the corner of West and Calvert Sts., the walker may continue one block on West St. to West Washington St. and Stanton School (90 West Washington St.), the second site of the first publicly supported school for African American children, which opened after the Civil War in 1867 at Camp Parole (near the intersection of West St. and U.S. 50). Named after Edwin M. Stanton, Lincoln's secretary of war, the school had moved here by 1900. Elementary school students from grades one to six attended the school until 1917; then high school students were admitted. (In 1933, Bates High School opened for black students.) When Anne Arundel County public schools were integrated in 1954, the Stanton School closed, but in 1975 it reopened as the **Stanton Community Center.** In 1994, the building was placed on the National Register of Historic Places, in recognition of its role as educational and cultural center for the region's African American residents.

Half a dozen blocks farther out West St. (left onto Amos Garrett Blvd., right onto Constitution Ave., at the end of Constitution) sits the **Maryland Hall for the Creative Arts.** When Annapolis High School moved to a new building, the Annapolis community turned this into a lively center offering artists' studios, exhibit and meeting spaces, classes and workshops, and theater and musical productions. The Annapolis Symphony Orchestra performs here.

Back at Church Circle, Northwest St. connects downtown Annapolis to U.S. 50 and the Severn River Bridge via Rowe Blvd. The **Post Office,** a 1901 brick building in the neo-Georgian style, is located on the circle just beyond Northwest St.

The final two spokes off Church Circle are College Ave., running behind the Governor's Mansion and past St. John's College, and School St., connecting Annapolis's two circles.

St. Anne's Church

Placement of this house of worship in the middle of Church Circle dates—in design—to 1695 and one of the early attempts officially to establish the Church of England in Maryland as the state church—a single denomination supported by public revenues and defended by the state. Parishioners could be fined for nonattendance, and the assembly declared it illegal for anyone to profane the sabbath with "drunkenness, Swearing, Gaming, fowling, fishing, hunting, or any other Sports Pastimes or Recreations whatsover."

The first church built here was for Middle Neck Parish, established in 1692. Appropriations were made in 1695, when Annapolis became the state capital, but construction proceeded erratically. The church was probably ready for use in 1704 and was definitely completed by 1706. A silver communion service, which bears the royal arms and cipher, was sent to the parish by King William III in 1696. As the city prospered, people began to comment negatively on the church's size and appearance.

A poet complained in the *Maryland Gazette*, "Here, in Annapolis alone, God has the meanest house in town." So plans for a new church were made, and the old structure was razed in 1775, while the new State House was also under construction. During the Revolution, many of the materials collected for the new church were taken for private or wartime uses, and the building was not completed for 17 years. In the interim, worshipers used King William's School and the nearby theater on West St. The second church, completed in 1792, burned in 1858. Construction of the current building incorporated the tower, doorway, and front wall of its predecessor and was completed in 1859. The Romanesque octagonal steeple contains a bell and clock that still mark the hours of the Annapolitan day.

St. Anne's Parish was relatively small compared to other Maryland parishes of the colonial period. Since the population of a parish—taxed at a flat rate per taxable head—determined the income of a rector, an unusually large number of rectors served St. Anne's, usually only until a richer parish opened. The notorious Bennet Allen, inducted in 1767, moved on to All Saints Parish in Frederick as a result of a feud with the Dulany family. Both families were close to the Calverts; Allen allegedly had won the sixth Lord Baltimore's favor for trying heroically to champion the proprietor during a rape proceeding (Sarah Woodcock having preferred the charges). In 1782 the Reverend Mr. Allen killed Lloyd Dulany in a London duel. Jonathan Boucher, another well-known rector, began service here in 1770. During the unrest that preceded the decision to declare independence, Boucher proved himself one of the great colonial spokesmen for submission to crown and Parliament.

The churchyard contains the graves of a representative number of early Annapolitans, including Amos Garrett, the first mayor of Annapolis, who died in 1727. The remains of Robert Eden, the last colonial governor of Maryland, were reinterred here in 1926. Eden, who was well-liked in Annapolis, had returned after the Revolution in 1783 to reclaim confiscated property, but he died shortly after his arrival.

The **Southgate Cross** and its fountain basin supply another circle landmark. Annapolitans erected the cross in 1901 as a memorial to Dr. William Southgate, who defied the old colonial pattern and served St. Anne's as rector for 30 years—from 1869 to 1899, longer than any of his predecessors. Horses used the fountain as a watering trough until World War II.

Duke of Gloucester and Side Streets

Duke of Gloucester St., named for the oldest surviving son of Queen Anne and Prince George of Denmark, forms triangular and polygonal blocks with Main and Compromise Sts. Side streets branch southwest, offering the walker opportunities for pleasant discoveries in this eastern part of the old city. Start from Church Circle, pass the Maryland Inn, and proceed to Charles St. on the right.

Turn right on Charles St. Only two blocks long, it runs between Duke of Gloucester St. and a small inlet of Spa Creek, Acton Cove, which in 1669 was the town's first port of entry. The **Jonas Green House** (124 Charles St.) once belonged to the publisher of the *Maryland Gazette*, which his family operated until 1840. Part of the gambrel-roofed house may date to the late 17th century; the large front section is an early-18th-century addition. Green, an apprentice to Benjamin Franklin, moved to Annapolis from Philadelphia in 1738 and established his newspaper seven years later. As public printer of the colony, he became a prominent figure in Annapolis, serving as a vestryman at St. Anne's and as a city alderman. He also belonged to the Maryland Jockey Club and acted as the official "Poet, Printer, Punster, Purveyor and Punchmaker" of the Tuesday Club.

At Charles and Cathedral Sts. turn left to Conduit St., so named in the 18th century because it connected Church (now Main) and Duke of Gloucester Sts. with the water at Acton Cove. Lloyd Dulany inherited the land at **162 Conduit Street** from his mother in 1766. Dulany, who had close ties to the Calvert proprietary government, was much criticized for his ostentatious display of the wealth he acquired from this association. A loyalist, he fled the state in 1776, his property was confiscated, and he fell victim to Bennet Allen in London. In 1783 the Commissioners of Confiscated Property sold Dulany's property to George Mann, who built this large brick house. Mann converted the house to a tavern. (George Washington stayed at Mann's when he came to Annapolis in 1783 to resign his commission.) The house later became the City Hotel, a fashionable hostelry, which after 1900 included an adjoining theater. In 1919 the complex—except for the old Dulany House—burned to the ground.

The 2½-story brick structure at **164 Conduit Street** (private) has been moved twice: first from its original site on College Ave. and then in 1972 from the St. John's College campus. Built about 1750 according to a design by John Callahan, it was sold in 1839 to Somerville Pinkney. St. John's College, which bought the house from the Pinkney family, used it as an infirmary.

Follow Conduit back to Duke of Gloucester St. There the **First Presbyterian Church** now occupies the **site of the City Theater** (1828–47), which replaced the 18th-century theater on West St.

Maynard-Burgess House

This two-story brick building (163 Duke of Gloucester St.) was originally built in the late 18th century as a one-story structure with no windows, then enlarged and moved to this location in the 1830s. John Maynard, a waiter at the City Hotel a block away, bought the house in 1847, thus joining the ranks of about 20 free African Americans who owned property in Annapolis. Maynard had purchased the freedom of his wife Maria, her daughter, and her mother. One of the stained-glass windows in the Mount Moriah Church is dedicated to him and his wife. John Maynard died in 1875, but his descendants occupied the house until 1914, when his granddaughter sold it to Willis Burgess, a former boarder. It then remained in the Burgess family until the 1990s and is now owned by the City of Annapolis, which is restoring and developing the house as a museum under the supervision of the Historic Annapolis Foundation.

City Hall

Across the street stands the **Municipal Building** (164 Duke of Gloucester St.) and Annapolis City Hall. This two-story brick building occupies the **site of the Assembly Rooms,** built in 1765 for social gatherings, which included card games and balls. The building burned during the Civil War, while it was being used as the provost marshal's headquarters. In the 1870s the city government moved from 211 Main St.

and occupied this structure, which incorporates portions of three original walls left standing after the fire. Inside, three murals depict early events in the city's history. They were created in 1997 to commemorate the 300th anniversary of Annapolis as state capital.

Across from the Municipal Building, turn down Market St. (named for a proposed market that was never built) and turn left onto Shipwright St., which ends at Spa Creek. The **Upton Scott House** (4 Shipwright St., private)—a square, hip-roofed building with two tall chimneys and a pedimented doorway—stands on land that once boasted extensive gardens and greenhouses. Dr. Upton Scott, who came to Annapolis in 1753 with the retinue of Gov. Horatio Sharpe, built this house around 1765. Scott had been a poor Belfast physician, but Governor Sharpe's patronage eventually made him a wealthy man. The popular doctor remained a loyalist during the Revolution, but he was not particularly vocal in his Tory views, and the new state government protected him. His friend Robert Eden, the former governor, stayed here after returning to Annapolis from England in 1783. Francis Scott Key lived here while a student at St. John's College. The house for many years served as a convent for the Sisters of Notre Dame.

Return to Market St. and then to Duke of Gloucester St., turning right (southeast).

The **William H. Butler House** (148 Duke of Gloucester St., private) probably dates from the 1850s. A prosperous carpenter and "free person of color," Butler resided in this three-story Victorian Italianate structure in 1873, when he won the race for alderman from the city's third ward, becoming the first African American elected to public office in the state of Maryland. His son William Jr. held the same office from 1893 to 1897.

The Ridout House and nearby town houses, Duke of Gloucester St., as they appeared in the 1930s

The **Ridout House** (120 Duke of Gloucester St., private), was built around 1765 by John Ridout, secretary and lifelong friend of Gov. Horatio Sharpe. He and Mary Ogle, daughter of Gov. Benjamin Ogle and Mary Tasker Ogle, began their marriage in this 2½-story mansion with massive end chimneys and a gable roof. The brickwork on the street facade is laid in all-header bond, accented by a projecting stringcourse. Rubbed brick arches accent the regularly spaced windows on the building, which has a wide, overhanging cornice. A flight of stone steps with wrought-iron handrails ascends to a Doric entrance under a simple pediment with dentils and modillions. The garden facade is even more elaborate than the front. The property still belongs to Ridout descendants, who also retain in their possession a nightcap left behind by Martha Washington.

John Ridout built the three town houses at **110–14 Duke of Gloucester St.** in 1774 as rental properties. When a serious effort was made in 1786 to move the capital from Annapolis to Baltimore, Ridout confessed "uneasiness on account of my houses in this place. . . . makes me regret I ever built them." Long since passed into separate ownership, the three houses supply the earliest surviving examples of English urban row house construction in America. Few of their kind still stand in England.

St. Mary's Church

St. Mary's Church (107 Duke of Gloucester St.) has been a prominent Annapolis landmark since 1876, when the spire was completed on this Victorian Gothic structure. The property was acquired in 1852 from the Carroll family by the Roman Catholic Congregation of the Most Holy Redeemer (Redemptorists). A much smaller church, completed in 1822, stood on the site of today's elementary school building. Brothers of the Redemptorist Order did the carving and other decorations in the interior of the present church, which dates from 1859.

Charles Carroll House

The Annapolis mansion of the Carrolls stands behind St. Mary's Church, between Duke of Gloucester and Shipwright Sts. It faces Spa Creek on land that Robert Proctor sold for Anne Arundel Town in 1685. Three generations of Carrolls contributed to the construction of this massive brick mansion; the third and most famous, Charles Carroll of Carrollton, was probably born here in 1737.

Charles Carroll the Settler (1660–1720) arrived in Anne Arundel Town from Ireland in 1688 and acquired this property in the new Annapolis in 1701. At his death he left the land (and perhaps a modest house) to his son, Charles Carroll of Annapolis (1702–82), who in 1721 began construction of what is now the central portion of the mansion. His son, Charles Carroll of Carrollton (1737–1832) made substantial changes and expansions to the structure, adding a third floor and continuing work on the terraced gardens to Spa Creek, where he also created a sea wall. A chapel on the upper floor was the first Roman Catholic place of worship in Annapolis.

Charles Carroll of Carrollton, the only Catholic and the longest-surviving signer of the Declaration of Independence, divided his time between his west-county estate at Doughoregan Manor and this house until about 1820, when he moved to a town house in Baltimore. At Carroll's death, the Annapolis property went to his daughter Mary Caton, whose

The WPA archival photograph of the classical Carroll Mansion

daughters sold the property to the Redemptorists for a modest $6,000 in 1852. For more than a century, this Catholic order used the house as a residence and school for priests, a social center, and even recently as a shelter for the homeless. The Charles Carroll House of Annapolis, Inc., has leased the house and spent $1 million for its restoration, including work on three acres of gardens near the creek. In 1993 the house opened to the public for the first time.

Both Newman and St. Mary's Sts. provide shortcuts to Compromise St., where, turning left, one has a short walk to City Dock. On the way, to the left, notice the **Annapolis Summer Garden Theater,** which stages musicals and light dramas in the warm months.

At the foot of Duke of Gloucester St. the visitor has the option of turning right and crossing the Spa Creek Bridge to **Eastport.** Now a part of Annapolis, Eastport developed after the Civil War as a farming and maritime village. Exhibits at the **Barge House Museum** on Second St. tell the story of this hardworking community, today the site of restaurants, specialty shops, water-related industry, and affordable houses.

The Historic Chesapeake-Patuxent Peninsula: Anne Arundel and Calvert Counties

Md. 2 from Annapolis to Solomons and Return via War of 1812 Sites

Md. 2 offers one traditional entrance to Southern Maryland. It branches southwest from U.S. 50/301 outside Annapolis and travels 57 miles south to the tip of Calvert County, which is bordered by the Chesapeake Bay on the east and the Patuxent River on the west.

Parole

Known for its first 29 miles as **Solomons Island Rd.,** Md. 2 skirts the northwest portion of Annapolis and passes through **Parole,** once a place of open fields which in 1863 the War Department converted into **Camp Parole.** Union prisoners paroled by the Confederate government waited here until they could be exchanged and returned to duty. About 70,000 soldiers passed through Camp Parole during the war, most of them before Ulysses S. Grant assumed command of the Union armies in 1864 and ended the system of prisoner exchanges.

Today, major highways and widened streets and roads crisscross Parole, where shopping centers and office parks employ many local residents. To the west of Md. 2 (reachable via West St. [Md. 450]), Riva Rd. has become a major thoroughfare above the South River. The county board of education has offices along its northwest side, and **Annapolis Senior High School** lies next door. The first secondary institution in Anne Arundel County, Annapolis High School appeared downtown in 1898; more recently, the county's schools have produced a CBS broadcasting anchorperson, Mark McEwen; the major league baseball player Denny Neagle; and the television talk-show host Montel Williams. Farther along Riva Rd., one finds **Camp Woodlands,** a Girl Scout retreat that backs onto Broad Creek.

Highland Beach and Other Shore Points via Md. 665

From Parole, Md. 665 angles southeast from Md. 2. Follow it to Forest Dr., then turn right onto Arundel on the Bay Rd. and watch for a left-hand turn at Bay Highlands, which leads to **Highland Beach,** the first African American incorporated township in Maryland and one of only two incorporated municipalities in Anne Arundel County (the other is Annapolis). Maj. Charles R. Douglass, a Civil War veteran and son of Frederick Douglass, bought 44 acres of waterfront property just south of

Annapolis in 1893 and created a summer refuge for prominent black families, particularly from Washington, who were barred from Chesapeake Bay resorts because of their skin color.

Over the years, Douglass descendants and such notables as Paul Laurence Dunbar, Langston Hughes, Mary Church Terrell, and Paul Robeson spent time in the secluded cottages of this isolated community. After Major Douglass died, in 1921, residents incorporated to preserve the area from commercial development. In the segregated decades of the 1930s, '40s, and '50s, Highland Beach provided a haven for the light-skinned elite, while nearby Carr's Beach and Sparrow's Beach catered to larger African American crowds drawn from the cities by the water and the famous jazz orchestras that appeared there. Segregated beaches have disappeared, but Highland Beach remains a sanctuary with a permanent population of over 100. Visitors should see the small museum in the town hall, just inside the gate to the beach. Twin Oaks, a cottage designed by Frederick Douglass but not completed before his death, still stands, now owned by one of the few white families in the town.

Staying on Arundel on the Bay Rd., one reaches **Thomas Point,** whose lighthouse, off to the north and east—marking shoals dangerous to mariners—has become one of the most famous fixtures on Chesapeake Bay.

Back where Arundel on the Bay Rd. leaves Forest Dr., the main road becomes Bay Ridge Rd. and then Farragut Ave. and leads to the charming bayside community of **Bay Ridge,** once a highly popular resort. Baltimoreans traveled to the spot by steamboats that left from the Light St. wharves and discharged passengers onto the beach by way of a long pier, long since disappeared.

Londontown via Md. 253

Beyond Parole, Md. 2 crosses South River, a wide tidal estuary fed by numerous small creeks. Turn east on Md. 253 and left again on the Londontown Rd., which leads to the **London Towne House and Gardens** on the banks of the South River. Cabinetmaker and ferryman William Brown built this brick Georgian building in the late 1750s to provide accommodations for his ferry passengers. Eighteenth-century travelers passed through Londontown en route to Williamsburg, Annapolis, and Philadelphia. The Anne Arundel County Court met here from 1689 to about 1695, but thereafter the town declined as Annapolis prospered. The river silted; ships and travelers went elsewhere and, with the exception of the hostelry, the town disappeared. The county government purchased the house in 1828 and operated it as an almshouse until 1965. Now the structure serves as centerpiece of a 10-acre historical park with gardens and a transplanted 18th-century tobacco barn.

Side Trips on Md. 214 and Md. 468/255

Londontown Rd. angles southwest from the park to Md. 214, an east-west highway that links Washington, D.C., with Annapolis. To the right (west) of this intersection, Md. 214 passes through a mixed rural and suburban area to **Davidsonville,** a crossroads farm community. The rolling countryside here is known for such aristocratic sports as dove shooting

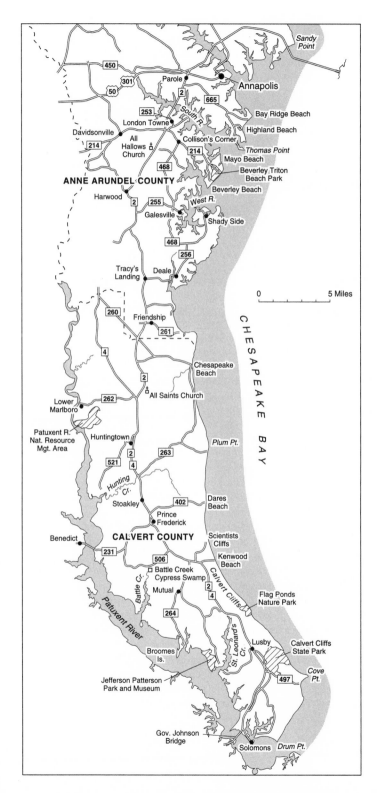

South River Clubhouse, which members still use, as it looked during the Depression

and point-to-point horse racing. Large, old houses dot the landscape to the south, accessible via smaller paved roads crisscrossing the area between Md. 2 and the Patuxent River. Queen Anne Bridge Rd. leaves Md. 214 just west of Davidsonville, passing **Friends Choice,** a small, 1½-story frame house on a brick foundation with brick gable ends, a gambrel roof, and a pair of massive end chimneys. Wayson Rd. forks to the left and then runs into Harwood Rd. The house known as **Roedown** is located to the right on Harwood Rd. near the Patuxent River. Built around 1750, this restored brick dwelling served as a honeymoon residence for Jerome Bonaparte and Betsy Patterson. Md. 214 continues its westward passage over the Patuxent River into Prince George's County and suburban Washington.

East of its intersection with Md. 2, Md. 214 first forms the northeastern boundary of a county educational complex that includes **South River Senior High School.** The road then follows a convoluted bay shoreline marked by small creeks, summer homes, and newer bayside residential developments, and ends at the small communities of Mayo and Beverley Beach, separated by the **Beverley-Triton Beach Park.**

Md. 468, known as Muddy Creek Rd., intersects Md. 214 at **Collison's Corner** and travels deeper into the Chesapeake countryside, its residential and recreational areas tucked away from main roads. A turn west on South River Clubhouse Rd. leads to the **South River Clubhouse,** a one-room frame building that houses what may be the oldest surviving private social club in America. The South River Club originated in 1722, when a group of Anne Arundel County gentlemen met for dinner every two weeks to enjoy convivial conversation and amusement. The question for July 6, 1786, introduced by the Rev. Mason Locke Weems, was "Is not the use of Spiritus Liquor, except in cases of ill health, an Idle and Unnecessary Practice?" The members apparently decided in the negative, because the club prides itself on making a powerful

Modest but comfortable Cedar Park, Cumberstone Rd., Anne Arundel County, in the 1930s

punch (a great silver punch bowl used since 1776 is kept at the house of each year's incumbent president). The clubhouse was built in 1742 and since then has served as headquarters for the club's meetings, held regularly except for a fallow period from 1875 to 1895. For the past century, a constant membership of 25 has held four dinner meetings annually, including every Fourth of July. On this occasion, the menu has always consisted of terrapin, soft-shelled crabs, oysters, duck, and other seasonal delicacies of the Chesapeake.

Contees Wharf Rd. turns south from Md. 468 to the Rhode River and the entrance to the **Smithsonian Environmental Research Center,** established in 1965. Now open to the public, this 2,600-acre facility offers trails, dock activities, and boat trips for individuals and groups interested in Chesapeake Bay ecology.

Md. 468 continues its southward course, crossing small creeks that empty into the nearby bay via the Rhode and West Rivers. Just before the intersection with Md. 255, Cumberstone Rd. angles sharply northeast for less than a mile to **Cedar Park** (private), an estate visible from the road. With its pitched roof and towering end chimneys, this old dwelling resembles an English Tudor country house; additions over generations give the house its idiosyncratic style. Richard Galloway, a Quaker, bought the tract in 1697 and built this house in 1704. John Francis Mercer, a governor of Maryland (1801–3), later lived here and made further changes. His daughter Margaret, an early abolitionist, operated the Cedar Park Academy, a boarding school for girls, on the property from 1825 to 1834. The "park," a virgin stand of timber from which the house took its name, lies farther down the road and may once have been part of an English-style deer park.

The entrance to **Tulip Hill** (private), one of Maryland's famous five-part Georgian mansions, is located on the east side of Md. 468, less than half a mile from the intersection with Md. 255. Named for the giant tulip poplars that surround it, this landmark on a ridge above the West River was constructed between 1756 and 1762. Samuel Galloway, a wealthy Quaker and merchant, built the center section, and his son John completed the wings in 1790. The double-hipped roof features two chimneys pierced by arches, a feature rarely found on colonial houses. Handcarved exterior and interior details, many of them with a tulip motif, contribute to the mansion's fame. Terraced gardens behind the house sweep down to the river. George Washington, an avid racing fan, dined here on several occasions with Samuel Galloway, owner of Selim, a celebrated racehorse of the colonial period.

Md. 255 intersects Md. 468 at the **West River Quaker Burial Ground,** where the first general meeting of Friends in Maryland was held in 1672, almost a decade before William Penn established his new Quaker colony of Pennsylvania. George Fox, the English founder of the Society of Friends, addressed this meeting during his tour of the North American colonies in 1672 and helped establish religious practices for the Maryland Quakers, who were located on both shores of the Chesapeake. Quakers predominated in this area during the 17th and early 18th centuries, but by the onset of the Revolution many had become members of the Anglican Church, through intermarriage. The West River meeting merged with the Baltimore Yearly Meeting of Friends in 1785. The earliest graves in the cemetery are unmarked, and the meeting house that once stood here burned during the Civil War.

Md. 255, a short east-west spur, links to Md. 2 three miles west of the intersection. The road's eastern terminus lies in nearby **Galesville,** originally called the West River Landing. The General Assembly designated the site for a town in 1684, but it developed slowly. Steamboats once used the landing; now it is a small fishing and boatbuilding village.

Md. 468 continues south for about another three miles and then hooks eastward, following the curve of a jagged peninsula formed by the West River and the bay. Md. 256 goes to **Deale,** a fishing and boating

Tulip Hill, Anne Arundel County. A formidable tobacco-wealth mansion as documented by the WPA

community, while Md. 468 traverses the neck to **Shady Side,** a waterfront and resort town. Early maps referred to the peninsula as "The Swamp" until it received the more fashionable "Shady Side" during the 1890s, when bay resort towns began to boom. Anne Arundel County watermen live in this area, tonging for oysters in the winter, crabbing in spring and summer, sometimes dredging for soft clams or guiding sport fishermen.

Below the South River, Md. 2 continues through charming rural countryside. **All Hallows Church** lies along the route about 1 ½ miles south of Md. 214 at the intersection of Brick Church Rd. Unusually elegant and symmetrical for a country church, All Hallows was built around 1729 and served as an early center of the established Anglican Church in Maryland. A square brick porch—common in England and found on several 18th-century churches near the Patuxent River—protects the entrance on one side. The Victorian interior was destroyed by fire in 1940; the present interior was modeled after existing churches from the same period. The churchyard contains a number of early graves, including that of William Burgess, a deputy governor who gave 100 acres of his land to establish nearby London Town in 1682.

The rector of All Hallows from 1784 to 1792 was Mason Locke Weems (1759–1825), an Anne Arundel County native widely known as "Parson Weems." Weems earned his living as an itinerant preacher, book salesman, and writer. Among his works was an influential book, *The Life and Memorable Actions of George Washington* (1800). Since not much was (or ever has been) known about George Washington's childhood, Weems simply invented incidents. The stories of the youthful Washington chopping down the cherry tree and throwing a rock across the Rappahannock River "at the lower ferry of Fredericksburg," and the image of Washington praying in the snow at Valley Forge—all sprang from Weems's fertile imagination. Thanks to Weems and other mythographers, most Americans still have difficulty understanding the man behind the monuments.

Obligation Farm (private), two miles south of All Hallows Church on the west side of the road, dates to 1743. The two-story brick house was enlarged in 1827.

Larkins Hill (private), a brick house with tall chimneys and a gambrel roof stands across the road. John Gassaway, a state legislator and South River Club member, probably built the house after he acquired the land in 1753. Seventy years earlier, Charles Calvert, the third Lord Baltimore, and his council had met the lower house of the assembly at Quaker John Larkin's house "on the Ridge," which must have been located here or nearby.

Etowah Farm (private), built around 1824, lies just beyond Obligation Farm; it follows a plan characteristic of English town houses. Anna Lee Marshall, sister of Robert E. Lee, once owned this house. William Penn and Charles Calvert met nearby in 1682 to discuss Maryland-Pennsylvania boundary disputes, which Penn later won for his colony.

Where Md. 2 joins Md. 408, it veers sharply southward. The countryside to the west along Md. 408 once was part of **Portland Manor,** 1,000 acres granted in 1697 by Lord Baltimore to Col. Henry Darnall, son of the secretary to George Calvert, first Lord Baltimore. The feudal manor

A sun-burned tobacco farmer, whom the WPA dutifully identified as Mr. Smith, and his daughter pose agreeably in a recently harvested field near Severn, Anne Arundel County.

system envisioned by Lord Baltimore's 17th-century cavaliers did not transplant well to Maryland. By the end of that century, new social classes, based on inherited wealth, business success, and slavery had emerged. The European model of manor lords, freeholders, and servants living in a family barony had disappeared.

Tobacco barns dot the countryside as Md. 2 takes one deeper into tobacco country. Many old barns, rotted with age, collapse into fields that in the 17th century produced Maryland's richest export crop. Most of the serviceable barns date to the late 19th or early 20th century and feature slats on the sides for air drying, a curing process distinctive but not unique to Maryland.

Just below its crossing with Md. 258, Md. 2 passes **St. James's Church** at **Tracy's Landing.** Finished in 1762 and later restored, this simple brick structure has a brick porch just like the one on All Hallows Church to the north. The church bell in the freestanding belfry is a 1706 gift from Queen Anne; tablets behind the altar, bearing the Ten Commandments, Apostles' Creed, and Lord's Prayer, were donated by William Locke in 1724 in honor of his wife.

At the junction of Md. 2 and Md. 256, one may travel east about two miles and visit **Fairhaven** on Herring Bay. Originally a small shipping port where farmers exported peaches, vegetables, and hogsheads of tobacco to Baltimore, Fairhaven now functions as a summer colony for Washingtonians.

South of the Fairhaven Rd. on Md. 2, Md. 261 angles off to the south and east and leads to **Friendship,** a village founded in 1804. A military company was formed here in 1821 after Nat Turner's rebellion in Virginia, but fears of a slave revolt—credible after Toussaint L'Ouverture's bloody revolt in Saint Domingue in 1791—proved exaggerated, and the local militiamen soon went home.

Following Friendship Rd. farther east takes one past **Holly Hill** (private). An early portion of this interesting house was built in 1698. Seventeenth-century buildings in the Chesapeake tended to be wooden structures, built on earthen foundations, and they decayed rapidly. Archaeologists have used the technique of dendrochronology—dating wood by counting the tree growth rings—to help determine the age of Maryland's oldest structures. This original clapboard frame house probably was built by Richard Harrison. It consisted of one room and a loft covered by a very steep roof. Typically, as owners became more prosperous and families expanded, their houses acquired additions, as well as brick veneers. The painted faux-marbelized paneling inside Holly Hill has attracted scholarly interest.

Maidstone and Chesapeake Beach via Md. 260

Md. 2 enters Calvert County at the intersection with Md. 260, which leads two miles east to **Maidstone** (private), an 18th-century house with a dramatic roof (rising at a 56-degree pitch) that covers both a second story and a 12-foot attic. Dr. Samuel Chew (1693–1744), only son of the noted Quaker Benjamin Chew, lived here until 1735, when he moved to Dover, Delaware. In 1741, the doctor was appointed chief justice for the Pennsylvania counties that now form the state of Delaware. Dr. Chew advocated military self-defense during King George's War (1740–48), when French-supported Indian warfare threatened the American colonies. His fellow Quakers, who always annoyed authorities by their pacifism, consequently read him out of the Friends Meeting. His son Benjamin (1722–1810), raised at Maidstone, became chief justice and later president of the High Court of Errors and Appeals of Pennsylvania (1791–1808). Benjamin's sister Anne married Samuel Galloway, of Tulip Hill.

Md. 260 east takes one to **Chesapeake Beach** (15' alt., 2,403 pop.), the largest incorporated town in Calvert County. In the late 1890s, as Victorians up and down the East Coast were discovering their shorelines, Otto Mears, a Colorado railroad builder, envisioned a resort on the Chesapeake. Mears gathered a group of Denver associates and created a railway between Washington and this spot on the bay. The group also built a 1,600-foot boardwalk, a band shell, dance pavilion, roller coaster, and other attractions in addition to a pier for steamboat passengers from Baltimore. The first train arrived on June 9, 1900. For the next 35 years, the "Honeysuckle Route" carried passengers and freight across the Southern Maryland landscape to the bay shore. Chesapeake Beach never developed into another Coney Island or Atlantic City, but it has survived as a slightly gaudy summer resort. The railroad folded during the Great Depression; the final train left the Chesapeake Beach Railway Station on April 15, 1935. The station is now a public museum.

Return to Md. 2 via Md. 260 and a secondary route, Mt. Harmony Paris Rd. Turn left and travel for about three miles.

All Saints Episcopal Church stands just east of the triangle formed by Md. 2, 4, and 262. Shaded by Canadian hemlocks, the rectangular brick church was constructed between 1774 and 1777. The congregation's original log church, built in 1693, stood on a different site. The interior, remodeled in 1857 and restored in 1950, features a gallery on either side. The sundial by the side of the road was presented to the church by Thomas John Claggett, rector from 1767 to 1776 and 1788 to 1792, to commemorate his consecration as the first Episcopal bishop of Maryland.

Lower Marlboro via Md. 262

From the church, the traveler may drive west on Md. 262 about 4½ miles and visit the once-busy port town of Lower Marlboro on the Patuxent River. During the early 19th century, silt from tobacco fields slowly rendered the spot obsolete as a shipping point. The **Harbor Master's House** lies at the intersecton of Md. 262 and Lower Marlboro Ln. A ferry also operated here. The Lower Marlboro Academy (ca. 1775–1860), one of few schools in 18th-century Maryland, was located in the village but closed at the outbreak of the Civil War. The **Graham House** (private), a 1½-story brick house, faces the river, in a field on the outskirts of town. Malcolm Graham built it in about 1744 on land that was part of the Patuxent Manor. To view the original paneling, one must visit the Winterthur Museum, near Wilmington, Delaware.

The junction of Md. 2 and Md. 4 marks the beginning of the Louis L. Goldstein Hwy., a modern, multilane expressway that bisects Calvert County and takes its name from a native son who became one of Maryland's most esteemed political figures. From the highway, smaller roads radiate east to the bay and west to the Patuxent River. The Patuxent, named for the tribe that once lined its banks, increases in width to as much as two miles on its relatively straight journey to the bay. Landings, wharfs, and summer cabins cluster along the waterway, whose banks have been farmed for centuries. Secluded beach communities lie sparsely scattered along the bay shore. Md. 263 branches from the highway east to one of them, **Plum Point**, an old landing where fishermen still congregate.

Md. 2 takes one south to **Calvert Memorial Hospital,** founded in the 1920s, on the outskirts of Prince Frederick. The community built the latest, 157-bed hospital in 1976. On the opposite side of the road, to the west, is the new **Islamic Center of Southern Maryland.**

East of the hospital, Md. 402 leads to **Dares Beach,** a bay resort made possible by a gap in the Calvert Cliffs (see below) which gives access to the narrow beach. A Quaker neighborhood in the 1670s, Dares Beach provides a lovely vista of the cliffs as they curve to the south.

Prince Frederick

Prince Frederick (150′ alt., 1,885 pop.), county seat since 1725, is located off the highway to the east on Md. 765. Virtually nothing remains from the 18th-century past of this old town, named for a son of King George II. British raiders burned it in 1814, and another fire, in 1882, destroyed the remaining old buildings. The present brick courthouse was built in 1915 and remodeled in 1948. Even the Goldstein General Store, which once served as informal bank and social center for the surrounding countryside, has been replaced by modern legal offices. The store belonged to an immigrant peddler who became a successful dry goods merchant. His son, Louis L. Goldstein, was born in 1913, became a lawyer, and first won elective office as a member of the House of Delegates in

1939. Goldstein won election as state senator in 1947 and in 1958 began a long tenure as the state's comptroller. Counting Harry W. Nice, who left office in 1939, Goldstein at his death in 1998 had served the state under eleven governors—three Republicans and eight Democrats.

Roger Brooke Taney

To the east and south, between the Patuxent River and Battle Creek, lies **Taney Place** (private), the ancestral home of Roger Brooke Taney (pron. Taw'nee), lawyer, cabinet officer, and U.S. Supreme Court chief justice from 1836 to 1864. The first Taney came to Calvert County as an indentured servant around 1660; after his term of service, he prospered as a planter, and he left a large estate when he died in 1692. By the time the future chief justice was born in 1777, five generations of Taneys had occupied the site. The British wrecked the family plantation in 1814. As a second son, Taney left the life of planting and learned the law, practicing in Annapolis, Frederick, Baltimore, and Washington. He married the sister of Francis Scott Key.

A celebrated Maryland lawyer by the 1820s, Taney also had become one of Andrew Jackson's staunchest supporters in the state. Taney served President Jackson as attorney general and, during Jackson's "war" on the second Bank of the United States, as secretary of the treasury before the president nominated him to succeed John Marshall as chief justice. As such, Taney spoke for the court in deciding such important cases as *Charles River Bridge v. Warren Bridge* (1837), which struck against monopolies.

Taney is best remembered for his opinion in the case, decided in 1857, of Dred Scott, a slave whose owner had lived for a time in free territory (Taney declared him still a slave and, as a black man, ineligible—according to principles embedded in the Constitution—for American citizenship). Taney's decision in *Dred Scott v. Sanford*, which also set aside the Missouri Compromise of 1820, enraged antislavery Americans at the time and has tainted his reputation since then. A former slaveowner who had freed his slaves and personally thought the system an evil, Taney often ran counter to popular opinion when he believed it conflicted with the law.

In one of his last opinions (*Ex parte Merryman*, 1864), in the heat of civil war, Taney championed the citizen's constitutional right to due process. The case involved a Southern sympathizer from Baltimore County whom Union troops had seized and held without benefit of a hearing, thus ignoring the writ of habeas corpus.

Taney died in Washington late in the war and is buried in Frederick, where his residence now serves as a museum. (On Taney's life in Frederick see Tour 18.)

Battle Creek Cypress Swamp via Md. 506

Drive south from Prince Frederick to Md. 506 and turn right to visit **Battle Creek Cypress Swamp,** a 100-acre sanctuary, free to the public, which guards a stand of bald cypress trees that has grown here for tens of thousands of years. Since this location is the northernmost area in which such trees naturally occur in the United States, the sanctuary has been registered as a National Natural Landmark. Visitors can walk through the deepest part of the swamp on a quarter-mile, raised boardwalk. The individual trees, which tower to a maximum height of 150 feet, can live for more than 1,000 years. "Knees," curiously shaped projections from the tree roots, rise above the standing water and probably help stabilize the conifers. A nature center displays examples of current flora and fauna.

Port Republic

Farther south, Md. 2/4 leads to Port Republic and a re-created one-room schoolhouse, **Port Republic School Number 7,** which first stood here about a century ago. Closed in 1932, the school was restored in 1977 under the auspices of the Calvert Retired Teachers Association. The school-museum displays original desks, slates, books, and a typical turn-of-the-century iron stove. One can imagine a fresh apple on the teacher's desk and eager pupils, varying in age from seven to seventeen, standing to recite the Pledge of Allegiance.

East and north of Port Republic, accessible via a road of the same name, lies the community of **Scientists Cliffs,** so-called because scientists gathered and bought property here partly to protect the chalky cliffs from vandals and fossil seekers.

Side Trip to Broomes Island via Md. 264 and to Jefferson Patterson Park and Museum via Md. 265 and Mackall Rd.

From Port Republic, turn south on Md. 264 for a journey to a Patuxent River waterfront community and marina, Broomes Island, beyond which lies one of Maryland's most interesting archaeological sites, Jefferson Patterson Park and Museum.

After half a mile along the way, **Christ Episcopal Church** comes into view on the right. It serves one of Maryland's original parishes. Construction of the present church began in 1769, using bricks of an earlier (1735) structure. The first church was built prior to 1692. Remodeled several times to the point where the lines of the old walls are difficult to see, this little structure illustrates the problems historians have dating buildings in Southern Maryland. The additional dates of 1772, 1881, and 1906 on the front of the church add to the confusion.

Brooke Place Manor (private), named for the first English family to settle in Calvert County, lies to the right on the south bank of Battle Creek. Robert Brooke came to Maryland in 1650 at the invitation of Lord Baltimore, bringing with him a wife, 10 children, 28 servants, and (according to legend) a pack of foxhounds. He was made "commander" of a new county called Charles and in 1652 established a county seat named Battle Town or Calvert Town on the creek bank. Brooke later became part of the Parliamentary insurgents, who briefly replaced Lord Baltimore's government. When the proprietary governor, Thomas Stone, was reinstated, he dismissed Brooke and declared that Charles County no longer existed. Patuxent County was established in its place in 1654 and renamed Calvert in 1658. Battle Town remained the county seat until 1725, but all traces of it have since disappeared. The Brookes and Taneys intermarried over the generations, an alliance that accounts for Roger Brooke Taney's middle name.

Md. 264 and Md. 265 meet in the small community of **Mutual,** the site of a famous summer tilt or "joust." This festival of horseback riding remains the state sport; in it riders armed with lances try to spear a ring suspended on a string about eight feet above the ground.

Md. 264 continues to **Broomes Island,** which actually is a long narrow neck jutting into the Patuxent. A place of charm and seclusion, it offers mile-long views up and down the river.

From Mutual, Md. 265 angles south as Mackall Rd. After about four miles it passes the entrance to **Cage** (private), an estate whose name (in roundabout fashion) honors its original owner, William Parrott, who settled here in 1650. The brick house along the river dates to the early 18th century.

The road continues to **Jefferson Patterson Park and Museum,** a remarkable green space covering 512 acres with two and a half miles of waterfront facing the Patuxent River and St. Leonard's Creek. A **Visitors Center,** converted from a cattle show barn, offers agricultural and biological exhibits as well as artifacts obtained from the archaeological sites within the park.

Jefferson Patterson Archaeological District

Archaeological evidence points to 12,000 years of continuous human habitation in the district surrounding the Jefferson Patterson Park and Museum, making this site along the Patuxent River and St. Leonard's Creek the oldest documented residence in Maryland. Placed on the National Register of Historic Places and administered by the state Department of Housing and Community Development, the Patterson district illustrates the increasing importance of archaeological techniques in the reconstruction of Maryland's past.

Careful digging, comparison of known tool techniques, and carbon-14 dating all have helped to date artifacts from the 35 prehistoric sites thus far identified within the district. The earliest discoveries from the so-called Archaic period (7500–1000 B.C.) have yielded mostly spear and arrow points, which have been catalogued by type. More Archaic sites probably lie underwater, submerged by rises in sea level over the past 5,000 years. Early Woodland period sites (1000–500 B.C.) have yielded pieces of "Accokeek Cord Impressed" pottery, as well as varying amounts of oyster shells, suggesting that the inhabitants then lived near the shoreline. High densities of shell have been found, and pottery, arrow points, and a cache of three green jasper blades have been recovered from Early Woodland sites. Inhabitants of the more numerous Late Woodland sites (A.D. 900–1600) left storage pits along the river from which archaeologists have extracted deer and bobcat remains, blue crab claws, hickory nut parts, and kernels of Indian corn carbon dated to 1400.

When in 1997 diggers discovered the skeleton of a 45–65-year-old woman at the base of one storage pit (radiocarbon dated to A.D. 400), they raised an issue that has become increasingly sensitive in Maryland archaeology—the care and disposal of excavated American Indian remains. Many of the early tribes considered ancestral bones sacred and even moved them when the tribe left the land. Their descendants have argued that excavated skeletons associated with a particular tribe should be reinterred with proper rites. In this instance, the woman's bones were reburied after a ceremony supervised by the Maryland Indian Affairs Commission.

Despite an abundance of artifacts, efforts to reconstruct tribal life in Maryland have been restricted by sketchy documentary evidence. Capt. John Smith visited this area in 1608 and described the people as Acquintanacksnak, Pawtuxunt and Mattapenient. The site of Quomocac, a village where Smith reported the presence of two hundred men and described the inhabitants as "most civil to give intertainement," may lie somewhere within the Patterson district. As other archaeological sites continue to be opened and catalogued, historians hope that the accumulated evidence will eventually illuminate this veiled portion of Maryland life.

Europeans settled this part of the countryside within five years after the founding of Maryland in 1634, leaving more extensive archaeological remains of human habitation. In the late 1650s, Richard Smith Sr., Lord Baltimore's earliest attorney general, acquired St. Leonard's, one of two 17th-century plantations identified within the Patterson district, and became the first documented resident. A site that has produced brick and shell remnants, Rhenish blue and grey stoneware, tin-glazed earthenware, and other ceramics marks the likely location of his main house, probably a wooden structure built on a brick foundation. Smith died in 1689, perhaps in King's Reach, a brick house his son Richard Smith Jr., surveyor general of Maryland, built between 1690 and 1714.

Most 17th-century Maryland houses were wooden structures that quickly deteriorated in the humid Chesapeake climate. Consequently, modern archaeologists depend primarily on artifacts to date structures in the ground. Post holes can be identified by characteristic stains and molds in the earth. Artifacts discovered in the backfill around the holes can often pinpoint the date of construction, since such items as nails, pottery, tobacco pipes, and table glassware have been extensively categorized and dated. Where the original wood has survived, investigators now take samples from the timber and study ring patterns, which vary annually according to climate. Using established "dendro patterns," which start from known years, researchers can establish a wood's age. Known as dendrochronology, this technique has resulted in later dates for many Maryland structures that had been thought to be 17th century.

The last two centuries within the Patterson district have been easier to document. Maj. Walter Smith, son of the surveyor general, inherited the properties and developed one of the area's largest farms. By the time of his death in 1754 he had become a prominent military and civic leader in Calvert County. The family farm was bequeathed to his grandson, Walter Smith, whose daughter, Margaret Mackall Smith, was born on the plantation and later married Gen. Zachary Taylor, 12th president of the United States. (She followed in the footsteps of Louise Catherine Johnson, niece of the revolutionary Maryland governor Thomas Johnson, who grew up nearby and in 1797 married John Quincy Adams, later the sixth president.) The Smith family had recently sold its Patuxent plantation to John Stuart Skinner when, in August 1814, a British fleet sailed up the river to attack Washington. Earlier that summer, when British vessels chased Commo. Joshua Barney and his small American flotilla into St. Leonard's Creek, artillery support from this side of the creek enabled Barney to break out and retreat farther up the river. The site of one battery has been identified through excavations and another site located through descriptions of the battle. Twenty-one ships from this battle lie in the river mud and await future investigation.

For the remainder of the 19th century, this Patuxent location settled into rural quietude. One Victorian house still stands along the river shore. Archaeological research indicates the presence of barns, privies, and wells typical of a large farming establishment. In 1932, Jefferson Patterson, a career diplomat, purchased the property for use as a residence and model farm. Patterson hired a Washington architect, Gertrude Sawyer, to design a series of buildings for Point Farm. The first female member of the American Institute of Architects, Sawyer chose a Colonial Revival design for the project. The current main house, a brick Tidewater Maryland–style structure with six asymmetrical bays, was completed in 1934 on the foundations of an older house. A number of barns, shops, other houses, and outbuildings also remain. In 1940 Patterson married Mary Marvin Breckinridge, who had worked as a war correspondent and CBS broadcaster with Edward R. Murrow in London. Forty-three years later, Mrs. Patterson donated the farm to the citizens of Maryland, the largest such gift in the state's history.

Since the museum opened to the public in 1984, more than 75 archaeological sites have been identified on the property. Additional sites in wooded sections of the property remain to be investigated. In 1994 the General Assembly approved funds to construct and staff an archaeological conservation laboratory at the museum to assess, restore, and display the more than seven million prehistoric and historic artifacts that have been accumulated throughout the state.

No bridge crosses St. Leonard's Creek, so a traveler must backtrack from the park to the main highway. To avoid the long way—Mackall Rd. to Md. 264 to Md. 2 and Port Republic—turn right off of Mackall Rd. onto Parran Rd. (about three miles north of the park) and rejoin Md. 2 about five miles south of Port Republic.

Below Port Republic, Md. 2/4 and the more leisurely Md. 765 pass three secondary roads leading east to private communities on the bay: Md. 509 to **Kenwood Beach;** Western Shores Blvd. to **Western Shore Estates;** and Calvert Beach Rd. to **Calvert Beach.** Farther south, Md. 765 parallels the shallow upper portion of St. Leonard's Creek while moving toward the narrowest part of the peninsula, where a distance of less than two miles separates the creek from the bay.

Flag Ponds Nature Park

About six miles south of Port Republic, a highway sign points east to Flag Ponds Nature Park, a 327-acre nature preserve on the bay. A major pound-net fishery operated at this location from the early 1900s until 1955, shipping herring, croaker, and trout to Baltimore. **Buoy Hotel Number Two,** a surviving overnight shanty, houses an exhibit center. Varied habitats—including the wooded Calvert Cliffs, freshwater ponds, and small beaches—make the park a haven for a great variety of wildlife. The park takes its name from the blue flag iris, a rare flower native to the area.

Calvert Cliffs Nuclear Power Plant

The entrance to the only electric-power–generating nuclear plant in Maryland lies off Md. 2/4 east of St. Leonard's Creek. The Baltimore Gas and Electric Company opened the facility in 1975, after seven years of construction; a second unit was completed in 1977. Two pressurized water reactors power steam turbines that generate 40 percent of the company's total electricity, enough to power 400,000 residential customers. A **Visitor's Center** includes a local museum and displays of fossils. Group tours are available.

The plant extracts water from the bay to cool the steam and discharges it 2–4 degrees warmer, but the facility lies away from fish spawning areas, and the heated discharge dissipates quickly. Extensive studies before construction indicated that the bay would suffer minimal damage from the plant, and they have proved accurate. Used nuclear fuel with high levels of radiation has been stored at the site since initial operation until it can eventually be moved to a permanent federal storage depot not yet constructed. Low-level waste materials such as clothing, tools, and resins are sent to a disposal site in South Carolina.

In 1988 the plant's safety procedures came under scrutiny from the Nuclear Regulatory Commission, which placed the facility on its "watch list" of problem plants until 1992. Calvert Cliffs is now off the list and presumably meets or exceeds current safety standards. There are currently 110 nuclear power units operating at 68 U.S. plants. They provide almost 22 percent of the nation's electricity. Besides Calvert Cliffs, nine other plants are located within a 150-mile radius of Baltimore: four in Pennsylvania, three in New Jersey, and two in Virginia.

South of Lusby, follow Md. 765, the old Solomons Island Rd. **Middleham Chapel** is located to the right of the road in a grove of shellbark hickory trees. In 1746 the vestry of Christ Church, far to the north, petitioned the assembly to levy 80,000 pounds of tobacco for a new chapel in this area of the parish. Two years later this one was built.

Calvert Cliffs State Park

Md. 765 passes the entrance (as does Md. 2/4) to a 1,600-acre park providing public access to a remarkable geological display from the Miocene Period (7–26 million years ago), one that John Smith first noted in 1608.

The Calvert Cliffs stretch 30-some miles along the western bay shore. For many years privately owned, the cliffs have not been a popular attraction (perhaps just as well). Now, at Calvert Cliffs State Park, authorities have made an exception to Maryland's general rule against removal of natural materials from state parks. The park offers a wide range of walking and cycling opportunities over hilly terrain and marshland; it also features a population of wild turkeys.

The park's main attraction lies where beach meets cliff, where the fossils are accessible. To get there from the parking area, visitors face a pleasant two-mile hike (in hot months beware of foreseeable thunderstorms). The three fossiliferous layers in the exposed cliffs are world famous among geologists and paleontologists. Whale bones, crocodile plates, shark teeth, and other prehistoric remains lie embedded in the exposed bluffs. The first fossil from North America described in European scientific literature came from these deposits (or nearby); an English volume published in 1658 supplied an illustration of *Ecphora quadricostata*, an extinct snail. In 1984 this *Ecphora*, which inhabited the bay 5–10 million years ago, became the official state fossil. When the snail proved in truth to have been a native of Virginia waters, the General Assembly made its close Maryland relative, *Ecphora gardnerae gardnerae*, the official state fossil.

After visiting the park, follow Md. 765 a short distance south, where at Bertha it branches east and becomes Md. 497, or Cove Point Rd. The road passes by parkland before ending at **Cove Point** and its assembly of cottages. The **U.S. Coast Guard Lighthouse,** built in 1820, is not open to the public. Its brick tower is the oldest of its type on the bay.

Solomons

From Calvert Cliffs and Cove Point, one may take either Md. 2/4 or the less traveled Md. 765 south to Solomons (10' alt., 800 pop.), an 18th-century waterfront community that has blossomed into a recreational and tourist attraction. Mariners long have known of its wonderful natural harbor along the Patuxent River (here two miles wide and in places more than 100 feet deep). The British used the harbor to block the river and the bay during the Revolution and the War of 1812.

Calvert Marine Museum

Established in 1975 at the site of the Solomons School House, this museum has become a major Southern Maryland cultural institution. The exhibition building, museum store, boat basin, and other attractions on this nine-acre facility offer educational exhibits, programs, and publications relating to marine paleontology of the Calvert Cliffs, estuarine biology of the Patuxent River, and local maritime history. In a 200-seat auditorium, completed in 1989, the museum stages musical and theatrical events.

The **Drum Point Lighthouse,** built in 1883, was moved onto the museum grounds in 1975. Until 1962, this hexagonal, Victorian structure marked the entrance to the Patuxent River; its screwpile light is one of only three that remain in the United States. The museum also operates the **J. C. Lore and Sons Oyster House** on the causeway leading to the island. This packing house from the 1930s contains exhibits from the Chesapeake's declining seafood industry. Cruises along the adjacent waterways are offered aboard the *Wm. B. Tennison,* an 1899 bugeye, now the oldest passenger vessel on the bay registered by the Coast Guard.

Governor Thomas Johnson Bridge

From Solomons, Md. 4 branches westward across the high Governor Thomas Johnson Bridge to St. Mary's County. Completed in 1977 and repaired in 1989, the bridge commemorates the state's first governor, a native of the St. Leonard's Creek area who was also a member of the Continental Congress and an associate justice of the U.S. Supreme Court. In 1776 Johnson nominated his friend George Washington to become commander in chief of the Continental Army. As president, Washington tried on several occasions to entice Johnson into his cabinet. Johnson eventually settled near Frederick.

Solomon's Island

Follow Md. 2 to its southern terminus on the island that Capt. Isaac Solomon made famous. Solomon came here after the Civil War, married a local woman, and established an oyster cannery that now bears his name. The island, shaped like a pipe with a long stem and briarlike bowl, is now connected by a modern causeway to the mainland. Its shoreline, deeply indented by creeks, offers anchorage for many small boats. Solomon settled the island with people from the Eastern Shore, who fished, canned, oystered, crabbed, and built boats. In 1885 Marcellus M. Davis established a shipyard here; for more than two generations it built some of the most elegant racing yachts in the country. They included the *High Tide,* an undefeated boat owned by Eugene Dupont. The *Manitou,* owned briefly by President John F. Kennedy, also was built here.

A quiet town with a school and three churches gradually developed on and around Solomon's Island. The U.S. Navy exploited its strategic location during the 20th century. The drydock *Dewey* was tested here in 1905 before its transfer to the Philippines, and in 1942 the deep waters were used for mine testing. A Navy Amphibious Training Base operated nearby during 1942–45, and thousands of marines practiced landings on the beaches of Cove and Drum Points before being sent to the Pacific theater. The **Naval Surface Weapons Center** is still located off Point Patience, just north of Solomons.

Here at Solomon's, Reginald V. Truitt in 1925 founded the **Chesapeake Biological Laboratory.** Since that time, the lab, now under the auspices of the University of Maryland, has grown into a major center for estuarine research. Housed in brick buildings at the foot of the island, the center continues to explore the bay's fragile ecosystems.

Setting a crab net in a Southern Maryland river, ca. 1938

After hectic naval activity during World War II, Solomons Island reverted to its quiet ways. In the past 20 years, however, it has become increasingly popular in warm weather. Boaters on the Inland Waterway stop here, as do Washingtonians, who patronize new restaurants, shops, and marinas. Although the small boardinghouses that once sheltered writers and artists have almost disappeared, the town retains its easy-going, rustic charm.

Rousby Hall, a relic of past passions and ambitions, stands across Mill Creek on the mainland. The British burned the original brick house in 1780, and it was replaced by this whitewashed, weatherboarded farmhouse with a steep roof. A tomb lies in the garden wherein "lies Interr'd the Body of Mr. John Rousby . . . who departed this Life the 28th day of January Anno Domini 1750, in New Style 1751, Aged 23 years and 10 months." His widow married Col. William Fitzhugh, a fiery lover who allegedly rowed her and her baby into the river and threatened to toss the babe overboard unless she consented to marry him. Fitzhugh later became a leading planter and political power in the colony. Gov. Robert Eden, who befriended Fitzhugh in the early 1760s, was a frequent visitor at Rousby Hall. A member of the 1776 convention that framed the first state constitution, Fitzhugh in 1778 became Speaker of the House of Delegates. In 1890 the property was laid out in lots for a proposed city, "Rousby on Patuxent," to be served by the Baltimore–Drum Point Railroad, but neither railroad nor city came to pass.

Returning north on Md. 2/4, the traveler can visit places that echoed with excitement in the summer of 1814. Just south of Lusby, take Sollers

Wharf Rd. to the west and follow it to the hilly countryside—an area off the trodden path but rich in Maryland history.

St. Leonard's Creek

A nest of military transports anchored at Solomon's Island, Calvert County, June 1938

West of Sollers Wharf Rd. lies **Morgan Hill Farm** (private), a restored frame house built in the early 18th century on dark red native "iron rock." The road continues southwest, passing **Spout Farm** (private), another early-18th-century home built on a cliff overlooking the creek. From this point, at the confluence of St. Leonard's Creek and the Patuxent River, Commo. Joshua Barney managed to hold off a superior British force in the Battle of St. Leonard's Creek.

After repeated British violations of neutral rights on the high seas, President James Madison, in the early summer of 1812, had asked Congress to declare war against Great Britain. Embroiled in a struggle against Napoleon for European, if not world, supremacy, the British responded in 1813 by blockading the Chesapeake and raiding coastal farms and towns along its length. Under the command of Rear Adm. George Cockburn, their primary mission was to harass shipping, seize anything of value, and badger the former colonials, while the larger war raged in Europe. Cockburn developed a robust disdain for his enemies: the militia ran when the British marines landed; many Americans accepted his money for services and information. There were notable exceptions, but he met little opposition—partly because, at the slightest resistance, the British arbitrarily burned any structures—town or farm—as an object lesson.

In the summer of 1814—with Cockburn continuing his raids, supported by schooners, barges, and a rocket boat—Commodore Barney, a native of Baltimore County and veteran of Maryland's Revolutionary War navy, accepted the challenge of countering Cockburn's squadron. Barney assembled a makeshift flotilla of 15 or 20 shallow-draft gunboats for the task, but the British soon bottled them up in the waters of St. Leonard's Creek. Then, on June 10, 1814, supported by a battery across the creek (see "Jefferson Patterson Park and Museum"), Barney's force pushed the British back long enough to escape the creek and hasten farther upriver.

A few months later, a major British infantry force of almost 5,000 veteran troops, under Maj. Gen. Robert Ross and the overall command of

Vice Adm. Sir Alexander Cochrane, joined Cockburn's Chesapeake squadron. Cochrane dreamed of arming the slaves and chastising the "corrupt and depraved" Americans. "They are a whining, canting race much like the spaniel and require the same treatment—must be drubbed into good manners," he wrote his superiors. On August 17, 1814, the British fleet anchored at the mouth of the Patuxent. Sir Peter Parker departed on a frigate for the upper Chesapeake, as a diversionary move (in Eastern Shore section, see "Caulk's Battlefield"); a small squadron had already sailed up the Potomac as another diversion. The main British force moved up the Patuxent the following morning toward Benedict, chasing Barney's boats northward as they went. (For the rest of the story, see "Benedict" below.)

Site of Preston-on-Patuxent

In the mid-17th century, on the neck formed by St. Leonard's and Hellen Creeks, Richard Preston built a house that served unexpectedly as the provincial seat of government from 1654 to 1657. An 18th-century house (private), once believed to be Preston's, still stands between Mears Creek and the Patuxent River. The writer Hulbert Footner (1879–1944) bought it in 1915 and in 1939 imaginatively reconstructed the Preston era in a book entitled *Charles' Gift*.

In 1649, only 15 years after the first English colonists settled in St. Mary's City, Puritans in the motherland, under the leadership of Oliver Cromwell, publicly beheaded Charles I, the Stuart monarch who had given the Calverts their Maryland charter. This regicide shocked Europe and created political confusion in the proprietary colony. In England, Cecil Calvert quickly expressed allegiance to the new Commonwealth, and the Maryland assembly allowed Puritans from Virginia to relocate in the province. An act supporting religious freedom soon followed. Unfortunately, the deputy governor in Maryland had first followed Virginia's example in proclaiming Charles II king after his father's execution. Governor Stone attempted to overturn that decision by proclaiming Maryland loyal to the Commonwealth, but Maryland came under suspicion and attack.

Parliament authorized commissioners to ensure the loyalty of Maryland and Virginia. One commissioner was the Virginian William Claiborne, who had always opposed the Calverts and now hoped to regain his property on Kent Island. In 1652 Claiborne and Richard Bennett, leader of the Maryland Puritans, used their influence to overthrow the "papist" government and reopen Virginia's old claim to the Maryland patent. In 1654 the commissioners deposed Governor Stone—who, though a Protestant, defended the proprietor's rights—and appointed 10 Puritan commissioners to govern Maryland. Richard Preston was one of them, and the colony's records were moved from St. Mary's City to his house, where the assembly and Provincial Court met until 1657.

Governor Stone meanwhile acted to retake the government in Calvert's name. His men temporarily retrieved the records from Preston's house and, on another occasion, raided it for arms. During these attacks some of the colony's records and the Great Seal of the Province were lost and never recovered. Writing a Maryland chapter in the English Civil War, Stone in 1655 led a small force of Calvert loyalists against the Puritans near their stronghold on the Severn River. He suffered a defeat, and Lord Baltimore did not regain complete control of Maryland until 1658.

Benedict via Md. 231

Rejoin Md. 2/4 and follow it north to Md. 231. There turn left and follow the road west, crossing the bridge to Charles County and Benedict. (For an alternate route, taking one past the cypress preserve at Battle Creek, drive west on Md. 506, turn right at Md. 508, and proceed to Md. 231 west.) **Benedict** was a river port, shipping center, and ferry location throughout the 19th century and into the 20th. The bridge now standing was built in 1950.

The British anchored here in 1812 while blockading the river. They used it again on August 19, 1814, as a landing and staging area for a determined attack on Washington. British troops marched up the western shore of the river to Nottingham and Upper Marlboro. On August 22 Commodore Barney, caught by Cockburn in the narrowing Patuxent southeast of Upper Marlboro, blew up his flotilla to prevent its capture. He then took his mariners to join the hastily assembled militia at Bladensburg.

On August 25, after sacking Washington, the British rejoined their ships at Benedict and by September 3 were on the Patuxent contemplating their next move. The diversionary force on the Potomac had taken Fort Washington, captured Alexandria, Virginia, without firing a shot, seized extensive property, and then escaped down the Potomac, eluding batteries in Virginia and Indian Head. For a few days, Cockburn's fleet anchored on the lower Chesapeake near its supply point on Tangier Island. Then, on September 7, the amphibious force moved to attack Baltimore.

Benedict is also the birthplace of Gen. James Wilkinson (1757–1825), soldier and adventurer. Wilkinson joined the Continental Army at the age of 19 and within a year was serving as adjutant to Gen. Horatio Gates. After the Revolution, like many other Southern Marylanders, he headed to Kentucky. On the western frontier he showed himself to be a man of unusual powers of persuasion and uncertain loyalties. He was instrumental in the Spanish decision to open the mouth of the Mississippi to American trade.

He also became a Spanish agent, "Number Thirteen," pledged to bring western settlements under the control of Louisiana authorities. Despite this commitment, Wilkinson in the 1790s served in the army of the United States; still on the Spanish payroll, he succeeded Gen. Anthony Wayne as army commander in the west upon Wayne's death in 1797 and in 1803 was one of the commissioners who accepted the Louisiana Purchase from the French. Two years later, with headquarters in St. Louis, he became governor of the northern portion of the vast Louisiana Territory. From this vantage point, Wilkinson conspired with Aaron Burr to seize Spanish claims south and west of the Louisiana Territory and set up an independent empire in the West. Wilkinson next informed President Thomas Jefferson of the Burr plot and placed New Orleans under martial law.

Wilkinson covered his tracks and during the War of 1812 was promoted to major general. His military career finally ended after blunders he committed during the campaign against Montreal. He died in Mexico City while seeking a Texas land grant. Only years later did his secret dealings with Spain become evident.

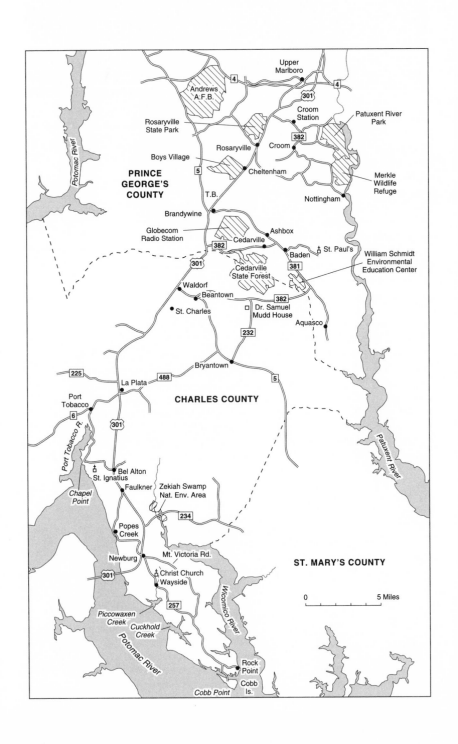

Tobacco Road: Eastern Prince George's and Charles Counties

U.S. 301 from Upper Marlboro to Lower Charles County

U.S. 301 generally follows the route of the railroad tracks laid in 1872 as the Pope's Creek Branch of the Baltimore and Potomac Railroad, later acquired by the Pennsylvania Railroad and now part of the Conrail system. Thanks to the B&O's influence in Annapolis, the Pennsylvania lacked a terminus in Washington. So, to avoid violating its state charter (allowing construction of branch lines no longer than 20 miles), it maintained a "main line" through Bowie to Pope's Creek and built a "branch" from Bowie to the District of Columbia. The line once served local farming and lumbering interests and now is largely unused except for occasional coal shipments to several power plants along the route, including one at Pasquahanna Creek near the Potomac.

U.S. 301 originates in Wilmington, Delaware, and on its way to Florida angles across both Maryland shores as the Blue Star Memorial Hwy. (named in tribute to servicemen and -women who gave their lives in World War II). Especially south of Upper Marlboro, the highway takes on the character of Main Street, Southern Maryland. It passes through a landscape of old tobacco lands with a heavy suburban overlay.

Prince George's and Charles, the two Southern Maryland counties 301 crosses, supply enduring evidence of the plantation economy that first accounted for their development. Colonial manors abound in the countryside; Prince George's residents boast that their county contains more 18th-century buildings than Williamsburg, Virginia. The region along the highway in these counties has been home to numerous distinguished families, including seven governors of Maryland. In many cases, their country estates have been preserved and restored; conscientious citizens struggle to maintain these bits of cultural heritage in the midst of rampant urbanization. The Maryland-National Capital Park and Planning Commission, established in 1927, has been a leader in such efforts, including a movement in the 1980s to recognize Prince George's County's African American past.

Slave labor, of course, supported the tobacco plantations and made the mansions possible. In 1860 the two counties led the state in numbers of slaves: more than 22,000. Many fled the large plantations during and after the Civil War, leaving the tobacco fields vacant and overgrown, swelling the populations of Washington and Baltimore. Others stayed and built churches and schools. A 1982 commission survey identified 60 historic sites associated with African Americans in Prince George's

County, including one benevolent lodge, one slave quarter, 15 private dwellings, 14 churches, and 17 school buildings.

Upper Marlboro

Bypassed by main roads and accessible via Md. 725, **Upper Marlboro** (39' alt., 745 pop.) lies northwest of the intersection of U.S. 301 and Md. 4. The town was first laid out in 1706 and named for John Churchill (an ancestor of Winston), the first Duke of Marlborough, who became a national hero when his forces defeated the French in 1704 at the Battle of Blenheim during the War of Spanish Succession. Upper Marlboro has been the Prince George's County seat since 1721 and a tobacco-marketing center throughout its existence. Politics, tobacco, and trade made Upper Marlboro a lively place during the 18th century, and the town produced some remarkable individuals—including Daniel Carroll and John Carroll.

Three branches of the Irish Catholic Carroll family have flourished in Maryland. Charles Carroll, the attorney general, arrived in Maryland in 1688. His descendants include Charles Carroll of Annapolis and Charles Carroll of Carrollton, a signer of the Declaration of Independence. Another branch started with Dr. Charles Carroll, who came to Annapolis around 1715 and abandoned his Catholic heritage, probably as a way to get ahead in a Protestant colony. His son Charles became a barrister and one of the wealthiest men in Maryland. Daniel Carroll I (1696–1751) started the third branch as a prosperous merchant in Upper Marlboro around 1720. He added to his growing fortune by marrying Eleanor Darnall (1704–96), daughter of a prominent family related to the Calverts and belle of the manor His Lordship's Kindness (see below). From this marriage came Daniel Carroll II (1730–96), friend of James Madison and signer of the U.S. Constitution, and his younger brother John Carroll (1735–1815), first bishop of the Roman Catholic Church in America, friend of Benjamin Franklin, and founder of Georgetown University. A marker on the courthouse lawn commemorates these famous brothers' contributions to their country.

Upper Marlboro grew into a political and economic center for the surrounding plantation society. In the mid-18th century, it was self-sufficient and somewhat cosmopolitan, similar to Chestertown and Easton on the Eastern Shore. Theatrical companies visited and horse races attracted large crowds. On a memorable day in 1768, Samuel Galloway's Selim, grandson of Godolphin Arabian, suffered its first loss to another undefeated horse, Figure, imported from England. Merchants like the Carrolls offered "European and West Indian" goods for sale and occasionally advertised "silks of the newest Patterns." As the plantation economy declined in the 19th century, improved transportation linked the little town to the urban centers of Baltimore and Washington, and it settled into a role as rural county seat with a distinctive past—a character it still retains amid extensive suburban expansion.

Darnall's Chance, the probable birthplace of Daniel and John Carroll, is located on Gov. Oden Bowie Dr. off Main St. (Md. 725). This restored colonial building was formerly known as the Harry Buck House, named for the family that lived there for nearly 70 years. The house was purchased by the Maryland-National Capital Park and Planning Commission in 1974 for potential use as an administration building. Subse-

quent research revealed a much older building beneath its 19th-century facade. Darnall's Chance was constructed between 1694 and 1713 by Col. Henry Darnall or his son on a 105-acre tract of the same name. At the time of his death in 1711, Col. Darnall, a Catholic related to the Calvert family, owned 27,000 acres in Prince George's County, in addition to large holdings in four other counties. Darnall's Chance was probably given to the colonel's granddaughter Eleanor when she married Daniel Carroll I in 1727. The couple and their growing family lived here until 1741. The house was rebuilt in the Italianate style in 1858, then restored to its colonial configuration in the 1980s and opened to the public in 1988.

Somewhere in Southern Maryland, the WPA captured this demonstration of tobacco harvesting—its hard and careful work and the sufficiency of mule power. The image also makes clear the division of labor.

The **Courthouse,** built in 1881 but remodeled and enlarged five times since, stands in the center of town on a lot deeded by Daniel Carroll I in 1730. The vacant post office across the street contains a mural depicting workers loading tobacco *leaves* onto wagons. Since everyone in this area knew that tobacco was harvested by the stalk, not the leaf, the mural—sponsored by the WPA in the 1930s—became a local symbol of well-intentioned government ignorance.

Beyond the courthouse, Elm St. intersects Main and ends at **Academy Hill,** location of the grave of Dr. William Beanes and his wife. The elderly doctor was the leading physician in Upper Marlboro, and the only man still in town when the British arrived on August 23, 1814, during their march to Washington. British Gen. Robert Ross and his staff used the Beanes's house, the best in town, as their headquarters. The invaders apparently enjoyed the good doctor's hospitality and departed cordially the next day. After the American defeat at Bladensburg and Britain's successful raid on Washington, the British returned to their fleet at Benedict, marching back through Upper Marlboro on August 27. The main body of troops caused no trouble, but British stragglers and deserters looted along the route. One of Dr. Beanes's Prince George's County neighbors, Robert Bowie, a former governor of Maryland, approached him for assistance in dealing with these derelicts, and they organized a group that jailed some of the offenders. Unfortunately for the doctor, one of the soldiers escaped and returned to the fleet. A party of British cavalry seized Beanes at his house in the middle of the night on August 28 and carried him off to the British flagship, where the offended general threw the 65-year-old doctor in the brig. Beanes's influential friends engaged lawyer Francis Scott Key, who obtained President Madison's permission to negotiate Beanes's release. Key and John S. Skinner, the American exchange agent for prisoners of war, caught up with the British fleet as it was preparing to attack Baltimore. The British admiral, Sir Alexander Cochrane, and Gen. Ross agreed to release Beanes but detained the other Americans until after their assault on Baltimore. Thus, from a British ship on the night of September 14, 1814, Beanes, Skinner, and Key together watched the bombardment of Fort McHenry, the event that inspired Key to compose "The Star-Spangled Banner."

Trinity Episcopal Church, designed by Baltimore architect Robert Cary Long Jr. and built in 1846, is located nearby on Church St. The Rt. Rev. Thomas John Claggett (1743–1816), the first Episcopal bishop consecrated on American soil, founded the congregation in 1810, after age had forced his retirement from the parish of St. Paul's at Baden (see below). Scion of an old county family, Claggett was consecrated bishop of Maryland in 1792. It is noteworthy that he wore a mitre, the first worn by any bishop in the Anglican Church since the Protestant Reformation. He was buried at his estate, **Croome,** but his remains were reinterred in 1919 at the National Cathedral in Washington. The frame house **Content** (private), built about 1787 and known for its pair of great exterior brick chimneys, stands across the street. **Kingston** (private), a frame building with double chimneys at each gable, is at the intersection of Church St. and Old Crain Hwy. David Craufurd, one of Upper Marlboro's founding fathers, probably built the house before the Revolution; it was renovated in the Gothic cottage style in 1859 and retains its Victorian trim.

Tobacco in Maryland

"Tobacco is our staple, is our all and leaves no room for anything else," Benedict Leonard Calvert wrote his father Charles, third Lord Baltimore, in 1729. "It requires the attendance of all our hands, and exacts their utmost labor the whole year round; it requires us to abhor communities in townships." Tobacco still stirs the economies of the five southern counties on Maryland's Western Shore. St. Mary's leads the area in acres harvested and production, followed by Charles, Calvert, Prince George's, and Anne Arundel. The latter two counties, most heavily influenced by suburban growth from Washington, continue to decline in acreage devoted to the cash crop, but some experts optimistically predict a stable Southern Maryland production of 10–12 million pounds a year for the foreseeable future.

Tobacco requires considerable care and attention. Thirteen to 15 months elapse from planting to market, and, except for the use of tractors and transplanting machines, the process has not changed much since colonial days. Tobacco still demands as much as 270 hours of labor per acre. (A scarcity of reliable hands has led most Southern Maryland growers to plant fewer than 12 acres each in tobacco.) In the spring, seeds are sown in protected beds and fields plowed in preparation for transplanting during the rainy season. A weeding period follows, when the young plants must be protected from assorted bacteria and pests, like cutworms and beetles. After flowering, the plants must be topped and pruned. In the fall, the stalks are handcut, speared on sticks, and hung in the curing barn, whose exterior walls let in just enough air. The smaller structures next to many of the barns are stripping sheds, where the cured tobacco leaves are stripped from the stalks and graded.

The Tobacco Inspection Act of 1747 created public warehouses where all tobacco was examined and graded before shipment to market. The leaves were tied in bundles called "hands" and packed in hogsheads (large barrels into which the leaves were pressed). From 1748 until about 1818, all locally grown tobacco was inspected at a public warehouse in Upper Marlboro. Shallow-draft boats carried the hogsheads down the Western Branch to the nearby Patuxent River for overseas shipment. Later the hogsheads went to Baltimore warehouses, where they sometimes sat for months awaiting sale. In 1939 two enterprising farmers from St. Mary's County investigated marketing methods in the Carolinas and returned to Maryland to establish the existing system of local auction houses at Hughesville, Upper Marlboro, Waldorf, and Wayson's Corner. The advantage of this setup lies in the fact that farmers receive their income immediately. Buyers come to the local warehouses from late March until mid-July to examine the leaf in daylight, provided by skylights. Shallow, flat baskets holding 140 pounds of tobacco—each marked by weight and grade—sit in long lines, as the auctioneer, chanting the bidding, moves rapidly up the rows. As many as 400 baskets an hour can be sold this way; a planter's entire income from a year's crop can be determined in minutes. If the grower feels that the offered price is too low, he has 30 minutes to void the sale by tearing the bid price off the basket's label. Then he can put the tobacco up for sale again.

Although smoking has declined in the United States and farm acreage continues to decrease, the foreign demand for tobacco has sustained the industry. More than half of Maryland's annual crop goes to European buyers, who each year journey to Southern Maryland in search of the high quality, thin-leaved, and even-burning Type 32 tobacco. The 1991 Maryland crop totaled 13 million pounds and was auctioned in 1992 for $20.7 million at an average of $1.62 a pound. State revenues from the tobacco tax and cigarette license sales annually exceed $60 million—a figure, the state argues, that fails to cover the medical and related public health costs that smoking carries with it.

Old Marlboro Pike (the old Washington-Marlborough Turnpike) parallels Md. 4 from its junction with Md. 223 east to the Patuxent River, passing through Upper Marlboro. **Mount Carmel Cemetery** lies on the south side of the pike west of the town. Gov. Thomas Sim Lee (1745–1819), the second elected governor of Maryland (1779–83 and 1792–94) is buried here. **Melwood Park,** a long narrow brick house once owned by Ignatius Digges, is visible from the road farther west. George Washington was entertained here several times during the early 1770s.

Old Marlboro Pike and Old Crain Hwy. briefly share a route east from Upper Marlboro, cross U.S. 301, and then fork. Bear right on the pike; the 18th-century brick chapel at **Compton Bassett** (private) is sometimes visible through the trees to the east. Catholic services were not permitted in Maryland between 1704 and the Revolution, except in private homes. This chapel continued the tradition of private family services and was built for the descendants of Clement Hill, surveyor general of Maryland. The pike ends at its intersection with Md. 4, near the Patuxent River. Old Crain Hwy. forks north to another intersection with U.S. 301. The **Clagett Family Burying Ground** is visible just before **Weston** (private), a brick dwelling on a tract owned by the Clagett family almost continuously since the 17th century. The house was built in the early 19th century on the foundations of an early 18th-century predecessor.

Side Trip on Croom Rd. (Md. 382)

From Upper Marlboro, go south on the Old Crain Hwy.—a 1920s-era road project that testified to the demands of the automobile age—for about four miles to U.S. 301 and then the intersection of Md. 382, known as Croom Rd. This scenic road travels through rich farmland along the Patuxent River. It crosses the old Pennsylvania Railroad tracks at **Croom Station** and then intersects Mount Calvert Rd., which bends northeast toward the river to **Mount Calvert** (private). A brick house of the late 18th century with exterior chimneys, Mount Calvert, with its spectacular view of the confluence of the Western Branch and the Patuxent, occupies the **site of Charles Town,** the Prince George's County seat from 1696 to 1721. The tract, Mount Calvert Manor, was surveyed in 1657, and Charles Town was established in 1683.

Elizabeth Fowler, the only person ever executed for witchcraft in Maryland, lived in Mount Calvert Hundred on this manor. A grand jury in 1685 reported that "having not the feare of God before her eyes but being led by the instigation of the Devil certaine evil & dyabolicall artes called witchcraft . . . (she) did use and practice & exercise in, upon & against one Francis Sandsbury . . . & several others." She was convicted and hanged. Only four other people were tried for witchcraft in Maryland, all before 1713. One of the four was reprieved, and the other three were acquitted.

Duvall Rd. forks south from Mount Calvert Rd. and passes **Waverly,** an elegant 1855 Italianate house (private), en route to Croom Airport Rd. and the entrance to **Patuxent River Park,** also known as the **Jug Bay Natural Area.** This riverfront environment is one of 11 limited-use parks scattered along the Patuxent's 110-mile run from Mount Airy to the bay. The Patuxent is the longest river wholly contained within Maryland boundaries. The state began acquiring land along its banks in 1963, and the park now contains more than 6,500 largely undeveloped acres. Private individuals have worked with the state to improve sewage treatment along the river during the past 20 years; the end result is a park system that encourages canoe trips, walking, and nature studies.

Md. 382 continues through the village of **Croom,** an English place name associated with the Clagett family. Duley Station Rd. goes west for about a mile to **Bellefields** (private), built on a tract formerly known as Sim's Delight. Dr. Patrick Sim, alleged to have been a refugee from the Scottish rebellion of 1715, may have built part of this brick house. Bellefields was the 19th-century home of the influential Oden and Bowie families.

St. Thomas Episcopal Church is located outside Croom at the intersection with Md. 382 and St. Thomas Church Rd. Finished in 1745 as a local chapel for St. Paul's Parish in Baden, the little brick church has remained basically unchanged for almost two and a half centuries. The bell tower was added in 1888 as a memorial to Bishop Thomas John Claggett, who served the chapel for 30 years before his death, in Croom in 1816. The shaded tombstones in the graveyard bear the names of many prominent local families, including Oden, Bowie, and Sim. Members of the Calvert family are buried under the church floor. Family relationships remain important in this part of Maryland; many long-time residents are cousins. A rector at St. Thomas once defined "Croomness" as a mixture of individuality, hardheadedness, and respect for the past.

The impressive Greek Revival entrance of Mattaponi, home of William Bowie, Prince George's County

St. Thomas Church Rd. continues toward the Patuxent River. Mattaponi Rd. and Creek take their name from the Bowie mansion **Mattaponi** (private), visible from the road, which William Bowie is believed to have constructed around 1745. It was greatly altered in 1820 with the addition of one-story wings and the finishing of the main block in the popular Federal style.

St. Thomas Church Rd. becomes Fenno Rd. at the **Merkle Wildlife Refuge,** adjacent to the Patuxent River Park. A visitor's center and observation deck at the refuge offer opportunities to view a wide variety of waterfowl, particularly during the migratory seasons. Fenno Rd. ends at Nottingham Rd., where a turn east leads to the **site of Nottingham,** an 18th-century river port that the British considered important enough to visit during their march to Washington in 1814. Now the location is little more than a name on the map.

A turn west on Nottingham Rd. takes the traveler back to Croom Rd.; driving north on Croom Rd., turning left on Mollyberry Rd., and then right on Van Brady Rd. will return one to U.S. 301 at Rosaryville.

Rosaryville State Park and His Lordship's Kindness via Rosaryville Rd. and Md. 223

Continuing south on U.S. 301, the traveler reaches Rosaryville, from which a turn to the west on Rosaryville Rd. leads to **Rosaryville State Park.** This 990-acre enclave was incorporated into the state system in 1975 and contains **Mount Airy,** an ancestral home built ca. 1740 by the Calvert family, descendants of the lords Baltimore. Mount Airy stayed in the Calvert family until 1903 and the death of 81-year-old Eleanora Calvert. The three-part brick building was destroyed by fire and rebuilt in 1931. In the 1980s it was remodeled as a country inn. The state now has opened it to the public.

Follow Rosaryville Rd. west, cross Piscataway Creek, and then turn south for three miles on Md. 223 (Woodyard Rd.) to visit **His Lordship's Kindness,** also known as **Poplar Hill.** Notable for its proportions and late Georgian detail, this five-part brick mansion was built in the 1780s by Robert Darnall. The property remained in the Darnall, Sewall, and Daingerfield families until 1928, since which it has had a succession of owners. Along with Montpelier, the mansion is one of two in Prince George's County that have been registered as National Historic Landmarks. The north wing was originally a Catholic chapel, later converted to a library; the south wing is a kitchen. The grounds contain a rare surviving complex of early outbuildings. A private foundation operates the estate, which has recently been opened to the public.

Backtrack to U.S. 301, which continues through **Cheltenham,** location of **Boys Village of Maryland** (formerly the Cheltenham House of Reformation). The institution, established privately in 1870 for delinquent boys, became a state institution in 1937.

At "**T.B.,**" a crossroads apparently named for an old boundary stone that marked the boundary between the lands of the Townshend and Brooke families, the highway intersects Md. 381.

Side Trip on Md. 381

Md. 381 curves into a rural, southeast corner of Prince George's County, near the Patuxent River, that is dotted with villages with quaint names. After Brandywine the road crosses a Conrail railroad junction and passes the Globecom Radio Station, a U.S. military installation with many radio towers.

Cedarville Rd., leading one back to U.S. 301, passes **Cedarville State Forest,** 3,000 acres of woodland and swamp to the south that offer five hiking trails and straddle the Prince George's–Charles county line. The headwaters of the **Zekiah Swamp,** Maryland's largest freshwater swamp, are located here as is a former winter camp of the Piscataway Indians.

Md. 381 continues to **Baden** and the Baden-Westwood Rd., which leads to **St. Paul's Episcopal Church,** built in 1735. According to specifications outlined in the vestry minutes, the church originally resembled St. Thomas Church at Croom. Projecting porches on both sides made the original structure cruciform. In 1794, the south porch was replaced by a large wing, which became the entry, thus reorienting the church on a north-south axis. The north porch was enlarged in 1882 to become the present chancel. The present east window is a memorial to Bishop Claggett, rector of St. Paul's 1780–86 and 1793–1806.

The state road continues south past Baden through **Horsehead,** passes the **William Schmidt Environmental Education Center,** crosses Croom Rd. (Md. 382), and continues to **Aquasco.** This small farming village, originally called Woodville, developed in the early 19th century and now boasts an outstanding group of Victorian dwellings (private), which are visible from the road. Nearby lies the Aquasco Speedway.

South of T.B., U.S. 301 leads across Mattawoman Creek into Charles County and the growing city of **Waldorf.** About half of the county's entire population and housing is concentrated in Waldorf and the nearby residential development known as **St. Charles** (pop. 28,717).

Waldorf (200' alt., 15,058 pop.) developed after 1870 as a railroad shipping center for tobacco, and it remains one of the four tobacco auction centers in Maryland. In 1949, when Charles County legalized slot machines, a "Million Dollar Motel Row" grew along U.S. 301 from Waldorf to the Potomac River, 20 miles to the south. Casinos, restaurants, motels, and other establishments catered to the gambling public; slot machine license revenues accounted for more than 20 percent of the county's budget in 1960. Some casinos contained as many as 250 of the machines, which rang night and day along the strip. Although illegal gambling undoubtedly continues in a county with a long tradition of marathon poker games, the slots were phased out during the early 1960s; by 1968, their clanking had ceased. Some of the establishments went out of business, but the strip along U.S. 301 retained its commercial character.

Meanwhile, people who worked in Washington flocked to Waldorf to live. In 1950 slightly more than 23,000 people lived in the entire county. In the 1970s, the population increased 53 percent to 72,751. The 1990 census counted 101,154 people, an increase of 39 percent since 1980.

St. Charles began in 1965 as a planned community, a project of Interstate General Company. It apparently was supposed to resemble Columbia in Howard County. By 2020, the town's population will likely stand at 80,000.

Below Waldorf and St. Charles, about two miles south of Md. 227, U.S. 301 crosses Mitchell Rd. Driving on it a short distance west and south leads to the site of **Mount Carmel** (on the left), founded in 1790 by four Carmelite nuns: Anne Matthews, her two nieces, and an English associate. The first three women were born in Charles County and like many Southern Maryland Catholics had gone to Europe to obtain the Catholic education they were denied at home. They joined the Carmelite order in Belgium and obtained permission in 1790 to establish a nunnery in Maryland, the first religious community for women in the United States. The four nuns stayed with Father Charles Neale at his family home at **Chandler's Hope** until they could establish a proper residence. By October 1790, they had moved into unfinished buildings on the site; slaves provided by supporters worked the farm, and Father Neale provided spiritual guidance. However, by the 1820s, some of the founders had died, and the farm no longer could support itself. The convent moved to Baltimore in 1831, and the buildings lay abandoned for a century. Two of the original seven buildings still stood in 1931. They were joined together and restored to create the frame house that stands here now. The larger section was the dormitory; the smaller was the infirmary. In 1954, the Restorers of Mount Carmel built the rose brick **Pilgrim's Chapel,** which is maintained as a shrine.

Charles County Community College, which includes a center for the study of Southern Maryland history and culture, is located across from Mount Carmel.

Mitchell Rd. leads to Md. 225. Turn left to La Plata.

La Plata

This town (192' alt., 5,841 pop.) owes its existence to the completion in 1872 of the Baltimore and Potomac Railroad along the 55 miles between Bowie and Pope's Creek. At first nothing more than a store, station, and post office, La Plata (pron. "la play'ta," a variation on Le Plateau, the original farm at this location) soon became the most important of the new towns along the railroad. It was incorporated in 1888. On August 3, 1892 (and after records had been removed), a suspicious fire destroyed the old county courthouse at Port Tobacco. Three years later a special election made La Plata the county seat. A new courthouse went up in 1896 and served the county well until 1956, when postwar growth (La Plata had only 488 inhabitants in 1940) called for a new structure. To reach the old county seat, which still rewards a visit, go west on Md. 6, known here as the La Plata–Doncaster Rd.

Port Tobacco and Chapel Point via Md. 6 and Chapel Point Rd.

As one departs La Plata, **La Grange** (private), a frame house with brick ends and brick nogging (pieces of broken brick wedged between inside and outside walls for insulation and fire protection), is visible from the road on the right. Dr. James Craik (1730–1814) bought the property in 1763 and probably built the house soon thereafter, naming it after the Marquis de Lafayette's chateau outside Paris. The property is listed on the National Register of Historic Places. A close friend of George Washington, with whom he served in the French and Indian War and in the Continental Army, Dr. Craik was a frequent visitor to Mount Vernon and also accompanied Washington on trips to the Appalachian interior to visit his western lands. Craik attended his friend and patient when Washington died, on December 14, 1799.

The **site of the McDonough Institute,** less than half a mile farther on Md. 6, is now occupied by the **Archbishop Neale School.** In the late 18th century, Maurice James McDonough, who lived in Pomfret, a few miles to the northwest of here, peddled goods all over the western portion of Charles County. In his will, probated in 1804, he stipulated that, upon his wife's death, his estate should be sold and the profits used to educate poor children in the "McDonough District." With the aid of an annual appropriation from the state, the trustees of his estate in 1903 opened the McDonough Institute, which taught children from kindergarten through 10th grade. Until 1924, the institute provided the only high school education in the county. Since the establishment of public high schools, the trustees have used the income to grant scholarships to children of the "district."

Port Tobacco

Port Tobacco (pop. 36), the former county seat and a thriving port during the 18th century lies off Md. 6 at the mouth of a silted river, less than two miles southwest of La Plata.

When Capt. John Smith sailed up the Potomac in 1606, noting navigational points and numbers of tribal warriors, he marked a "Potapaco" village with 20 men at this point. When Father Andrew White arrived with the Maryland settlers in 1634, he made the "Potopaco" village a center for some of his early missionary work. After the tribe disappeared— dispersed with remnants of other Potomac tribes to more westerly locations or intermarried with other ethnic groups—justices selected this river location for the Charles County seat, in 1727. Then being called Chandler's Town, the county seat was eventually named Charles Town; but residents must have used variants of the old Indian name: Potobac, Portabatoo, Portopacoo. The unofficial name "Port Tobacco" developed and finally became official in 1820.

Port Tobacco was a major river port before the Revolution and served as a station on the water and coach route between Philadelphia and the southern states. However, soil runoff from upriver plantations gradually silted the river, and a traveler observed in 1775 that Port Tobacco Creek "only carried small craft now." The town remained viable into the 19th century, due to local commerce and politics. Before the Civil War, Port Tobacco had 50–70 homes, several hotels, at least one newspaper, and numerous small businesses. An active Confederate underground and smuggling operation flourished here during the war.

After the war, the development of railroads contributed to a serious decline in Port Tobacco's population. When the courthouse burned in 1892, the county seat was moved to La Plata; and, like many of Maryland's 17th- and 18th-century river towns, Port Tobacco almost disappeared. Tobacco grew where the 25-room St. Charles Hotel had once served 200 people in its dining room. When the Society for the Preservation of Port Tobacco was formed in 1949, only a handful of houses remained, mostly near the **site of the Old Courthouse.** The society purchased the courthouse land and constructed the current replica on the old foundations. The **Charles County Museum** is located on the second floor.

Three 18th-century houses and the reconstruction of a fourth occupy the borders of what was once the town's public square. **Chimney House** (private), a two-story frame dwelling, dates to about 1770; an

Taking the crop to market during the Depression: workers unload a flatbed truck —canvas having covered the tobacco en route—at an auction barn in Upper Marlboro

enormous double chimney with a two-story brick pent almost covers one gable. Next door, **Stagg Hall** (private), with its steep gambrel roof, appears older than Chimney House but may be slightly later in date. **Quinsell House** (private) across the green is a reconstruction of the salt box frame house that once stood on the same foundations. **Cat Slide House,** another 18th-century dwelling, has been converted into a children's museum. A small brick well house stands on the site of the hydrant that once supplied the village with fresh water piped from nearby springs. The structure was built in 1958 to celebrate the Charles County Tercentenary. The **Port Tobacco School** (1870s) has been restored and is operated as a museum by the Charles County Retired Teachers Association. Port Tobacco is listed as a historic district on the National Register.

The Escape of John Wilkes Booth

The younger son in a distinguished family of actors from Harford County, John Wilkes Booth originally planned to kidnap President Abraham Lincoln and hold him hostage. In 1864, Booth organized a motley group of conspirators that included John Surratt, a pro-South Prince George's Countian, and George Atzerodt, a fervent friend of Southern rights who lived in Port Tobacco. Booth counted on using boats belonging to Southern sympathizers in Port Tobacco to ferry the bound and gagged president across the Potomac.

This wild scheme never materialized, and Lee's surrender on April 9, 1865, ended Booth's dream of a Confederate victory. Distraught and desperate, he quickly concocted a plan to murder Lincoln, Vice President Andrew Johnson, Gen. Ulysses S. Grant, and Secretary of State William H. Seward. Some of the plotters backed away from the idea of murder. On the night of April 14, 1865, only Booth succeeded in the deed. Armed with a knife, David Herold wounded and disabled Secretary Seward in his home.

From Washington to about Waldorf, Md. 5 (Branch Ave.) roughly follows the route Booth took after he assassinated President Lincoln in Ford's Theater. As Booth, his leg broken by his fall from the presidential box to the stage floor, and Herold rode out of the capital, they passed along farms and tobacco fields now occupied by residential developments, shopping centers, and government installations like the headquarters of the U.S. Census Bureau in Suitland and the **Paul E. Garber Aviation Museum** at the intersection of Md. 5 and Md. 458. (Operated by the Smithsonian Institution, the museum includes five buildings open to the public; about 140 aircraft are on display, ranging from vintage World War I biplanes to World War II fighter planes and one-of-a-kind experimental models.)

Booth and Herold next crossed Henson Creek and rode by the site of Andrews Air Force Base. Union troops occupied the church now known as **Chapel No. 2,** but they paid the pair no heed. Booth eventually stopped at the **Surratt House,** a red frame house in the modern-day suburb of Clinton. To reach it, leave Md. 5 at Jenkins Corner and bear right onto Old Branch Ave. Cross Md. 223; the house is on the left just before Surratts Rd. Mrs. Mary Surratt, John's mother, owned this combination tavern, store, and post office and there, for much of the war, had presided over a circle of discontented ex-Confederate soldiers and pro-Confederate stay-at-homes. In 1864 she and John rented out the property and moved to Washington. Here Booth and Herold changed horses, rearmed, and gathered themselves for a run to the Potomac. (In 1976 a local-history group restored the house, which has grown into a museum center with a gift shop and research library. A 12-hour bus tour leaving from this point and tracing Booth's escape route through Southern Maryland to Virginia has become a popular annual event.)

Booth and Herold continued south along Brandywine Rd., through the village of that name, and then through what is now Cedarville State Forest, possibly via St. Peter's Church Rd. or Cedar Forest Rd., to the **Dr. Samuel Mudd House,** located on Doctor Samuel Mudd Rd. off Poplar Hill–Beantown Rd. about two miles east of Beantown. Booth and Herold arrived here early in the morning of April 15 to seek Mudd's help in setting Booth's broken leg. The Mudds later claimed that they did not know of the murder or recognize the assassin (he may have been disguised), who once had been a guest in their home. (The frame house, filled with furniture and mementoes from the period, is operated as a museum by the Dr. Samuel A. Mudd Society.)

The two fugitives then traveled south along the **Zekiah Swamp** to the marshy woods south of **Port Tobacco** and east of **Bel Alton** and **Faulkner** on what is now U.S. 301. Federal troops used the **Brawner Hotel** in Port Tobacco as a field headquarters during the hunt for Booth. Thomas A. Jones, a native of the town, helped supply and shelter the fugitives for five days; a wartime Confederate secret agent and mail runner, Jones remained silent about their hiding place despite a $100,000 reward the War Department promised to pay for information leading to Booth's arrest.

Booth and Herold hid in the marsh until Jones could provide them with a boat for the river crossing to Virginia, where they apparently expected to fade into the ex-Confederate population. On the night of April 22, making their way quietly to **Pope's Creek,** Booth and Herold got across the Potomac. Twelve days after the assassination, Federal troops caught up with the pair at a farm just south of the Rappahannock River, near Port Royal, Virginia. Soldiers captured Herold. Trapped in a tobacco barn, Booth was shot and killed.

Early that summer, the War Department convened a military commission to try the conspirators. It found eight of them guilty and sentenced four, including Herold and Mrs. Surratt, to hang. On July 7, 1865, in Washington's old penitentiary building, all four conspirators died at the gallows. Mrs. Surratt may have been guilty only of owning the tavern where Booth's schemes were hatched. The military commission found Dr. Mudd guilty as an accessory, for aiding the fugitive, and sentenced him to life imprisonment at Fort Jefferson Prison in the Dry Tortugas. There Dr. Mudd rendered great service during a yellow fever epidemic. President Andrew Johnson pardoned him in 1869, and he returned to his Maryland farm. He lectured around the country on yellow fever in his later years and died of pneumonia in 1882.

John Surratt had taken part in the kidnapping scheme but denied any role in the assassination plot. He escaped to Europe and remained a fugitive until 1867. The Supreme Court's *Ex Parte Milligan* decision assured him of a civilian trial, during which the impaneled jury failed to agree on a verdict. Surratt went free and lived in Maryland until his death in 1916. Thomas Jones, the secret Confederate agent, was never caught, and he lived undisturbed for another 30 years in his native Charles County.

Chapel Point State Park

Chapel Point Rd. leaves Port Tobacco and follows the east bank of the Port Tobacco River as it flows south to the Potomac. Less than a mile outside the old town, a road rises to **Chandler's Hope,** which commands a view of the Port Tobacco valley below. Job Chandler acquired land on both sides of the river in 1651. During the late 18th and 19th centuries, the Neale family occupied the brick-nogged frame house located here and produced a generation of sons who became famous in American Catholic life. Father Leonard Neale (1745–1817) succeeded John Carroll as archbishop of Baltimore. His brother Francis Neale became vice president (1799) and then president (1809) of Georgetown College. Father Charles Neale helped found the Mount Carmel Convent and at the time of his death in 1823 was superior of the Jesuit Mission in America. During the prerevolutionary period when public Catholic worship was prohibited in Maryland, candles were allegedly put in the windows at

Chandler's Hope to inform worshipers in the river valley when masses were to be held.

The entrance to **Mulberry Grove** (private; visible from the road) is farther down Chapel Point Rd. The original house burned in 1934, but a similar building was erected on the foundations with a chimney made from bricks of the first house. John Hanson, whom Congress elected president of the United States in 1781, purchased the property in 1747 and lived here about 20 years. A Swedish benevolent order, the Sons of Vasa, erected a monument to Hanson at the edge of the steep bluff overlooking the Port Tobacco and Potomac Rivers.

Chapel Point Rd. continues to the source of its name at **St. Ignatius Roman Catholic Church** and the **St. Thomas Manor House,** part of a Jesuit mission established on the Port Tobacco River in 1662. Similar missions existed on St. Inigoes Creek and Newton Neck, but the one on Port Tobacco River seems to have been the largest and most influential. The Calverts supported these religious efforts but strongly opposed development of the Jesuit missions as tax free, independent church states with their own courts and laws. To protect his property, Lord Baltimore invoked the medieval English statute of mortmain, forbidding corporate bodies to acquire land. The Society of Jesus adjusted to this strategy by acquiring land through the proprietary under the names of individual priests or members of their households. Father Thomas Copley, returning from England after Ingle's Rebellion, assigned the manor to Thomas Matthews, who held the land in trusteeship until 1662, when Father Henry Warren took possession and built the first chapel. The original property included Cedar Point Neck (more than 3,000 acres on the peninsula between the west bank of the Port Tobacco River and Nanjemoy Creek) and more than 500 acres on the river's east bank.

With the help of slave labor, the Jesuits developed what they viewed as a model plantation. It included a water-powered gristmill, tannery, and buildings for hogs, horses, and cattle. St. Thomas flour, cheeses, and cured hams set standards of excellence, and planters from throughout the lower Potomac visited the Jesuits to share ideas about farm management. The existing manor house seems unlikely to be the "palace" begun in 1741 to the displeasure of other Jesuit priests, who preferred more austerity. Yet Gov. Thomas Sim Lee's statement in 1781 that the British had "burnt Priest Hunter's house at the mouth of Port Tobacco Creek" suggests that this building postdates the Revolution. A fire in 1866 gutted the interior and destroyed the hipped roof of the manor house and the interiors and roofs of the hyphens and church.

The present church building dates to 1790. The hyphen connecting the church and the house, ca. 1741–90, was once a chapel, built because of the Maryland law banning "public buildings of Catholic worship."

In 1784 an English traveler visited this part of Maryland and wrote the following in London:

> Port Tobacco is not much larger than Piscataway, neither of them containing more than forty or fifty houses, but it carries on much more and considerable trade which consists of some wheat, but chiefly tobacco. Near the town of Port Tobacco upon a commanding eminence overlooking the Potomack is a seat belonging to the late society of the Jesuits in

occupation of a Roman Catholic priest named Hunter in a situation the most magnificent, grand and elegant in the whole world. The house itself is exceedingly handsome, executed in fine taste and of a very beautiful model; but imagination cannot form the idea of a perspective more noble, rich and delightful than this charming villa in reality is. And as the best description I could give of it would come so far short as even to disgrace the place itself, I shall not hazard the attempt.

The Catholic Church had suppressed the Society of Jesus in 1773, except in the White Russian provinces, so a "Corporation of Roman Catholic Clergymen" was formed to hold St. Thomas Manor. The few surviving Jesuit priests in the United States reestablished the order in America by joining the Russian Province in 1805. The first three Jesuits to do so, one of whom was Father Charles Neale, took their priestly vows here in August 1805.

Following the Revolution, the Jesuit farms along the Potomac declined, as the order issued more profitable short-term leases instead of the previous life-term leases, which had encouraged farmers to conserve the land. The Chapel Point Farm was occupied throughout the Civil War by Union troops, who vandalized much of the property. All the tombstones in the graveyard were shot or knocked down except the one erected for a man who had seven wives, their names chiseled onto the stone in the order they died. After the war, the farm resumed its profitable activities, and the Jesuits even operated a steamboat between their stations along the Potomac. Beginning in the 1890s, the priests allowed a popular entertainment center to develop along the Point. During the Depression, a roller skating rink and slot-machine casino were added to a dancing pavilion and other attractions; variations on the operation continued until 1961. The state of Maryland purchased 828 acres at Chapel Point from the Society of Jesus in 1970 and has been developing the site as a state park with limited recreational facilities.

Chapel Point Rd. turns sharply east near the church and leads to U.S. 301 at **Bel Alton.** Turn right upon reaching U.S. 301 (or choose the slower, older Faulkner Rd.). Both routes soon pass Mt. Air Rd., which angles west toward the river and **Mount Air** (private), a large, brick-nogged frame house (ca. 1806) built by Luke Francis Matthews on a bluff overlooking the Potomac.

Pope's Creek

Pope's Creek Rd. intersects U.S. 301 and veers to the confluence of the Potomac River and a small creek named for Francis Pope, a 17th-century settler. A wharf community known for seafood and crab houses developed here during the 1940s, the most recent manifestation of the creek's ancient attraction as a feasting place. Archaeological excavations have uncovered artifacts of people who lived here long before the Europeans arrived. The tribes apparently gathered at Pope's Creek to eat oysters. Shell heaps at this location once covered 30 acres and in places were 15 feet high—obviously the accumulation of centuries. Most of the shell has been trucked away for use as fertilizer, road building material or cultch (material for new oyster beds to which larvae can attach). For the involvement of Pope's Creek in post–Civil War railroading, see headnote to this tour. The rail line, now part of the Conrail system, still occasionally carries coal to power plants, including one at Pasquahanna Creek. John Wilkes Booth escaped into Virginia from about this spot.

One may follow Pope's Creek Rd. on its eastwardly loop and turn right onto Edge Hill Rd.

Rock Point via Md. 257

Just below Newburg, U.S. 301 intersects Md. 257 or Rock Point Rd. (from Pope's Creek Rd., Edge Hill continues as Md. 257). Md. 257 travels for about 10 miles down a narrow, indented neck between the Potomac River on the west and Wicomico River on the east.

Mt. Victoria Rd. branches from Md. 257 at Newburg to the Wicomico side of the neck, which includes several old estates. **Society Hill** (private), a frame house built in the early 19th century, overlooks the river valley. **West Hatton** (private), on a road of the same name, was built on the banks of the river about 1790 by Maj. William Truman Stoddert, brother of Benjamin Stoddert, first secretary of the navy. The road passes through **Mount Victoria,** the place name once associated with a 15,000-acre estate that produced and shipped tobacco, grain, livestock, and lumber. The road rejoins Md. 257 at **Tompkinsville.**

Md. 257 follows the Potomac side of the neck and passes **Mount Republican** (private), a large two-story house overlooking the Potomac, built in 1792 then altered and expanded by subsequent owners. At **Wayside,** one can view **Christ Episcopal Church,** off the road and behind a low brick wall in a churchyard planted with cedars. This plain brick rectangular building with a steep gable roof was constructed before 1750 and remodeled in 1871. The communion service was imported from England in 1740. Md. 257 crosses Ditchley Prong, which empties into Piccowaxen Creek. An Indian oyster shell field similar to the one at Pope's Creek extends from this creek south along the Potomac for about two miles. Waverley Creek and Waverley Point on the west side of Piccowaxen took their names from the Waverley estate and the mansion, now restored, of the same name.

Md. 257 continues past Cuckhold Creek, which the Jesuits originally named St. James Creek. According to local lore, English tobacco factors in 1793 wrote their home office that "deer here are as numerous as cuckholds in Liverpool." Down the narrowing neck, the road links small waterfront communities known for boating, fishing, seafood, and summer vacations. Md. 254 branches south from Md. 257 and travels less than two miles to **Cobb Island,** once a summer resort, at the confluence of the Wicomico and Potomac Rivers. Md. 257 ends at **Rock Point,** another favorite place among Wicomico fishermen.

Gov. Harry W. Nice Memorial Bridge

U.S. 301 crosses the Potomac River into Virginia over this toll bridge, opened in 1940. Harry W. Nice, one of Maryland's rare Republican governors, served during—and supported—the New Deal. Born in Washington, he was living in Baltimore when elected. This bridge affected Southern Maryland's isolation much as the William Preston Lane Jr. Memorial Bridge across the Chesapeake would change the Eastern Shore.

Racing log canoes in the 1930s, when they were still work as well as pleasure boats

PART II

THE EASTERN SHORE

Maryland's Eastern Shore as a geographical definition began when a near war with Virginia in 1668 established a southern boundary, cut through the trees from Pocomoke Bay to the Atlantic Ocean, and ended nearly 100 years later when two scientists, Charles Mason and Jeremiah Dixon, surveyed Maryland's border with Pennsylvania. The Eastern Shore's boundaries are as arbitrary and idiosyncratic as its residents are alleged to be. Carved out of a peninsula shared today by three states—Delaware (formerly three counties of Pennsylvania), Virginia, and Maryland—its principal borders are the Susquehanna River and the Chesapeake Bay on the west, Virginia on the south, Delaware and the Atlantic Ocean on the east, and Pennsylvania on the north. The names of eight of the nine Eastern Shore counties—Cecil, Kent, Queen Anne's, Talbot, Caroline, Dorchester, Somerset, and Worcester—recall 17th-century English origins, remnants of which linger in the customs and even the speech of its residents.

Until the first span of the Bay Bridge was opened in 1952, almost all contact with the Shore was by water or rail, although from earliest times cattle, carts, and then cars and trucks did make their way to and from Philadelphia by land. In all, until recent times, the Shore remained rural and isolated. Its residents liked it that way and have yet to get over the massive intrusion into their lives that bridges and superhighways have inflicted upon them. Tradition still remains strong here; fact and fancy mingle creatively. Families have remained for generations, spinning out their stories of successes and tragedies. More than a few Eastern Shore natives became part of the national heritage. Others contentedly lived and died in isolation and anonymity. Particular houses evoke myths and ghost stories, and guarded family recipes contribute to the Eastern Shore's reputation for good cooking. In contrast to Western Maryland, where the Civil War left an enduring legacy, the Eastern Shore (like Southern Maryland) mainly remembers struggles against the British and their sympathizers during the Revolution and in the War of 1812. The land and waters of the Shore provided the scenes of exploits involving patriots, picaroons, pirates, and other colorful characters.

Over the past 20 years, an influx of retirees and other "foreigners" has diluted and altered life on the Shore, but the people still cling to an Eastern Shore identity. It grows out of a reliance on farming, working the water, and, increasingly, employment in small business and industry. Shore people—many of them—also tend to follow the teachings of old-time Methodism. In all, they take a critical view of much that other Marylanders take for granted. It long has been so; more than a few times between 1700 and 1850, Eastern Shore politicians tried to secede from Maryland. Today bumper stickers still declare "There's No Life West of Chesapeake Bay."

The Upper Shore—coursed by the Northeast, Elk, Bohemia, and Sassafras Rivers—has a slightly higher elevation than the lower part of the peninsula; its rolling hillsides, with dairy farms and fields of soybeans and grain, contrast noticeably with the flat fields of the Lower Shore, which are marked by corn fields and broiler chicken houses. Major ground transportation routes for centuries have passed along the head of the bay, linking Baltimore and other cities south of the Mason-Dixon line to Philadelphia, New York, and Boston. Thus, the Upper Shore has never been as isolated as the southern portion of the peninsula.

Swedish and Dutch settlers penetrated this upper region, giving it a permanent tilt toward Pennsylvania and Delaware. The Susquehannocks, the tribe that lived along the river now named for them, were perceived as different from their southern neighbors. An Iroquoian people with ties to and rivalries with tribes of the Five Nations to the north, the Susquehannocks terrified their Algonquian neighbors to the south with periodic raids. Capt. John Smith described them as "the strangest people of all those Countries, both in language & attire," who seemed "like Giants to the English."

The middle portion of the Eastern Shore, between the Sassafras and Choptank Rivers, lies across the bay from the urban centers of Baltimore and Annapolis. Here developed a rural plantation society augmented by the rise of shipbuilding and fishing along a deeply indented coastline. Sophisticated towns like Chestertown and Easton grew along rivers in the 18th century as market centers and homes for a small but influential merchant class.

The largest Indian villages in early Maryland developed along the rivers and creeks of the Lower Shore, particularly those of the Nanticokes, who lived along the river named for them. Related to the Lenni Lenape in Pennsylvania and Delaware, the Nanticokes had a reputation as sorcerers—marshland wizards who possessed secrets that could hurt you. The region has also had a strong African American presence. Almost 40 percent of the population in 1860—four years before Maryland abolished slavery—was black, almost evenly half free and half slave. Only Southern Maryland, across the bay, had a higher percentage of Americans of African descent (58 percent), but almost 80 percent of them remained enslaved until abolition.

Quakers and other religious nonconformists originally settled the Lower Shore, moving up from the Virginia portion of the peninsula. Col. Edmund Scarborough, a Virginia Anglican notorious for his hatred of both Indians and Quakers, tried unsuccessfully to claim the territory along the Annemessex and Manokin Rivers for Virginia in the 17th century. In the absence of Anglican (or other) denominational strength in the Lower Shore, Methodism, with its highly effective system of circuit-riding preachers (among them Joshua Thomas, the great waterman "preacher of the islands"), left a deep imprint on local culture.

Strong women emerged from the Lower Shore. Harriet Tubman, pillar of the Underground Railroad, was born on the Lower Eastern Shore, from which she escaped slavery to become the "Moses of her people." The region also provided a haven for the knavish Patty Cannon, leader of a gang that kidnapped both free and slave blacks for sale in the South. Anna Ella Carroll, born in Kingston Hall near Westover, served during the Civil War as a publicist for the Union cause and allegedly as a private advisor to Abraham Lincoln.

The Lower Shore always has been especially isolated and quiet. Not as sophisticated and generally poorer than its neighbors to the north, the Lower Shore rewarded fierce independence. Watermen and their families knew the swamps and marshes, the rivers and creeks, and went about their business. They were not above breaking the law. After the Civil War, oystermen based on the islands and inlets of the Lower Shore fought Maryland police and Virginia rivals for access to protected oyster beds. Outsiders were wary. Roads remained poor well into the 20th century, and few travelers found their way here. One could get lost; the people were clannish. After a spate of lynchings in the 1930s, H. L. Mencken derided the Lower Shore as "trans Choptankia."

The Eastern Shore, even more so than Southern Maryland, illustrates the impact of railroads, bridges, and highways on local economy and culture. By 1870 railroads linked all major towns of the Shore, and in the 1880s, thanks to rail connections to Chesapeake steamboat landings, Ocean City began to draw people to its beaches.

With rail links to Delaware and Pennsylvania, the farming of vegetables on the Shore—tomatoes, snap beans, sweet potatoes, and sweet corn—became a significant industry. Fruit trees and strawberries became money crops on the Upper and middle Shore. With the invention of the refrigerated railroad car in 1901 and the rise of truck transportation, the Lower Eastern Shore became a produce center for nearby metropolitan areas.

Increased traffic, agricultural competition, and the civil rights movement continued to alter established patterns of life after World War II. Kent Island, separated only by a narrow channel from the flat peninsula of Queen Anne's County and thus serving as a stepping stone from the Western Shore, became the logical point for the first major bridge crossing of the bay, in 1952. The first Bay Bridge created a gateway to the Atlantic Coast beaches and assured the rise of Ocean City as a major resort. The bridge effectively ended the historic segregation of the Eastern Shore from the rest of the state, bringing new money, residents, and customs. To the dismay of traditionalists, the trend only gained momentum. In 1964 Virginia completed a bridge and tunnel connecting Cape Charles to Cape Henry and greater Norfolk. Maryland completed a second span over the bay in 1973.

So the Shore continues to change. Millions of dollars have been invested in Ocean City and related tourist attractions. Year-round California agriculture has forced Eastern Shore fruit and vegetable growers to emphasize quality control. Processors now contract for crops in advance, provide farmers with seed and fertilizer, supervise the growing, and promote mechanical harvesting. The small cannery, once a village fixture on the Shore, has virtually disappeared. Migrant workers, who once came here by the thousands in the summer and fall, have steadily decreased in number as farms have become larger and more mechanized. The remaining small truck farmers have discovered that soybeans are more practical and profitable than the traditional garden vegetables.

Poultry has become an increasingly important cash crop, more than doubling in value in the past 30 years. Long, low broiler barns dot the countryside, which is often cultivated in grain that is used for feed. Perdue Farms, based in Salisbury and founded by Franklin S. Perdue, is now the largest privately owned poultry company in the United States, with more than $1 billion in annual sales. Spurred by such industry, Salisbury has become a mini-metropolis in a rural setting.

Even with all the growth fostered by these "improvements" (as the Western Shore saw them), three of the five lowest population densities among Maryland's 23 counties (Dorchester, Worcester, Somerset) are found on the Eastern Shore. The Malkus bridge over the wide Choptank River dramatically carries one into Cambridge and toward Salisbury, progressive urban areas that reflect the modernity of a new Eastern Shore. South of those cities lie marshlands and farmlands with long histories of hardship and outlawry.

Chesapeake Bay

Roughly 75 percent of the total population of Maryland (4,781,468 in 1990) lives within 30 miles of Chesapeake Bay, making it the literal as well as figurative heart of Maryland. This relatively shallow, 195-mile-long estuary divides the state into two convoluted "shores," the eastern and western, with a total shore length estimated at more than 8,000 miles of curved coves, inlets, creeks, and rivers. On each shore the tributary rivers create multiple peninsulas, isolated from each other but linked by water to the rest of the world.

If the bay were drained, the deep groove of the original Susquehanna River channel would lie exposed on its slightly sloping route to the sea. Around 15,000 years ago, as the ice caps of the Wisconsin glaciation began to melt, the ocean started its slow rise through the river valley, creating islands and "necks" of land above the encroaching sea. The river and its tributaries fought back with massive flows of fresh water, producing fluctuations in salinity levels that were ideal for spawning fish and other species.

The unsung, largely unnavigable Susquehanna ranks among the great rivers of the East Coast. Its north branch rises in Otsego Lake near Cooperstown, New York, and flows 316 miles across the Appalachian Plateau to Northumberland, Pennsylvania, where it joins with the West Branch, which has already meandered 228 miles across coal and timber country. The two then flow together as the mighty Susquehanna through 116 miles of Pennsylvania and 12 miles of Maryland before opening into the bay. Even though dammed at Conowingo and points farther upstream, the river still carries billions of gallons of fresh water into the bay, creating a net flow to the sea. The silt from this 27,000-square-mile watershed may eventually fill up the bay.

On a map the Chesapeake Bay resembles a twisted cypress tree. It shelters and nurtures life ranging from microscopic phytoplankton and copepods to marsh plants, waterfowl, fish, crabs, oysters, muskrats, and humans. Its depths vary from inches to 175 feet, averaging slightly more than 21 feet throughout the system. The cycles, patterns, and migrations of life within these saline, sedimentary waters have been measured scientifically for the past 30 years, but they still challenge scientists. The natural pulses vary both predictably and randomly from day to day, season to season, year to year.

Influenced by the motions of earth, moon, and sun, two tides every 24.8 hours undulate from the ocean up the gradual slope of the bay and its tributary rivers. Each tide, 1–2 feet high, takes about 13 hours, moving on a progressive surface wave accompanied by underwater currents that vary in speed, temperature, salinity, and turbulence.

A two-masted bugeye, bearing downwind, and tacking skipjacks work over an oyster bed during the Depression.

The tides represent only one of the beats in the polyrhythmic Chesapeake. The animals, too, go through cycles and migrations. One summer the jellyfish plague swimmers; the next year they seem to disappear. Oysters become abundant in one place, followed by a shortage of clams in another. The life cycle of the famous blue crab plays like a natural symphony in movements: Male and female mate throughout the summer in the middle and upper bay and its tributaries. Then the females migrate to the lower bay to spawn, while the males winter in fresher waters, preferring the muddy bottoms of deep channels. Several million eggs, the "sponge," attach themselves to the female's body in the early fall, then become "zoeae," small larvae that swim away and live like plankton. The larvae then molt, becoming more complex in structure after each molt to emerge as a "megalopa," a lobsterlike creature less than one-quarter inch long, which crawls along the bottom with claws. The megalopae migrate up the estuary and molt successively, each time emerging as a larger blue crab. After about a year and a half, the crabs become legal size for someone's feast.

American eel come from the Sargasso Sea in the southwestern Atlantic as larvae, turn into "elvers" during a year-long migration to Maryland waters, and live in the Chesapeake several years until a biological code triggers their return to the ocean. Striped bass, the famous rockfish, come to the same Chesapeake rivers every year to spawn. Until blocked by 20th-century dams, the American shad came from the Atlantic to spawn hundreds of miles up the Susquehanna—at one time the longest and largest fish run in the eastern United States. Canada geese and whistling swans, the great winged migrants from the north, winter along the tributaries of the Eastern Shore.

These cycles we can observe fairly easily. Geological cycles—longer and less visible—are harder to perceive. The bay's basic shape is only about 3,000 years old. If global temperatures continue to increase, the oceans will rise, and today's islands and rivers will begin to disappear. When the next ice age arrives, on the other hand, the Chesapeake will recede and the Susquehanna will reclaim its valley.

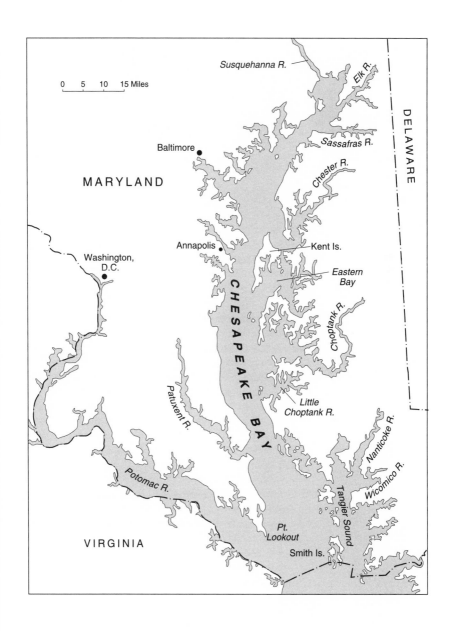

0   5   10   15 Miles

Susquehanna R.

Elk R.

DELAWARE

MARYLAND

Baltimore

Sassafras R.

Chester R.

Washington,
D.C.

Annapolis

Kent Is.

Eastern
Bay

CHESAPEAKE BAY

Choptank R.

Patuxent R.

Little
Choptank R.

Nanticoke R.

Wicomico R.

Potomac R.

Tangier Sound

Pt.
Lookout

VIRGINIA

Smith Is.

Checking an oyster catch in the 1930s. Not always did Maryland watermen smile in the presence of marine police.

The bay's history of human habitation is also partially hidden from view. No undisputed human or protohuman remains older than 15,000 years have yet been discovered in North America. Paleo-Indian tribes existed in small groups all over the continent 11,000 years ago and presumably near the emerging Chesapeake Bay. These people hunted and fished in small groups, spoke many localized languages, and lived in villages along the rivers. By the time Capt. John Smith made his epic explorations of the bay in 1607–9, the diverse tribes were highly organized and settled in a manner that has since disappeared. Only the native names endure on the landscape: mispronounced, misspelled, and not completely understood. In 1585 the English called the bay "Chesepiooc," perhaps after a village or a tribe. John Smith's map of 1608 spelled the word as "Chesapeack"; Marylanders dropped the *c* and added the *e* a few decades later. Some of the early settlers explained the meaning of the word as "great shell fish bay." Each of the native languages had a different name for a particular portion of the whole.

Smith—the doughty adventurer, explorer, and pioneer, who died in 1631—predicted that the Chesapeake area, if fully "manured" and "inhabited by industrious people," would outshine "the most pleasant places knowne." Inspired by such glowing 17th-century descriptions, thousands of Europeans migrated to the bay. Twentieth-century promoters and advertisers have borrowed from his vocabulary and called the Chesapeake region the "land of pleasant living."

After 358 years of exploration and exploitation, however, no one imagines that current or future numbers of trees, oysters, crabs, fish, and waterfowl will ever match what existed four centuries ago. More than 15 million people now live within the 64,000-square-mile watershed of the bay, more than 368,000 of them (as of 1995) on Maryland's 3,365-square-mile Eastern Shore. Suburban growth over the past 50 years has increased use of the Chesapeake for residence and recreation while decreasing its viability as a "protein factory." The bay still remains hospitable and amenable for human beings, but its ecology has been permanently altered.

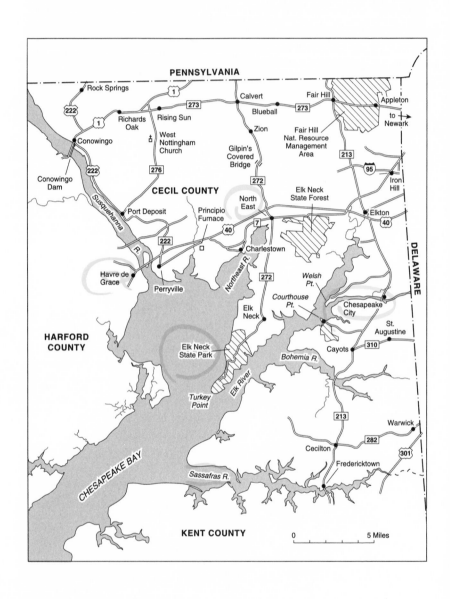

PENNSYLVANIA

Rock Springs

222

1

273   Calvert

Fair Hill

273   Appleton

to
Newark

Richards
Oak

Rising Sun

Blueball

Zion

Fair Hill
Nat. Resource
Management
Area

213

Conowingo

West
Nottingham
Church

Gilpin's
Covered
Bridge

95

Iron
Hill

Conowingo
Dam

222

276

CECIL COUNTY

272

Elk Neck
State Forest

Elkton

40

Port Deposit

Principio
Furnace

North
East

222

40   7

Charlestown

Welsh
Pt.

272

Havre de
Grace

Perryville

Courthouse
Pt.

Chesapeake
City

Elk
Neck

St.
Augustine

HARFORD
COUNTY

Elk Neck
State Park

Bohemia R.

Cayots

310

Turkey
Point

213

Warwick

Cecilton

282

301

Fredericktown

CHESAPEAKE BAY

Sassafras R.

Susquehanna R.

Northeast R.

Elk River

DELAWARE

KENT COUNTY

0   5 Miles

The Maryland countryside at the head of the Chesapeake Bay lies hidden from hurried travelers on I-95. Travelers must seek roundabout routes properly to explore Cecil County and the upper edge of the Eastern Shore. The following loop takes one around the countryside via a series of federal highways and state roads that connect the Conowingo Dam, Rising Sun, Appleton, Elkton, North East, Perryville, and Port Deposit—with a side trip to the Sassafras River.

Conowingo Dam

Begin by heading north on U.S. 1 at the edge of Harford County and follow the road over the Susquehanna River on top of this engineering achievement, which the Philadelphia Electric Company built as a power-generating plant in 1927–28. The old dam is 4,648 feet long, 105 feet high. It backs up the river for more than 14 miles to the north, forming Conowingo Lake—150 billion gallons of impounded river water. Both *Conowingo* and *Susquehanna* have Indian origins. *Conowingo* is Algonquian, possibly referring to the shallow, rocky rapids that mark this part of the river; the latter name derives from the Susquehannocks, the Iroquoian tribe that so impressed John Smith in 1608.

The 18th-century river crossing at **Bald Friar,** about four miles north of Conowingo Dam, has disappeared, commemorated only in the name of a secondary road. Bald Friar lay on the main route to Philadelphia; Lafayette's troops and the Comte de Rochambeau's heavy baggage and artillery used the crossing on their way to Yorktown in 1781. Rochambeau's aide-de-camp, Baron Von Closen, described the ford as *diabolique* because of the slippery rocks and potholes that crippled his horses and wrecked his wagons. The submerged **site of Mile's Island**—where American Indians carved images of fish, crabs, and other animals on the rocks—lies about half a mile below Bald Friar. Some of the carvings are preserved at the Maryland Academy of Sciences in Baltimore.

U.S. 1 above the Conowingo Dam follows Indian trails that became wagon and cattle roads joining settlements. With the advent of motor transportation, this highway became a lifeline for Eastern Seaboard states from Maine to Florida. By the onset of World War II, the worst of the curves had been eliminated and the roadway widened, but the highway remained a relic of horse-and-buggy days. After the war, attempts to improve U.S. 1 were abandoned in favor of building completely new parallel superhighways.

Line Pits via U.S. 222 and Old Mill Rd.

For the first mile beyond the dam, U.S. I and U.S. 222 rise from the river. Just before the road crosses the state line, Old Mill Rd. angles left at Rock Springs to a dirt track that branches right to the Line Pits, one of several chromium mines along the Maryland-Pennsylvania border east of the Susquehanna. Isaac Tyson of Baltimore developed most of these mines, which were active between 1828 and 1850, when most of the world's chromium ore originated here. Hauled by wagon to Port Deposit, the ore was then shipped to Baltimore by water. After the late 1850s, when the Philadelphia, Wilmington, and Baltimore Railroad built a branch through Rising Sun, shipments went by rail. Operations slowed after richer chrome ores were discovered in Asia Minor in 1848, and little of this region's chromium was shipped overseas after 1860. Mining here virtually ceased by 1886. In 1890, prospectors believed they had found gold in the serpentine formations containing the chromium. A brief gold rush followed, but prospectors found no commercial deposits.

U.S. I continues east and crosses Octoraro Creek at **Richards Oak,** named for a great tree whose branches once spanned the road. The tree had a trunk circumference that exceeded 22 feet and a spread of more than 125 feet; now only a stump remains. According to a plaque erected by the Hytheham Club of Port Deposit in 1922, the Marquis de Lafayette and his troops camped here on April 12, 1781, just before crossing the Susquehanna at Bald Friar.

The Colonial Path to Philadelphia via Md. 273

In colonial times, the main road from Bald Friar to Philadelphia followed what today is Md. 273 (Telegraph Rd.) across Cecil County to New Castle, Delaware. U.S. I follows this historic route for only a short distance before striking off to the northeast. At the branch, continue straight on Md. 273 for a scenic and historic journey through northern Cecil County.

Md. 273 traverses land that was a source of bitter contention between the Penns and the Calverts from 1681 until 1768, when Mason and Dixon completed their famous line. In 1680 Lord Baltimore granted a 32,000-acre tract known as Susquehanna Manor to his kinsman, George Talbot. As a member of the council and a colonel of the rangers in this area, Talbot was one of the most important residents of Cecil County. The northern boundary of Talbot's grant reached five miles into what later became Pennsylvania. Countering Lord Baltimore's grant to Talbot, William Penn, proprietor of Pennsylvania, claimed much of Cecil County by issuing grants in his own name for the Nottingham Lots and a tract on Iron Hill, Delaware. By 1700 Quaker settlers from Pennsylvania and Scotch-Irish Presbyterians from New Castle had begun arriving in numbers, and both proprietors maneuvered to obtain their loyalty. In 1738, the two provinces agreed to a temporary dividing line.

West Nottingham Church and Academy via Md. 276

Before Md. 273 reaches Rising Sun, it crosses Harrisville Rd. and Md. 276 (Jacob Toome Rd.). Turning south on either one and turning right again on Firetower Rd. after almost two miles, leads one to West Nottingham Presbyterian Church and West Nottingham Academy. Early Scotch-Irish settlers had established a Presbyterian congregation here by

1724, but evangelist George Whitefield's visit to Cecil County in 1739 split the congregation into New Light (revivalist) and Old Light groups. In 1744 the New Lights built their own church, near Rising Sun, and called the Rev. Samuel Finley to be their minister. Finley immediately established what is now the West Nottingham Academy, attracting pupils from a wide area. Among them were Richard Stockton and Benjamin Rush, signers of the Declaration of Independence from New Jersey and Pennsylvania respectively. Finley left Cecil County in 1761 to become president of the College of New Jersey (now Princeton University), and the New Light Church soon declined. In 1792 members of the church joined forces with the other congregation, and in 1804 the reunited group finished the present brick church, remodeled later in the century. The school benefited from the reunion, receiving a charter from the assembly in 1812. Nine years later the academy moved to its present location. The oldest academy building still standing is the low, multigabled brick structure with a small carpenter-Gothic frame bell tower, which dates from 1865. Today West Nottingham is a Presbyterian coeducational boarding and day school known for its innovative teaching methods.

Continue on Md. 273 east to **Rising Sun** (1,263 pop.), a trading center for grain and dairy farmers. Known as Summer Hill in 1807, it had been renamed by 1817, probably after Sunrise Tavern. The name Rising Sun was fairly common in 19th-century America; the Maryland community bears no known relation to the New Orleans bordello.

Nottingham Lots and Meeting House

East of Rising Sun, the route passes the site of the Nottingham Lots, at the junction of Md. 272 around the crossroads town of **Calvert,** where in the early days a branch of the main road between Baltimore and New York, now known as Post Rd., turned north toward Philadelphia. In 1792, William Penn granted the land to 18 Quaker families who created a township of 18,000 acres laid out in 37 lots of about 500 acres each. According to tradition, Penn himself selected the site for the **East Nottingham Friends Meeting House,** now restored and located on Md. 272 just south of the junction. The meeting house was originally made of logs; a 2$\frac{1}{2}$-story brick portion was added in 1752. After a fire in 1810, the interior was remodeled. Artifacts and documents in the meeting house illustrate the establishment of the Nottingham Lots, the boundary disputes they engendered, and the resulting Mason-Dixon survey. For about three months in 1778, Gen. William Smallwood used the building as a hospital; some of the soldiers who died here are buried in the graveyard.

Blueball

Md. 273 continues east through this crossroads community, named after a 2$\frac{1}{2}$-story stone tavern, now a private residence, which is visible from the road. The main routes from Lancaster County, Pennsylvania, and New Castle, Delaware, once met at this intersection. Near this location, at the edge of the Nottingham Lots, Andrew Job in 1710 established a tavern. According to legend, he bought an indentured servant named Elizabeth Maxwell, who had run away to America from England at age 18. After seven years of servitude, she married his son, Thomas. When Elizabeth finally wrote home, she found that her mother had died and that she had inherited her mother's furniture and other personal property, which were later sent by her uncle, Daniel Defoe, author of *Robinson Crusoe*.

Three roads intersect Md. 273 where it crosses Little Elk Creek. **Rock Presbyterian Church,** believed to have been built in 1761, lies less than two miles north along Rock Church Rd. (the second road on the left). In 1844 the interior was renovated in Gothic-Revival style. The adjacent stone **Session House** served for many years as a schoolhouse.

Md. 273 intersects Md. 213 at **Fair Hill,** where, on the northeast corner of the crossroads, one may view the **Mitchell House** (private), a considerably altered stone dwelling believed to have been built in 1764. To the north, Md. 213, called Lewisville Rd., crosses northern Maryland into a part of southern Pennsylvania famous for its mushrooms.

Follow Md. 273 east through the **Fair Hill Natural Resource Management Area,** formerly a 7,000-acre Du Pont estate, where the Fox Catcher Hound Hunt Club has built three overpasses in the three miles between Fair Hill and Appleton to enable hunters to cross the highway without danger to dogs, horses, or hunters.

Md. 273 leaves Maryland and crosses into Newark, Delaware, an atmospheric university town tracing its origins to the New Worke Meeting House of the 1680s.

In Newark, follow Del. 2 (Elkton Rd.) southwest past the Newark City Hall for the brief journey to the Maryland line, where the road becomes Md. 279.

Mason-Dixon Tangent Stone

Soon after crossing back into Maryland, turn south on Iron Hill Rd., following the railroad tracks to the Mason-Dixon Tangent Stone. This weathered marker in a pasture was set by Mason and Dixon in 1765; it still bears the Calvert and Penn coats of arms. A stone inscribed "Tangent" was placed beside the older stone in 1849 by the Graham Resurvey. Both stones mark the point at which the boundary between Maryland and Delaware is tangent to an arc centered at New Castle (a 12-mile tangent-line reference appeared in one of the original deeds of enrollment by which the Duke of York granted his Delaware territory, captured from the Dutch, to William Penn in 1682). The Calvert and Penn heirs debated for more than 50 years whether the 12-mile dimension referred to radius or circumference. The line was finally settled after Mason and Dixon made their survey between 1763 and 1768.

Iron Hill is on the Welsh Tract—30,000 acres William Penn granted to Welsh Baptist miners in 1701 to substantiate his claim to this part of Maryland. Iron was mined here beginning in the early decades of the 18th century. Follow Md. 279 across Interstate 95 to its intersection with Md. 7 outside Elkton.

Elkton

Originally known as "Head of Elk," Elkton (29' alt., 9,073 pop.) grew up between Big Elk and Little Elk Creeks, two streams that converge here to form the Elk River. As land transportation improved, the settlement developed into an important stop along the paths between Philadelphia and the southern colonies. There was a post office here in 1776, testifying to the town's business as a shipping point for wheat grown on the upper Eastern Shore and southern counties of Pennsylvania.

As a strategic location, Elkton also saw much activity during the Revolution. The British under General Howe passed through in force in August 1777, intent on capturing Philadelphia. They were welcomed by local Tories, whom patriots may barely have outnumbered. According to one local legend, Robert Alexander, who resided at the **Hermitage** (now a private apartment building on East Main St.), prepared dinner for Howe after his troops landed at Elk Neck. While he was delivering the invitation, Continental soldiers assigned to watch his house confiscated the supper. Until then a supposed patriot, Alexander angrily changed sides and fled to the protection of British troops. Revolutionaries then confiscated his landholdings and sold them.

In March 1781, Lafayette's troops embarked on ships from Elkton bound for Annapolis and Yorktown; they returned in early April, unable to pass the British ships that were on the bay. On April 11 Lafayette departed again, this time by land. Other troops, under Washington and Rochambeau, passed through the town that September. The Cecil County seat moved to Head of Elk in 1786, and the town officially became Elkton a year later. Francis Asbury, the first American Methodist bishop, visited the rough-and-ready town in 1815 and sadly concluded that "it may be visited by the Lord in the fourth or fifth generation."

As the closest Maryland county seat south of New York, New Jersey, and Pennsylvania, Elkton profited in the early 20th century from couples unwilling to wait the time those states required to obtain a marriage license. The Pennsylvania Railroad also passed through Elkton by this time, so weddings became big business. Taxi drivers met couples at the station and for a set fee took them to the courthouse for a license, then to a minister for the ceremony. Signs lining Main St. advertised "marrying parsons." Maryland finally adopted its own 48-hour waiting period in 1938, and the flow of elopers ebbed. People still come to Elkton to get married, perhaps because of this tradition, but the town no longer calls itself the "Gretna Green of the East."

Wartime industry built the town's population during World War II. Now surrounded by shopping centers and suburban developments, Elkton serves as home and service center for residents who work as far away as Baltimore and Wilmington. Elkton High School claims two graduates of distinction in music—Bernard "Pretty" Purdy (1960), the jazz artist, and Janie Clewer (1976), who sings with Julio Iglesias. Diana Milbourn (1976) is a professional artist in New York.

Follow Md. 279 to Md. 213, which passes through Elkton as Bridge St., and turn left toward the center of town; the intersection of Main and Bridge Sts. marks the town's east-west dividing point. Turn onto East Main St., which features structures of historic interest.

The **Cecil County Public Library,** at 135 East Main, offers the visitor a small historical museum and exhibits. Immediately to the west is the **Residence of Dr. Abraham Mitchell** (private), who built the house in 1769 and, according to tradition, treated wounded Continental soldiers here. (The Maryland alcove in the chapel at Valley Forge is dedicated to Mitchell.) The house later belonged to his son, Dr. George Mitchell (1785–1832), a prominent member of the Pike Expedition to Canada in 1813. Later, as a congressman, Mitchell introduced the resolution that invited Lafayette to return to the United States and led to his triumphant tour in 1824.

The **Courthouse** on East Main, just east of North St., was constructed in 1938 on the site of the 18th-century Fountain Inn. **Cecil Center** occupies a large 2½-story brick mansion with a hip roof, believed to have been built before 1802 by Maj. James Sewall. During the War of 1812, Sewall commanded a battalion at Fort Defiance, a fortification hurriedly constructed a mile below Elkton after the British attacked Elk River points in 1813.

Col. Henry Hollingsworth, who served as commissary (or military buyer) for the Eastern Shore during the Revolution, lived in **Partridge Hill,** the brick house at 129 East Main St. (private). The Hollingsworth family acquired Elk Landing, once the port at Head of Elk, in 1735. Family account books from the early 19th century show that boats carrying flour, nails, bar iron, lumber, and pork departed Elk Landing for Baltimore and returned with coal, coffee, molasses, and whiskey.

A force from Admiral Cockburn's Chesapeake flotilla attacked Elkton in April 1813 but retreated under the guns of the local militiamen who met them at a small redoubt built at the landing. Now on private property, the **site of Fort Hollingsworth** lies off Landing Ln., which branches from Md. 7 just west of the town.

Side Trip to Fredericktown via U.S. 213

Rte. 213 beyond Elkton becomes the Augustine Herman Hwy., named for a remarkable 17th-century gentleman whose legacy and name permeate the Upper Shore.

Augustine Herrman

Born in Prague around 1621, Augustine Herrman, a trader and adventurer, made his way to the New Netherlands in 1642. There he became one of the "Nine Men of New Amsterdam" who opposed Peter Stuyvesant's arbitrary rule on Manhattan Island. His politics got him in trouble with the volatile Stuyvesant, but his business networks, which included agents in Virginia, usually kept him out of jail. The Dutch in New York used "Heermans" as ambassador to the New Englanders, with whom they feuded over trade rights and land ownership. Herrman, a surveyor who spoke several languages, found ways to profit from the controversies.

Maryland's charter included "that part of the Bay of Delaware on the North which lieth under the fortieth degree of north latitude from the Equinoctial, where New England is terminated." When Maryland representatives threatened force to gain citizens among the Dutch and Swedish settlers along the Delaware, Stuyvesant sent Augustine Herrman to Maryland in 1659 to protest. Herrman reminded the Marylanders that their charter applied only to areas not previously settled by "Christians." While the English pondered this astute challenge Herrman spent the winter here. Charmed by the hospitality of the Tidewater, he applied the next year for permission to own land. In exchange for agreeing to make an accurate map of Maryland, the Bohemian received, in 1662, his first 4,000 acres, along the shores of one of the rivers he had passed on his diplomatic journey. He named his property Bohemia Manor, and the river became the Bohemia on his map, which was finally completed in 1673.

Herrman and his family were listed in the first Act of Naturalization passed in 1666 by the Maryland assembly, which expressed concern that the lack of legal rights for "aliens" was "Foreslowing the peopleing of the Province with useful Artificers & handicrafts men." By this time, the English had seized New Amsterdam and named it New York. When he died in 1686, Augustine Herrman owned more than 20,000 acres in Maryland and was among the largest, most aristocratic land-owners in America. Legends about his hospitality and horsemanship still linger in this portion of the Upper Shore.

Frenchtown

Just outside the Elkton city limits, Rte. 213 crosses Frenchtown Rd. Go right on this road to the **site of Frenchtown** and the remains of an 18th-century tavern on the banks of the Elk River.

Swedes first settled this area in the 17th century, when they established a village called "Transtown," derived from a Swedish word for "crane." French Acadians, refugees from Nova Scotia, occupied the site around 1755 and renamed the village, calling it La Ville Francaise, which was subsequently Anglicized. Until 1837, Frenchtown was a busy port and a relay station on the main routes between Baltimore and points north. The land trip of 16½ miles between Frenchtown and New Castle, Delaware, greatly shortened the water journey to Philadelphia and New York, avoiding the trip around the Delmarva Peninsula. Freight lines took goods by sloop (later by steamboat) to Frenchtown and transported them by wagon and stagecoach to New Castle. The British bombarded French-town on April 29, 1813, plundering and burning the wharf, fishery, ware-house, and five vessels in the harbor. A garrison behind a redoubt re-treated, but a group of stagecoach drivers twice repulsed the enemy before being forced to withdraw. The town itself was spared, and only two months later, on June 21, 1813, the *Chesapeake*, the first steamboat on the Chesapeake Bay, docked at Frenchtown on her maiden voyage from Baltimore.

In 1815, the New Castle and Frenchtown Turnpike Company opened a toll road between the two cities, and in 1827 became the New Castle and Frenchtown Turnpike and Railroad Company. The railroad line opened on July 4, 1831, but for the first year the cars were pulled by horses. On September 10, 1832, a locomotive named the *Delaware* made its first trip, with two cars. When the locomotive approached a stop, the engineer would shut off the power and send up a signal of steam from the safety valve. Several men at the station would then grab the engine with their hands, while the station agent thrust a fence rail between the spikes of the *Delaware*'s wheels to stop the train. With completion of a Baltimore-to-Elkton-to-Philadelphia railroad line in 1837, business in Frenchtown declined. The New Castle and Frenchtown Railroad made its last trip in 1854.

Only remnants of the old dock remain, along with the site of the tav-ern, which burned in 1964. Cranes occasionally visit the marshes along the river.

Below Point and Williams Rds., Md. 213 crosses Elk Forest Rd., a right turn on which leads to **Welch Point.** Local legend describes the capture and execution here of 19 deserting Hessians during the Revolutionary War. A depression in the ground at their presumed common grave is called The Hessians' Hole. **Canal National Wildlife Area** now occu-pies Welch Point.

Chesapeake City and the C&D Canal

Md. 213 leads to Chesapeake City (735 pop.), which occupies both sides of the Chesapeake and Delaware Canal, a coastal transportation link that shortens the water route between Baltimore and Philadelphia by 296 miles. As early as 1661, Augustine Herrman predicted the construction of such a waterway. In 1799, Maryland chartered a canal company, and construction began in 1801 under the supervision of Benjamin H. Latrobe. Work was suspended in 1803 and not resumed until 1824, but the canal finally opened for navigation in 1829. One of the most difficult tasks confronting the builders was lock construction, necessary to compensate for a difference of several feet between the water levels of the bay and the Delaware River.

The canal, which allowed the passage of Northern troops to Washington at the beginning of the Civil War, may have prevented that city from falling to the Confederacy. (Railroad lines were disrupted in those first critical weeks, and the Confederates controlled the lower bay.) Recognizing its strategic and economic value, the federal government purchased the canal in 1919 for $2.5 million and lowered the channel to sea level in 1927 at a cost of more than $10 million. During World War II, the canal enabled shipping to escape German submarines in the Atlantic. In 1962, construction began on a project that made the waterway 35 feet deep and 400 feet wide throughout its entire length.

Chesapeake City grew around the C&D Canal. When the lock system was changed to the current sea-level course, a new main street was established. Maryland pilots hand over their charges to Delaware pilots at this location, a process which occurs while the ships are moving. The ocean-going cargo vessels, which never stop in the busy ditch, glide slowly, with incongruous maritime grace, through the rural countryside. The chief business of the town, besides maintenance of the canal itself, is servicing boats, including thousands of pleasure craft that annually use the waterway for the cruise north to Maine or south to Florida and the Caribbean. The town also supplies many small craft that cruise on the Chesapeake Bay. Antique shops, restaurants, and small inns give the village additional distinction.

Md. 213 crosses city and canal on a high bridge opened on September 20, 1949. The height was necessary to permit large ships to pass without requiring a draw span. The current structure replaced a bridge demolished on July 28, 1942, by the tanker *Franz Klasen*. Fortunately for wartime shipping, the canal was completely closed for only a week and returned to full service after a month.

Turn right on the bridge's south side to visit Chesapeake City South and the U.S. Army Corps of Engineers Station. The stone **Pumphouse** (1837) is a national historic landmark with a one-room museum containing the large wooden waterwheel (1851) that once ran day and night to replace water lost every time a vessel passed through the lock. A plaque commemorates the opening of the canal and describes difficulties overcome in its construction. Tours are available to the public.

In 1910 Stephan Ortynsky of Philadelphia, the first Ukrainian Catholic bishop in the United States, bought a tract of land along the canal, to establish a farm to raise food for the rectory and convent of St. Basil in Philadelphia. The convent sisters established an orphanage on the north side of the canal, and the bishop purchased 700 acres of swampy land for 40 Ukrainian families. Additional families arrived from Pennsylvania and created a self-sufficient community of small farms. They built **St. Basil's Ukrainian Catholic Church** in 1920. Its onion-shaped dome can be seen above the treetops from the main highway.

Courthouse Point via Courthouse Point Rd.

Beyond Chesapeake City, a road of the same name leads to the Elk River and the site of Cecil County's second courthouse. It provided the seat of county business from 1719 to 1781, superseding the first courthouse at Oldtown on the Sassafras River. According to local tradition, bricks from this structure were used in building its successor in Elkton. During the 18th century, the ferry running from this point to Elk Ferry on Oldfield Point across the Elk River was one of the most important in the county.

The place proved its value in wartime. Gen. William Howe and his troops landed at Elk Ferry on August 25, 1777, soon proceeding to Head of Elk. As part of this campaign, British and Hessian forces crossed to Courthouse Point, removed some court records, but left the building intact. **Courthouse Point Wildlife Management Area** is just south of its namesake.

Rte. 213 continues south through the hamlet of **Cayots** on the northern edge of the **Labadie Tract,** some 3,700 acres of fertile farmland that in the 17th century belonged to followers of Jean de Labadie, a religious mystic who advocated community ownership of property. In

A poor rural family near St. Augustine, Cecil County, during the Depression

1679 Labadists in the Netherlands sent Jaspar Dankers and Peter Sluyter to New Amsterdam in search of land for a New World community. There they met and converted Ephraim Herrman, son of Augustine Herrman, who was at that point planning to establish a town at Bohemia Manor. Ephraim, who was interested in attracting as many settlers as possible, agreed to grant a tract to the Labadists, who returned to Holland and came back in 1683 with a group to take up the land. Herrman refused to honor his promise, however, and the Labadists had to take their case to court before a deed was executed in their favor in August 1684.

Most of the Labadists came from Holland, a few came from New Amsterdam, and some were recruited from the surrounding countryside. The group never exceeded 100. Hardworking members followed a rule of silence at meals; men and women ate at separate tables. Each gave all of his or her belongings to the community and in return was issued only bare necessities. All shared equally in the work without regard to their former station in life. The cult raised corn, hemp, flax, and cattle, and used slaves to cultivate tobacco. In violation of the rules of the mother church in Holland, Sluyter made himself a dictator, and the community disintegrated before the end of the 17th century. One colonist complained, "Sluyter would not allow them to have any fire in order to harden them and mortify and subdue the sins of the body . . . but . . . had his own hearth well provided night and day." In 1698 Sluyter divided the property among the more prominent members of the community, keeping for himself a portion upon which he grew wealthy. By five years after his death, in 1722, the colony had completely disappeared.

St. Augustine via Md. 310

Follow Md. 310 east at Cayots to St. Augustine and the small frame **St. Augustine Episcopal Church of Bohemia Manor.** North Sassafras Parish obtained permission to build a chapel of ease here in 1695; a brick chapel replaced the early structure in about 1735. This church fell into decay in the early 19th century, when Methodism began to attract large numbers on the Eastern Shore, and by 1816 only the arch of the chancel stood. The present simple frame church was built in 1838 and consecrated by Bishop William R. Whittingham in 1841. From 1893 to 1924, and from 1930 to 1962, the church fell into disuse. In 1963 the Episcopal Church restored it, and regular services have resumed.

According to local tradition, a walled grave in the cemetery contains the remains of a dissolute young man who in 1861 requested that his coffin lid be left unscrewed and a brick wall set around the grave with one brick left out—all this so that he could escape if the devil came after him. Bricks mortared into the space from time to time by church sextons reportedly always disappear.

Md. 213 continues through land originally patented by Augustine Herrman. A roadside sign identifies the approximate site of the original **Bohemia Manor,** now private property. Herrman's broken gravestone, reset in marble, is also here, but the exact site of his grave is unknown.

The highway then crosses the Bohemia River, marked by small sandy beaches, a few docking areas, and scattered houses along the shore. Just beyond the river and visible on the west side of the road, the traveler passes **The Anchorage** (private), home of the Lusbys in the early 1700s. Col. Jacob Jones, commander of the sloop *Wasp* during the War of 1812, married Ruth Lusby in 1821. The couple lived here and enlarged the house in 1835.

Bohemia Church via Bohemia Church Rd.

About three miles below the Bohemia River, a turn to the east on Bohemia Church Rd. ends within a few minutes at **St. Francis Xavier Church,** also known as **Old Bohemia,** whose bell tower rises above farmland on a hill above Little Bohemia Creek. Built around 1790, this brick church originally served a Roman Catholic mission established in 1704 by the Jesuit Thomas Mansell. The mission secretly opened Bohemia Academy around 1745, a time when Catholic schools were illegal. Students included John Carroll, who became the first American Catholic archbishop, and perhaps Charles Carroll of Carrollton, signer of the Declaration of Independence. John Carroll also founded Georgetown University; Leonard Neale, his Bohemia classmate, became the fourth president of the university. The brick rectory, to one side, was erected in 1825 from the bricks of the old schoolhouse. At the back of the church, under a great clump of trees, are the graves of eight of the early Jesuit priests of the mission. Nearby is the tomb of Kitty Knight, remembered for her heroism in the War of 1812 (see under "Georgetown" in Tour 8). The Jesuits turned the church and buildings over to the Wilmington Diocese in 1898. A fire gutted the interior in 1912, but the church was rebuilt within the old walls. Regular services discontinued in the 1920s, but the adjacent cemetery remained in use. The Old Bohemia Historical Society now maintains the church, which is open by request and during selected Sundays in the summer.

The traveler who continues east on Church Rd. through the flat farmland reaches **Warwick,** near which is the **birthplace of James Rumsey** (1743–92), inventor of an early marine steam engine. On two occasions in 1787, Rumsey's steam pump successfully propelled a boat against the current on the Potomac River south of Sharpsburg. Robert Fulton operated his "Clermont" on the Hudson 20 years later, but as far as is known, Rumsey's experiment was the first application of the principle of jet propulsion by steam.

Turn west at Warwick and continue on Md. 282. Visible from the road is the brick **Daniel Charles Heath House** (private), which Heath built for his son in about 1750. The original house consisted of a passageway along one gable which opened into one large room downstairs, with two small rooms above. The house was extended to make the long, narrow 2$\frac{1}{2}$-story building that now stands.

Md. 282 returns to Md. 213 at **Cecilton** (489 pop.), the third and only surviving Maryland town honoring Cecil, second Lord Baltimore.

To see **Rose Hill** (private), one of eight Maryland houses to bear this name, follow Md. 282 west from Cecilton about two and a half miles and bear right when the road forks. Thomas Marsh had built the small frame, gambrel-roofed section by about 1683. In 1830 Gen. Thomas Marsh Forman (1758–1845) added the brick town house, which boasts molded plaster ceilings and marble fireplaces. General Forman, who joined Washington's army at the age of 18 and served in the War of 1812, lies buried in the family graveyard. Follow Md. 282 another mile to **St. Stephen's Episcopal Church,** built in 1873, which serves what was once North Sassafras Parish, one of the original parishes of Maryland. The third rector of St. Stephen's, the Rev. Hugh Jones, arrived here in 1731 after many years teaching mathematics and natural philosophy at the College of William and Mary. At St. Stephen's he wrote one of the earliest histories of Maryland's southern sister, *The History and Present State of Virginia*, published in London in 1734. One century later, St. Stephen's supplied the scene for the ordination of William Douglass, the first African American to receive Anglican orders south of the Mason-Dixon line.

To the north of the church, on Cherry Grove Rd., **Cherry Grove** (private), a gambrel-roofed house built in the second half of the 18th century, illustrates three wooden-contruction methods of the period—hewn log, timber frame, and post-and-hewn plank. It has brick end walls.

From Cecilton, Md. 213 continues south toward the Sassafras River, passing **Greenfields** (or Greenfield Castle, private), visible on the left at the end of a tree-lined lane in the middle of the fields. This large, hip-roofed brick mansion may have been built in the 1740s on a tract of land patented to John Ward about 1674.

Fredericktown

The traveler reaches the Sassafras River at Fredericktown, laid out in 1736 as a stop along the post route from Annapolis to Philadelphia via Rock Hall. This area was once the home of 30 or more Acadian families, people of French descent who came as refugees from Nova Scotia in 1755 during the French and Indian War. The town is now a center for boat-building and -repairing. Dozens of small boats of all kinds lie at anchor in the tranquil water, which attracts ducks and geese.

Builders of the new Chesapeake Bay bridge (1987) preserved a stone monument commemorating Capt. John Smith's explorations of this river in 1607–9. The marker identifies the river as Smith's "Tockwough," named for the Indian tribe that lived along its banks; it also claims that "tockwough" was the Indian name for the sassafras root. But the connection with sassafras, which the Europeans knew, is undoubtedly false (see Tuckahoe State Park).

From Fredericktown, Md. 213 leads to Chestertown and the Bay Bridge. The Cecil County tour resumes on the western side of Elkton.

To North East via Md. 7 (Philadelphia Road)

West of Elkton, one may travel on U.S. 40, known as Pulaski Hwy. (for the Polish hero of the Revolution) from the Delaware line to Baltimore, but this heavily traveled, dual-lane highway offers little except convenience. A scenic alternative, Md. 7 follows the original route of U.S. 40 and passes through historic small towns.

Take Md. 7 west from Elkton across the top of Elk Neck, a hilly, wooded peninsula formed by the Elk River on the east and the Northeast River and the bay on the west. The road passes the northern edge of **Elk Neck State Forest** nearly parallel to the Amtrak railroad tracks.

The old industrial community of **North East** (20' alt., 1,913 pop.) stands at the head of the river from which it takes its name. A flour mill and early forge had appeared at this site by 1716; the Principio Company established a forge here that remained in operation until 1780. Another forge and a rolling mill were constructed on the same site and flourished from 1829 to 1893. Most of the town's buildings date to the late 19th and early 20th centuries. **St. Mary Anne's Episcopal Church,** a brick, gambrel-roofed structure with wide roundheaded windows, on South Main St., was built in 1742. The Georgian bell tower was added in 1904 by Robert Brookings, founder of the Brookings Institution, in memory of his parents, who are buried in the churchyard.

An attractive municipal park and marina sit on the river bank. Adjacent to the marina, the **Cecil County Hunters' Association** operates the **Upper Bay Museum,** dedicated to the locale's outdoor heritage. Fishing along the Northeast River was unexcelled in the 18th and 19th centuries. During a 26-day period in 1819, one haul of the seine each day from the same place produced 2,600 barrels of herring. Hunting is permitted in season in the nearby state forest.

A little more than three miles north of the center of town, on Md. 272 just beyond I-95 and Cecil Community College, **Gilpin's Covered Bridge,** the longest (119') covered wooden bridge still standing in Maryland, crosses Northeast Creek. A bowstring type, its arches are made from single timbers that stretch from bank to bank to provide support. The timbers were warped to shape by balancing them on stumps and gradually pulling down each end with chains.

Elk Neck via Md. 272

From North East, Main St. leads to Turkey Point Rd. (Md. 272), which descends Elk Neck, a surprisingly rural and undeveloped area. The road travels along the Northeast River through hilly, rugged countryside more reminiscent of Western Maryland than the familiar flatlands of the Eastern Shore. Just beyond the junction with Old Elk Neck Rd. and Elk River Ln., the road reaches the Elk River and provides a broad vista of the 1777 British landing sites on both banks.

Md. 272 continues to **Elk Neck State Park,** part of which was presented to the state in 1936 by Dr. William L. Abbott, a naturalist who had established a game preserve here. Visitors on the Elk River side of the neck have a splendid view of the freighters that travel the Chesapeake and Delaware Canal. The western shorelines and Susquehanna River bridges are clearly visible from the bay side. The road passes through a private area, then ends in a section of the park that includes the **Turkey Point Lighthouse** (1834), a 35-foot tower on a 100-foot bluff. Visitors may park cars in a lot and walk to the lighthouse across high, windy bluffs and rolling wooded pastures that drop down to sandy beaches. More than seven miles of trails in the park offer a walker more geographic diversity than any other state park on the Eastern Shore. Return to North East via Md. 272.

West from North East, Md. 7 takes one to **Charlestown** (578 pop.), laid out on the shore of the Northeast River in 1742. Benjamin Mifflin in 1762 described the village as "a miserable forlorn place" with a landing too shallow for 50-ton vessels. An attempt to make it the county seat after the Revolution failed when construction of a courthouse was delayed four years, so Charlestown developed as a fishing center. A traveler in 1793 reported that 2,000 wagons of salted herring were transported from here to the back country every spring. The village now boasts a quiet waterfront and a few buildings that may date to the 18th century.

Md. 7 briefly joins U.S. 40 outside Charlestown and then angles southwest, crossing Principio Creek, which empties into Furnace Bay. This little creek valley contains the **site of the Principio Iron Works** (private), which British capitalists first developed in 1719. Ironmaster John England arrived in 1723, finished the furnace, located iron deposits on the Patapsco River, and in 1728 arranged an alliance with Augustine Washington (George's father) to acquire more iron lands in Stafford County, Virginia. At his death in 1734, England had made the Principio Furnace one of the most successful in the colonies, capable of producing high-quality iron that would sell on the London market. In the 1740s the Principio properties at this location, in North East, and at Accokeek, Virginia, supplied almost half of all the pig iron exported to England. Thomas Russell Jr. came from England to run the furnace for a while in the 1760s and returned shortly before the Revolution. During the Revolution he made bar iron and cannonballs for the Continentals. When Principio was confiscated as British property in 1780, Russell was given the forge at North East as compensation. New owners built another furnace here after the Revolution, but British troops destroyed it in 1813. In 1837, the Whitaker Iron Company built a third furnace, which produced pig iron until 1889. Iron coke furnaces in Alabama and the Lake Superior region eventually made Maryland's charcoal iron industry obsolete, but a forge here continued to make high-quality iron for steam boiler tubes until 1925. All that remains from the 200-year-old history of this industry are a few ruins covered with honeysuckle and poison ivy.

Perryville

Beyond Principio Furnace, Md. 7 enters this old community (20' alt., 2,456 pop.) at the mouth of the Susquehanna River (known in the 18th century as the Susquehanna Lower Ferry). Railroads and highways converge at this historic site, where Washington's and Rochambeau's troops crossed in 1781 on their way to Yorktown. By 1837 a railroad linked Baltimore and Philadelphia, but a steam ferry had to transfer the rail cars across the river. During the winter of 1852–53, the river for several weeks froze hard enough to lay tracks across the ice. The first railroad bridge crossed the river in 1866. When the present railroad bridge was constructed in 1906, the older bridge became the first highway bridge at this site.

Rodgers Tavern, a stone building near the Amtrak railroad bridge, may have been standing as early as 1745. William Stephenson operated a tavern here before John Rodgers, father of Commo. John Rodgers (naval hero of the War of 1812), acquired it in 1780. The building appears to be the tavern mentioned by Benjamin Mifflin, who wrote in 1762 about "a Fine dish of the Largest Oldwives [herring] that Ever I Eat." George Washington mentioned stopping here many times, especially during the 1780s and '90s.

The entrance to the **Perry Point Veterans Administration Medical Center** is just beyond the Amtrak bridge. This property was patented in 1658 by John Bateman and later named Perry Point, after Richard Perry and his two sons, who owned the land from 1710 to 1729. The Thomas family then purchased the land and during their ownership (1729–1800) built the hip-roofed, stuccoed brick building, formerly occupied by the hospital superintendent. In 1800, John Stump bought the manor and 1,800-acre farm, which the family turned over to the Union

Army during the Civil War. In 1918, the U.S. government bought the farm from the Stump family and converted Perry Point to a rehabilitation center and psychiatric hospital for veterans, and a supply depot. The VA hospital was established in 1930.

The **Thomas J. Hatem Memorial Bridge** (toll) used by U.S. 40 and the CSX Railroad bridge also cross the Susquehanna at Perryville. Both cross **Garrett Island** on their way from Cecil County on the Eastern Shore to Harford County and Havre de Grace on the Western Shore. Originally called Palmer's Island, this wooded isle near the river's mouth may be the site of one of the earliest English settlements in Maryland. Sometime between 1612 and 1616, Edward Palmer, nephew of Sir Thomas Overbury (poet and essayist, who was murdered in a famous intrigue at the court of James I), presumably came here from Virginia to trade with the native tribes. Palmer dreamed of establishing a university and reportedly willed the island to Oxford University at his death in 1625. William Claiborne (of Kent Island renown) established a trading outpost here before Lord Baltimore's colonists arrived in the lower bay in 1634. According to a local historian, when the first Maryland agents arrived to claim the island in 1637, they found four servants and six books in the middle of a wilderness. No physical evidence has ever been discovered on the island to confirm its legendary past. The island was later known as Watson's Island and then named for John W. Garrett (1820–84), president of the Baltimore and Ohio Railroad during the Civil War.

Perryville residents recently have taken pride in the academic achievement of pupils at **Perryville High School,** whose team took first place on the competitive scholastic television program "It's Academic!" in both 1996 and 1997.

From the center of Perryville, take Md. 222 north to complete the Cecil County loop. After crossing over I-95, the road turns west. On the left, the Mt. Ararat Farm Rd. leads to a large dairy farm on the heights above the river. The **Physick House** (private), a 2½-story stone building

Where Capt. John Smith first encountered the falls of the Susquehanna, as the site appeared in the 1930s

(ca. 1830) with a hipped roof, is visible from the road. George Talbot, to whom Lord Baltimore had made extensive land grants in northern Cecil County, came to grief in 1684 when he murdered a royal tax collector. It is said that after the deed he hid for months in a cave at the foot of the nearby cliffs, sending his trained falcons out to hunt for him. He eventually turned himself in. Sentenced to death by a Virginia court, Talbot received a pardon from King James II and returned to England. His vast landed estate reverted to the lord proprietor.

As Md. 222 descends from the Susquehanna bluffs to Port Deposit, it passes the entrance to the former **Bainbridge Naval Training Center.** Nearly 350,000 sailors passed through Bainbridge during World War II. It closed in 1947, partially reopened in 1951, and by 1964 was about one-third operational as a WAVES training center, the home of the Service School Command, and the location of a prep school for the Naval Academy. Also, the Navy Bureau of Personnel kept records and equipment here. It closed again in 1976.

Port Deposit

This old river port (16' alt., 685 pop.), set dramatically against the Susquehanna bluffs, occupies a narrow strip of land along the river. The cliffs rise more than 200 feet, leaving space along the shore for only a single street and the railroad track. One other small street has been quarried out of the rock near the southern end of the town.

Port Deposit and the Market Economy

As early as 1729 Thomas Cresap operated a ferry near this spot, which by the early 19th century was known as Creswell's Ferry. George Washington took Creswell's Ferry on May 8, 1775, on his way to Philadelphia for the session of the Continental Congress that chose him to be commander in chief of the American army.

A settlement developed here after completion in 1808 of the Susquehanna (or Maryland) Canal, which ran from the highest point of navigation, just below Smith's Falls, to the Pennsylvania line. In that prerailroad era, canal backers hoped to make the bay accessible for transport of grain and other products from the rich Pennsylvania hinterland. In 1812, Philip Thomas, who owned most of the site, laid out the town, and the assembly named it Port Deposit. When the marauding British entered the river in 1813, the town was still too insignificant to attract their attention; they burned a warehouse across the river.

The new canal gradually brought traffic to the river port. Great wooden flats (later known as scows) and rafts carrying flour and wheat, whiskey, iron, pork, slate, and other products flowed down from Pennsylvania; their cargo was then transferred to ships, and the rafts were broken up and sold as lumber. In 1822, Port Deposit handled $1,337,925 worth of commodities. Nearly 1,000 scows and rafts came down the river and canal; 128 vessels entered from the bay and cleared the port.

Herring and shad fisheries—once Maryland mainstays—also added to the town's wealth. The great silver shad once entered the river in unimaginable numbers to travel hundreds of miles inland for their annual spawning. In 1827, near the Pennsylvania line, Thomas Stump caught about 15 million shad in a single haul, an amount that filled 100 wagons.

Beginning in the 1830s, local stone quarries provided another important industry for the young town. An iron foundry established here in 1849 produced the popular Armstrong stove in the 1870s. The economic landscape of Port Deposit then changed for the worse. The arrival of railroads helped close the canal in the 1890s. In 1910 a dam across the Susquehanna in Pennsylvania ended the rafting and blocked the spawning shad, as did other dams, most notably the Pennsylvania Electric's massive Conowingo. The Susquehanna was no longer navigable in any sense of the word. After the 1930s, quarrying, the navy's presence at Bainbridge, and a barge and scow construction yard had kept the town alive. But quarrying played out in the 1970s, when the navy closed Bainbridge. In the past 15 years the town's population has declined by almost 25 percent.

So, clearly the regional, then national, and now global economy have not always been kind to little Port Deposit, where, to show how fickle nature as well as market forces can be, winter floods in early 1996 wreaked havoc (townspeople complained that the operators of Conowingo Dam gave inadequate warning before releasing millions of gallons of pent-up water). The tough river folk may survive, as luck would have it, by catering to out-of-town tourists.

Md. 222 supplies Port Deposit's single street. The river and railroad tracks lie to the west; houses and churches, some built of stone, hug the nearby bluffs on the east. A two-story stone house built in 1816 sits across the street from a marina for sport fishing boats. **Washington Hall,** a large brick building with brownstone trim, was built in 1894 to house a free school that Jacob Tome (1819–98), a native of York County, Pennsylvania, established for the children of Port Deposit. Tome had arrived here penniless on a raft, at the age of 14, and entered the lumber business. He finished his life as one of the leading financiers in Maryland, extending his investments as far as timberlands in Michigan. Tome felt deeply grateful for the town's role in his financial success.

While he lived, Tome gave his institute $1.5 million; he bequeathed his residuary estate, worth almost as much, for a town school system, which opened in 1894. At his death, about 600 children attended Tome's schools, which functioned in place of public education. With the development of the county school system, enrollment declined. The institute's trustees used Tome's additional endowment to open a boarding school for boys, the Tome School, in 1902 on the bluff above Port Deposit. Income from the boarding school helped support the free schools for a generation, but the school never recovered from the Great Depression, and it closed in 1941. Opposite Washington Hall, a great brick and stone staircase climbs to the former Tome School; a waterfall cascades beside the steps, creating a scene unique to Maryland's small towns.

North of the staircase, the cliff has been terraced to accommodate a second row of houses. The **Gerry House,** believed to have been built in 1813, is a three-story stone building with a three-story wooden gallery across the front. Lafayette is supposed to have stopped here in 1824. Nearby is another stone house, thought to have been built before 1818. At the junction with Md. 276, a hollow in the cliff has been laid out as a public square.

A short distance north, Md. 276 leads to the entrance lane to **Anchor and Hope Farm** (private). The old stone house on this farm, probably built in the late 17th century, stands on a great bluff above Port Deposit and the Susquehanna River. During the 18th and early 19th centuries, the ferry-operating Creswell family owned the farm, which included what is now the upper portion of Port Deposit.

Rock Run Mill, at the northern edge of Port Deposit, where Rock Creek descends to the river, may be "the merchant's mill" that appeared in a petition for a road to this point in 1731. A marker notes the location of

Smith's Falls, named in 1606 by Capt. John Smith, who ascended the Susquehanna to this point. Rocks blocked further passage, and on his famous map of Virginia, the explorer marked "Smith's Fals" with a cross to indicate the limit of his trip.

Opposite the falls, the **Port Deposit Quarries** extend 200 feet up the face of the cliff. Quarrying began here after a bridge was built across the river in 1816–17. The bridge was rebuilt after a fire in 1829 and finally destroyed by a drove of crossing cattle in 1854. Extensive quarrying operations began in 1829 and lasted well into the 20th century. Port Deposit granite has been widely used as a building stone in New York, Philadelphia, Baltimore, Washington, and other cities. Examples can be found at the Naval Academy in Annapolis, the Maryland State Penitentiary in Baltimore, St. Thomas Episcopal Church in Washington, and Haverford College near Philadelphia.

Md. 222 continues northwest along the Susquehanna riverbank through a flat, wooded area. Traces of the old canal are visible along the route; the river, dotted with rocks and small islands, can be glimpsed through the trees. **Susquehanna State Park** adjoins Octoraro Creek, which empties into the river after cutting a deep gorge immediately to the east. A Susquehannock fort lay along the creek in this area. The Susquehannocks, related by language and culture to the Iroquois, caused early Marylanders much concern. Capt. John Smith had been impressed by their stature and military manner, guessing their numbers to include 600 warriors. The Maryland Algonquian tribes to the south—such as the Piscataway in Southern Maryland and the Nanticoke on the Lower Eastern Shore—feared the Susquehannocks, who lived in palisaded forts, fought the Five Nations to the north, and raided the tribes to the south. Within 50 years of European settlement, however, the tribe had been reduced to a few refugees. Only the tribal name remains on the landscape.

Md. 222 returns the traveler to the starting point of this loop around the Susquehanna at Conowingo.

The Charms of the Upper Shore: Kent and Queen Anne's Counties

Bay Bridge to Centreville, Chestertown, and Eastern Neck
via Md. 18, 213, 313, and 404

Bay Bridges

A triumph of vision and engineering after years of debate and doubt (in 1949, a Talbot County senator filibustered against it), the first Chesapeake Bay Bridge—today the southern span—opened in 1952. Still one of the largest continuous overwater steel structures in the world, the bridge stretches with imposing grace from Sandy Point on the Western Shore to Kent Island. Renamed in 1967 for William Preston Lane Jr. (governor of Maryland 1947–51), the original bridge cost $45 million to construct and spans 4.35 miles of water. Elevated, curved roadways lead to two 385-foot-high suspension towers, 2,922½ feet apart. The span between them provides a 198½-foot clearance for ocean-going vessels moving in the channel to and from Baltimore port facilities. On clear days, the view from the bridge is spectacular; during hazy, foggy periods, the structure becomes mysterious—a ghostly, steel apparition.

For more than three centuries, travel from the Western to the Eastern Shore involved boarding a boat or taking the road to Elkton from which other roads descended the peninsula. As late as 1840, no railroads existed on the Eastern Shore. Many of the wagon roads were primitive affairs paved with oyster shells. Steam and sail boats traditionally did most of the transportation work on the bay. For much of the 20th century, a state-run ferry service connected the shores, but the system could serve only a limited number of motorists.

The Bay Bridge permanently ended the Eastern Shore's historic isolation from the rest of Maryland. Traffic has become intense, particularly in the summer, when Marylanders make their annual vacation runs to the Atlantic beaches; so a second, parallel bridge seemed the answer. It opened to traffic on June 28, 1973, at a cost of $120 million.

KENT ISLAND

From the Western Shore, U.S. 50 and 301 cross the bridge to Queen Anne's County and first touch land on **Kent Island,** separated from the Eastern Shore mainland by a small "narrows." Although nothing visible from the road would so indicate, Kent Island is the site of the first permanent European settlement within the present borders of Maryland.

Passengers alight from the state-operated ferry Albert C. Ritchie at Claiborne, Talbot County.

In 1631, three years before Lord Baltimore's settlers landed at St. Mary's, William Claiborne established a trading post here and presumably named the island after his home county in England. Claiborne had obtained a license from the crown to explore the bay and trade with the Chesapeake Indian tribes. When Lord Baltimore received his patent, which included the Kent Island trading post, Claiborne decided to resist the Calverts and uphold the Virginia Company's claim to the island. Thus, Maryland began its history with a boundary dispute that soon erupted into a small war, on land and—in 1635, when Claiborne defiantly sailed into Maryland waters—on the sea.

George Evelin arrived from England in 1636 to take over Claiborne's post on Kent Island, and Claiborne returned to Virginia to confer with his trading partners. Evelin made peace with the Calverts and helped a small "invasion" party subdue the island for Maryland in 1638. Claiborne reclaimed the island for himself and Virginia in 1645, after a Puritan rebellion led by Richard Ingle briefly overthrew the Calverts. When the Puritans succumbed to the proprietary government the following year, Claiborne retreated to Virginia and waited for another opportunity to pursue his claim. The chance arose six years later, when a frigate arrived to "reduce all the plantations within the Bay of Chesapeake to their due obedience to the Parliament of the Commonwealth of England." Claiborne helped the process occur peacefully in Virginia then came aboard to help subdue the Maryland "royalists" and "papists." For the next six years, the Puritans and Claiborne controlled the colony and Kent Island. Finally, in 1658, an agreement in London restored Maryland to Lord Baltimore, and Claiborne returned once more to Virginia. He apparently never again set foot on Kent Island, although just before his death in 1677, he petitioned Charles II to have it restored to him.

Claiborne's settlement on his "Isle of Kent" has completely disappeared, but it likely lies under water west of the existing shoreline. Farming and fishing are the chief sources of income for those residents who don't commute to work in nearby Annapolis, Baltimore, or Washington. Sport fishing and sailing have also become island attractions.

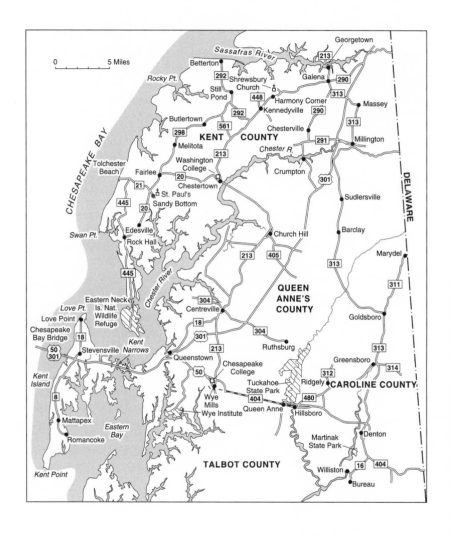

Love Point via Md. 18

From U.S. 50/301 take Md. 18, which goes north toward **Stevens-ville,** named for Stevens Adventure, the tract on which it was built. About a mile farther, **Scillin** (private), a 2½-story brick house, is visible from the road. Built in three stages, the house consists of what seems to be a 17th-century cottage surrounded by 18th-century additions. Md. 18 ends at **Love Point,** a small village at the northern tip of the island, from which a ferry to Baltimore operated until after World War II.

Kent Point via Md. 8

Md. 8 proceeds south from U.S. 50/301 shortly after the bridge, passing small farms, a few large estates, and recent residential developments. Just after the **Bay Bridge Airport,** the road passes **Broad Creek.** Kent Island's importance as a transportation link began early: when the Maryland assembly established the postal route in 1695, a Broad Creek settlement became a postal stop. By the mid-18th century, Broad Creek was the terminus for two ferries from Annapolis, and an inn here served the travelers who used the main route between the southern and northern colonies. By the time of the Revolution, the traffic pattern had shifted, and Kent Island became a backwater. Because Anglican worship services have been held here since Claiborne's time, this part of Kent Island can also be considered the cradle of the Anglican Church in Maryland. An Anglican house of worship stood at Broad Creek by 1651. A later building was still in use in 1880, when the present church in Stevensville was built.

Md. 8 continues by **Matapeake State Park,** a small preserve located on the bay and named for one of the tribes that once inhabited the island. In 1650 the settlers passed a law prohibiting nonresident Indians from coming onto the island without giving notice. Violators could be shot, killed, beaten, or taken prisoner. The last of the natives, the Matapeakes, left the island shortly before the Revolution, heading west.

Md. 8 swerves eastward at the fork with Kent Point Rd./Kent Fort Manor Rd. and ends at **Romancoke,** once a ferry stop on the route from Claiborne in Talbot County to the Western Shore. A small park and fishing pier are all that remain. The county road passes **Kent Fort Manor,** an old estate that encompasses Claiborne's original settlement on Eastern Bay. The road ends at **Kent Point,** site of a small residential area with piers that shelter a few oyster boats.

Kent Narrows

When U.S. 50/301 leaves the east side of the island, it crosses **Kent Narrows** and carries one to the Eastern Shore. A drawbridge at this point caused infamous traffic bottlenecks until the modern by-pass was completed in 1990. Several packing plants process the catch from a large oyster, crab, and clam fleet based at Kent Narrows. Soft clams grow three times faster in the Chesapeake than in New England waters. In 1951, when a fisherman in the Eastern Bay–Miles River area perfected a hydraulic dredge that sucks the clams out of the mud, soft-shell clamming dramatically increased. Since clam dredging kills oysters within 25 feet of the dredge site, the General Assembly passed strict regulations on the new industry in 1955. Maryland's soft clam industry, led by Queen

Anne's County watermen, produces revenues exceeded only by those from blue crabs.

After crossing over the Narrows, U.S. 50 forks southeast to Easton while U.S. 301 splits northeast toward Wilmington, Delaware. U.S. 301 has functioned as a main route between New York and Washington since World War II. Its route through the flat, rural countryside offers quick passage; but to reach points of interest one must follow state roads off either side. Take the Md. 18 exit off U.S. 50 to reach Queenstown.

Queenstown

This small town (453 pop.) was the first seat of Queen Anne's County. Like virtually all significant settlements on the Eastern Shore, it is on a creek that was navigable in the 18th century, when the town was a shipping center for cargoes of grain, hemp, and tobacco as well as a receiving point for manufactured goods. The British considered the location important enough to attack by land and sea when their fleet sailed up the Chesapeake during the War of 1812. Two miles south of the town, they encountered pickets who, although greatly outnumbered, briefly checked their advance at Slippery Hill. British forces entered the town but here did little plundering and no damage.

St. Peter's Roman Catholic Church, on the north side of U.S. 50 outside Queenstown, dates from the early 19th century. Its apse, nave, and vestibule were added in 1877. The congregation traces its origins to the first Jesuits who came to Kent Island, around 1639.

Bloomingdale (private), called Mount Mill when it was built by the Seth family in 1792, is also visible on the north side of U.S. 50. This large, hip-roofed brick house has an unusual two-story, octagonal portico.

Follow Md. 18 north and east to its intersection with U.S. 213. **Peace and Plenty** (private) stands a short distance south on the eastern side of the road. A handsome two-story brick house, it dates from just before the Revolution. Turn left (north) on U.S. 213.

Centreville

Incorporated in 1794, Centreville (2,097 pop.) is the county seat and largest town in rural Queen Anne's County. Its business consists chiefly of supplying the needs of public officials and farmers. The original county seat was at Queenstown, but in 1782 the assembly authorized construction of a new courthouse and jail at this site at the head of the Corsica River. The **courthouse,** at 120 North Commerce St., was completed in 1792 after many delays, and in 1794 the town of Centreville was laid out. The Flemish-bond brick courthouse, set on a tree-shaded square, is one of only two 18th-century courthouses left standing in Maryland and may be the oldest in continuous use. A handsome iron balcony, added in the 19th century, ornaments the second story; hip-roofed wings complement the central structure. The interior of the building has been completely remodeled. In 1977 H.R.H. Princess Anne helped dedicate a bronze statue that stands in front of the courthouse, Elizabeth Gordon Chandler's *Queen Anne.*

Md. 213 divides in Centreville: southbound traffic flows on Liberty St., northbound traffic on Commerce St. Along with Water St. (Md. 304), which crosses them one block below the courthouse, these are the original streets of Centreville. A few houses built in the town's early years still stand along the traffic arteries. The **Yellow Brick House** (private), at the northeast corner of Water St. and **Banjo Lane** (one block east of Commerce St.), is believed to have been built in the late 18th century.

Judge Richard Bennett Carmichael (1807–84) lived in this 2½-story brick house with double chimneys. During the Civil War, though believing that Maryland should remain in the Union, Carmichael as a state circuit court judge supported the Confederate states' right to secede and instructed grand juries to indict law officers guilty of illegal search and seizure. In May 1862, while he sat in court at Easton, Union soldiers arrived to arrest him for treason. His obituary in the Baltimore *Sun* described the incident in gruesome detail: "Marshal McPhail gave the order to seize the judge and drag him from the bench. Deputy Marshal Bishop at once seized the judge by the throat, but was repulsed. The other deputies then closed in upon the judge and beat him over the head with the butts of their revolvers. Deputy Marshal Cassell interfered for his protection, but not until five wounds had been inflicted, and the judge, stunned and bleeding, had been dragged from the recess behind the desk at which he was sitting." No warrant was ever served on the judge and no specific charge ever made against him. He was finally released from prison on December 2 and at once resumed his judicial duties.

Wright's Chance, 119 S. Commerce St., a frame, gambrel-roofed house, was probably built in the 1740s on a site some miles away. It now houses the Queen Anne's County Historical Society, which restored the building and furnished it with period pieces.

St. Paul's Episcopal Church on Liberty St., built in 1834–35, serves St. Paul's Parish, created in 1692 with the other original Anglican parishes in Maryland. The transept and chancel were added in 1862 and enlarged in 1892, when the interior was remodeled.

Just to the east of town, on the north side of Md. 304, one will find **Queen Anne's County High School.** Private interests founded an academy in Centreville as early as 1869, and in 1890 the county assumed responsiblity for what then became a public high school. Queen Anne's High owes its existence to academic consolidation and racial integration; it formed in 1963 out of Centreville High (white), Sudlersville High (white), and Church Hill High (African American).

TO CHESTERTOWN AND GEORGETOWN VIA MD. 213

From Centreville, follow Md. 213 north toward the Chester River into flat, mostly fenceless country rich in cash crops of grain and feed crops for dairy cattle. Much earlier, in the 18th century, these farms turned from the tobacco culture of the early Tidewater settlers to wheat, vegetables, and fruit orchards. Dairy and soybean farms became more prominent in the early 20th century. Many of the residences visible from the road silently testify to intricate family trees with roots deep in the land. The road reveals only a portion of the landscape's character, because often one can view only the backyard of the brick and frame houses, for many houses along the Chesapeake waterfront are built facing the water. The water route—up the rivers and creeks, past the landings that slope down gently to the shores—remains the best way to sense the history of these Eastern Shore counties.

Church Hill

Church Hill (pop. 481), a crossroads community at the intersection of Md. 213 and Md. 300, derives its name from **St. Luke's Episcopal Church**. St. Luke's Parish was created in 1728; this brick church was finished in 1732 at a cost of 140,000 pounds of tobacco. A heavy gambrel roof covers brick walls laid in Flemish bond. During the early 19th century, St. Luke's fell into disrepair, but it was restored in 1842. The interior was wrecked during the Civil War, but the church was restored again in 1881, when the entrance was moved from the south to the west end, where the present bell tower was erected. In 1957, the stained-glass windows were replaced by panes of hand-blown clear glass which let in a flood of light. Behind the church is a small brick parish house built in 1817 and used as the first public school in the county.

Not far to the east, **Readbourne** (private) overlooks the Chester River from a small knoll. Col. James Hollyday (whose wife, Sarah Covington Lloyd, was the widow of Edward Lloyd of Wye House) built the original house in 1734. The family made additions in 1791 and 1948. The original staircase and most of the building's 18th-century wood paneling are now on display at Winterthur Museum near Wilmington, Delaware.

CHESTERTOWN

Chestertown (22'alt., 4,005 pop.) is an unusually distinctive and gracious town on the broad and tranquil Chester River. The town was born in 1706, after Kent County moved the county seat to this location from

The riverfront houses of Chestertown as pictured from the bridge over the Chester River in the 1930s

New Yarmouth on Eastern Neck Island. Annapolis developed during the 18th century as the aristocratic and cultural center of Maryland's Western Shore; the same could be claimed—with apologies to Easton—for Chestertown and the Eastern Shore.

A block of 18th-century brick houses overlooks the Chester River, evoking memories of a maritime, mercantile society dominated by transplanted English gentlemen and supported by African slavery. A row of one-story law offices on Courthouse Square bespeaks the generations of lawyers who have practiced the profession here. Traces of the town's aristocratic past remain in aspects of its yachting and hunting traditions, but the modern town has become more diverse and reflective of the variety of newcomers to the Eastern Shore in recent decades.

Twenty years ago, African American neighborhoods in Chestertown—like many throughout Maryland—were disgracefully dilapidated, the legacy of a segregated past that endured until the 1960s. Despite obstacles, however, African American residents of such small Eastern Shore towns distinguished themselves in many professions. The town's elementary school is named for James Garnett, an African American educator from Chestertown. A new generation of residents has tentatively come together to address past social and economic injustices. The predominantly black **James Methodist Church** (1914), at Cross and Cannon Sts., was recently restored after a fund-raising effort that involved all segments of the community.

The first lots in Chestertown were laid out in 1707. A year later, Newtown, as it was then called, was made a port of entry for Cecil, Kent, and Queen Anne's Counties. By 1750 trade with the British West Indies flourished, and, as the merchants prospered, Chestertown became a center for horse racing, theatrical performances, and other lively pursuits. In his journal for the year 1786, the ubiquitous Francis Asbury noted: "Sunday

9. I preached at Kent Old Chapel . . . in the afternoon and at night in Chestertown. I always have an enlargement in preaching in this very wicked place." Perhaps due to such preaching, the town became a center of early Methodism on the Eastern Shore.

A Chestertown tea party was staged here on May 13, 1774, when tea brought into port by the brigantine *Geddes* was thrown overboard after an indignant meeting of citizens. A short while later, Chestertown sent vessels loaded with provisions to the people of Boston, who were suffering from the effects of the Boston Port Act.

After the Revolution, Chestertown, like other bay ports, lost its foreign trade to Baltimore; only the Georgian mansions along the water evoked its cosmopolitan past. Four U.S. senators from the 19th century were intimately associated with Chestertown: Philip Reed; Ezekiel Foreman Chambers, who wrote legislation that established the Smithsonian Institution; James Alfred Pearce, whose No vote in May 1868 helped save President Andrew Johnson from conviction in his impeachment trial; and George Vickers. During the same century, sailing packets and steamboats carried grain and passengers to Baltimore. When the railroad finally arrived after the Civil War, Chestertown established closer links to Wilmington and Philadelphia, a pattern that holds today. Many residents commute to jobs in northern Delaware.

Walking Tour

Md. 213 intersects Md. 20 three blocks after crossing the Chester River. To begin a walking tour—the best way to appreciate Chestertown—turn left on Md. 20 to the town square and find a place to park. (Parking is also available along the river at the foot of High St.) A courthouse and Episcopal church have stood on the square since 1698 and 1768, respectively. The present **courthouse** was built in 1860, and although numerous additions have been made since, its facade has remained unchanged. In front of the courthouse is the **Civil War Monument,** erected in 1917 to honor the soldiers of Kent County who fought on both sides. The inscription for the Federals faces north, that for the Confederates south. **Emmanuel Episcopal Church,** at High and Cross Sts., was built in 1768; it became the Chester Parish church in 1809. Several additions, new windows, and a completely altered interior largely conceal the church's 18th-century identity; but the original walls, two laid in all-header bond, remain visible.

In 1780 the Rev. Dr. William Smith became rector of Chester Parish. He had come from Scotland to the colonies in 1751 and been first provost of the College of Philadelphia (now the University of Pennsylvania), making him a close associate of Benjamin Franklin. In November 1780, at a convention that met at Chestertown, Smith led the effort to reorganize a church that could no longer be headed by the King of England. It was not an easy task. Of 54 Anglican clergy active in Maryland in 1775, only 16 had taken the Oath of Allegiance to the revolutionary government. Three clergy and 24 laymen attended the Chestertown convention, which adopted a new name: the Protestant Episcopal Church of America. Smith's participation in the 1785 revision of the *Book of Common Prayer* cost him popularity. He was forced to withdraw his name from nomination as bishop of the new church in Maryland and in 1789 returned to the University of Pennsylvania.

High Street descends a hill to the Chester River, providing pedestrian vistas that reveal the town's distinctive architecture. Some of the small privately owned frame houses along this street are among the oldest surviving buildings in the town, although many have been changed over time and have lost their chimneys. Six 18th-century houses have been identified along the stretch from the square to the stone **Palmer House,** at 532 High St. (between College Ave. and Kent St.). A representation of this house was embossed on the silver service presented to the battleship *Maryland.* Four 18th-century houses can be found between Palmer House and the river. At **411 W. High St.** (between Kent and Mill Sts.) is a house with Flemish bond brickwork and large chimneys that may have been built soon after the Revolution. The dwelling at **414 W. High St.** resembles the other 18th-century houses but has many Victorian details.

Part way down the hill, Mill St. turns off High St. to the right. Numbers **101 and 103 Mill St.** are frame houses with large chimneys and old window sashes. Mill St. runs into **Cannon Street,** and one block east on Cannon St. is a large brick house of considerable interest. The common bond of the brickwork and its very steep roof and heavy chimneys with elaborate multiple hips are characteristic of 18th-century styles.

Back on High St., the plain brick building at **320 W. High St.** on the northwest side of the town square was raised in 1803 as the second Methodist meeting house in Chestertown. (The first was created in 1780, when a congregation acquired the distillery adjoining Worrell's Tavern.) The **White Swan Tavern,** 231–35 E. High St., a white brick building across from the courthouse, has been restored as a bed and breakfast inn. This glazed header brick structure, laid in Flemish bond, was built in the early 18th century and subsequently enlarged. The roof slopes from a height of two stories in front to one story in the rear.

The **Masonic Building** has stood on the southeast corner of the courthouse green since 1827. Queen St. crosses High St. one block east of the green. Walk to the Queen St. block between High and Maple Sts., where a number of old, private houses still stand. Both **109 Queen St.** and the **Nicholson House, 111 Queen St.,** brick town houses with brick cornices, were probably built soon after the Revolution. Number 109 was the Episcopal rectory from 1850 to 1910. On Church St., a very short alley from Queen St. to the courthouse green, stands the **Geddes-Piper House,** a handsome three-story brick house built between 1730 and 1754. The house was restored and is occupied by the **Kent County Historical Society. 135 and 137 Queen St.** are 18th-century frame houses, now being restored. The former was built by 1760 and owned by John Bolton, a merchant who served as commissary for the Kent County Militia during the Revolution.

The mid- and late-18th-century mansions for which Chestertown is famous lie in the block of East High St. between Queen St. and the waterfront and along Water St., which borders the Chester River. The first floor of the **William Barroll House,** 108–10 E. High St., is believed to have been built about 1735; the line of the old catslide roof can still be seen in the brickwork. The first floor of the **Wickes House, or Johnstone House,** 102 E. High St. (at the corner of Water St.), may have been a pre-Revolutionary tavern operated by Samuel Beck. The formal garden at this location was created by the Burrell family, former owners.

High St. ends at the river just beyond Water St. **The Abbey** or the **Hynson-Ringgold House,** now the official home of the president of Washington College, stands one block to the right on the corner of Front and Cannon Sts. The rear portion of the house on Cannon St. was built in 1767 by Thomas Ringgold, who also bought the house on Water St., erected in 1738 by Dr. William Murray, and connected them. Ringgold, a prominent Chestertown merchant and member of the Stamp Act Congress of 1765, installed in the central hallway a beautiful divided staircase, probably designed by William Buckland, whose woodwork decorates several famous Annapolis houses. Buckland may have designed one of the two front rooms in the earlier wing; the initials "W.B." and the date 1771 were found on the back of the paneling in 1932, when the woodwork was lent to the Baltimore Museum of Art. In 1854, U.S. senator James Alfred Pearce (1805–62) bought the house, and his descendants lived here until the 20th century.

The **Chestertown Customhouse** at 103 High St., a long, three-story brick building, was once a dwelling and warehouse owned by the Ringgolds. The earliest section was built sometime after 1719, and the remainder was completed before the Revolution. The Ringgolds are supposed to have rented a room here to the port authorities, hence the building's name.

Widehall, 101 Water St., an imposing brick mansion with double-hipped roof and facade laid in all-header bond, was probably built sometime in the 1760s. The Georgian doorway, with its fluted engaged columns and carved pediment, is a beautiful example of 18th-century craftsmanship. Modern owners removed Victorian modifications that had been made to the house and added the Ionic portico on the river front. A former owner, Col. Thomas Smythe, was an influential Chestertown merchant who became a member of the Council of Safety during the Revolution.

103 Water St. is a late-18th-century house once occupied by Charles Hackett, watchmaker and silversmith. **River House,** 107 Water St. (private), stands on land purchased by the merchant William Trimbrill, who purchased the land in 1737. The present three-story house is believed to have been finished by 1782 by lawyer Peregrine Leatherbury. The woodwork from one of the bedrooms is now installed as "The Chestertown Room" in the Winterthur Museum near Wilmington, Delaware. The privately owned house at **110 Water St.** is believed to have been built about 1780; the one at **115 Water St.** may date to 1736.

One may either walk up Washington Ave. or drive northward out Md. 213 to visit the 50-acre campus of **Washington College,** a coeducational, nonsectarian liberal arts institution that stands on a ridge overlooking the town. The Reverend Doctor Smith founded this college in 1782, making it the oldest institution of higher education in Maryland and the tenth oldest in the country. Smith was serving as director of the Kent County Free School, which dated from about 1723 (some evidence suggests 1707), when the Maryland assembly offered an endowment of 100 acres of land for a free school in each county. By 1782 the Free School had 140 pupils, and the assembly agreed to charter it as a college if a $10,000 endowment could be raised within five years. Dr. Smith collected the money within five months. The college conducted its first commencement in May 1783, when four graduates delivered their orations in both Latin and French. The name of the college of course honored George Washington, who visited in 1784 as a member of the board of governors. In 1789 the college gave Washington the honorary degree of doctor of laws, the first he received after becoming president. Presidents Franklin D. Roosevelt (in 1933) and Harry S Truman (1946) accepted the same honor. Each year the college makes national news by granting the largest literary prize in the country to a graduating senior, the Sophie Kerr Prize.

At one point it was hoped that Washington College and St. John's College in Annapolis would become the highest reaches of a state-supported system of public education, but in 1805 Maryland curtailed such subsidies, striking serious and long-felt blows to both institutions. After 1839 the state provided scholarships to selected Washington College students. In 1827 the original building of Washington College burned, but classes continued in other quarters until the construction of **Middle Hall** in 1844. **East** and **West Halls** were erected in 1854.

The **William Smith Building,** on College Ave., which runs parallel to Md. 213, forms part of a complex that includes classrooms and administrative offices. The president's office, in **Bunting Hall,** features a portrait of George Washington by Rembrandt Peale (1778–1860), painted in 1803, while Peale was studying in the London studio of the American painter Benjamin West. Peale devoted much of his life to painting portraits of Washington. His father, Charles Willson Peale (1741–1826), born near Chestertown, was a good friend of Washington and painted several portraits of him from life. Rembrandt Peale's grandfather, Charles Peale, was headmaster of the Kent County Free School from 1742 until his death, in 1749. Next to these buildings are the library and science buildings. Nearby are the college commons, auditorium, art center, swim center, gym, and more dormitories.

Md. 213 continues north, crossing Md. 297 at Hopewell. A left onto Rte. 297 leads to Catts Corner and the **Kent County High School,** founded in 1971 and state 1A football champions in 1988–89. Congressman Wayne Gilchrist once taught citizenship at the school; David A. Kergaard was honored as state principal of the year in 1993.

Farther along Md. 213, near Kennedyville and the junction of Md. 448, a community of Amish settled in 1954. Just beyond the junction with Md. 292 on the right stands the **Thomas Perkins House** (private). In 1720 Thomas Perkins built most of this long, narrow, whitewashed brick dwelling with steep gabled roof. His son, Col. Isaac Perkins, was known as the "Flaming Patriot" during the Revolution. Colonel Perkins was one of the commissioners of the Maryland Council of Safety, appointed to raise supplies for Washington's army, and much of the flour supplied from the Eastern Shore was ground in the mills on his property. On June 29, 1780, Perkins wrote the council that "the precarious supply that our Army has had for some time past and the Considerable Consequence my Mills has been in the Manufacturing such large Quantitys of grain for the Army and french fleet . . . has caused those Villains [the Tories] to hire some Abandoned Wretch to set those Mills on fire."

Rock Hall and Eastern Neck Island
via Md. 20 and 298

From Chestertown, one may take Md. 20 west for a jaunt on the Chester-Chesapeake neck, once the site of summer resorts and still a haven from the busy life.

At Fairlee, Md. 20 turns south, passing Sandy Bottom. There, a short distance on Sandy Bottom Rd. leads to **St. Paul's Episcopal Church,** which sits on the left among great oaks and sycamores. The trees may have been standing in 1713 when the brick building opened (it replaced an earlier structure on Eastern Neck). Laid in Flemish bond and marked by great roundheaded windows, St. Paul's probably is the oldest Maryland church building in continuous use. The vestry house, a small brick building with the date 1766 in one gable, stands nearby. In 1714 the parish installed 34 new pews, which one could rent or, at 1,000 pounds of tobacco, purchase free and clear. One family has used the same pew for 10 generations. In 1801 the parish vestry agreed to rent the church as a schoolhouse on condition that the schoolmaster keep the building in good repair and immediately replace broken windows. The Alabama-born star of early film, Tallulah Bankhead (1902–65), is buried in the churchyard. (Her sister Eugenia, who owned a farm in Kent County, is also buried here.)

Just beyond the church, the road forks, and a right turn leads to **Remington Farms.** The Remington Arms Corporation took possession in 1957 of a game sanctuary established here by Glenn L. Martin. The company has since developed a demonstration program for raising and harvesting field crops to provide food and cover for game birds. **Broadnox** (private)—a restored, two-wing brick house believed to have been built between 1704 and 1708 by Robert Dunn—is located on the property. The house is named for Thomas Broadnox, who surveyed the land in 1659. Broadnox, a notoriously cruel master, was one of only three people in Maryland history known to have been subjected to the so-called "blood test." He had beaten one of his servants to death and, according to the ancient English procedure, was forced to put his hand on the victim. If the corpse bled, then the suspect was the real murderer. Broadnox thrust his thumb into the body to show "how the flesh did dent"; but no blood appeared. He passed the test but died during the trial.

West of Sandy Bottom, Md. 21, or Tolchester Beach Rd., takes one toward the bay. On the way, Caulk's Field Rd. branches right to **Caulk's Battlefield,** site of a skirmish between British and American forces in late August 1814. Sir Peter Parker, commander of the ship *Menelaus,* landed here with a force of 260 men to engage in what he termed a "frolic with the Yankees." The British twice attacked the assembled militiamen, who held on despite being dangerously low on ammunition. While the Americans waited anxiously for an attack that never came, the British retreated, having lost 13 and with 29 wounded. Among the latter was their brash commander, who died from his wounds. Militia casualties numbered only a few wounded. A simple granite marker in the middle of a field indicates the site of what some have called the only true land battle ever fought on the Eastern Shore—and a fairly rare American victory in the War of 1812.

Caulk's Field House, built in 1743, is visible from the monument. With its steep gable roof on two stories, the structure resembles many other old houses in Kent County—simple but eloquent—like the granite marker.

Both Md. 21 and Caulk's Field Rd. (after a left turn on Bay Shore Rd.) lead to the **site of Tolchester Beach,** a Victorian bayside resort and amusement park. Opened in 1877, Tolchester was particularly popular during the steamboat era and especially among Baltimoreans, who were only about 20 miles away by water. Follow Md. 445 south of Tolchester.

Rock Hall (pop. 1,584), a simple watermen's town, once served as the Eastern Shore terminus of the main post road linking the northern and southern colonies. George Washington crossed here many times. Here Col. Tench Tilghman began his famous ride to Philadelphia to announce the British surrender at Yorktown. In 1790 Thomas Shippen, of Virginia, wrote of eating "delicious crabs" in Rock Hall while awaiting the ferryboat in the company of Thomas Jefferson and James Madison.

The Rock Hall waterman, known for his independence and salty wisdom, has long been a fixture on the bay. A carved, wooden statue in a small **city park** off Main St. commemorates him as standing, arms at side, in slicker and hat, observing the horizon—patient, tough, enduring. Nearby marinas and remnants of the "water business" remain in Rock Hall, but most of the town's young people have found jobs elsewhere. New residences are developing along the water, undoubtedly to take advantage of the view of the Chesapeake that extends from Sparrows Point, near Baltimore, to the Bay Bridge.

Follow Md. 445 south from Rock Hall down Eastern Neck, a narrow peninsula created by Grays Inn Creek and the Chester River on the east and the bay on the west. The road passes the **site of New Yarmouth,** a 17th-century settlement that between 1679 and 1696 gave Kent County its first courthouse. In 1674 Charles Calvert had ordered the removal of court sessions from Eastern Neck Island. When the court later moved to New Town (later Chestertown), New Yarmouth rapidly declined and then disappeared.

Md. 445 reaches the end of the peninsula and crosses over a bridge to the **Eastern Neck Island National Wildlife Refuge.** Wooden walkways extend into wetlands of marsh grasses, cattails, and other plants that thrive in brackish water. The setting is classic Eastern Shore: flat, marshy land mixed with pastures and woodlands, waterfowl, amphibious reptiles and mammals, insects, salty water, silence.

Eastern Neck Island Rd. ends at the **site of Wickliffe,** the home of the Wickes family for many generations. Maj. Joseph Wickes settled the island around 1658 and served as chief judge of the Kent County Court, which met here on occasion before 1674. His great-grandson, Lambert Wickes, was born here and spent his early years on the island. As captain of the *Reprise* he carried Benjamin Franklin to France. After capturing 17 British merchant ships, Capt. Wickes went down with his ship in a storm off Newfoundland in 1777. A plaque commemorating his birthplace was placed here in 1975.

From Eastern Neck Island, return to Rock Hall and then follow Md. 20 north to Fairlee and Md. 298.

Md. 298 passes through flat, rural countryside never more than a few minutes from the bay or one of the creeks that indent the Kent County peninsula. Some large estates on this part of the Shore maintain prize-winning herds of Aberdeen Angus beef cattle.

The **site of the Cecil Meeting House,** built by Friends in 1696, is on the left just beyond the junction with Md. 297 at Butlertown.

A short distance beyond the meeting house site, Coopers Ln. turns northwest to **Drayton Manor,** an original manor of 1,200 acres granted in 1677. The brick house here was built from an 18th-century plan and contains paneling from an old Rhode Island house. An anonymous buyer gave the property, which once supported prize cattle and fruit orchards, to the United Methodist Church for use as a Retreat Center.

Rocky Point, at the mouth of Still Pond Creek, is visible from the gardens on the bluff. This rounded bit of land was the site in 1849 of the prize fight in which Tom Hyer defeated Yankee Sullivan for a purse of $10,000. The fight was originally scheduled to be held on Poole's Island off Harford County on the Western Shore, but the state of Maryland dispatched militia via steamboat to break up the event. The steamboat went aground, and many of the more devoted fans went across the bay to Rocky Point for the fight. Hyer thrashed his opponent so severely that Sullivan had to be sent to the hospital.

Betterton via Md. 292

At Md. 292, turn left and pass through **Still Pond,** whose natives for generations told "foreigners" that their locale's name came from a neighboring pond, now mostly a marsh, supposedly bottomless and haunted by an Indian chief. Augustine Herrman's map of 1673 labels this site "Steel Pone Creek."

At the Edwardian summer resort of **Betterton,** steamboats once tied up to discharge eager visitors. The road to the beach and pier descends a steep hill, taking the visitor past mansard-roofed houses and sprawling, white-painted residences. Baltimoreans once made excursions to shore

Jousting on the Eastern Shore during the 1930s

towns like this one and Rock Hall for swimming and sport fishing. Sportsmen from all over the East come to shoot the ducks and geese that flock here by the hundreds of thousands to winter in the fields and creeks.

Follow Md. 292 and 298 to Harmony Corner and Md. 213.

Back on Md. 213, just east of Harmony Corner, a left turn on **Shrewsbury Church** Rd. leads to a fine old church that serves one of the original Anglican parishes of Maryland, "laid out" in 1692 when the assembly passed the first act establishing the Anglican Church. This plain brick church dates from 1832; it went on the site of the original one, erected in 1692–93. In the churchyard are the graves of parishioners buried over a period of two centuries. One stone marks the grave of revolutionary general John Cadwalader (1742–86), a close friend of George Washington. Cadwalader challenged the leader of the "Conway Cabal," Gen. Thomas Conway, to a duel and wounded him in the mouth. When Cadwalader saw Conway lying on the ground with blood gushing from his mouth, he is supposed to have said, "I have stopped the damned rascal's lying tongue, at any rate."

Md. 213 continues to **Galena** (pop. 342), formerly known as Georgetown Crossroads and the **site of Down's Cross Roads Tavern.** The tavern had appeared by 1763, serving the stage route between Annapolis and Philadelphia. George Washington stopped here in 1774 on his way to and from the first Continental Congress. The tavern burned in 1893.

The landscape here reminds one of the Midwest: flat fields of corn, soybeans, and wheat with occasional dairy farms, homesteads surrounded by silos and outbuildings, country towns that are clusters of frame houses with front porches on tree-lined side streets. Visible hints of the nearby rivers belie the illusion, however. Scattered brick "manors" remind travelers that they're moving through the original agricultural United States.

Georgetown

From Galena drive north two miles to Georgetown, opposite Fredericktown on the south bank of the Sassafras. Georgetown was laid out at the same time as Fredericktown and developed into an active port during the 18th century. On May 6, 1813, a British landing party from Adm. George Cockburn's fleet badly damaged both Sassafras towns (militia had apparently fired on the British from the shore and then fled). Because of the pluck of a Kent County grand dame, Catherine "Kitty" Knight, two brick houses on top of the hill in Georgetown still stand. Knight followed the troops to rescue a sick old lady trapped in one of the structures. After much pleading, she persuaded the commanding officer to spare both houses, then she put out the remaining flames herself with a broom. Kitty died in 1855 at a ripe old age, famous for her conversation and knowledge of the British classics. The two structures—now joined—are part of the **Kitty Knight House,** a rambling brick building with a gambrel roof now used as an inn. It overlooks the river near the bridge.

One may return to the starting point at the Bay Bridge by picking up U.S. 301 South, two miles southeast of Galena on Md. 313, or choose the slower, more scenic option below.

Md. 313 roughly parallels U.S. 301 in Kent and Queen Anne Counties, then sweeps south, crossing the Mason Branch of Tuckahoe Creek, the Tubmill Branch of the upper Choptank River, Marshyhope Creek, and the Nanticoke River. This is not a spectacular route marked by historic houses and churches, but the road reveals the rural interior of the Delmarva Peninsula. The highway parallels railroad tracks from Massey to Barclay and again from Goldsboro to Greensboro. Villages along this route have changed little since 1900; the countryside is crisscrossed by side roads that run through pine woods to the marshy shores of creeks where waterlilies bloom in season.

Md. 313 leaves Galena headed southeast and crosses U.S. 301 to **Massey,** a railroad junction named for Daniel Massey, an 18th-century settler. The road then turns south to Millington.

Located at the headwaters of the Chester River, **Millington** (409 pop.) was once called Head of Chester. Fire destroyed half the village in 1872, but a few surviving structures indicate its 18th-century origins. The **Higman Mill** on the river bank has foundations that may have been constructed in the 1760s. Dating from a period when the presence of six or more mills probably spawned the town's name, this waterpowered mill faithfully ground corn until the 1950s. Now the town serves as a shopping and supply center for the surrounding farms.

Sudlersville (428 pop.) grew up around an 18th-century church named for a pioneering local family. The railroad arrived here in 1869, and the community sported a small train station surrounded by granaries, canneries, and a milk plant. The automobile and 1920s-era highways diminished the town's importance. Rail passenger service ceased in 1939, but the freights continued to run intermittently. J. Wilbur Stafford, one of the last station agents, retired in 1961 after 47 years with the Pennsylvania Railroad. The station closed four years later. Mrs. Stafford bought the station and donated it to the town, a "betterment club" raised money to establish a town museum, and now, visiting it, one can learn all about Sudlersville, its railroad heritage, and its favorite son—Baseball Hall of Famer Jimmie Foxx. The museum displays a ball autographed by the Philadelphia Athletics of 1932, the year Foxx hit 58 home runs.

Md. 313 diverges from the railroad tracks at **Barclay** (132 pop.) and continues south across Long Marsh Ditch, which becomes the Mason Branch of the Tuckahoe, to **Goldsboro** (185 pop.). Originally a crossroads called Oldtown, the community was renamed in 1870 after Dr. G. W. Goldsborough, who owned most of the surrounding land. When the railroad arrived from Delaware in 1867, this little town became a canning center. Tomatoes, once a huge crop in this part of the Eastern Shore, are disappearing as a cash crop and the canning industry has declined accordingly. **Castle Hall** (private), a brick "telescope" house with four sections, is visible from the road north of Goldsboro on Md. 311. Robert Hardcastle acquired the tract in 1748, and his eldest son Thomas, a county justice, finished the house in 1781. The family was prominent in colonial Maryland's military, legal, and medical affairs.

Marydel via Md. 311

Md. 311 proceeds north from Goldsboro and ends at **Marydel** (143 pop.), named for its geographical position on the Maryland-Delaware line. This sleepy village, which dates to the 1850s, suddenly became notorious in early January 1877, when James Gordon Bennett, owner of the *New York Herald*, and Frederick May, a well-known explorer, fought an illegal duel here. They had quarreled in New York City after May broke his engagement to Bennett's sister. Both men fired wildly, as was often the case in such "affairs of honor," and neither was hit. Bennett later exiled himself to Paris.

Greensboro

Md. 313 continues south from Goldsboro to Greensboro (1,253 pop.), one of the oldest inland towns on the Eastern Shore. Near the headwaters of the Choptank River, this townsite was first proposed in 1732 but did not materialize until 1783. Known as Choptank Bridge, then as Bridgetown when it competed against Pig Point for the county courthouse, the town was resurveyed in 1791 and renamed "Greensborough" by legislative act. Sailing packets once made their way up the Choptank to this river port, which now harbors an occasional oil or fertilizer barge. When the railroad arrived after the Civil War, Greensboro became a small industrial and trading center.

From Greensboro, a turn west and south on Md. 480 leads to Boonsboro and—north of the highway—to **Ridgely** (1,034 pop.), a forwarding and processing point for farm vegetables to the northwest of Denton. The town was laid out in 1867 as a joint land speculation of the Maryland Baltimore Land Association and the Rev. Greenbury W. Ridgely, who owned several thousand acres of land in the area. Ridgely, whose home **Oak Lawn** (private) is off Md. 312 north of town, was briefly a law partner of Henry Clay in Lexington, Kentucky, before he became a clergyman. The promoters persuaded the Maryland and Delaware Railway to extend its line from Greensboro, but by the time the track was finished, in 1868, the land company had gone bankrupt. Eventually, as the surrounding farmland became more heavily populated, the town developed along the lines of the original plan, which included the broad Main St. In 1959 the county opened **North Caroline High School** here. Enlarged in 1975, the school has produced girls' state champions in track (1975), volleyball (1990), and softball (1988, 1991) and boys' state champions in basketball (1987) and golf (1997).

Denton

Follow Md. 313 six miles south of Greensboro to Denton (2,977 pop.), the county seat of Caroline County, which also lies along the Choptank River. In 1773 the assembly called for establishment of the new county seat at Pig Point, a landmark formed by a bend of the river. The Revolution postponed construction of the courthouse, and competition for the seat later developed from nearby Goldsboro. A local referendum settled the issue in 1790, when Denton, a town established adjacent to Pig Point around 1783, emerged the winner. The original courthouse, finished in 1797, was replaced in 1895 by the present, late-Victorian building on a tree-lined public square elevated above the river. The courthouse

Potter House and grounds at Williston Landing, Caroline County

square remains the most distinctive part of Denton. The rest of the early town, which grew up around the square, was largely destroyed in 1863, when Union soldiers celebrating the Fourth of July set off skyrockets that started a serious fire.

Two-masted schooners once sailed up the Choptank to Denton; they were replaced by steamboats after 1850. Railroads became the freight carriers after the Civil War, but the steamboats continued to carry passengers until the 1930s. County government, visible in the many lawyers' offices and support businesses here, gives the town its style and culture. Harry Hughes, two-time governor of Maryland (1978–86) was born in Denton and grew up in a Victorian house with a big front porch which still stands.

Martinak State Park and Environs

A short distance south of Denton, Md. 313/404 takes one to Deep Shore Rd., a right on which leads to the only public land on the Choptank River. Located where Watts Creek empties into the river, **Martinak State Park** may encompass the site of a Choptank Indian village. Distinct from the Nanticokes, the Choptanks lived in small groups along the river from which they took their name. *Choptank* may mean "flowing in the wrong direction," a reference to the tides that surge back and forth every day in the river. Outnumbered and outmaneuvered by the European settlers, the small tribe appealed for aid from the General Assembly, and the Choptank Reservation was created downriver in 1698. The settlers' incursions on their traditional way of life continued, however, and the peaceful natives slowly moved into the marshes. By 1800, the Maryland Choptanks had disappeared.

About two miles farther south on Md. 313/404, Md. 16, also on the right, runs roughly parallel to the Choptank River past several points of interest. Williston Rd. branches west from Md. 16 to **Williston,** also known as **Potters Landing,** after Zabdiel Potter, a Rhode Island sea captain. Captain Potter, the first settler, built the small log wing of the **Potter**

Mansion (private) on the riverbank, where he also established a commercially significant landing. The captain's grandson, William Potter, built the brick house about 1808. Col. Arthur John Willis—for whom the village is named—bought the mansion in 1849 and maintained a line of sailing packets that traded with Baltimore. As late as 1900, two steamboats a day stopped here. **Williston Lake,** created in part by a mill dam (1778) that Gen. William Potter enlarged, lies just east of where Williston Rd. meets it. A local 4-H club has established a park near the lake.

Md. 16 continues to the crossroads created by Two Johns Rd. and American Corner Rd. Although no buildings stand here, maps still indicate its name as Bureau. The foundations of a center built after the Civil War by the Freedman's Bureau are visible in the field on the southwest corner of the intersection. When the federal center for education of emancipated slaves was discontinued in 1870, the building was used as an African American school and then as a church until destroyed by fire in 1938. The Freedman's Bureau center may have been erected at this location because a river captain unloaded lumber at a nearby wharf instead of at Denton, as intended. Another reason for the location in this predominantly pro-Confederate region may have been its proximity to Potter's Landing, where Col. A. J. Willis raised Union companies during the Civil War.

Two Johns Rd. branches from the crossroads to a private landing on the Choptank named for John Stewart Crossey and John Hart, the "Two Johns." During the 1880s, these vaudevillian comedians, each of whom weighed over 300 pounds, turned a simple farmhouse into a Victorian mansion with a roof-top observatory overlooking the river. Their landing became a regular stop for the Baltimore-Denton steamers, and trains brought show folk from around the country for dancing and theatrical performances. The performers once invited the whole town of Denton to attend one of their Sunday extravaganzas. Such excitement didn't last long: the two Johns went broke and disappeared, and the mansion declined to ruins and was later demolished.

WEST ON MD. 404 AND ALT. 404

A principal link between U.S. 50 and the Delaware resort beaches of Rehoboth and Dewey, Md. 404 carries heavy traffic during the summer months. It nonetheless rewards the devotion of a little time to its own attractions, some of them a bit off the beaten path. The countryside is tabletop flat, and the road runs straight for miles through farmlands planted in wheat, corn, soybeans, and hay. Other important local industries produce meat animals, broiler chickens, milk, and vegetables.

Driving west from Denton, take the turnoff onto Alt. Md. 404 to Hillsboro.

Hillsboro

A chapel stood in this old community (164 pop.) as early as 1694. A bridge has crossed the creek at this location since the mid-18th century. Francis Sellers, a Scottish merchant, is believed to have built the sand-colored brick house near the present bridge just after the Revolution, when a tobacco warehouse and tavern could also be found here. During the steamboat era, steamers unloaded four miles south and smaller vessels carried freight up the creek to the town wharf. In 1797 local citizens founded Hillsboro Academy, which offered classical education to the white farmers' children and was absorbed into the county school system in 1878.

Tuckahoe Rd. runs south from Hillsboro into a farming region known as **Tuckahoe Neck. Daffin House** (private), visible from the road, is a long, narrow brick house decorated with Victorian Gothic icing trim that was retained during its modern restoration. Charles Daffin is believed to have begun the house in 1774 and to have finished it just after the Revolution. Andrew Jackson, while visiting here, first met Charles Dickinson, Rebecca Daffin's brother. In 1806 Jackson and Dickinson quarreled over payment of a racing bet and met in a duel on the banks of the Red River in Kentucky. Jackson allowed Dickinson, known as an excellent shot, to fire first; then, ignoring his own wound, took deliberate aim and killed Dickinson. Even in rough frontier society, Jackson's act seemed brutal, and it clouded his reputation for some years.

Driving farther east on Alt. 404, the traveler leaves Hillsboro and crosses Tuckahoe Creek.

Queen Anne

This small community (250 pop.) straddles the creek's east and west banks and thus the Caroline-Talbot county line. About 75 percent of the town's population lives in Queen Anne's County, the other 25 lives in Talbot.

The **birthplace of Frederick Douglass** lies on private property south of Queen Anne off of Md. 303, just south of **Tappers Corner** at the edge of a wooded ravine. A roadside marker farther south at the Tuckahoe Bridge on Md. 328 describes Douglass but has no physical connection to his birthplace. Douglass spent the first six years of his life along the creek with his slave grandmother, Betsey Bailey, who had a local reputation as midwife, gardener, fisherwoman, and child nurturer.

Tuckahoe State Park

Located along the stream valley to the north of Queen Anne, this park takes its name from a beautiful, low-lying stream that rises from the German and Mason Branches in Queen Anne's County and flows south to the Choptank River. The name *Tuckahoe* itself derives from a marsh plant whose roots native tribes used in making a kind of bread.

Continuing west on Md. 404 brings the traveler to Wye Mills, described at the beginning of Tour 9, and back to U.S. 50 and the bridges across the bay.

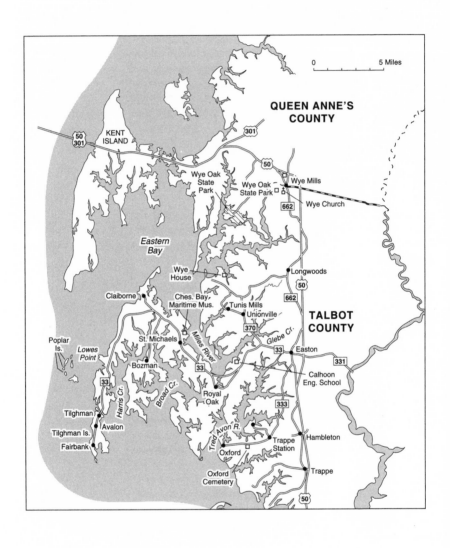

Land of the Lloyds: Talbot County

Md. 662, 33, 333

From the west and the bay bridges, follow U.S. 50 east for a little more than two miles beyond the point where U.S. 301 breaks to the north.

Wye Natural Resource Management Area via Carmichael Rd.

After passing Bloomingdale Rd. on the left, turn right on Carmichael Rd. and follow it to the **Wye Institute** (off Cheston Ln.), an experiment station of the University of Maryland established in 1964. Research is conducted here on vegetables, corn, soybeans, and other field crops. The **Aspen Institute at Wye,** an East Coast branch of the Colorado think tank, sponsors seminars on environmental and cultural issues and conducts research on public policies.

Carmichael Rd. continues into a deeply indented countryside marked by the convolutions of the Wye River(s). The gates of the **Wye Plantation** (private) are visible at Wye Neck Rd., named for the thin strip of farmland between Wye Narrows and the Wye River East. The original Wye Plantation, dating in part to the 17th century, was owned by the Tilghman family. It was inherited by Julianna Tilghman Paca, wife of John Philemon Paca, whose father William Paca was a signer of the Declaration of Independence and three-term governor of Maryland. A monument to the signer was erected in 1911 by the Maryland Society of the Sons of the American Revolution, in the family graveyard in front of the house. William Paca owned half of Wye Island across Wye Narrows, where he built **Wye Hall** in the 1790s. The house was finally lost in 1879 when workmen repairing the roof accidentally started a fire.

As owner of both properties through his marriage to Julianna Tilghman, John Philemon Paca bequeathed Wye Hall to his eldest son, William B. Paca, and Wye Plantation to another son, Edward. Already divided by personality, the two brothers and their families split further during the Civil War. Edward died before the war, but his oldest son joined the Confederacy, leaving another son to run the plantation with their mother. Their uncle William, at Wye Hall, became a Unionist and used wartime dislocations to seize Wye Plantation. In the ensuing family feud, two members of Edward Paca's family were killed. William Paca and three of his sons, including two who were mentally ill, were indicted for murder but acquitted. William Paca's family was ostracized from society, and he died shortly thereafter. Two of his sons committed suicide; a daughter died of accidental poisoning; his wife and the rest of their children were confined to mental institutions. Then Wye Hall burned.

The spreading Wye Oak, the official state tree, in 1997

No Aeschylus sang the bloody songs of the Wye; and the traveler encounters no tangible reminders of this family tragedy. Prize Angus cattle are now raised on Wye Plantation. **Wye Island** is now a state natural resource management area, accessible via Wye Island Rd., which crosses the narrows.

Beyond Carmichael Rd. on U.S. 50, turn south on Md. 662 and drive a short distance, passing **Chesapeake College,** to the junction with Queen Anne Hwy. (Md. 404).

Wye Mills

Here, on the border between Queen Anne's and Talbot Counties, a mill has stood since early colonial days. The date of the existing building is uncertain. Old records reveal that the mill ground grain for General Washington's troops during the Revolution; it remained in private ownership and continuous operation for an estimated 250 years, finally closing in 1953. The state then acquired the structure, and a local organization, the Old Wye Mills Society, restored it. Preservation Maryland now operates the mill in the summer, when flour is still ground as it was during the revolutionary period.

Wye Oak House, opposite the junction of Md. 404 and Md. 662, may have been built about 1720 as a schoolhouse. The building has been restored by the garden clubs of Talbot and Queen Anne's Counties.

Wye Oak State Park surrounds the largest white oak in Maryland and one of the largest in the United States. Believed to be nearly 450 years old, the **Wye Oak** is 107 feet high with a spread of 160 feet and a trunk circumference of 32 feet. The state acquired the tree and the park's 1.5 acres in 1939. In 1941 the General Assembly named the Wye Oak the official state tree. The American Forestry Association lists it among national tree "champions." In August 1959 a massive limb crashed to the ground, and another one fell in June 1984. Some of the wood was dried and sold as souvenirs; and a two-ton section was sculpted into a monument now on display at Martinak State Park. In 1991, the oak dropped thousands of acorns after a five-year dormant period. Forestry specialists speculated that the monumental tree, now a hollow shell held together by wire, was making a final effort to perpetuate itself before dying.

Old Wye Church (or Wye Chapel) also lies at the intersection with Md. 404. This small brick church was consecrated on October 18, 1721, as a local chapel for St. Paul's Parish, Centreville. Restored in 1949 by the Boston firm of Perry, Shaw, and Hepburn, the church is now regarded as a near-perfect example of rural colonial church architecture, featuring brick floors, box pews, a slave gallery, and a hanging pulpit and pulpit canopy. The chancel contains two chairs dating from the time of James II. The Baskerville Bible at the reading desk is contemporary with the church. A reconstructed vestry house, erected on the original 1763 foundations, and an 18th century–style parish house built in 1957 are located nearby.

From Wye Mills, take Md. 662 south to U.S. 50 and follow the highway for about two miles. Return to Md. 662, here named Longwoods Rd. The traveler soon reaches the village of Longwoods, to the north of which, on Wye Heights Rd., lies **Wye Heights,** or **Cleghorne-on-Wye** (private), a three-story house the Lloyds built in 1823 and enlarged in the 1930s. Its gardens along the river include some of the most beautiful boxwoods in Maryland.

About two miles farther south, Md. 662 crosses Hailem School Rd., on the right. From here, to the west on Goldsborough Neck Rd., **Myrtle Grove** (private) overlooks Goldsborough Creek. Robert Goldsborough of Myrtle Grove (1704–77), a county justice of the peace, built a small log house here in 1734. Although now covered with clapboards the house retains its original interior paneling. In 1790 the builder's son, Robert Goldsborough IV (1740–98) put a $2^{1}/_{2}$-story brick addition on the original house. This portion features a modillioned cornice, oval windows in the gables, molded ceilings, plaster cornices, and a hanging staircase. A member of the House of Delegates during the Revolution, Goldsborough at the time of his death owned 78 slaves and held other property assessed at more than £2,000.

Miles River Neck

The traveler now reaches deeper into proud old Talbot County, whose borders are mostly water: the Chesapeake Bay on the west, the Choptank River on the south and east, and Tuckahoe Creek on the east. Miles Neck—with the Wye East River to the north and Miles River to the south—contains long stretches of twisting secondary roads never more than a mile from tidewater. Sometimes—as a boat navigates a low creek—one will glimpse the sight of a mast or a sail seemingly gliding across the landscape. Md. 662, a slow road south toward the county seat of Easton, travels through fields and woodlands that make up ancient estates. Generally, the houses remain private residences either closed to the public entirely or viewable only during historic-house tours. Such tours have become a favorite means of fund-raising among Eastern Shore cultural organizations.

To reach **Gross's Coate,** begun in the mid-18th century, turn right on Sharp Rd. and at the next fork go straight on Little Park Rd. At Todds Corner Rd., turn right and follow Gross Coate Rd.

Gross's Coate occupies a tract Lord Baltimore granted to Roger Gross in 1658. The Tilghmans acquired the land in the 18th century, and the family held on to it for more than two centuries. In 1790 Charles Willson Peale visited and painted three portraits, all of which hung in the house until this century. Peale completed the portrait of Mary Tilghman, one of his finest, when he was a 49-year-old widower with six children and looking for another wife. He fell in love with Mary, but her family expected her to marry within her social class, and so she finally refused him.

Wye House (private), one of the most distinctive residences on the

Wye House, as documented by the WPA

Eastern Shore, stands across Lloyd Creek from Gross's Coate (the entrance lies on the north side of Bruff's Island Rd., reachable via Todds Corner Rd.). This property has belonged to the Lloyd family since 1658, when Edward Lloyd received a grant of thousands of acres. Beyond the entrance gates, a formal avenue lined with oaks and beeches leads to the Palladian portico of the mansion three-quarters of a mile away. The fourth Edward Lloyd started to build Wye House in 1770, when he inherited the plantation. The first building was destroyed by the British during the Revolution and rebuilt around 1784, for which occasion some of the present furnishings were ordered from England. (Two of his three children scratched their initials and the date "1792" on a window pane.) The Orangery, a stucco-covered brick building in a French style, is behind the house, which faces a bowling green. Large arched windows admitted sunlight and heat for the lemons and oranges once planted here in square tubs modeled after those at Versailles.

The Lloyds of Maryland and Frederick Douglass

One of the oldest family graveyards in America is at Wye House, beyond the Orangery, through an arched gate, and behind a high brick wall. Twelve generations of Lloyds are buried there. The graveyard's earliest stone dates to 1684, and the latest graves date to the modern era. From 1664 to 1907 seven successive Edward Lloyds owned Wye House, all seven served in the provincial or state legislature, and all but one are buried here along with other members of the family. The first Edward, a Puritan of Welsh ancestry who aided Lord Baltimore in retention of his colony, died in 1696 in his native England. His son Philemon married Henrietta Maria Bennett (1647–97), a local widow who became the social progenitor of the Eastern Shore's most prominent families.

Henrietta Maria, supposed to be a noblewoman with ties to the English crown, had a dozen children by two husbands. She was the forebear of generations of Lloyds, Tilghmans, Goldsboroughs, Chamberlaines, Hollydays, and other families who intermarried and constituted the Eastern Shore branch of an aristocratic, social oligarchy that ruled Maryland society and politics before the Revolution. Her son Edward II (1670–1718) served as acting governor of Maryland from 1709 to 1714. Edward IV (1744–96), "the patriot," was a member of the first Council of Safety, a delegate to the Continental Congress, and from 1781 until his death, a member of the Maryland Senate. Edward V, "the governor" or "Colonel Lloyd," was governor of Maryland in 1809 and a U.S. senator from 1819 to 1826. His son-in-law, Confederate admiral Franklin Buchanan is buried at the left of the entrance gate (Confederate general Isaac R. Trimble, who was a confidante of General Lee and who participated in most of the war's major battles, was also a Lloyd son-in-law). Here also is the grave of Edward V's grandson, Confederate brigade commander Charles S. Winder, killed at the Battle of Cedar Mountain on August 9, 1862.

Before the Civil War, the Lloyds were the largest slaveowners on the Eastern Shore. In 1824, when a little slave boy named Fred Bailey walked 12 miles from Tuckahoe Creek to work for his master at Wye House, the Lloyd family became intimately connected to one of the greatest antislavery spokesmen of the 19th century: Frederick Douglass. The story of these two families, linked by slavery, contains a quintessence of the Eastern Shore.

The Baileys, buried in unmarked graves in Talbot County, can trace their ancestry on the Shore to at least 1701. The man who would become Frederick Douglass was born in 1818, the son of Harriet Bailey and an unknown white man, possibly his master, Capt. Aaron Anthony, overseer for the 13 farms and 550 slaves of Colonel Lloyd. Because of Fred Bailey's unusual appearance (he had African, European, and Indian ancestors), Anthony called him "my little Indian boy." After only a few years at Wye House, the boy was shipped to Fells Point, at the age of 8, then to St. Michaels at the age of 15, and back to Baltimore at 18. He escaped slavery two years later and embarked on multiple careers as abolitionist, newspaperman, writer, orator, diplomat, and statesman. By the time of his death in 1895, Douglass was considered by many the leading 19th-century American spokesman for human rights.

In 1877, a wealthy and prominent Douglass returned to St. Michaels and told an integrated audience: "I am an Eastern Shoreman, with all that name implies. Eastern Shore corn and Eastern Shore pork gave me my muscle. I love Maryland and the Eastern Shore." Four years later, he visited Wye House, walked in the atmospheric family burial ground, and sipped wine on the veranda with the great-grandson of Colonel Lloyd. (Ten years previously, Jefferson Davis had been entertained there while promoting his history of the Confederacy.) In a burst of nostalgia and good will, Douglass toasted the Lloyd family with the hope that "God, in his providence, would pour out the horn of plenty to the latest generation."

Douglass is buried in Rochester, New York, where he published his antislavery newspaper. Cedar Hill, his mansion in the Anacostia section of Washington, D.C., is a national monument administered by the National Park Service. His Maryland birthplace is marked by an inaccurate road sign.

Following either Todds Corner Rd. south or Bruff's Island Rd. east, turn south on Unionville Rd., which becomes Md. 370.

The Anchorage (private), a five-part frame house that incorporates in its central section a house built in the mid-18th century, lies just before the Miles River bridge. In the 1830s, Edward Lloyd V gave the property to his daughter Sarah and her husband, Lt. Charles Lowndes. The Lowndeses added the two-story portico, hyphens, and wings, converting the house into an antebellum mansion. Lowndes retired from the navy just before the Civil War but remained a Union sympathizer in a strongly pro-Southern family. In 1862 he was awarded the rank of commodore on the retired list.

From The Anchorage, Sarah Lloyd Lowndes could look across the river to **The Rest** (private), home of her sister Ann Catherine, wife of Adm. Franklin Buchanan (1800–1874). The first superintendent of the

U.S. Naval Academy in Annapolis (appointed in 1845), Buchanan joined the Confederates during the Civil War. On March 8, 1862, he commanded the ironclad *Virginia* (earlier the USS *Merrimac*) in its first foray among Union blockaders at Hampton Roads. (Wounded in action, Buchanan missed the next day's famous battle with the *Monitor*.) He became the highest-ranking officer of the Confederate Navy. It was his force that Admiral Farragut defeated at the Battle of Mobile Bay, August 5, 1864. After the war, Buchanan returned to The Rest, where he died in 1874.

A concrete bridge now spans the Miles River, originally called St. Michaels in honor of the saint whose feast day marked one of the dates when the semiannual rents were due to the lord proprietor for land grants. The word *Saint* was later dropped, perhaps after objections from local Quakers; and the river's name was gradually corrupted to "Miles." As early as 1677, this crossing site featured a ferry—first "a canowe" and later a flat scow pulled by a rope. The General Assembly authorized some of the Miles River planters to build a toll bridge, which was finished in 1859.

From the bridge the tract once known as "Ending of the Controversie" can be seen to the north where Glebe Creek branches from the river to the right. The land was granted to Wenlocke Christison in 1670. On three separate occasions in the 1660s, this famous Quaker was whipped through the streets of Boston, then banished for "Rebellion, which is as the Sin of Witchcraft." Like many others, he found Maryland more tolerant and was soon active in the Third Haven Meeting. At his death, around 1679, he was a delegate to the state assembly.

Beyond the bridge, follow signs to Easton.

EASTON

U.S. 50 provides the fastest, most direct route to Easton from the bay bridges. Just north of the Talbot County seat, the highway passes the **Talbot County Chamber of Commerce and Information Center,** located in a restored building that originally stood on a tract named Tilghman's Fortune. The Ocean Gateway (U.S. 50) bypasses downtown Easton, so the traveler must take Md. 322 to get to the marked historic district in town.

Easton (35' alt., 9,372 pop.) now serves the surrounding region as county seat and commercial and cultural center. In addition to a growing industrial capacity, the town boasts banking and medical facilities that make it the trading and distribution point for a four-county area. In contrast to many other Eastern Shore towns, Easton's population has increased in recent years. Since the end of World War II, new residents from such cities as New York, Pittsburgh, and Cleveland have bought waterfront plantations in the county. The "newcomers" have actively supported local cultural and philanthropic affairs. This "gentrification" has encouraged the growth of restaurants and other specialty stores.

Also unlike many Eastern Shore towns, Easton is situated inland, with the nearest waterfront, **Easton Point on the Tred Avon River,** a mile away. The old docks and warehouses at the point have largely been supplanted by modern oil company installations. Easton developed around the Talbot County Courthouse, which was erected in 1710–12 near what was then known as Pitt's Bridge. The bridge spanned a small arm of the Tred Avon on the main road north from Oxford; its location is now marked by a plaque on the wall of a shopping center on North Washington St. At the time the original courthouse was built, the only other structure of importance in the neighborhood was the Third Haven Quaker Meeting House, erected in 1682–84. The courthouse provided impetus for growth; by 1723 the justices were forced to forbid "the Publick Houses at the Court House" from "keeping their nine pins in the streets during the sitting of this Court."

Early in its history, the village was known as Talbot Court House. For convenience, the name was later shortened to Talbot Town or Talbottown, and still later to Talbotton or just plain Talbot. The village grew very slowly in colonial times, and not a single prerevolutionary building survives except the old Quaker meeting house. Resisting the British-imposed stamp tax in 1765, the freemen of Talbot County met in the courthouse and adopted a resolution declaring that they would "detest, abhor, and hold in the utmost contempt" anyone involved with enforcement of the obnoxious Stamp Act. When revolution broke out 10 years later, the Declaration of Independence was read from the courthouse steps and Talbot County troops drilled on the dusty road in front of the courthouse before marching off to join Washington's army.

After the Revolution, the village developed rapidly. Because of the town's central location on the peninsula, the state located administrative offices for the Eastern Shore counties here. Talbot became in effect the "capital" of the Eastern Shore. In 1788, the assembly named the town Easton, a contraction of East-town. The old courthouse was too small for the Court of Appeals, the federal courts, and state offices; so in 1794 a new courthouse was finished at a cost of £3,000, with the state providing five-sixths of the cost. Some Eastern Shore residents hoped that the Maryland legislature would hold alternate sessions in Easton and Annapolis, but it never did so. The government presence did help make Easton the largest, most important, and most progressive town on the Eastern Shore for the next century. The first newspaper on the Eastern Shore was established here (1790), the first bank (1805), and the first steamboat line to Baltimore (1817). Most of the buildings facing the courthouse, in the heart of the business section, were built between 1790 and 1820, although their fronts have since been remodeled. The checkerboard street plan of the central section of Easton dates to 1785. Col. Jeremiah Banning, a wealthy landowner of Talbot County, "had the honour" of naming the streets, giving the name of Washington to the principal business thoroughfare.

The Episcopal Diocese of Easton, covering the nine counties of the Eastern Shore, takes its name from the town and has its cathedral here. The headquarters of the Easton District of the Peninsula Conference of the Methodist Church is also located in town. The Talbot County Free Library has an especially good Maryland collection and children's library. The Easton Players, a veteran little theater group also performs here. Numerous other recreational and civic clubs add substance to the town.

The **Talbot County Courthouse,** on the courthouse green in the center of town, is the state office and court building of 1794, enlarged in 1958 by the addition of north and south wings. Its second-floor courtroom was the scene of Judge Richard B. Carmichael's military arrest during the Civil War (see Tour 8). In the middle to late 1950s, citizens and businesses, supported by a variety of public agencies, began a project to restore the buildings on this courthouse square to their approximate appearance during the Federal period. The restoration project aroused such interest that many new buildings beyond the square have since been built in the Federal style, including a shopping center, a hotel, various office buildings and stores, and even service stations.

The **Thomas Perrin Smith House,** 119 N. Washington St., was built in 1803 by the founder of the newspaper from which the present *Easton Star-Democrat* developed; since 1912 the building has been the home of the Chesapeake Bay Yacht Club. The **Brick Hotel** on the corner of Washington and Federal Sts., completed in 1812, was used as a hotel until the late 19th or early 20th century, when it was converted into an office building. The former **Old Frame Hotel,** believed to be more than 150 years old, is in the same block, on the corner of Goldsborough and Washington Sts.

The **Stevens House,** 29 S. Washington St., one block south of the courthouse, is home to the Historical Society of Talbot County, which restored the building (ca. 1800) during the late 1950s. In its small museum, the society mounts exhibits of furniture and other Talbot artifacts. The **Hughlett-Henry House,** 26 South St., just off S. Washington St., dates to the 1790s. Well-proportioned brick buildings at 105–109 S. Washington St. (private) retain attractive, original external woodwork.

The **Third Haven Quaker Meeting House,** off S. Washington St. immediately beyond the railway overpass, is one of the oldest frame houses of worship in the United States. The clapboard structure was erected between 1682 and 1684 and enlarged in 1792. The Friends, deri-

Inside the Third Haven Meeting House, near Easton, in the 1930s

sively called "Quakers" by their many enemies in the 17th century, have been active in Maryland for more than 300 years. George Fox, one of the denomination's founders, visited the colony in 1672 and established the Maryland Yearly Meeting, the second in America. William Penn visited meetings on both the Western and Eastern Shores; he once held meeting under one of the massive oaks on the parklike grounds here. The original broad-plank floors and straightback benches in the old meeting house have been preserved. The stove was a source of contention in 1781; some members thought that religious zeal should give sufficient warmth without artificial heating. The Third Haven Meeting still functions but no longer uses the historic house, meeting instead in the adjacent brick building. The Maryland State Archives now protects the meeting's records, which date from the mid-17th century.

The **Old Market House,** a small 1½-story stuccoed brick building erected in 1791, sits at Harrison St. and Magazine Alley. The Grand Lodge of Maryland of the Masonic Order, organized in Easton in 1783, held its first meetings in the old courthouse but moved to the Market House while the courthouse of 1794 was being constructed. A monument here commemorates Dr. John Coats, the first Grand Master, and the building houses a small museum.

The cannon in front of the **American Legion home** on Dover St., east of the **Tidewater Inn,** is believed to have been part of the armament of Fort Stokes, built in 1813 on the Tred Avon River opposite Easton Point to protect the town from the British fleet. The 2½-story **Bullitt** or **Chamberlain House** at Dover and Harrison Sts., was erected about 1790 by Thomas James Bullitt, progenitor of the famous Bullitt family of Philadelphia. One of his descendants, William C. Bullitt (1891–1967) served as American ambassador to the USSR (1933–36) and to France (1936–41). **Foxley Hall,** an imposing brick building located at North Aurora and Goldsborough Sts., was built about 1794 by Mrs. Henry Dickinson.

Trinity Cathedral, on Goldsborough St. east of Aurora St., functions as the primary church of the Episcopal Diocese of Easton. Consecrated in 1894, this stone, Romanesque building has notable stained-glass windows. The small, one-story frame building behind it, now used as a parish house, was the original cathedral, built in 1876.

St. Michaels and Tilghman Island via Md. 33

From Easton, the traveler must explore an example of the creeks and waterfronts that typify the Eastern Shore. Centuries of "following the water" have produced a distinctive water-oriented culture with its own dialect, work ethic, and regard for the bay.

Md. 33 was once part of the main route between Ocean City and the ferry terminal at Claiborne, which connected the Eastern Shore to Annapolis. With construction of the Bay Bridge, ferry service ended, and the road now represents the principal entrance to the **St. Michaels** and **Bay Hundred** districts of Talbot County—areas famous among hunters, fishers, writers, and boaters. The road angles northwest from downtown Easton over the headwaters of the Tred Avon River and then follows the Miles River on its way to St. Michaels, a trip of 10 miles.

Less than four miles from Easton, the road passes the **Calhoon**

M.E.B.A. Engineering School, where Md. 329 (Royal Oak Rd.) forks south to Deep Neck and Ferry Neck. The latter is named for the ferry that has operated from the small community of **Bellevue** since 1760. The toll boat, perhaps the oldest "free-running" ferry in the United States, crosses to Oxford daily during daylight hours but is closed December 16 through March 1. The sites of many 17th- and 18th-century shipyards are scattered throughout the coves and creeks of the two necks.

St. Michaels (8' alt., 1,301 pop.), a waterfront landmark, occupies a narrow piece of land between the Miles River and Broad Creek. This picturesque village has become a major summer tourist attraction and one of the best-known yachting centers on the East Coast. Thousands visit here annually in early August for a variety of regattas and boating festivals held on the wide Miles River west of the town. The **Chesapeake Bay Maritime Museum** attracts thousands more with its indoor and outdoor exhibits of bay vessels, the local shipbuilding industry, and the life of the 19th-century waterman. The collection includes more than 80 examples of bay craft, ranging from the log canoe to the skipjack. The complex occupies 18 acres along the water and features the Hooper Strait Lighthouse (1879), a cottage-style structure built on stilts, which once raised this relic above the bay mud. The Waterfowling Building illustrates the hunter's arts, and the Chesapeake Bay Building traces the history of the bay and its inhabitants since the last Ice Age. The museum stages craft demonstrations during warm weather months. Its library of 4,000 volumes is open to the public.

Once heavily timbered, the St. Michaels area has been a shipbuilding center since the last half of the 17th century, although the town itself did not develop until the American Revolution. One of the first buildings on the townsite was an Anglican church, built in the late 1680s by Edward Elliott. An English merchant, James Braddock, bought land beside the church in 1778 and had it surveyed into lots. By 1805, the village had grown sufficiently to incorporate as a town. About 1810, when ship construction was at its height, sailing craft of all kinds were built here, including schooners of the type later known as the "Baltimore Clipper," reputedly the fastest sailing vessel afloat. This activity captured the attention of the British, who invaded the Chesapeake in 1813 to attack the privateers, or "pirates," wreaking havoc on British trade during the War of 1812. A fleet under the command of Rear Adm. George Cockburn slowly advanced up the bay that summer, to punish the newly independent upstarts who dared to challenge the world's most powerful maritime empire. In the darkness of August 10, 1813, 300 British marines landed in an assault on the town, but they sustained heavy losses when the local militia fired a cannon into their ranks at point-blank range in the early morning mist. British barges on the Miles River bombarded the town, but it escaped serious damage. Local tradition relates that the residents extinguished all lights near the ground and hung lanterns in upper-story windows and treetops to draw off the enemy fire. Two weeks later, a larger British force disembarked to capture St. Michaels but unexpectedly turned back without a battle.

By 1820 local timber supplies had been depleted, and Baltimore was becoming the major shipbuilding center on the bay. However, oystering became a new source of income in 1829, when the Chesapeake and Delaware Canal provided access to northern markets. The St. Michaels shipyards began to concentrate on smaller watercraft designed for local bay commerce. The pungies, sloops, and two-masted schooners built in St. Michaels and other bay villages contributed vitally to Maryland's 19th-century economy. These sailing vessels provided fast, low-cost transportation for shipping Eastern Shore grain, farm produce, and seafood to Baltimore markets.

After the Civil War, when oyster dredging under sail was made legal in Maryland waters, St. Michaels' shipbuilders produced "buckeyes," or "bugeyes." These long, low vessels with two raked masts developed from the smaller log canoes that had been used for more than a century in oyster tonging. The bugeye was heavy enough to haul a dredge, and its thick log hull could withstand the sharp edges of the oyster shells. The shallow bottom enabled watermen to transport farm crops along the bay's shallow tributaries during the off season. A few bugeyes and other locally built sailing vessels have survived as pleasure craft or in museum collections. Power boats have become the predominant commercial vessels on the bay. Sailing in St. Michaels is now recreational.

Md. 33 in St. Michaels is known as Talbot St. The **Cannon Ball House** (1800–1810), an elegant 2$^1/_2$-story brick house laid in Flemish bond, stands on Mulberry St., four houses on the right off Talbot. The house received its name after a cannonball from the 1813 bombardment dropped through the roof and bounced down the stairs past the owner's wife. The **Amelia Welby House,** a frame house at the foot of Mulberry St. on the left, was the birthplace of Amelia Ball Coppuck (1819–52), a poet praised by Poe for her "true poetical qualities."

The Cannon Ball House stands at the corner of a lane leading to **St. Mary's Square,** the original public square of St. Michaels. A rectangular brick structure in the middle of the green was built in 1832 for the **Methodist Episcopal Church,** a denomination that has flourished here since the late 18th century. A small cannon in front of the structure is reputed to be one of two presented to St. Michaels by Jacob Gibson in apology for a prank; it may have been used in the defense against the British. The **St. Mary's Square Museum** includes the St. Michael's Bell, cast in 1842 and for a long time used in local shipyards to signal the beginning of the workday, lunch break, and quitting time.

The **Christ Episcopal Church** (1878) on Talbot between Mulberry and Willow Sts. is situated on the site of a church built by Edward Elliott in the 17th century. The Rev. John Gordon, one of the few Church of England rectors who kept his parish during the Revolution, served here from 1749 until his death in 1790. True to the spirit of the Tidewater, Gordon reputedly was a racing enthusiast as well as patriot. He is said to have maintained a track near his church, where he and the members bet on each other's horses after services. At one time the harbor came up to the back of the church, but during the 19th century, the townspeople dumped their refuse into the water, and the area was finally filled. A town office and the fire department now occupy the reclaimed land.

The prerevolutionary part of St. Michaels begins at Willow St. beyond the church. Small brick and shingled-over log houses bespeak their early origins. The brick house at Willow and Locust Sts. was reputedly built by Edward Elliott about 1680. Md. 33 passes the Chesapeake Bay Maritime Museum on Navy Point and then leaves St. Michaels to Claiborne and Tilghman Island.

Md. 33 forks south at the junction with Md. 451, which leads to **Claiborne,** named after Lord Baltimore's 17th-century nemesis. This village was established in 1866 by the Baltimore and Eastern Shore Railroad as a ferry point on its boat-and-rail line between Ocean City and Baltimore. The town later became the terminus of a state-operated ferry line to Annapolis. When the ferry's Eastern Shore terminus moved to Matapeake, on Kent Island, an auxiliary ferry ran from Romancoke on Lower Kent Island to Claiborne. After the ferry finally ceased operations following completion of the Bay Bridge, the site became a quiet residential area.

As Md. 33 continues down the narrow neck of land between Harris Creek and the bay, the road passes **Webley** (private), an old house with modern wings. Dr. Absalom Thompson purchased it in 1826 and four years later converted the house into the first hospital on the Eastern Shore. Contemporaries described this famous surgeon riding bareback and barefoot on a mule to visit patients, carrying a jar of calomel, a lancet, and a syringe with a nozzle as big as a gun barrel.

A right turn onto Lowes Wharf Road leads to a view of the bay which includes **Poplar Island,** two miles offshore. Richard Thompson, a Claiborne kinsman, patented the island in 1640; he lost his family a few years later in an Indian attack. Alexander D'Hinoyossa, the director of Dutch settlements in Delaware, who came to Maryland in 1644 when the English captured New Amstel (New Castle), purchased the island in 1699 and lived there a few years. The original patent, a 1,000-acre tract, has been eroded by time and tides; it now consists of three small islets.

Md. 33 crosses Knapp Narrows to **Tilghman Island,** a flat expanse of low, sandy ground that protrudes into the water where the bay and

Unloading fish for processing at Avalon, Tilghman Island

the large estuary of the Choptank River merge. Three small watermen's villages—**Tilghman, Avalon,** and **Fairbank**—occupy the island.

Oxford via Peach Blossom Rd. (Md. 333)

Md. 333 leaves Easton from Washington St. south of Md. 33 and enters farming, fishing, and yachting areas where water, land, and sky form the flat continuum characteristic of bay country. Locally known as the Oxford or Peach Blossom Rd., Md. 333 crosses three small peninsulas created by the Tred Avon River and its tributaries. This river has been variously known since the 1600s as Tiedhaven, Trudhaven, Treaqvon, Third Haven, Tread Haven, Trade Haven, and Thread Haven. No one knows for sure how it received its present name.

Paper Mill Pond, which once had a factory on its banks, is the first branch of the river, just outside Easton. A concrete bridge crosses Peach Blossom Creek, a tidal tributary where country houses peek from behind dense woods. Beyond the creek, the road intersects Country Club Rd., which leads to the **Talbot Country Club,** located on land formerly called Llandaff, once owned by Richard Tilghman Goldsborough. Md. 333 then crosses Trippe Creek, which runs into the Tred Avon River at **Turner's Point,** granted in 1659 to the Quaker William Turner. Following Turner's death, in 1663, and for about 34 years afterward, Thomas Skillington built ships here. According to local lore, the yard built and supplied ships for buccaneers. Legend further tells of pirates and various fugitives taking advantage of the Chesapeake's countless coves and creeks, and the facts support more than a few such stories.

Trappe Station, a former railroad shipping point, is at the junction of Md. 333 and Otwell Road, which leads to **Otwell** (private) and an associated woodland preserve. The gambrel-roofed wing predates the main section of the house, which was part of a Goldsborough estate for more than two centuries.

Anderton (private) can be seen from Md 333. The old part of this frame house was built in two sections of 1½ stories each, one weatherboarded, the other covered with wide fitted boards. The weatherboarded section, which may have been built sometime in the early 18th century, has an outside door only four feet high and an interior "cell" 19 feet long but only five feet wide.

Jena (private) presents a dramatic appearance from the road because of the high peak of its dormered roof. This small 1½-story, yellow brick house was built after 1700 with a catslide roof. Each window is a different size, but they all have the same number of panes. The frame wings, built about 75 years ago, replaced a much older frame house. The 2½-story main block, laid in Flemish bond and painted yellow, appears to have been built after the Revolution. The property was christened "Jena" by Jacob Gibson, a well-known Talbot County eccentric who named his various county estates after Napoleon's victories; others were Marengo, Austerlitz, and Friedland. During the War of 1812, Gibson owned Sharp's Island near the mouth of the Choptank River. When British cruisers under Adm. John Borlase Warren raided the island and carried off some of the cattle, Gibson persuaded the admiral to reimburse him. Gossips claimed that Gibson had sold out to the enemy. With animosity against him at its height and at a time when the people of St. Michaels were fearing an attack any minute, Gibson sailed up Broad Creek with a red bandana at the masthead of his boat and an empty rum barrel on its deck. The town thought the attack had come; women and children were sent to the country, and the militia had assembled before Gibson's prank was discovered. Angry soldiers nearly shot Gibson, but after a public apology and explanation he was allowed to depart. He then presented the town of St. Michaels with two cannon for its defense.

Md. 333 also passes **Plinhimmon** (private), which sits in a grove of great old trees at the end of a lane. It was purchased in 1719 by John Coward, whose son John, a merchant and sea captain, sailed the *Integrity* between Oxford and London. Folklore credits the *Integrity* as the ship on which a young gentlewoman, disguised as a sailor, sailed away to America. According to the story, when the captain learned that he had been deceived, he angrily took her home to his plantation in the vicinity of Oxford and banished her to kitchen chores with the slaves. Later, with the help of a more gallant seaman, the girl stowed away on a tobacco ship and returned to London. A visitor seems to have heard the legend while visiting Plinhimmon in about 1825; Catherine Maria Sedgwick, a well-known writer of the day, embroidered the adventure tale and published it as "Modern Chivalry" in the Philadelphia *Atlantic Souvenir* in 1827.

Capt. John Coward's son Thomas was captain of the *Choptank*, one of the last ships to trade out of Oxford before the Revolution. In 1786, Thomas sold Plinhimmon to Matthew Tilghman, who gave it to his daughter Anna Maria, widow of Washington's aide-de-camp, Col. Tench Tilghman (1744–86; see below); she may have built the remaining brick wing of the house. Upon her death in 1843, Anna Maria willed the estate to her grandson, Gen. Tench Tilghman (1810–74), who was the first Talbot County farmer to fertilize with Peruvian guano, as well as the first Marylander to use the newly invented Hussey reaper (in 1836). In the 1850s, he also built on Tilghman Island the first steam-powered sawmills on the Eastern Shore. His son Tench was an aide to Jefferson Davis during the Civil War. This Tench Tilghman left a diary describing the flight of Davis and the Confederate cabinet in the last days of the war, his own capture by African American troops, and his determination to leave the scene of past humiliations to seek his fortune in South America.

The **Oxford Cemetery,** a Tilghman family burying ground once part of Plinhimmon, occupies an area between World Farm Rd. and Evergreen Rd. just north of Md. 333. Here is a monument to the memories of Col. Tench and Anna Maria Tilghman. Colonel Tilghman was born at Fausley, near the Miles River in Talbot County, but moved with his father James to Philadelphia in 1762. There he became a merchant, acquiring a great fortune before the outbreak of the Revolution, when he liquidated his business. Though his father was a firm loyalist, Tench Tilghman warmly supported independence and from 1776 until the end of the war served as Washington's secretary, then as his aide-de-camp. After the victory at Yorktown, it was Tilghman who carried the news to Congress, traveling by boat via Annapolis to Rock Hall, then overland to Philadelphia. Tench Tilghman's ride ranks with that of Paul Revere, although celebrated in lesser poetry. Legend relates that he rode without a break, stopping every three or four hours at the nearest farmhouse with the cry "Cornwallis is taken; a fresh horse for the Congress!" He arrived in Philadelphia at night, where his news prompted a celebration. After the

Revolution, Tilghman went into business in Baltimore with wartime financier Robert Morris, a partnership that terminated with Tilghman's death in 1786. Washington said of him, "He had as fair a reputation as ever belonged to a human character."

Just inside the town limits of Oxford a left turn leads to the **U.S. Bureau of Commercial Fisheries Biological Laboratory,** established in 1960 on Boone Creek to study oyster culture and diseases. The steady, drastic decline of the oyster catch in Chesapeake waters has threatened the whole industry; research here may determine how bay fishermen can create oyster "farms" similar to those successfully operated in Japan. Shells with spat (baby oysters) are strung on ropes, which are lowered into the water to a point a few inches above the creek floor. The suspended shellfish grow much faster than those on natural oyster beds.

Oxford

Oxford (699 pop.), on the southern tip of a peninsula formed by Town Creek and the Choptank and Tred Avon Rivers, harbors a fishing and oyster fleet. Trees and lawns line its main street; small, well-kept, white frame houses reflect its maritime heritage; historic brick structures bespeak its past importance. Once rivaled only by Annapolis among prerevolutionary Maryland ports, Oxford became an official port of entry into the colony in 1683. The town was laid out in 1684 and again in 1694, when its name was changed briefly to Williamstadt, in honor of King William. Large London and Liverpool commercial houses established branch stores here, exchanging articles of necessity for cargoes of tobacco. Slaves from the West Indies were also delivered here. Two record books kept by the port collectors between 1747 and 1775 show almost 200 vessels registering at the customs house.

The outbreak of the Revolution and subsequent rise of Baltimore accelerated the town's decline as a major port. Before his death in 1798, Jeremiah Banning, a sea captain who had long sailed out of Oxford, wrote in his diary: "Oxford's streets and strands were once covered by busy crowds ushering in commerce from almost every quarter of the globe. The once well-worn streets are now grown in grass, save a few narrow tracks made by sheep and swine; and the strands have more the appearance of an uninhabited island than where human feet have ever trod."

Oxford's municipal government had ceased to function by 1825, when the town was incorporated and surveyed again to revive local affairs. After the Civil War, shipbuilding returned; oystering and fishpacking became important occupations, and summer visitors came to enjoy "the salubrity of the air." A branch of the Maryland and Delaware Railroad reached Oxford in 1871. Boatbuilding and fishing remain occupations of some Oxford residents, but retirees, other newcomers, and summer tourists have bolstered the town's economy. Every August, the Tred Avon Yacht Club holds a three-day regatta, which includes races for log canoes.

Oxford's main street is named for Robert Morris Sr. (1711–50) and for his son and namesake (1734–1806), who played a large role in building the financial support—domestic and foreign—necessary for waging the War for Independence. The senior Morris arrived in Oxford in 1738 as a factor for the Liverpool house of Foster Cunliffe, Esq. and Sons and became a successful merchant in his own right. He died accidentally from a wound received after a cannon salute upon his departure from one of the company ships. At least one contemporary attributed Oxford's subsequent decline to Morris's death. Robert Morris the younger is believed to have come to Oxford at age 13 and to have attended school here briefly before entering the Greenway countinghouse in Philadelphia. He became one of the wealthiest merchants in the colonies, a signer of the Declaration of Independence, and finance minister for the Confederation. Morris raised the funds, including money from his own pocket, that made it possible for Washington to move his army from New York to Yorktown. After the Revolution, he served in the U.S. Senate representing Pennsylvania from 1789 to 1794. He later lost everything and spent three years in a debtor's prison until his release in 1801, five years before his death at the age of 72.

Remnants of the **Morris House** (1774) at the end of Morris St. are incorporated into the **Robert Morris Inn,** a three-story frame hotel with a mansard roof, restored and refurnished in 1952. Large, wooden beams in the basement, evidently part of the original house, support the old portion of the building. During the restoration, many hand-wrought iron nails and a few English copper coins were found. The inn is on "The Strand," a roadway along the Tred Avon which also fronts a small dockside park at the terminus of the **Tred Avon Ferry.** This local landmark may be the oldest ferry in the United States that runs "free," not attached to a cable. The ferry line, which connects Oxford and Bellevue, was started in 1760 by a woman, Elizabeth Skinner.

The **Grapevine House** is across from the inn on the south side of Morris St. The building takes its name from an ancient but still productive grapevine believed to have been planted about 1808 by John Willis, who introduced many new and improved varieties of fruit into Talbot County.

The gray clapboard **Academy (Bratt) House,** four doors farther up Morris St. from The Strand, features a pilastered facade and cupola atop a low hipped roof. The original structure was built around 1848 as the officers' residence for the Maryland Military Academy, a preparatory school established under the sponsorship of Gen. Tench Tilghman of Plinhimmon. The main house, which stood in what is now the box garden, burned down in 1855; shortly thereafter the school closed.

The town's oldest boatyard occupies a site at the end of Tilghman St. and dates to colonial times. **Byberry,** the town's oldest residence, built around 1695, sits at the water's edge. This shingled, settler-type house with a long sloping roof was moved to its present site in 1929 and named for a Pennsylvania village.

The small **Oxford Museum,** located at the corner of Morris and Market Sts., contains artifacts and memorabilia from the town's history.

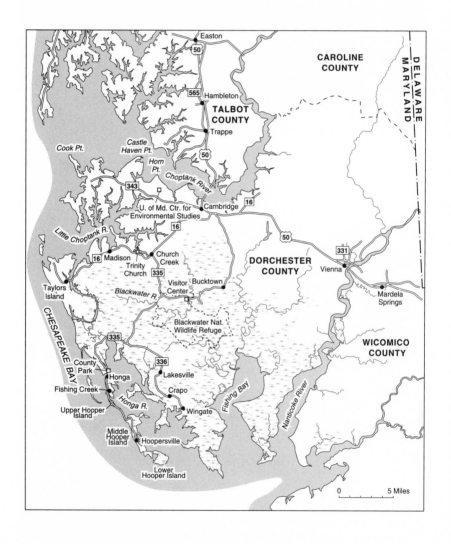

From the Chesapeake to the Atlantic: Dorchester, Wicomico, Somerset, and Worcester Counties

Easton to Ocean City via U.S. 50

After by-passing downtown Easton, U.S. 50, a dual highway conspicuously identifying itself as "Ocean Gateway," runs through a cluster of roadside businesses and continues south through farmland. About half a mile south of the Maryland State Police barracks lie the remains of a small hexagonal frame structure, **Peachblossom Church,** built in 1881. According to folklore, the devil can make himself invisible by hiding in a right-angled corner. This six-sided, wide-angled edifice was built "so that the devil would have no corner to sit in and hatch evil." Methodist, Reformed Lutheran, Swedenborgian, and Church of the Brethren congregations once used the church on alternating Sundays.

Follow signs immediately on the right to Md. 565, the old Easton-Trappe Rd. The visitor passes through Stumptown and then reaches **Hambleton,** a building known locally for more than two centuries as **Hole-in-the-Wall.** The name may have come from an inn that operated here about 1750. An Eastern Shore yarn relates that sailors sold smuggled goods at the inn through a hole in the wall. A shingled telescope house has stood on the northeast corner for more than 200 years.

To the east on U.S. 50, just above the point where the highway crosses Almshouse Rd. (which becomes Manadier Rd.), the visitor will find the **ruins of White Marsh Church** and its well-tended graveyard. The original church may have been built as early as 1685; parish records indicate that White Marsh had an Anglican rector by 1690. The brick church was abandoned during the Civil War and partly burned in 1896. The grave of Robert Morris Sr., a Liverpool native and father of the Revolutionary War financier, is here. His epitaph reads in part:

> His hospitality was enhanced by his Conversation
> Seasoned with cheerful wit and a sound judgment
> A Salute from the cannon of a ship
> The wad fracturing his arm
> Was the signal by which he departed
> Greatly lamented as he was esteemed
> In the fortieth year of his age,
> On the 12th day of July MDCCL

The Rev. Thomas Bacon (1700–68) served as a provincial rector of White Marsh between 1746 and 1768. His compendium of Maryland colonial statutes entitled *Laws of Maryland at Large* (1765) but commonly known as "Bacon's Laws" served as an authoritative guide to colonial legislation for many decades. It included the definitive translation of Maryland's original Latin charter. Another 18th-century rector, the Rev. Daniel Maynadier, was believed to be a Huguenot. A gothic Eastern Shore legend relates that the night after his wife died, two strangers opened her grave to steal a valuable ring. Unable to slip it off, they cut off her finger. Revived by the shock, she rose up and walked to the rectory for a few more years of life.

Trappe

Md. 565 meanders on to this village (56' alt., 974 pop.), which is known to baseball fans as the home of J. Franklin "Home Run" Baker. Born here on March 13, 1886, Baker played third base in the "$100,000 infield" of the Philadelphia Athletics. He won two games with home runs during the 1911 World Series against the New York Giants and is now enshrined in the Baseball Hall of Fame at Cooperstown, New York.

The **Dickinson House** on Maple St. is a frame residence marked by a gambrel roof with picturesque chimneys; it once belonged to the family of John Dickinson (1732–1808), whose "Letters from a Pennsylvania Farmer," written in 1767 after he had moved to Delaware, attacked British taxes and contributed to anti-British feelings in the colonies. Dickinson served as president of the state of Delaware in 1781 and president of the state of Pennsylvania from 1782 to 1786. South of Trappe—down Howell Point Rd. to Grubin Neck—lies the **site of Crosiadore,** Dickinson's birthplace. Crosiadore remained in the Dickinson family for nearly three hundred years, until 1959. The dwelling was destroyed in 1976.

Compton, which belonged to the Stevens family from 1679 to 1860, is also on the neck. William Stevens was a prominent Quaker; but his great-grandson John was expelled from the meeting in 1759 for having "a dark and Libertine spirit" that allowed "fiddling and dancing . . . and also the poppets to be shown in his house." John inherited Compton in 1782 and may have built the present brick house in which he is said to have continued his libertine ways. His son, Samuel Jr. (1778–1860) served three terms as governor of Maryland (1822–26).

Beyond Trappe, follow U.S. 50 to the wide (1.5 miles at this point) and imposing **Choptank River.** Named for the tribe that once lived along its shores, the Choptank is the longest river on the Eastern Shore; it rises from creeks in Delaware and winds southwestward through Caroline County and then between Talbot and Dorchester on its way to the bay.

The highway no longer crosses the low-lying Gov. Emerson C. Harrington Bridge, now a public fishing pier. When President Franklin D. Roosevelt attended its dedication in 1935, the old bridge represented a public investment of $1.5 million, one-third paid by the state, the remainder by the federal Public Works Administration. The new Senator Frederick C. Malkus Jr. Bridge was completed in 1987 at a cost of $37.2 million. It is named for a veteran Maryland legislator who represented the Lower Eastern Shore in the assembly from 1947 until 1994.

Cook Point via Md. 343

U.S. 50 by-passes downtown Cambridge and intersects Md. 343
(Washington St.), which heads west toward the bay along a narrow,
deeply indented, flat neck of land formed by the Choptank River and its
cousin, the Little Choptank River, to the south of the larger river.
Thomas Coleman Du Pont (1863–1930), U.S. senator, industrialist,
and leader of one of the country's most famous business families, developed **Horn Point,** two miles west of Cambridge. The late Francis P. Du
Pont donated the 720-acre site to the city of Cambridge, which in 1971
conveyed the property to the state. Here the University of Maryland now
operates its **Center for Environmental and Estuarine Studies.**

Three miles farther west look for **Spocot** (private), visible during the
winter from the road along the Little Choptank. This house likely dates
from the early 18th century. Stephen Gary patented the property in 1662.
A self-contained community once existed here, complete with shipyard,
sawmill, blacksmith shop, and large slave quarters. The buildings have
disappeared except for two slave houses, which at some point were combined into a single tenant house.

Castle Haven Road turns north from Md. 343 to **Castle Haven
Point.** The road passes a private estate that was part of a grant made in
1659 to Anthony LeCompte, a French Huguenot who came to Maryland
from England in 1655 and settled in Dorchester.

Md. 343 continues to the towns of Hudson, James, and Thomas
(near Hills Point). North of Hudson, **Cook Point** juts into the bay at its
confluence with the Choptank. This spit of land received its name from
Sir Andrew Cooke, father of Ebenezer Cooke, deputy receiver-general to
the fifth Lord Baltimore and Maryland's first poet laureate. Ebenezer published two books of rhymed, rambling verses in London—*The Sot-Weed
Factor* (1708) and *Sot-Weed Redivivus; or The Planter's Looking Glass*
(1730). John Barth, a native of nearby Cambridge, took Cooke's humor-
ous looks at the tobacco planter's life as the start for his own book, *The
Sot-Weed Factor,* published in 1960. Barth's bawdy, picaresque novel—
written in the style of the time—provides a deft look at 17th-century
Maryland, a counterweight to more glorified versions of that past.
Retrace your route and rejoin U.S. 50.

CAMBRIDGE

Cambridge (20' alt., 11,514 pop.), seat of Dorchester County, is one
of the oldest towns in Maryland. The General Assembly in 1684 authorized a town "in Dorchester County Att Daniell Joansis plantation on the
south side of the Great Choptancke." The Choptank tribe had already
moved to a reservation a few miles up the river, in 1669, so the site on
Daniel Jones's land must have seemed practical as a port of entry for the
surrounding plantations. When a supplementary act to build a courthouse was passed in 1686, the name *Cambridge* was used for the first
time. Most of the legislated towns in Maryland never materialized, but
Cambridge took root. The Great Choptank Parish, one of the 30 officially
established by Maryland in 1692, built an Anglican church here in 1696.
The courthouse and church stood on High St. near their present sites,

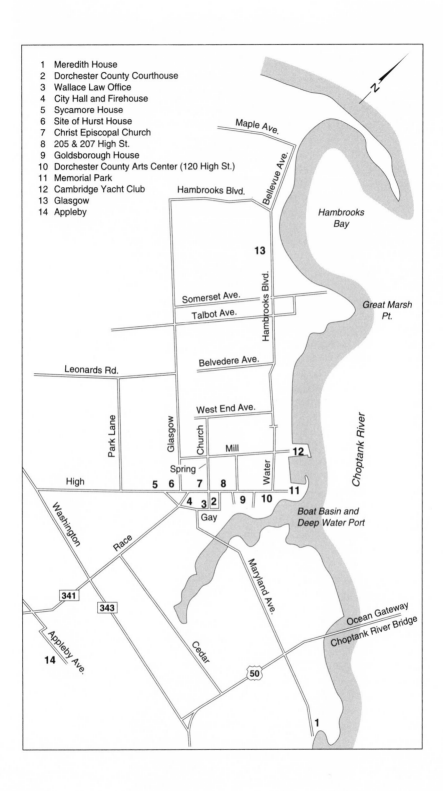

1 Meredith House
2 Dorchester County Courthouse
3 Wallace Law Office
4 City Hall and Firehouse
5 Sycamore House
6 Site of Hurst House
7 Christ Episcopal Church
8 205 & 207 High St.
9 Goldsborough House
10 Dorchester County Arts Center (120 High St.)
11 Memorial Park
12 Cambridge Yacht Club
13 Glasgow
14 Appleby

Maple Ave.
Bellevue Ave.
Hambrooks Blvd.
Hambrooks Bay
Hambrooks Blvd.
Somerset Ave.
Talbot Ave.
Great Marsh Pt.
Belvedere Ave.
Leonards Rd.
West End Ave.
Park Lane
Glasgow
Church
Mill
Water
Choptank River
Spring
High
Gay
Boat Basin and Deep Water Port
Washington
Race
Maryland Ave.
341
343
Ocean Gateway
Choptank River Bridge
Appleby Ave.
Cedar
50

but early in the 18th century, the town contained few other buildings. John Kirk purchased the 100-acre town site from Jones and laid out lots on High St., but they sold slowly.

In 1771, Henry Murray advertised a house for rent near the courthouse, suitable for a tavern, with 15 acres of "Pasture ground on the opposite side of the Street." That same year, Michael Burke advertised a consignment of European, West Indies, and country goods for which he would take "Cash, Wheat, Flaxseed, Corn, Pork, Staves, Plank and Feathers," the kind of goods used in the extensive West Indian–Chesapeake trade. Tobacco, noticeably absent from the barter list, had already been largely replaced on the Eastern Shore by grain.

One might assume that a plantation society committed to slavery would have universally opposed abolitionists and supported the Confederate cause during the Civil War, but Cambridge provided some exceptions. Harriet Tubman was assisted by Quakers and others in Cambridge during her many trips to transport slaves to freedom on the Underground Railroad. Gov. Thomas H. Hicks (1798–1865), born in East New Market, a few miles northeast of Cambridge, helped keep Maryland in the Union at the outbreak of the Civil War. At the request of Governor Hicks, Col. James Wallace (1818–87), a Dorchester County lawyer, raised and then commanded the 1st Maryland Eastern Shore Volunteer Infantry. The unit served in the 12th Corps, Army of the Potomac, and was commended for gallantry at the Battle of Gettysburg, where it fought against Confederate Maryland troops at Culp's Hill early on the third day of battle.

At the city's bicentennial celebration on July 4, 1884, Wallace, who also owned a cannery and had established the town's first oyster shucking and steaming plant, reflected nostalgically on the city's history:

> From 1700 to 1776 the town grew very slowly, but its population was very select and society highly polished. Here were located the Judges of the Court, the clerks, the lawyers, the physicians, the teachers—the cultivated people of the land. Hither came those who sought asylum and rest; some from sunny France, fleeing from persecution after the revocation of the edict of Nantes, some from old England, some from Virginia, some from Scotland and the green Emerald Isle. . . . They came here to rest, and they found it; they lived the life of gentlemen of the olden time. They were gallant, chivalric, polite, cultivated and hospitable; they had no mails, no newspapers, no politics, no heated discussions; they devoted themselves to literature and leisure.

At the start of the Civil War, the population of Cambridge was about 1,800. By 1890, the number of residents had increased to more than 4,000; the town had a railroad to Delaware, and steamboats linked Cambridge to the Western Shore. At the turn of the century, Cambridge was second only to Baltimore as an oyster packing center. Fruit and vegetable canneries thrived along with a cottage shipbuilding industry. Duck and goose hunting—for both sport and commerce—contributed to the town's reputation; the famous sharpshooter Annie Oakley lived in Cambridge briefly, shooting geese from the roof of her house. Cambridge retained its basic character and economy, slowly but steadily growing about 15 percent every 10 years, until the decade of the 1960s. In 1961, the biggest packer closed down completely, putting 1,200 people out of work, nearly a third of all those employed in the town. This economic crisis stimulated a diversification of small industry and changed the town that Colonel Wallace had eulogized. The state and federal governments spent more than $1 million to build a marine terminal, which opened in 1964. Deep-sea vessels immediately began to use the newly dredged river channel to deliver frozen tuna for processing. The Maryland Port Authority spent another $2 million in 1973–74 to expand new port facilities at Cambridge and Crisfield. Vegetable and shellfish processing remain the principal industries in Cambridge, but a wide variety of small factories now supplement the town's economy.

The 1960s also revealed the simmering presence of what virtually every Maryland town has tried to keep in its backyard—a minority African American community with strong churches and weak economies. On June 14, 1963, Cambridge made the national news when Gov. J. Millard Tawes sent National Guard troops to quell disorders that arose from demonstrations against segregated schools, restaurants, and jobs. The Guard remained in town for almost a year. Cambridge erupted again on July 24, 1967; after a ringing provocative speech by H. Rap Brown, fires broke out. National Guard troops again patrolled the streets, and another Maryland governor, Spiro T. Agnew, appeared on national television from Cambridge. Such outbursts of frustration and violence called attention to legitimate grievances and resulted in public programs and private committees to address them. In 1992, the Committee of 100 of Dorchester County announced plans for **Sailwinds Park,** a $35 million project to transform the Cambridge waterfront into a smaller version of Baltimore's Inner Harbor. The project includes a marina, 300-room hotel and conference center, restaurants, historical exhibits, and excursion trains from Cambridge to Hurlock. At the time, the remarks of an African American county commissioner pointed to new hope for Cambridge: "We as a race have never before been let in on a project like this in Dorchester County. We've always had to read about it in the newspaper. But we're involved in this, and it's going to bring housing and jobs to the area. That's what people are looking for."

Walking Tour

To reach the historic center of Cambridge, drive across the Choptank River over U.S. 50 and look for the first intersection, which is Maryland Ave. There a left leads to **Meredith House,** a 2½-story brick house that was built around 1760 and serves as home to the **Dorchester County Historical Society** and its museum (open Sunday afternoons 1:00–5:00 and by appointment). A right onto Maryland Ave. takes one over **Cambridge Creek**, which divides the town east and west and is lined with fishwharves, crab plants, canneries, and warehouses. The avenue leads to the confluence of Market, Academy, and Muse Sts., with city parking ahead and to the left on Academy. One may begin at the eastern end of Gay St. (where it meets Court Lane) and the **Dorchester County Courthouse:** built in 1853, it retains its Italianate facade despite later changes. A predecessor burned in 1851. To the left stands the **old law office** (ca. 1852) of the town's Civil War hero, Colonel Wallace. His mansion, The Hill, once stood behind the office. Built in the late 18th century and earlier home to a proprietary officer, Sir Roger Woolford, who with his wife lies buried here, the house came down in 1971 to make way for the **Dorchester County Public Library.** Farther along Gay St. is the **Cambridge City Hall and Fire House,** a Georgian structure dating from the 1930s. On its walls hang a few paintings by popular artist John Moll.

Following Gay St. to the left, the visitor reaches High St. A short distance to the left, on the north side of the street, one finds **Sycamore House** (417), a small, gambrel-roofed frame house. It was moved here from another site, restored, and is now used by the Cambridge Women's Club. About half the lots in the original town, laid out in 1706, were in the High St. blocks northeast of Christ Church (see below) and the courthouse. No early-18th-century houses remain, and on most of the land there may never have been any. In 1739, when Dr. William Murray leased the area on the west side of High St. between the church and the river, the 25 acres were described as "the Pasture." Most of the town's 18th- and early-19th-century buildings were destroyed in the fires that devastated the downtown in 1882, 1892, and 1910. The stately Victorian and Edwardian structures that still line High St. nonetheless testify to the prosperity that oystering and canning once brought to Cambridge.

Writer John Barth, born in Cambridge in 1930, described a walk down High St. from Christ Church in his first novel, *The Floating Opera* (1955):

> High Street, where I walked, is like no other street in Cambridge, or on the peninsula. A wide, flat boulevard of a street, gently arched with edge-laid yellow brick, it runs its gracious best from Christ Church and the courthouse down to Long Wharf, the municipal park, two stately blocks away. One is tempted to describe it as lined with mansions, until one examines it in winter, when the leaves are down and the trees gaunt as gibbets. Mansions there are—two, three of them—but the majority of the homes are large and inelegant. What makes High Street lovely are the trees and the street itself. The trees are enormous: oaks and cottonwood poplars that rustle loftily above you like pennants atop mighty masts; that when leaved transform the shabbiest houses into mansions; that corrugate the concrete of the wide sidewalks with the idle flexing of their roots. An avenue of edge-laid yellow bricks is the only pavement worthy of such trees, and like them, it dignifies the things around it. Automobiles whisper over this brick like quiet yachts; men walking on the outsized sidewalk under the outsized poplars are dwarfed into dignity. The boulevard terminates in a circular roadway on Long Wharf—terminates, actually, in the grander boulevard of the Choptank. Daniel Jones, upon whose plantation the city of Cambridge now rests, put his house near where this street runs. Colonel John Kirk, Lord Baltimore's Dorchester land agent, built in 1706 the town's first house near where this street runs. There are slave quarters; there are porch columns made of ships' masts; there are ancient names bred to idle pursuits; there are barns of houses housing servantless, kinless, friendless dodderers; there are brazen parades and bold seagulls, eminence and imbecility; there are Sunday pigeons and excursion steamers and mock oranges—all dignified by the great trees and soft glazed brick of the street. The rest of Cambridge is rather unattractive.

Today's visitor can nearly repeat the walk described above. Walk past the corner of Glasgow St., where the Hurst sisters once owned a frame cottage that featured a garden of ancient boxwood, and proceed to

Christ Episcopal Church, a granite structure built in 1883. It stands across High St. from the courthouse. The first church here was constructed from logs by the Great Choptank Parish in 1696 and was rebuilt with brick in 1794. A fire destroyed the second church in 1882. Buried in the graveyard are five governors of Maryland: John Henry (1797–98), Charles Goldsborough (1819), Henry Lloyd (1885–88), Phillips Lee Goldsborough (1912–16), and Emerson C. Harrington (1916–20).

Farther down, on the left, **205 and 207 High St.** apparently date from the mid-18th century, when they would have been owned by John Caille, a merchant and clerk of the Dorchester County Court. Number 207, a weatherboarded frame house, was reputedly transferred from Annapolis by boat and rebuilt on this ground, which Caille leased from the Great Choptank Parish in 1750. (Its brick chimney fulfilled the requirement written into the lease that "no Fire shall be kept or made in any wooden chimney.") The first floor of 205 High St. is believed to be the brick house required by the terms of the lease Caille had from David Murray in 1762. The present roof was erected about 1884, but the interior retains original corner fireplaces and paneled chimney pieces.

The **Goldsborough House,** closer to the water and across the street at 200 High St. must have been standing when Charles Goldsborough sold the property to Henry Dickinson for $4,000 in 1800. With its wooden keystone lintels over the windows and fanlight over the door, this house stood out from its contemporaries. In the late 19th century, it housed the first yacht club in Cambridge.

The **Dorchester County Arts Center,** founded in 1970, occupies 120 High St.; its members include potters, photographers, quilters, stained-glass artists, and basketmakers. A large statue of a blue heron, at the High and Water Sts., the work of John Neal Mulligan, commemorates the founding of Blackwater Wildlife Refuge (see below). High St. ends at the "grander boulevard of the Choptank."

Memorial Park occupies three blocks along a waterfront area that once included the Long Wharf that Barth referred to. After World War II, the town cleared and landscaped the spot to commemorate veterans of both world wars. A large marina for pleasure craft and workboats borders the park between High and Mill Sts. The **Cambridge Yacht Club,** which resembles the deck and bridge of a large vessel, is located nearby at the foot of Mill St. Every summer, the club sponsors a regatta which is visible from the park. Sailwinds Park occupies the waterfront area to the southeast between Cambridge Creek and the Malkus Bridge.

Driving Tour

From the High St.–Gay St. historic area, depart Memorial Park on Water St., following it as it jogs a bit at Choptank Ave. and becomes Hambrooks Blvd. Two blocks beyond Belvedere, one may turn left onto Talbot Ave. and visit the **Brannock Maritime Museum,** which focuses on local personalities, the 19th-century oyster wars, and Chesapeake shipbuilding traditions. **Glasgow,** a large, white brick house set back on a broad lawn, stands on the left, across Somerset Ave., at the city line. Dr. William Murray, "Chirurjeon" (surgeon), fled Scotland after the failure of the Stuart Pretender in the rebellion of 1715. He settled in Cambridge, made a fortune in his practice, and in 1739 bought about a third of the land on which Cambridge stands. His grandson, William Vans Murray (1765–1803), won election to Congress at the age of 25. He served as American foreign minister to Holland during the John Adams administration and was named one of the three negotiators to meet with Napoleon Bonaparte and end America's undeclared war with France. In 1801, after the inauguration of President Jefferson, the State Department sent Murray to Glasgow, Scotland, where he survived only another two years.

To visit **Appleby,** the home of Gov. Thomas H. Hicks, one travels south from the High St.–Gay St. area on Race St. (Md. 341) and follows Race St. south to East Appleby Ave. Hicks remodeled this Georgian house into a Greek Revival structure; later owners added the Queen Anne towers and porches. Son of a slave-owning plantation family and self-made businessman, Hicks became governor of Maryland in 1858, thus serving during the onset of the Civil War. Both sides abused him for what seemed a vacillating, conciliatory posture, but his policy helped keep Maryland from joining the secessionists. Appointed U.S. senator in 1863, to fill a vacancy caused by the death of James Alfred Pearce, Hicks died in office on February 13, 1865.

East from Cambridge, U.S. 50 passes the **Eastern Shore Hospital Center,** an institution of about 100 beds, on its way to the Nanticoke River. Md. 16 leads south from the hospital center.

Side Trip to Church Creek, Blackwater National Wildlife Refuge, and Lower Dorchester via Md. 16, 335, and 336

Below the city of Cambridge stretches a flat, thinly populated landscape with watery, dreamlike vistas. Marshes, farmlands, rivers, and trees form a wild, spacious panorama where water, land, and sky converge on a horizontal plane that dwarfs the observer. Popularly known as the Dorchester Marshes, these wetlands are home to fish, muskrats, and migratory birds—all of which vastly outnumber human inhabitants.

The nocturnal nutria—large, muskratlike South American rodents introduced to the marshes in the 1930s to stimulate the fur industry—have multiplied faster than people here. Trappers still catch both nutria and muskrats, but the market for their fur and meat has diminished. One occasionally finds "marsh rabbit" in local markets, but no one has been able to popularize the meat for the modern diet. The musquash—or muskrat, as Europeans later named the creature (*Ondatra zibethicus*)—is native to the marshes, an aquatic mammal that builds a cone-shaped lodge about three feet above the marsh. These houses—built of mud, grasses, and sedges—have underwater entrances and are connected to feeding areas by tunnels. Where muskrat and nutria have overpopulated, the devegetated land quickly erodes, turning the marsh back to water. In recent decades, thousands of acres have disappeared in this manner.

Church Creek

Md. 16 takes the traveler south and west from Cambridge on a path paralleling the Little Choptank River and crossing its tributary creeks— Fishing, Church, Woolford, Parsons, and Slaughter—and passing Madison Bay. At the junction with Md. 335, the old houses of **Church Creek** stand along both sides of the junction like timeworn sentinels from a forgotten war.

This settlement probably developed around Trinity (Dorchester) Church in the late 17th century. Town lots in Church Creek were mentioned in the land records as early as 1700; a 1766 deed records a shipyard, which operated until native oak and pine were overcut in the first half of the 19th century. Portions of older houses have been incorporated into newer buildings; brick chimneys bespeak other eras. The two-story frame **Gibson House** (private), opposite the **Methodist Episcopal Church** at the east end of town, was built just after the Civil War. Daniel T. Owen, ardent abolitionist and delegate to the Republican convention that nominated Abraham Lincoln, supposedly modeled the house after Lincoln's dwelling in Springfield, Illinois.

Taylor's Island via Md. 16

From Church Creek, Md. 16 continues westward, passing the frame telescope structure **Wyvill House** (private), named for Dr. Dorsey Wyvill, one of the founders (in 1799) of the Medical and Chirurgical Faculty of Maryland.

Trinity Episcopal Church, the oldest church building still standing in Maryland, sits on the shore of Church Creek about a mile west of the town on Md. 16. Built before 1692 as Dorchester Church, the brick church served the English settlers who moved across the bay to establish homesteads during the 25 years after founding of the Maryland colony

Trinity Church,
Dorchester County

in 1634. They named their county and parish Dorchester after Charles Sackville, sixth Earl of Dorset, composer of heroic couplets and friend of Charles II and the Calvert family. The name also evoked the original Dorchester in southern England, county seat of Dorset, later home of poet and novelist Thomas Hardy. When Hardy wrote of the "singularly colossal and mysterious . . . untameable Ismaelitish" heaths around Dorchester, he could have been describing Maryland's Dorchester marshes. Trinity Church has served as a beacon on these heaths for more than three centuries.

In 1956, Col. Edgar Garbish restored the church as a memorial to his father-in-law, Walter P. Chrysler, founder of the automobile corporation that still bears his name. When excavations revealed that a T-wing had been added about 100 years after construction of the main section, the church was restored without it. The north wall, bulging dangerously, was torn down during the restoration process and rebuilt to match the original precisely. All the church's walls were laid in Flemish bond. The altar table is believed to be original, although the top was apparently replaced sometime during the church's long history. Trinity still possesses a communion chalice presented by Queen Anne. Another prized possession, a cushion supposedly used by the same queen at her coronation in 1702, was destroyed in a fire in 1939.

The tree-shaded graveyard at Trinity contains the remains of Gov. Thomas King Carroll and his daughter Anna Ella Carroll (see below). Millstones mark the grave of an early miller.

Md. 16 continues westward through **Madison,** a small waterfront town that dates from before 1760, when it was called Tobacco Stick after the creek that flows into the Little Choptank River at this location. Local lore traces this unusual name to an unidentified Indian who vaulted over the creek with a tobacco stick (a long pole on which planters hung bundles of leaves to dry) to escape pursuers. (Another legend tells of a stubborn white mule on a nearby farm who resisted every attempt to harness him. Said to have been an incarnation of the devil, he galloped the marshes at night until he sank from the view of a pursuing posse. Sighting the mule's ghost allegedly cured the town drunk, who became a parson.) One fact about Madison remains undisputed: Emerson C. Harrington (1864–1945), governor of Maryland from 1916 to 1920, was born here.

Beyond Madison, the road travels across flat marshes punctuated by clusters of groundsel trees (*Baccharis halimifolia*), shrubs that bloom yellow-white during September and October. The marsh grasses here seem to float on air, creating a dreamlike landscape of plant, water, and sky. The **site of the Hodson House** is on the northern side of the road about a mile from Madison. Named for an early justice, John Hodson, the house served as the first Dorchester County Courthouse, in the 17th century. As late as 1814 the building was used as a jail. That year, men from Madison and Taylor's Island captured the 18-man crew of a British tender from the ship *Dauntless* and detained them in this jail until they were marched to Easton the next day. As Md. 16 crosses Slaughter Creek to Taylor's Island, the **Becky-Phipps Cannon**—named for Lt. Phipps, commander of the British crew, and Becky, a slave whom they had taken prisoner—serves as a reminder of that incident.

The road ends at **Taylor's Island,** a little community named for the isle on which it stands. Western Shore pioneers cultivated crops here as early as 1659; the residents built ships from 1700 until the virgin timber stands were depleted around 1850. Since the mid-19th century, the principal island livelihoods have been commercial fishing, sport fishing, hunting, and farming.

Just west of Taylor's Island, Hooper Neck Rd. goes north to the **Chapel of Ease, Grace Episcopal Church.** This simple, one-room frame building with a freestanding chimney is probably the original chapel built after 1709 for Dorchester Parish. The only older frame church in Maryland is the Third Haven Meeting House in Easton. The Dorchester chapel was moved here in 1959 from its original site about a mile away and then restored by the Grace Church Foundation.

Blackwater National Wildlife Refuge

From Church Creek, follow Md. 335 past the **Church Creek Fire Tower** and through the **Kentuck Swamp.** About four miles below Church Creek, look for a Y intersection and bear to the left on Key Wallace Dr., which heads east to the entrance of the **Blackwater National Wildlife Refuge.** This 17,121-acre federal retreat, established in 1933, abounds with "watchable wildlife." The refuge provides haven to more than 232 species of birds. Canada geese using the Atlantic Flyway winter here by the thousands, as do migratory ducks. With the exception of Florida, Blackwater Refuge has the largest density of nesting bald eagles in the eastern United States. The rare Delmarva fox squirrel can also be found here.

A **Visitor Center** located off Key Wallace Dr. sells admission to a paved, 5-mile "wildlife drive," open daily from dawn to dusk, which passes through unfenced marsh, ponds, and fields filled with waterfowl. Great blue herons often stalk along the embankments, and eagles can be seen perching on man-made nest sites. The U.S. Fish and Wildlife Service administers the refuge, which also serves as a research station for the study of muskrats and nutria.

Four rivers—the Blackwater, Little Blackwater, Transquaking, and Chicamacomico—meander through the refuge on their way to Fishing Bay, a wide estuary that empties into Tangier Sound. Their twisting routes outline a maze of waterways where an inexperienced boater without a guide could easily become lost. A few secondary roads crisscross the marshlands, but this part of Maryland belongs to the water creatures and the people who husband them.

Harriet Tubman

Beyond the entrance to Blackwater Refuge, one may continue east on Key Wallace Dr. to Maple Dam Rd., turn left and go a short distance, and then turn right on Greenbrier Rd. to **Bucktown.** This crossroads community between the Little Blackwater and Transquaking Rivers makes a good spot to reflect on the life of one of Maryland's truly illustrious women, Harriet Tubman (ca. 1820–1913).

Harriet ("Minty") Ross was born a slave on a nearby plantation. In 1844 she married John Tubman and five years later managed to escape to Philadelphia. She worked there before volunteering to return to Maryland to help other slaves escape on the Underground Railroad. During the 1850s—

traveling with small groups from Dorchester County northward, occasionally going as far north as Canada—she guided more than 300 slaves, including her own parents, to freedom. Known as "Moses," Harriet Tubman was short and muscular, skilled in woodcraft, and possessed of uncommon courage. She suffered periodic blackouts from an old head injury inflicted by an overseer, but she also experienced dreams that seemed to help her avoid capture. She used hidden routes through woods, marsh, and swamp and had the assistance of a network of friendly white farmers. Tubman's exploits drew the angry attention of slaveholders, but she was never caught, in nearly twenty trips—one as late as 1860, two years after she began speaking at antislavery rallies in the North.

During the Civil War, Tubman nursed the wounded and acted as a spy for the Southern Department of the Union Army near Charleston, South Carolina. After the war, she lived simply in Auburn, New York, and cooperated in the writing of a book about her eventful life. Frederick Douglass said to his friend and fellow Marylander, "I have wrought in the day—you in the night. I have had the applause of the crowd and the satisfaction that comes of being approved by the multitude, while the most that you have done has been witnessed by the few trembling, scarred, foot-sore bondsmen and -women, whom you have led out of the house of bondage."

Because she never actually had enlisted as a soldier, Congress refused to recognize her services or grant her a pension. Tubman farmed and eventually peddled vegetables from door to door in Auburn, where she died on March 10, 1913, in her nineties. The following year, her fellow citizens erected a bronze tablet in front of the courthouse. It reads in part: "She braved every danger and overcame every obstacle. Withal she possessed extraordinary foresight and judgment so that she truthfully said 'On my underground railroad I nebber run my train off de track an' I nebber los' a passenger.'"

The Hooper Islands

Md. 335 continues beyond Key Wallace Dr. across the Blackwater River and through a portion of the wildlife refuge on its way to the **Hooper Islands.** The road veers sharply to the right at the junction with Md. 336 and crosses two creeks before passing **Applegarth House** (private). Richard Tubman, an early Catholic settler from St. Mary's County, received a patent for this land in 1670, as a reward for fighting Indians. Part of the present sprawling frame house may have been built by Tubman, although most of it dates to the 19th century. The road crosses Great Marsh Creek just beyond this house and enters **Meekins Neck,** an area settled by 17th-century Catholics, including the Tubmans, Meekins, and Hoopers. **St. Mary's Star of the Sea Church,** a white frame building erected in 1872, serves their descendants; it stands near the site of the first Catholic church built in Dorchester County, reportedly by Richard Tubman II in 1769.

A county park occupies the ancient **site of Plymouth,** where Md. 335 crosses Fishing Creek to Upper Hooper Island. Plymouth owed its brief existence to colonial efforts to support tobacco exports by means of legislative-fiat towns. In 1707, a year after the second such act, the town of Plymouth was laid out on "Philips his pointe." During the first three years, only 8 out of 100 legislated lots were sold to the tradesmen and skilled workers who received tax inducements to settle there. In 1748 the assembly ordered a public tobacco warehouse built at Plymouth Town, which later became known simply as Plymouth Warehouse. The tobacco inspector operated only three days a week, and in 1773 the warehouse was sold. A militia company that formed in 1776 called itself the Plymouth Greens, but after the Revolution the name disappeared from the records.

Road along the Hooper Islands, Dorchester County, during the Depression, when residents still farmed

The three **Hooper Islands,** named for one of the pioneering families, form a narrow, 8-mile-long archipelago separated from the mainland by the Honga (formerly Hunger) River. Concentrations of wild geese and ducks accentuate the wildness of the surrounding marshlands. Originally, the islanders were farmers, but local families now make a living as crabbers, oyster tongers, and seafood packers. The folks of this isolated area once spoke their own back-of-the-throat dialect. Improved transportation after the Civil War linked the islands to seafood markets; 20th-century roads made them accessible by commercial trucks. Now the islanders seem not much different from anyone else—except for their stubborn hold on a water-oriented culture.

The villages of **Honga** and **Fishing Creek** occupy **Upper Hooper Island.** Retaining walls along the shore allow trucks to back up to the water to receive catches from the boats. The backyards of houses in Fishing Creek merge with the bay; the front yards border the river. Crab houses along the water punctuate a landscape of fishermen's cottages and gardens.

Md. 335 ends at Honga. A secondary road passes through Fishing Creek, winds through the flat marshland, and passes over a narrow causeway to a one-way plank bridge that crosses to **Middle Hooper Island.** The road ends at **Hoopersville,** another waterfront town, with its familiar oyster boats, tonging craft, and crab houses. No road goes farther south, to **Lower Hooper Island,** which has been isolated since a connecting bridge washed away during a great storm in 1933. **Applegarth,** a small village on the last island, was abandoned after World War I.

Lakesville and Lower Dorchester via Md. 336

Md. 336 travels southeast from the crossroads with Md. 335 and enters a peninsula formed by the Honga River on the west and Fishing Bay

A stretch of the same Hooper Island roadway today

on the east. Numerous necks formed by small creeks and coves jut outward from the peninsula like fractal clusters. The highway crosses World's End Creek and terminates at **Lakesville,** which takes its name from a local family. Capt. Henry Lake fought in the Revolutionary War, during which his daughter Lavinia ("Lovey") became a legendary heroine. According to tradition, as a young teenager she fought off Tory "picaroons" (a 17th-century English word for brigand and pirate), who were attempting to steal the silver buckles off her shoes while ransacking the house in search of her father. Locked in a room when the marauders set fire to the house, she escaped and put the blaze out herself. Then she ran for help to members of her father's militia company, who chased the picaroons back to their boat. During the Civil War, 21 of Captain Lake's descendants supposedly fought for the Confederacy.

Secondary roads branch from Md. 336 through the marshlands to destinations with names that make local poetry. Andrews Rd. travels east to Maple Dam Rd., which winds northward across the marshes to Cambridge. The Lakesville Crapo Rd. heads south across Hell Hook Marsh to the village of **Crapo,** where it becomes Wingate Bishops Head Rd., which travels to **Wingate,** a center for oyster shucking and seafood packing. This is the land of **Jimson Weed Marsh, Crab Point Cove, Tedious Creek,** and **Crocheron.** Here one finds no roadside stands or fast food restaurants—just blood-sucking flies in the summer, damp chill in the fall, and a year-round, wild beauty that sings to the senses.

East of Cambridge, about two miles beyond Eastern Shore Hospital Center, Whitehall Rd. turns north from U.S. 50 to **Whitehall** (private). According to local legend, one of Patty Cannon's gang of slave catchers owned this long, narrow, three-story brick house and hid kidnapped African Americans in a barred basement room. A tunnel supposedly led from the basement to Whitehall Creek.

U.S. 50 crosses flat, marshy countryside and numerous small creeks, including the trickling beginning of the Chicamacomico River. A modern by-pass and bridge, completed in 1988, skirt Vienna, an old village on the

Bean pickers near Cambridge gather their baskets for the trip to market. The FSA captured the scene in 1936 or 1937.

Nanticoke River. The twin smokestacks of the **Eastern Shore Public Service Company,** a plant built in 1927–28, tower above the flat marshlands.

Vienna and the Nanticoke via Md. 331

To reach **Vienna** (264 pop.), the traveler must exit U.S. 50 before the bridge and take Md. 331 into town. A settlement may have existed here before the 18th century, but no mention of the place occurs in official records until 1706, when the General Assembly ordered the site laid out "for the advancement of trade." Earlier, the spot had been known as Emperor's Landing, presumably named for the Nanticoke chiefs whose tribe lent their name to the river. (The name "Vienna" probably refers to Vinnacokasimmon, a 17th-century tayac, or emperor, of the Nanticokes.) By 1709 some houses and a chapel existed here, and by 1768 it had become a port of entry with its own customs official. During the Revolution the British considered Vienna's shipyards worth attacking; they burned a brig here in 1781. Levin Dorsey, killed during the skirmish, became the only man to die in battle on Dorchester soil in the war.

Vienna developed as a stopping point on the inland route linking the upper and lower Eastern Shore. A ferry operated across the river until 1828, when a wooden bridge was built. By this time, however, steamboats had become ubiquitous on the bay; and the bridge was eventually destroyed, considered a menace to navigation. Ferry service resumed in 1860 and lasted for 70 years. After considerable agitation from residents of the area, a new bridge and low causeway over the marshes were constructed in 1931. A flood of telegrams supporting the project supposedly drove Gov. Albert C. Ritchie to wire in return, "For God's sake stop the telegrams; we'll give you the damned bridge." Now the old bridge stands isolated and unused, supplanted by the new by-pass, part of an effort, when William Donald Schaefer served as governor, to improve traffic flow from the Western Shore to ocean resorts. Vienna sits quietly on the Nanticoke River, slowly losing population. A row of frame houses fronting the river along Water St. appears to antedate the Civil War. Some of the buildings must be older. The small **Customshouse,** built in 1791 and used until 1866, is at the end of Water St.

The **site of the Nanticoke Reservation** is along Indiantown Rd., which branches from Md. 331 just north of Vienna. The former reservation was established in 1698 along the river between Chicone and Marshyhope Creeks. Throughout the 17th century, colonists and tribe members regarded each other with mutual suspicion. Maryland had declared war on the Nanticokes in 1642, but a treaty the next year prevented widespread bloodshed. The Nanticokes often petitioned the General Assembly for redress against various trespasses by farmers and their livestock. Establishment of the 4,000–5,000-acre reservation didn't stop complaints of illegal liquor sales or occasional armed clashes between individuals. In 1742 a widespread fear of a general uprising exacerbated matters, and in 1744 the Nanticokes began to leave their Eastern Shore river for new homes in Pennsylvania, New York, and Canada. True to custom, the tribe gathered the bones of its ancestors and departed in small groups; by 1800 virtually all Nanticokes had left the state. A small group remained in Sussex County, Delaware, intermarrying with African Americans of the area. In 1852, a group of Canadian Nanticokes petitioned the Maryland General Assembly for return of their reservation land. After deliberation, the Select Committee on the Claims of the Nanticoke Indians concluded that the tribe had forfeited all rights to its former homelands. Nothing visible now remains of the former Indian presence.

Mardela Springs

After crossing the Nanticoke River, U.S. 50 continues east to **Mardela Springs** (360 pop.), formerly the village of Barren Creek. The octagonal spring house covers a natural spring that made this location a stopping place for American Indians long before European settlers arrived. During the 19th century, the village became a small health resort, due to the alleged benefits of the water. The General Assembly in 1906 incorporated the town as Mardela Springs, coined from *Maryland* and *Delaware.*

Nanticoke-Wicomico Neck Country

U.S. 50 continues to a junction with Quantico Rd. (Md. 347). **Spring Hill Church** is located northeast of this intersection on Spring Hill Ln. near the Delaware line. This simple white-frame structure was built in 1771–72 as an Anglican chapel. The unpainted pine interior retains some of the original woodwork, and the old hand-pegged box pews have been restored. A narrow band of paneling rises about 12 feet to a small canopy over the altar, similar to the canopies found over the pulpits of many prerevolutionary churches.

Hebron (665 pop.), a railroad village dating to the 1890s, is on Md. 347 at the entrance to a low, pine-wooded neck between the Nanticoke

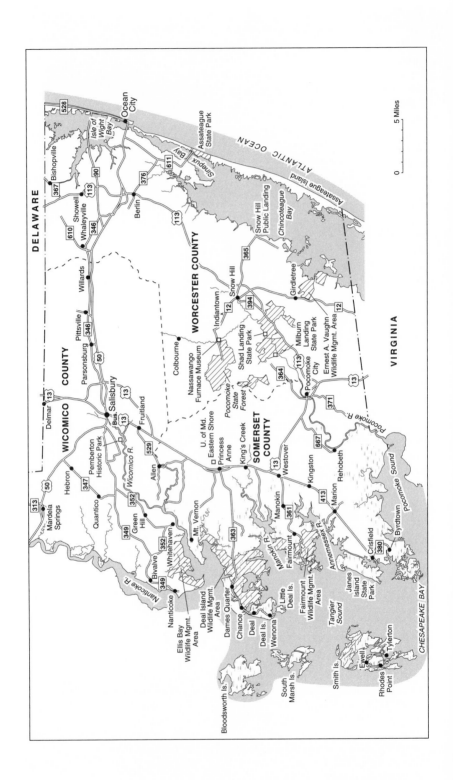

and Wicomico Rivers. Deeply indented by creeks flowing to both rivers, this land has been farmed for more than two centuries. A few old houses still dot the landscape; watermen's villages cluster around marshy creeks with names like Rewastico, Rockawalkin, Wetipquin, and Manumsco. To explore the neck, continue on Md. 347 through the village of **Quantico** to Md. 349, the Salisbury-Nanticoke Rd. A southwest turn on Md. 349 leads past the **University of Maryland Experiment Station** on Quantico Creek and continues to the waterfront villages of Bivalve and Nanticoke, where oystering, fishing, and muskrat trapping remain viable occupations. The **Ellis Bay Wildlife Management Area** is southwest of these villages on the Wicomico River estuary.

The northwest route on Md. 349 roughly parallels the Wicomico River toward Salisbury. Less than a mile in this direction, the road intersects Md. 352, Whitehaven Rd., which leads to Green Hill Church Rd. and the **Green Hill Episcopal Church,** built on the banks of the Wicomico in 1733. Virtually unchanged, the church's walls and unpainted interiors are all original. **Whitehaven,** at the end of White-haven Rd., was once an active fishing and fish packing center. A three-car ferry crosses the Wicomico River at Whitehaven into Somerset County. Several yachting groups have their clubhouses along the river; residential developments have also expanded into this area, from nearby Salisbury.

After Md. 349 crosses Rockawalkin Creek, Crooked Oak Ln. turns south to Pemberton Dr. and **Pemberton Historic Park.** The small brick house here was built in 1741 by the Handy family, founders of Handy's Landing, the forerunner of Salisbury. The brick is laid in Flemish bond under a cove cornice, one of the few remaining on a Maryland building. According to local tradition, Capt. Allison Parsons, a Confederate sympathizer, occupied the house during the Civil War. His practice of firing a cannon whenever he heard about a Rebel victory brought him repeated warnings from Union commanders in Salisbury, who finally raided the house. Although the captain claimed to have stashed a hidden supply of arms for Confederate sympathizers, the armaments were never found.

New Nithsdale (private), a fine colonial brick house with a colorful legend, lies farther down Pemberton Dr., overlooking the Wicomico River. Capt. Levin Gale, a planter, trader, and merchant, built the $1\frac{1}{2}$-story structure, with three-bay interior, end fireplaces, and dormer windows, in about 1735. According to the story, Captain Gale was homeward bound from Glasgow, Scotland, in 1730, when he stopped in Bermuda for water and supplies and found the island embroiled in a slave revolt. A desperate planter persuaded him to transport his family to Maryland, and that night, a four-year-old boy and a six-year-old girl arrived with some baggage. He waited for the parents but finally hoisted sail and departed without them. The children knew their names only as John and Frances; the name "North" appeared on some of their possessions; other articles bore a family crest. Gale brought the children here and returned the next year in search of their parents, who had disappeared. John was lost at sea as a young man. Frances married Capt. William Murray, a Scottish sea captain, who is believed to have named this place after his native Nithsdale. Gale served as one of the commissioners who laid out the town of Princess Anne in 1733. His son of the same name supported the Revolution; collateral descendants served in Congress.

*New Nithsdale,
Wicomico County,
offering a fine example
of 18th-century
Flemish-bond
brickwork*

U.S. 50 enters Salisbury as a limited-access highway that crosses the narrow Wicomico River and then by-passes the central business district.

SALISBURY

Salisbury (23' alt., 20,592 pop.), the most industrious town on the Eastern Shore and a retail center for the Delmarva Peninsula, owes its success to a convergence of highway routes and individual entrepreneurs who saw opportunities to attract customers and make money. Fires in 1860 and 1886 destroyed most material reminders of earlier history. Nondescript in architecture, its buildings reflect an automobile culture that has driven the town during the 20th century. When in the 1990 census Salisbury registered more than 20,000 residents, it was the first time any Eastern Shore town had reached that population level. Salisbury stood 11th among Maryland cities.

Salisbury Town was laid out in 1732 on 20 lots around Handy's Landing at the forks of the Wicomico River. Ten years later, when Worcester County was created from Somerset, officials drew the county line through Salisbury, roughly following what is Division St. today. Local farmers and merchants had to travel to the courthouses in Snow Hill or Princess Anne to conduct their legal affairs. The census of 1800 counted 240 people, including 61 slaves, distributed in 32 families living in 34 houses. The town served as a river trading port, where farmers and timber men gathered to do business.

During the Revolution, Tory picaroons, smugglers, and other pirates occupied the marshes and creeks around Salisbury. According to legend,

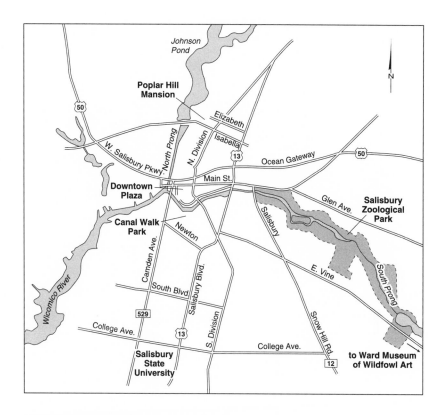

the most fearsome of these was Ben Allen, an illiterate giant of great strength. He supposedly lived in a cave in what is now Municipal Park. The story goes that he was eventually caught, and executed by a patriot firing squad. When excavations were made for St. Peter's Episcopal Church, a century later, the bones of a huge man, believed to be Allen's, were discovered. By January 1777, Salisbury citizens had petitioned the Continental Congress for military assistance against such predators, and Gen. William Smallwood took a company of militia to Salisbury and nearby Princess Anne. Alexander Roxburgh, a Scot who served with General Smallwood, became Salisbury's Revolutionary hero. He was promoted to captain for conspicuous gallantry in the Battle of Long Island and ended the war as a major. After the war, Roxburgh eloped with Frances Handy, granddaughter of Col. Isaac Handy of Pemberton Hall. Local intrigues and escapades subsided after the Revolution, and Salisbury settled down to business.

Several travel routes along the peninsula converged on Salisbury; a survey from 1817 shows three taverns in the town. Even in the early 19th century, local merchants demonstrated merchandising flair with a street fair held at Whitsuntide which attracted the whole countryside. In 1852, the steamboat *Wilson Small* began running twice a week between Baltimore and the "Cotton Patch," a landing two miles below Salisbury. At each high tide after the steamer's arrival, flat-bottomed scows removed cargo before the low tide returned. After the Civil War—which had no great impact on the town—Salisbury's 2,000 citizens petitioned for creation of a separate county. Despite bitter opposition, this movement suc-

Main St., Salisbury, in the 1930s

ceeded in 1867, when Wicomico County was created, with Salisbury as its county seat. The Philadelphia, Wilmington and Baltimore Railroad reached Salisbury from Delaware about the same time, and the Wicomico and Pocomoke Railroad linked Salisbury and Berlin in 1868. In the 1890s, the federal government helped dredge a channel in the river to the town landing, and by 1906 a small harbor had been created. When the refrigerated railroad car came into service in 1901, the stage had been set for Salisbury's rise as the leading shipping and commercial center on the peninsula. Fresh produce, including poultry and vegetables, could be moved great distances, and Salisbury became chief mart for the trade.

The automobile accelerated Salisbury's economic development past its Eastern Shore competitors. The first motor car arrived in Salisbury in 1900, and by 1910 perhaps a dozen cars sputtered down its streets. By 1920, Salisbury had a slightly larger population than Cambridge (6,660 vs. 6,407) but within the next 10 years had widened the margin significantly (10,977 vs. 8,544). Trucks gradually replaced the railroad as primary carriers, and farmers started driving to Salisbury to buy supplies they had formerly ordered from mail-order houses. The retail trade in consumer goods became big business, and Salisbury became the town of the promoter, salesman, and merchandiser with customers not just in Maryland but on the whole Delmarva Peninsula.

The poultry business, along with fertilizer and feed production, dominates industry in Salisbury. Poultry business leader Franklin Perdue dropped out of Salisbury State College at the age of 19 to join his father's two-man egg business in the 1930s. With a combination of single-mindedness, astuteness, hard work, and promotional flair, he built Perdue Farms, a company that in 1990 employed 12,000 people and sold $1.2 billion worth of chickens. Vegetable and fruit packing plants, clothing fac-

THE EASTERN SHORE

A view from the same spot in the 1990s, when Main St. had become a pedestrian mall

tories, lumber mills, and other light industries add to the manufacturing base, which remains dependent on local agriculture. Numerous truck lines use the two interstate highways (U.S. 50 and U.S. 13) and four state roads that converge on Salisbury. Conrail (old Penn-Central) still operates here, and the city serves as a distribution point for oil, gasoline, and coal, which small freighters and barges bring up the Wicomico River. The county and city also operate and maintain an airport southeast of town. All this activity has led to the frequent comment that Salisbury is "the busiest city in America for the area it covers."

Despite the racial segregation that was in place during most of the city's history, Salisbury's African American community has also demonstrated exceptional enterprise. A meeting house and school were established in 1838 at Ellen and Broad Sts. The first African American high school on the Eastern Shore was created in Salisbury in 1919, and black and white ministers exchanged pulpits as early as 1930 on "race relations day." As in most Eastern Shore towns, blacks waited tables, canned fruit, plucked chickens, and operated shoeshine parlors—but in Salisbury they also established businesses and in the 1960s joined multiracial business associations. In Salisbury, organizations that combined blacks and whites, Jews and Christians largely succeeded in creating a progressive social climate.

The presence of the Peninsula Regional Medical Center (more than 370 beds and 16,000 admissions a year), two state nursing and convalescent homes (Deer's Head Center and Holly Center), and a large concentration of practicing physicians have made Salisbury the major medical center of the lower Eastern Shore. The town has many churches, a civic arena, county library, two newspapers, four radio stations, two television stations and a well-regarded municipal zoo. Although officially a county seat with fewer than 21,000 people, Salisbury is unofficially the capital of a growing metropolitan area that includes part of three states and more than 100,000 people.

The Salisbury Parkway (U.S. 50) crosses the North Prong of the Wicomico River and continues through the heart of the city, where it intersects Salisbury Blvd. (Bus. U.S. 13). To explore Salisbury, follow signs to Main St. and stop at the **Downtown Plaza,** a pedestrian shopping area created in 1969 on two blocks of Main St. between Market and Division Sts. (the original site of the town). Local government and business groups cooperated to create the plaza in response to construction of the Salisbury Mall outside the city. The 30-foot, polished metal obelisk in the plaza was created by Alfredo Haleugua, a sculptor from Silver Spring, Maryland. Across the South Prong of the Wicomico, **Canal Walk Park** supplies downtown green space and a hint of how the town appeared in its earliest years. Just as the North Prong of the river leads upstream to Johnson Pond, the upper reaches of the South Fork produce an amenity in Park Lake.

From the plaza, take Division St. north to **Poplar Hill Mansion,** 117 Elizabeth St., an attractive frame house built in 1795 for Maj. Levin Handy. This structure remains the only pre-Victorian house in the city. Poplar Hill is within the Newtown Historic District, established in 1975 to preserve the Victorian architecture saved from disastrous fires in 1860 and 1886.

Follow Elizabeth St. to Salisbury Blvd. (Bus. U.S. 13) and follow the boulevard south to the campus of **Salisbury State University.** In 1922, the General Assembly established a teacher's college for the Eastern Shore and selected this Salisbury site; the two-year institution opened in 1925 as the State Normal School at Salisbury. The school was renamed the State Teachers College at Salisbury in 1935, became Salisbury State College in 1963, and Salisbury State University in 1988. It is now a nationally accredited four-year liberal arts institution with an enrollment of about 6,000 students, more than 4,000 of them full time. The graduate school includes programs in business administration and nursing. The university's theater and music programs have won an avid regional audience.

From the university campus, follow East College Ave. across Md. 12 (Salisbury–Snow Hill Rd.) and past Parkside High School to **Schumaker Park** and Schumaker Pond, which bear the name of an early 19th-century gristmill operator who lived and worked nearby (the park dates to 1966). The **Ward Museum of Wildfowl Life** preserves the work of Lem and Steve Ward, the late Eastern Shore decoy carvers who turned a utilitarian craft into a decorative art. The museum opened in 1992 with about 4,000 objects and 30,000 square feet of exhibition space. Salisbury architect Michael Wigley designed the complex, which includes a three-story glass atrium that overlooks the pond. One gallery re-creates the Ward brothers' workshop and displays examples of their world-famous craftsmanship. The Championship Gallery contains winners in the Ward carving competitions, held every spring in Ocean City. Paintings and video presentations supplement the displays, which range from ancient lures and decoys to decorative carvings. The Ward Foundation, established in 1974, operates the facility, which cost more than $5 million to build.

From the Ward Museum, follow Schumaker Dr. west to Churchill Ave., a right on which leads to **Salisbury Zoological Park,** along the South Prong of the Wicomico River. Since opening in 1954, it has developed into one of the finest small zoological parks in the country. Almost 500 species of birds, mammals, and reptiles native to the Americas inhabit a quiet, imaginatively designed landscape of winding trails, ponds, and natural enclosures. City taxes support the park; improvements are funded by civic groups and the Friends of the Salisbury Zoo.

Side Trip to Princess Anne, Deal Island, and Crisfield via U.S. 13, Md. 363, and Md. 413

Beginning in Wilmington, Delaware, U.S. 13 travels the length of the Delmarva Peninsula to Cape Charles and across the Chesapeake Bay Bridge-Tunnel to Newport News, Norfolk, and Virginia Beach, Virginia. With the completion of the Virginia bridge-tunnel in 1964, U.S. 13 became a through highway, and the Lower Eastern Shore was no longer a cul-de-sac to travelers.

U.S. 13 crosses the three Maryland counties—Wicomico, Somerset, and Worcester—that fall between the Chesapeake Bay and the Atlantic Ocean. Somerset—named for Cecil Calvert's sister-in-law—was created in 1666 to serve the Quakers, Presbyterians, and other "non-conformists" from Virginia, who settled around the Annemessex and Manokin Rivers. These pioneers cleared small patches of pine forest on the necks; but their settlements progressed more slowly than those to the north, where the land was generally richer and better drained. With soil ill-suited for high-quality tobacco, local farmers developed a trade in grain and livestock with New England and Barbados. Proximity to the bay also stimulated shipbuilding and fishing. In response to this gradual growth before the Revolution, Worcester County, named after the Earl of Worcester, was created from Somerset in 1742.

When the railroad from Delaware penetrated the area after the Civil War, the undeveloped spaces east of U.S. 13 filled with farmers, who exploited the woodlands and created truck farms that produced beans, tomatoes, melons, peppers, and potatoes. Wicomico County, named after the river, was created from Somerset in 1867. Migrant workers joined the local farm workers at harvest time, but their primitive living conditions prompted media outrage and government insistence on decent housing. Many farmers have subsequently shifted to crops such as corn and soybeans which do not depend on seasonal labor.

U.S. 13 enters Maryland just east of **Delmar** (57' alt., 1,430 Md. pop.), a town on the state line with two governments and school systems but one Delaware post office. State St., the main thoroughfare, forms the boundary line. The Delaware Railroad opened repair shops here in 1858, and the town grew out of the adjacent pine forest. Delmar became a more important stop after 1884, when the New York, Philadelphia and Norfolk Railroad extended its line southward to Cape Charles and established a ferry line to Norfolk, Virginia. The town's economy declined with the growth of truck transportation in the 1920s; it now functions as a service area for the surrounding countryside.

U.S. 13 by-passes the city of Salisbury just north of the city limits. Business U.S. 13 runs through the city and passes through **Fruitland** (3,511 pop.) before it rejoins the main by-pass near Passersdyke Creek. This dense commercial area is a canning and freezing center. Holly and other Christmas greens from all over the Lower Eastern Shore are sold here at two great auctions every year.

Princess Anne

U.S. 13 crosses Passersdyke Creek into Somerset County and within five miles intersects Md. 675, the main route to **Princess Anne** (18' alt., 1,666 pop.), named for Anne (1709–59), daughter of George II. Laid out in 1733, the town became the Somerset County seat in 1742, when the assembly created Worcester County (the seat of old Somerset County had been Dividing Creek).

As late as 1900, three-masted schooners could sail up the Manokin River almost to the main street in Princess Anne, but increased development along the river has caused siltation up the waterway. Agriculture, lumbering, poultry, and county government still support the town's economy, but the growth of the nearby **University of Maryland Eastern Shore (UMES)** has wrought the largest change. The university began in 1886 as the Delaware Conference Academy, a preparatory branch of the African American Centenary Bible Institute in Baltimore, which became Morgan College in 1890. The Delaware Conference Academy became a land-grant college in 1890 and changed its name to the Princess Anne Academy. The University of Maryland assumed control of the college in 1919, and in 1935 the state acquired full title. In the 1937–38 academic year, total enrollment at Maryland State was 90. The location of the school may or may not have affected its size and drawing power, but it could not have helped matters that in 1933 a mob of 5,000 in Princess Anne lynched and then tore apart and burned the body of a black man accused of attacking an elderly white woman. H. L. Mencken added to his unpopularity on the Eastern Shore when he attacked the mob in print as brutal assassins and described the Lower Shore as beneath civilization. Ironically, Princess Anne has always had a rather high degree of culture for its size and location. Littleton D. Teackle, a Princess Anne banker, railroad investor, and merchant, was among the first Marylanders to call for a statewide system of public education. In the 1991–92 academic year enrollment at UMES was almost 2,400 and growing both larger and more diverse.

In 1801 Littleton Teackle built the center part of a large brick house at the foot of Prince William St., a broad street of Federal and Victorian houses lined with high sycamores. He added the wings two years later. **Teackle Mansion** has since become the most famous house in Princess Anne. George Alfred Townsend, whose pen name was "Gath" (see Gathland State Park in Tour 19), chose the mansion as one of the central locations for his 19th-century novel of the Eastern Shore, *The Entailed Hat; or, Patty Cannon's Times* (1884). Olde Princess Anne Days and the Somerset County Historical Society now occupy the mansion. The former organization, founded in 1958, sponsors an annual October event that features tours of the area's historic houses and buildings.

Princess Anne house tours always include the **Washington Hotel** on North Somerset Ave., which has been used as an inn since the late 18th century, and **Beckford** (private), a Georgian brick mansion built on a sumptuous scale around 1776 by merchant Henry Jackson. Other significant visual attractions in the town include the **Handy Garden,** a formal box garden planted in 1842 on Somerset Ave., and the **County Courthouse,** built in 1905, which features a portrait of Queen Anne attributed to Sir Godfrey Kneller. **Tunstall Cottage** (private), at Corner and Broad Sts., is a picturesque 18th-century frame house. **Nutter's Purchase,** a restored 18th-century house, stands just beyond the bridge over the Manokin River.

The Manokin Presbyterian Church, near the bridge, serves a congregation founded in 1683. The first church on this site was described

The stately Teackle Mansion in Princess Anne as photographed by the WPA

to Gov. Francis Nicholson in 1697 as a "plain country building" belonging to the "dissenters." Only the walls of the current structure date to the 1760s; the tower was added in 1888, and many other alterations have been made. The other colonial church in town was for the established "conformists," **St. Andrew's Episcopal,** on Church St. one block south of Prince William St. The Somerset Parish vestry contracted for a chapel of ease on this site in 1767. The brick walls, laid in Flemish bond, still stand, but the apse has been enlarged and the interior remodeled in the Victorian style. While rector here, the Rev. Clayton Torrence wrote *Old Somerset on the Eastern Shore of Maryland* (1935), a standard source for local history and genealogy.

Deal Island via Md. 363

An excursion from Princess Anne to Deal Island transports the traveler to primitive marshlands punctuated by watermen's villages and sailing vessels. Md. 363 travels west across a peninsula—the Wicomico River to the north and the Manokin to the south—on which farmlands and forested lowlands gradually recede into marshes.

South of the junction of Md. 363 and Md. 627 is the **site of Almodington,** which was one of Somerset County's best-known houses until it burned in 1993. Woodwork from its colonial dining room and a mantel from the early Federal period were salvaged and are on display in the American wing of the Metropolitan Museum of Art in New York City. Arnold Elzey, who died in 1733, built the long, narrow brick house. John Elzey, Arnold's father, who patented the tract in 1661, served as one of the Maryland commissioners appointed to govern the Manokin and nearby Quaker Annemessex settlements, established by English migrants from Virginia's Eastern Shore. Col. Edmund Scarborough, surveyor general and treasurer of Virginia, demanded that Elzey acknowledge the Virginia government and pay fees for his land grant. Elzey sent a vaguely worded reply and begged Lord Baltimore "to consider our condition, how we lye between Sylla and Charibdis, not knowing how to gett out of this labarith." The Maryland government, only 27 years old, protested to Virginia's Governor Berkeley but sent no assistance. Scarborough invaded the two settlements with 40 horsemen in 1663 and placed "ye broad arrow" of confiscation on the doors of all who opposed him. The Quakers resisted, and Elzey stalled for time. The Virginia government refused to support their renegade cavalier, notorious for his bigotry, and within a few years the Virginia-Maryland boundary was set well to the south. Scarborough retained his position in Virginia, and Elzey kept his place on the Maryland commission until his death in 1664.

Elmwood (private), a brick house built about 1800 by another member of the Elzey family, is south of the Almodington site on the Manokin River. **Clifton** is visible on the other side of the river.

Md. 363 continues west through portions of the **Deal Island Wildlife Management Area,** miles of flat marshland that almost reach the road. One of 32 such areas in Maryland, this 10,000-acre preserve is managed by the Wildlife Program of the Department of Natural Resources. The route continues through **Dames Quarter,** a small fishing village once named Damned Quarter, perhaps because of its proximity to Deal Island, originally known as Devil Island and probably altered by postal clerks. Nearby **Chance** may be named for an early land patent.

A wooden bridge crosses a narrows named Upper Thorofare (pronounced "furfrer") to this island, one of about 50 islands scattered around the bay. Constantly changing shape and size as their shorelines erode, many of these islands have no human residents. Inhabited islands like Deal, populated since the 17th century, have spawned a distinctive, insular life that is fast disappearing. **Bloodsworth Island** and **South Marsh Island,** a wildlife management area, are visible to the west. Between them lies Holland Straits, the primary location of a major state experiment to revive the oyster beds. Researchers planted millions of bushels of oyster shells here in 1961 to create seed beds for oyster larvae. After they had "set" and grown for about a year, the seed oysters were moved to natural bars for further growth. The experiment was successful and led to a propagation program now supervised by the Department of Natural Resources.

The skipjacks moored in the Upper Thorofare belong to the few tough, hard-working men who still dredge for oysters. The skipjack, perhaps named for bluefish, which seem to skip over the water, is a relatively recent baycraft, varying in length from 30 to 60 feet. The sight of its raked mast, white hull, and colorful bow sailing in the wind evokes the romance of the Chesapeake. After the Civil War, responding to the threat of dwindling oyster beds, the state restricted dredging to sailing vessels. Versions of the simple, sloop-rigged skipjack appeared on the bay in the 1890s. One man could handle the tiller, and only a small crew was needed to operate a dredge lowered overside to scrape the bay bottom. The annual oyster catch by log canoes, sloops, pungies, schooners, and bugeyes soared to a high of 15 million bushels in 1884; then started a general decline that has never stopped. (The official 1989 oyster harvest was 395,000 bushels.) In 1940, about 150 skipjacks docked at Deal Island; now they cluster in small groups of twos and threes. America's last com-

Oyster tonging,
Somerset County, ca.
1935

mercial sailing fleet has declined to fewer than 10 vessels. No new skip-jacks have been built for many years, and the men who sail them are getting old. Deal Island skippers nonetheless still race on Labor Day and on Chesapeake Appreciation Day every fall before the oyster season begins November 1.

Tonging boats also anchor at Deal Island. Watermen use giant hand tongs to harvest oysters in shallow waters from these low, power-driven craft. The tongs lift as much as 50 pounds at a time, requiring considerable physical strength and endurance in the winter months of the season. An occasional, unmasted sailing canoe called a "cunner" may sometimes be seen among the tongers; but most of the old-time baycraft are now visible only in photos at the state archives or in museums like the ones at St. Michaels and Solomons.

In recent years, crabbing has become more important to watermen as a livelihood than oystering. The soft-crab season runs from May to October. The crabs are caught in latticed shedder-floats, then stored until they shed their old shells. While soft, they're packed in seaweed and crushed ice, then shipped live to market.

Most of the island's watermen and their families live in **Deal,** at the northern end, and in **Wenona** on the southern end. Their white-painted frame houses sit on a "high" strip of land about a mile wide on the western side, surrounded by water and marshland. Nearly all make their living by catching, packing, or shipping oysters and crabs, trapping muskrats, and catering to fishermen and hunters in season. Retirees and vacationers have discovered this part of Maryland, which retains the simplicity and serenity of a bygone era.

On its brief traverse of the island, Md. 363 passes three Methodist churches and adjoining graveyards, where the dead lie in sarcophagi that rise above the surface of the marshy ground. The white frame chapel behind one of the churches was built in 1850 for Joshua Thomas (1776–1853), famed "Parson of the Islands," who lived here for more than 30 years. A fisherman, this Somerset County native began his ministry after a conversion experience in 1807 at a Methodist camp meeting. From his base on Tangier Island in the Virginia portion of the bay south of Smith Island, Thomas spread evangelistic fervor throughout the lower Chesapeake, particularly among the watermen. Like the fishermen of the Gospels, Joshua Thomas was illiterate but full of the spirit. His reputation as a "shouting preacher" spread further after he preached to the British soldiers who occupied Tangier Island in 1814 during the War of 1812: he told the encamped army of his experiences, thanked them for sparing the meeting ground, and warned them that the Almighty wouldn't let them take Baltimore.

Thomas moved to Deal Island in the 1820s and made the camp meetings here famous throughout the Eastern Shore. He traveled on a log canoe, *The Methodist,* to communities along the coves and creeks preaching, praying, officiating at weddings and funerals, trading, and spreading the evangelical gospel. The stone above his grave, placed near the church so he could hear the Sunday sermons, reads:

Come all my friends as you pass by
Behold the place where I do lie
Once as you are, so was I
Remember, you are born to die.

Md. 363 ends in Wenona. An anchorage for skipjacks and other small craft marks the Lower Thorofare, which separates Deal Island from Little Deal Island, where Joshua Thomas lived until his death.

Return to Princess Anne and continue south on U.S. 13. The highway crosses Jones Creek at a point near the **site of Washington Academy,** chartered in 1779 and housed in a new brick building in 1803. The academy apparently served the entire lower peninsula. Representatives from Virginia's Accomack and Northampton Counties, Delaware's Sussex County and Maryland's Somerset, Worcester, and Dorchester Counties were appointed to the governing board in 1785. The 1819 curriculum for the 45 male students reflected the period's notion of a gentleman's education: mathematics, Latin grammar, Greek testament, rhetoric, Homer, Horace, Cicero, and Virgil. Student visits to billiard or gaming rooms in Princess Anne were regarded as major offenses, but despite the town's temptations, the school moved to Princess Anne in 1843. The venerable academy closed in 1872, but county school commissioners reopened it as a public high school. Contractors used bricks and timbers from the "Old Academy" near the creek as well as the buildings in Princess Anne in construction of a new public school building, which in turn was demolished in 1939. The bricks were used again as backing for the wall of the present Washington High School.

U.S. 13 continues across **King's Creek** and its namesake town, a crossroads community. Just beyond lies the mansion known as **Beverly of Somerset** (private), so named to distinguish it from Beverley in Worcester County. Nehemiah King II (1755–1802), scion of an old family and wealthy slaveowner, completed this house in 1796 as a monument to his patrimony. His family subsequently lost both house and property, and the interior was destroyed by fire in 1938. The restored edifice has become a county landmark and subject of an Eastern Shore legend. According to the tale, when Napoleon was confined to St. Helena after his defeat at Waterloo in 1815, a plot was hatched in New Orleans to free him. The plotters would build a fast sloop, overcome the island fortifications, and whisk Napoleon across the Atlantic to Beverly, where he would be hidden in a secret room until he could safely travel to New Orleans. Just before the sloop was to set sail in 1821, word was received of Bonaparte's death. In the 1930s such tales still lingered around the isolated old houses of the Lower Shore, like a summer breeze—welcome, mysterious, leaving no evidence.

Raccoon Point Park via Revell's Neck Rd.

Beyond King's Creek, Revell's Neck Rd. turns west off U.S. 13 to a long-settled area between the Manokin River on the north and west and Back Creek on the south. Randall Revell, one of the earliest Somerset County settlers, patented a large tract here with the name Double Purchase. Somerset Town, established as the county's first town in 1668, was constructed on Double Purchase; it included a courthouse, but the exact site remains unknown. The town may have stood on what is now called **Clifton Point,** where an old brick house, **Clifton** (private), still stands. The house does not appear old enough to date to the first settlement, even if some people claim it has stood here since 1700.

Randall Revell and John Elzey (see Elmwood and site of Almondington, above) were named in the first commissions for granting land and enforcing law in this region (1661–62), before the establishment of a county government. Revell later lost his position when he was suspected of supporting Edmund Scarborough, a Virginia official who invaded Maryland in 1663. However, he continued to reside on Double Purchase; he held the office of sheriff of Somerset County in 1670.

The road ends at Revell's Point, where there is a small park for picnicking.

Down Md. 413

Md. 413 branches south from U.S. 13 just south of the **Eastern Correctional Institution** and leads down a Somerset County neck that juts into Tangier Sound—a deep portion of the Chesapeake Bay lying between the Lower Eastern Shore and Bloodsworth, South Marsh, Smith, and Tangier Islands (a small portion of Smith Island and all of Tangier Island belong to Virginia).

Westover, on Md. 413 slightly more than a mile from the above intersection, is a rail and highway shipping point for regional agricultural products. More than 100 years ago, migrant workers assembled here every spring to work the strawberry fields. A writer for *Harper's Magazine* in 1879 remarked that the pickers were "merry, jolly and happy-go-lucky, taking no thought of the morrow, finding food in the berry fields, where they work." The migrants still come to the Westover area in season, although the numbers aren't as large and the crops are more diverse. Twentieth-century observers have also not been so cavalier about the pickers' lives and working conditions. In 1959, after years of periodic exposés and complaints, the state of Maryland finally mandated improvements for the living quarters and community services available to migrant workers. The Governor's Committee for the Regulation and Study of Migratory Labor in Maryland was created to develop and recommend standards for housing, sanitation, health, and welfare.

Maryland lies in the middle of the East Coast migrant labor stream. Pickers travel as families in their own cars or in crews on trucks; they work the winter crops in Florida and move north through the Carolinas, Virginia, Maryland, and New Jersey during the summer and fall. Depending on the crop, the workers are paid by the hour or by the quantity harvested. In recent years, neither farmer nor picker has made much money in this system, and the use of migrant labor has declined in Maryland as farmers have mechanized or changed to more profitable crops.

Md. 361 leaves Md. 413 just south of Westover and travels west across **Fairmount Neck,** with the Manokin River and Back Creek on the north and the Big Annemessex River on the south. A number of old brick and frame houses line the shores of the Annemessex, reflecting this area's 17th-century settlement by Virginia Quakers and other dissenters. Early maps indicate that the road to Fairmount was a major county route; now a byway, it passes through **Manokin,** a crossroads hamlet, and **Fairmount,** a small village of farmers and watermen. A paved secondary road proceeds farther west, to the **Fairmount Wildlife Management Area,** created from flat marshes that line the surrounding creeks and rivers.

Kingston

This town recalls an old Somerset County family that left its name on the map as well as in the Lower Eastern Shore's genealogical history.

Kings, Carrolls, and Pretenders

Robert King settled in lower Somerset County around 1682 in the area of King's Creek, south of Princess Anne and about four miles north of Kingston. He built an estate he called "Kingsland," where his son Robert II was born and raised. Robert II became wealthy, acquired more land, and established the base for his descendants' lavish, slave-based living. One grandson, Nehemiah King II, inherited Kingsland and built the mansion called Beverly near Princess Anne. Another grandson, Thomas King, inherited land to the south and in the latter half of the 18th century built **Kingston Hall** at the head of the Annemessex River.

Thomas King Carroll (1793–1873), grandson of Thomas King, grew up at Kingston Hall. Trained by his grandfather to become a gentleman politician, he rose to become governor of Maryland (1830–31). His first child, Anna Ella Carroll, was born at Kingston Hall in 1815. Similarly trained in law and politics, she became one of the most famous women in 19th-century America. Financial difficulties, partly the result of Carroll's unwillingness to sell slaves or free them without adequate provision, forced the sale of Kingston Hall after the Panic of 1837.

Anna Ella Carroll, who never married, then embarked on a career that would be described today as "public relations." She moved to Baltimore and Washington, where her eminent social connections gave her unquestioned entrée to influential society. Her ability to write and her knowledge of the law also enabled her to overcome the era's prejudice against women in public life. At first she wrote and lobbied for various railroad interests. After 1850, she became an active participant in Whig and American (Know-Nothing) politics as well as a low-key abolitionist who freed her own slaves. When the Civil War broke out, she turned her talents to helping the Union. Her 1861 pamphlet, "Reply to Breckinridge," accused Southern leaders of preparing for secession as early as 1850. The document was considered so effective in persuading Marylanders to stay in the Union that the federal government bought 10,000 copies for distribution throughout the North. Carroll and her friends later claimed that she became one of President Lincoln's secret advisors at this time, an "unacknowledged member of Lincoln's cabinet."

Commissioned as a writer for the War Department during the war, Carroll never was able to collect more than token payment for her work. Her "War Powers of the General Government" (1862) contained the first published justification for the extraordinary executive powers Lincoln exercised during the war. She traveled to St. Louis in the summer of 1861 to assist in devising a plan for invading the South. Her advice (not hers alone) was to advance through the Tennessee Valley rather than the heavily fortified Mississippi River, a plan that went into effect during the winter of 1862. When the capture of Vicksburg seemed impossible, she suggested plans for attacking it by land—a strategy that eventually succeeded by fits and starts in 1863. Carroll's admirers claimed that her contributions to the war strategy were a well-kept secret that Lincoln would have revealed had he lived. Despite their support and her own agitation, Congress never acknowledged her role in the war. Documentary evidence for her claims was slim. Much of the correspondence with Lincoln that would have supported her story apparently disappeared in a misplaced trunk. Perhaps it never existed.

Anna Carroll was finally granted a small pension and lived in Washington, a poor and paralyzed old woman, supported by her sister, who worked as a government clerk. By the time she died in 1894, the King fortunes on the Eastern Shore had declined and largely disappeared. The land had been sold; Kingston Hall had deteriorated. She and her father are buried alongside each other in the Old Trinity Church yard on the shore of Church Creek.

South of Kingston, Md. 413 intersects Md. 357 at **Marion,** an auction center for strawberries. To the west, Md. 357, as Charles Cannon Rd., takes the visitor to **Coulbourne Creek,** where Stephen Horsey—the first known European settler in Maryland below the Choptank River—patented the tract Coulbourne in 1663. Horsey, a cooper, arrived around 1643 in Northampton County, Virginia, when he was in his early 20s; nine years later he became one of the Committee of Six, who drafted the Northampton Protest. This document, written more than a century before the Declaration of Independence, opposed taxation of Eastern Shore settlers without representation in the Virginia assembly. A year later, Horsey was elected a burgess by "ye common Crowd" but then was "thrown out of ye Assembly for a factious and tumultuous person; a man repugnant to all Government." After several arrests for refusal to pay taxes to support the Church of England, this factious commoner, in about 1661, moved across the line to Maryland. He became a leader of the Maryland settlements along the Annemessex, opposed Col. Edmund Scarborough's efforts to expand Virginia's boundaries to this area, and lived on his own terms until his death in 1671.

Crisfield

Md. 413 ends at a small community near the southernmost tip of Maryland. Originally known as Somers Cove, Crisfield (5' alt., 2,880 pop.) now bills itself as "The Seafood Capital of the Country." The upper part of town resembles many other Eastern Shore villages, with tree-lined streets, small frame houses, businesses, churches, and municipal buildings. The arrival of a railroad spur after the Civil War and the booming oyster industry of the 1880s transformed the waterfront into a boom town, a rough-and-ready place that attracted water prospectors and bold entrepreneurs.

Trailboard of the Seagull, *Crisfield harbor, 1930s*

Crisfield and the Oyster Boom

John Woodland Crisfield, a lawyer and congressman with deep Eastern Shore roots, helped found the Eastern Shore Railway and brought a spur to the wharf at Somers Cove in 1868. The rails went down Main St. and eventually reached the water on a bed of oyster shells. In 1872, grateful for the new business opportunities, the area's leading citizens named the newly incorporated town Crisfield, and it soon established itself as a leading port and processing center. Hundreds of watermen from lower Maryland and Virginia competed for and frequently fought over the oyster harvest. To prevent New England boats from exploiting the oyster beds, Maryland in 1820 banned dredging in state waters. Lawmakers reinstated the practice in 1865 but restricted oyster dredging to Maryland sailcraft.

Thereafter, cheap processing, improved canning methods, and rail access to metropolitan areas converged to create a huge demand for oysters. Crisfield filled with locally crafted workboats of all descriptions—bateaux, skipjacks, bugeyes, log canoes—all individually painted and marked by small variations visible to the trained eye. By the turn of the century, more than 600 sailing vessels were registered in Crisfield. They lined the Little Annemessex River from sunset to sunrise, anchored like graceful resting birds on the water.

When the dredgers, crabbers, and fishermen returned to port, they found businesses ready to receive them. Thousands of shuckers and pickers worked in the waterfront sheds for low wages. Bars, saloons, and bawdy houses beckoned. The boat captains and their crewmen—some of whom had been shanghaied from Baltimore waterfronts—blew off steam in places like Goodsell's Alley, where fights were common. Occasional gunshots echoed in the alleys and over the water. For a decade or two, Crisfield rivaled Western gold rush towns for lawlessness.

Maryland and Virginia finally set a boundary line along the Chesapeake in 1877, and marine police from both states struggled to restore order. Crisfield's many churches worked to reduce the civic violence. Seven disastrous fires also swept through the town's frame buildings and sheds, the first in 1883, the last in 1928.

But the oysters started to give out. The oyster harvest reached its peak at 15 million bushels in 1884–85; in 1900 the level was only about 5 million. With money no longer so quick and easy, calm returned to Crisfield once again. By 1900, the town's population had dwindled from a high of perhaps as many as 10,000 in the 1880s to less than half that number.

Most of the commercial sailing vessels have disappeared from Crisfield, but **Somers Cove Marina,** built with the assistance of the Maryland Port Authority, is a modern marine facility with berths for more than 500 boats. Hundreds of workers still process seafood in the wooden and concrete block buildings along the waterfront. No machines have yet been devised to shuck oysters or pick the meat from hard crabs, so these operations are still done by hand. Dexterous, female "pickers" at long, stainless-steel tables pick the flesh, graded from back to claw, from steamed hard crabs. Shuckers, both men and women, use oyster knives, prying open the oysters in one quick motion. Fertilizer makers pick up the shells and other residue; and the fresh seafood moves out of Crisfield daily by truck. The railroad that first linked the town to the rest of the world no longer runs.

The size of the crab catch and oyster harvest fluctuates from year to year. Small catches bring higher prices for the watermen, but workers in the processing plants lose their jobs when yields are low. For almost a century, Maryland has attempted with mixed results to preserve its seafood resources and keep the annual harvests flowing. In 1906, the Haman Act provided for a state survey of oyster beds and a program that enabled people to lease unproductive oyster beds if they would seed them. The survey, described as one of the most thorough made of any natural resource, took six years to complete. Experts believed that the submerged beds could produce 40 million bushels of oysters a year through private management.

But local oystermen feared—with some reason—that large corporations would reduce them to mere employees. Political pressure from the Eastern Shore kept the oyster beds public and preserved the watermen's independence. Since 1912, the state has engaged in "oyster farming," financed by a tax on yields taken from "planted" areas. However, the program has never proved profitable, and the new acreage did not affect the oyster yield. From 1915 to 1950, the annual oyster harvest averaged slightly under 3 million bushels, but from 1950 to 1961 the quantity dropped to less than half this amount. In 1960, the state decided to embark on a major effort to create new oyster beds and preserve the public fishery. The program has proved successful, and Maryland now has a major shellfish propagation effort under way.

Maryland watermen rely now almost entirely on state "planted" oyster beds, but the harvest continues to decline, lately because of a mysterious disease known as DSX; the harvest reached its lowest ebb in 1987–88, at 363,000 bushels. In 1991–92 it still fell below 400,000 bushels.

As late as the 1890s, the bay's blue crabs were considered more a nuisance than a commodity, because they fouled fishing nets. Yet crabs have

Workers during the Depression load oyster shells for planting on seed beds

become the major seafood commodity on the bay, followed by soft clams. The annual crab catch fluctuates dramatically from year to year, but the supply does not seem to be declining. The dockside value of the 44 million or so bushels caught in 1989 was slightly more than $26 million, almost half the total value of Maryland seafood products that year. The fin-fish catch is also important to Crisfield, although subordinate to shellfish. In the spring and summer, hundreds of barrels and boxes of shad, herring, croakers (hardhead), and other varieties, both fresh and frozen, leave Crisfield for market. Sportsmen may charter boats that run to the fishing grounds of Tangier Sound.

Crisfield has always had its share of strong, interesting individuals. The late J. Millard Tawes (1894–1979), two-term governor of Maryland between 1959 and 1967, was born in Crisfield. The **Tawes Visitors Center and Museum,** opened at Somers Cove Marina in 1983, features memorabilia from his long career as well as artifacts and models from the region's past. The museum also exhibits decoys and tools from the workshop of the Ward brothers, Lem and Steve. The Wards won international acclaim in the 1960s as "wildfowl counterfeiters in wood"; collectors and customers swamped their work shack with orders they were unable to fill before retiring in 1970. (See under Salisbury, above.) Harry Clifton ("Curley") Byrd, who built the University of Maryland into an international institution in the 1940s, was born near here and graduated from Crisfield High School. James Wesley Nelson, who created the Del Monte fruit company in California, was also born in Crisfield. Charles D. (Charlie) Briddell Sr., a talented mechanic, opened a blacksmith shop in the area in the 1890s and started making oyster knives and tongs. The business grew into **Carvel Hall,** which still manufactures knives and other equipment in Crisfield.

As the town's population continues to decline (19 percent between 1980 and 1990), citizens increasingly turn to tourism as a means of livelihood. Building on the informality and originality that characterized its famous citizens, Crisfield now sponsors crab bakes, music festivals, and fishing competitions during the summer. On Labor Day weekend, the tourist season reaches its peak at the Hard Crab Derby, which pits quick crustaceans carrying famous political names in a race for the "Governor's Cup."

Crisfield is surrounded by marshlands and islands near the southern border of the state. The only state road to travel farther south is Md. 380, which branches off Main St. and descends a few miles to the village of **Byrdtown.** Johnson Creek Rd. branches east from Md. 380 to **Makepeace** (private), a 17th-century landmark that overlooks the green marshes of Johnson's Creek, a tributary of Pocomoke Sound. This early Virginia-type house with walls laid in Flemish bond stands on the 150-acre tract that John Roach called "Makepeace" in his 1663 patent. According to tradition, Roach chose the name to commemorate the peace negotiated with the American Indians when Virginians first settled around the Annemessex.

South and slightly west of Byrdtown lies the low, marshy ground (now part of Cedar Island Wildlife Management Area) that Capt. John Smith in 1612 named Watkins' Point—perhaps the most famous point in Maryland that turned out not in fact to be a cartographically true point. It became the center of long-lasting Maryland-Virginia boundary disputes, because the Maryland Charter of 1632 established this "point" as the Chesapeake Bay dividing line between the provinces. Not until 1877 did a joint commission agree on the spot Smith meant when he wrote "Watkins' Point."

Janes Island State Park

Janes Island, 3,200 acres of marsh and flatland, is across the Little Annemessex River from Crisfield. Indian artifacts are sometimes discovered on its beaches, and farmers once lived here, but the island has been uninhabited for decades. Accessible only by boat, Janes Island remains an isolated refuge with miles of sandy beaches and wetland trails for the solitary walker. The diamondback terrapin, once cultivated in Crisfield as a delicacy, crawls wild here, and the osprey fly free. The state purchased the property in 1961–62 and created Janes Island State Park. The park's southern portion marks the entrance of Crisfield's harbor with a 50-foot brick smokestack, a remnant of a large, 19th-century fish fertilizer factory that operated here through the 1920s. The northern section of the island juts into the Big Annemessex River and is connected by the **Daugherty Creek Canal** to the Little Annemessex, creating a water shortcut to Crisfield. The **Hodson Memorial Recreation Area,** named for a native son who became a rich New York broker, occupies the small, mainland portion of the park just north of Crisfield. Pontoon boats provide service to the island during summer months.

Smith Island

Every day, a boat carrying mail, freight, and passengers (and in summer several cruise vessels) leaves Crisfield for **Smith Island,** the most remote and distinctive of all Maryland islands in the Chesapeake. Many of the island's 750 residents, almost entirely of British ancestry, can trace their ancestry to the original 17th-century settlers. Part of the "Russell Isles" charted by Capt. John Smith in 1608, Smith Island is actually a compact group of islets located about 11 miles west of Crisfield across Tangier Sound—almost in the middle of the bay. Most of the land consists of eroding salt marsh or meadow, a few feet above sea level, cut and indented by "thorofares," "guts," creeks, ditches, and coves. The northern group of islets composes the **Martin National Wildlife Refuge.** The southern group contains three villages: **Ewell, Tylerton,** and **Rhodes Point,** each separated from the others by marsh and water.

Approached by water, the villages have a simple, time-worn character. Frame houses cluster around a Methodist church; crab houses—where soft-shell crabs are packed in ice for shipment to Crisfield—extend on pilings into the water. Scores of latticework "shedding floats" lie behind fences between and around the crab houses. Thousands of blue crabs growing in the floats are carefully separated each day according to their progress in shedding their hard shells. A road connects Ewell, the largest town, to Rhodes Point, which was known as Rogue's Point until the people got religion. Because the islanders maintain their own roads, the state does not enforce the law requiring license plates. Abandoned, rusted vehicles occasionally mar the flat, watery vistas. Tylerton is accessible only by water.

Fires, storms, floods, and invasions—by pirates, ships' crews, and the British navy—have taken their toll on generations of Smith Islanders, who have always derived their livelihood from the water. Isolation from the mainland produced an island dialect, punctuated with unusual, often archaic words and grammatical constructions. Until about 1800, the people of Smith Island lived alone, largely neglected by government and church alike. The men battled the bay for a living, a task both difficult and dangerous in the winter months, and the women kept the windswept households together. The clannish islanders supported each other, distrusted strangers, danced, occasionally got drunk, and sometimes fought with their neighbors. Joshua Thomas of Deal Island reached these islands around 1807 and turned the sinners into staunch Methodists. The camp meeting replaced the tavern, and the church became a powerful unifying force. One preacher, who also acts as public arbiter and counselor, serves all three congregations. The minister heads the church council, which governs the island without jail, mayor, or city council. Children attend public school in Crisfield, commuting by boat every day.

Religious fervor captured the islanders' spirits but did not diminish their independence of mind or skepticism about the law. In 1877 the Black and Jenkins Award forced Maryland to cede Virginia 23,000 acres of fine oyster bottoms, to the advantage of watermen on Tangier Island about eight miles to the south. But the Smith Island men kept dredging there for more than 30 years, despite repeated attacks by Virginia patrol boats and interisland battles in which oystermen on both sides were killed. The sporadic warfare ended about 1910, when the oysters in the disputed area died, a calamity that some islanders interpreted as an act of God. Although the killing of wild ducks for market was outlawed by international treaty in 1918, islanders continued the slaughter for years thereafter. Game wardens risked their lives when they entered these marshes, where the islanders used powerful swivel guns to kill ducks by the hundreds. Such self-sufficiency has long been typical of watermen on the Lower Shore but has diminished in recent years. Now linked to the rest of the world by radio and television, Smith Island has become a summer tourist attraction, complete with several restaurants. The watermen have reluctantly conceded the need for conservation measures, and they now talk of their traditional way of life in the past tense.

Alternate Route East from Salisbury via Pocomoke City and Snow Hill on U.S. 13 and 113

Most travelers rush to Ocean City, but if one can leave home a day early, a southern loop from Salisbury to Princess Anne, the Pocomoke State Forest, Pocomoke City, Nassawango Furnace, Snow Hill, Berlin, and back to U.S. 50 richly repays the extra time and mileage.

To take this option, follow the directions to Crisfield (via U.S. 13) as far as Princess Anne. After visiting Princess Anne, remain on U.S. 13 south, rather than taking Md. 413 to Crisfield, and head through farmland and woodland toward the Pocomoke River.

Rehoboth Presbyterian Church

Turn southwest on Md. 667 (Rehobeth Rd.) for about six miles to see the oldest Presbyterian house of worship in the United States which has remained exclusively Presbyterian. Col. William Stevens (1630–87), wealthy landowner and influential politician, named his Pocomoke River plantation, patented in 1665, Rehoboth. The Hebrew word (occasionally spelled Rehobeth) means "enlargement" or "there is room" and appears in Genesis 26:22. Devout Protestants have applied it to more than one place on the Delmarva peninsula.

Just before Md. 667 crosses Rehobeth Branch, a sign marks a road that leads to the river, where one encounters the ruins of **Coventry Church,** not far from a broiler shed. Placed on the National Register of Historic Places in 1984, the ruins date to 1784–92, when the brick church was built next to the site of an earlier, late-17th-century church. Both structures belonged to Coventry Parish of the then-established Anglican Church. The 18th-century building was used until about 1900, when it began to deteriorate. Preservationists capped the walls with cement in 1928 and built a brick altar within the roofless rectangle; foundations of the 17th-century church were excavated in 1933 and marked with four cement posts. Old gravesites cluster around the ruins.

Rehoboth Presbyterian Church, built in 1705–6 and still used as a house of worship, is located within sight of Coventry Church along the river to the north. This Presbyterian landmark traces its origins to Francis Makemie (ca. 1658–1708, pronounced M'Kemmy), born of Scottish parents who emigrated to the Eastern Shore in 1683. Colonel Stevens of Rehoboth, himself an Anglican, had requested a Presbyterian minister to service the growing unchurched population in Somerset County. Makemie acquired land along the Pocomoke River and was followed within a few years by other ministers, including Samuel Davis, William Traile, and Thomas Wilson. Makemie preached extensively in the colonies and built the meeting house at Rehoboth despite the opposition of the Anglican ministry, which protested to the governor and council the erection of a "dissenting church" within half a mile of an established church (Coventry Church lay fewer than 200 yards away). Pending action by the Bishop of London, temporary permission was granted to Makemie "to preach in his house according to the Tolleration [Act of 1689]." The county court later certified the meeting house, in 1708, without waiting for the bishop's reply. In 1706, around the same time that the brick church was completed, Makemie helped organize the presbytery of Philadelphia, which united scattered churches in Maryland, Virginia, Pennsylvania, and New Jersey, setting the pattern for organized Presbyterianism in America. The active preacher later settled in nearby Accomack County, Virginia, and ministered to Presbyterians in both colonies.

Rehoboth Church, bricked in Flemish bond with random glazed headers and surrounded by gravestones, was partially restored in 1954–55. The stained-glass windows were added during a Victorian remodeling, but much of the interior—with its plain walls, paneled pews and reading desk—reflects the simple character of an early-18th-century dissenters' house of prayer.

Pocomoke River State Forest

Just before crossing the Pocomoke River, U.S. 13 intersects Md. 364, which heads north to the largest portion of this forest. Md. 364 parallels the river about a mile from its banks. This region along the Pocomoke has been reclaimed by the forest—not the virgin timber stands that once towered along its banks, but acres of semicultivated loblolly pines that have grown over agricultural fields. Farmers deserted these fields in the 1930s because of depleted soil and the Great Depression; the state has since acquired more than 12,000 acres, scattered throughout Worcester County, for conservation projects and development of a timber industry. Overgrown cemeteries and even a few plowed furrows remain from those who abandoned the land. Oral tradition claims that escaped slaves and their guides followed the river north along the Underground Railroad to Pennsylvania and New Jersey. During the Civil War, the adjacent swamps offered a natural haven for deserters, bootleggers, and assorted outlaws. **Milburn Landing State Park,** reached by following River Rd. and the signs off Md. 364, offers walking, camping, fishing, and picnicking facilities.

Pocomoke City

Md. 675 crosses the Pocomoke River on a picturesque whitewashed bridge that leads to downtown **Pocomoke City** (8' alt., 3,922 pop.). A navigable landing on this deep river has been located here since the 17th century; sailing vessels and oil tankers still moor along the riverbank. The site was called Newtown when first laid out about 1780, but the name was changed in 1878 after the town became an incorporated city. The arrival of the Eastern Shore Railroad, after the Civil War, stimulated growth, and Pocomoke City became a commercial center for the surrounding rural countryside. Fires in 1888, 1892, and 1922 destroyed most of the old structures, but Pocomoke City retains the aura of an old river town. Population has risen about 10 percent over the past 15 years.

Fourth St. in Pocomoke City becomes Md. 371 (Cedarhall Wharf Rd.) and angles southwest to **Beverly of Worcester** (private; visible from the road), a two-story 18th-century mansion on the Pocomoke River. Constructed around 1774, the brick house has the balanced, propor-

tioned appearance of its Georgian era; the Greek Revival portico on the land approach is a later addition.

A classic steamer plies the Pocomoke River near Pocomoke City, ca. 1930

Until this century, the Dennis family owned the Beverly tract, which once extended into nearby Virginia. Donnoch Dennis moved here from Accomac, Virginia, in 1669; his great-grandson, Littleton Dennis, started work on the house. Descendants served on Maryland courts and in Congress. John Dennis, elected to Congress at the age of 25, was one of the five Federalists who switched their vote to Jefferson in the presidential election of 1800, thus breaking the deadlock with Aaron Burr. John Upshur Dennis (1797–1851), an exporter of cypress and molasses, sired 21 children and allegedly won his third wife in a competition with his oldest son. According to family tradition, a tombstone for his second wife arrived on the same ship as a carriage for his new spouse. The family graveyard, surrounded by a brick wall, is near the house.

After visiting Pocomoke City, drive northeast on U.S. 113, which slants across the heart of Worcester County toward the Atlantic Coast.

This flat countryside, heavily wooded with loblolly pines, supports a local timber industry. Since the 17th century, when Eastern Shore Virginians settled in this region, farmers have taken advantage of its long growing season (more than 200 days). Most of the hard-shell clams harvested in Maryland come from Worcester County. Disease, pollution, and over-harvesting have taken their toll on the water creatures of the Chesapeake and the people who have depended on them. Despite the hardships Worcester Countians have endured, they have a reputation for friendliness and hospitality. Long-time residents occasionally use archaic words, and their speech contains rhythms foreign to an urban ear.

About five miles northwest of Pocomoke City, U.S. 113 begins to skirt a large portion of the Pocomoke River State Forest. On the left, accessible from the highway, **Shad Landing State Park** fronts a bend of the river and offers a good taste of the Pocomoke's charms.

A boat landing on the
Pocomoke River,
Worcester County,
during the early 1930s

Snow Hill

To reach the center of this distinctive old town (24' alt., 2,217 pop.),
one of the oldest on the Eastern Shore and seat of Worcester County
since 1742, depart U.S. 113 and follow Md. 394. Col. William Stevens,
owner of Rehoboth plantation, patented a tract here in 1676 and named
it Snow Hill, presumably after the section of London bearing that name.
Located at the head of navigation on the Pocomoke River, the town was
laid out in 1686 and became a commercial center for the Lower Eastern
Shore. The proximity of Chincoteague Bay (only seven miles east from
the river) and its access to the Atlantic Ocean added to the town's geographical advantage. Scottish Presbyterians from Northern Ireland were
among the early settlers and merchants. By 1687, Samuel Davis, one of
the pioneer Presbyterian ministers in Somerset County, was preaching to
a congregation here.

Snow Hill merchants developed an active trade with England and Barbados in the late 17th and early 18th centuries. Gristmills and a tobacco
inspection station, established in 1753, added to the town's prosperity.
During the Revolution, the region harbored local loyalists who couldn't
return to England and found sanctuaries in the nearby Pocomoke
swamps. Yet Snow Hill also produced patriots; sixty leading men from the
county met here on July 26, 1775, to join the Association of Freemen.
Shipping in Snow Hill declined after the Revolution, as Chesapeake Bay
commerce gravitated to Baltimore, the new republic's fastest growing city
in the early 1800s. Although 18th-century residents had regular contacts
with London, 19th-century townspeople lived in an isolated, rural-county
seat. During the Civil War, the town became known as a center of Confederate sympathies.

After the Civil War, Snow Hill experienced decades of peaceful living.

Generations of stability led one native to write in 1970 that "the absence of abrupt change over a long period of time . . . has fostered and perpetuated a sense of security and a feeling of orderliness that are foreign to city dwellers, whose landmarks tumble, whose neighbors and co-workers change, seemingly, with every shift of the wind." Snow Hill's population in 1970 was 2,201. Twenty years later, the 1990 census listed the population as 2,217.

Destructive fires in 1834 and 1893 burned most of the old town, but the remaining mixture of colonial, Federal-period, Greek Revival, and Victorian architecture testifies to an economically stable and aesthetically rich environment. Except for the brick business section squeezed between the courthouse and the river, Snow Hill has a predominantly Victorian flavor—shingled frame houses with ornamental trim, homes with front porches, tree-lined streets. Earlier houses can be identified by large outside chimneys and separate kitchen buildings connected to the main house by "curtains"—all characteristics of early-19th-century houses on the Lower Shore.

The brick **Makemie Memorial Presbyterian Church** at the junction of Market St. (U.S. 113) and Washington St. (Md. 12 West) occupies a site used since 1742. Built in 1890, the present church serves a congregation that traces its roots to a plain country church built in Snow Hill sometime between 1686 and 1697. The **All Hallows Episcopal Church,** on Market St. at the corner of Church St. (Md. 12 East), blends Georgian and Victorian features. The brick walls stand as they did when the building was completed in 1755 after seven years of work. Remodeling in the 1870s removed the belfry and added the chancel and a slate roof. In 1899 the parishioners installed amber and purple panes in the great roundheaded windows. A Bible, printed in London in 1701 and given to the church by Queen Anne, sits in a glass case on one wall.

The **Julia Purnell Museum** is located beyond the church, at 208 Market St. When Mrs. Purnell died in 1943 at the age of 100, she had embroidered more than 3,000 pieces, some of which are on display here. The museum also houses various artifacts and memorabilia from Snow Hill's past. Federal St., heavily shaded by old trees and lined with lovely houses, runs parallel to Market St. Many structures on this street display small details, visible only to the stroller, that reveal the personalities and idiosyncrasies of their builders and owners.

From the center of Snow Hill, Md. 365 branches east a little more than five miles to **Public Landing,** on the shore of Chincoteague Bay. This road follows a 19th-century wagon route, a portage between the town and sailing vessels small enough to negotiate any passages from the bay to the ocean. (Assateague Island during this period may have been pierced by several inlets, allowing access to the mainland from the ocean.) Concealed behind shrubbery, the **Mansion House** (private) was built in stages during the 18th and 19th centuries by the Spence family. The building served for many years as a hotel when Public Landing was a small summer resort.

Bayside Rd. travels south from Public Landing for slightly more than three miles along Chincoteague Bay, the only road which does so. Other roads to Chincoteague's coastline terminate at marshy creeks. Pirates may well have used this isolated, sheltered bay between the Worcester County coast and Assateague Island. Small islands and coves offered numerous hiding places. A pirate legend is associated with **Mount Ephraim,** an old brick seaside house (private; visible from the road). The occupants supposedly paraded the shore with cornstalks to simulate a large force of soldiers and thus spared themselves a raid. The Worcester shore may be the "Arcadia" described by Giovanni da Verrazano, a Florentine navigator who explored the East Coast north of North Carolina in 1524 for the king of France. The explorer described a place that fits this locale, where he landed and walked eight miles inward.

East and south from Snow Hill, Md. 12 leads to **Girdletree,** the **Ernest A. Vaughn Wildlife Management Area,** and **Stockton,** once a railroad shipping point for Chincoteague oysters and crabs. To the east, Md. 366 (George Island Landing Rd.) ends at a bayshore landing only two miles from Virginia. The oyster houses that once flourished here were famous throughout several counties.

Site of Nassawango Furnace via Md. 12

Take Md. 12, which passes through the heart of Snow Hill, west and north across the Pocomoke River and through flat farmland, marshes, and woodland. A marker at the junction of Rte. 12 and Md. 354 identifies the **site of Askiminokonson,** reputedly the largest American Indian town in 17th-century Maryland. Members of the Nanticoke, Pocomoke, Annemessex, Manokin, Massawattex, and Acquintica tribes allegedly lived here before they left the state during the early 1700s. Nothing visible remains of their presence. Old Furnace Rd. leads southwest from Md. 12 across Nassawango Creek to the **site of Nassawango Furnace.**

Nassawango Furnace

Nassawango Creek rises east of Salisbury in Wicomico County and winds slowly south through Worcester County until it meets the Pocomoke River. In its 10-mile course, the creek crosses the marshy, wooded landscape of Maryland's coastal plain, where the soils are composed mostly of clay, sand, and gravel. Smaller waterways along its route offer havens for wildlife and native cypress trees. The creek appears sleepy, but in terms of geology and history, Nassawango has surprising secrets.

Over eons, a hematite variety precipitated out of ground water and gradually formed deep sediments along the creekbed. These iron oxides and adjacent "bog ore" make up one of the few mineral deposits on the Eastern Shore. We now know that early Indians discovered and made use of the oxide, for in 1973 a bulldozer accidentally uncovered evidence of an ancient society near Colbourne. Eventually its four gravesites and five hearths yielded the first archaeological evidence that, in the period 750 to 250 B.C., mid-Atlantic Indians developed a culture above the subsistence level. One hearth appears to have been used for processing the red ochre found in all four graves. (Contemporary tribes still manufacture the pigment by burning the iron oxide in leaves and then extracting the residue.) In the burial sites, researchers found cremated bones, loose copper beads, a copper cup, and the skeleton of a child buried with a pendant and necklace of graduated copper beads. Such copper artifacts suggest a trading network that may have extended to the Ohio River Valley.

Apart from these mysterious remains, nothing is left to tell us about the Indians who lived along Nassawango Creek. From 1670 to 1686 a reservation named Askiminikansen was located along the creek's confluence with the Pocomoke. In 1698 Thomas Chalkley, a traveling Quaker, visited the town out of "a desire to see these people, having never seen any of them before." He reported that the Indians "were kind to us, spoke well of Friends, and said they would not cheat them as others did." A historical marker now marks the approximate site of Askiminikansen at a spot locally known as Indiantown.

About the time of the Revolution, European settlers penetrated the marshy forests to build grist and saw mills along the Nassawango and its tributaries. A Philadelphian reportedly discovered the bog ore deposits in 1788 and made an unsuccessful attempt to smelt them for iron. His holdings were sold to members of the Maryland Iron Company, incorporated in 1829, which bought a mill complex created by Joshua Morris and his descendants. The company later purchased thousands of acres of adjacent forest, built a fieldstone and brick furnace with support buildings, constructed a small company town, and imported workers to extract the iron.

The Nassawango Furnace represented an early application in the United States of the iron smelting technology developed in England. Workers hauled dredged bog ore from the swamps and stored it with oyster shells from Chincoteague Bay; trees were cut and burned for charcoal. Men carted loads of charcoal, shells, and ore and dumped them into the stack in alternating layers until the furnace was "charged." When the charcoal was ignited the shells acted as agents to draw off impurities, and the melted iron dripped to the bottom, where it cooled and was cut into "pigs" about two feet long and four inches square.

Nassawango ore varied in composition, depending on the chemistry of the water, but it never produced top-quality iron. The Maryland Iron Company, the only operation in the state to use bog ore, got in trouble with its creditors; and in 1835 the furnace's assets—including 7,000 acres, two grist and saw mills, and 1,650 tons of ore—went to sale at auction. Thomas A. Spence, who later became a county justice of the peace, bought the property in 1837 and during the next 10 years spent much of his Baltimore-born wife's fortune trying to make the furnace profitable. Under his ownership, the plant produced as much as 700 tons of pig iron annually for shipment via the Pocomoke River to Baltimore and Philadelphia. But better iron ores were discovered in the west, and Spence abandoned Nassawango in 1847.

Variously known as Furnace Town, Furnace Hill, and Furnaceville, the industrial village soon fell to ruin. The wooden buildings—a Methodist church, a tavern, workers' housing, a 14-room superintendent's house, outbuildings—all disappeared. Only the furnace stack remained. The abandoned property excited the romantic imaginations of generations of later residents, including George Alfred Townsend, an Eastern Shore native who incorporated the Nassawango Furnace into his 1884 novel, *The Entailed Hat*. Townsend used Judge Spence and his family as a model for an aristocratic, cavalier social order that was as doomed as the Indian. "Money is becoming a thing and not merely a name," the judge tells his daughter in the story, "and it captures every other thing—land, distinction, talent, family, even beauty and purity." Another character, a self-made man whose parents worked at the furnace and who marries the judge's cherished daughter, revisits the abandoned village and reflects: "The earliest fools who turned up the bog ores for wealth released the miasmas which slew all the people roundabout. They killed all my family, but set me free."

John Walter Smith (1845–1925), a Worcester County native who served as governor of Maryland from 1900 to 1904 and as a U.S. senator from 1913 to 1919, acquired the furnace property in 1912. Half a century later, his family deeded a 12-acre site around the old furnace stack to the Worcester County Historical Society, which began restoring the Nassawango Furnace as a historical attraction. The Furnace Town Foundation, established in 1978, now operates a several-building museum on the site from April to October as part of its efforts to promote tourism.

Like many other locations on the Eastern Shore, the swampy landscape along Nassawango Creek, even its very name, evokes the ghosts of previous users and occupants. Prehistoric people used the red soil to paint their dead; European Americans dredged and smelted the land to make money; the living have restored the site. Visitors have an opportunity to savor the enigmas of this region and wonder at the passions of Marylanders over the centuries to use the land and trade its resources—even in the middle of a bog.

Above Snow Hill, U.S. 113 continues through flat, sometimes marshy countryside, crossing creeks that empty into Chincoteague Bay only two to three miles east. At the Conrail tracks, the highway crosses the old U.S. 13 roadbed, which angles up to the railroad junction town of **Newark** and its **Queponco Station.** The railroad used this Indian name to distinguish the stop from other Newarks along its Eastern Shore route.

Berlin

U.S. 113 cuts through the center of Berlin (45' alt., 2,616 pop.), a 19th-century village that grew around a public stable, blacksmith shop, and tavern. Berlin was built on land patented as "Burleith" in 1677 by Col. William Stevens, holder of the patents on Rehoboth and Snow Hill. The town's current name derives from a contraction of "Burleigh Inn"; residents pronounce the name "ber'lin." Many of the frame houses—which radiate on shady, winding streets from the compact business center— date to the antebellum period. **Buckingham Presbyterian Church,** on the west side of Main St., is the fourth church to serve the congregation, organized soon after 1683 by Francis Makemie. The first church, in use by 1696, stood in the cemetery at the southern end of town, on land that was then part of a tract named Buckingham. A later church was blown down by high winds during a blizzard in 1857. The present church dates to 1906.

Stephen Decatur High School on Seahawk Rd. (east on Md. 346 and U.S. 50, south side of the highway) dates from 1952. A nationally recognized Blue Ribbon School in 1997, when one of its faculty received a Milken Teacher Award, the school has sent graduates to the naval and merchant-marine academies and recently supplied the state doubles (1996) and singles (1997) tennis champions. Accomplished alumni include Maryland Court of Appeals judge Dale R. Cathell, the artist Patrick Henry, and the college basketball coach Oliver Purnell.

From Berlin, Md. 376 takes one eastward to Md. 611, the highway that leads to Assateague Island National Seashore.

North of Berlin, U.S. 113 intersects U.S. 50 and Md. 90, both of which cross the Isle of Wight Bay to **Ocean City,** about seven and a half miles to the east.

Most travelers from the west have the beach as their destination, but those who continue north on U.S. 113 enter **Showell,** named for one of the largest slaveholding families of the region. **Ocean Pines,** a modern residential development, lies on the east along St. Martin's River. **St. Martin's Episcopal Church** stands alone on the edge of a pine woods just south of Showell. The specifications for the 44-by-54-foot structure, signed in 1756 by the builder James Johnson, mention no decoration of any kind, and the interior of the brick church, seldom used, is indeed austere.

About two miles south of the Maryland-Delaware line, Md. 367 (Bishopville Rd.) angles northeast from the highway to **Bishopville,** originally Milltown. This village grew up at the dammed headwaters of St. Martin's River, an estuary of Isle of Wight Bay. As late as 1900, small sailing vessels carried lumber and farm products out to sea from this location.

East of Salisbury, U.S. 50 cuts across flat farmland marked by occasional stands of woods, grain fields, and modern "br'iler plants"—the long, low buildings that house hundreds, sometimes thousands of broiler chickens. To explore this countryside, take Md. 346, the Old Ocean City Rd., which branches from U.S. 50 in Salisbury and parallels the newer highway to the Pocomoke River.

Pittsville (602 pop.), about eight miles east of Salisbury, is named for Dr. H. R. Pitts, president of the Wicomico and Pocomoke Railroad, a small line completed in 1869 from Salisbury to Berlin. During the Christmas season, the village attracts shoppers for holly and other evergreens. **Willards** (708 pop.), also a former rail depot, is named after Willard Thompson, of Baltimore, a railroad officer. The city limits form a perfect circle.

Great Pocomoke Swamp

East of Willards, Md. 346 enters a swampy, forested area along the Pocomoke River. The Pocomoke, here little more than a small stream separating Wicomico and Worcester Counties, rises in an area along the Maryland-Delaware border which has been variously called Burnt Swamp, Cypress Swamp, and the Great Pocomoke Swamp. Bear, deer, and wildcats survived in this region until the middle of the 19th century, long after they were virtually extinct in the rest of the peninsula. Bootleggers and escaped slaves also found refuge within the 50 square miles of this flooded forest.

A Worcester County sawmill in the 1930s

From early colonial days, bald cypress trees provided a living for those living near the swamp. Residents used the wood to make shingles, which were riven out by hand with heavy iron blades called "frows" and then drawknifed to the required thinness. Most old-time Pocomoke cypress shingles were 30 inches long or more (modern shingles are 18 inches) and were used for roofs and siding. Many houses on the Lower Eastern Shore still have shingled walls more than a century old; the handshaved cypress shingle wears paper thin with age but never decays.

By 1860, however, most of the old-growth timber suitable for shingles had been cut. Then enterprising swampers discovered layers of bald cypress and white cedar protected within the deep peat of the swamp floor. Felled by prehistoric winds, their trunks had been perfectly preserved for hundreds of years by rotting vegetation and sphagnum moss. Men with oxen drove into the swamps and scooped the muck off the logs, which then floated to the surface. The logs were dragged to nearby sawmills and cut into large cylinders that were split into blocks. An expert workman with a drawknife could cut 500 long shingles a day from such shingle blocks; when he had produced 1,000 shingles, he traded them at the store in Whaleyville for calico, sugar, tobacco, whiskey, and other commodities. The wood was also used for shipbuilding and coffins. In 1930, after drainage and drought had lowered water levels, a great fire—allegedly started by an exploding moonshine still—burned for several months in the swamp, searing through 5–10 feet of the peat and destroying the remaining logs. The fire ruined the Eastern Shore cypress shingle industry. Redwood shingles from the West Coast now supply most of the nation's demand. Foresters estimate that it will take several thousand years for the swamp to regenerate itself.

The Pocomoke River grows in width and depth as it winds 33 marshy miles through Wicomico, Worcester, and Somerset Counties on its way to Pocomoke Sound in Chesapeake Bay. Pine, gum, white cedar, bald cypress, and holly trees line its banks, protected in several places by state forests.

Whaleyville, slightly north of Md. 346 on Md. 610, named for Capt. Seth Whaley, who settled here in the 18th century, once was a center of the Pocomoke Swamp shingle industry. The town also touted itself in the 1930s as the birthplace of P. Dale Wimbrow, an entertainer who called himself "Old Pete Daley of Whaleysville." Wimbrow put on a benefit performance in 1926 that paid for the expansion and painting of an African American Methodist Church on nearby Shepards Crossing Rd.

Md. 346 rejoins U.S. 50 after passing the northern outskirts of Berlin. Md. 90, the Ocean City Expressway, splits from U.S. 50 and Md. 346 and takes one directly through Ocean Pines, across St. Martin's River, and then across Isle of Wight Bay to 62nd St. in Ocean City.

Side Trip down Sinepuxent Neck to Assateague via Md. 611

Stephen Decatur Memorial Rd. (Md. 611) branches southwest from U.S. 50 after crossing Herring Creek and before the bridge to Ocean City. Stephen Decatur, one of the country's truly dashing naval heroes, was born on a nearby farm on January 5, 1779. His father, a revolutionary naval officer, had sent his wife here for safety during her "confinement";

she returned to Philadelphia with their young son when he was four months old. Following his father's footsteps, Stephen entered the navy as a midshipman in 1798 and in 1804–5 participated gallantly in naval attacks against Mediterranean pirates. He fought the British fleet with equal vigor during the War of 1812. In 1815 he made his famous toast at a dinner in Norfolk: "Our country! In her intercourse with foreign nations may she always be in the right; but our country, right or wrong!" Decatur later commanded the squadron that forced Algiers to end its practice of exacting tribute from American ships in the Mediterranean. His distinguished career came to an abrupt end on March 22, 1820, when a fellow officer, incensed at Decatur for recommending his suspension from service, killed him in a duel held in a Bladensburg cemetery. His body lies in St. Peter's churchyard, Philadelphia.

The Stephen Decatur Rd. travels down the wooded, marsh-fringed Sinepuxent Neck. Only about nine miles long and less than two miles wide, the narrow peninsula is defined by Sinepuxent Bay on the east and Ayer and Trappe Creeks and Newport Bay on the west. Many old Worcester families (Fassitt, Cropper, Whaley, Robins, Purnell, Henry, Spence) trace their ancestry to the early colonists who planted corn, flax, and tobacco here three centuries ago. A few of the original plantation houses still stand; poor soil conditions caused many farms to deteriorate and disappear. Before World War II this neck was known chiefly to a few tenant farmers, moonshiners, duck hunters, and trappers. Now it provides the site of the Ocean City Airport, a golf course, and tourist attractions.

At Lewis Corner, take Md. 376 west toward Berlin. Just after the road crosses Ayer Creek, **Golden Quarter** (private) becomes visible. The name of this historic estate may refer to yellow English daisies planted by a woman of the Ayres family, which built the house here. The prerevolutionary, brick wing is shaded by the Ayres Elm, once a landmark for boaters.

Just south of Lewis Corner on Md. 611 one may see the **Fassitt House** (private). This 17th-century house was probably built by William Fassitt, an early Presbyterian follower of the Rev. Francis Makemie. The brickwork—with its elaborate patterns of glazed headers—is typical of many English houses of the early 16th century. One Fassitt family legend concerns an ancestor who may have shot Gen. Edward Braddock during the British attack on Fort Duquesne in 1755. Braddock supposedly ordered a Fassitt shot for breaking ranks when the British and colonials were ambushed; another member of the family presumably avenged his death by shooting the general in the back.

On the west side of South Point Rd., a short distance from the turn Md. 611 takes to the east for Assateague Island, one may see **Genesar,** an early 18th-century house, modified over the years.

Md. 611 crosses Sinepuxent Bay to **Assateague Island,** the sandy, 35-mile-long barrier reef that extends down the coast from the Ocean City Inlet to Chincoteague, Virginia. Named for American Indians who inhabited the Chincoteague Bay shoreline, this narrow island remains an ocean wilderness, alive with waves, wind, and moving sand dunes. The air smells clean and salty; the light is clear and brilliant; marsh plants, mammals, and sea life abound.

Wild ponies, descendants of horses that 17th-century colonists allowed to graze freely, roam the length of the island. Assateague also supports more than 275 species of birds, including the American oyster-catcher, the only bird of its type in the eastern United States. Only the stinging and biting insects that thrive during the summer months diminish the pleasure evoked by miles of uncluttered ocean shoreline. No one ever settled on the island. Except for an occasional pirate or explorer, it remained wild and vacant. In 1650 a Col. Henry Norwood was stranded on the northern part of the island with 19 other persons, who resorted to cannibalism to stay alive. The survivors, including Norwood, were found by Assateague tribesmen and guided to Virginia's Eastern Shore.

Spurred by the success of Ocean City, a real estate speculator created hundreds of lots for a resort development on the island in the late 1940s. Worcester County business and political leaders built the Md. 611 bridge with state aid. By 1962 the Ocean Beach Corporation owned most of Assateague and had sold almost 6,000 lots along a paved Baltimore Ave. Then for three days in March, the tides and winds of a great nor'easter totally demolished the improvements, moving the shore line in places more than 400 feet. Federal studies indicated that costs to protect the island were prohibitive and impractical; the U.S. Army Corps of Engineers declared Assateague unsuitable for commercial development.

In 1965 Congress created the **Assateague National Seashore,** which encompasses a 700-acre state park. Park rules restrict regular automobile traffic to a short, paved highway. Hikers, campers, canoeists, and fishermen flock to the island's dunes, unencumbered beaches, and ocean surf. The National Park Service uses the **McCabe House,** built in 1949 at the island's northern end. The **Chincoteague National Wildlife Refuge** occupies the island's southern end, 12 miles of which lies in Virginia; the refuge personnel manage the resident herd of wild ponies.

OCEAN CITY

U.S. 50 crosses the Harry W. Kelly Memorial Bridge to the oldest section of Ocean City (5' alt., 5,146 pop.), located near the southern tip of Fenwick Island, which extends north into Delaware. During the summer season, Ocean City becomes Maryland's second largest city and its largest seaside resort. On hot summer weekends, temporary residents and visitors swell the population to as many as 300,000, most of whom come from the metropolitan areas of the Western Shore.

Ocean City perches precariously on a barrier island on which more than $2 billion worth of recreational and residential property has been constructed, generating about $85 million in taxes every year. Memorial Day usually brings the first great migration of summer visitors, and Labor Day ends the cycle. During the winter, Ocean City shrinks to a small number of permanent residents who tend the properties and a growing number of visitors who enjoy the less crowded off-season and walk the winter beaches.

Less than 130 years ago, only a Coast Guard station occupied these Atlantic beaches. A narrow, 60-mile island of sand stretched unbroken from Indian River Inlet in Delaware to Toms Cove, Virginia. People in Delaware and the upper part of Worcester County called their portion Fenwick Island; those further south called it Assateague. Similar islands, created by constant wave action, stretched along the entire Middle Atlantic Coast, sheltering small bays off the mainland. The island sands shifted dramatically during severe storms; adjacent wetlands provided shelter for a rich variety of wildlife.

After the Civil War, a few people ventured into this special environment and patented some sand under the name, "The Ladies Resort to the Ocean." Nothing came of this venture, but in 1875, another group of promoters, from Salisbury, built the Atlantic Hotel—a 400-room, four-story Victorian frame building with wide porches. When the hotel opened on July 4, 1875, news and promotional accounts referred to the site as Ocean City. By 1878, the railroad from Salisbury had reached Sinepuxent Bay; completion of a railroad bridge in 1881 enabled guests to embark directly in the newly fashionable resort town. Other hotels followed the crowds; touts and hacks clustered around the train depot to corral the sun worshipers. The *Maryland Gazette* in 1749 had reported storm tides that reached two miles inland into Worcester County, but the Victorians, buoyed by their faith in progress, ignored such potential danger. By 1891, Ocean City had been laid into plats up to 32nd St.; other subdivisions followed and had filled the beach to 118th St. by 1917. Jetties built at the turn of the century helped retain the wide, gently sloping beach for which the town was becoming famous. Baltimoreans discovered the attractions and by the 1920s were driving their Model-Ts or crowding excursion trains to the beach. By 1930, the town had a population of 946 permanent residents and had become established as a major summer resort.

Then, on August 22, 1933, a hurricane washed away the railroad bridge, the small boardwalk, three streets, and all the fishing camps that had clustered near the bridge. The storm cut an inlet to Sinepuxent Bay which had been closed since 1819. After this disaster, state and federal funds were provided to shore up the inlet, giving permanent ocean access to the fishing boats on the bay. In addition to tourists, Ocean City

Fishermen proudly display their catches of marlin, Ocean City, ca. 1937

The beaches and high-
rises of Ocean City,
1997

now had the ingredients of a fishing center. No one bothered to replace
the railroad bridge, and the town rebuilt. Until 1962, Ocean City developed like many other East Coast beach towns—with a boardwalk, refreshment stands, small hotels and motels, fishing boats, and crowded
beachfront shops. All these clustered to the south; open dunes stretched
to the north. The town was not as gawdy as Virginia Beach or as sophisticated as Rehoboth Beach in Delaware. Ocean City pursued a middle
way; its promoters touted the family atmosphere, and the predictable
crowds came every summer, growing larger with completion of the first
Chesapeake Bay bridge in 1952.

On March 5, 1962, a three-day storm ravaged the barrier islands; and
on July 22, 1962, Bobby Baker, then President Lyndon Johnson's personal
assistant, opened the Carousel Hotel just below 120th St. in North Ocean
City. These two events set the patterns for the rise of modern Ocean City.
The storm washed much of the sandy beach into the town, destroyed
the boardwalk and ruined many ocean-front buildings. Only three stories
high, the new hotel reflected Washington money and influence; its glamorous night club pointed the way for other investors, who looked at the
beachfronts and dreamed of Atlantic City or Miami Beach. Property owners repaired the storm damage but soon found themselves at odds with
environmentalists, who questioned the wisdom of beach construction.

While developers reaped profits from the growing crowds, the state invested public funds to protect a valuable tax base.

With the construction in 1970 of the first high-rise condominium, below the Carousel Hotel, Ocean City boomed. "High-Rise Row" emerged during the '70s, giving the town a skyline. Thereafter, people would speak of two Ocean Cities: the older, homier town to the south and the more expensive, glamorous city above 91st St. The city now stretches almost 10 miles, from the Ocean City Inlet to the Fenwick Island Lighthouse at the Delaware state line. About 500 apartment buildings, 38 hotels, 81 motels, 158 restaurants, and 33 banks border the single main highway that travels a narrow strip of sand ranging from 1,050 feet to a mile wide. A two-mile boardwalk, lined with refreshment stands, souvenir shops, and amusement centers, begins on the city's southern edge.

Ocean City has also become a major center for deep-sea fishing and hosts an annual white marlin tournament in early September. In 1988, the state and federal governments began the multimillion-dollar Beach Replenishment and Hurricane Protection Project, which has created sand dunes by dredging and pumping sand from offshore. A northeaster in 1993 caused more than $12 million worth of damage.

Historical Attractions

U.S. 50 (Ocean Gateway) crosses the **Harry W. Kelly Jr. Memorial Bridge** at the south end of Fenwick Island, the original entrance to Ocean City. (The newer Ocean City Expressway [Md. 90] branches off from U.S. 50 and enters the city near the middle of the island, above 60th St., via the Assawoman Bay Bridge.) To reach the older, southern portion of Ocean City, continue on U.S. 50 across the Kelly Bridge. Harry Kelly, who died in 1985 at the age of 66, served in the city council for 16 years prior to becoming mayor of Ocean City for 15 years. He presided over city government during the boom years of the 1970s and achieved national attention for his single-minded promotion of his native town.

Turn right (south) on Philadelphia Ave. to the **Coast Guard Station,** one of the oldest in the United States. The station has occupied this site since August 4, 1790. An **Ocean City Museum** is to the south, near the **Inlet Boardwalk.** The area immediately north of the boardwalk bespeaks Ocean City before its high-rise development. **City Hall** stands between 2nd and 3rd Sts.

Drive north on Ocean Hwy. (Md. 528) to the **Convention Center,** built in 1970, above 40th St. **High-Rise Row** and the **Carousel Hotel,** the latter considerably expanded from its initial size, are located between 90th and 120th Sts.

Continue on Md. 528 to the Delaware line and the no-longer-used **Fenwick Island Lighthouse,** location of the **first Maryland-Delaware boundary marker.** The stone, erected in 1751, marks the survey made by John Watson and William Parsons of Pennsylvania and John Emory and Thomas Jones of Maryland. Their line due west from the stone across the Delmarva peninsula partially settled a long dispute between the Calverts and the Penns over the boundaries of their respective colonies.

The controversy between the two proprietors began in 1682, when William Penn, looking for a sea outlet for his new colony, bought the lands on the western shore of the Delaware River from the Duke of York. In 1685, the English Privy Council established Cape Henlopen as the southern boundary of Pennsylvania; but the map used by the council, published in 1651 by Nicholas Visscher, showed the cape at the location of Fenwick Island. On his map of 1670, Augustine Herrman had drawn the correct location of Cape Henlopen (15 miles north of Fenwick Island); but the Penns persisted in using the map more favorable to their cause. In 1750 the Court of Chancery settled the dispute in favor of the Penns.

Watson and his colleagues began the official survey in December 1750. Watson's diary records storm tides that nearly drowned the surveyors and a fire from which they barely escaped with their lives. After surveying about 6 miles during 22 midwinter days, they found the icy swamps impassable and postponed the rest of the work until April 1751. Commissioners appointed by the two proprietors then met and accepted the line, which defined the southernmost boundary between the two states. The carved Penn coat of arms occupies the northern side of the stone, that of the Calverts the southern. In 1952 the state of Delaware had the badly weathered stone recut.

Return from Salisbury to Easton
via Md. 313, 318, 331

Returning from the beach, travelers often opt for directness. If time permits, one may take a leisurely route that breaks up the trip between Salisbury and Easton.

Parts of the route follow the former main road between Salisbury and the Talbot County seat, which runs through northern Dorchester County and southern Caroline County. In the spring, the road passes through rye and wheat fields; in summer and fall, one sees corn and soybeans. Although the acreage devoted to vegetable crops has diminished in recent years, canning and freezing remain important sources of income in the area. Evidence of chicken farming is everywhere. The road passes more than a few steep-roofed cottages with large chimneys, indicating considerable age, under the disguise of modern shingles or siding.

Md. 313 angles north from U.S. 50 at Mardela Springs and, after a short distance, Md. 54 branches east to the **Mason-Dixon Middlestone,** establishing the southwestern corner of Delaware. A small, unsigned brick structure shelters four stones which mark the midpoint of a line surveyed in 1750–51 from Fenwick Island on the Delaware Bay due west to the Chesapeake Bay. From this midpoint, the east-west boundary between Maryland and Delaware was to be formed, by running a line north to a point where it would be tangent to a circle with a 12-mile radius centered in New Castle. The midpoint could not be determined, however, until the states agreed where the line ended in the Chesapeake. The Maryland commissioners claimed that Slaughter Creek, which separates Taylor's Island from the Dorchester County mainland, should be the end point. The Pennsylvania commissioners (Delaware did not separate from Pennsylvania until 1776) argued that since water in the creek at low tide was less than two feet deep, the bay shore of Taylor's Island should be the end point. The question was settled in favor of the Penns in 1760. When Charles Mason and Jeremiah Dixon resumed their survey in 1763, they placed the midpoint on this transpeninsular line, marking it with a double crown stone in 1768. The worn stones sheltered here faintly show the Calvert arms on the south and Penn's on the north.

Farther north, Md. 313 reaches the village of **Sharptown** (609 pop.) and then crosses the Nanticoke River into Dorchester County.

A striking country church at **Eldorado** (49 pop.) dominates the intersection with Md. 14, where a marker points the way to yet another **Rehoboth** (private), patented in 1673 to John Lee, son of Col. Richard Lee, founder of the Lee family of Virginia. The family built the house around 1725 and lived here until 1787.

Side Trip to East New Market and Secretary via Md. 14 and 16

At Eldorado, the explorer may take a side trip that rejoins the main route near Preston. Take Md. 14 west to Brookview, Rhodesdale, and then to **East New Market,** which dates from the late 18th century. Its houses, set back from the road, are almost concealed by great trees, and travelers can easily drive through the town without realizing they have passed such an old settlement. Visible from the road just before the junction with Md. 16 is **Friendship Hall** (private), a 2½-story brick mansion built about 1790 by James Sulivane, quartermaster general of Dorchester County during the Revolution. **Maurice Manor** (private), a smaller 18th-century frame house, is also visible, across the street. The **Old House of the Hinges** (private), locally known as the **Brick Hotel,** lies just beyond the blinker light, to the left on Md. 16. Behind the kitchen wing is an old meat house with enormous hinges, which accounts for the house's name. Said to have been built in the late 18th century, the building housed the East New Market Hotel in the 1920s. Farther along Md. 16 is the **Smith House** (private), a small frame structure built before 1797 with a very steep roof and outside end chimneys with elaborate pyramidic hips. According to local legend, a 19th-century owner swapped this house and his nagging wife for a new wife and a feather bed.

Md. 14 west from East New Market leads to **Secretary,** a small fishing village situated along the Warwick River where it meets the wide Choptank. **My Lady Sewall's House,** a small brick structure, occupies the end of Willow St. Local lore has long ascribed the house's construction to Henry Sewall, secretary of Maryland under Gov. Charles Calvert in 1661. "My Lady Sewall" married Charles Calvert, later the third Lord Baltimore, shortly after her first husband's death in 1664. The house's fine interior paneling, installed in the early 18th century, is now housed in the Brooklyn Museum of Art.

Beyond Secretary, Md. 14 crosses Secretary Creek and intersects Green Point Rd., which leads to **Indian Purchase** (private), formerly known as Goose Creek Farm. The farm was originally part of a tract reserved for the Choptank Indians; Chief Hatchwop and his queen signed the deed transferring the land to Francis Taylor in 1693. The brick house—with the entrance at the gable end and a hall running across the front—is typical of many houses built in this area at the end of the 18th century.

Follow Md. 14 back to Md. 16 and north through East New Market to Preston (see below) via Md. 16 and 331.

_____

West and East of Finchville on Md. 392

From Md. 313 at Finchville, one may travel west on Md. 392 to **Hurlock** (45' alt., 1,706 pop.), a town that developed around a railroad station built in 1867. John M. Hurlock erected the first store here in 1869 and the town's first dwelling in 1872. The town was incorporated under his name 20 years later. The **Hurlock Free Library,** established in 1900 and now a branch of the Dorchester County Library, is the oldest public library on the Eastern Shore.

East on Md. 392, after four miles, one reaches a place on the Maryland-Delaware line where three jurisdictions come together—the Maryland counties of Dorchester and Caroline and the Delaware county of Sussex. In the old days, before SWAT teams and federal agents, this location proved ideal for outlaws. A plain-frame building at **Reliance** may be the **site of the Patty Cannon Gang headquarters.**

An Eastern Shore legend, Patty Cannon was a handsome woman of extraordinary charm and physical strength. Reportedly born in Canada as Lucretia Hanly, she married a Delaware man, Alonzo Cannon, as a teenager at the end of the 18th century. The two operated a successful ferry on the Nanticoke River south of Seaford, Delaware. Legend has it that she poisoned her first husband and then assembled a gang of cutthroats that included her son-in-law, Joe Johnson. Patty and her gang then created a minor industry of kidnapping free and slave African Americans and selling them to slave traders—whom she entertained and sometimes robbed.

Sheltered by bought politicians and feared by the common folk, the gang operated with relative impunity in this isolated region between the Nanticoke River and Marshyhope Creek. According to local tradition, because the state line ran through the tavern, a combined Delaware and Maryland sheriffs' raid was finally necessary to arrest Patty. Johnson escaped, but Patty and other gang members were tried at Georgetown, Delaware. In 1829, sentenced to be hanged, she committed suicide in jail. Later in the century George Alfred Townsend, a native of the region, wrote of Patty's crimes in his novel, _The Entailed Hat; or, Patty Cannon's Times._

From Reliance Md. 577 angles northwest to Federalsburg in Caroline County, created in 1773 and named for Lady Caroline Eden, the sister of the last Lord Baltimore.

Federalsburg

Md. 313 and Md. 557 enter Federalsburg from the south. In the 18th century, the site of this community (2,365 pop.) on upper Marshyhope Creek was known as Northwest Fork (of the Nanticoke River). Cloudsberry Jones opened a general store in 1789 at the bridge here, and a settlement developed. Ordinaries, or taverns, were authorized at "Northwest Forks Bridge," but in 1793 the name of the settlement appears on maps and documents as "Federalsburgh," probably the reflection of townsmen's allegiance to the political party of Washington and Hamilton.

Although the creek was too shallow for launching boats, a ship-building business, using top-grade white oak, flourished through the mid-19th century. Hulls were conveyed on lighters and scows to a point about four miles down the creek, where they could be launched. Other lumber and mill products added to the town's prosperity. A large slave-trading station was located in an old tavern at the east bridgehead. After the Civil War, the railroad from Seaford, Delaware, reached the town, and the new depot center served various small and agricultural industries, a position it still enjoys.

Northwest of the town, Laurel Grove Rd. crosses Richardson Rd., which leads to **Colonel Richardson High School,** named for William Richardson (1735–1825), revolutionary officer, state district court judge, and resident of what became Caroline County. The school was founded in 1963, when Caroline County merged Federalsburg High School (white) and Preston High (black). Richardson High claimed the state Group 1 Marching-Band Championship every year between 1987 and 1997.

The **Idylwild Wildlife Management Area,** just northeast of Federalsburg, features about 24 miles of walking trails along Marshyhope Creek and its tributaries. Quiet and relatively unused except during hunting season, this 3,000-acre preserve offers many opportunities for bird watchers, wild flower enthusiasts, and canoeists.

For half a dozen miles or more west of Federalsburg, Md. 318 follows the boundary between Caroline and Dorchester Counties to **Linchester,** on Hunting Creek, one of the oldest settlements in Caroline County. A gristmill, established here in 1681, became the center of a settlement known as Murray's Mill. Since the creek forms the boundary between Caroline and Dorchester Counties, a legislative act renamed the town Linchester (from Caroline and Dorchester). An old mill still sits to the side, opposite a millpond. A newspaper editor from Preston has argued that the present structure is the reconstructed original mill, swept from its foundations to its present site during a spring flood. During the 1960s, he waged a national campaign to have it recognized as the oldest continuous manufacturing business in the United States. When reporters arrived to investigate the claim, the last miller, a grizzled Shoreman from Denton who had bought the structure in 1914, told them, "I ain't worrying over it."

Preston

After the Civil War, this railroad town (509 pop.) helped to open the interior of the Delmarva Peninsula to outside markets. Preston still serves as a commercial center for a broiler-raising and truck-gardening district. Canning factories and associated brokerages, supported by a locally based trucking firm, have made this little town known in markets along the Eastern Seaboard. The **Bethesda Methodist Church,** at the junction of Md. 16 and Main St., occupies the site of one of the first Methodist churches in America, the Bethesda Chapel. William Frazier (1756–1807), a captain in the Revolution, had built a house near Dover. Bishop Francis Asbury made frequent visits between 1801 and 1813 to the Frazier household and preached in the little settlement, then known as Snow Hill. Local authorities date the change in name to 1856 and ascribe the new one to Alexander Preston, then a prominent Baltimore lawyer.

West of Preston, Md. 331 passes through the villages of Bethlehem and Tanyard, which seems to have origins as a tannery. Resplendent wetlands line the road. (The Choptank Wetlands Preserve, inaccessible by automobile, lies to the southwest at a bend in the river.)

Md. 331 crosses the Choptank River from Caroline into Talbot on the **Dover Bridge,** built in 1860. Until 1865, when the counties bought the company stock and made this bridge free, foot passengers, horses, and cows were charged a five-cent toll; a sheep or pig cost three cents. The **site of Dover,** reportedly a port of considerable foreign trade during the 18th century, is two miles below the bridge, on the west bank of the Choptank. Seagoing vessels once tied up at Dover's wharves to allow the fresh river water to kill barnacles on their bottoms. In 1778, the General Assembly authorized construction of a courthouse and prison at Dover for use by the state General Court, which met on the Eastern Shore in alternate years. The law was not heeded, however, and the General Court continued to use the county courthouse at Talbottown, later renamed Easton. During the Revolution, when the Eastern Shore began its long agitation for autonomy from the rest of the state, this site was even proposed as a capital for the Shore. Dover did not become a capital, of course (secession efforts have so-far failed). New shipping routes developed. The harbor shoaled. Dover disappeared.

The Baltimore Beltway from the I-70 overpass

PART III

CENTRAL MARYLAND

If Maryland deserves the nickname "America in Miniature," then Central Maryland well illustrates the country's early-20th-century urbanization and late-century suburban sprawl. More than 80 percent of Maryland's 4.8 million people live within 40 miles of Baltimore or Washington. More than 90 percent of the state's African American citizens live in Central Maryland, where they form the majority in Prince George's County and Baltimore City. Suburban Baltimore and Washington residents have subdivided and spread into the surrounding countryside at a rate that has devoured farmland and green space. The U.S. Census Bureau has joined the two metropolitan areas—Washington with 3.92 million people and Baltimore with 2.38 million—forming a single Consolidated Metropolitan Statistical Area (CMSA), now the fourth largest such unit in the United States, following New York, Los Angeles, and Chicago.

At the beginning of the 19th century, Maryland, like the rest of the country, remained about 95 percent rural. Rapidly growing Baltimore had become one of America's largest cities, but the rest of the state retained a pastoral or plantation character. Frederick, Cumberland, Hagerstown, and Annapolis were fairly small towns.

In the past 50 years, the state's population has more than doubled. More than four out of five citizens now live in urban areas. Rockville, Gaithersburg, Bowie, College Park, Greenbelt, Laurel, Takoma Park, Hyattsville, New Carrollton, Aberdeen, and Westminster have all mushroomed, bringing to 18 the number of Maryland towns with 10,000 or more residents. Since 1940 Rockville, the state's second largest city, with 44,835 people, has experienced a population increase of 3,005 percent.

Baltimore and Washington—the two poles in this new urban landscape—have progressed at uneven paces, although their growth curves, plotted over the past two centuries, look remarkably the same. In 1830 Baltimore had 80,620 people and had successfully withstood British attack. Burned extensively by the same troops, Washington was still a struggling small town, one-fourth the size of Baltimore. When Charles Dickens visited the region in 1842, he found the Barnum Hotel in Baltimore "the most comfortable of all the hotels of which I had any experience in the United States." Washington, however, he described as having "spacious avenues that begin in nothing and lead nowhere; streets a mile long that only want houses, roads and inhabitants; public buildings that need but a public to be complete; and ornaments of great thoroughfares which only need great thoroughfares to ornament."

Close by Confederate lines and threatened more than once by invasion, both cities were armed camps during the Civil War. The cannon were always pointed outward in Washington, whereas in Baltimore they pointed in both directions to contain the city's many Southern-leaning citizens who were rankled by martial law. Washington grew three times faster than Baltimore in the decade of that war. Both cities grew dramatically, and at about the same pace, during the decade of World War I. By 1920 American population had shifted from mostly rural to mostly urban, and Washington, still smaller than its Patapsco sister (437,571 vs. 733,826), had defied Dickens and become a "city beautiful," having benefited from the turn-of-the-century urban beautification movement by that name. During the New Deal years of the 1930s, Washington grew four times faster than Baltimore, exploding with new bureaucracies and the people who staffed them. Growth continued during World War II—Baltimore, with its war industries, at an 11 percent rate and Washington, capital of the most powerful Allied nation, at 27 percent. In 1950 the cities reached their population peaks and near parity (Baltimore, 949,708 persons; Washington, 802,178).

Since 1950 both cities have steadily lost residents, while their suburbs have grown. The 38-mile distance between the two city lines has filled with highways, shopping centers, residential developments, and suburban offices. In the 20-year period between 1952 and 1972, 13 of the 15 major highways constructed in Maryland (at a cost of more than $100 million) were built to link the two cities and their suburban satellites. The result has been a sprawl of urban clusters extending north toward Pennsylvania, south well into Charles County, east to the Susquehanna River, and west nearly to Frederick. Small towns once surrounded by farms now find themselves surrounded by town- and ranch-house developments, commercial strips, and malls, all within an encompassing suburban culture dependent on automobile, television, telephone, and computer networks. Slightly more than 1.8 million people lived in Maryland in 1940, more than 13 percent on 42,100 farms. In 1990 the state counted about 4.8 million people, less than 1 percent of whom lived on 15,200 farms. Fifty years ago, about two-thirds of Maryland's total land acreage was farmland; now the total is about one-third.

These developments outline something extraordinary in American history: the emergence of a region that one U.S. Census Bureau demographer has called "the largest merger of metropolitan areas in world history." Similar areas—Minneapolis/St. Paul, Seattle/Tacoma, San Francisco/Oakland, St. Petersburg/Tampa—have been linked by a shared body of water and developed along common economic and other paths. Central Maryland divides itself between two quite different cities. Baltimore is an old, hardworking, blue-collar Maryland town—a place H. L. Mencken celebrated for its charm and "whole hierarchy of peculiarly private and potent gods." From his perspective, Washington—like New York—was a place of vagabonds, filled with people who were "highly sophisticated and inordinately trashy." From the Washington perspective, Baltimore is like a dowdy maiden aunt—slow-moving, sly, a bit frayed—but full of surprising mysteries, like crab cakes, the Orioles, Arabbers, seaport smells, ethnic neighborhoods, and waitresses who call patrons "Hon." In the 1950s and '60s, AM radio stations in both Washington and Baltimore aired evening jazz programs. Tellingly, the Baltimore station played classic big-band sounds and Dixieland favorites (the disk jockey described the

A sturdy and independent lot, Arabbers continued to sell fresh produce in the streets of Baltimore at the end of the 20th century.

broadcasts as originating "just a little south of the Mason and Dixon Line"); in Washington, introducing his listeners to the latest and most sophisticated jazz in the world, Felix Grant almost single-handedly started the Bossa Nova craze.

Maryland's portion of the Washington-Baltimore CMSA includes pockets and fringes of rural countryside but consists largely of urban and suburban landscape.

Baltimore City

Baltimore (20' alt., 736,014 pop.), Maryland's metropolis, emerged in 1729 as a tobacco town on the Patapsco River and after mid-century grew rapidly as a wheat and flour entrepôt. The town benefited from the commerce of the Revolutionary War and from trading with various belligerents during the Napoleonic period. It briefly rivaled New York City as the premier port on the East Coast; in 1830 it had grown into the second largest city in the country. During the Civil War, Federal authorities placed the city—some of whose citizenry were notorious for their Southern sympathies—under martial law. By contrast, the world wars of the 20th century rewarded Baltimore, as an aircraft, shipping, and clothing center. Since 1950, however, the city has steadily yielded population and wealth to the surrounding suburban counties. In 1996 its population, estimated at 675,401, was the lowest it had been in eight decades. In 1930 Baltimore was the sixth-largest city in the United States; as the century closed, the city stood as only the fourth-largest political subdivision in Maryland.

English, Africans, Irish, and Germans first gave Baltimore its character. After the Civil War came Italians, Russians, Poles, Ukrainians, and Lithuanians, with sprinklings of other nationalities and traditions as well. A pattern developed in the ethnic neighborhoods: individual leaders—usually attorneys, sometimes teachers or social workers—rose to prominence, became city council members, and claimed pieces of the municipal pie. During the 1970s, when two such native sons—Spiro T. Agnew, the first Greek American vice president of the United States, and Marvin Mandel, the first Jewish governor of Maryland—fell afoul of corruption charges, outsiders sneered at the morality of Baltimore and Maryland politics. Russell Baker, *New York Times* columnist and erstwhile Baltimorean, spoke more philosophically. "Baltimore tolerates sin," he wrote in 1973. "The pleasures of the flesh, the table, the bottle and the purse are tolerated with a civilized understanding of the subtleties of moral questions that would have been perfectly comprehensible to Edwardian Londoners."

H. L. Mencken, one of the better-known products of Baltimore ethnic upbringing, claimed that his charming native city had "a feeling for hearth, for the immemorial lares and penates" that survived better in Baltimore than in any other large American city; Baltimore exemplified, he said, "a tradition of sound and comfortable living." The heart of Baltimore experience encompasses fine foods, love of baseball, the sport of lacrosse, old churches, pioneering hospitals and medical schools, the first American research university, libraries, theaters, concert halls, and world-famous museums (the first museum being Peale's Baltimore Museum and Gallery of Fine Arts, which opened in 1814). A seaport lying between the intellectual traditions of the North and the sporting heritage of the South, Baltimore has shared elements of both.

Aristocrats, plutocrats, and artists have given Baltimore cultural distinction, but its blue-collar residents have supplied its gritty authenticity. Sailors, millers, stevedores, storekeepers, and traders manned the bustling port that linked the city to the sea. Shipbuilders, canners, refiners, truckers, railroad men, and steel workers established the city as a manufacturing center. Generations of clerks, secretaries, lawyers, and bureaucrats have been added with its growth as a metropolitan service center and secondary location for federal government offices. All these citizens have given Baltimore a character that its people share by way of crab feasts, painted door and window screens, club basements, Pimlico races, neighborhood festivals, and Oriole baseball games. Neither phony nor sophisticated, Baltimore graces the Patapsco like a brawny sailor: friendly, likable, sunburned, full of prejudices, ready for the sudden squalls that surge along the Chesapeake.

Founding

The future site of Baltimore stood on the imaginary fall line along the East Coast, where Piedmont plateau meets coastal plain and falling water provides the easiest source of mechanical energy. Capt. John Smith first noticed this location during his 1608 expedition up the Chesapeake Bay; he mistakenly believed the area uninhabited and named the river he found here, presumably the Patapsco, the "Bolus," after the red mineral clay along its banks. When Baltimore County was laid out in 1659, meadows and marshes surrounded the inner harbor, where an unruly creek, later named Jones Falls, emptied from the north into a broad cove, later named the Northwest Branch of the Patapsco River. Another creek (Gwynn's Falls) flowed into the Middle Branch, while the Patapsco itself formed a wide basin connecting the two branches and flowed 14 miles southeast to the bay. A low peninsula named Whetstone Neck lay between the river's two tributaries, which provided sheltered harborage and a constant flow of fresh water, which would rid ocean-going wooden ships of boring shipworms. Urban development has altered and tamed much of this original terrain, but the rough outlines remain the same. Travelers still ascend northward from the harbor; the land still slopes sharply on either side of the Jones Falls; and the harbor still attracts ocean-going vessels.

David Jones, who gave the Jones Falls its name, surveyed land on its east bank in June 1661 and there established a homestead that grew into the village of Jones Town (later Old Town). In 1696 Charles Carroll the Settler (grandfather of the famous Catholic signer of the Declaration of Independence) and his brother Daniel resurveyed and patented 1,000 acres on the west bank of Jones Falls, including part of an earlier patent called Cole's Harbor. By 1726 a gristmill owned by Edward Fell operated on the east bank near the present intersection of Hillen St. and Fallsway, forming the nucleus of a small settlement composed of three dwellings, a store, and some tobacco warehouses—Fells Point.

Local tobacco growers, anxious to develop a nearby port and customs house, joined the Carrolls in petitioning the Maryland assembly for a town on Carroll land north of the Patapsco River. The bill to establish "Baltimore Town" passed, and Gov. Benedict Leonard Calvert signed it August 8, 1729. (*Baltimore,* the name of the small Irish land grant from which the Calverts took their title, apparently derives from a Celtic word,

Beal-t-more, meaning "great place" or "circle" of the sun god "Beal" or "Baal.") Seven commissioners met in 1730 to select and lay out an irregular, 60-acre site shaped roughly like an arrowhead pointing west.

Colonial Growth

The founders may have hoped that the two major north-south street names, taken from Charles Calvert, fifth Lord Baltimore (1699–1751), would enhance the town's potential for growth in Baltimore County, which then included most of northern Maryland east of the Susquehanna River. At first slow to develop, Baltimore eventually prospered, because of a combination of geography and the industriousness of maritime traders who vigorously pursued their economic interests. When in 1750 Dr. John Stevenson (1718–85), a surgeon from Ireland, successfully sent a consignment of flour back to Ireland, he opened the eyes of planters, who quickly saw the commercial connections between wheat, water-powered mills, flour, and foreign markets.

As a flour port, Baltimore grew rapidly. A retaining wall was built to prevent further silting into the harbor, and by 1752 Baltimore had 25 houses, two taverns, one church, and about 200 people. French-speaking Acadians, deported by the British from Canada and Nova Scotia, arrived in 1755, adding their numbers to the English, Irish, Scots, Germans, and Africans who already lived here.

In 1756 a Baltimore ship sailed for the British West Indies with a mixed cargo of flour from the Jones Falls and Patapsco mills, corn, beans, hams, bread, iron, barrel staves, peas, and tobacco. It returned with sugar, rum, and slaves, thus creating a commerce that lasted for a century. As German and other European immigrant farmers filled the Piedmont valleys, Baltimore traders traveled through the hinterlands, dealing for the wheat crops. The grain shipped through Baltimore, stimulating the growth of flour mills and such related industries as timber for barrel staves and iron for barrel hoops.

Breaking Free of Britain

Baltimore's rise as an exporter of staples and importer of molasses from French and Spanish possessions in the New World ran directly counter to Great Britain's mercantile policies for its colonies. The city soon found itself allied with major colonial ports against the various taxes and duties periodically imposed by George III and his parliaments. In 1765, Baltimoreans hanged in effigy the man who had been appointed stamp distributor for Maryland, and they later passed a resolution not to trade with Rhode Island, when that colony violated the intercolonial non-importation agreement. In 1774 a Committee of Correspondence passed resolutions recommending that all trade with Great Britain and the West Indies cease, even though the West Indian trade represented the port's most profitable traffic.

A company of militia, the Baltimore Independent Cadets, formed in December 1774, "impress'd with a sense of the unhappy (state) of our Suffering Brethren in Boston." Seven companies were drilling in Baltimore by the time, six months later, when news of Lexington and Concord reached the town. Hundreds of Baltimoreans volunteered, and many fought with distinction during the war. One of them, Mordecai Gist, joined the famed Maryland Battalion, under the command of Gen.

William F. Smallwood, and led it during its gallant rear-guard action at the Battle of Long Island in 1776; as a brigadier general, Gist five years later commanded Marylanders at the Battle of Yorktown and the surrender of Cornwallis. Gen. Samuel Smith, wounded at the Battle of White Plains in 1776, heroically defended Fort Mifflin in the Delaware River in 1777. He received special commendation from Congress. John Eager Howard served with other Maryland troops who distinguished themselves in the southern-campaign battles of Cowpens, Eutaw, Camden, and Guilford Court House (all of which produced Baltimore street names) in 1781.

Other Baltimoreans—merchants—made money during the Revolution while pulling the tail of the British lion on the high seas. Baltimore, no stranger to the sailors of the fledgling U.S. Navy (its first two cruisers, *Hornet* and *Wasp*, were fitted out in Baltimore in 1775), became a haven for the risky but profitable business of privateering. (Carrying government-issued licenses, or letters of marque and reprisal, private vessels could attempt to seize—and then profit from the sale of—enemy shipping.) Between April 1, 1777, and March 14, 1783, a total of 248 vessels, most owned by Baltimoreans, sailed from the city to capture British merchant vessels. Well prepared after years of evading various embargoes and blockades, Baltimoreans built fast schooners (the classic "Baltimore Clipper" schooner featured two raked, or backward-tilting, masts, low freeboard, and lofty sails). Baltimore raiders captured, burned, or sank ships and cargoes with an estimated value of a million pounds. Even fellow patriots looked askance at the boomtown. When the Continental Congress met in Baltimore from December 1776 to February 1777, John Adams wrote that "the object of men of property here, the planters &c., is universally wealth. Every way in the world is sought to get and save money." "If you desire to keep out of the damnedest hole on earth," said a Virginia delegate, "come not here."

Nest of Pirates, Monumental City

Whatever its odor, Baltimore thrived during and after the Revolution. From a population of 6,700 in 1776, the city by 1790 had increased to 13,503, including 1,255 slaves and 323 free African Americans. The federal census of 1800 revealed another doubling in population; the city had grown to 45,000 persons by 1810. Conestoga wagons became the land equivalent of the Baltimore Clipper, constantly flowing in and out of the port, following the increasing number of turnpikes spreading out like fingers from Baltimore into the hinterlands. Freed from British restrictions, Baltimore's merchants exploited European and West Indian markets from the outbreak of the French Revolution to the close of the Napoleonic Wars. Grain flowed in from the west and north, tobacco from the south, all of it to be loaded onto ships that returned with sugar, molasses, coffee, and fruit, much of it later exported to Europe in exchange for manufactured goods. By the turn of the 19th century, the port had its first sugar refinery, a glass factory, brickworks, a handful of public markets, 10 insurance companies, and at least three banks. In its 1796–97 session, the Maryland assembly passed an act elevating Baltimore Town to an incorporated city. A mayor and city council took office in 1797.

Hostility against the British lingered. The master of a vessel landing in Baltimore in 1808 had paid duty in an English port. Citizens destroyed his cargo of barreled gin. In the summer of 1812, a mob attacked the office of a partisan newspaper vocal in opposing the Madison administration and the declaration of war against Britain. In the ensuing riot, both sides sustained injuries and even deaths. One staunch Federalist, revolutionary veteran Gen. "Light-Horse Harry" Lee (father of Robert E. Lee), was crippled for life. The *New Bedford Mercury* referred to Baltimore as "that sink of corruption, that `Sodom' of our country."

Baltimore privateers again plied the seas in search of plunder. The first 10 letters of marque the government issued in June 1812 went to Baltimore ship owners, and within four months, 42 privateers, carrying 330 guns and about 3,000 men, had put out from the city. Capt. Thomas Boyle, master of the privateers *Comet* and then the *Chasseur,* preyed on enemy shipping near the British coast and in August 1814 sent a written message to London, in which he proclaimed the coasts of the United Kingdom of Great Britain and Ireland "in a state of strict and rigorous blockade." Not surprisingly, the British spoke of Baltimore as "a nest of pirates," "the great depository of the hostile spirit of the United States against England." London papers called for the taming of its "truculent" citizenry.

In the summer of 1814, a British force of 24 vessels and about 5,000 veteran troops under the command of Vice Adm. Sir Alexander Cochrane entered Chesapeake Bay. After routing a disorganized American militia force near Bladensburg, Cochrane's men burned Washington and turned their attention to Baltimore. City fathers appointed Samuel Smith, former general and then U.S. senator, commander in chief of the forces assembled to defend Baltimore. Smith correctly predicted the British plan of attack. Little federal help being available and big guns being scarce, the locals repaired Fort McHenry and borrowed guns from an abandoned French frigate. The defenders built furnaces to make the 42-pound balls and stationed 40 pieces of artillery on elevated ground east of the city. Few able-bodied men escaped military duty.

The highly confident British land and sea force arrived on Baltimore's Chesapeake doorstep Sunday, September 11, 1814. When the alarm guns sounded, more than 16,000 citizen soldiers hurried to their posts. During the early morning hours of September 12, 4,700 British troops and marines, veterans of the war against Napoleon, landed on the North Point peninsula and marched toward the city from the southeast. About halfway up the peninsula, at its narrowest point, the redcoats faced a force of militiamen determined at least to slow their advance and inflict punishment. In this they succeeded, by happenstance killing the troop commander, Gen. Robert Ross, before falling back to the strongpoint at Hampstead Hill. There (now the site of Patterson Park) the British at the end of the day faced double their number, miltiamen gathered where they felt most comfortable—behind earthworks. Drenched by cold rain, the British during the night decided against a frontal attack and withdrew. Meanwhile, the British fleet stood beyond range of the guns at Fort McHenry and fired at it more than 1,500 bombs and 700 rockets.

Francis Scott Key, detained by the British while on a mission to obtain a prisoner's release, anxiously stood on deck during the bombardment and, at dawn's early light, saw that the fort's over-sized flag still waved. The fort had held, and within a few days the British force retreated down the Chesapeake. Baltimoreans celebrated, congratulated themselves, and sang Key's published poem, "The Star-Spangled Banner," to the tune—a bit ironically, or suitably—of an old English drinking song.

The Committee of Vigilance and Safety disbanded in March 1815 but called on citizens to erect a memorial to the defenders who died in the Battle of Baltimore. Work on Battle Monument began later that year, when the city council authorized Rembrandt Peale to paint portraits of the city's military heroes. On July 4 citizens gathered for the laying of the cornerstone of a towering monument to George Washington. It would stand on land General Howard had donated for the purpose—a hill overlooking the city and harbor. No other American city had yet erected such impressive memorials to revolutionary and military heroes, so, when President John Quincy Adams visited to attend a public dinner in 1827, he raised his glass and proposed a toast "To Baltimore, the Monumental City." The tribute became popular coinage, and the city's official seal proudly bears the image of Battle Monument.

Regional Hub, Eastern Terminus

On July 4, 1828, Charles Carroll of Carrollton—then 91 years old and the last surviving signer of the Declaration of Independence—took part in ceremonies that launched the Baltimore and Ohio Railroad. During his lifetime, Baltimore had risen from an insignificant tobacco port to a city of 80,000 people, making it the second-largest city in the world's newest and largest republic. Though it continued to grow, Baltimore had peaked in terms of most national indexes, and the geographic and population center of the nation was moving steadily westward. Baltimore's South American and Caribbean trade remained strong, but after 1815 the city lost ground to New York as an Atlantic-rim seaport. Baltimore thrived as a regional exchange center. It retained its inland markets and built western ones, by means of the enormously successful B&O, which, along with turnpikes and coastwise shipping, fostered manufacturing, encouraged wholesaling, and created steady demands for labor, skilled and unskilled alike. The percolating economy also rewarded banking, although after disestablishment of the federally chartered national bank in 1832–33, speculative tendencies among local banks and other currency-issuing institutions worsened dangerously. The collapse of Baltimore's Bank of Maryland in 1835 drove ruined and angry investors into the streets and into the homes of the bank directors, whose belongings they heaped in piles outside and set afire.

Politically and morally, Baltimore clung to middle ground. A slaveholding city, it nevertheless had the largest free black population in the country; it also relied, in northern fashion, on interstate transportation, factories, and commerce. Baltimore sent mostly moderates to Congress. Because it stood on the border between north and south, it supplied the site of a series of national party conventions. In 1831–32—during the first presidential election in which opposing party delegates met, published platforms, and made a carnival of their business—all three parties (Antimasonic, National Republican, and Democratic) met in Baltimore. The Democrats did so again in 1836, 1840, 1844 (when the proceedings were reported by telegraph along the B&O line to Washington), 1848 (when the slavery issue surfaced), and 1852; the Whigs met there in 1840, 1852, and 1856 (when the party threw its weakening support behind the anti-foreign, nostalgic Know-Nothing Party and warned against sectional animosity).

In the late 1850s, Baltimore on a local level exemplified the severity of American tensions. Still divided white and black, slave and free (the number of slaves had dropped precipitously), the city continued to grow in population. Many of the newcomers—12,000 in 1846 alone, more after the European upheavals of 1848—were foreign born (mainly German). The police force consisted of only one uniformed constable per ward by day and a night watchman by night. The volunteer fire companies amounted to rival gangs that sometimes set fires to entrap and attack one another. They evolved into political clubs with fearful names like Rips Raps, Plug Uglies, and Blood Tubs (who dumped slaughterhouse offal on incorrect voters).

The viciousness of street politics grew legendary. The Know-Nothings hardly invented electoral violence or fraud in Baltimore. Voters at the time could not easily hide which party-produced ballots they dropped into the box. Election-day assaults were commonplace. For years party thugs "cooped" or ganged voters and forced them to vote repeatedly along party lines; Edgar Allan Poe, who had struggled to make a living in Baltimore from 1831 to 1835 and received a prize there for his "MS. Found in a Bottle," died in Baltimore in 1849, possibly while being "cooped." But the Know-Nothing ascendancy in city politics in the 1850s owed much to voter intimidation and incited more of the same from the Democratic side. Newspapers in Baltimore and elsewhere decried the situation. In 1859 the "rowdyism," smashed ballot boxes, and pistol shots of a typical Baltimore primary election provided fodder for the derisive London *Illustrated News*. Baltimore continued to earn the title "Mobtown."

By 1860, with an ethnically diverse population of about 200,000 and as the country's third-largest city, Baltimore reflected all the divisions and ambiguities that eventually divided the country and brought on war. Having adjourned their Charleston, South Carolina, national convention in disarray, a faction of Democrats reconvened in Baltimore to nominate Stephen A. Douglas, and then they split again. In that crucial election, Baltimore voted a bit misleadingly. German Republicans gave Lincoln a few votes. Moderates chose Douglas or the pro-peace Constitutional Union ticket (this party also had held its 1860 nominating convention in Baltimore). Baltimore's plurality went to the radical Southern-rights Democratic candidate for president, in large part because his supporters aligned him with the local contest against nativist violence and in favor of electoral reform.

"The Warsaw of the United States"

Baltimoreans debated secession, but in the spring of 1861—to paraphrase President Lincoln—they did not control events, events controlled them. Baltimore lay astride the cortex of rail and telegraph lines necessary to maintain Washington as the capital of the federal union. After the fall of Fort Sumter in Charleston harbor on April 13, Lincoln called for troops to suppress the rebellion, and they came down the Philadelphia, Wilmington and Baltimore Railroad. Two days after the secession of Virginia, an early contingent arrived in Baltimore at President Street Station and began moving by foot and horsecar to the B&O's Camden Street Station (now famous for forming part of the Orioles' ballpark). There the men would climb aboard cars for Washington.

A mob of Southern sympathizers set upon them, however; shots rang out, and there, on Pratt St., Americans shed the first blood of the war.

Four soldiers of the 6th Massachusetts and 11 citizens died, and many more were injured. To prevent further unrest—and to the dismay of federal officials—city fathers ordered the destruction of railroad bridges to the north of Baltimore. As a temporary measure, Lincoln agreed to route reinforcements to Washington by water instead of by rail. Steamboats unloaded at Annapolis. Under cover of a severe thunderstorm, some of these troops marched into Baltimore the night of May 13 and occupied Federal Hill. For the following four years, the city lay under martial law. A ring of Federal forts encircled Baltimore, but this time, unlike in 1814, their guns were aimed inward, toward a city that was contributing fighting men to both sides. Visiting Baltimore early in the war, William Howard Russell of the London *Times* described the divided, sullen city as resembling nothing so much as Warsaw, the Polish capital that the Russians had occupied since 1813. (While he correctly judged the depth of divisions within Baltimore, he vastly underestimated the Unionism of the city's manufacturers, workingmen, and shopkeepers.)

James Ryder Randall, a Baltimorean teaching in New Orleans, expressed his solidarity with his fellow citizens and tried to rouse them to the Southern cause by writing a hearty poem, "Maryland, My Maryland." Put to the German melody of "Lauriger Horatius" (also "O, Tannenbaum"), it urged Marylanders to "avenge the patriotic gore / That flecked the streets of Baltimore"; the poem referred to the Federal Hill garrison and other men in blue as "Northern scum." (In 1939, over some objections, "Maryland, My Maryland" became the official state song.)

Despite provost-marshal's supervision and the disruption of normal commerce with the South, Baltimore became an important depot during the war, and many firms profited from the traffic in military supplies. The B&O Railroad played a major role in the movement of Union troops and supplies; its crews and repair shops worked overtime throughout the conflict. Though never an object of a campaign, citizens braced for possible attack during Gen. Robert E. Lee's invasion of Maryland in September 1862 and of Pennsylvania in 1863; in July 1864, Gen. Jubal Early's Confederate raid gave the divided citizenry another rush of either hope or terror. As part of the expedition, Harry Gilmor's Confederate Maryland cavalry came as close to Baltimore as any "enemy" did during the war. Gilmor, who had grown up near Towson, north of the city, rode south toward the city's northern limits after destroying Unionist governor Bradford's home in southern Baltimore County.

When the war ended the following April, Baltimore stood in an excellent position to aid the defeated states, and it did so in the years of Reconstruction. Baltimore banks invested in Southern transportation, industry, and agriculture; businesses extended credit to erstwhile customers. Members of Southern families arrived in Baltimore, hoping to recoup fortunes, resume professions, and create new lives. Freed slave families also came to the city; they sought jobs, looked for lost relatives, hoped for a better life in freedom.

Queen City of the Patapsco

In 1870 the population of Baltimore stood at 267,354, still much larger than Washington's (109,199), despite that Washington had been growing three times faster. During the 1870s, industry and business continued to thrive in Baltimore. Exports of Western Maryland coal led to improved port and railroad facilities. The Baltimore coffee trade recovered. West Indian pineapples and bananas rose suddenly in demand. Steamboat lines helped to maintain Baltimore's role as a regional trading hub. A visitor to the harbor might have noticed that steam gradually was replacing sail in ocean-going and even coastal shipping, though sail was still important among Chesapeake workboats; the Baltimore Clipper evolved into the rugged pungy. Isaac Myers, an African American who had been born free and had attended school in Baltimore, succeeded in establishing a cooperative black shipbuilding company at the foot of Federal Hill. He hoped to organize a national black labor union. The government offered no protections to unions, and laboring men and women at the time struggled for fairness; Baltimoreans did not share prosperity equally. In 1873 a depression produced wage cuts at the B&O, and four years later railroad workers mounted a violent strike, one that returned armed troops to Baltimore streets, led to serious casualties, and left no doubt of the city's industrial cast.

Clothing, grain, lumber, chemical fertilizer, and iron and steel became increasingly important Baltimore products in the last years of the 19th century. With the rise of the western wheat belt, Baltimore's rank among flour milling cities declined, but its vegetable- and oyster-canning houses hummed with activity. By 1880 Baltimore was the chief oyster packing center in the world. This prosperity had noteworthy social consequences; canning in general relied on the cheap labor of women, children, and new immigrants. Baltimore industry grew southward and eastward, following the waterfront and railroad lines. Southwest Baltimore, Canton, Locust Point, and Curtis Bay joined the Jones Falls valley as industrial sites. The bonding, banking, accounting, and legal professions also grew, in service to the expanding business community. Proud of being a "city of firsts," Baltimore claimed the first Linotype machine (Ottmar Mergenthaler, a German immigrant, invented it) in 1884. The following year, a local company began the first commercial electric streetcar line in the United States.

In 1888 Baltimore succeeded in expanding the city limits to incorporate areas east, north, and west of the existing boundaries—an area that contemporaries called "the Belt."

Extraordinary philanthropy accounted for the emergence of several highly important institutions in Victorian Baltimore. Earlier, the arts had lagged behind the civic impulse to make money. When Ralph Waldo Emerson visited the city in 1837, he wrote his wife that "Charles Carroll the Signer is dead and Archbishop Carroll is dead, and there is no vision in the land." When he returned in 1872 to give a series of lectures at the new Peabody Institute, the visionary landscape had improved, and it continued to improve to the point that Baltimore became the site of some of the most important cultural institutions of modern America. George Peabody (1795–1869), Emerson's fellow New Englander and earlier a Baltimore businessman, gave the city an institute that originally included a library, museum, and conservatory of music. The war delayed its completion, but after 1867 the conservatory, collections, and library all flourished. In 1878 the library moved into the magnificent skylighted home that it still occupies, one of the handsomest interiors in the city. When the Anne Arundel County native Johns Hopkins (1795–1873) died, the city learned that he had chosen to follow Peabody's example. Hopkins left an endowment for a university and hospital to bear his name. Adhering to his will, trustees opened the earliest purely research university in the United States in 1876, a hospital—revolutionary in its design—in East Baltimore in 1889, and then in 1893 a school of medicine, the first to require a baccalaureate degree and to admit women. Massachusetts-born Enoch Pratt (1809–97) contributed his fortune to establish the first truly free public library in the country. Its 28,000 volumes became available to borrowers in early 1886; branches in every part of the city encouraged all classes and ethnic groups to read and educate themselves. Meantime, a wealthy father and son who combined the disparate interests of railroading and art collecting, William T. and Henry Walters, amassed one of the premier art collections in private American hands. The elder Walters expanded his home on Mt. Vernon Place to house his magnificent collection, which he periodically opened for public viewing (and later donated to the city). Henry built public baths for Baltimore's poorest citizens.

Baltimore's version of the Great Chicago Fire broke out on the windy Sunday morning of February 7, 1904, when a warehouse fire at the corner of Liberty and Redwood Sts. flared and quickly burned out of control. All Baltimore fire companies came to the scene; others arrived from as far away as New York City and Richmond. Nothing worked to slow the flames, not even the deliberate destruction of buildings in their path. On Monday, when the wind shifted to the southeast and fire halted at the Jones Falls, 1,343 buildings in an area of almost 140 acres had been destroyed. Baltimore's original downtown lay in smoldering ruins. Estimates of damage ranged between $125–150 million. Remarkably, no loss of life occurred. The city nonetheless faced an enormous rebuilding task. The mayor committed suicide. His successor appointed a Burnt District Commission to oversee relief and reconstruction. As part of the reconstruction, critical streets were widened, straightened, and regraded.

Eventually, about 800 buildings worth $25 million replaced 1,400 destroyed structures that had been assessed at $13 million. "Physically," the urban geographer Sherry Olsen has observed, "the city was rebuilt much as it was before."

Arsenal on the Chesapeake

Baltimore after 1900 continued to grow as an exporter of manufactured goods, even as its traditional agricultural exports declined. Raw materials like petroleum and ores entered the city for refining and processing. Inland from the sea, though not far from open water, Baltimore always offered advantages in wartime; the city's heavy industry, shipbuilding, and transportation links to the interior especially recommended themselves in modern war. In 1917, when the United States entered the three-year-old general conflict in Europe, Baltimore shipbuilders moved into full-scale production of metal vessels. The city churned out steel and chemicals, grains, and military apparel. Between 1910 and 1920, the city's population-growth rate tripled over that of the preceding decade; among American manufacturing cities, Baltimore rose from 11th in 1914 to 7th in 1919.

Baltimoreans in uniform shipped to France, as part of the army's new 29th (Blue-Gray) Division of national guardsmen from both sides of the Mason-Dixon line. At the beginning of the 1918 Meuse-Argonne offensive, the 313th Infantry, "Baltimore's Own," turned the tide in the battle for the height of Montfaucon. At home, Baltimoreans planted vegetable gardens, sang patriotic songs, and fell under pressure to hate "the Hun." Members of the city's strong German American community felt uneasy. German St. became Redwood St., renamed to commemorate an officer who lost his life in combat. Baltimore's German-language newspaper ceased publication. H. L. Mencken, fiercely proud of his German heritage, stopped writing his weekly *Evening Sun* column and stayed out of the limelight.

In 1918 Baltimore again annexed adjoining territory, most of it to the east (Highlandtown and environs) and along the southeastern and southwestern waterfronts (thus for the first time expanding at the expense of Anne Arundel County).

During the 1920s, Baltimore continued to prosper. After 1922 a large sugar refinery gave the harbor a distinctive building and, at night, a colorful sign. Other industries ebbed and flowed. Prohibition (1920–33) placed only a slight damper on the city's traditional tolerance for entertainment, because Maryland's Baltimore-bred governor refused to pass state laws to help enforce the federal Volstead Act. Baltimore may have been the wettest big city in the Union. When the stock market crashed in 1929 and Depression set in, Baltimore's varied industrial base saved it from the degree of suffering that befell other American cities. Trade with South America remained strong. Baltimore had the good fortune to produce the straw hats that were all the rage among middle-class men in the day. Glenn L. Martin's decision in 1929 to move his aircraft-building plant to eastern Baltimore County shored up the metropolitan economy, particularly when France and Great Britain began to place large aircraft orders in the late 1930s.

A working city, Baltimore in these years grew only one-fourth as quickly as the District of Columbia, which burgeoned with people who

Pratt and Light Sts., looking south, 1930s

arrived to fill New Deal offices and staff new federal programs. By 1940, Washington boasted 633,091 residents, Baltimore 859,100.

World War II revitalized Baltimore industry, particularly in steel, ship-building, and machinery. Hundreds of aircraft and Liberty ships were turned out during the war. Munitions and chemical manufacturing resumed on an even larger scale than they had reached during World War I. Military bases soon ringed the city, providing new avenues for employment. War workers, including many women, thronged to the factories, jammed public transportation, and stimulated demands for public housing. Baltimoreans once more went to France, many of them again as soldiers in the 29th Division, the only National Guard division to wade ashore at Omaha Beach on D-Day, June 6, 1944.

When they and their comrades returned home in 1945, looking for work and a place to live, they set in motion a train of events that ensured that cities like Baltimore would never be the same.

Mother of Suburbanites

After the war and a period of economic and domestic adjustment, Baltimore families increasingly succumbed to the lure of the suburbs. The metropolitan region continued to grow, but as a city, Baltimore (as well as Washington after 1960) experienced negative growth rates. A trend began, which continues still, of the leading transportation, financial, communications, and manufacturing institutions of earlier Baltimore becoming branches of larger corporations based elsewhere (Baltimoreans long have fretted over their "branch-office" status). In 1986, the A. S. Abell Company, owner of the venerable Sunpapers, sold out to the Times-Mirror Company, based in Los Angeles, and the next year the B&O Railroad lost its identity within the CSX Transportation System. Maryland National Bank became part of Sovran (later NationsBank) in 1993; four years later, Alex. Brown and Sons, the nation's oldest brokerage house and a Baltimore institution since 1808, merged with Bankers Trust New York Corp.

Baltimore's political and business leaders responded to the suburban challenge by downtown redevelopment projects that surprised observers, first because they were so ambitious and then because they appeared to be so successful. In 1954 a group of merchants who included J. Jefferson Miller organized the Committee for Downtown, which raised money for a downtown master plan. A year later, chief executives of the largest metropolitan corporations, utility companies, and law firms formed the Greater Baltimore Committee. The GBC set out to rescue the center of the city from its postwar decline, address problems of dilapidated housing, and seek solutions to transportation problems. Eventually Miller's group and the GBC joined forces. They found political allies in Theodore H. McKeldin—the Republican governor and a former (and future) Baltimore mayor—and in the incumbent Democratic mayor Thomas A. D'Alesandro Jr. Hiring architects and planners, the consortium developed plans for a signal urban renewal project, Charles Center, which eventually demolished 251 properties and replaced them with almost $130 million of new downtown construction. An inner harbor redevelopment plan followed in the late 1960s and early 1970s, when William Donald Schaefer served as a nationally prominent and highly flamboyant mayor. Civic leaders who helped shape plans for renewing the downtown included James W. Rouse, a builder of enclosed shopping malls and the planned community at Columbia, Maryland, and the businessman and former school board chair Walter Sondheim.

International visitors from harbor cities around the world have come to Baltimore to study the public-private financial arrangements that made such revitalization possible. Critics nonetheless pointed to this "renaissance" as a deceptively bright spot in a large tapestry of typical American inner-city problems that include increasing poverty and urban decay. The decade of the 1980s, with its decreasing federal support for cities, was not kind to Baltimore. Kurt Schmoke, who became the city's first elected African American mayor in 1988, has continued vigorously to support downtown development.

Throughout the city's long history, the port on the Patapsco has been the abiding factor in its prosperity. Baltimore's port now ranks number one nationally in automobile and truck exports. The highly automated Seagirt Terminal ships containers around the world, and the Canton facility handles 1 million tons of dry bulk cargo a year. Appalachian coal moves in a steady stream. Connected now via computer to other international ports, Baltimore has become an "inter-modal" center where ships, trucks, and railroads create complex transportation webs throughout North America and around the globe. Amid this constant motion, Baltimoreans keep trading, playing, making money, and hoping for the best.

Baltimore's relatively low-rise, high-density cityscape offers the pedestrian opportunities to explore much of the city's downtown within an hour's walking radius. Planners of the Charles Center and Inner Harbor developments considered the walker, so pedestrian bridges, plazas, and promenades offer some relief from vehicular traffic.

Numerous garages along Baltimore and Pratt Sts. offer normally ample downtown parking; parking is also available at some piers east of the inner harbor basin and at metered lots near the Convention Center and Oriole Park at Camden Yards. The downtown area experiences morning and afternoon rush hours, when traffic slows, but they are milder than similar periods in Washington, Philadelphia, and New York. As of 1996, a subway system, called the Metro, connects Owings Mills and the Johns Hopkins Hospital, with a central station at Charles Center. A light rail system from Timonium to Camden Yards opened in 1992 and reached Glen Burnie by 1993. Further extensions include lines to BWI Airport, Penn Station in Baltimore, and Hunt Valley. These rail systems, combined with regular bus lines, provide an increasingly efficient way to move around the city. Routes and schedules are available from the Mass Transit Administration, a state agency, and at a few public venues, like the central branch of the Pratt library. Planners envision a 21st-century rail transit system that eventually will link the Baltimore and Washington subway networks.

The walking tours described below presume that the visitor has found downtown parking or taken public transportation to the Inner Harbor, which remains the city's chief tourist focal point. City streets are well marked. In the past 10 years, specialized guidebooks and tours have emerged that will direct the traveler to information not included below. For example, Frank Shivers' *Walking in Baltimore, An Intimate Guide to the Old City* (Johns Hopkins University Press, 1995) offers distinctive pedestrian maps and descriptions.

The following five walking tours, beginning at the Inner Harbor, give the visitor a sense of Baltimore's history and character. Additional tours carry one to outlying neighborhoods and other attractions. Headnotes outline the availability of public transportation.

A. EAST FROM THE INNER HARBOR TO LITTLE ITALY AND OLD TOWN

The structures that had accumulated along the northern edge of what is now called the **Inner Harbor** (labeled "Bason" on an 1801 map) disappeared in the Great Fire of 1904. None of the prerevolutionary town remains, and only one 18th-century building still stands in the entire downtown area. Marsh and water once covered the sections of Pratt and Light Sts. that border the current Inner Harbor.

Pratt St., which by 1780 ran west of the Basin, was named in honor of Charles Pratt, first Earl of Camden, an English statesman who supported the American cause during the Revolution. In the early part of the 19th century, commercial shipping still dominated this inner harbor area, ranging from ocean-going ships to schooners bearing watermelons and oysters from the Eastern Shore. Before World War II, bay craft of all kinds

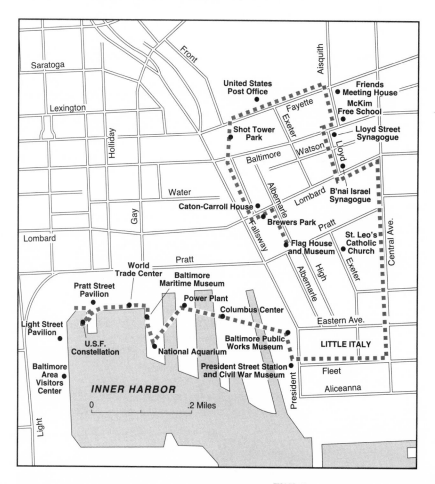

brought fish and produce to supply downtown markets, and occasionally freighters docked at one of the narrow slips. The regular steamboat service that for more than a hundred years linked Baltimore to many bay and river towns on the Chesapeake ended in 1960. By the early 1960s, before the inner harbor development project was launched, cargo docking had moved to other parts of the harbor, and the basin had become dingy and rat-infested, an embarrassment to the city and a symbol of urban decay. Eventually the impetus of the successful Charles Center project spread to the inner harbor. Bond issues and federal money enabled the city to buy and clear land around the water. The *Constellation* arrived at Pier 1 in 1969, and the Maryland Science Center opened in 1976.

By 1980, when **Harborplace** opened to the public, the basin had been transformed. This Rouse Company project, which in 1978 passed a public referendum by a majority of only 54 percent, cost $18 million and was stimulated by the vision of James Rouse and municipal leaders. Benjamin Thompson and Associates, architects from Cambridge, Massachusetts, created two low glassy pavilions for the three-acre site. The **Pratt Street Pavilion** contains a few restaurants but mostly retail shops, while the **Light Street Pavilion** houses many small shops but focuses on food. In all, 12 restaurants and cafés are sprinkled throughout the pavilions, including high-volume eateries at the ends of the buildings. More than 100 merchants and their 2,000 employees earn income here, supported by about 250 employees who maintain the 234,000-square-foot complex. Harborplace continues to draw visitors, more than half from the immediate five-county region, and has become one of the attractions to which city dwellers take their out-of-town guests.

A walk along the harbor past the Light Street Pavilion at Harborplace takes one to the **Baltimore Area Visitors Center,** which dispenses useful maps, brochures, and schedules.

Between the two Harborplace pavilions is the berth of the **USF Constellation,** a monument to the first frigate of the U.S. Navy and reputedly the oldest ship in the world continuously afloat. Josiah Humphrey, a Philadelphia Quaker, designed the ship; but David Stodder, a local shipwright, substantially altered the vessel for speed. The warship was

Light Street Pavilion of Harborplace, 1997

launched from Harris Creek in 1797, the same year Baltimore became an incorporated city. In 1799, the *Constellation* captured the *L'Insurgente,* the first prize ship won by a U.S. vessel. In subsequent years, the frigate fought Barbary pirates, engaged the British during the War of 1812, and served on the Union side during the Civil War. President Roosevelt commissioned her as flagship of the Atlantic fleet during World War II, when she was moored at Newport, Rhode Island.

In 1852–53 the navy lengthened *Constellation* by 12 feet and redesigned her as a sloop of war, leading to subsequent doubts that she remains an artifact of the 18th century (the navy may have intended to rebuild the old ship secretly, at a time when Congress prohibited new construction of naval craft). Whatever the ship's pedigree, in 1955 a volunteer committee of sailing enthusiasts moved the ship to Baltimore from Newport, restored it, and operated it as a floating museum of early naval warfare. In 1996, the ship left its Inner Harbor berth for much-needed repairs, and marine historians soon determined without doubt that the ship as we know it dates from the 1850s. For further information, call 410-539-1797.

The **World Trade Center,** designed by I. M. Pei and home of the Maryland Port Administration, stands tall just beyond the Pratt Street Pavilion. When it opened in 1977, the building won attention as the highest (423 feet) pentagonal structure in the world. **The Top of the World Observation Level and Museum** on the 27th floor offers panoramic views of the entire harbor area. For information, call 410-837-4515.

Continue east to Pier 3 and the first of several structures that attract millions of visitors each year.

The National Aquarium in Baltimore

Owned by the city and operated by a nonprofit organization, the National Aquarium (111 Market Place) opened in 1981. It quickly became a premier attraction, one of the highlights of a visit to Baltimore. Outside, a 70,000-gallon seal pool provides a home for a collection of playful harbor and gray seals.

The **original building,** a striking tetrahedron topped with glassed pyramidal structures, houses a series of stunning exhibits. "Wings in the Water" features sea turtles, small sharks, and the largest collection of stingrays in the United States, all of which the visitor views from above. A "North Atlantic to Pacific" gallery takes one from Atlantic sea cliffs to an undersea kelp forest and a brilliantly colored Pacific reef. A deep 335,000-gallon tank contains an Atlantic coral reef. Hundreds of fish swim around as the viewer descends a long, winding ramp deeper and deeper into the sea. An "Open Ocean" tank—ring-shaped and 220,000 gallons in size—houses an impressive assemblage of large sharks and sawfish. The Aquarium also features a gallery demonstrating how marine life adapts to survive in extreme conditions and a four-part exhibit that depicts the various aquatic habitats of Maryland—mountain pond, tidal marsh, coastal shore, and continental shelf. Climbing up into the glass pyramid of the original structure, the visitor explores a tropical jungle filled with colorful birds, poisonous frogs, lush greenery, and vigilant piranhas.

The **Marine Mammal Pavilion** opened in 1990 on the adjacent Pier 4. There bottlenose dolphins prove their grace and agility in daily performances. The amphitheater seats 1,300 persons, some of whom are so close to the action that they often get wet. The "Exploration Station" supplies hands-on, high-tech learning exhibits.

Open July–August: 9 a.m. to 6 p.m. Sunday–Thursday, 9 a.m. to 8 p.m. Friday and Saturday;
March–June and September–October: 9 a.m. to 5 p.m. Saturday–Thursday, 9 a.m. to 8 p.m. Friday;
November–February: 10 a.m. to 5 p.m. Saturday–Thursday, 10 a.m. to 8 p.m. Friday. Closed Thanksgiving Day and Christmas Day.
Admission: $11.95 for adults, $10.50 for seniors, $7.50 for children ages 3 to 11, children under 3
free. Parking on lots east of Pier 5 and on nearby streets.
Gift shop and snack bar in the Pier 4 pavilion. For information call 410-576-3800.

The **Baltimore Maritime Museum** operates three historic vessels,
all of which are available for inspection. The *Torsk*, a World War II submarine, sank the last Japanese combatant ships. The *Chesapeake*, a 133-foot lightship, once marked the entrance to the bay at the Virginia Capes.
These two vessels are moored at Pier 3, next to the main building of the
Aquarium. The *Taney*, a 327-foot Coast Guard cutter, is the last survivor
of the Japanese attack on Pearl Harbor still afloat. Decommissioned in
1986, the cutter lies at anchor off Pier 4, near the Marine Mammal Pavilion. For further information call 410-396-3453.

The city acquired the **Power Plant,** a monolithic, three-part brick
building, from the Baltimore Gas and Electric Company in 1977. Its four
idle stacks, which once belched smoke from coal-powered turbines, still
dominate the eastern skyline of the basin. After several unsuccessful attempts to transform its interior spaces into entertainment centers, an $18
million "Metropolis at the Power Plant" opened in 1997 and includes a
Baltimore version of one of the most successful nostalgia-bar franchises
in the world.

The **University of Maryland at Columbus Center,** a maritime
research laboratory, occupies a site of approximately 11 acres on Piers 5
and 6. Between 1995 and 1997 this attractive modern building housed
the Columbus Center, an ambitious program that combined marine
biotechnology, underwater archaeology, and public education. The University of Maryland aims to pursue largely the same agenda—cutting-edge research in the field of marine science that helps to develop products that will be attractive to private industry and contribute to the
common good. In the summer of 1997, on the Lower Eastern Shore, an
outbreak of *Pfiesteria piscida,* a fish-killing microorganism, underscored
the importance of the university's research at this facility.

A $20 million restaurant-hotel complex is located at the end of Pier
5. The **Seven Foot Knoll Lighthouse,** which once stood at the mouth
of the Patapsco River, stands south of the restaurant.

The open-air, tentlike **Pier 6 Pavilion** serves as the site of the Harborlights Music Festival, a series of summer events, begun in 1981 and featuring concerts of jazz, pop, country, and light classical music. The Jones
Falls empties into the harbor at Pier 6 and forms the basin's natural eastern
boundary. The stream, now covered with concrete, divided the original
Baltimore Town from its older predecessors, Jones Town and Fells Point.

A few steps across Pratt St. on Albemarle St. would lead the pedestrian into Little Italy. Instead, first walk west to President St. and then
south along the Jones Falls, which has emerged at this point from its underground flow beneath the Fallsway. At the southwest corner of the intersection of Eastern Ave. and President St., is a statue of Christopher
Columbus, in a small park dedicated in 1984 by Baltimore's Italian-Amer-

icans. **Scarlett Place,** a huge structure of apartments and commercial enterprises, looms over the park from the north.

The **Eastern Avenue Pumping Station** occupies the southwest corner of the intersection. Completed in 1912, the brick pumping station marked the beginning of Baltimore's modern sewage system. Before the Great Fire of 1904, city residents relied on cesspools and privies; the harbor served as the great drain for animal and vegetable wastes, and it stank in the summertime. Nineteenth-century citizens either visited the outhouse, or, if they were rich, servants carried the household's eliminations from the "dressing room." During the massive reconstruction efforts after the Great Fire of 1904, the Sanitary Commission decided to create separate drains and pipes for sewage and storm water, a more expensive and unusual system for cities but one which prevents overflows at sewage treatment plants. By 1912, the city had laid the pipes and created the Back River Waste Water Treatment Plant on 450 acres near Essex in Baltimore County; at that time it was the largest "trickling filter" treatment facility in the world. About a third of the sewage lines were too low to drain by gravity to Back River, so the Eastern Avenue Pumping Station was created to force the sewage up 72 feet to Bond and Fayette Sts., where it joins the main gravity drain. In 1961, the three great, steam-driven Corliss pumps that accomplished this task were replaced by five turbine pumps, which still handle 72 million gallons a day.

Baltimore's Department of Public Works restored the pumping station in 1980, thus making it eligible for the National Register of Historic Places. In 1982, the **Baltimore Public Works Museum,** a nonprofit group within the department, organized and moved into part of the building. The museum—the first one in the United States dedicated to educating the public about the hidden history of public works—has attracted considerable interest from other cities. Multimedia presentations and graphic displays reveal the street lights, tunnels, bridges, roads, water and sewer systems, and other public works that have contributed to the city's essential amenities since 1730. (Baltimore became the first city lit by gas lights, in 1816.) The museum also honors past engineers and such public servants as Johns Hopkins sanitary engineer Abel Wolman (1892–1989), who pioneered the use of chemicals for chlorinating water, a process begun in Baltimore. An outdoor streetscape displays the pipes and conduits underneath a typical city street. For further information, call 410-727-4806.

President St. continues south to Fleet St., where only the **President Street Station and Civil War Museum** remains in a cleared, 20-acre section of Inner Harbor East under commercial development. The Philadelphia, Wilmington and Baltimore Railroad built this small brick structure with its unusual domed roof between May 1849 and February 18, 1851, when it opened. Frederick Douglass escaped slavery after embarking from this station, and the museum includes artifacts and information on the Underground Railroad. Here troops of the 6th Massachusetts debarked before the riot of April 19, 1861. Many of the Italian immigrants who populated nearby Little Italy arrived at the President Street Station during the 1850s, 1870s, and 1880s. The station continued to serve passengers until the early 20th century; its yards (now gone) remained active with freight cars until about 1980. The renovated headhouse (station without the train shed) reopened as a museum in 1997.

Little Italy

From the President Street Station, walk back to Eastern Ave., which forms the informal southern boundary of Little Italy between President St. on the west and Central Ave. on the east. Walk east on Eastern Ave., from which Albemarle and High Sts. branch north into a neighborhood of restaurants, cafés, grocery stores, and residences redolent with the sights, sounds, and tastes of Genoa, Naples, Sicily, and the province of Abruzzi. Although smaller than it was 50 years ago and threatened by the movement of young families to the suburbs, Little Italy has remained a viable ethnic center, while Baltimore's Little Bohemias, Polands, and Ukraines have largely disappeared.

Turn north on Exeter St. to **St. Leo's Catholic Church,** the heart and spiritual center of Little Italy, consecrated in 1880, at the corner of Exeter and Stiles Sts. A city bench on Exeter next to the church is dedicated to Tommy D'Alesandro Jr. (1903–87), three-term Maryland congressman and mayor of Baltimore (1947–59), who spent his entire life—and based his considerable political support—in Little Italy.

Old Town

Settlers made homes on the east bank of the Jones Falls well before they did in what became Baltimore Town. In 1732 some of them claimed 10 acres along the stream whose name, like that of "Jones Town," recalled an earlier settler, David Jones. Lots were laid along Front St., which even now roughly traces the lines of the original town from Hillen St. on the north to Lombard St. on the south. A bridge across the Jones Falls and its marshes eventually went up where Gay St. now crosses Fallsway. Jones Town merged with Baltimore Town in 1745. "Old Town" thereafter referred to that portion of downtown immediately east of the Jones Falls.

Exeter St. ends at Pratt St. Turn east on Pratt and follow it to Central Ave., a wide, once-busy commercial street. It runs for almost two miles, connecting Harford Rd. to Inner Harbor East. Walk one block north on Central Ave. to Lombard St. and then return west to Lloyd St., once the center of a thriving Jewish community.

The Jewish Museum of Maryland

In this quarter of the city lived immigrants, mostly from Eastern Europe and Russia, who crowded into Baltimore at the turn of the century. A small-scale version of New York's famous Lower East Side, it teemed with Jewish life as late as the early 1960s, when Hasidim walked the streets and merchants sold corned beef and live chickens. A few remnants of that life remain, including the **B'nai Israel Synagogue, the Russisheh Shul,** at the corner of Lloyd and Lombard Sts. Lovingly restored in the mid-1980s, this structure boasts stained-glass windows and a brass gas chandelier. Henry Berge built the synagogue in 1876 for the Chizuk Amuno Congregation, created in 1871 when Jonas Friedenwald and others became upset at the addition of women to the choir and changes in ritual at the Baltimore Hebrew Congregation. Chizuk Amuno sold its synagogue to B'nai Israel in 1895, moved to McCulloh and Mosher Sts., then in 1957 to Stevenson Rd. and the Beltway in Baltimore County. B'nai Israel, founded in 1873 as the second Eastern European congregation and now the oldest Orthodox group continuously functioning in the city, still uses Berge's building.

Walk up Lloyd St. to the low brick building that houses the Jewish Museum of Maryland (15 Lloyd St.; originally the Jewish Historical Society of Maryland). Opened in 1987, the center preserves 150,000 documents, photographs, and other artifacts from Maryland's Jewish heritage.

Farther up Lloyd St., at Watson, one finds the **Lloyd Street Synagogue,** the first synagogue erected in Maryland and the third oldest surviving one in the United States. The Baltimore Hebrew Congregation (organized in 1829), which had first met above a grocery store at Bond and Fleet Sts., commissioned the noted architect Robert Cary Long Jr. to design this building in 1845. Rabbi Abraham Rice (1800–1862), the first ordained rabbi to arrive in America, had come from Bavaria in 1840 to serve Baltimore Hebrew. His strong orthodoxy soon conflicted with American laxness over the sabbath and led to formation, in 1842, of the Har Sinai Congregation, the oldest Reform congregation in continuous existence in the United States. Despite such internal frictions, the Baltimore Hebrew Congregation prospered. It accepted Long's design for a Greek Revival building. Beyond the four heavy Doric columns of the portico, the building's simple interior features fluted columns supporting a gallery that runs along three sides. A railed beam, the platform from which the Torah is read, stands in the middle of the room. Two great crystal chandeliers hang from the ceiling.

The Jewish Heritage Center offers tours of both synagogues and also makes the Lloyd Street Synagogue available for weddings and bar and bat mitzvahs. For further information, call 410-732-6400.

Continue on Lloyd St. to Baltimore St., from which the granite Doric pillars of the **McKim Free School** (1822) become visible immediately to the east. Isaac McKim founded the school to educate poor children. The architects, William Howard and William Small, took inspiration from the facade of the temple of Hephaestus in Athens; the flanks seem modeled after the north wing of the Propylaea on the Acropolis. The single large room has been renovated several times, and the exterior shows wear, but the school stands as a monument to the ideal of free education. After 1829, other public schools in Baltimore used modified versions of the same design.

Walk north on Aisquith St. to Fayette. The **Friends Meeting House,** another monument to free expression, stands just behind the McKim Free School at the southeast corner of Fayette and Aisquith Sts. This plain, two-story brick building (1781) was the first Quaker meeting house built in the city and now ranks as the oldest religious meeting place in Baltimore. In 1819 dissension over rights to the burial ground once located here led to the demotion of the Old Town meeting to a branch of the Lombard Street meeting. Religious observances continued here, however, until 1891, when the building was sold. According to early Quaker custom, many of the graves in the cemetery were unmarked, but 77 simple stones were moved to another Friends graveyard, at 2506 Harford Rd. The city restored the building in 1967 and has created a small park around it. In 1991 city officials and private citizens cooperated again, restoring the building as a community meeting place. In 1996, for the first time in 75 years, local Quakers again met here in a joint worship service with members of the New Covenant Tabernacle Church. From this location, walk west on Fayette St. back toward the Jones Falls to Front St. and what remains of Old Town.

At Fayette St., turn left. The mammoth **United States Post Office** at Front and E. Fayette Sts. dates from 1971 and covers most of the 24 acres bounded by Fayette St., the Fallsway, Orleans St., and Calvin St. This blocky, six-story concrete structure, the largest public building in Baltimore, supplies more than 883,000 square feet of interior space.

E. Fayette St., looking west toward the Shot Tower, 1930s

St. Vincent de Paul Church, across Front St. from the Post Office, once dominated this part of Old Town. A Baltimore native who was first priest of this Roman Catholic parish, John Baptist Gildea, designed the structure, apparently making use of pattern books showing neoclassical designs. The former president of St. Mary's College, then Bishop of the Diocese of Natchez, John Chanche, dedicated the church in December 1840. Built of stuccoed brick, it features a three-tiered, octagonal domed tower that has been a city landmark for more than 150 years. Inside, four pairs of engaged columns repeat the design of the facade. Named for the French saint who established charitable organizations for the poor in Paris (and an outgrowth of an earlier benevolent association in Old Town), the church has served a similar role in Baltimore ever since.

The small **Shot Tower Park**—constructed around a 234-foot high, tapered brick cylinder—occupies the southeast corner of Front and Fayette Sts. across from the post office. Charles Carroll of Carrollton laid the cornerstone for this structure, built by Jacob Wolfe in 1828 for the manufacture of shot that the newspaper advertised as "not excelled in the world." Workers poured molten lead through a sieve from platforms at various heights in the tower. As the lead fell, it formed into round pellets that hardened into shot in a tank of water at the bottom. The tower foundation, 17 feet deep, rests on solid rock. The walls, which contain more than one million handmade bricks, taper from 4.5 feet to 1.75 feet in thickness and were built from the inside out, freeing the tower from vibration, a condition necessary for perfect shot. Shot towers were common in the 19th century, but few remain. The Shot Tower was restored in 1976.

9 North Front Street, located just south of the Shot Tower, illustrates the popular Federal architectural style that appealed to Baltimoreans after the Revolution. This restored merchant's house was built around 1794. Thorowgood Smith, the second mayor of Baltimore, lived here

from 1802 to 1804. The Women's Civic League maintains the isolated brick dwelling, once one of many houses that stood along the east bank of the Jones Falls. Tons of concrete have replaced them. For information call 410-837-5424.

The Baltimore skyline from about the same point in 1997

From the Shot Tower, cross Baltimore St. and continue down narrow Front St. to the cluster of buildings located just north of Lombard St. They belonged to the Baltimore City Life Museums, a nonprofit corporation that administered seven municipal museums in the city until falling victim to financial difficulties in 1997. The **Caton-Carroll House** stands at the corner of Front and Lombard Sts. Mary Carroll Caton, daughter of Charles Carroll of Carrollton, and her husband, Richard Caton, bought this Federal town house in 1818 from a merchant who had expanded the original property, built in 1808. The three-story brick dwelling, with its gabled roof and paneled recesses under the third-floor windows, represents an enlarged version of the house at 9 North Front St. Charles Carroll bought out Caton's interest in 1824 and lived here every fall and winter until his death in the third-floor bedroom in 1832. The city acquired the property in 1915, almost demolished it in the 1950s, and then, with the aid of dedicated volunteers from the Carroll Society, eventually restored it. Furnished in the French Second Empire fashion popular after 1815, the house accurately reflects the taste of the Catholic patriot and successful businessman who lived there.

The Carroll House had been a museum since 1931; in the 1980s other attractions of historical interest joined it, and the entire block between Front and Albemarle Sts. north of Lombard became a city park. The **1840 House** at 50 Albemarle St., a row house restored in 1985, recreated the city home of John Hutchinson, a wheelwright in the 1840s. Nine people lived here, including Sarah West, a free African American woman, and her child, who boarded in the basement.

In 1996 City Life Museums opened the **Morton K. Blaustein Exhibition Center,** a 30,000-square-foot building on Front St. It incorporated the cast-iron facade of the Fava Fruit Company building (1869), demolished during construction of the Convention Center.

Brewers Park, added to the City Life complex in 1989, lies across Lombard St. The city acquired the brewery site in 1970; in 1983 its excavation became the first project of the newly formed Baltimore Center for Urban Archaeology. Digging and archival research revealed that Thomas Peters came to this location from Philadelphia during the Revolution to create the Baltimore Strong Beer Brewery for American and French troops, as well as for the general public. Fire destroyed the brewery in 1812, but later owners rebuilt and expanded the operation. Under the ownership of Eli Clagett, the brewery in 1850 produced 10,000 barrels of beer, leading the city's 11 breweries. The Clagett family sold the business in 1879, and the property became part of the National Casket Company. Markers indicate the sites of the brewery's warehouses and malthouses, the brewer's house and kitchen, and a warehouse used by the casket company.

The **Baltimore Brewing Company,** a private enterprise established in 1990 by Theo de Groen, faces Albemarle St. adjacent to the park. When visitors ask why a European operation came to Baltimore to establish a bar and restaurant that makes its own beer on the premises, the Dutch brewmaster points to the city's long brewing tradition. The first Baltimore brewery opened in 1748; since that time, at least 115 breweries have operated in the city. Prohibition (1920–33) forced the brewers' art underground, creating many amateur chemists, but the traditions of the master brewers have slowly returned, on a smaller scale.

Walk south from Brewers Park to the **Star-Spangled Banner Flag House and Museum,** which occupies the northwest corner of Albemarle and Pratt Sts. Mrs. Mary Pickersgill, maker of "ships banners and flags," moved here from Philadelphia in 1807 with her small daughter Caroline and widowed mother, Rebecca Young. Mrs. Young had made the Grand Union Flag of 1775, requested by Gen. George Washington after he assumed command of the Continental Army on June 16, 1775. In 1814 Maj. George Armistead, commander of Fort McHenry, commissioned Mrs. Pickersgill to make a battle flag, an "American ensign 30 by 42 feet of first quality bunting" with 15 stars and stripes. Too large to complete in her small brick house (1793), she and her assistants assembled the 80-pound flag in the nearby brewery. The huge flag required nearly a dozen strong men to raise. It flew from the fort during the British attack on Baltimore and became the "star-spangled banner" of Francis Scott Key's poem (to see the original banner, visit the National Museum of American History in Washington, D.C.). By act of Congress, the Flag House may fly the current American flag and the original banner at any time, day or night. The brick, Federal-style house, once part of a group of four, is furnished as it may have been in 1814. A museum in the rear, on the site of the original kitchen, displays family papers, Key mementos, relics of the War of 1812, and the original receipt for the flag. It cost $405.90. For further information, call 410-837-1793.

From this point, the visitor may walk west until reaching Harborwalk, an urban trail that takes one beyond Pier 5 all the way to Canton, or simply walk west on Pratt St. to return to the Inner Harbor.

B. SOUTH *FROM THE* INNER HARBOR *TO* FEDERAL HILL, OTTERBEIN, *AND* RETURN

Beyond the visitors kiosk see the berth of the *Pride of Baltimore II*, a reproduction Baltimore Clipper schooner that serves as the city's maritime ambassador. Constructed at the Inner Harbor in 1976, the first *Pride of Baltimore* slipped into the water with great fanfare on February 27, 1977. During her nine years of operation, that graceful vessel traveled more than 125,000 miles to ports throughout the United States, South America, and Europe. On May 14, 1986, she was lost at sea during a violent windstorm off the coast of Puerto Rico. Capt. Armin Elsaesser and three other crew members died in the accident. A memorial to them and their vessel stands in Rash Field, below Federal Hill at the southern end of the basin. Baltimoreans rallied and in April 1988, launched the *Pride of Baltimore II*. The best months to catch her in port are April, May, and October.

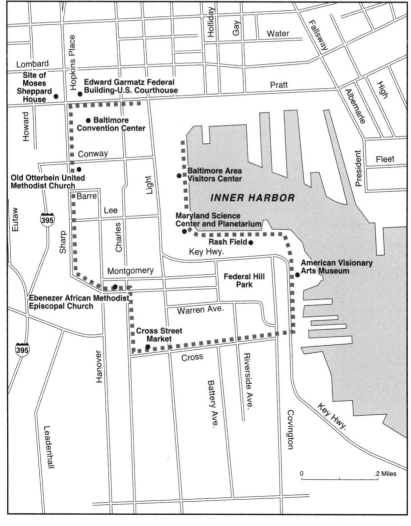

At the south corner of the basin one comes to an ultra-modern structure that houses the Maryland Academy of Sciences.

The Maryland Science Center and Planetarium

The oldest scientific research institution in the state, the Maryland Academy of Sciences formed in Baltimore in 1797. In its early years, when housed on South Charles St., it combined the attractions of zoo, freak show, wax-figure display, natural history museum, and meeting place for avid amateurs. In 1976, its purpose having evolved into teaching scientific fundamentals, the center moved into a specially designed new building on the southwestern edge of the Inner Harbor.

Here the Maryland Science Center (Light St. and Key Hwy.) maintains three floors of scientific exhibits that provide both family entertainment and a basic introduction to the world of science. Permanent displays examine the nature of numbers, the complexity of the Chesapeake Bay ecosystem, and the phenomenon of physical energy (objects spark, crackle, spin, and glow). Visitors may conduct their own experiments at a station that demonstrates how scientists think. In cooperation with the Johns Hopkins Space Telescope Science Institute, the center also offers one a view of the universe through the "eyes" of the Hubble Space Telescope. More than 8,000 stars twinkle on the dome of the Davis Planetarium, whose instructional films exploring astronomy and cosmology circulate worldwide. Yet another "hands-on" exhibit—featuring building blocks, paper models, and electronic simulation—teaches principles of civil engineering and architecture.

In 1987 the center added an IMAX Theater to its interior attractions. Five stories tall, the theater screen and multiple speakers surround the viewer with the sensations that accompany film topics like space and undersea exploration, flying, peeking inside the human body, and crawling in caves.

A number of sculptures surround the center, including a granite lantern and garden stones—gifts from one of Baltimore's sister cities, Kawasaki, Japan.

Open 10 a.m. to 5 p.m., Monday–Friday; 10 a.m. to 6 p.m. Saturday and Sunday. Closed Thanksgiving Day and Christmas Day.

Admission: $9.50 for adults, $7 for children, $6 for Saturday and Sunday evening IMAX double features (7:30 p.m.), children under 4 free. Special rates for school groups. Parking at nearby hotels and on streets.

Gift shop and snack bar. For information call 410-685-5225.

Rash Field, adjacent to the Science Center, commemorates a former director of the city park commission, Joseph H. Rash, whose service began in 1965. Originally a high school sports field, it still supports recreational activities that include ice skating in the winter and kite flying in the summer. A carousel operates in warm weather months. Several commercial firms offer boat tours of the harbor from the basin, and water taxis serve the Inner Harbor area during the summer season. Commercial boat slips line the south edge of the basin, where once shipyards built and launched schooners for the Brazilian coffee trade.

From Rash Field, one may proceed past the *Pride of Baltimore* memorial and then follow Harborwalk south and east along Key Highway (eventually the walk will extend to Locust Point and Fort McHenry).

A short distance down Key Hwy., at the intersection of Covington St., the visitor finds a museum specializing in the quirky.

The American Visionary Art Museum

Born of pure imagination the world over, the objects in the American Visionary Art Museum (800 Key Hwy.)—scrap-metal flying machines, embroidered rugs, whirligigs, perpetual-motion machines, and miscellaneous ingenuities—reflect the visions, pastimes, and obsessions of untrained artists from many backgrounds.

Opened in 1995, the museum makes adaptive reuse of a late-19th-century whiskey warehouse, which it has fashioned into its large Tall Sculpture Barn. This space, its ceiling 45 feet high, opens onto a wildflower and sculpture garden and a central, granite-paved plaza that features a 55-foot-tall, three-ton whirligig that an elderly farmer built as a salute to Federal Hill, Life, Liberty, and the Pursuit of Happiness. The Baltimore *Sun* referred to it as "Baltimore's most joyous piece of public sculpture."

Open Tuesday–Sunday, 10 a.m. to 6 p.m. Closed Mondays, Thanksgiving Day, and Christmas Day. Admission: $6 for adults; $4 for seniors, students, and children. Ample parking in metered spaces and in a lot across from main entry.

Museum shop. Café (open Tuesday–Sunday, 11:30 a.m. to 6 p.m.). For information call 410-244-1900.

South Baltimore

The original South Baltimore lies between the Northwest and Middle Branches of the Patapsco River on a peninsula (Whetstone Point, now occupied by Fort McHenry, on the east) that shelters the Inner Harbor. A walk down S. Charles and Hanover Sts. west of the Inner Harbor leads to the area where Acadian refugees settled in 1755. In 1824, these streets were known collectively as Frenchtown. Eighteenth-century houses still stand on Montgomery St. Around Sharp and Leadenhall Sts., one of the city's oldest free African American communities formed in the 19th century. Between the Civil War and World War I, the interior of the peninsula south of Montgomery and east of Hanover filled with row houses whose owners worked along the bustling waterfront. A newer South Baltimore, on the south bank of the Middle Branch, became part of Baltimore in 1918.

Comparatively isolated, South Baltimore developed its own independent character. Not as ethnically diverse as other parts of the city, South Baltimore tended to be self-sufficient and proud of its stubborn adherence to tradition. This quality changed dramatically during the 1970s, when wealthier, more liberal citizens moved into the old neighborhoods, renovated houses, and contributed to what came to be known as "gentrification." Boutique retail shops and restaurants developed along Light St., and the area near Federal Hill has become a fashionable address.

Federal Hill and the Cross Street Market are within walking distance of Rash Field. (Other portions of South Baltimore require private auto or public transportation.) Walk across Key Hwy. to Battery Ave., the western boundary of the actual Federal Hill. Go one block to Warren Ave. and turn left into a driveway that leads to the park and its vistas.

Federal Hill

Federal Hill Park—bounded by Key Hwy., Covington St., and Warren and Battery Aves.—dominates the southern border of the Inner Har-

The view of Baltimore from Federal Hill— a favorite perspective of artists and photographers— in 1997

bor and offers a view that many tour guides choose as the best place to begin an exploration of downtown Baltimore. This hill has undergone many transformations since Capt. John Smith first sailed up the Patapsco in 1608 and noticed its red clay banks. Shipyards had clustered at its feet by May 1788, when Baltimoreans celebrated Maryland's ratification of the federal Constitution. A parade wound through city streets and ended on the hilltop with a spirited picnic. Thereafter Capt. John Smith's Hill became Federal Hill.

On May 13, 1861, soon after Southern sympathizers had attempted to raise the Confederate flag on Federal Hill, Union troops under Maj. Gen. Benjamin F. Butler occupied the site and turned it into a fort. General Butler called his maneuver "the capture of Baltimore," and throughout the war the hill bristled with cannon aimed at the city. Tunnels under the hill, originally created to mine sand for glass and clay for pipes, filled with ammunition and military supplies.

In 1962, government planners proposed construction of an expressway that would have cut through Federal Hill and crossed the inner harbor through Fells Point. Residents of both neighborhoods rose up to defeat the plan. The struggle created grassroots leaders, some of whom, U.S. senator Barbara Mikulski among them, went on to high station. Now part of a protected, historic district, the hill offers a magnificent view of the harbor, including eastern vistas that only hint at the maritime activity that once enveloped both banks of the Patapsco River. Still visible is the **site of the Bethlehem Steel Company Yards,** closed in 1983, on which more than 2,600 ships were built and repaired during World War II.

Cross Street Market

From Federal Hill, walk south down Riverside Ave. from Warren Ave. The two 1½-story brick houses (ca. 1800) with single dormers at 1124 and 1126 Riverside, just beyond Cross St., may be the only ones extant from the time Baltimore became an incorporated city (1797). Go back to Cross St. and follow it west to the **Cross Street Market,** one of six municipal markets operated by the city, located on Cross St. between Light and S. Charles Sts. Like its counterparts in other parts of the city, this market, founded in 1846, serves as a focal point for the surrounding neighborhood. Merchants typically know many of their customers; patrons faithfully return year after year. The original wooden buildings of this market burned in 1951. The rebuilt market anchors surrounding bars, cafés, and food establishments. From the market, walk east to Charles St. and follow it north to Montgomery St.

Turn left, walking west on Montgomery St. to the **Ebenezer African Methodist Episcopal Church** between Hanover and Charles Sts. The congregation claims the current brick building, constructed in 1865 on the site of an earlier church (1848), to be the oldest surviving black-built church in the country. Bishop Daniel A. Payne, a prolific writer and founder of Wilberforce University in Ohio, once served as pastor here. Follow Montgomery St. to Sharp St. and the square in front of the refurbished, brick **Church of the Lord Jesus Christ,** which Methodists built in 1889.

Continue north on Sharp St. into an area of restored row houses that in 1980 won a design award from the local chapter of the American Institute of Architects. Urban "homesteaders"—people who paid the city

Two-and-a-half-story row houses, once a staple of Baltimore workers' housing, ca. 1940

$1 for their houses with the promise to restore and live in them—transformed this area in the 1970s. Newly constructed housing has been added to the old to create a modern neighborhood with brick Federal, Classical Revival, and modish styles.

The **Federal Reserve Bank** (1981) stands on the west side of the street opposite Barre, Welcome, and Lee Sts. Excavation for it yielded more than 3,000 household artifacts (bottles, plates, thimbles, chamber pots, etc.) from old basements and privies. A few of them are on public display in the lobby.

Continue on Sharp St. to the **Old Otterbein United Methodist Church,** the oldest church building in Baltimore. This gem of 18th-century craftsmanship now stands alone in a cleared area where Sharp St. crosses Conway St. In 1785 Jacob Small Sr., a local carpenter, earned about $5,000 for building the two-story brick church. He placed two tiers of round-headed windows with clear glass around the structure and topped it with a squat, square tower with belfry. Completed with the proceeds from a lottery in 1789, the tower was adorned with bells imported from Germany.

It takes its name from the Rev. Philip William Otterbein (1726–1813), who came to Maryland from his native Prussia in 1752 and served various German Reformed congregations—one in Frederick from 1760 to 1764—until he assumed the pastorship of the Second Evangelical Reformed Church in Baltimore in 1774. He soon befriended Francis Asbury, founder of American Methodism. The bilingual Otterbein became noted for his cooperation with Methodist and Mennonite groups. At Frederick in 1800 he cooperated in forming a Methodist-like sect of German speakers, the United Brethren in Christ. Otterbein remained in Baltimore until his death. In 1968 the successor to Otterbein's United Brethren merged with the Methodists to form the United Methodist Church. Otterbein lies buried in the churchyard. Inside an iron fence stands the three-story brick parsonage, built in 1811. For information call 410-685-4703.

Sharp St. no longer extends north of Pratt St., so continue the walk on Pratt St. Opposite the Convention Center, at the northwest corner of Pratt and Sharp Sts., one can see what once was the **Moses Sheppard House** (1795), now a sports bar. Sheppard (1775–1857), a wealthy Quaker merchant and philanthropist, purchased the 3 1/2-story brick house in 1821. His humanitarian projects ranged from work on behalf of the Six Nations and protection of free African Americans to sponsorship of the Maryland State Colonization Society. Sheppard paid for the medical education of Dr. Samuel McGill, who then practiced medicine in Maryland's ex-slave colony in Liberia and in 1851 became its governor. Sheppard's largest gift, a bequest of $565,000, led to the establishment of the Sheppard Asylum for the insane, later Sheppard and Enoch Pratt Hospital, which continues to be a major regional mental health resource. The Katzenstein family owned a picture-framing business at this location until 1983 and restored the property.

Long before the heyday of Pennsylvania Ave., Sharp St. ran through the heart of the African American community in Baltimore. Quaker antislavery advocates and the first black teachers and preachers of the 18th and early 19th centuries lived and worked along Sharp St. Tradition ascribes the street name to Horatio Sharpe, governor of Maryland from 1753 to 1769; but in spirit it more appropriately honors Granville Sharp

(1735–1813), an English antislavery activist who corresponded with his American counterparts in making common cause. Elisha Tyson (1750–1824), whom a local 19th-century historian called "the great champion of the rights of the sable sons of Africa," led early Quaker humanitarian efforts in Baltimore and lived just south of the Otterbein Church. Tyson had come to Harford County from Pennsylvania to work as a miller before the Revolution and then moved to the city with his family in 1781. He established mills on the Jones Falls, became wealthy, and retired about 1800. In 1797 he and his brother Jesse established the African Academy, a school for free blacks, at 112–116 Sharp St., between Pratt and Lombard. The Days Inn on Hopkins Place now occupies the site.

In 1787, experiencing problems within integrated congregations, black Methodists from Baltimore, Philadelphia, and New York decided to establish their own churches. The Baltimore group broke off from the Lovely Lane Meeting House on German St. and established the Colored Methodist Society, which in 1802 opened the **Sharp Street Methodist Church** at the old African Academy. This pioneering congregation built a second church on the same site in 1860 and in 1898 built a Gothic-style church at the corner of Dolpin and Etting Sts., where it has kept the Sharp Street name.

Not all the African American Methodists, however, chose to stay within the fold. Daniel Coker (1780–1846), born a slave on the Eastern Shore of Maryland, escaped to New York, received a Methodist education, and returned to Maryland to teach at the Sharp Street Church. He published pamphlets against slavery and in 1816 played a key role in the Philadelphia convention that founded the African Methodist Episcopal Church. Coker later traveled to Liberia as a missionary.

The **Baltimore Convention Center** occupies the block bounded by Pratt St. on the north (main entrance being One West Pratt), S. Charles St. on the east, Conway St. on the south, and Howard St. on the west.

This three-level glass, steel, concrete, and stone structure, built in 1979, conceals a highly sophisticated design that encompasses over 400,000 square feet. The architects (Naramore, Bain, Brady and Johanson; and Cochran, Stephenson and Donkervoet) worked with a Seattle structural engineering firm to create a building using computer-aided techniques borrowed from suspension bridge construction. In 1993 the Maryland General Assembly approved a $150 million expansion of the center, to attract larger conventions to the city. The expanded convention center stretches a full block farther west than the original structure did. Completed in the fall of 1996, the addition provides 305,000 square feet of exhibit space on one level, in addition to a 40,000-square-foot special events room seating 3,000–5,000 people.

A walk on Pratt St. east of the Convention Center offers an opportunity to view several examples of the city's public art. In 1964, Baltimore became the second U.S. city (Philadelphia was first) to pass a "1% for art" bill, which mandated that public construction projects set aside funds for artistic enhancements such as murals, sculptures, fountains, and mosaics. As a result, 148 contemporary sculptures have been placed throughout the city since 1960, bringing the total of such creations to 246.

Reuben Kramer's sculpture *Thurgood Marshall* (1980) stands near the northeast corner of Pratt St. and Hopkins Place as part of the **Edward**

Garmatz Federal Building–U.S. Courthouse, constructed in 1976. (The main entrance of the building, located at Lombard and Hanover Sts., features George Sugarman's painted aluminum work entitled *Baltimore Federal* [1978].)

The public art program also stimulated such privately funded donations as Thomas A. Todd's 1980 piece at the corner of Pratt and Charles Sts. Seven rough stone monoliths of varying heights, surrounded by a low circular wall, bear the names of Maryland's counties.

Mary Ann E. Mears' *Red Buoyant* (1979), a painted aluminum sculpture, lies a block away at 100 East Pratt St. on the **IBM Building Plaza.**

C. NORTH FROM THE INNER HARBOR VIA GAY ST. TO CITY HALL AND MONUMENT SQUARE

The area Baltimoreans refer to as "downtown" largely encompasses the portion of the city west of the Jones Falls, north of the Basin, and downhill from Mulberry or Saratoga, bounded on the west by Park or Howard. Fire destroyed much of this quarter in 1904. Today, it remains home to banks, business, and courts.

To see an eastern chunk of it, begin at the corner of Pratt and Gay Sts. and walk north to the corner of Lombard, where the **United States Customs House** (1900–1908) occupies the site of the first U.S. Customs offices, established in Baltimore in 1786. The **Call Room** (open to the public only by appointment), where captains once delivered their manifests and clearing papers, dominates the first floor. Murals on the 35-foot ceiling and walls include a 30-by-68-foot painting depicting the arrival in Baltimore of 10 sailing vessels. The painter, Francis D. Millet, died in the *Titanic* disaster of 1912. The building became a National Historic Landmark in 1972.

Cross the street from the Customs House to a **Memorial to the World War II Holocaust,** first dedicated in 1980, then dismantled and redesigned in 1997 after vandals and street people misused the space. Concrete monoliths, abstractions of boxcars, are inscribed with names of all the concentration camps in which six million European Jews and members of other minority groups were systematically exterminated by the Nazis. A bronze monument by Joseph Sheppard now dominates an open plaza fronting Lombard St. It depicts bodies consumed in flames, with a quote from George Santayana: "Those who cannot remember the past are bound to repeat it."

The **Harbor Campus of the Baltimore City Community College** occupies two buildings east of the Holocaust Memorial on 5.3 acres north and south of Lombard St. The school traces its origins to 1946, when returning veterans began college preparatory courses at Baltimore City College, a public high school. This program developed into a two-year college and moved to the former campus of Park School at 2901 Liberty Heights Ave. The college expanded to the inner harbor in 1976 and in 1990 became a state institution with about 7,200 students in more than 30 fields, including computer information, nursing, and business. A number of notable Baltimoreans, including Oscar-winning director Barry Levinson and Congressman Kweisi Mfume have graduated from BCCC. A shuttle bus links the Liberty Heights campus with the harbor campus,

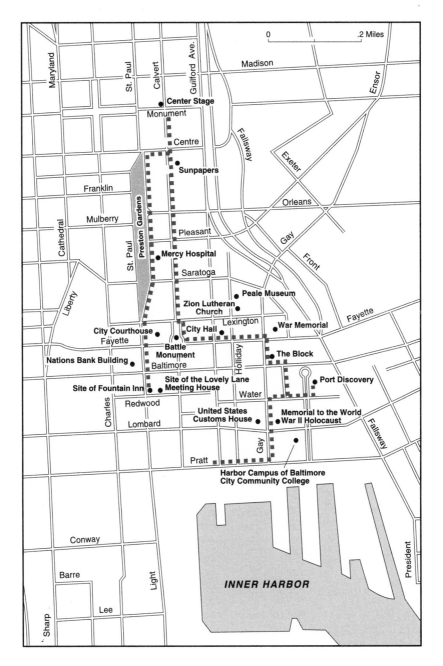

which serves students primarily from East Baltimore. As part of an ambitious expansion plan for the 1990s, the school will add a commercial hotel and additional classrooms on the site across Pratt St. from the Columbus Center.

From the memorial, walk east on Water St. past the Brokerage to Market Place and the new Port Discovery Children's Museum. This part of the downtown area, from Holliday St. east to the Jones Falls, was known as Harrison's Marsh before the Revolution. A causeway crossed the marsh to a bridge over the Jones Falls, approximately where Gay St. now crosses the expressway. By 1785 the city had drained and filled the marsh and established a market on the site. Known to all as Marsh Market, it occupied what is now an attractive public square known as Market Place. Most of the original buildings in this area were destroyed during the Great Fire of 1904. During the 1980s the city attempted with only limited success to develop the Market Place area as an entertainment center. In 1983 the **Brokerage,** a three-acre, multistory retail and office complex, replaced 19 buildings that had housed brokers of produce and other market goods. The **Eubie Blake National Museum** maintains temporary headquarters at the Brokerage while searching for a permanent city location. The museum showcases the accomplishments of Eubie Blake, the great ragtime pianist-composer who was born in Baltimore in 1883 and continued to perform almost to the year of his death in 1983, five days after reaching his 100th birthday. For information on the museum call 410-396-8128.

A wholesale fishmarket stood on Market Place for more than a century, until the mid-1980s, when the post-fire brick fishmarket became part of a private "entertainment mall" with theme night clubs and a concert hall. The new "Fishmarket" closed in 1989. More recently, the Rouse Company, in partnership with a subsidiary of the Walt Disney Company, converted the site into a $25 million nonprofit children's museum, **Port Discovery.**

From Market Place walk north a block via Frederick St. or Gay St. to Baltimore St. and what remains of the once notorious "**Block**"—a dwindling strip of pawnshops, striptease joints, X-rated book and video stores, theaters, hidden gambling rooms, and bars between Holliday St. and the Jones Falls. As late as the early 1960s, The Block featured live burlesque shows that included comics, dancers, and musicians and attracted seamen, conventioneers, college students, and others seeking relief from respectability. The famous stripper Blaze Starr—friend to all, but special to a sitting Louisiana senator—became a Block icon in the 1950s. She had inspired other young women who, during WWII and afterward, left rural communities seeking fame and fortune in the big city. Only a short distance from City Hall and police headquarters, The Block made visible the sordid Baltimore of waterfront dives, snake pit bars, jazz clubs, and whorehouses. The Broadway gambler and the Harlem hustler could disappear here for a while, while local police made the area generally safe for visitors. During its heyday, The Block became a tourist attraction and even won grudging admiration for its sinful vitality. The theaters no longer operate, and The Block has now become a mere shadow of its former self. A few bar and peep-show owners fight City Hall to stay in business.

City Hall and War Memorial Plaza

From The Block, walk north on Gay St. to **Memorial Plaza,** a municipal square dominated by **City Hall** on the west and the **War Memorial** on the east. The War Memorial—a neoclassical marble hall with wide entrance steps leading to a portico of Doric columns—occupies a large block directly across the plaza from City Hall. Ferdinand Foch, marshal of France and commander in chief of Allied forces in the last months of World War I, broke ground for the memorial in 1921. Designed by Laurence Hall Fowler, the building was dedicated in 1925. The names of Marylanders who died in the "Great War" are carved on the marble walls of the main hall. Two urns of black Belgian marble contain the names of all previous battles in which Maryland soldiers played a role. On the wall over the stairs leading to the first floor is a mural by Baltimore artist R. MacGill Mackall, who depicted Victory standing over the tomb of an unknown soldier.

Walk across the plaza, around which sit municipal buildings that house the police and fire departments, the district court, and other city agencies. On the second day of the 1904 fire, obliging winds spared **City Hall** (1867–75), a Beaux-Arts landmark combining French and American influences. The four-story iron, brick, and marble structure contains an interior rotunda topped by an exterior dome that rises 227 feet above the ground. City Hall was substantially renovated and refurbished in 1975–77 and now features two public gallery spaces. The **Courtyard Gallery** contains changing exhibits on Baltimore historical and cultural themes; the **Circle Gallery** on the lower-level rotunda exhibits creative projects by local schoolchildren.

Zion Lutheran Church sits across from City Hall at the northeast corner of Holliday and Lexington Sts. This structure succeeded George Rohrbach and Johann Mackenheimer's building of 1807. The congregation built this Gothic church within the original walls after a fire in 1840. The pews of varnished oak retain the nameplates of their first owners, and portraits of former pastors hang in the vestibule, beginning with Johann Daniel Kurtz (1763–1856), pastor from 1785 to 1833 and first president of the General Synod of Lutherans in America. German Lutherans established this congregation in 1755, only 25 years after the town had been laid out. Services remained exclusively in German until after World War II. During the long pastorate (1835–96) of Heinrich Scheib (1808–97) the church served as a center of German American life in Maryland. Scheib created a nondenominational and progressive school, which reached an enrollment of more than 800 children in the 1860s (it closed in 1895). In the 1880s young Henry Mencken attended F. Knapp's school across the alley and later recalled a friendly rivalry. The Scheib school bell stills hangs in the garden on the Gay St. side of the church, and more than one city mayor has regarded the church's chimes as a temporary respite from civic duties. A walled garden surrounds the parish house, which fronts on Holliday St. The garden, too, offers repose to civil servants.

The Peale Museum

One of Baltimore's truly eminent structures, the old Peale Museum stands at 225 Holliday St., once a bustling avenue. It embodied the high hopes of Rembrandt Peale (1776–1860), son of Charles Willson Peale (1741–1827). The elder Peale, a native of Maryland's Eastern Shore, had founded the young nation's first museum, in Philadelphia in 1786, and become famous as a painter of the Founding Fathers, particularly of George Washington. Inspired by his example, Rembrandt and his brother Rubens (they also had brothers named Raphael and Titian) decided in 1813 to establish in Baltimore a "scientific institution such as the population and wealth of this city demands." Robert Cary

*Frieze on exterior of the
Peale Museum*

Long Sr. (1770–1833) designed the building, the first in America specifically planned as a museum. Having no precedent, Long designed a typical three-story town house to which he added a square wing on the rear. The wing consisted of two large rooms, the first floor lit by windows and the second by a skylight.

Peale opened his new establishment in August 1814, proclaiming it "an elegant Rendezvous for taste, curiosity and leisure" where he exhibited "Birds, Beasts, Fishes, Snakes, Antiquities, Indian Dresses and War Instruments, Shells and Miscellaneous Curiosities." The oddities included

*Mural depicting the
triumph of the natural
gas industry in
Baltimore, interior of
Peale Museum*

mastodon bones he and his father had dug up on a New York farm in 1801 and a Rembrandt Peale original, "The Court of Death" (13 by 24 feet), "the figures larger than life." Two years later, Peale pioneered the use of "Carburetted Hydrogen Gas" lighting in his museum (Rubens had experimented with this artificial light in Philadelphia). The Baltimore museum rightly claimed to offer the first practical use of gaslight in Baltimore. Later in 1816 Peale, Long, and others formed the first gaslight company in the country and obtained a contract for lighting the city streets.

Despite all the hoopla and invention, Rembrandt's museum lost money. He turned the museum over to Rubens in 1822 and returned to Philadelphia to paint and write. Eight years later Rubens sold the building to the city and moved the collection to a building that subsequently burned, in 1833. The original museum building served as City Hall from 1830 to 1875. Thereafter, it became a school, the water board office, and factory space. In 1928 the city condemned it as unsafe. Baltimore then restored the building, using hardware and building materials from nearby period structures for interior details, and in 1931 reopened it as a modest municipal museum.

In that role, the Peale Museum housed the bones of the mastodon Rembrandt Peale originally exhibited here, along with his father's 1806 painting "Exhuming the First American Mastodon." Other paintings in the gallery included a portrait of Charles Calvert, fifth Lord Baltimore, painted by Van De Rhyn and brought to Maryland by Calvert himself in 1732. On the third floor were six portraits of heroes of the War of 1812, which the City of Baltimore had commissioned in 1817–18 and Rembrandt Peale had painted. The museum also housed a valuable collection of historic prints and photographs of Baltimore, which, along with the Peale masterworks, the city in 1998 turned over to the Maryland Historical Society.

Monument Square

From City Hall, walk one block west on either Fayette or Lexington to Monument Square. There **Battle Monument** (1815–27), the first substantial war memorial built in the United States, faces south toward the inner harbor. The Committee of Vigilance and Safety sponsored this commemorative structure shortly after the city's successful defense against a British land and sea attack on September 12–14, 1814. Citizens laid the cornerstone a year later. Maximilien Godefroy—a French officer and architect who came to Baltimore in 1805 to teach at St. Mary's College and went on to design some of the city's most treasured structures—used an Egyptian motif for the first time in Baltimore (it had become popular in Europe in the wake of Napoleon's Egyptian campaign). A Roman fascia rises above a marble base shaped like an Egyptian cenotaph; the cords around the fascia list the names of 36 soldiers killed in the city's defense; the names of three lost officers appear above. A classical female figure, by Antonio Capellano, crowns the monument. She holds a rudder with one hand, raising a laurel wreath in the other.

The monument occupies the site of the Baltimore County Courthouse, built in 1768 and razed in 1809. When the expanding city graded the hill on which it stood in 1784, engineers built a 20-foot stone arch and diverted Calvert St. under the courthouse, creating an unusual landmark that stands out in early prints. Battle Monument dominated its space in early years, but in this century the increase of automobile traffic and rising buildings gradually obscured the memorial's original splendor. In an effort to enhance this public area, the city in 1964 landscaped the square.

At the other end of the plaza, facing north on Calvert St., stands a **Memorial to the Black Soldier,** the work of Baltimore sculptor James

Lewis. Lewis began work on this bronze figure in 1969. It was the first monument in the country specifically to memorialize black soldiers, and its placement here, in 1971, drew some public protest. The nine-foot figure, dressed in World War II uniform, holds a wreath with a ribbon listing 18 conflicts in which black troops participated between 1775 and 1970.

The **Baltimore City Courthouse** (1894–99) occupies the block between Calvert St. and St. Paul St. The design of J. B. Noel Wyatt and William G. Nolting, it is in the French Renaissance style. In 1985, it was renamed for Clarence M. Mitchell Jr. (1911–84), a Baltimorean who worked in Washington for decades as a lawyer and lobbyist for the NAACP. Mitchell was frequently called the "101st senator" for his work in advancing civil rights legislation in Congress. His family, including brother Parren Mitchell (Maryland's first African American congressman), wife Juanita Jackson Mitchell, and two sons played prominent roles in the legal battles of the 1950s and 1960s to end segregation.

Inside the elaborate marble building, one will find a number of murals by American painters from the late 19th century. On the walls of the Court of Equity, Edwin Blashfield's "Religious Toleration" shows Lord Baltimore recommending Wisdom, Justice and Mercy to the colonists. His portrait of "Washington Surrendering His Commission" decorates the wall in the Court of Common Pleas. Charles Yardley Turner's murals "Burning of the Peggy Stewart" and "Barter with the Indians for Land in Southern Maryland in 1634" highlight the vestibule of the Criminal Court and nearby corridor. French artist Jean Paul Laurens painted the four panels in the Orphans' Court, "Surrender of Cornwallis at Yorktown." John La Farge's "Lawgivers" depicts Justinian, Moses, Mohammed, Lycurgus, and Confucius inside the St. Paul St. entrance. Here the visitor also will find an exhibit honoring the Mitchell family and Albert Weinert's statue (1908) of Cecil Calvert, second Lord Baltimore. Weinert supposedly modeled Calvert after the silent film star from Baltimore, Francis X. Bushman.

North from Battle Monument

From the Battle Monument, one may continue north on Calvert St. for five blocks to see several noteworthy sights. Walk past **Mercy Hospital,** an architecturally striking building first constructed in 1963 and expanded in the 1970s.

North of the Orleans Street Viaduct, which carries U.S. 40 across the Jones Falls tunnel, the Baltimore Sunpapers main offices occupy an entire block on the east side of Calvert St. When New Englander Arunah S. Abell issued the first edition of *The Sun* for a penny on May 17, 1837, the city had six other daily newspapers, nine weeklies, and two monthlies. In 1851, the newspaper built a landmark headquarters at the southeast corner of Baltimore and South Sts.—the "Iron Building," the first structure in America to distribute weight on cast-iron columns instead of masonry walls. The building did not survive the Great Fire, and the paper then rebuilt at the southwest corner of Baltimore and Charles Sts., where it remained until moving to this site in 1959. Conglomerate-owned since 1986, the *Sun* is now the city's only daily newspaper.

Center Stage, Maryland's premier theater group, occupies the west side of the 700 block of N. Calvert St. The block-long building complex where the theater now flourishes once housed Loyola College and High School—both now moved north to different locations on Charles St. St.

Ignatius Church occupies the northern end of the block. The Jesuit order offered the southern portion of the block to the theater in 1975, and architect James R. Grieves converted the space into a 500-seat facility that received an American Institute of Architects Honor Award in 1978. A second theater, named after benefactor Howard Head, was added in 1992. The state's only regional, professional theater held its first production in Heptasoph Hall, in the Mount Royal district, in 1963 and occupied a smaller North Ave. location before moving here.

Walking west one block on Centre St. leads one to St. Paul St., a north-south artery that extends from Baltimore St. into the old suburb of Guilford. Turn left and follow it to the point where it splits to form **Preston Gardens,** a five-block strip of greenery between St. Paul St. and St. Paul Place. The garden blooms with multicolored tulips every spring. It represented a major downtown renewal achievement during World War I, when it opened in honor of James Harry Preston. Baltimore mayor for seven years after 1911, Preston lent city support to the Baltimore Symphony Orchestra, the first municipal orchestra in the country, and established a popular summer music-in-the-parks program.

South from Battle Monument

The city's Financial District lies south of the Battle Monument along Calvert St. and the side streets that link Calvert with the parallel St. Paul–Light St. thoroughfare (the street changes name at Baltimore St.). Most of this area was destroyed in 1904 by the Great Fire. The **Alexander Brown and Sons** brokerage house at the southwest corner of Calvert and Baltimore Sts. was the only building (1900, Parker and Thomas) at the intersection to survive that disaster. Alexander Brown, a New Englander, arrived in Baltimore in 1800 and built one of the city's strongest financial institutions. Its offices have moved to the southeast corner of Baltimore and South Sts.

The brick, Romanesque Revival exterior of the **Mercantile-Safe Deposit and Trust Building** (1885, J. B. Noel Wyatt and Joseph E. Sperry) on the northeast corner of Calvert and Redwood (earlier German) Sts., also survived the fire. The offices of the bank are now part of Charles Center (see below). Redwood St. once formed the heart of the city's banking and stock brokerage community. Next door to the Mercantile-Safe Deposit building, at 206 E. Redwood St., stands an impressive building that once housed the Merchants' Club, an elegant and exclusive businessmen's society that was renowned for its luncheons and holiday dinners. The club closed in 1989.

Quite by contrast, this address is also the **site of the Lovely Lane Meeting House** (1774–96), birthplace of the Methodist Church in America. Representatives of Methodist societies met here in December 1774 and organized the Methodist Episcopal Church of the United States of America. At the suggestion of John Wesley, the English leader of the Methodists, Francis Asbury was chosen superintendent of the church in America and adopted the title of bishop.

The **site of the Fountain Inn,** which opened in 1773, lies across the street at the northeast corner of Redwood and Light Sts. For more than 50 years, the inn enjoyed a high reputation among travelers. George Washington stayed here in September 1781 and again in April 1789 en route to New York to assume the presidency of the United States. The Marquis de

Lafayette, Thomas Jefferson, Winfield Scott, and Andrew Jackson also were among the guests. The Fountain Inn's successor, the Carrollton (1872), burned down in the 1904 fire. The Southern Hotel, which replaced it in 1917, closed in 1964. Today the property awaits redevelopment.

When it opened in 1929 as the Baltimore Trust Building, the **NationsBank Building** at the southwest corner of Baltimore and Light Sts. was the city's first skyscraper. The 34-story building, 780 feet tall, features a two-story banking room accented with multicolored marble columns, a mosaic floor, and painted ceiling. The Art Deco exterior reflects the ideas of modernism that prevailed in the 1920s and provides an interesting contrast with its more recent, austere neighbors. After its construction, downtown building languished until the late 1950s and early work on the Charles Center project.

The **Baltimore International Culinary College,** which Roger Chylinski founded in 1972, moved to 25 S. Calvert St. in 1978. The 500 students major in professional cooking, baking, and pastry, innkeeping management, or restaurant and food service management and receive an associate degree after two years. The college occupies 19 downtown buildings and offers a catering service at its Redwood Center. Open to the public are a cooking demonstration theater at 206 Water St., the Harbor City Diner at 15 S. Gay St., and the Baltimore Baking Company at 19 S. Gay St.

D. NORTH FROM THE INNER HARBOR VIA SKYWALK AND CHARLES ST. TO MT. VERNON PLACE

Charles St. near Fayette in the 1940s

Charles Street, the city's best-known artery, cuts through Baltimore as Broadway does through Manhattan and Michigan Ave. through

CENTRAL MARYLAND

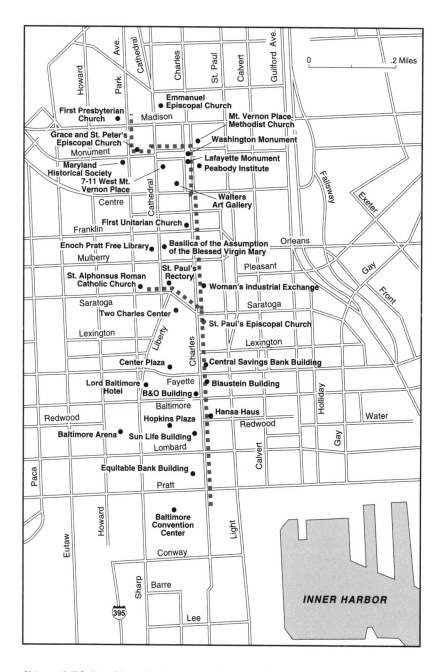

Chicago. Still fashionable and both cultural and commercial, the street originated with the town and now—lengthened over the centuries—runs more than 10 miles, from Middle Branch and South Baltimore to the Beltway in Baltimore County.

The monumental **U.S. Fidelity and Guaranty (USF&G) Building** occupies a block bounded by Charles, Pratt, Light, and Lombard Sts. The **Baltimore Convention Center** lies to the southwest. These buildings mark the start of a walk up Charles St. to Mt. Vernon Place, a journey into the heart of 19th-century Baltimore. The pedestrian may choose to walk up Charles St. or, for part of the way, take the Skywalk. The Skywalk leads from the Light Street Pavilion at Harborplace west over Light and Charles Sts. to the Convention Center and north to Lombard St. It rewards one with sweeping vistas of downtown architecture. Begin at Harborplace and follow the walkway north across Pratt St. *through* the **Equitable Bank Building.** Cross Lombard and ascend the stairway to **Hopkins Plaza,** one striking feature of the Charles Center redevelopment project.

To reach Hopkins Plaza at street level, go up Charles St. as far as Redwood (on the right) and the plaza will be on your left. A towering office building, **Charles Center South** forms the southeastern corner of this white-collar plaza, which the city recently renovated with new paving and landscaping (in the process tearing down a portion of the 1960s-era Skywalk). Federal offices occupy the southwestern corner of Hopkins Plaza, and the **Mercantile-Safe Deposit and Trust Company Building** (1969) the northwestern corner. On the Charles St. side stands the **Sun Life Building** (1966, Peterson and Brickbauer of Baltimore; Emery, Roth and Sons of New York), a striking 12-story building of glass and black Canadian granite. The first-floor design includes an open terrace and lobby with a Dimitri Hadzi sculpture hanging from the ceiling. The half-timbered **Hansa Haus** at Redwood and Charles Sts., visible across the street to the east, dates from 1907. It once served as local headquarters for the North German Lloyd Steamship Company, which in the 19th century brought thousands of European immigrants to Locust Point.

On the northeastern corner of the plaza, note the **Morris Mechanic Theater** (1967). John M. Johansen, architect of the theater, labeled his building an example of "functional expressionism." The sculpted, concrete structure, which seats slightly more than 1,600, takes its name from the real estate developer who purchased historic Ford's Theater (sister to the infamous Washington house) in the 1940s and demolished it for a parking garage in 1964. As if to atone for destroying a 93-year-old cultural landmark, the Mechanic family contributed heavily to building of the Mechanic, which the quasi-public Baltimore Center for the Performing Arts operates. With more than 20,000 subscribers from throughout the region, the Mechanic now ranks among the most successful theaters of its kind in the United States. It has rejuvenated Baltimore's historic role as a New York "tryout" town and given touring stock companies a reliable billing.

Although not part of the plaza, the **Baltimore Arena** (1962) looms above it to the west. Earlier known as the Baltimore Civic Center, the municipally owned exhibition center, concert hall, and sports facility occupies about four acres and seats more than 10,000 people. A plaque on the building notes that the land here includes a historic site. In the winter of 1776–77, when the British threatened Philadelphia, the Continental Congress repaired to Baltimore, and the legislators met in a building at Liberty and Baltimore Sts. that naturally became known as Congress Hall.

Exit Hopkins Plaza on its north (Baltimore St.) side. Straight ahead, with a main entrance on quiet Hanover St., stands the old Lord Baltimore Hotel (now part of the Hilton chain). The building dates to 1928, and its interior public spaces and larger rooms—the Calvert Ballroom and Versailles Room—recall the Jazz Age and the height of 1920s luxury. Turn right to reach Charles St. The sculpted former home office of one of Baltimore's greatest companies, the **B&O Building** stands on the northwestern corner of Charles and Baltimore Sts. The **Savings Bank of Baltimore** building (now housing First Union) (1905-7)—directly modeled after the Erechtheum, an Ionic temple of Athena on the Acropolis in Athens—stands on the southeast corner.

Until 1998, walking north the visitor could view on the left a strange building that bridged Fayette St. on three-story trusses sheathed in buff-colored brick. Constructed in 1963, it originally housed Hamburger's, a local clothing firm which, like so many family-owned, downtown retail establishments, went out of business. Then, in the late 1990s, city authorities tore down the bridge part of the building to open up the Fayette St. corridor. Across Fayette St. a seven-story dark brick, glass, and aluminum tower was one of the low-rise structures of the original Charles Center complex. Vermont Federal Savings and Loan first occupied the building; in 1998 it was home to Harbor Bank of Maryland.

The **Macht Building** (1908), with its elaborate decorations and mansard roof, stands across Charles at 11-13 E. Fayette. Ephraim Macht had come to Baltimore in 1886 from Russia with his wife Annie, who sold hats from a pushcart in Fells Point. To avoid antisemitism, Macht, in organizing a construction company, adopted the name John Welsh. The company, which eventually included Macht's son Morris and nephew Morton, built more than 8,000 houses in Baltimore.

After crossing Fayette St., the walker turns left to **Center Plaza.** More intimate than Hopkins Plaza, this circular space is surrounded by the towers of **Two Charles Center** (1965-69) on the north, the **Baltimore Gas and Electric Company Building** (1916, additions in 1966) to the west, and **One Charles Center** (1962) on the southeast. One Charles Center, the first structure completed in Charles Center, was also the first office building to go up in downtown Baltimore in 30 years. Ludwig Mies van der Rohe (1886-1969), one of the 20th century's best-known architects, designed the 24-story tower with its glass and aluminum exterior. Renovated in 1993, the building won the "25-Year Award" from the Baltimore chapter of the American Association of Architects as an older building that has retained its distinction. Miffed that the Charles Center building contract went to a Chicagoan, the Blaustein family of Baltimore constructed a look-alike building at Charles and Baltimore Sts. The **Blaustein Building,** all 30 stories, matched construction of One Charles Center almost floor-by-floor.

Only five structures in the renewal area survived the redevelopment. Two of them—the **Central Savings Bank Building** (1890) at the southeast corner of Charles and Lexington Sts. and the **Fidelity Building** (1894) at the northwest corner—just escaped the Great Fire of 1904.

A two-acre retail area occupies the southwest corner of Charles and Saratoga Sts., the northern tip of Charles Center. It clusters around two apartment towers faced with dark-brown brick. Small shops and restaurants occupy this space, as does the downtown branch of the continuing studies program of Johns Hopkins University.

The open plaza faces historic **St. Paul's Church.** The Protestant Episcopal parish has owned this prominent property since shortly after the city's founding. The red-brick building, the fourth house of worship on the site, represents the work of New York architect Richard Upjohn, a founder of the American Institute of Architects and exponent of the Gothic Revival. Upjohn used the walls and space of the previous church (1814–17), which had burned in 1854, to construct a basilica modeled after forms from 12th-century Lombardy. Antonio Capellano, who also made the figure atop the Battle Monument, carved the bas-relief stone panels on the entrance front. Louis Comfort Tiffany made several of the interior stained-glass windows, including the one under the chancel vault. Original plans called for a campanile at the corner, but it was never constructed. The third church building was designed by Robert Cary Long Jr. Long and his father, both native-born architects, made important contributions to 19th-century Baltimore.

A Bit of Saratoga St.

The trace for what later became Saratoga St. (many downtown street names commemorate revolutionary victories or heroes) marked the northernmost limit of Baltimore when it was laid out in 1730. Walk west from Charles St. to **St. Paul's Rectory** (1789–91), one of the few 18th-century buildings still standing in the downtown area. The parish dates to 1692, when the Anglican Church became tax supported. John Eager Howard conveyed the land along Saratoga St. with the stipulation that it should always be used for the rectory. Then located at the edge of town, this late-Georgian country house—only one room deep—occupies a hill that overlooked the harbor (now obscured by much larger buildings). The Society for the Preservation of Maryland Antiquities (Preservation Maryland) has restored the rectory and uses it as an office. A portion, including the secluded, rear courtyard garden, provides space for meetings, parties, and weddings.

Proceed another block west on Saratoga to Park Ave. and **St. Alphonsus Church** (1841–45), which stands on the northeastern corner. Robert Cary Long Jr. designed this Gothic Revival structure. Note that the tapered, 200-foot spire stands 50 feet higher than the church's length. German and Austrian Redemptorist fathers maintained the church for the large numbers of German-speaking immigrants who settled in Baltimore during the 1840s. Father John Nepomucene Neumann (1811–60), later bishop of Philadelphia and leader in the development of parochial schools in America, served this congregation as a priest in 1851–52. Beatified in 1963 and canonized in 1977, Neumann was only the second American to become a Roman Catholic saint. In 1917 a Lithuanian Catholic congregation (which had purchased the Lloyd Street Synagogue building in 1889) moved to St. Alphonsus, and since then the church has served as the home of a Lithuanian parish started by immigrants in the 1880s and later, in the 1940s, supported by wartime refugees. The parish also supports a Catholic school in the brick **St. Alphonsus Halle** (1873) across the street, the only parochial school still operating in downtown Baltimore.

Rejoin the main tour by walking back to Charles St. or, at Liberty St., turning left up the hill to the Basilica of the Assumption.

Farther North on Charles to Mt. Vernon Place

Walk up Charles St. on the west side, passing specialty shops and eating places, some of which have been located at the same address for generations. On the opposite side of the street, where Charles crosses Pleasant, note the **Women's Industrial Exchange.** This dining room with gift shop loaded with hand-made collectibles dates from the late 19th century, when women of breeding who had fallen on hard times (some of them Civil War widows) opened this still-charming means of earning modest income. Baltimoreans who work downtown enjoy its simplicity and honesty—and the food does not disappoint. Recently in danger of closing because of high maintenance costs, the Exchange seems to have rallied enough of its old friends to save it. It has become a downtown institution.

Basilica of the Assumption

At Mulberry St., cross and turn left to Cathedral St., then right to position yourself in front of a building that in 1976 was one of four to receive bicentennial recognition on U.S. postage stamps as the most distinguished achievements of American architecture. The **Basilica of the Assumption of the Blessed Virgin Mary** (1806–21) occupies the east side of Cathedral St. between Mulberry and Franklin Sts. Architects praise its exterior proportions and interior design. In 1805, Archbishop John Carroll asked Benjamin Henry Latrobe (1762–1820) to submit plans for the first Roman Catholic cathedral in the United States. Latrobe, an English engineer who had also worked as an architect for the U.S. Capitol, submitted both a Gothic and classical plan. When the latter was approved, in 1806, construction began, and it continued intermittently until 1818. Neither Carroll nor Latrobe lived to see the dedication of the cathedral in 1821. On September 1, 1937, Pope Pius XI elevated the cathedral to the rank of minor basilica, a title bestowed on historically significant churches.

The modest, granite-faced exterior has a cruciform shape with short transepts and a great dome over the intersection of transepts and nave. The two towers, part of the original design, were added in 1832, although their current onion domes are not original. The bells in the south tower, cast at Lyons in 1830, sound to a clock made by the French clockmaker M. Colin. The Ionic portico, also part of Latrobe's design, was added during the Civil War; and in 1890, the building was extended 40 feet to the east. Pale shades of gray, blue, and gold dominate the cool, quiet interior. The remains of John Carroll (1735–1815), first Roman Catholic bishop of the United States, lie under the large rotunda.

Baltimore became the first Roman Catholic episcopal see in the United States on November 6, 1789: when Carroll was ordained as archbishop on April 8, 1808, the city automatically became see of the first American archdiocese. Since Carroll's death, 12 other prelates have presided over the see of Baltimore, James Gibbons serving the longest term (44 years). Only the second North American cardinal, Gibbons (1834–1921) was born to a Baltimore Irish family, educated at St. Mary's Seminary, then on Paca St., and ordained a priest in June 1861. He was named archbishop of Baltimore in 1877. Pope Leo XII anointed him cardinal in 1886. In 1917, his friend President Theodore Roosevelt called him the most respected and venerated citizen in America. Following Maryland tradition, the cardinal became a strong advocate of religious toleration and interdenominational cooperation, as well as defender of American democracy. In 1889, when the Catholic University of America was established in Washington, D.C., Gibbons became its chancellor and president of the board of trustees. His books include *The Faith of Our Fathers* (1877, over 100 editions in many languages), *Our Christian Heritage* (1895), and *The Ambassador of Christ* (1896).

The **Archbishop's House** (1830), a five-part, neoclassical building designed by William Small, faces Charles St., connected to the cathedral by a sheltered walkway. The garden was a favorite retreat of Cardinal Gibbons, who is said to have planted some of the crocuses that appear there every spring.

Our Daily Bread, a public kitchen that Catholic Charities opened here in 1981, stands on the southeastern corner of Cathedral and Franklin Sts. It reaches out to the increasing number of homeless people who come to the basilica for help. The kitchen now serves about 800 meals a day, seven days a week, to any hungry person who comes to the door. The building, completed in 1991 and bearing the names of the principal donors, Harry and Jeanette Weinberg, went up despite opposition from local historical and cultural groups.

Enoch Pratt Free Library

This secular shrine to literacy proudly stands directly across the street from the basilica. When the current, three-story limestone building was finished in 1933, its 12 large display windows facing Cathedral St. set a national precedent for library design.

Enoch Pratt came to Baltimore from Massachusetts in 1831 and organized a wholesale hardware company specializing in nails and horseshoes. A pillar of the Unitarian Church and a notorious pennypincher, Pratt accumulated a fortune as businessman and financier. He was also a staunch Unionist during the Civil War and a supporter of education for the city's African Americans. Probably inspired by the examples of his friends, George Peabody and Johns Hopkins, Pratt in 1882 offered to build a library on Mulberry St. He would construct the facility and provide an endowment of $833,333.33 if the city would establish a $50,000 perpetual annuity to be administered by a Pratt-appointed board of trustees. The city accepted, and on January 5, 1886, the central library opened its doors with 28,000 books and four branch libraries in every quadrant of the city. Pratt's free library, universally praised by everyone from Andrew Carnegie to the poorest cardholder, became an instant public success. When the current central library on Cathedral St. replaced the original Victorian building, the library system had more than 1 million books and 100,000 cardholders. The central branch became a State Library Resource Center in 1971. The Pratt now has 28 branches, 2 million volumes, 6,500 films and videos, 28,000 recordings, and 300,000 cardholders. Millions more may access the library's catalogue on the World Wide Web. H. L. Mencken bequeathed his own library, papers, and time-locked manuscripts to his beloved Pratt when he died in 1956.

The building retains its democratic splendor. In the great two-story central room, beautifully restored under current leadership, patrons find computer terminals that have replaced catalogues, loan desks, and reading tables. Adjoining rooms make available reference works, periodicals and newspapers on microfilm, and the literature and social science collections. Two murals by George Novikoff illustrate Johannes Gutenberg with his press and William Caxton, the first English printer, presenting his first book to his patroness, the Duchess Marguerite. Behind the loan desks hang full-length portraits of the six Lords Baltimore and of Gov. Benedict Leonard Calvert, presented to the library in 1940 by Dr. Hugh Hampton Young, a Baltimore surgeon who assembled them from several English auction buyers.

On the second floor, the Maryland Room houses books, pamphlets, maps, and other publications relating to Maryland, including such rare items as the George Cator Collection of pictures and engravings. Baltimore artist Lee Woodward Ziegler painted the wall murals, which depict scenes from Edmund Spenser's ode, *The Faerie Queene*. The Music and Fine Arts Room houses books and periodicals and also audio recordings. The Edgar Allan Poe Room contains likenesses of the poet and provides a meeting space for literary groups. On the third floor the library maintains circulating film and video collections as well as the H. L. Mencken Room, open to serious researchers upon request.

Across Franklin St., the **Franklin Street Church,** a Gothic Revival building designed by Robert Cary Long Jr. in 1844, faces the library. Listed on the National Register of Historic Places, this distinctive structure— with its English Tudor towers—originally housed a Presbyterian congregation. Woodrow Wilson occupied pew 11 during his graduate student days at Johns Hopkins University in the 1880s. The congregation merged with the First Presbyterian Church in 1973 and sold its old home to the New Psalmist Baptist Church in 1977. That thriving congregation outgrew the facility and moved in 1995. A nondenominational group has occupied the building since 1996.

Walk east one block on Franklin to Charles to see the **First Unitarian Church,** a classical domed structure—similar on a smaller scale to the nearby basilica. It dates to 1817, when a small number of Baltimoreans, many of New England origin, met to form the First Independent or Unitarian Church of Baltimore. The group hired Maximilian Godefroy to design the church, whose chief outside ornamentation is a reddish terracotta relief figure of the Angel of Truth on the pediment above the recessed Tuscan portico. Over time, weather took its toll on the original, designed by Simon Willard and executed by Antonio Capellano; Henry Berge supplied an exact copy in 1954.

In 1819 the congregation hired the Rev. Jared Sparks, later to become publisher of the *North American Review* and president of Harvard College, as their first pastor. In May of that year William Ellery Channing delivered the ordination sermon entitled "Unitarian Christianity," which laid out doctrinal differences with the Congregational Church. Later translated into seven languages, the sermon marked the beginning of the Unitarian movement and formed the basis for this church's claim to being "The Birthplace of Unitarianism in the United States."

Godefroy's beautiful interior proved acoustically unsound—so much so that no one behind the first three rows heard the famous sermon; according to legend, one minister of a nearby Trinitarian church told his congregation, "There has been a new Church erected in our city for the dissemination of pernicious doctrines, but by the grace of God, nobody can hear what the minister has to say." In 1893, to improve the acoustics, Joseph E. Sperry substantially redesigned the interior spaces. He placed the barrel ceiling under a dome and replaced the original organ, which was shaped like a lyre. Godefroy's original pulpit remains, and people in all of the pews can now hear what issues from it.

Follow Charles St. north as it slopes downhill from Franklin St. to Centre St. On the northwest corner of Charles and Centre the visitor finds one of Baltimore's most famous museums.

The Walters Art Gallery

William T. Walters, a Pennsylvania native of Scotch-Irish ancestry, came to Baltimore in 1841 as a trained civil engineer. He soon entered the wholesale produce business while also gaining control of the Baltimore and Susquehanna Railroad and developing Southern rail networks that eventually became the Atlantic Coast Line Railroad. A Southern sympathizer, Walters sat out the Civil War in Paris, where he collected art. At his death, he owned a significant collection of 19th-century French paintings and sculptures as well as a pioneering assemblage of Far Eastern porcelains.

His son Henry (1848–1931) continued his father's career as railroad magnate and patron of the arts, expanding the collection to include virtually all fields of art from predynastic Egypt to Tiffany. Henry Walters pursued collecting with passion, spending around $1 million a year for objects that accumulated in crates and boxes in the Walters family mansion at 5 W. Mt. Vernon Place. After he purchased the Don Marcello Massaranti collection of Italian art in 1902, he commissioned the New York firm of Delano and Aldrich to build a private gallery with an interior court modeled after the University Palace at the University of Genoa. In 1909 he opened the gallery to the public, charging a small admission fee that he donated to charity. At his death Henry Walters bequeathed the gallery and its 22,000 pieces to his native city "for the benefit of the public." The gift stands as one of the country's most impressive acts of cultural philanthropy.

Since 1931 the Walters Art Gallery (600 N. Charles St.) has earned renown as one of only a few museums worldwide whose holdings offer a comprehensive view of art history from the third millennium B.C. to the early 20th century. Among its thousands of treasures, the Walters holds the finest collection of ivories, jewelry, enamels, and bronzes in America and a spectacular reserve of medieval and Renaissance illuminated manuscripts. The Egyptian, Greek and Roman, Byzantine, Ethiopian, and Western-medieval art collections rank among the best in the nation, as do those of Renaissance and Asian art. The Walters has examples of every major trend in French painting during the 19th century.

Until 1974, when the gallery expanded along Centre St., most of this rich collection could not be displayed. The **contemporary addition** (Shepley, Bulfinch, Richardson and Abbott of Boston) contains four levels for an auditorium, ancient civilizations, medieval, Romanesque, Islamic, Byzantine, Coptic, Gothic, and 19th-century paintings. The old building, which has also been refurbished, houses Renaissance sculpture, jewelry, bronzes, and European paintings from the 16th to the 18th centuries. In 1991 the museum opened **Hackerman House** at 1 W. Mt. Vernon Place to display more than 1,000 objects from China, Japan, India, and Southeast Asia. This restored town house, originally built in 1850, connects to other parts of the gallery by means of a restaurant pavilion that occupies what once was the backyard of the mansion.

The Walters Art Gallery is known not only for its collections but also for its longstanding traditions of scholarship, conservation research, and education. The museum emphasizes a contextual, humanistic approach in its exhibits and programs; its wide-ranging collections enable visitors to learn about the artistic accomplishments of many of the world's civilizations.

Open Wednesday–Friday 10:00 a.m. to 4:00 p.m., Saturday and Sunday 11:00 a.m. to 5:00 p.m. Admission: $6.00 for adults, $4.00 for senior citizens, $3.00 for students with valid identification, $2.00 for children ages 6 to 17. Museum members and children under 6 years enter free. Admission is free on the first Thursday of every month between 5:00 and 8:00 p.m. Attended parking at Centre and Cathedral Sts.; additional lots at the Peabody Garage, Centre and St. Paul Sts., and on West Franklin St.

Museum shop and restaurant. For further information, call 410-547-9000.

Mt. Vernon Place

Farther north, Charles St. climbs again through the southern arm of a cross-shaped park that radiates from the Washington Monument. Although locals long have referred to the entire area as Mt. Vernon Place, this name technically belongs only to the two east-west blocks of Monument St. between St. Paul and Cathedral Sts. Washington Place lies along the two blocks of Charles St. between Centre and Madison Sts.

When John Eager Howard (1752–1827) donated part of his wooded hillside for the Washington Monument in 1815, the site lay well beyond the city limits. After Howard's death his heirs laid out lots facing rectangular parks around the monument. The first substantial houses appeared in the 1840s, and by the time the city expanded to this area in the 1850s, the squares had become prime properties lined with distinguished residences. The houses reflect Greek Revival simplicity and—more of them—Italian Renaissance style with flat brick or brownstone fronts trimmed with elaborate stone cornices and balconies. Various landscape styles have graced the parks; Thomas Hastings created the current design in 1916.

When the automobile changed the city's character in the 1920s and affluent families moved farther north, Mount Vernon declined. Only thanks to devoted attention on the part of early preservationists—that of the late Douglas H. Gordon being a premier example—does this lovely and unique urban setting survive. In 1964 Baltimore created the Mount

Iron-balconied town houses dating from the 19th century, the original Peabody Institute building, and Mt. Vernon Place Methodist Church, seen from Charles St. as it ascends toward the Washington Monument

Vernon Historic Preservation District, an area around Mt. Vernon Place from Centre to Read Sts. and between Howard and St. Paul Sts. Civic guardians have been particularly zealous in protecting the district's architectural heritage.

Washington Monument

This 164-foot, unfluted Doric column dominates Mt. Vernon Place and was once visible from the inner harbor. With the exception of a humble homemade memorial in Boonsboro, Maryland, Baltimore's was the first monument to George Washington constructed in the new republic. Baltimoreans laid plans for it in 1809. After wartime delays, a design competition was held, and judges selected Robert Mills's design. Citizens decided to place the smaller Battle Monument on the site of the old courthouse on Calvert St. and to accept John Eager Howard's offer of a rural (and presumably safer) site for the monument to Washington. Private and public lotteries raised nearly $178,000 for the monument. Mills (1781–1855), an eminent American-born professional architect, placed the column on a 50-foot square base, 28 feet high, with inscriptions on each side identifying key elements of Washington's military and political career. A circular iron fence with Roman military motifs surrounds the base. A small observation deck caps the column, which is made from Baltimore County marble. Italian sculptor Enrico Causici created the 16-foot statue of Washington that stands on the stepped dome. Baltimoreans laid the cornerstone in elaborate ceremonies on July 4, 1815; workmen installed the last piece of the statue November 25, 1829.

The monument was closed to the public in 1985 and then reopened in 1993 after extensive interior restoration. A museum inside the base contains exhibits relating to the construction; 228 steps lead up to the observation platform.

The Peabody Institute of the Johns Hopkins University

A native of South Danvers, Massachusetts, George Peabody came to Baltimore in 1815 to establish a wholesale dry-goods business. It developed into one of the largest mercantile firms in the country. While in England on business in 1835, Peabody successfully negotiated an $8 million loan for the state of Maryland, then virtually bankrupt. Two years later, he moved to London and began a career as an international banker.

Then in 1857 Peabody returned briefly to Baltimore and set in motion long-held plans for endowing a private institute "useful towards the improvement of the moral and intellectual culture of the inhabitants of Baltimore, and, collaterally, to those of the State, and, also, towards the enlargement and diffusion of a taste for the Fine Arts." His proposal included establishment of a noncirculating library, a lecture series, an academy of music, and a painting-and-sculpture gallery supervised by a board of trustees to whom he eventually entrusted $1.4 million. The trustees organized in 1858 and by 1861, a marble building for these enterprises had been completed at 1 E. Mt. Vernon Place. After the Civil War, in 1866, Peabody formally and pointedly dedicated the institute as "a common ground" for "political tolerance and charity." His example profoundly influenced the cultural growth of Baltimore. Johns Hopkins consulted him. Enoch Pratt was the long-time treasurer of the Peabody Institute, and William T. Walters served briefly as its president. Peabody thus helped transform "mobtown" into a place *Harper's Magazine* in 1896 called the "Athens of America."

The music conservatory opened on Mulberry St. in 1868, joining the rest of the institute 10 years later; a new, adjoining library building was completed to house the growing research collections. With its six stories of book shelves, all facing a skylighted central open space featuring ornate cast-iron columns and railings, the Peabody Library supplies one of the city's most dramatic interior spaces. Daniel Coit Gilman (first president of Johns Hopkins University), Sidney Lanier, H. L. Mencken, and John Dos Passos used reserved desks here. Peabody's philanthropy stimulated Johns Hopkins, a Peabody Institute trustee, to bequeath $7 million for establishment of a university and hospital after his death in 1873. The university opened its doors nearby at N. Howard St. near Centre St. in 1876 and used the Peabody Library facilities almost exclusively until moving to its Homewood Campus in 1915. In 1966, the financially pressed Peabody trustees handed control of the library's 300,000 volumes to the Enoch Pratt Free Library. Eleven years later the Peabody Institute became a division of Johns Hopkins University, and in 1982 the historic Peabody Library became a department within the Special Collections of the university's Milton S. Eisenhower Library.

The **Conservatory of Music,** the nation's oldest by founding date (1857), grew dramatically under its second director, Danish composer and conductor Asger Hamerik, who attracted internationally known musicians to the school. The Peabody Symphony Orchestra became the city's first professional orchestra and contributed to the establishment of the Baltimore Symphony Orchestra in 1915. The conservatory now has an enrollment of about 600 undergraduate and post-baccalaureate students from throughout the world. The **Peabody Preparatory,** which occupies **Leakin Hall** (1926) and four regional satellite branches, has a student body of more than 2,000. This pre-college program for both children and adults was founded in 1894 by May Garrettson Evans, Baltimore's first female newspaper reporter.

In 1990, the conservatory opened the **Arthur Friedheim Library,** repository of 100,000 books, scores, and recordings. Open to the public, the library also contains extensive materials relating to Maryland musicians and composers. Borrowing privileges are restricted to members of the Hopkins community. The conservatory library building is accessible from Charles St. via a landscaped plaza that connects the older buildings to dormitories designed by Edward Durrell Stone in 1969. The **Peabody Inn,** opened in 1993, was created from four 19th-century rowhouses at 601–607 S. Washington Place to house senior citizens who participate in the popular International Elderhostel program at the conservatory.

When George Peabody founded his Gallery of Art on the second floor of the original building's east wing (**North Hall**), it became the nation's third oldest art gallery, antedated only by the Peale Museum and the Philadelphia Academy of Fine Arts. The Peabody gallery housed accessions of the Baltimore Museum of Art (begun in 1914) until 1923, when the BMA established its first home at 101 W. Monument St. The neighborly association between the two institutions lasted until 1929, when the museum moved to Wyman Park. During the 1940s, as the conservatory expanded, the gallery's collection—featuring sculptures by

William Rinehart and paintings by such American artists as Winslow Homer and Mary Cassatt—moved to other exhibit spaces. The entire Peabody art collection went to the Maryland State Archives in 1996 in exchange for a $15 million contribution from the state to the institute's endowment. A complete inventory of the collection is available on the archives' web site; works from it circulate within the state on request.

Mount Vernon Place Methodist Church

This Victorian Gothic building of green serpentine marble (1873, Dixon and Carson) occupies the corner of E. Mt. Vernon Place and N. Washington Place, site of the Charles Howard mansion, where Francis Scott Key died in 1843. **Asbury House,** an Italianate Renaissance rowhouse designed by John R. Niernsee and J. Crawford Nielson around 1855, stands immediately next to the church at 10 E. Mt. Vernon Place. Niernsee, a Viennese architect, came to Baltimore around 1845 and worked with Nielson, a Baltimorean, to create a number of local structures, including Hackerman House and its neighbors on the south side of W. Mt. Vernon Place.

The Squares

Walk up S. Washington Place from Centre St. between the Peabody Conservatory and Walters Art Gallery. The fountain features an enlargement of **Sea Urchin,** by Edward Berge, a German American artist from Baltimore who studied at the Maryland Institute before going to Paris to study with Auguste Rodin. In 1961 Henry Berge, Edward's son, completed this copy, a gift of Frederick R. Huber; the smaller original now graces a lily pond on the Homewood campus of Johns Hopkins University. The **Schapiro House** at 609 S. Washington Place (ca. 1848) offers an outstanding example of the ornamental cast ironwork that Baltimore manufactured and shipped as far away as New Orleans.

The **Lafayette Monument** (1924)—an animated bronze equestrian figure of the Marquis de Lafayette by Andrew O'Connor Jr. on a base designed by Thomas Hastings—stands just south of the Washington Monument at the top of the square. Field Marshal Joseph Joffre, commander of the French armies in World War I from 1914 to 1916, broke ground for the monument in 1917. President Calvin Coolidge attended its unveiling on September 6, 1924, when speakers recalled both American troops sent to France in 1917 and the French troops who fought in the American Revolution.

In keeping with the martial spirit of the place, four bronzes by Antoine Louis Barye (**War, Peace, Force, Order**), presented to the city by William Walters, stand on pedestals at the corners of the Mt. Vernon Place parks nearest the Washington Monument.

Turn right on E. Mt. Vernon Place to the park that lies between the Peabody Institute and Mt. Vernon Methodist Church. A replica of the **statue of George Peabody,** a seated figure facing the monument, is located across from the Peabody Library. American sculptor William Wetmore Story did the original, unveiled by the Prince of Wales in London shortly after Peabody's death. Robert Garrett presented this copy to the city in 1890. Below the fountain at the bottom of the park, facing St. Paul St., stands a **statue of Severn Teackle Wallis,** the work of Laurent Marqueste in 1906. Wallis (1816–94), a noted lawyer and wit, spent fourteen months in prison during the Civil War for his Southern sympathies and outspoken objections to arbitrary Union authority. After the war he became a leader in the movement for city political and civil-service reform. The elegant row of brownstone houses on the other side of the park reflects a style that became popular in eastern cities during the second half of the 19th century.

The park on N. Washington Place provides a setting for the bronze **statue of Chief Justice Roger Brooke Taney.** William Walters gave this replica to the city in 1887; the original, the work of William Henry Rinehart (1825–74), sits in front of the State House in Annapolis. Rinehart, a native of Union Bridge, willed his property to the Peabody Institute to "aid in the promotion of a more highly cultivated taste for art." His trustees founded the Rinehart School of Sculpture, now located at the Maryland Institute College of Art. A bronze equestrian **statue of John Eager Howard** (Emmanuel Fremiet, 1904) faces Madison St. at the north end of the park. The granite pedestal contains a copy of the medal Congress awarded Howard for valor at the Battle of Cowpens in South Carolina. Howard led Maryland and Delaware soldiers in a bayonet charge that turned the tide of the battle. A plaque on the **Stafford Hotel** on the west side of the park commemorates the formation here on May 9, 1911, of the American Psychoanalytic Association. Ernest Jones and seven other doctors thereby aimed "to further the knowledge of Doctor Sigmund Freud's pioneering work." Charles E. Cassell designed the hotel as well as the ornamental, chateau-like house (ca. 1895) at the corner of Washington Place and Madison St.

The park on W. Mt. Vernon Place contains the bronze **Lion** (1885), another Barye work that William Walters, who had assembled a large collection by the popular French sculptor, donated to the city. The statue in the fountain, Henri Crenier's **Boy and the Turtle,** was originally part of an exhibit the Baltimore Museum of Art arranged on this square in 1924. A bronze replica of Paul Dubois's figure entitled **Military Courage** (1885) commands the Cathedral St. end of the park. The **Mount Vernon Club,** a private women's club, has occupied the Greek Revival town house at 8 W. Mt. Vernon Place since 1942. Built around 1842, the house is a fine example of the Baltimore town houses built by the well-to-do in the first half of the 19th century. Noted diplomat David K. E. Bruce grew up in this house.

The most expensive town house ever built in Baltimore lies across the street at **7–11 W. Mt. Vernon Place.** Robert Garrett, president of the Baltimore and Ohio Railroad, and his wife, Mary Sloane Frick, hired New York architect Stanford White to design the house in 1884. When Garrett died in 1902, his widow married Dr. Henry Barton Jacobs and in 1905 hired John Russell Pope to add an extension—including library, theater, and art gallery—which incorporated two adjacent houses. Embellished with carved wood, marble, and Tiffany glass, the 40-room mansion and its furnishings cost an estimated $1.5 million. From this princely establishment Mrs. Jacobs ruled as the grande dame of Baltimore society. Dr. Jacobs died in 1939, and the house went through a series of owners until 1961, when the Engineering Society of Baltimore acquired it. The society has restored the building, which is open to the public by appointment. For information call 410-539-6914.

Walk on Monument St. one block west of Mt. Vernon Place to the

Enoch Pratt House, a three-story brick house built for Enoch Pratt in 1846. The fourth floor and mansard roof of his house, designed by Edmund G. Lind, were added in 1871. Mrs. H. Irvine Keyser bought the house in 1916, added the library and main gallery (designed by J. B. Noel Wyatt and William G. Nolting) to the rear, and presented the building to the Maryland Historical Society in memory of her husband. The society now occupies most of the block.

The Maryland Historical Society

The Maryland Historical Society (201 W. Monument St.), founded in 1844, collects, preserves, and interprets materials that illuminate the story of Maryland. The society owes its origins to the cultural-preservation interests of some of the city's leading gentlemen, who in 1844 secured a charter from the General Assembly. The founders then raised $35,000 to build an "Athenaeum" at the corner of St. Paul and Saratoga Sts., in which they presented exhibits of Maryland art and gave papers on state history. George Peabody, a longtime member, had originally proposed that the society manage the Peabody Institute. While this scheme proved impractical, his support enabled the society to begin publishing works on Maryland history and collecting documents from the colonial and revolutionary past. The society produced the first of 72 volumes of *The Archives of Maryland* in 1882 and began publishing the *Maryland Historical Magazine* (still appearing quarterly) in 1906.

Collections range widely and include paintings, silver, textiles, ceramics, crystal, French porcelain, antique toys, and sports memorabilia. These collections increased dramatically in 1998 when the society acquired the holdings—some 300,000 paintings, prints, and photographs—of the defunct Baltimore City Life Museums. Now, more than 500,000 objects, as well as 6.2 million documents and books record and elucidate Maryland's rich heritage since before European settlement. Gallery space includes the three floors of the Thomas and Hugg Building (which visitors enter from Monument St.), the first floor of the adjoining Pratt House, the Robert T. Merrick Wing (1981), and, as of 1997, a renovated bus barn that lies along Centre St. and adds some 21,000 square feet of temporary and permanent exhibit space.

On display in the galleries, visitors can see one of only three Revolutionary War officer's uniforms still in existence. Also on view are the original manuscript for Francis Scott Key's "The Star-Spangled Banner" and paintings by Joshua Johnson, Baltimorean and America's first professional African American artist. Baltimore album quilts, some of the best examples of 19th-century American needlework, tell of women's experiences. The society holds the nation's richest collection of paintings by the famous American artist (and father of artists) Charles Willson Peale. Displayed objects on the second floor of the Thomas and Hugg Building include stellar examples of Federal-period furniture—some of it commissioned by the Ettings, one of Baltimore's oldest Jewish families—and representative pieces from the country's largest collection of 19th-century American silver. Permanent second-floor exhibits explore Maryland's experience in the War of 1812 and Civil War. Pieces from the Eubie Blake collection shed light on the achievements of this legendary African American ragtime pianist and jazz composer. Below the first floor, the ship models, paintings, prints, pennants, and re-created ship chandlery of the Radcliffe Maritime Museum offer a clear and colorful overview of Maryland's experience in waterborne commerce.

Children may visit the Darnall Young People's Gallery of Maryland History on the first floor of the Thomas and Hugg Building and also the hands-on colonial kitchen and playroom in the lower level of the Pratt House.

The library, a major resource to historians and genealogists, preserves the papers of such nationally significant figures as Charles Carroll of Carrollton, signer of the Declaration of Independence, and Benjamin Henry Latrobe, architect of the U.S. Capitol (whose drawings form an important part of the collection). Other highlights include Capt. John Smith's map of the Chesapeake (1607), a dictionary of the Delaware Indian language (1856), broadsides and pamphlets debating slavery, Civil War photographs of Alexander Gardner and Mathew Brady, and immigrant debarkation lists. Here one also finds a file of newspaper clippings, miscellaneous prints and photographs, and the papers of Marylanders who shaped four centuries of state history.

Museum open Tuesday–Friday, 10 a.m. to 5 p.m., Saturday 9 a.m. to 5 p.m., and Sunday, 1 to 5 p.m. Library open Tuesday–Friday, 10 a.m. to 4:30 p.m., Saturday 9 a.m. to 4:30 p.m. Closed Mondays and major holidays. Parking on street and in nearby lots.

Admission: Free to members, $4 for adults, $3 for seniors, children under 12 free. A family rate of $6 is available for two adults and two children. Admission is free Saturdays 9 to 11 a.m.

Museum shop. For information call 410-685-3750.

Two Royal Ladies

Among its many artifacts, the historical society owns furniture and other belongings of Elizabeth ("Betsy") Patterson (1785–1879), one of two Baltimore women who created upheavals in European royal circles.

Betsy was an 18-year-old belle from one of Maryland's wealthiest families when she met 19-year-old Jerome Bonaparte, youngest brother of Napoleon Bonaparte, on his visit to Baltimore from the French West Indies in 1803. Despite opposition from both families, the two lovers pursued the romance to marriage, which Bishop John Carroll performed on Christmas Eve 1803. Napoleon, who planned to marry his relatives to European royal families, suspended his brother's allowance and ordered him back to France at once. While his new bride waited in England, barred from Continental Europe, Jerome allowed himself to be persuaded to abandon Betsy in favor of his brother's dynastic plans. Their son, Jerome Napoleon, was born in 1805 in Camberwell, England. Pope Pius VII refused Napoleon's demand to dissolve the marriage, but the Maryland General Assembly, at the urging of Betsy's father, William Patterson, passed a special act of annulment. Betsy eventually accepted an annual French pension of 60,000 francs. She returned to Baltimore, where, a miserly landlord, she lived in the hope that her descendants would either succeed to the French throne or marry into European aristocracy. "My ruling passions have been love, ambition and avarice," the aging Betsy told her Baltimore confidantes. "Love has fled, ambition has brought disappointment, but avarice remains." She died at the age of 94 in a Cathedral St. boarding house.

Bessie Wallis Warfield (1896–1986), though also born into a prominent Maryland family, grew up in genteel poverty in a row house at 212 East Biddle St. Her father, Teackle Wallis Warfield, died when she was an infant, and her mother, Alys Montague Warfield, struggled to make ends meet. Richer family members insured that she received a fashionable education, and she was presented to Baltimore society at the Bachelors Cotillion in 1914. Two years later, she married first a new lieutenant from the U.S. Naval Academy and then, after a divorce in 1927, Ernest Simpson, a shipping broker who did business in Great Britain. The Simpsons became part of the social circle around the Prince of Wales during the early 1930s. During her husband's absences on business trips, a romance developed with the prince, who became King Edward VIII on January 20, 1936. Wallis Warfield Simpson was granted a preliminary divorce decree in October, but both church and government officials opposed her marriage to the king. On December 11, 1936, the British monarch astonished the world by abdicating the throne for the "woman I love." H. L. Mencken called their love "the greatest story since the resurrection." The couple married in France the following spring. When they visited Baltimore in 1941, thousands jammed the route of their downtown motorcade to a reception at City Hall. They remained together for 35 years, living in France with the titles Duke and Duchess of Windsor, until the duke's death in 1972. The duchess died at the age of 89, a rich recluse in Paris.

A Walk to Three Gothic Churches and Antique Row

The hearty walker may proceed north on Park Ave. to see a few more Gothic churches within the Mt. Vernon Historic District and to visit a colorful neighborhood. The churches testify to the northward expansion of the city during the 1850s. **Grace and St. Peter's Episcopal Church** (Niernsee and Neilson, 1852), at the northeast corner of Monument St. and Park Ave., deliberately resembles a rural English church. One block north, **First and Franklin Street Presbyterian Church,** at Madison and Park, dominates the sky with its 273-foot Gothic spire, the tallest in Baltimore. Nathan Starkweather designed the church in 1854, but the steeple, which rests on a great cast-iron frame, was not erected until 1874. Walk east one block to Cathedral and then north (left) for a block to Read St. and **Emmanuel Episcopal Church** (1854), another Niernsee and Neilson Gothic edifice in granite. The facade changed considerably in 1920, when John Kirchmayer ornamented the tower with sculpture representing the Christmas story.

A literary sidelight: H. L. Mencken lived, with his wife Sarah Haardt, at 704 Cathedral St.; they married in 1930, and she died of tuberculosis only five years later.

Read St. forms the northern boundary of the Mt. Vernon Historic District. Walking up Read and crossing Park Ave., one reaches Tyson St. Named for Elisha Tyson, the Quaker abolitionist, the small street became a highly publicized object of private urban renewal activity in the early 1950s. Artists and others bought the little houses, originally constructed for Irish immigrants, painted them in pastel colors, and created a lively urban space. It remains a charming community given to alternative styles of life.

Farther on, the walker reaches Howard St. Turn left and proceed down Antique Row, a succession of galleries, shops, and cafés that will lead to West Monument St. From that point, looking up Monument to the west, lies the site of the Johns Hopkins University's first campus. Down Howard a block, also on the west, note the large Victorian brick building—the late-19th-century site of Baltimore City College—the premier academic high school for boys, now located near Memorial Stadium. One block south on the east side of Howard, a restored transcontinental bus station houses the Metropolitan Regional Planning Council, the Maryland Arts Council, and the Maryland Humanities Council.

One can return to the Inner Harbor by walking south on Howard St. (once Baltimore's premier shopping and entertainment avenue, lined with department stores and movie theaters, most of which closed during the

1960s and '70s); or go left two blocks to Charles, then right to backtrack the walk north; or simply take the Light Rail down Howard St. to Pratt St.

E. WEST FROM THE INNER HARBOR TO CAMDEN ST., LEXINGTON MARKET, AND SETON HILL

This walking tour explores part of Baltimore's sports history, the city's oldest medical and professional schools, famous gravesites, a historic marketplace, and religious shrines both Catholic and Protestant. From Harborplace walk west on Pratt St. past the Convention Center. On the northeastern corner of Pratt and Howard Sts., at 250 West Pratt, a 25-story structure provides offices to bankers and airlines and impresses the viewer with its corrugated, glistening surface. Across the street, at 300 West Pratt, architects in 1989 combined the construction of a new, metallic-appearing building of five stories with preservation of an adjacent old office building with a locally made iron front. It belonged to the furniture maker William Wilkens.

Continue west on Pratt to Eutaw St. Look to the north and admire the Bromo-Seltzer Tower—now the **Baltimore Arts Tower**—which dominates the city skyline in these blocks. The 308-foot clocktower rose in 1911, testimony to the fancy of Capt. Isaac E. Emerson, founder of the Emerson Drug Company and father of the heartburn remedy, Bromo-Seltzer. Fascinated by the Palazzo Vecchio in Florence, Emerson commissioned architect Joseph E. Sperry to build a replica next to his factory. Still not content, Emerson, in true American fashion, placed on top of the Florentine tower a 51-foot revolving replica of the blue Bromo-Seltzer bottle, crowned with lights. The bottle came down in 1930, and the factory fell to the wrecker's ball in 1967 after a Pennsylvania firm bought the business. Preserved, the tower now shelters the offices of the Mayor's Advisory Committee on Art and Culture. The **John Steadman Fire Station,** commemorating a longtime chief, occupies the factory site, on which also stands Roger Majorowicz's fanciful sculpture, *Fire Chariot* (1972).

At Pratt and Eutaw one can see both the Pratt St. and Camden Yards Stations of the Light Rail system, which opened in 1992 and connects Hunt Valley in Baltimore County with Baltimore-Washington International Airport in Anne Arundel County.

Camden Station

Turn left one block to Camden St., which gave its name to the old B&O station (Niernsee and Neilson, 1857) that served as the railroad's principal passenger and freight depot. The center portion, which was crowned with a 180-foot tower, was designed to resemble the grandest stations in London. Two wings with 80-foot towers were added between 1865 and 1867. By the turn of the century, the towers were gone, and the building itself gradually deteriorated. During construction of the Baltimore Orioles' new ballpark, the station enjoyed a renaissance—and obtained shorter, near-replica towers.

Abraham Lincoln boarded a train here in February 1861, traveling to Washington for his inauguration. He had intended to reach Baltimore

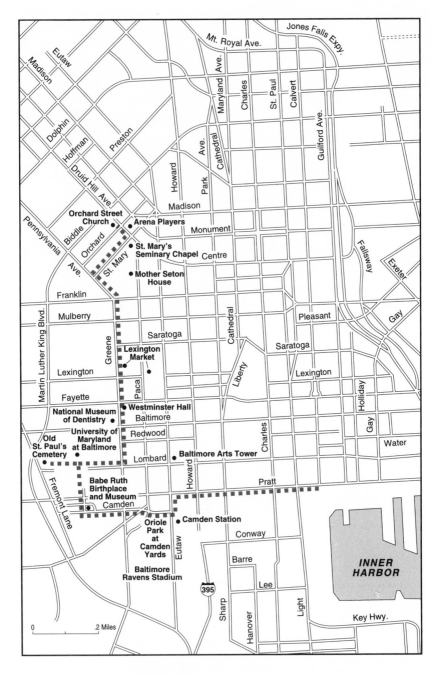

from Harrisburg, Pennsylvania, by the Northern Central Railroad and then transfer to Camden Station by horse-drawn rail car. Allan Pinkerton, founder of the detective agency and later an intelligence agent during the Civil War, informed Lincoln's advisors of a plot to assassinate the president-elect in Baltimore. Pinkerton recommended that Lincoln travel first to Philadelphia, where he could ride the Philadelphia, Wilmington, and Baltimore Railroad (one of Pinkerton's employers) to the President St. Station in Baltimore. From there, horses could pull his sleeping car to Camden Station and thus avoid daylight provocation of Southern sympathizers. Although unconvinced of the danger, Lincoln accepted Pinkerton's advice and passed through Baltimore at 3:30 a.m. without leaving his car. The press, particularly in the South, ridiculed Lincoln's "skulking" passage through Baltimore, and the president subsequently considered it a political mistake. In any case, two months later a similar transfer, then of troops, led to the Pratt Street riot.

During the B&O Railroad strike in July 1877, Gov. John Lee Carroll ordered the Fifth and Sixth Maryland National Guard regiments to Cumberland to control the disorder that followed the railroad's use of strikebreakers. Labor sympathizers jeered and stoned men of the Sixth Regiment as they left their armory at Fayette and Front Sts., and many of the citizen soldiers opted to return home. About half the unit reached Camden Station—at point of bayonet. A mob of thousands then besieged the station, setting fire to several railroad cars and part of the station itself. During the confrontation, the remaining members of the Sixth killed 10 protesters and wounded 13 more. Regular troops from Fort McHenry relieved the militia the next day, and the mob eventually dispersed.

Oriole Park at Camden Yards

A professional baseball team has played in Baltimore since at least the end of the Civil War. By the 1880s, a team was calling itself the Baltimore Orioles. The Orioles joined the National League in 1892 and under manager Ned Hanlon won consecutive pennants in 1894, '95, and '96. After the first championship, crowds gathered at Camden Station to pay tribute to their returning heroes, a team with a batting average of .328 and such players as John McGraw and Wee Willie Keeler. These "Old Orioles" won lasting fame as technicians who either invented or refined the practices of hit-and-run, base stealing, place hitting, sacrifice hits, and bunts. The team declined after Hanlon's departure to New York. The Orioles briefly belonged to the American League in 1901–2, then descended to the minor leagues. In the minor league era—between 1903 and 1953—the Orioles often finished at or near the top of what became the International League, winning "the little World Series" from 1919 to 1925 and again in 1944. When the St. Louis Browns, of the American League, moved to Baltimore in 1954 and again put major league Orioles on the field, Baltimore baseball fans entered heaven's gate. The club won the 1966 World Series handily and afterward claimed so many league pennants that bumper stickers declared the city to be "Flag Town, USA." The Orioles again prevailed in the Series in 1970 and 1983.

Before the mid-1950s, local African American players also performed with high quality professional teams. The Baltimore Elites, later the Baltimore Elite Giants, of the Negro American League, arrived in the city in 1936. After Jackie Robinson broke the color barrier in 1947, the Negro leagues began a decline, and by the time the Browns came to Baltimore, major league baseball had become racially integrated on the field.

In early 1984 the Baltimore Colts secretly left town for Indianapolis and then, if not before, Baltimoreans realized that fan support alone cannot hold a professional team. Two years later the state created the Maryland Stadium Authority to acquire and operate sports facilities for professional football and baseball. The authority selected Camden Yards, the old railroad and industrial facility in downtown Baltimore, as the location for two stadiums. The Orioles agreed to a long-term lease in 1988, and, with a large measure of state funding, construction of a new baseball park began a year later. The Kansas City architectural firm of Helmuth, Obata and Kassabaum patterned the asymmetrical, steel-and-brick structure after such famous early parks as Ebbets Field in Brooklyn, Fenway Park in Boston, and Wrigley Field in Chicago. The B&O warehouse (1895–1905) —a narrow, four-block-long brick building incorporated into the new design—forms a mammoth backdrop for right field. Separated from the ballpark by a 60-foot promenade, it houses the offices of the Orioles and other businesses.

When Oriole Park at Camden Yards opened on April 6, 1992, a sellout crowd of 44,568 watched the Orioles defeat the Cleveland Indians 2-0. Since that time, Orioles fans have set a major league record for consecutive sold-out games. The intimate, old-fashioned park has won virtually unanimous praise. Under what is now the playing field, archaeologists discovered the remains of a French Revolutionary War encampment and also the foundations of the tavern Babe Ruth's father owned in the late 19th century.

Babe Ruth Museums

No description of Baltimore baseball would be complete without a tip of the cap to George Herman Ruth (1895–1948), born in a row house at 216 Emory St. Susan Luery's nine-foot statue of "the Babe" stands near the Eutaw St. entrance to Camden Yards. A new $10 million **Babe Ruth Baseball Center** opened at Camden Station in 1997, complete with such modern exhibits as the "Negro Leagues in Baltimore," "Women in Sports," and "History of Baseball along the Chesapeake." It also includes exhibits and video materials covering the history of the Orioles.

To visit the **Babe Ruth Birthplace and Museum,** carefully cross busy Paca St. on the west edge of the ballpark complex, then cross Washington Blvd. and continue on Portland St. to Emory St. Turn right; the Ruth house stands on the west side of Emory. Babe Ruth learned to play baseball at St. Mary's Industrial School. He started his career with the minor league Orioles, moved on to set pitching records for the Boston Red Sox, and then excelled, especially as a hitter, for the New York Yankees. The museum showcases photographs and all manner of memorabilia from Ruth's colorful career. A clubroom commemorates the Babe's 714 home runs (a mark only Henry Aaron has exceeded). For information call 410-727-1539.

Baltimore Ravens Stadium

Just south of Oriole Park, a new football stadium seating nearly 70,000 spectators stands on 85 acres that the Maryland Stadium Authority purchased in 1989. The impressive new facility, which a Baltimore sportswriter has likened to an aircraft hanger in drydock, replaces Memorial Stadium on 33rd St. as home to professional football in the city. For 31 story-filled seasons after 1953, the Colts rewarded Baltimore fans every Sunday, winning league championshps in 1958 and 1959 and Super Bowl V in 1971. The brilliance and come-from-behind courage of Colts players—John Unitas, Lenny Moore, Raymond Berry, Alan "The Horse"

Ameche, and Art Donovan among them—became legendary. Baltimore's fans of professional football seethed after the Colts' departure (the Colts Marching Band never disbanded) and then reacted with mixed emotion in 1994 when, lured by the prospect of a new stadium, Arthur B. Modell moved the Cleveland Browns to Baltimore—thus visiting on Cleveland fans the same heartbreak Baltimore had felt in 1984. The public opted for the "Ravens" name, inspired by Edgar Allan Poe's famous poem. The team has played in the new stadium since the fall of 1998.

University of Maryland at Baltimore

One block west of Camden Street Station lies Greene St. (named for the revolutionary general Nathaniel Greene). Walking north on Greene, one soon reaches the extensive University of Maryland at Baltimore, which covers the area from Pratt St. north to Saratoga St. and from Eutaw St. west to Martin Luther King Jr. Blvd. This professional branch of the University of Maryland includes schools of medicine, nursing, physical therapy, pharmacy, dentistry, dental hygiene, medical and research technology, law, and social work. The complex also includes the **University of Maryland Medical System, the R Adams Cowley Shock Trauma Center,** and a **Veterans Affairs Medical Center.**

Davidge Hall (Robert Cary Long Sr., 1812), the oldest still-standing medical-school building in the country, occupies the northeast corner of Greene and Lombard Sts. Named for a founder of the College of Medicine of Maryland, John Beale Davidge, this eminently classical structure (Long modeled it on the Roman Pantheon) underwent restoration in 1979. Its principal room, a circular anatomy theater with domed roof and steeply tiered seats, reminds us of a time when dissection of human cadavers provoked popular distrust and even hostility. Before establishment of the medical school, Davidge, a Scottish-trained physician, delivered lectures and supervised dissections at a private laboratory on Liberty St. The destruction of his lab at the hands of a "dissection mob" in November 1807 prompted the General Assembly to charter, and partially extend

Davidge Hall (right), the oldest building of the University of Maryland School of Medicine, and (left) some of the most recent additions, 1997

protection to, the College of Medicine of Maryland (the nation's fifth oldest). Dissecting the dead remained a public relations issue; as a precaution, cadavers were brought to the anatomy theater through back entrances and hidden passageways.

In 1812, Maryland lawmakers created a University of Maryland, with the medical college at the center. A far-sighted lawyer, David Hoffman, designed a revolutionary curriculum and started the law school in 1822 (it lapsed in 1843 and then reopened in 1869). A college of pharmacy merged with the university in 1844, and dentists created their own school in 1882. Every attempt to create an undergraduate division failed; the chartered University of Maryland did not absorb the Maryland State College of Agriculture in College Park until 1920. The **Baltimore College of Dentistry,** a separate institution established in 1840—the first dental college in the world—merged with the university's dental school in 1923.

To visit **Old St. Paul's Cemetery** (open only on Saturday) follow Lombard St. west from Greene. On the way, one passes the university student union, residence halls, the nursing school, and other classroom and administration buildings. St. Paul's Protestant Episcopal Church established the cemetery, located between Lombard and Redwood Sts., in about 1804. Bodies earlier interred in the churchyard at Charles and Saratoga Sts. were moved here in about 1817. Among those buried here are Daniel Dulany the Younger (1722–97), Supreme Court Justice Samuel Chase (1741–1811), Col. George Armistead (1780–1818), and John Eager Howard (1752–1827).

From the professional schools, walk north on Greene St. to the **University of Maryland Hospital** at Greene and Redwood Sts. Constructed in 1933–34, the core teaching hospital now has the benefit of numerous additions. The tiered park plaza at this location provides a good view of the complex as well as pedestrian maps.

Continue to the **National Museum of Dentistry,** 31 S. Greene St., a $5.8 million, 7,000-square-foot exhibition space dedicated in 1996. Named after Samuel D. Harris, a major benefactor who practiced children's dentistry in Detroit, its exhibits highlight human dental cares and woes—including those of George Washington and Queen Victoria—from the beginning of recorded history.

At Greene and Fayette Sts., **Westminster Hall,** formerly Westminster Presbyterian Church (1852), serves as a performing arts center and meeting place. Still partially surrounded by a brick wall with ironwork, the churchyard contains the graves of a number of notables, including **Edgar Allan Poe,** whose gravesite one can see from the southeast corner.

Poe died mysteriously on October 7, 1849, four days after being found ill and incapacitated on an East Baltimore street. Many stories circulated about his death, including one that he was dragged—either drunk or drugged—by political thugs from polling place to polling place as a repeat voter. His body was originally buried in the rear of the church, but Baltimore schoolteachers, aroused by neglect of the grave, collected pennies from their pupils to pay for the current gravesite and marker. Walt Whitman, visiting nearby Washington, attended the reburial and dedication in 1875. He sat silently on the platform and later recalled a dream of a storm-tossed ship with a slender, beautiful figure on deck. "That figure of my lurid dream might stand for Edgar Poe, his spirit, his fortunes and his poems—themselves all lurid dreams" he told a small audience after the Baltimore ceremonies. Literary pilgrims will visit the grave e'ermore.

Also buried in the churchyard: Poe's grandfather, David Poe (1743–1816), a cabinetmaker who served in the army during the Revolution; Col. James McHenry (1755–1816), Washington's and John Adams's secretary of war, after whom the famous Baltimore fort was named; James Calhoun (1743–1816), first mayor of Baltimore from 1797 to 1804; and Gen. Samuel Smith (1752–1839), who organized the defenses of Baltimore in 1814.

Continue north on Greene to Lexington St. For a visit to two architectural history sites, take Lexington St. west about three blocks. The university has renovated **Pascault Row,** a set of eight three-story houses that Louis Pascault built in about 1816, and has modified the historic row for student housing. At Pine St., look to the right for the **Pine Street Police Station.** This Victorian structure, dating from 1870 or so, escaped destruction in the mid-1970s, during construction of the nearby expressway. It now houses campus police.

Lexington Market

To the east, one sees the oldest still-operating urban market in America. **The Lexington Market** (for nonwalkers, the Baltimore Metro stops here between the Charles and State Center stations). The site has undergone a number of changes since its establishment in 1782 on land John Eager Howard donated. The East and West markets replace a three-block-long shed surrounded by street stalls, which fire destroyed in 1949.

Lexington Market East (1952) and its adjoining Arcade (1982) between Eutaw and Paca Sts. compose Baltimore's largest and most famous market establishment. Many food stalls in the East Market have been leased by the same families for generations; others are the pride of new immigrants. The raw bar and seafood cases will delight any visitor. (One boasts, "If it lives in the water, and you want it, we got it.") The East Market also features a colorful 100' × 8' wall mural by Bob Hieronimus entitled "E Pluribus Unum" (1983–85). It depicts famous Baltimoreans.

The Municipal Market Administration, one of the city's oldest agencies, used to administer Lexington Market, but it is now operated by a quasi-public corporation. The city continues to run other markets—Bel Air, Broadway, Northeast, Hollins, Cross St., and Lafayette—each a gathering place for its surrounding neighborhood.

To the east, Lexington St. has become a pedestrian mall.

Seton Hill and St. Mary's Seminary

From Lexington Market East follow Paca St. north to the historic district known as Seton Hill. Many of the small houses date from 1820–50, when French-speaking people from the mother country as well as refugees from Santo Domingo settled here. A community of free African Americans also grew up in this neighborhood, where slave families lived in alley dwellings adjacent to their masters. According to local tradition, the area provided a temporary haven for runaways heading north via the Underground Railroad.

At the persuasion of Bishop John Carroll, four priests of the Society of St. Sulpice arrived in Baltimore with five seminarians in 1791 to establish the first Roman Catholic seminary in the United States. The Sulpicians also opened St. Mary's College (1799), which offered a liberal education for boys. The school was incorporated as a university in 1805. Here Maximilian Godefroy became the first professional teacher of architecture in Baltimore and perhaps in the country. The buildings of both schools have been razed, and now Godefroy's **St. Mary's Seminary Chapel** (1806–8) stands alone in the park off 600 North Paca St. Surrounded by trees and highlighted by open spaces, the little chapel has a national reputation for being the first notable Gothic Revival church in the United States. Robert Cary Long Jr. added a tower and interior decorations in 1840, but the tower fell down in 1916. The firm of Cochran, Stephenson and Donkervoet restored the interior to its original Gothic simplicity in 1967, and it has subsequently been remodeled to reflect the church's new liturgy.

The **Mother Seton House,** at 600 Paca St., stands next to the entrance to Godefroy's chapel. Built around the same time, this 2¹/₂-story structure, restored in 1963, is open to the public by appointment.

Elizabeth Bayley Seton (1774–1821), a Catholic convert, conducted a school here during 1808–9. A widow with five children, she came to Baltimore at the invitation of Father Dubois, director of St. Mary's Seminary, who wanted to establish a Catholic school for girls. Aided by a gift from Samuel Cooper, a seminarian, Mother Seton founded an American branch of the French order of St. Vincent de Paul. Called the Sisters of Charity, the order was established in 1809 with Mother Seton as mother superior. The first sisters, along with Mother Seton, took their vows in St. Mary's Seminary Chapel. That same year, the new order moved to Emmitsburg, where Mother Seton established St. Joseph's College. Pope Paul VI canonized Mother Seton in 1975, making her the first American-born Roman Catholic saint.

Another woman, Elizabeth Clovis Lange, a French-speaking refugee from Haiti, came to Baltimore to teach the refugee children clustered around the seminary. As a person of mixed racial background, the daughter of a white planter and black mother, she worshiped in the African Americans' "Chapelle Basse," in the basement of the chapel. Under the guidance of Father James Joubert, she and three companions took their vows as Oblate Sisters of Providence in 1829. Sister Mary Elizabeth Lange, foundress of the first Catholic order for African American women, died in 1882 at the age of 98. A guild has been established for her beatification and canonization.

One may proceed on Paca St. to the southern end of Druid Hill Ave. Nearby (on the southwest corner of Druid Hill Ave. and Eutaw St.) for 82 years stood the offices of the *Baltimore Afro-American,* founded in 1892 by John H. Murphy Sr. "The Afro" lobbied for the rights of African American citizens during the long decades of "Jim Crow" laws and in the process achieved national recognition. The newspaper sold its converted brick row house establishment in 1992 and moved to roomier quarters at 2519 N. Charles St.

Across Druid Hill Ave., at McCulloch St., turn left to 801 McCulloch, home of the **Arena Players,** which may be the oldest, continuously running African American community theater in the country. Sam Wilson, artistic director, and others started the theater in 1953 with a production of William Saroyan's "Hello Out There." Hampered by social and legal segregation, the integrated players performed in various places throughout the city until 1961, when they acquired an old warehouse at this site. The group slowly renovated the building, which now seats 300 persons.

From the Arena Players theater, walk northwest on McCulloch to Orchard St. and turn left to the brick **Orchard Street Church,** built in 1839 by a congregation of free blacks headed by Truman Pratt. Presumably, some of the African Americans in this 19th-century neighborhood were Catholic, but this church was Protestant, one of at least 10 black Protestant churches scattered throughout the city. The congregations of the Sharp St. United Methodist Church and Bethel African Methodist Episcopal Church are older but have moved from their original locations. The Orchard Street Church has been rebuilt several times (1853–59, 1882); virtually nothing remains of the original building, but the site has been identified with African American congregations for more than a century and a half. In 1970 the last congregation merged with another and abandoned the structure. The Baltimore Urban League renovated the building in 1991 and adopted it as its home office. The old sanctuary has been transformed into a museum and performance space to "present the inspiring story of the Black Church in Baltimore."

From the church, follow Tessier St.—named for Sulpician Father Jean Marie Tessier—which branches southeast from Orchard St. and returns one picturesquely to St. Mary's Park. To return to the Inner Harbor, either retrace your steps on Greene or Paca, or proceed east on Franklin to Howard St. and ride south to Pratt on the Light Rail.

Some of the places that truly "make Baltimore Baltimore" lie to the east of the Inner Harbor—old hard-working, no-nonsense communities of people who fly the flag and love life. A famous hospital stands on Broadway, the last stop in the tour that follows. One may, however, reach it directly via the Metro; the ride from Charles Center to the Johns Hopkins station takes only a few minutes.

Funky Fells Point

To reach this historic, more or less gentrified, waterfront community, one may take a water taxi from the Inner Harbor during warm weather. By car or cab, follow Pratt St. east to President St., turn right, then make a left onto Eastern Ave. and proceed to Broadway. At Broadway turn south toward the water.

Edward Fell established this port in 1763 on family land that already included a small shipyard. By 1781, when the settlement became part of Baltimore Town, Fells Point (its water deeper than that farther up the

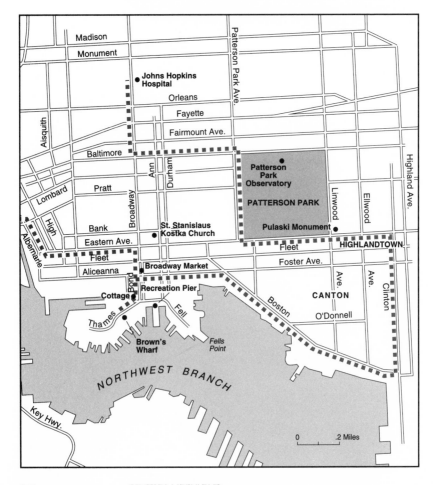

Northwest Branch) had grown into an active waterfront, with wharves and yards scattered along an irregular neck and shipbuilding an active industry. Many of the privateers that sailed from Baltimore during the Revolution and War of 1812 were built here. By the 1790s Fells Point had developed into a rowdy, robust village where sailors delighted in the nearly 50 taverns and inns. On the continuum of accommodations, rooming houses shaded into houses of ill repute. All the while, wealthier ship's captains and merchants built handsome brick dwellings and financed churches.

For 140 years, the tip of Fells Point—the western end of the hooked peninsula that separated the point from the basin—was home to a chrome plant that Isaac Tyson Jr. had established in 1845. The first plant of its kind in the United States, it later formed part of Allied Chemical Corporation, which transformed it into the largest facility of its kind in the world. The plant closed in 1985, a victim of foreign competition, leaving the port with its most difficult environmental cleanup problem.

The African American abolitionist Frederick Douglass worked in the Fells Point shipyards as a slave. He eventually escaped servitude, disguised as a seaman, on September 3, 1838. After the Civil War, Isaac Myers organized the Chesapeake Marine Railway and Dry Dock Company in Fells Point (1866–84), probably Baltimore's first significant black-owned business. It employed several hundred African American caulkers near Chase's Wharf, east of the chrome plant.

Polish Catholic immigrants arrived here in the 1870s, the men finding work as stevedores, the women often laboring in canning factories. The Poles formed the St. Stanislaus Kostka Society in 1875 and by 1879 had raised enough money to finance a church. **St. Stanislaus Kostka Church** at the southwest corner of Ann and Aliceanna Sts. (from Broadway turn east on Aliceanna and go two blocks) has been a center of Polish American life in Baltimore ever since. At one time, the blocks on Eastern Ave. just east and west of Broadway—lined with taverns, building and loan associations, real estate and insurance offices—were known as the "Polish Wall Street." The once tightly knit Polish community, centered around four churches (St. Stanislaus, Holy Rosary, Holy Cross, and St. Casimir's) since has dispersed, but remnants, like meat shops, remain in Fells Point and the surrounding cityscape.

In 1969, when Fells Point became a nationally registered historic district, it won praise for being one of the few colonial waterfront communities on the East Coast still surviving largely intact. The designation helped local residents win their fight in the late 1960s and early 1970s against plans to run an expressway through the neighborhood. This traditional, working-class section of the city has since become increasingly gentrified. Restored houses, bars and restaurants, marinas, condominiums, and pedestrian promenades make up for lost maritime revenue.

Broadway divides at Fleet St., a block south of Eastern Ave., to make room for the **Broadway Market,** which has stood here since 1783. (Facing narrow streets and crowded quarters, the motorist should find street parking and walk.) Shakespeare St. branches west from Broadway for about two blocks. The **Cottage,** a double brick house, occupies the corner of Bond and Shakespeare Sts. One section, built by John Smith (ca. 1781–98) at 1608 Shakespeare, has been joined to 1600 Shakespeare, which dates from the 1790s. The **Fell Family Tomb** lies across the street

A view of Baltimore harbor from Fells Point in the late 1930s

at 1607. A horizontal stone marker records that Edward Fell came to Maryland in 1723 from Lancaster, England, acquired land in Jones Town, and died in 1743. His brother William (not buried here), a shipbuilder, came to Maryland in 1730, bought a thousand acres, and became a commissioner of Baltimore Town. Named after his uncle, William's son Edward laid out the town of Fells Point.

The heart of Fells Point lies at the foot of Broadway, where the street meets the water. Shops, taverns, and galleries face the open square. Community theater has thrived here; the Vagabond Players (1916), housed at 806 S. Broadway, claim to be the oldest survivor of the little-theater movement that revitalized American drama in the early 20th century.

The restored **Admiral Fell Inn,** 888 S. Broadway, was formerly the Anchorage Hotel, where seamen seeking temporary lodgings parted with their wages. From the foot of Broadway, Thames St. travels east and west along the water, past historic piers and wharves now modified for recreation and boat storage.

The **Recreation Pier** (1914), just to the east on Thames, began as a municipal dance hall, one of the first in the United States (and much later served as "police headquarters" for the television series *Homicide*). Just north of the pier, at 812 S. Ann St., stands the **Robert Long House,** a 2¹/₂-story brick house built in 1765 by a warehouse owner. Fell St. angles southeast from Thames St. to an area where several 18th-century structures have been restored. The **Captain Steel House,** 931 Fell St., was built for a wealthy shipbuilder around 1784, a date that makes it one of the few intact houses left in Baltimore from the revolutionary period.

A turn west from Broadway onto Thames leads past **Brown's Wharf,** a retail and office complex reconstructed from a coffee warehouse with components dating to 1822. George S. Brown—son of Alexander Brown, founder of the banking firm of Alexander Brown and Sons—bought the property in 1840 and expanded it for the coffee and flour trade with Brazil. Norman G. Rukert (1915–84), whose family shipping business acquired the property in 1947, turned the old warehouses into a maritime museum; in 1988 the wharf once again became part of a

commercial enterprise. Thames St. continues west to Philpot St., where Frederick Douglass lived with his owners, Hugh Auld and family. Only rough cobblestone and a few derelict buildings remain.

Essex and Foster Sts., Fells Point, during the Depression

Canton

Follow Broadway north to Aliceanna St., make a right turn, and follow Aliceanna east to Boston St., which enters the waterfront area known as Canton. In 1785, a mysterious Irish sea captain, John O'Donnell (1749–1805), arrived in Baltimore with a cargo of exotic goods from Canton, China. On hearing announcement of the ship's arrival, George Washington was so intrigued that he sent his friend, Col. Tench Tilghman, to the cargo sale to look for bargains. Captain O'Donnell must have been impressed with the port. He married the daughter of a Fells Point sea captain and by 1800 had built a 2,000-acre plantation named Canton, which included all the southeastern waterfront from Fells Point to Colgate Creek. His home, near what is now Boston St. between Clinton St. and Highland Ave., became famous for its hospitality. After the captain's death, the family rented out the plantation; in 1829 his son Columbus joined with six other investors to form the Canton Company, a real estate development company, which controlled 3,000 acres of waterfront property from Fells Point to Lazaretto Point.

The Canton waterfront became the home for a wide variety of industries: fertilizer, poultry feed, iron, oil, coal, shipping, canning, packing, brewing, licorice and dye manufacturing, and copper smelting—to name a few. Row houses for the workers mushroomed north and east of the harbor, neat brick structures with polished marble steps that sported painted screens in the summer. During the past two decades, however, Canton's heavy manufacturing character has changed, yielding to residential areas spreading east from Fells Point.

Follow Boston St. east along the water. At the turn of the century, the 2300–2600 blocks were known as Canner's Row; now they are lined with new apartments, condominiums, and marinas. Just before its intersection with O'Donnell St. (which passes through the heart of residential Canton), Boston St. crosses a concrete viaduct over the vestige of Harris Creek, which once flowed through Patterson Park and emptied into the Northwest Branch. The rusting, vacant buildings of the former American Can Company face residential complexes built in the late 1980s. **Tindeco Wharf,** a condominium project opened in 1986, occupies the former home of the Tin Decorating Company, once one of the world's largest manufacturers of lithographed tin boxes. Just to the east of Tindeco and another apartment complex, called **Canton Cove,** lies the **Maryland Korean War Memorial,** dedicated in 1990 on a waterfront park that faces the harbor. The memorial names the 525 Marylanders killed in that conflict and describes its history on engraved stones built in a circle around an inlaid map of Korea on the paved ground. The visitor here has a commanding view of **Canton Hollow**—the bend to the east where the shoreline turns south—once a favorite anchorage for sailing ships. The low shoreline along the curve was also known as "Baptizing Shore," a favorite locale for mass baptisms. The North Locust Point Marine Terminal and Fort McHenry are clearly visible across the river.

Just to the north of Boston St., at 1301 S. Ellwood Ave., one finds the **Clarence "Du" Burns Arena,** a multipurpose sports establishment with an indoor soccer and lacrosse field. It recalls a veteran East Baltimore politician who became the first African American to serve as mayor (1987–88).

Boston St. intersects Clinton St. near the presumed site of Captain O'Donnell's plantation home. Clinton St. continues south down the waterfront past commercial piers. One of them, Pier 1, has been home to the Liberty ship *John W. Brown* since the summer of 1988. A local volunteer group, Project Liberty Ship, acquired the vessel with the idea of restoring and sailing it as a memorial museum ship honoring the men and women who built and served on supply ships during World War II. In the Bethlehem Steel shipyards, across the Patapsco River in Fairfield, Baltimore workers constructed 384 of them, plus 94 Victory ships, before war's end. Groups of school children visit the *John W. Brown* to learn of Baltimore's industrial heritage and the sacrifices of World War II. The ship also takes summer cruises; in 1994 she took passengers to New York, Boston, and Halifax. At the end of Clinton St. the visitor reaches **Lazaretto Point,** now occupied by the Lehigh Portland Cement Company. From 1831 to 1926 a landmark lighthouse marked the point, known as Gorsuch Point until an isolation hospital for smallpox victims was located here around 1801. The hospital moved in 1870 to a quarantine station on Leading Point west of Fort Armistead, where it operated until 1961. In 1985, Rukert Terminals erected a replica of the old lighthouse at the end of Mertens Ave., to honor Norman G. Rukert and his father, who founded the shipping firm in 1921.

Highlandtown

East Baltimore offered more room for 19th-century immigrants, many of whom got off the boat at Locust Point and ferried across the harbor to find jobs and to gather in neighborhoods where their native languages were spoken. In the 1830s and 1840s, Broadway north of Eastern Ave. developed as a major residential street. Intensive development east of Patterson Park occurred during the 1880s with a new tide of immigration from Eastern Europe and the Mediterranean. Germans, who settled in large numbers in Highlandtown, joined building and loan associations, which permitted them to make small down payments on long-term mortgages for $800–1,000 row houses. This pattern of home ownership, combined with the practice of selling ground rents, enabled immigrants to avoid the tenements that emerged in other large eastern cities. Southeast Baltimore provided residential opportunities for the workers who manned the expanding industries around Dundalk, Essex, and Middle River.

Turn north onto Clinton St. from Boston St. As Clinton St. crosses Foster Ave., the traveler passes from Canton into Highlandtown. In 1861, when Union troops established Fort Marshall as part of a chain of garrisons that protected Baltimore from attack and guarded against internal insurrection, locals knew this area as Snake Hill. It consisted of pastureland overlooking the city. The fort lay unused after the Civil War. German immigrants began to move to the area in numbers, establishing breweries, taverns, and meat markets. During the 1870s the growing settlement changed its name to "Highland Town" and developed into a country village east of Patterson Park. By 1881 nearby Canton claimed 2,084 residents, Highlandtown only 644. New immigrants—including Finns, Poles, Ukrainians, and Italians—added to the German-Welsh-Irish mixture of the neighborhood, which became part of Baltimore in 1918. Most Highlandtowners opposed annexation. Like Hampden, Highlandtown retains many small-town mannerisms in the middle of a metropolis.

The oldest family-owned restaurant in Baltimore, established in 1926, stands at the northwest corner of Clinton St. and Eastern Ave. Its German food and eclectic art collection have made it a landmark in Highlandtown. The commercial district along Eastern Ave. suffered during the growth of regional shopping centers but has rebounded in recent years.

Turn west on Eastern Ave. and follow it to Patterson Park.

Patterson Park

The intersection of Eastern Ave. and Ellwood Ave. marks the southeast corner of Patterson Park, a 155-acre recreational area bounded by Patterson Park Ave. on the west and Baltimore St. on the north. In 1814, the northernmost section of the present park was called Hampstead Hill and was the target of the British land forces that approached Baltimore from the east after scattering local militia at the Battle of North Point. Rodgers' Bastion, named after the auxiliary naval forces of Commo. John Rodgers, fortified the hill, strategically located in the center of a defensive line that ran from the Northwest Branch to Belair Rd. About 120 cannon, supported by as many as 12,000 men behind trenches and redoubts, faced down the British troops.

William Patterson, wealthy merchant and father of Betsy Patterson, gave five acres of this pasturage to the city in 1827. Following further acquisitions of adjacent land, the park opened to the public in 1853. The 7th Maine Regiment established Camp Washburn here in August 1861, and federal troops camped here throughout the Civil War. One of seven Union military hospitals in Baltimore stood on the parkland. For the past century, Patterson Park has served as a recreational center for the surrounding neighborhoods, providing playing fields, tennis courts, swimming pool, and ice skating rink in the winter.

Continue west on Eastern Ave. along the park to Linwood Ave., where the **Pulaski Monument** is visible in the park, on the right. In 1951, Hans Schuler created this great bronze plaque, which commemorates the services of Casimir Pulaski (1748–79), the Polish count who became a hero of the American Revolution. Pulaski raised part of his special volunteers, the Pulaski Legion, in Baltimore, uniformed them here, and died the following year at the Battle of Savannah.

Opposite the park, at the corner of Eastern and Montford Aves., **St. Michael Ukrainian Catholic Church,** dedicated in 1991, makes a striking visual landmark. Modeled after a design from Kiev, this modern reconstruction with its five onion domes serves a congregation founded in 1893.

Turn north from Eastern Ave. on Patterson Park Ave. and follow the western boundary of the park. The **Patterson Park Observatory,** popularly known as The Pagoda, towers above the Lombard St. entrance to the park. Charles H. Latrobe designed this 60-foot octagonal structure in 1891, an example of the late Victorian fascination with the Far East. In 1965, following years of vandalism, the city restored the tower. It offers a magnificent view of the harbor from its balconies. The Pagoda occupies the site of Rodgers' Bastion on the highest point in the park, marked by a line of cannon and the **Star-Spangled Banner Monument** (1914, A. Maxwell Miller). Baltimore school children contributed to the fund for this statue in commemoration of the centennial of the National Anthem. A plaque on a cannon to the right of the monument describes the bastion's role in the defense of Baltimore.

Continue north on Patterson Park Ave. and turn west on Baltimore St., which descends to Broadway. Turn north on Broadway to the Johns Hopkins Hospital.

Johns Hopkins Hospital

(Reachable from downtown via the Metro.) Broadway, a wide boulevard with a grass median strip, is lined with 19th-century brick rowhouses, some dating from the 1830–50 period. The **Church Home and Hospital,** located at Broadway and Fairmount Ave., dates to 1833, when it was known as the Washington Medical College. Edgar Allan Poe was taken here after being found semiconscious in Old Town and died in a ward four days later. The **Wildey Monument,** a plain shaft topped by a statue of Charity, stands a block to the north, at Fayette St. and Broadway. Raised in 1865, the landmark commemorates Thomas Wildey (1783–1861), who founded the fraternal order of Odd Fellows in America in 1819.

Broadway crosses Orleans St. (U.S. 40) and passes the main entrance to Johns Hopkins Hospital, centerpiece of a growing medical complex that includes medical and nursing schools, a school of public health, more than a dozen centers offering specific medical services, and 200 separate clinics spread over 10 city blocks. The hospital and its associated schools and laboratories operate 24 hours a day, employing the skills of 1,600 physicians, 1,500 nurses, and 500 residents caring for thousands of patients while pursuing an almost equal number of research projects.

Johns Hopkins (1795–1873), a bachelor, Quaker, and merchant-banker with little formal education, bequeathed $7 million to trustees charged with creating a university, hospital, and medical school. He stipulated that the latter two institutions were to be closely related, and in

The rotunda, Johns Hopkins Hospital, 1997

doing so he established a precedent for American medical education and research. The university opened near W. Monument and Howard Sts. in 1876. Hopkins had wanted the hospital to be built on his Clifton country estate, but the trustees chose the site at Broadway and Monument, earlier occupied by a state "lunatic" asylum. John Shaw Billings (1838–1913) designed the hospital with pioneering light and airy spaces. Formal ceremonies dedicated the new hospital on May 7, 1889, a year when most Baltimoreans, who had an average life span of about 43, died of consumption, pneumonia, cholera, and measles. Today, the famous domed administration building alone remains of the original design; the hospital occupies almost 30 buildings and continues to grow.

The medical school might never have opened without a $500,000 gift from Mary Garrett and her Women's Medical School Fund Committee, which insisted on two conditions: that the new school admit women on the same basis as men and that the female students meet the same requirements as any other Hopkins graduate candidate. After much debate, these innovative criteria were accepted, and the first class—13 men and 3 women—gathered in 1893. During the past century, the Johns Hopkins Hospital and the medical school have acquired a worldwide reputation for patient-centered work in the medical sciences.

In the main hall of the **Welch Medical Library,** at 1900 E. Monument St., hangs ***The Four Doctors*** (1907), John Singer Sargent's famous group portrait (1907) of the physicians who started the hospital on its road to international recognition. William Osler (1849–1919) came to Hopkins at the age of 44 as professor of the principles and practices of medicine; he established the residency system that became the norm in American medical schools. William Halsted (1852–1922) served as the hospital's chief surgeon and professor of surgery from 1889 until his death. Howard A. Kelly (1858–1943), professor of gynecology from 1888 to 1919, pioneered the use of radium therapy for cancer and invented the cystoscope. The work and personality of William H. Welch (1850–1934), professor of pathology and hospital pathologist from 1889 until 1930, persuaded the Rockefeller Foundation to establish the first school of public health in the United States at Hopkins in 1916. A larger, more recent group portrait would probably include two women—Isabel Hampton and Adelaide Nutting, who started the nursing program—and two more men, Dr. Jesse Lazear, who died while seeking the cause of yellow fever, and Dr. Frederick H. Baetjer, who died as a result of X-ray experiments. The presence of such men and women over generations has exerted subtle but powerful influences on Baltimore's public and private society.

The **John F. Kennedy Childrens' Center** fronts on Madison St., a block north of the Welch Library.

To return to the area of the Inner Harbor, either take the Metro to Charles Center or drive east on Orleans (a block south of E. Monument) to St. Paul, there turning left. (Note that at this point, one is close to some early features on the driving tour of northeast Baltimore. To pursue that tour, drive east on Orleans to Ensor St., there turning right to the Number 6 Fire Engine House.)

G. TOURING NORTHEAST BALTIMORE

From the Inner Harbor, drive east on Pratt to Gay, there turning left. Gay passes underneath Fallsway and crosses Orleans, becoming Ensor St. (Md. 147).

Number 6 Fire Engine House and Old Town Mall

The Number 6 Fire Engine House stands at the intersections of Orleans, Gay, and Ensor Sts. and marks the beginning of the Old Town Mall. In 1853–54, the Independent Fire Company added a 103-foot Venetian Gothic bell tower to an older building to create the current engine house. The company was one of many independents that operated in the city before Baltimore's public fire department was organized in 1858. Such early volunteer companies wielded considerable influence as grassroots political and social organizations, but their rivalries often detracted from public safety. Householders subscribed to particular fire companies; if another company arrived on the scene first, its fire fighters might watch the building burn rather than risk a fight with the "home" company. Some of the independents were even accused of setting fires to create business. The old engine house was threatened with demolition in 1960, but has since been restored and now houses the **Baltimore City Fire Museum.** For information call 410-727-2414.

Gay St. once carried vehicles between Orleans and Monument Sts. As part of an East Baltimore renewal and redevelopment effort in the af-

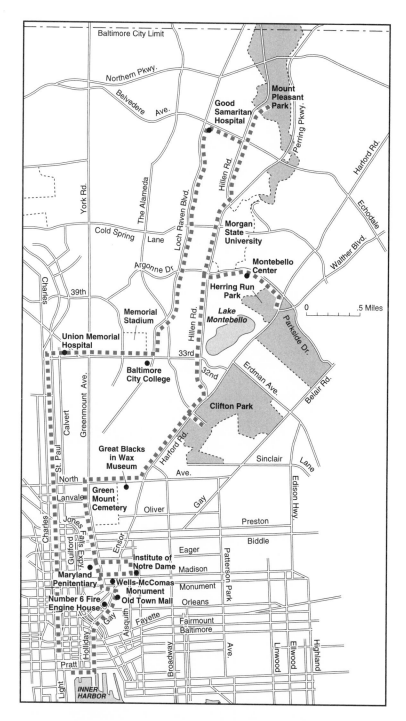

termath of riots in April 1968, it became the **Old Town Mall,** a neighborhood attraction lined with shops and encompassing the **Bel Air Market** (1835). Political violence in Baltimore may have reached its peak here in November 1856, when Democrats and Know-Nothings fought each other on election day. Ten people were killed and 250 injured (the nativist Know-Nothings won by 9,000 votes). Two years later, in a city election, most Democrats avoided the polls, and their candidate withdrew at noon on election day in the hope of preventing further bloodshed. State legislators intervened in 1860, refusing to seat delegates from Baltimore until the city's police force submitted to the control of a gubernatorially appointed commission. It would take another 116 years before the mayor would be legally permitted to appoint the city police commissioner.

Old Town Mall ends at the intersection of Aisquith, Gay, and Monument Sts., where the **Wells-McComas Monument** has stood since 1871. This plain obelisk marks the graves of Daniel Wells and Henry McComas, the young riflemen believed to have killed the British general Robert Ross during the Battle of North Point. Apprentices in the saddlery business, they lost their lives when the British quickly returned fire.

City Jail and State Penitentiary

From the mall, take Forrest St. north across Hillen St. to Front, where, bearing slightly right, Forrest becomes Greenmount Ave. Follow Greenmount to Madison St. and the southern edge of the Baltimore City Jail and the Maryland State Penitentiary, unmistakable landmarks on the eastern bank of the Jones Falls. The old Baltimore City Jail **Gatehouse,** at Buren and Madison Sts., is the only remnant of the original granite structure that James and Thomas Dixon completed in 1859 (an earlier city jail had stood on the spot since 1768). The Maryland Penitentiary, north of the jail, dates from 1811, making it the oldest prison in the state and the second oldest in the United States. Jackson C. Gott designed the dark granite fortress section at Forrest and Eager Sts., built between 1893 and 1899. Many of the buildings have been altered since that time.

Institute of Notre Dame

To visit this venerable Catholic girls' high school, travel north on Greenmount to Eager St., make a right and then another right on Aisquith St. The school occupies the block defined by Eager, Aisquith, Somerset, and Ashland. Over the entrance at 901 Aisquith are inscribed the words of a familiar Catholic American motto, "Pro Deo et Patria" ("For God and Country"). The School Sisters of Notre Dame established this academically strong program at this site in 1847, the time of the Mexican War. Well-known graduates include Barbara Mikulski, the first female U.S. senator from Maryland.

Green Mount Cemetery

From the Institute, travel south on Aisquith St. and make a right on Madison, looping back to the penitentiary. Then travel north on Greenmount Ave. (Md. 45) to **Green Mount**—the city's most visually interesting cemetery and a National Register of Historic Places landmark. In 1838 the cemetery proprietors bought the country estate of wealthy shipper Robert Oliver (1757–1834) and created the fourth garden cemetery in America. Many of the most famous and infamous people from Baltimore's long history rest here: philanthropists Enoch Pratt, William and Henry Walters, Johns Hopkins, and Moses Sheppard; B&O president John Work Garrett; Sunpapers founder Arunah Abell; the Georgia-born poet Sidney Lanier; and the assassin John Wilkes Booth. Here also lie nine

Maryland governors, six Baltimore mayors, and 15 Civil War generals from both sides. In 1846 Robert Cary Long Jr. designed the solitary entrance, a granite gateway, at Greenmount Ave. and Oliver St., a Tudor Gothic structure with two 40-foot towers. The octagonal chapel, designed in 1856 by Niernsee and Nielson on the site of the Oliver mansion, rises above elaborately carved gravestones like a Gothic fantasy.

Great Blacks in Wax Museum

From Greenmount Ave., turn east (right) onto North Ave., which marked the northern city limits between 1818 and 1888. Follow it west to the Great Blacks in Wax Museum, the first and only wax museum dedicated to the study and preservation of African American culture. The museum developed as the brainchild of a couple who in 1983 started with four figures, Frederick Douglass and Mary McLeod Bethune among them, which they exhibited in churches, schools, and malls. With the aid of public funds, the museum moved to an old firehouse at 1601 E. North Ave. in 1988. It now features more than 100 figures arranged in scenes that carry the visitor from the African past to the modern civil rights movement. For information call 410-563-3404.

From North Ave., turn left on Harford Rd. (Md. 147) to continue the tour of northeast Baltimore, which above North Ave. developed largely as a residential area early in the 20th century, accelerating after World War I.

An 18th-century Quaker burial ground lies at 2506 Harford Rd.

Clifton Park

Turn right on St. Lo Dr. into Clifton Park, which the city acquired in 1895 from the estate of Johns Hopkins. Hopkins bought the property in 1836 and later expanded the original farmhouse, built around 1800, into an Italian-style villa with a six-story square tower and arched arcades on three sides. From this location, set in a landscaped park adorned with statuary, the philanthropist conducted his business, pursued his hobby of horticulture, and entertained visitors in style. The city maintains the mansion, which houses park offices, and an 18-hole public golf course. **Lake Clifton–Eastern High School** occupies the site of the old Clifton reservoir.

Just to the east of the tract where Hopkins would soon build Clifton, the Baltimore Hebrew Congregation in 1832 established a cemetery that by 1898 was the largest Jewish cemetery south of New York City.

Return to Harford Rd., turn right and then left, after a few blocks, onto Hillen Rd. At 33rd St., an 18-foot statue of Martin Luther, by Hans Schuler, stands in a small park on the southeast corner of the intersection. After crossing 33rd St., look to the left for one of the city's foundation technical high schools, Mergenthaler Vocational-Technical High School (named for the inventor of the Linotype machine). On the right, notice **Lake Montebello,** a retaining reservoir built between 1874 and 1881. It stores water delivered via a tunnel from the Great Gunpowder River in Baltimore County. The **Montebello Filtration Plant,** north of the reservoir, marked the continuation of a water-supply system that began with Druid Hill Park. The eastern group of buildings was constructed in 1915 and the western group in 1928.

At Argonne Dr., one may turn right and drive a short distance back toward Harford Rd., first passing **Montebello Center,** a state rehabilitative facility opened in 1953 and operated by the University of Maryland Medical System for patients with disabilities from strokes, head and spinal injuries, and other trauma, next to the **Columbus Monument** (1792), a plain stuccoed brick obelisk in a park at the intersection of Argonne and Harford. It may be the first monument to Columbus in the Americas. Charles François Adrian de Paulmier, Chevalier d'Anmour, the French consul in Baltimore during and after the Revolution, laid the cornerstone on August 3, 1792, the 300th anniversary of the date Columbus set sail from Spain. The monument was moved to this site in 1913; earlier it had stood on North Ave. opposite Bond St., originally part of de Paulmier's estate, Villa Belmont.

Herring Run Valley

From Argonne at Harford, turn sharply right into a drive leading to parking for Herring Run Park. From this spot one can appreciate the greenspace that follows the winding course of Herring Run as it falls through the northeastern corner of Baltimore to Back River. Most of this stream valley within the city limits has been incorporated into the 323 acres of Herring Run Park, crisscrossed with nature trails, bike and jogging paths, exercise points, picnic areas, and playing fields.

Morgan State University

Return to Hillen Rd., turn right (north), and drive to Cold Spring Ln. On the right, above and below Cold Spring, lies the campus of a historic African American institution. In 1867, the congregation of Lovely Lane

Morgan State University, especially renowned for its choir and its engineering school, in 1998

Meeting House, supported by other members of the Methodist Episcopal Church, established the Centenary Bible Institute for African American students. In 1890, the institute changed its name to Morgan College, in honor of Dr. Lyttleton Morgan, a pastor at Lovely Lane whose endowment enabled the school to offer college courses. The college moved to its current location in 1917 and remained under Methodist auspices until 1939, when it was purchased by the state of Maryland. In 1918, Zora Neale Hurston (1891–1960), writer, folklorist, and free spirit of the Harlem Renaissance, graduated from the Morgan Academy, then the institution's high school division. She received an honorary degree from the college in 1939.

The natural stone buildings date to the early 1940s, when the state began a construction program that continues. The college became a university in 1975 and is governed by an independent board of regents appointed by the governor. The predominantly black university has over 5,000 students of all ethnic heritages, enrolled in schools of business and management, education and urban studies, engineering, graduate studies, and a college of arts and sciences.

The **Carl Murphy Auditorium and Fine Arts Building** (1950, Gaudreau and Gaudreau), named for Carl James Murphy (1889–1967), son of the founder of the Afro-American Company, contains departments of music, drama, and the fine arts. The building also houses the **James E. Lewis Museum,** named for a noted local sculptor and professor emeritus of art. Over a period of 40 years, Dr. Lewis (1923–97) assembled the museum's permanent collection of valuable paintings and sculptures by African and African American artists.

Morgan Park

Just beyond the campus, Montebello Terrace turns left (north) from E. Cold Spring Ln. to the small neighborhood known as **Morgan Park.** A number of distinguished members of Morgan State's faculty have lived here as well as other prominent members of Baltimore's African American community. W. E. B. Du Bois (1868–1963), a founder of the NAACP (1910) and leading civil rights advocate of the first half of the 20th century, maintained a residence here for many years.

Mount Pleasant

North of the campus, the main artery becomes Perring Parkway, which takes one north and east to Parkville; Hillen Rd. bears to the left, soon reaching more green space, **Mount Pleasant Park,** a 264-acre development with a municipal golf course. This rolling countryside once belonged to the Taylor family, builders of the Mount Pleasant estate in the 1760s. A service road on the right leads from Hillen Rd. to the golf course's clubhouse and **Taylor's Chapel,** a small stone church erected in 1853 on the site of a log meeting house built by Quakers about 1770. The small cemetery around the chapel, which has served many denominations, contains the 18th-century graves of Taylors and Hillens, among others. The city acquired the Mount Pleasant property in 1925; St. John's of Hamilton United Methodist Church maintains the chapel and cemetery.

Rather than leave the city, return south on Hillen Rd. to Belvedere Ave. and turn right to Loch Raven Ave., there turning left to continue south. On the southeast corner of that intersection, notice **Good Samaritan Hospital,** an independent Catholic institution that opened in 1968 through the generosity of Catholic philanthropist Thomas J. O'Neill, whose munificence was also responsible for the Cathedral of Mary Our Queen (see below). Knowing, he said, of "many so-called charitable hospitals where God's poor receive scant treatment," O'Neill envisioned a hospital expressly for the needy. Now specializing in orthopedics, rehabilitation, and rheumatology, "Good Sam" fulfills its original purpose through a wide variety of charitable interventions made possible by the O'Neill Catholic Health Care Fund.

Loch Raven southbound takes the visitor through the community known as Northwood past town houses that date from World War II and the period soon after.

Loch Raven joins The Alameda and shortly intersects 33rd St. **Baltimore City College** (1924–28), a Gothic building that houses the oldest high school in Baltimore, occupies the southwestern portion of the intersection. Opened in 1839 as the Male High School, with a student body of seven, the school acquired the name City College in 1866 and moved here about a dozen years after the Johns Hopkins University migrated to the nearby Homewood campus (for many years the two institutions had shared a neighborhood in the area of Howard, Centre, and W. Monument Sts.). Among its graduates are *New York Times* columnist Russell Baker and former Baltimore mayor and Maryland governor William Donald Schaefer.

Turn right (west) to drive past **Memorial Stadium** (1950–54), once home of the Baltimore Colts and the Baltimore Orioles and later temporary playing field of the Baltimore Ravens. Built of reinforced concrete and faced with brick, the stadium commemorates those who died in this century's two world wars; it replaced an earthwork stadium constructed in 1922.

The simple charm of this stadium—placid rowhouses visible beyond center field—became familiar to sports fans in the 1960s, '70s, and early '80s. The Orioles played in World Series games here in 1966, 1969, 1970,

This Dutch Colonial row, pictured in the early 1930s, typifies new construction in Baltimore during the 1920s. Much of the building took place in northeast Baltimore.

1971, 1979, and 1983, winning all except the painful classics of 1969 (lost to the New York Mets) and 1971 and 1979 (to the Pittsburgh Pirates). The Colts played any number of memorable home games in Memorial Stadium. Then the Ravens' colors of purple and black dominated the signage. The future of the stadium remains unclear in 1998.

Continue west on 33rd St., crossing Greenmount Ave. (where Asian restaurants and "down home" food outlets offer good meals, and many pubs cling to orange and black bunting and baseball memorabilia). On the north side of the street, where 33rd crosses Calvert, one passes **Union Memorial Hospital.** This institution dates from 1854, when it opened downtown as a 20-bed haven for "the sick, the poor and the infirm." The hospital moved to this part of the city in 1923. Here Al Capone underwent treatment for syphilis in 1939; he had hoped for a bed at Johns Hopkins, but staffers at that institution had declined him admission, fearing trouble from the kingpin's enemies. (A grateful Capone later donated the flowering Japanese cherry tree that stands next to the hospital's Calvert St. entrance.) Today a comprehensive hospital with about 425 beds, Union Memorial also specializes in treating spinal disorders and sports injuries.

To return to the Inner Harbor, go another block west to St. Paul St., there turning left. The drive to Pratt St. takes about 10 minutes.

H. THE MOUNT ROYAL CULTURAL DISTRICT

Mt. Royal Ave. lies at the outer limit of most pedestrians who begin at the Inner Harbor—nearly two miles away. Both the Light Rail (the University of Baltimore / Mount Royal station) and the Metro (State Center) stop nearby, however, and buses run north on Charles to Mt. Royal, as well. Drivers will find metered parking on Preston St. and on Mt. Royal Ave. and unmetered spaces north of the Light Rail crossing.

Mount Royal takes its name from the home of Judge Hugh Lennox Bond, which still stands in modified form at the end of Reservoir St. City commissioners laid out Mt. Royal in 1816, when the city limits were extended to North Ave. The street commissioners, faced with a hilly geography and the angle of Reisterstown Pike to the west, shifted the street grid 45 degrees, beginning at the corner of Greene and Franklin Sts. Thus, the streets run northwest to southeast and northeast to southwest between Pennsylvania Ave. (the intown extension of Reisterstown Rd.) and Cathedral St. This skewed street pattern ends at Druid Hill Park.

Institutional development in this area started around 1890, when the Bryn Mawr School for Girls (1885) was built on the present site of the Joseph Meyerhoff Symphony Hall (Cathedral St. between Preston and Biddle). By 1925, when the University of Baltimore was founded, the Mount Royal area had assumed its basic character. Over the past 30 years, with expansion of the university, the Maryland Institute College of Art, and other cultural attractions, Mount Royal has become a lively artistic and educational enclave. Since 1982, Mt. Royal Ave. between Cathedral and Mosher Sts. has provided the site for Artscape, an annual three-day festival for the performing and visual arts, held in July and sponsored by the Mayor's Advisory Committee on Art and Culture.

The walker enters the Mount Royal Cultural District at the junction of Mt. Royal Ave. and N. Charles St. Metro passengers alight near

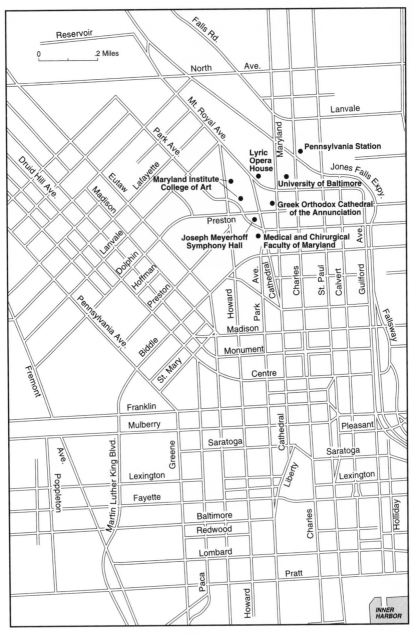

Howard St. and may walk east on Preston, then north to Mt. Royal. Light
Rail riders get off at a station a few blocks west of Charles on Mt. Royal.

Starting at Charles and Mt. Royal, the visitor to Mount Royal might
well begin by appreciating **Pennsylvania Station** (1911), Baltimore's
last major railroad station, at 525 N. Charles St. Off a bit to the north and
east, the station calls for a mere five-minute walk and repays the effort.
Renovation work done in 1976 revealed the quality of New York architect
Kenneth W. Murchison's fine Beaux-Arts design. It also exposed three
domed skylights of colored, leaded glass that World War II blackout paint

had obscured for decades. The marble walls, mahogany benches, iron balconies, terrazzo floors, and installations of Rookwood ceramic tiles cannot match the mass or grandeur of Washington's Union Station, but this restoration befits a city that became nationally known for historic preservation during the 1960s and 1970s. A new plaza and parking garage in front opened in 1997.

University of Baltimore

Walk south on Charles St. from Penn Station to this unusual school, founded in 1925 as a modest night school for the study of business and law. Since that time, it has grown into a campus of 10 buildings. One of them, the **Academic Center** at the corner of Mt. Royal Ave. and Charles St., won recognition for architect Allen Hopkins, who in 1971 converted the building from an automobile emporium to academic offices, classrooms, and an upstairs gymnasium. The University of Baltimore is one of only 15 upper-division universities (juniors and seniors only) in the country. About 3,400 of its 5,800 students are enrolled in the **Robert G. Merrick School of Business** and the **Yale Gordon College of Liberal Arts.**

The **Peggy and Yale Gordon Plaza** at the corner of Mt. Royal and Maryland Aves. fronts the university's **Law Center,** which houses offices and classrooms, the law library, and Poe's Publick House, a dining complex. The **Poe Monument,** designed by Moses J. Ezekiel in 1921, faces Mt. Royal from the plaza; it originally stood in Wyman Park. The **Langsdale Library,** at the corner of Maryland Ave. and Oliver St., has a collection of 300,000 books, periodicals, CD-ROM indexes, maps, prints, and government documents, along with archival records that are particularly strong in local history. It includes tapes of television newscasts. The first floor includes a 400-seat auditorium.

Lyric Opera House

Cross Maryland Ave., walking west-northwest, and on the right, at 128 W. Mt. Royal, notice the **Lyric Theater** (1895). Architect Henry Randall modeled it after the *Gewandhaus* in Leipzig, Germany. Home of the Baltimore Symphony Orchestra until 1982, the Lyric has been remodeled and renamed the **Lyric Opera House.** It now accommodates a rich assortment of musical productions each season. The **Maryland Line Monument,** a narrow shaft topped by a figure of Liberty sculpted by A. L. van der Bergen, stands in front of the Lyric. The Maryland Society of the Sons of the Revolution erected the memorial in 1901 to honor Maryland soldiers who fought in the War of Independence.

Maryland Institute College of Art

This school originated in 1826, when citizens who included John H. B. Latrobe incorporated the Maryland Institute for the Promotion of the Mechanic Arts. The school held classes in the Athenaeum, which was at the southwest corner of Lexington and St. Paul Sts., until 1835, when fire totally destroyed the building and its contents. After a decade of inactivity, the institute reorganized in 1847 and in 1851 moved into a new Great Hall, which occupied a block near today's intersection of Baltimore St. and Market Place. The Rinehart School of Sculpture was established there in 1896. George A. Lucas bequeathed to the institute his collection of hundreds of Barye bronzes, James McNeil Whistler etchings, rare porcelains, and thousands of prints, photographs, and paintings—now on indefinite loan to the Walters Art Gallery and Baltimore Museum of Art. The Great Fire of 1904 destroyed the historic hall, and once again the institute searched for a new home. This time, Andrew Carnegie and the state provided funds to rebuild it as the School of Art and Design, at the corner of Lanvale St. and Mt. Royal Ave. on land that Michael Jenkins donated. The marble, Roman classical building, designed by the New York firm of Pell and Corbet, opened in 1908.

To reflect its growing importance as a fine arts institution, the school in 1960 changed its name to Maryland Institute, College of Art; and since 1963, all the institute's offices and studios have resided in the Mount Royal area. A shoe company warehouse across the street from the main building was renovated for studios and gallery spaces in 1980 and renamed the **Fox Building.** The main building itself underwent renovation in 1990–92, and in 1992 a new student apartment complex, **The Commons,** opened on a five-acre plot between McMechen St. and North Ave. in adjacent Bolton Hill. The institute now enrolls more than 900 full-time students from 40 or more states and a similar number of countries. They study for bachelor's and master's degrees in the visual arts.

Corpus Christi Church, located next to the main institute building, at Lafayette and Mt. Royal Aves., has shared in the area's rejuvenation. In 1891, when Cardinal Gibbons dedicated the church, he called the Gothic Revival building "a beautiful work of art." It commemorates Thomas E. Jenkins.

Just beyond the church, on the other side of the street in the 1400 block of Mt. Royal, stands the **Confederate War Memorial,** designed by J. Wellington Ruchstuhl and erected in 1903. In contrast to more triumphant memorials scattered around the city, this small statue depicts a life-sized, wounded youth supported by a comforting angel.

Return south-southeast down Mt. Royal Ave. and turn right on Cathedral St. to the **Mt. Royal Street Station** (E. Francis Baldwin and Josias Pennington, 1896), a landmark since it first appeared, replacing Camden Station as the principal Baltimore stop on the B&O Railroad. The architects placed the granite Romanesque building in a hollow at the entrance to the tunnel that carries the tracks beneath the downtown area to Camden Station. At the time of its construction, the station—with its lofty, oak-paneled waiting room—was the largest built by a single railroad for its passengers. The high tower, with its still-functioning clock, dominates the long, two-story building. The railroad sold it to the Maryland Institute in 1964; using an award-winning design by Richard Donkervoet, the institute converted the interior spaces in two renovations (1964 and 1984) to accommodate three floors of studios, offices, a library, and lecture hall while retaining many original features.

Proceed farther south on Cathedral to the **Joseph Meyerhoff Symphony Hall,** the most recent landmark in the Mount Royal Cultural District. It dominates the intersection of Preston and Cathedral Sts. Named for the principal benefactor of the Baltimore Symphony Orchestra, the unusually shaped, 2,462-seat hall was designed by Pietro Belluschi with acoustics by Bolt, Beranek and Newman. From the air, the $10.5 million brick and glass building resembles a terraced ziggurat cut in half to form a large, sloping oval roof. The warm, wood-appointed interior with its sculpted box seats gives the orchestra an elegant modern home. It first opened to the public on September 16, 1982.

The Baltimore Symphony Orchestra was organized in the winter of 1915–16 by the city of Baltimore, with Gustav Strube, a Peabody faculty member, as the first conductor. The nation's first municipally sponsored symphony orchestra, it continued in that form until 1942, when a nonprofit board took over its management. Since that time, it has developed into one of the top ten orchestras in the United States.

The **Medical and Chirurgical Faculty of Maryland** stands across the street from the Meyerhoff at 1211 Cathedral St. It has occupied this location since 1909. The faculty, founded in 1799, serves as the state medical society. Under the leadership of Dr. William Osler, who served as president in 1896–97, the faculty supported founding of the American Public Health Association and advocated other Progressive-era public health measures. The faculty's collection of paintings and antique medical instruments speaks to the state's medical history. The library, open to the public, contains rare medical books dating to the 17th century. With 312 journals, 110,000 volumes, and a website (PubMed), the library also serves as an up-to-date repository for medical research reports.

The restored **Heptasoph Hall** occupies the corner of Preston and Cathedral Sts. next to the "Med-Chi" building. In 1896 the Improved Order of Heptasophs, a fraternal group of craftsmen, built this multipurpose brick hall with stained-glass windows to be a regional meeting place and dance hall and to house their insurance business. After the Heptasophs went bankrupt in the 1920s, the structure served a variety of needs, until 1963, when it provided the first home for Center Stage.

The Baltimore Theatre Project, an experimental troupe founded by Philip Arnoult in 1971, bought the building from the city in 1977 and then in 1983 sold it to a private group that soon developed a 200-seat theater on the top floor and a restaurant–music club on the two renovated floors below. The Theatre Project, now associated with Towson University, continues to feature avant garde thespian and dance groups from around the world. A successful restaurant occupies the spaces created for the music club.

Greek Orthodox Cathedral

Walk east on Preston St. to Maryland Ave. and the **Greek Orthodox Cathedral of the Annunciation,** a granite Romanesque church originally designed by Charles Cassell in 1889 for the Associate Congregational Church of Baltimore. That congregation abandoned the church in 1934, and a gasoline station nearly went on the corner. The Greek Orthodox Church "Evangelismos" acquired the building in 1937. Purchase of the church signaled the growing prosperity of a Greek American community, which continues to thrive. In 1905 the Baltimore Greek community numbered not more than two hundred newcomers, many from the province of Laconia. In 1906 they organized a parish, and soon a priest arrived from Athens. This Greek Orthodox church became a cathedral in 1975 —the spiritual and cultural center for Greek orthodoxy in the state of Maryland. In 1978, the congregation purchased five row houses across from the church on Preston St. and converted them into the **Orthodox Center,** which includes archives, library, chapel, and social center for the elderly.

The walker may continue east down Preston St. to Charles St. and bus transportation or return west on Preston St. past Pearlstone Park to Howard St. and both Light Rail and Metro stops. Note that from this point, one could easily proceed to the Eutaw Place–Bolton Hill tour, which follows.

I. EUTAW PLACE AND BOLTON HILL

This walk begins at State Center, which one may reach via the Mount Royal tour (State Center is across Howard St. opposite Preston St.), via the Metro from Charles Center downtown; by taking the Light Rail to the University of Baltimore / Mount Royal station; or by driving from the Inner Harbor (north on Charles to Franklin, left on Franklin, right on Eutaw until it crosses Martin Luther King Jr. Blvd.).

Maryland State Office Center

This 18-acre office complex, completed in 1960, demonstrates the power and scope of urban-renewal efforts in postwar Baltimore. The Mount Royal Plaza project demolished most structures in a 74-acre area bounded by Cathedral, Madison, Biddle, and Dolphin Sts. The seven-story **State Office Building** (Fisher, Nes, Campbell), a six-story **State Highway Administration Building,** and the **Employment Security Building** make up the original grouping. The **Herbert R. O'Conor Building,** opened in 1975, occupies the corner of Howard and Preston Sts.

Fifth Regiment Armory

The Fifth Regiment Armory occupies the block bordered by Preston, Howard, Hoffman, and Bolton Sts. This fortresslike structure (Frank E. and Henry R. Davis, 1903) underwent interior remodeling (J. B. Noel Wyatt and William G. Nolting) in 1933 following a fire. In 1912 the Democratic Party met here in convention to nominate (after 46 ballots) Woodrow Wilson for president. Then governor of New Jersey, Wilson had earned a Ph.D. in history and political science from Johns Hopkins University. H. L. Mencken, who reveled in American political theater, delighted at the spectacle of William Jennings Bryan swinging crucial votes to Wilson (the grateful Wilson named Bryan his secretary of state). Mencken later called Wilson "an inflated pedagogue with messianic delusions" and Bryan "an oily fellow" who was "consumed by the natural heat of his own dreadful fury against his betters."

The armory now serves as headquarters for the 175th Regiment of the Maryland National Guard, a direct descendant of Mordecai Gist's Baltimore Independent Cadets, organized in 1774 and later part of Smallwood's Maryland Battalion. The unit reassembled in 1794 as the Fifth Regiment of militia, and its members again fought the British, at the battles of Bladensburg and North Point in 1814. During the Civil War, most of its members served in the 1st Maryland Infantry (CSA). The Fifth Regiment merged with the First and Fourth Regiments during World War I to form the 115th Infantry Regiment; in 1940, it became the 175th Infantry Regiment. On Tuesdays, 10 a.m. to 2 p.m., volunteers maintain a basement museum of Maryland National Guard memorabilia.

From the armory, follow Preston or Hoffman a short distance to Eutaw and turn right a block or two to Dolphin St.

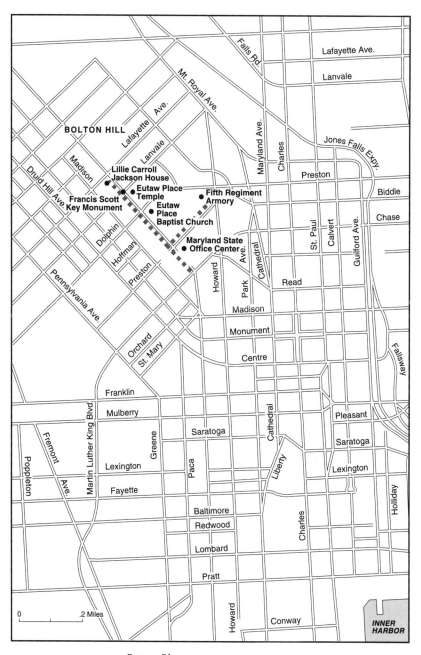

Eutaw Place

Eutaw St. becomes Eutaw Place—a wide, landscaped boulevard that begins just north of the State Office Center and extends to Druid Hill Park. Highly fashionable in the late 19th century, the street boasted some of the most expensive and elaborate town houses of the period. It also forms the southwestern boundary of the historic district known as Bolton Hill. Drivers will find on-street parking near the office center. Pedestrians should take the Metro to the State Center Station.

Storied Eutaw Place in
the 1930s

On the corner of Dolphin and Eutaw stands **Eutaw Place Baptist
Church** (1871), a white-marble Gothic Revival structure with a tower
190 feet high. The architect, New Yorker Thomas U. Walter, also designed the dome and wings of the U.S. Capitol.

One block to the north, the exotic, tiled domes of the marble **Eutaw
Place Temple** give the intersection of Eutaw Place and Lanvale St. a
Middle Eastern appearance. The Oheb Shalom Congregation hired Joseph
E. Sperry to build this structure in 1893, when Eutaw Place attracted
many of Baltimore's German-speaking Jewish families. Oheb Shalom
(1853), the city's third synagogue after Baltimore Hebrew Congregation
(1830) and Har Sinai (1842), served the immigrants who settled in Baltimore after the General Assembly passed the 1826 "Jew Bill," allowing
non-Christian Marylanders to vote and hold office. In 1859, Oheb Shalom
appointed Rabbi Benjamin Szold (1829–1902) to lead the temple. His
daughter Henrietta Szold (1860–1945) grew up in Baltimore and later
founded Hadassah and became a leader of the Zionist movement in America. The congregation sold the building to the Prince Hall Masons in 1961.

Continue along Eutaw Place to the **Lillie Carroll Jackson House,**
just above Lanvale St. at 1320 Eutaw Place. "Ma" Jackson (1889–1975)
lived the last 20 years of her life here, and in recent years the house has
served as a museum commemorating the formidable civil rights leader,
who traced her descent to Somalian chiefs and Charles Carroll of Carrollton. At age 45, having retired from teaching school, she reorganized the
small Baltimore branch of the National Association for the Advancement
of Colored People and turned it into an effective instrument of social
change. By 1946, with more than 17,000 members, the Baltimore chapter had become the largest in the country. With Thurgood Marshall as
her advocate, she galvanized Baltimoreans in a constant struggle for civil
rights during the 1930s, '40s, and '50s. "We must go ahead with our work
on faith," she told faltering followers, "because God's storehouse is full."

The **Marlborough Apartments** (1907), 1701 Eutaw Place, a 10-story building located at the northeast corner of Eutaw Place and Wilson St., once ranked among the grandest apartment buildings in the city. Etta and Claribel Cone lived in side-by-side apartments on the eighth floor from 1908 until their respective deaths in 1929 and 1949. Their private collections of Matisse, Picasso, Renoir, and other Parisian painters, which overflowed the rooms, became the basis of the world-famous Cone Collection at the Baltimore Museum of Art.

Return to the intersection of Lanvale St. and Eutaw Place and the **Francis Scott Key Monument** (1911). This elaborate statuary group by Jean Marius Antonin Mercie shows Key (in bronze) seated in a boat (stone) offering the manuscript of "The Star-Spangled Banner" to a bronze Columbia standing on a marble pedestal.

Bolton Hill

The Key monument serves as a convenient entrance to a neighborhood that takes its name from the mansion that once stood on the site of the Fifth Regiment Armory. Bolton Hill lies within the area between Eutaw Place on the southwest, Mt. Royal Ave. on the northeast, Dolphin St. on the southeast, and North Ave. It has received protection as a historic and architectural preservation district. The town houses of Bolton Hill, especially those at its southern end, have provided homes to a number of distinguished residents over the years. F. Scott Fitzgerald (Francis Scott, named after Key) (1896–1940) and his wife Zelda lived at 1307 Park Ave. for several years during a five-year sojourn in Baltimore. "Baltimore is warm but pleasant," he wrote in a 1935 letter. "I love it more than I thought—it is so rich in memories—it is nice to look up the street and see the statue of my great uncle and to know that Poe is buried here and that many ancestors of mine have walked in the old town on the bay. I belong here, where everything is civilized and gay and rotted and polite."

Lanvale St. descends northeast from the monument to houses built shortly after the Civil War, when Southerners come to the city seemed

The southern tip of Bolton St., as it appeared in the 1930s. The Fifth Regiment Armory looms in the distance.

to prefer the ambiance of this neighborhood over any other. Walk through the street park and continue to Bolton, a tree-lined avenue that has been homey and cultured since before Fitzgerald's day. Within a few blocks on either side of Bolton St. have lived writers as diverse in tone and purpose as Gerald W. Johnson, James Cain, Edith Hamilton, Dr. Lewis Thomas, Gertrude Stein, Felix and Christopher Morley, Hulbert Footner, Elliott Coleman, William Manchester, and Russell Baker. Accomplished residents included university presidents, professors, medical school faculty, and directors of Baltimore businesses.

To appreciate the care lavished on the restoration of these large brick row houses, the walker should turn left on Bolton and ascend the hill to the 1400 and 1500 blocks. At Bolton and McMechen, enjoy the quiet and character of the neighborhood restaurant and visit one of the specialty shops. A leisurely stroll through the neighborhood continues on Bolton to Laurens St. There, make a right for two blocks to Park Ave., turn right again and return to Lanvale St.

The country house at the corner, 232 W. Lanvale St., dates to a period earlier than the fashionable rows and is probably the oldest in the neighborhood. Mrs. Nancy Howard DeFord Venable lived here in the period of World War II; after the war, she entertained, among other literati, W. H. Auden and Tennessee Williams. She may have been Williams' model for Violet Venable in *Suddenly Last Summer.*

Walk downhill past the 1200 block of Bolton to Dolphin Ln. The small, brick-walled park at the end of the block on the right commemorates "the spirit of neighborliness" of two 1200-block Bolton St. residents, William Gaines Contee and Edward Wilson Parrago. Neighbors dedicated the park in 1971. Turn left on Dolphin and walk past the venerable Bolton Swim and Tennis Club to Park Ave. Turn right on Park and walk down to Howard St. The small park at the corner on the right contains a monument (1939) to two Marylanders who won the Congressional Medal of Honor for bravery during World War I—Ens. Charles H. Hammann, a navy flyer who in his seaplane rescued a downed compatriot in a small Austrian lake, and Pvt. Henry G. Costin, a soldier in the 115th Infantry, who died in battle.

Walk south (right) down Howard St. to return to the Maryland State Office Center or the University of Baltimore–Mt. Royal Avenue Light Rail stop.

J. SEEING SOUTH BALTIMORE

In 1913 the city built Key Highway to connect Light St. to the heart of a peninsula formed by the Northwest and Middle Branches of the Patapsco River. The highway provided improved street transportation to the busy shipyards that clustered along the northern side of the peninsula. From Light St. on the southern edge of the Inner Harbor, follow Key Highway past the old Bethlehem Steel yards to one of the city's leading attractions, a museum devoted to working people and the making of things. (Note that in warm months one may also reach the museum via water taxi.)

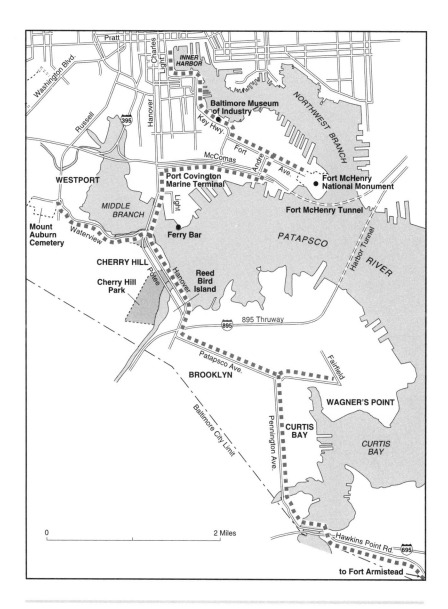

The Baltimore Museum of Industry

Housed in the historic Platt Oyster Cannery (ca. 1870), the Baltimore Museum of Industry (1415 Key Highway) invites visitors to explore the machinery and work experience of bygone days when Baltimore boasted hundreds of factory smokestacks, teemed with shipping, and offered decent-paying jobs to incoming families from places as far away as the Carolinas and the mountains of West Virginia.

The equipment in a painstakingly restored machine shop still operates—with all the clatter and whirring belts that eventually gave rise to the worker-safety movement. Vintage printing presses date from the 1820s. Exhibits, many of them interactive, deal with early radio, commercial trucking, aircraft manufacturing at Glenn L. Martin, cargo moving, blacksmithing, marine transportation, canning, and the needle trades. Outside, go aboard the museum's fully operational tugboat, pulled from the bottom of the Sassafras River in 1981. A privately owned oyster buyboat, *The Halfshell,* normally lies tied up at the BMI pier.

Children of all ages may participate in the BMI's award-winning hands-on activities. In the Childrens' Motorworks Assembly Line, youngsters come to realize the importance of mass production in the development of modern industry and experience something of the routine, pace, and problems of assembly-line work. In the Kids' Cannery, children assume the roles of workers in a turn-of-the-century oyster cannery. Doing so, they learn the history of the oyster-packing industry (including the costs of unbridled harvesting) and the story of the people who made their lives in the plants.

Besides work-related equipment, the museum collects and preserves company records, printed materials, and photographs. Housed in a second-story research center, they are available to serious researchers by appointment.

Between Memorial Day and Labor Day, the BMI is open Tuesday–Friday, noon to 5 p.m. (and Wednesday evenings, 7 p.m. until 9 p.m.); Saturdays 10 a.m. to 5 p.m.; Sundays noon to 5. During the rest of the year, it is open Thursday, Friday, and Sunday, noon to 5; Saturday 10 a.m. to 5 p.m.; and Wednesdays 6 p.m. to 9 p.m. Closed Mondays, Thanksgiving Day, Christmas Eve, and Christmas Day. A side lot offers ample off-street parking; one may also reach the site by water taxi.

Admission: free to members; $3.50 for adults; $2.50 for students and seniors; $12 for families. The Kids' Cannery costs an additional $3.50, the Assembly Line $2.

Museum shop. For information call 410-727-4808.

Farther south and east, Key Highway intersects Fort Ave., which passes through the community of **Locust Point** on its way to Fort McHenry. The Baltimore and Ohio Railroad developed this area after 1845, when it received permission to extend its lines to the harbor and develop deep-water loading points. The railroad first built on Locust Point, the local name for the current site of the **Domino Sugar** and **Procter and Gamble** plants. As the port expanded to the east, the entire peninsula became known as Locust Point, site of a nationally significant sea-rail complex for the export of coal and grain. After the Civil War, Piers 8 and 9 became an immigrant debarkation center second only to Ellis Island in New York. Tens of thousands of Germans, Irish, Italians, Scandinavians, Russians, Poles, Lithuanians, Ukrainians, and Bohemians arrived at Locust Point before World War I and either boarded westward trains or found work in Baltimore. The Maryland Port Administration took over the Locust Point facilities in 1964.

Fort McHenry National Monument

Fort Ave. continues east to the entrance of **Fort McHenry,** a National Park Service site famous for its role in the defense of Baltimore in 1814 and as the birthplace of the National Anthem.

The fort lies on the tip of the peninsula, at a spot once known as Whetstone Point and a location ideal for protecting Fells Point and the inner Basin. Engineers had built an earlier structure here, Fort Whetstone, during the Revolution. In 1794 the Washington administration, developing the country's defenses under the Constitution, set Maj. John Jacob Ulrich Rivardi, who later taught at West Point, the task of designing the outer batteries. Others designed the fort itself, following the ideas of French military engineer Sebastien Le Prestre de Vauban (with whom Rivardi disagreed). Work on the fort was complete in about 1803 (it underwent major alterations in 1824 and again in 1837). The fort's name

honors James McHenry (1755–1816), a Marylander who served as an army surgeon and later George Washington's secretary during the Revolution and as John Adams's secretary of war from 1796 to 1800.

A bronze figure of *Orpheus*, the mythological Greek musician, sculpted by Charles Neihaus in 1922, stands inside the monument's outer gate. Pathways offer panoramic views of the harbor as freighters coming up the bay pass into the river branches. During the Civil War, these open spaces were filled with barracks for Union troops who guarded prisoners-of-war and suspected Maryland secessionists who had been rounded up, including Baltimore mayor George Brown, state senators and delegates, and newspapermen. Confined inside the fort, the political prisoners shared quarters in spaces first built as powder magazines.

After exploring the visitors center, one may enter the fort through an arched sally port that opens onto a parade ground. At one side of this ceremonial space rises the wooden staff from which the 15-star American banner flew during the British attack in September 1814. Baltimorean Mary Pickersgill, her daughter, and her niece made the special 80-pound battle flag oversized, so the British would have no trouble seeing it. They didn't, and neither did Francis Scott Key. The parade ground also contains three cannon used in the defense of the city, one bearing the seal of King George III of England. At the time of the Battle of Baltimore, the buildings within the fort were only one-and-a-half stories high; their existing shed roofs date from 1829. The first building to the right of the sally port served as quarters for the commanding officer; next to it is the powder magazine, hit by a 186-pound bomb that failed to explode during the bombardment. The park superintendent now occupies the building that once housed junior officers. Two enlisted men's barracks offer military displays and models describing the defense of the fort.

At dawn on September 13, 1814, the British anchored 16 warships in

In the mid-1930s aged housing stock and references to blacksmiths coexisted with automobiles, their accompanying signage, and freshly painted notices on behalf of post-Prohibition beer.

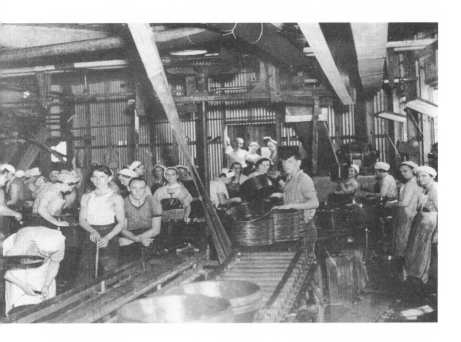

Workers at a Baltimore canning factory, ca. 1930

the Patapsco River, about two miles below Fort McHenry. The distance placed the fleet beyond range of the fort's guns, but it also hindered the accuracy of the ships' cannon, bombs, and Congreve rockets. Shortly after midnight on the 14th, a landing force made its way up the Middle Branch (then called Ferry Branch) to attack Baltimore from the south and support the main British attack at North Point. Eleven of the boats mistakenly turned into the Northwest Branch and beat a retreat when a shore battery opposite Fort McHenry discovered their position. The other nine boats continued up Ferry Branch but withdrew when they were attacked by the guns at **Fort Covington,** which stood about a mile and a half west of Fort McHenry. These failures led to the withdrawal of the British on the 16th and Fort McHenry's place in American legend. Two of the buildings were damaged during the British attack; but there were few casualties, and the heavy guns of the outer battery were never silenced. A brick walk leads to outer batteries constructed between 1850 and 1877 as replacements for those built in 1794.

After the Civil War, Fort McHenry became an infantry post, which was abandoned in 1900. Baltimore leased the grounds from the federal government for a park, but during World War I, the war department reclaimed the property for use as a military hospital. In 1925, Congress designated the fort and surrounding acreage a national park (in 1939 it became a national monument and historic shrine). Because of the fort's historic association with the flag, new versions of the American flag have been inaugurated here. On July 4, 1958, after Alaska was admitted to the Union, the first 49-star flag was raised here, as was the first 50-star flag a year later, when Hawaii joined the Union.

For further information, call 410-962-4290.

While history buffs flock to Fort McHenry, engineers come from around the world to inspect the **Fort McHenry Tunnel,** located underwater just south of the fort (at about the place where the British ships anchored for the attack). When completed in 1985, this $825 million project represented the largest project in the history of the federal Interstate Highway program. At the time of its construction, it was the world's widest motor vehicle tunnel and the only one in the world that turns in two directions simultaneously: down, so ships above have clearance, and around the point. The tunnel carries eight lanes of I-95 traffic.

Ferry Bar

From Fort McHenry, the visitor may return on Fort Ave. to Reynolds St., there turning left (south). Across the street lies Latrobe Park, named for Ferdinand C. Latrobe, who was elected mayor of Baltimore seven times in the late 19th century. Reynolds St. leads to McComas St. Turn right for a tour of industrial development that includes the **South Locust Point Marine Terminal.** In 1903 the Western Maryland Railway established the **Port Covington Marine Terminal,** named for the fort which once stood here; it is now operated by the Maryland Port Administration. To the south lies **Ferry Bar**—the point of land jutting into the water at the foot of Light St.

In 1859, from approximately this convenient spot on the river, the B&O designer Ross Winans launched a steam-powered, all-metal "cigar ship." A huge iron wheel amidships propelled the narrow steamer (180-by-16 feet), which was supposedly able to cross the ocean in four days. Like several other of Winans's ventures, the ship failed; Winans had better success with devices that enabled railroad cars to move around curves. Simon Lake (1866–1945), another inventor, set out from Ferry Bar on December 16, 1897, with 10 passengers on the maiden voyage of the *Argonaut,* an experimental submarine he built on the peninsula. The submarine skimmed along the river bottom on wheels, powered by a gasoline engine vented to the surface by a 20-foot pipe, The craft made successful voyages up the East Coast and established Lake's reputation among the pioneer submariners who earned the praise of Jules Verne. In the 1890s, Ferry Bar also flourished as a fashionable local resort.

McComas St. reaches Hanover St. (Md. 2). There turn left and cross the **Hanover Street Bridge,** which dates from 1914 and replaced a wooden structure. Until the city's annexation of 1918, this bridge linked Baltimore City to south Baltimore County. Recreational boat basins now nestle below the bridge.

Brooklyn and Curtis Bay

After crossing the bridge, the visitor may bear right onto Waterview Ave., passing a park on the right. Driving a mile and a quarter takes one underneath Russell St. to the gates of **Mount Auburn Cemetery,** the last surviving African American burial ground in Baltimore. The Sharp Street Methodist Church established it in 1872. Its 33 acres shelter the remains of both escaped slaves and members of socially and politically prominent families. The first black lightweight boxing champion of the world (1902), Joe Gans, lies here.

A newer South Baltimore—Cherry Hill, Brooklyn, Curtis Bay, and Fairfield—lies on the south banks of the Middle Branch and the wide estuary of the Patapsco River.

South from Middle Branch, Hanover St. passes **Harbor Hospital** and skirts **Cherry Hill,** a public housing project dating from the post–World War II years. At one time, with nearly 1,600 units, Cherry Hill was the largest project of its kind on the East Coast. The road then crosses a narrow inlet of the Patapsco River. The high banks of two parks—Cherry Hill Park and Reed Bird Island—help protect this bit of water. One hundred and fifty years ago, this area consisted of marshy lowlands along the water; now railroads, streets, and expressways crisscross the land. Hanover St. passes under the Harbor Tunnel Thruway, opened to traffic on November 30, 1957, as a bypass for interstate traffic. The thruway (now I-895) crosses under the Patapsco River in two, 1.7-mile tunnels that link this part of the harbor with Canton on the other side. The point where the thruway enters the tunnels marks the site where, during World War II, Bethlehem Steel Corporation built Liberty and Victory ships.

Follow Hanover St. to Patapsco Ave. and turn left (east) through the community of **Brooklyn,** the site of the Patapsco Company, developer of this land in the 1850s. Streets of neat row houses, churches, and taverns share landscape with docks, factories, former canneries, and storage tanks. Patapsco Ave. intersects Pennington Ave. (Md. 173), which breaks due south through the community of **Curtis Bay,** once separate from Brooklyn but now virtually indistinguishable. Patapsco Ave. continues east under railroad tracks to **Wagner's Point,** an industrial region where the small residential pockets seem like western frontier towns surrounded by a vast industrial wilderness. The point now contains the city's **Patapsco Waste Water Treatment Plant** and oil company terminals. Fairfield Rd. branches north from Patapsco Ave. to the community of Fairfield, whose residents mostly work for, or have worked for, nearby industries. Pennington Ave. crosses Curtis Creek at the border line between Baltimore City and Anne Arundel County. On a clear day, the CSX coal piers can be seen to the north, where the creek empties into Curtis Bay. The wrecked hulks of steamers, schooners, and other baycraft are visible from both sides of the bridge over Curtis Creek.

Beyond the bridge, the road crosses under the Baltimore Beltway (I-695) and branches east as Hawkins Point Rd. Follow it south as it becomes Fort Smallwood Rd. and then makes an odd loop onto Fort Armistead Rd., which travels east past a chemical factory to **Hawkins Point** and **Fort Armistead,** built at the time of the Spanish-American War. The fort lost its cannon in 1903, and the army abandoned it altogether in 1921. Since then, with exceptions during World War II and the Red Scare of the 1950s, when the federal government reclaimed it, Baltimore has managed the site as a park. The city renovated it in 1983–84, adding boat ramps, picnic tables, and walkways to enhance its commanding view of the Patapsco River. **Fort Carroll**, an artificial island built around 1850 under the direction of Robert E. Lee, rises from the middle of the Patapsco. **Sparrows Point** and **Fort Howard** are clearly visible on the opposite shore. Fort Armistead lies almost directly under the **Francis Scott Key Bridge,** opened in 1978 to complete the Baltimore Beltway.

Retrace the route to the Hanover Street Bridge and follow Md. 2 north to the Inner Harbor.

The southwest part of the city offers the delights of railroad history, scenes from the life of one of Baltimore's best writers, and a wonderful park that gives the visitor an inkling of life in 18th-century Baltimore. From the Inner Harbor, follow Lombard St. west.

The B&O Railroad Museum

At Poppleton St., turn left to the B&O Railroad Museum (901 W. Pratt St.), not far from the point where Baltimoreans in 1828 laid the first tie of the Baltimore and Ohio Railroad, the pioneer line in the United States and at the time a highly risky venture. The 35-acre site includes five historic buildings, one of them the B&O's old eastern terminal, **Mount Clare Station** (this version 1851), and the richest railroad collection in the Western Hemisphere—more than two hundred full-size original or replica locomotives, passenger and freight cars, and railroad artifacts, plus historical archives.

Outdoors, in front of the depot, one finds an impressive grouping of 20th-century steam locomotives, diesel-electric and electric locomotives, 20th-century passenger cars, switchers, cabooses, and a variety of historic freight cars. The outdoor lot also gives one an idea of the size and variety of railroad repair equipment; a giant Pennsylvania Railroad steam wreck crane weighs two hundred tons.

Guests enter the museum through the Mount Clare station. The first mile and a half of track ran from this station to the Carrollton Viaduct across the Gwynns Falls. The directors made the first trip in a horse car in 1829, and soon the public could ride for nine cents a trip. The track was finally finished across the Patapsco River to Ellicotts' Mills, and on May 24, 1830, tickets for the first regularly scheduled railroad trip in the United States went on sale at the Mount Clare Station. The first horse-drawn passenger cars, including *Pioneer,* covered the 13-mile, one-way distance in one hour and five minutes. Steam engines—already running in England, where the Baltimoreans had acquired their railroading ideas—soon replaced the horses. On May 24, 1844, the world's first official telegraph message passed through the station to the nearby Pratt Street Station (now destroyed) when Samuel F. B. Morse sent the words "What hath God wrought?" from the chambers of the old Supreme Court building in Washington, D.C.

An **Annex Building** (E. Francis Baldwin, 1891) adjoining the station contains a working replica of the *Tom Thumb* in addition to displays of early engines and rolling stock. On August 25, 1830, Peter Cooper, a New York inventor and industrialist, demonstrated this locomotive, constructed from an old engine found in his New York glue factory and tubing made from gun barrels. Three days later, he made the trip to Ellicotts' Mills in 75 minutes, arriving 10 minutes later than the horse. But the return, downgrade, trip required only 61 minutes, including a four-minute stop for water. According to legend, sometime during this early period the *Tom Thumb* lost a race with a horse-drawn car. Upstairs, the annex houses an HO-scale model railroad that depicts typical B&O-region scenery and delights railroaders of all ages.

The spectacular **Roundhouse** (Baldwin, 1884) measures nearly 240 feet across and 123 feet high from the wooden roundtable on the floor to the cupola and has 22 polygonal sides. This experimental industrial building stood at the center of **Mount Clare Yards,** one of the largest railroad shops in the world and one of Maryland's major 19th-century employers (the thousands of skilled laborers who worked here lived in the surrounding neighborhoods). Originally the home of locomotives, the Roundhouse later housed a repair shop serving the B&O's passenger car fleet. Today, the turntable lies at the center of a fascinating assortment of equipment, both original and

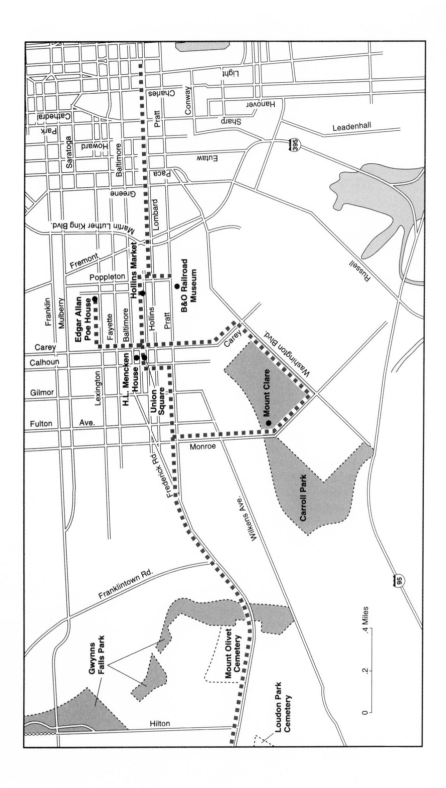

replica, dating from the 1820s and including two replica and nine original 19th-century locomotives and cars from the Civil War era.

A large part of the museum's collection originated from a railroad-history exhibit that Joseph G. Pangborn, a former newspaperman, prepared for the 1892–93 Columbian Exposition in Chicago. When in 1927 the B&O celebrated its centennial, the company used many of the same cars and locomotives in staging an elaborate pageant at Halethorpe, near Baltimore (now a suburb), entitled "The Fair of the Iron Horse." The fair proved so successful that the railroad considered maintaining the site as a permanent museum. Not until 1953 did the B&O public relations department acquire the Mount Clare complex and open a public museum. In 1987, incorporated and privately endowed, the B&O Railroad Museum embarked on a building program that has made it one of the premier American transportation museums.

Open 10 a.m. to 5 p.m. daily; closed only on Thanksgiving, Christmas, and Easter. Admission: $6.50 for adults, $5.50 for senior citizens, $4.00 for children 3–12. Children age 2 and under enter free. Off-street parking.

Train rides are available on weekends for an additional charge of $2.00 per person (children 2 years old and younger ride free). The half-hour excursion carries passengers to the site where the B&O first laid track. During the trip, guides supply sidelights on the history of the railroad and its eastern terminus.

The museum also includes a museum shop and research library. For information call 410-752-2490.

Hollins Market

From the railroad museum, travel north on Poppleton to Hollins St., which parallels Lombard, and look for on-street parking. To the left stands the Hollins Market. Named after a family that once had extensive land holdings in West Baltimore, the market dates to 1835. The brick Italianate addition to the low market sheds, built in 1863–64, is the oldest market structure still in use in the city. An artistic community—supported by coffee houses, small restaurants, and cafés—has grown up in this neigh-

Looking west along the B&O tracks, with the Roundhouse in the foreground, 1930s

borhood, adding a new element to its earlier mixture of German, Lithuanian, and Irish influences.

Union Square and the Mencken House

Continue west on Hollins St. to Union Square, one of many community squares that enhanced West Baltimore in the 19th century. This one, bounded by Hollins, Calhoun, Lombard, and Carey Sts., dates from 1847. It acquired some fame because Henry Louis Mencken made his home at **1524 Hollins St.** Baltimore's most famous newspaperman and cultural critic, Mencken (1880–1956) moved to this three-story brick house when he was three years old and lived here virtually all his life.

Largely self-educated, Mencken was born "a larva of the comfortable and complacent bourgeoisie" into a German American family that owned a cigar factory on Baltimore St. At the age of 18 and soon after his father's death, he became a full-time newspaper reporter. By the time he died, at the age of 75, he had written thousands of articles, critical essays, and columns, as well as numerous books, including a definitive study of the American language. As co-editor with George Jean Nathan of the *Smart Set* (1914–23) and editor of the *American Mercury* (1924–33), Mencken became a national literary and cultural arbiter, admired by intellectuals and abhorred by the puritanical citizenry he categorized as "boobus Americanus." Virtually every major American writer in the 1920s and '30s either paid Mencken a visit at Hollins Street or corresponded with the "Sage of Baltimore," who assiduously organized his volumes of private papers and memoirs. He may have appreciated his own importance, but he said that he wished his tombstone to read simply, "If, after I depart this vale, you ever remember me and have thought to please my ghost, forgive some sinner and wink your eye at some homely girl."

Mencken would likely not have enjoyed visitors snooping around his private quarters, admiring his desk, scattered reference books, homely parlor, and comfortable sitting room. Out back, he kept a tidy garden and, to protect his privacy, built a brick wall around it. Nonetheless, his home was a public museum for 14 years until the City Life Museums folded in 1997. The secular sage spent the unhappy last eight years of his life here—immobilized by a massive stroke and largely unable to read or write—watched over by his brother August, who died in 1967.

Restored and sometimes the backdrop for films shot in Baltimore (notably a rendition of Henry James's *Washington Square*), Union Square merits a walk. A fountain bears the titles of Mencken's books.

A Trip to Two West Baltimore Cemeteries

Two old cemeteries, Mount Olivet and Loudon Park, lie a manageable distance to the west. To visit them, drive south from Union Square two blocks to Pratt, there turning right. Pratt eventually merges with Frederick Rd., on which continue driving west. Soon after crossing the bridge over the Gwynns Falls, Mount Olivet will appear on the right.

Mount Olivet Cemetery, a historic burial ground (1849) located at the 2500 block of Frederick Ave., contains the remains of Francis Asbury (1745–1816), "Father of American Methodism." Asbury, who shared honors with Thomas Coke as the first superintendents of the Methodist Episcopal Church in America, traveled the country's backroads as a circuit rider for more than 40 years. A few months before his death, he gave his address to an English correspondent as "America," claiming that any postmaster would hold the letter in the knowledge that Asbury would eventually pass through the area. Asbury's body lay in a vault at the Eutaw Street Methodist Church until June 16, 1851, when church members reinterred the body at Mount Olivet. Beside his grave in the **Bishop's Lot** on the north side of the cemetery is the grave of Robert Strawbridge (d. 1781), founder in 1764 of the first Methodist church in Maryland.

A short distance farther out Frederick Ave., across the Hilton-Caton intersection, lies the city's largest public cemetery, **Loudon Park,** with more than 200,000 gravesites. In 1852, when the city set aside its 365 acres, this area appeared likely to remain rural countryside indefinitely. But the city's growth overtook it. After the Civil War it became such a fashionable resting place that more than a few families exhumed the remains of loved ones and reinterred them here. Maryland Confederates like Brig. Gen. Bradley T. Johnson and Col. Harry Gilmor lie here, as does H. L. Mencken.

To return to the main tour, drive east on Frederick Rd. to Pratt St. and follow it to Monroe St. (Md. 3). There turn right and follow Monroe to Washington Blvd. Turn left to reach the entrance to Mount Clare.

Mount Clare

From Union Square, take Carey St. south to Washington Blvd. and there turn right toward **Carroll Park** and **Mount Clare,** the only 18th-century plantation still extant within the limits of a major American city and site of the sole colonial building remaining in Baltimore. The property once belonged to one of the lesser-known of the Carrolls of Maryland, the descendants of Dr. Charles Carroll, a surgeon who left Ireland in 1715. Dr. Carroll settled in Annapolis, where he renounced his Catholicism—a practical business decision in a colony that prohibited public practice of Catholic worship. Dr. Carroll's oldest son, Charles (1723–83), became a barrister in London and later, after the death of his younger brother John in 1754, returned to Maryland to manage the family's affairs. Between 1757 and 1760 the barrister tore down his brother's modest house on the 800-acre plantation, which faced the Middle Branch of the Patapsco, and built the brick mansion that survives today. For several years, the wealthy barrister-at-law did not marry (he thus paid a special tax for remaining "a persistent bachelor"). In 1763, wedded to Margaret Tilghman, he settled into the typical tidewater gentleman's roles as lawyer, statesman, and farmer. Charles Carroll "the Barrister" played an active part in the Revolution, as a principal author of Maryland's Declaration of Rights; in 1776 he also wrote much of the state constitution. A member of the Continental Congress, he declined the post of chief judge of the General Court of Maryland but served in the upper house of the General Assembly until his death.

The prerevolutionary mansion has been considerably altered. At one time, counting hyphens and other additions, the entire building was about 360 feet long. Now, only the center portion remains; the present wings date to 1906. Great brick pilasters dominate the corners of the main block on the garden front, and the entrance side features a Palladian front with portico and windows. The interior contains many original furnishings. During the 19th century, the railroad acquired the northern section of the plantation; the southern portion disappeared with development around Washington Boulevard. The city acquired the mansion and remaining property in 1890 and created Carroll Park, a 110-acre park with assorted playing fields and a nine-hole golf course. Mount Clare, maintained by the National Society of the Colonial Dames in America in the State of Maryland, became a National Historic Landmark in 1970. During the Christmas season Mount Clare plays host to special holiday social events.

A visitor standing on the hill overlooking the park and distant Baltimore landmarks can easily imagine the terraced gardens that once sloped downhill and the paths that must have meandered to the river a mile away. The Carrolls experimented with a great variety of plants, including broccoli, oranges, lemons, and pineapples. Excavations have pinpointed locations of the gardens and outbuildings, including an orangery that George Washington admired. Mrs. Carroll sent him some prized plantings. For information call 410-837-3262.

Edgar Allan Poe House

From Mount Clare, return to Carey St. and follow it north to Lexington St., there turning right and following it four blocks to Amity St. (If coming from Mencken's old neighborhood, drive north on Schroeder St.—one block east of the Hollins Market—to Lexington, then right for a short block to Amity St.) To the left at **203 N. Amity** (facing west), stands the Edgar Allan Poe House, where the often unhappy poet and critic lived between 1832 to 1835. In addition to the struggling writer, this narrow, steeply gabled brick structure housed his grandmother, Mrs. David Poe; his father's sister, Maria Poe Clemm; and her daughter Virginia. Poverty-stricken, estranged from his well-to-do stepfather in Richmond, Poe (1809–49) won a literary contest in Baltimore and also won the patronage of one of the city's leading cultural figures, John Pendleton Kennedy, who secured a job for him in Richmond as assistant editor of the *Southern Literary Messenger.* Poe moved there in the summer of 1835, obtained a marriage license that fall in Baltimore to wed his 13-year-old cousin Virginia, and probably secretly married her in this city. The two then returned to Richmond. Poe never again resided in Baltimore. For information call 410-396-7932.

Return to the Inner Harbor by driving south on Poppleton St. and east on Pratt St.

L. OLD WEST AND NORTHWEST BALTIMORE

Addresses in Baltimore are north, south, east, or west depending on their relationship to the intersection of Baltimore and Charles Sts. Before the city's expansion in 1888, the portion of the city lying to the northwest of the downtown and inside of the city limits at North Ave. came to be known as "West Baltimore," afterward as "Old West."

At first heavily Jewish, this quadrant of the city since World War II increasingly has become home to African American families who have moved northwesterly in search of better schools, more convenient shopping, and the good life of a nice house and yard. Earlier, during the 19th century, the densely settled neighborhood along Pennsylvania Ave. in West Baltimore had developed into a vibrant though segregated black community.

Pennsylvania Ave.

Drive west from the Inner Harbor on Lombard, turning right on Martin Luther King Jr. Blvd. and following it to Pennsylvania Ave. There turn left. (Pennsylvania Ave. is also accessible via the Upton or Penn-North Metro stations.) "The Avenue," as it was known, runs in a northwesterly direction from this starting point. The site of the **Royal Theater,** a mecca for black entertainers and their fans, stood on the east side of Pennsylvania Ave., between Dolphin and Lanvale Sts. Built in 1921, it featured all the jazz, comedy, and dancing acts that were famous in the 1920s, '30s, and '40s, including such native-Baltimore performers as Eubie Blake, Billie Holiday, Chick Webb, Cab Calloway, Avon Long, and Baby Lawrence. In the segregated Baltimore of the time, the Avenue flourished, by all accounts—lined with stores, eateries, and music clubs. Now, after urban riots and flight of the black middle class to the suburbs, the street—urban renewal efforts notwithstanding—looks dowdy and disappointing.

A statue of Billie Holiday (1915–59), the work of James Earl Reid, stands in a small park at the northwest corner of Pennsylvania and Lafayette Aves. Dedicated in 1985, the figure sings to (or chastises) the spires of downtown Baltimore. Born out of wedlock in a Philadelphia hospital as Eleanora Fagan, the young singer grew up poor in East Baltimore. She absorbed her musical ideas from recordings of Bessie Smith and Louis Armstrong which she heard in local "good time houses," as well as from her father, Clarence Holiday, a Baltimore guitarist and banjoist who traveled with such well-known groups as the Fletcher Henderson Band. "Lady

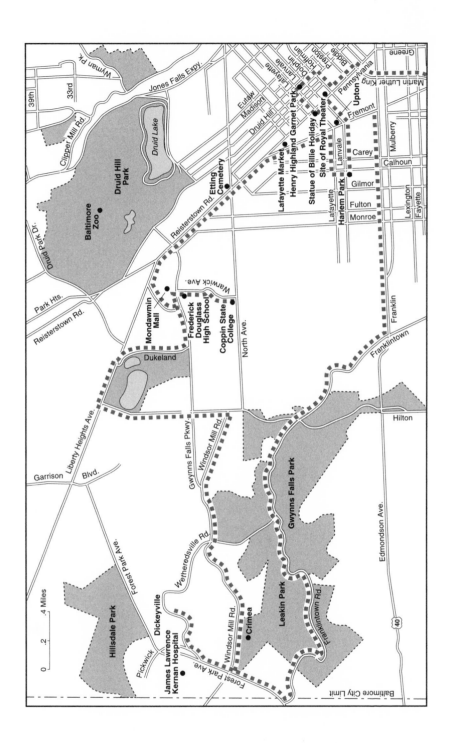

Day" moved to Harlem as a streetwise teenager, "jammed" with major musicians, made her first record in 1933, and by age 21 had become a major jazz singer. At the time of her death in New York from drug abuse and associated ills, many critics rated her as the best female jazz singer who ever lived.

Druid Hill Ave. and Dolphin St.

Turn right (northeast) on Lafayette Ave. and follow it to Druid Hill Ave. The **Henry Highland Garnet Park** occupies the southeast corner of Lafayette and Druid Hill, a memorial to a man who rose from slavery to become U.S. Minister to Liberia. Garnet (1815–82) was born in Kent County on the Eastern Shore, escaped from slavery, became a leader in the abolitionist movement, and served as pastor of Presbyterian churches in Washington and New York.

The **Bethel A.M.E. Church,** which traces its origins to a congregation led by Daniel Coker in the early 1800s, stands at the northwest corner of Druid Hill Ave. and Lanvale St., one block to the right. The legal and real estate office of the Mitchell family, whose members were central figures in the civil rights movement, occupies the southeast corner. Continue down Druid Hill Ave. and turn right on Dolphin St. The venerable **Sharp Street Methodist Church** now meets in the church at the corner of Dolphin and Etting Sts. Follow Dolphin past Division St. to Pennsylvania Ave., turn right and continue north.

Turn left (southwest) on Lanvale St. and follow it almost to its meeting with Fremont. **Upton,** a Greek Revival house built in 1838, stands at 811 W. Lanvale. An unknown architect built this brick, 2½-story country house for David Stewart, who in 1849 served briefly as a U.S. senator from Maryland. The original portico faced the harbor, a view now obscured by urban development. Since Stewart's death, in 1858, the house has been used as a private home, hospital, radio station, music conservatory, and special public school. The name Upton now applies to the surrounding neighborhood.

Lafayette Square and Harlem Park

Continue on Lanvale past **Lafayette Park,** a square block of greenery that the city acquired in 1857. During the Civil War, companies of Union troops camped here. The large mansions and churches that surround the park reflect the social prominence it originally enjoyed. Col. J. Thomas Scharf, in his *Chronicles of Baltimore* (1874), included Lafayette Park among "the favorite pleasure grounds of Baltimore." In the 1920s, a large influx of African Americans from the South migrated to the city and were forced by legal segregation and restrictive real estate codes into Baltimore's first "black belt"—roughly the area bounded by Druid Hill Park on the north, Madison Ave. (the northwesterly extension of Madison St.) on the east, Gilmor St. on the west, and Franklin St. to the south. White residents fled formerly fashionable Lafayette Park, and it disappeared from written descriptions of the city.

Follow Lanvale to Calhoun St., which forms the eastern boundary of **Harlem Park.** Once the site of an ambitious late-19th-century housing development scheme, this neighborhood later, in 1960, became the focal point of one of Baltimore's first urban renewal projects. For the first time, local officials, supported with federal funds, attacked the related

On a Sunday afternoon in about 1937 a WPA photographer happened upon this well-dressed girl sitting on her well-scrubbed Baltimore stoop.

problems of absentee landlords and substandard housing in a predominantly black neighborhood only minutes from downtown. Then the city battled "white flight"; now the problem seems to be "black flight." The struggle against poverty and urban decay continues.

The Avenue Market (Lafayette Market)

Turn right on Calhoun St. for a short block and turn right (east) on Lafayette Ave., which returns one across Fremont Ave. to Pennsylvania Ave. There turn left and drive to **Lafayette Market,** originally built in 1869, which serves the surrounding community from 1700 Pennsylvania Ave. The Upton Metro Station features a tile mosaic by Romare Bearden entitled "Baltimore Uproar, An American Sound Heard Around the World." Bearden (1914–88), a jazz fan, had begun his artistic career as a collegian by sketching cartoons for the Baltimore *Afro-American.* His colorful work portrays a female singer surrounded by a small, racially integrated orchestra. In 1996 an independent, nonprofit group renovated the building, giving it an Afrocentric theme, and changed its name to the Avenue Market. City officials and community leaders hope that the new market will help stem decline along the Pennsylvania Ave. business corridor and stimulate economic development in the surrounding communities of Sandtown-Winchester, Upton, Penn-North, Harlem Park, and Druid Heights.

Two blocks east of the market at Laurens and Division Sts. is the street corner where Frizzell Gray, known as "Pee Wee," experienced an epiphany and began a new life as Kweisi Mfume, Baltimore city councilman, Maryland congressman, and national executive director of the NAACP.

Etting Cemetery

Five short blocks northwest of Lafayette Market, Pennsylvania Ave. crosses North Ave. and becomes Reisterstown Rd. Just to the east of this

intersection, on the north side of the avenue, one finds Etting Cemetery, the city's oldest Hebrew burial ground. An ancient brick wall and locked iron gate—through which some of the graves are visible—identify the small site. A plaque on the wall indicates that the earliest burial among the 25 graves, most from the Etting family, dates to 1799 and the latest to 1881. Solomon Etting (1764–1847) came to Baltimore from York, Pennsylvania, in 1790, prospered as a merchant, and helped found the B&O Railroad. Soon after passage of an act that permitted non-Christians to hold office in Maryland, Etting and Jacob I. Cohen Jr. won election as the first Jewish members of the Baltimore City Council. At that time, only about 200 Jews lived in the entire state, most of them in Baltimore.

An archetypal Baltimore row, late-19th- or early-20th-century vintage

Continue north on Reisterstown Rd., climbing high ground and then bearing left onto Liberty Heights Ave. Turn left again at Tioga Pkwy. An early shopping center, Mondawmin Mall, lies on the left.

Mondawmin

This diverse neighborhood takes its name from what once was the estate of banker George S. Brown and, until his death in 1949, his son Alexander. Brown family legend has it that the place acquired its name when Henry Wadsworth Longfellow paid a visit; Longfellow's "Song of Hiawatha" praises Mondawmin, the Corn God. Nearby neighborhoods that also take their names from old estates include Walbrook, to the south, and Ashburton, to the north.

James W. Rouse and his development company acquired the Brown estate in the early 1950s and in 1956 opened 46-acre **Mondawmin Mall,** a pioneer "regional retail center." Mondawmin forecast the suburban malls that eventually mushroomed in and around Baltimore, as elsewhere. The Rouse Company still manages the mall.

Close by, one finds schools at every level, from elementary to college. Where Tioga Pkwy. ends in Gwynns Falls Pkwy., turn left to see **Freder-**

ick Douglass High School, located in a building formerly home to the (then white) Western High School for girls. Douglass, the state's oldest African American high school, traces its origins to 1883, when high school courses were added to the Grammar School for Colored Children, on Holliday St. In 1889, the first graduating class received its diplomas from Mayor Ferdinand C. Latrobe, and the city designated the institution "Colored High School"; it remained the only black high school in Maryland for almost three decades. The school moved to a building on the corner of Pennsylvania Ave. and Dolphin St. in 1901. In 1925, renamed for Frederick Douglass, the school moved into a new building, constructed for it at Calhoun and Baker Sts., the first school in Maryland to be built for African American high school students. Its dedication drew a large crowd of dignitaries. Douglass—which features a long list of graduates who became prominent in Maryland as well as national life, the late Justice Thurgood Marshall among them—moved to its current location in 1954.

The quiet campus of **Coppin State College** lies south and west of the high school off Warwick Ave., with its main entrance on North Ave. Coppin opened in 1900 as a normal school for teachers—a part of Douglass High School—and became a separate institution in 1909. In 1926 it was named the Coppin Normal School in honor of Mrs. Fannie Jackson Coppin, a former slave who purchased her freedom and reputedly became the first African American woman to graduate from an American college. In 1952, still a teacher's college, Coppin moved to North Ave. Eleven years later it became an unrestricted, degree-granting college with five divisions. Now part of the University of Maryland system, Coppin State College enrolls about 1,700 full-time students.

Gwynns Falls Parkway continues west beyond the Mondawmin Mall, passing **Gwynns Falls Elementary School,** which sits adjacent to the **William H. Lemmel Middle School.** Turn right on Dukeland St. and follow it to Liberty Heights Ave. **Hanlon Park**—named for Ned Hanlon, sometimes called the "father of modern baseball"—lies immediately to the left. **Lake Ashburton,** a city reservoir, stands on high ground west of the intersection. On the right, note the **Liberty Heights Campus of Baltimore City Community College.** The **Liberty Medical Center,** formerly Provident Hospital, stands just beyond the college on the north side of Liberty Heights Ave. It originated in 1894 when a group of African American physicians established their own hospital.

Turn left (west) on Liberty Heights Ave. and drive to the traffic light at Hilton St. Make a left turn and drive south, past Lake Ashburton, to Windsor Mill Rd. There turn right and follow it west to the Gwynns Falls Valley.

Gwynns Falls Valley

Gwynns Falls rises just south of Reisterstown and flows southeast through Baltimore to the Patapsco River, where it helps to form the Middle Branch. In 1672 Richard Gwynn acquired the rights to trade with the Americans Indians here, and in 1719 his son-in-law built a mill along the stream that now bears the family name. Like the Patapsco River and the Jones Falls, the Gwynns Falls and its valley became the site of much early Maryland industry.

A good portion of the valley has remained undeveloped, particularly within **Gwynns Falls Park** (686 acres), the largest public park in the city, which adjoins **Leakin Park** (324 acres). In 1995 the city announced plans for Gwynns Falls Trail, a 14-mile bicycle and hiking trail to follow the stream from Leakin Park to the Patapsco River. The trail remains under construction.

Follow Windsor Mill Rd. and enter Leakin Park at the entrance opposite Tucker Ln. A narrow road winds back to **Crimea,** the estate built by Thomas D. Winans in 1855. Winans and his brother had recently returned from Russia, where Czar Nicholas I had employed this railroad engineering family from Baltimore to build a line from Moscow to St. Petersburg. At one time, this estate encompassed 1,000 acres of surrounding countryside. The city acquired several hundred acres in 1948 through funds provided by J. Wilson Leakin, a wealthy attorney who, at his death in 1922, willed the city money for a large park. The park includes the Winanses's original stone mansion house—its three verandas overlook Dead Run valley—as well as a nearby wooden chapel, carriage house, and caretaker's house.

Windsor Mill Rd. continues west to N. Forest Park Ave., which forms the eastern boundary of the **James Lawrence Kernan Hospital,** established in 1895 as the Hospital for Deformed and Crippled Children. Kernan, a colorful Baltimore hotel and theatrical entrepreneur, endowed the hospital in 1910 and purchased the 65-acre estate on which it still stands.

Turn right and northeast on Forest Park, drive by the hospital on the left, and bear right on Wetheredsville Rd.

Dickeyville

Wimbert Tschudi erected a gristmill and house at the Dickeyville location in 1762. The Franklin Paper Mill, established around 1811, followed; and in 1829 the Wethered family converted the mill to the manufacture of woolens. John Wethered served as a one-term congressman from 1843 to 1845; in 1844 his wife Mary received only the second telegraph message ever sent from Washington, a greeting from her friend Dolley Madison. The Wethereds built the Ashland Mill downstream, and a village known as Wetheredsville grew up around the woolen mills, which manufactured uniforms during the Civil War. The village name changed after 1872, when William J. Dickey (1814–96) bought the mills. Born in the northern Irish town of Ballymena, Dickey in 1877 helped organize a Presbyterian congregation that eight years later built the **Dickey Memorial Presbyterian Church.** The nearby **Hillsdale United Methodist Church,** a stone Greek Revival structure, had stood since 1849.

In the early part of this century, after the Dickey family sold its interests, Dickeyville declined. The old Franklin mill burned in 1934. Then, in 1954, the family purchased the old Ashland Mill, renamed it Ballymena Mills, and resumed woolen manufacturing. Hurricane Agnes, in 1972, produced a devastating flood that ended this operation. The mills reopened in 1975 as a craft and small business center. Meantime, over the past 50 years, residents have restored, rebuilt, and remodeled the old stone houses and other buildings along Wetheredsville and Pickwick Rds. Insulated by surrounding parks, Dickeyville retains a Brigadoon-like quality—a rustic anachronism in the middle of a 20th-century city.

To continue these rural-within-urban reveries—and to return to the Inner Harbor—exit Dickeyville onto N. Forest Park Ave., turning left, and follow it south to its end at Franklintown Rd. There make a left and follow Franklintown Rd. for a pleasant trip through Gwynns Falls Park. At Edmondson Ave. (U.S. 40), turn left (east). Follow U.S. 40 to Martin Luther King Jr. Blvd. There turn right and, at Pratt St., left to the harbor.

M. FOLLOWING FALLS RD. TO THE ZOO AND MOUNT WASHINGTON

The Jones Falls Valley—lined with mills and small company towns, its banks providing many points of interest—divides the city between east and west. The Jones Falls rises in the Greenspring Valley, joins Deep Run near Brooklandville, and then "falls" on a southeasterly course to the Patapsco River. In the 18th and early 19th centuries, the flour mills it powered made large contributions to the rise of the port. Later, steam-powered cotton mills in the same locale gave rise to the villages of Hampden, Mount Vernon, Clipper, Druidville, Sweetaire, and Woodberry. After the Civil War, the mills expanded; in the 1890s the narrow valley became a world leader in the manufacture of cotton duck, and in so doing attracted thousands of men, women, and children from the countryside. Workers lived in company towns in a semirural setting.

Transportation, as well as industry, affected the valley. Before the Civil War, the Northern Central Railroad followed the Jones Falls into Baltimore. In 1912, both to speed automobile traffic and to prevent flooding, the city used the Fallsway to cover the stream from Penn Station to Lom-

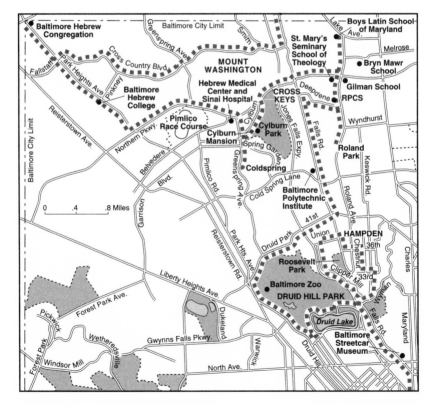

bard St. The Jones Falls Expressway, completed in 1962, placed millions of tons of concrete roadway in the valley and created a companion to the park-lined Rock Creek Parkway in Washington, D.C. Now light rail service, following old railroad track, courses through the valley from Mount Royal Station to Mount Washington before leaving the city on its way to Lake Roland, Timonium, and Hunt Valley.

From the Inner Harbor, drive north on Charles St. just past Penn Station to Lafayette Ave., there turning left. Lafayette drops one onto Falls Rd. (Md. 25) headed north.

Baltimore Streetcar Museum

Falls Rd. follows Pennsylvania Railroad tracks along the flood plain to the Baltimore Streetcar Museum, 1901 Falls Rd. Here a car barn houses restored examples of city streetcars and other urban transportation memorabilia. On Sundays during warm weather months, the museum offers rides—complete with a clanging bell and uniformed conductor—on its adjacent tracks.

Hampden-Woodberry

Continuing north on Falls Rd., the visitor passes beneath two overpasses and then arrives at a point where Falls Rd. takes a sharp left uphill. Continue straight and left on Clipper Mill Rd., which follows the Jones Falls. It passes **Mount Vernon Mill #2** and the former **Clipper Mill** (now a brush company). The Hooper Hotel, a boardinghouse for young women, stood at the corner of Ash St. and Clipper Mill Rd., now occupied by a pumping station. Clipper Mill Rd. ends at Union Ave., one of the few pre-expressway streets that still cross the Jones Falls. Turning left and west on Union Ave., one crosses the stream under the expressway and over railroad tracks, where, to the immediate northwest, Park and

The Jones Falls Valley as it appeared in the 1930s, from atop what now is Television Hill. The Roland Park water tower stands like a sentinel far to the east.

Woodberry Mills once flourished. The mill village of **Woodberry,** now a cluster of houses and industrial buildings, occupies this west bank of the Jones Falls.

Turning right on Union Ave., the visitor ascends to the village of **Hampden,** a conservative, self-sufficient community that developed above the mills. Hampden did not become part of Baltimore until the annexation of 1888, so it retains many elements of a small town—its own churches, businesses, and community groups. In recent years the neighborhood has added artists, small publishers and booksellers, Hopkins students and faculty, and young professionals to its rich bed of skilled tradespeople and specialty merchants. Turn right on Falls Rd. and, if time permits, park. On the west side of Falls, below 36th St., see **Roosevelt Park.** Special shops and local restaurants abound on 36th St., Hampden's Main Street, known to Hampdenites as The Avenue. To resume the tour, follow 36th St. east to Chestnut, there turning right and following it to 33rd, where through traffic veers left to Keswick Ave. Turn right on Keswick and follow it to the next light, then take a right onto Wyman Park Dr., crossing over the Jones Falls Expressway and into Druid Hill Park.

Druid Hill Park

During the 19th century, the green, rolling countryside in northwest Baltimore between the Gwynns Falls and the Jones Falls supplied the setting for dozens of country estates. As the city expanded beyond North Ave., developers altered most of the land for denser residence, typically row-house neighborhoods, whose street names and patches of green recalled the nearest defunct summer home. Fortunately, the city converted a few of the estates to parkland.

In 1860 Lloyd Nicholas Rogers sold his family estate, Druid Hill, to Baltimore for $475,000. His father Nicholas Rogers (1753–1822), an aide-de-camp to Baron de Kalb during the Revolution, had built a Federal-style mansion here in 1801 and landscaped the property after models from English private parks. The city added picnic areas, pathways, playing fields, a swimming pool, and lakes—including **Druid Lake** (1864–70), a public water-supply reservoir 1.5 miles in circumference. Some of the restored pavilions, once stations of a small railway that ran through the park, may be the oldest park buildings in the United States. Although not quite the city's largest, at some 600 acres, Druid Hill Park exemplifies the mid-19th-century foresight that led to an enlightened parks movement in Baltimore and other eastern cities. Thirty city parks now preserve 6,566 acres of public land throughout Baltimore.

Follow the drive until Druid Lake comes into view (the path becomes Druid Park Lake Dr.) and, along it, skirt the northern bank of the antebellum water reservoir. The city Department of Recreation and Parks has its offices in a brick building near the massive gateway at Madison Ave. visible across the lake and to the left. A rough stone monument there may be the only one in the country to commemorate the repeal of the Eighteenth Amendment; John Monroe, an English sculptor who worked on the Albert Memorial in London, had carved the stone for the doorway of Baltimore's old Post Office. When that building came down in 1932, William H. Parker bought the carving—cherubs operating a distillery with corn and grapes—and gave it to the park board. According to *The Sun* of

April 6, 1933, the stone was placed at this location "as a memorial to the return of beer at 12.01 tomorrow."

Where Druid Park Lake Dr. meets an extension of Madison Ave., notice a **statue of George Washington,** donated to the city in 1892. Follow signs to the Baltimore Zoo, which will put the visitor on a roadway leading past the **Conservatory** (1886), a Victorian greenhouse built for tropical plants and in the 1990s painstakingly renovated. At that point, the roadway to the right leads to a marble **statue of Christopher Columbus** at the northwest corner of Druid Lake. Local Italian Americans presented the monument—copied by Albert Weinert from Achille Canessa's statue in Genoa—to the city on Columbus Day, October 12, in 1892. The **William Wallace Monument,** a replica of D. W. Stevenson's statue of the Scottish hero at Abbey Craig, Scotland, overlooks the lake; a descendant presented it to the city in 1892.

Nearby, note the **Grove of Remembrance,** a cluster of oak trees that the National Service Star Legion dedicated October 8, 1919, in memory of all those who died in the Great War. The legion planted one tree for each state, for Baltimore, the Allies, and Woodrow Wilson.

From the Columbus statue, more signs point the way to the Baltimore Zoo.

The Baltimore Zoo

Chartered in 1876 and now the third-oldest zoo in the United States, the Baltimore Zoo (Druid Hill Park) is home to more than 2,250 mammals, birds, and reptiles. The zoo's 180-acre park offers a unique combination of some of the nation's finest naturalistic animal exhibits. It also features conservation and public education programs. It acts as a refuge for many endangered species.

Guests enter through the main gate and then wander the "main valley," where open-air exhibits enable them to watch and admire animals as varied as Kodiak bears, small birds, snow leopards, Arctic foxes, red pandas, wallabies, peacocks, and kangaroos. Farther along, more permanent exhibits allow visitors to see prairie dogs chattering, polar bears swimming, and flamingos and other waterfowl strutting in spacious, naturalistic settings.

All these attractions lead naturally to the Lyn P. Meyerhoff Maryland Wilderness and Maryland Farmyard—48 innovative "immersion" exhibits that cover eight acres. Known collectively as the Children's Zoo, this award-winning area delights everyone, regardless of age. The Maryland Wilderness exhibit includes a marsh aviary, beaver lodge, limestone cave, life-filled tree, and meadow. Animals appear in simulations of their native habitats—from the western mountains to the marshes of the Eastern Shore. These exhibits allow visitors to get an "animal's eye" view of natural habitats.

Open spring through fall, the Maryland Farmyard engages visitors in more interactive learning. It includes a petting zoo and a dairy barn with a mechanical milking cow, chicken coop, and other hands-on stations. On weekends, pony rides and demonstrations in the Farmyard Meeting Barn add to the excitement.

The nearby African exhibit—an expansive wonderland featuring a naturalistic re-creation of an African savannah and watering hole—is home to hippos, flamingos, vultures, sitatunga antelopes, porcupines, white rhinos, African elephants, Angolan giraffes, zebras, pelicans, storks, and sable antelope. Leopards lie in their lair. An exciting replica of an African village invites one to watch pigmy goats. Lions stalk their turf. Chimpanzees, endangered in the wild, play in a re-created forest; the Baltimore Zoo chimpanzee family consists of one male and six females, including baby Raven, born

August 1995. "Africa" also features African slender-snouted crocodiles, African mud turtles, Diana and red-tailed monkeys, an aardwolf, and a feature called Rock Island, home to the African black-footed penguin—the world's second-largest and America's most successful breeding colony of black-footed penguins. The African camel exhibit features Jake, a baby camel born May 1997, and his extended camel family (camel rides are available during the summer). The African collection makes up the largest indoor and outdoor exhibit in the history of the Baltimore Zoo.

The Reptile House, with 24 exhibits, displays creatures from such diverse parts of the world as Sri Lanka, the Solomon Islands, South America, New Guinea, Africa, North America, Australia, and China. The Herpetology Department takes part in a wide variety of breeding programs for endangered species and has registered noteworthy successes with the threatened Egyptian tortoise and Madagascar tomato frogs.

Guests may also experience "behind the scenes" at the zoo. The new Keeper Encounter program offers a passport to adventure, bringing guests into personal discussions with the men and women who take care of the zoo's animals and plants. Guests also see first-hand how the staff care for live animals.

The Baltimore Zoo offers a variety of seasonal events that include Bunny BonanZoo, an Easter egg party; Zoo BOO!, a safe alternative to trick-or-treating; and ZooLights, an annual winter spectacle of lights.

The original **Rogers Mansion House,** now zoo offices, stands on the hill that dominates the park. The city has substantially altered this structure over the years, replacing the center section and adding enclosed pavilions around the building. On an adjacent hill, see the pavilion that houses Maryland exhibits from the Philadelphia Centennial Exposition of 1876; reconstructed, it now serves the Baltimore Zoological Society.

Open 10 a.m. to 4 p.m. every day but Christmas. Summer hours 10 a.m. to 8 p.m. Admission: $7.50 for adults, $4.00 for children ages 2–15, and $4.00 for adults ages 62 and over. Children under 2 are admitted free. On the first Saturday of each month, between 10 a.m. and noon, all children are admitted free. Rides require tickets. Ample free parking.

Gifts shops, cafés. For information call 410-366-LION.

From the zoo, take the drive on the right and follow signs for any exit to Druid Park Dr. On reaching it, turn right and follow it to its end and the light at 41st St., where most traffic turns sharply left. Straight ahead and to the right Woodberry descends into the Jones Falls Valley; on the left, the tower on Television Hill broadcasts the signals of three Baltimore commercial TV stations. Proceed east on 41st St. across the Jones Falls Expressway to Falls Rd., there turning left. The houses and street-corner grocery stores along this stretch of Falls typify Baltimore communities.

Falls Rd. crosses Cold Spring Ln. at the base of a steep hill and on the left passes the most recent locations of two of Baltimore's better public schools, **Baltimore Polytechnic Institute** ("Poly") and **Western Vocational-Technical Center for Girls** ("Western"). Early in the century, Poly enjoyed one of the best reputations in math, science, and engineering teaching among preparatory schools in the nation; its graduates typically moved directly into a college or university's second-year curriculum. Among Poly's famous graduates are H. L. Mencken, who needed no college training to become a leading newspaperman and literary critic in his generation.

Farther up, on the left, at the traffic light, notice the entrance to the **Village of Cross Keys.**

Cross Keys

Once the site of the Baltimore Country Club golf course (the club itself thrives atop a hill on the eastern side of Falls Rd.), these 72 acres between the road and the Jones Falls became part of a Rouse Company project in 1964—the creation of a "new town" in the city. About 2,500 people live in Cross Keys, which takes its name from an inn that once stood near the intersection of Falls Rd. and Cold Spring Ln. The development contains a "village square," which in good weather serves as a fine place to have an outdoor lunch or simply meet with friends. When the Orioles played at Memorial Stadium, visiting teams often stayed at the Inn at Cross Keys.

Each Baltimore neighborhood once had its own grocery store, like this one ca. 1940.

Roland Park

After seeing Cross Keys, one may take Springhouse Path, opposite the entrance and slightly to the right, and drive up to Edgevale Rd., there making a left onto Deepdene Rd., which intersects Roland Ave. at the top of the hill. (Across the street, see shops that appeared in the film version of Ann Tyler's *Accidental Tourist.*) Or from Cross Keys one may return along Falls Rd. to Cold Spring Ln., turn left, and then make a left on Roland Ave. Either path leads to Roland Park, one of the country's oldest and most pristine urban neighborhoods.

The land roughly between Roland Ave. and the Jones Falls once formed the Oakland estate of Robert Goodloe Harper, a South Carolina native and son-in-law of Charles Carroll of Carrollton. Harper moved to Baltimore in the early days of the republic, opened a law practice, and later supported creation of an African colony for freed slaves and thus helped found the republic of Liberia. In 1891, an English syndicate bought 800 acres north of the hills east of Jones Falls and employed Frederick Law

Olmsted Jr., son of the fabled landscape designer and commentator on the pre–Civil War South, to lay out Roland Park. Schools, churches, and clubs also acquired segments of the wooded and grassy landscape. Where Roland Ave. crosses Wyndhurst Ave. (the first light up Roland Ave. from Cold Spring), the traveler enters the original section of Roland Park, which lay mostly between Roland Ave. and Stony Run to the east. William Edmunds owned about 100 acres of this land in 1890 and, through intermediaries in Kansas City, approached the Lands Trust Co. of England for capital to develop the property. Edmunds and friends formed the Roland Park Company; Edward H. Bouton, a young promoter from Kansas City, arrived in Baltimore to manage the project.

During the 1890s, things went slowly, but Bouton proved his abilities as an innovator. In an era without zoning and public sewers, he required that land deeds contain restrictions limiting property to a single house with no outbuildings and setting a minimum price level. The house had to be set back from the street at least 30 feet, and the owner had to contribute to a common fund for maintenance of sewer, water, and lighting systems. The restrictive covenants also barred Jews and African Americans, part of the company's desire to create an exclusive haven for a southern-style "society." (In 1942 Maryland author Hulbert Footner claimed that "the society of North Baltimore is one of the pleasantest in the world"; "people know where they are at.") In 1893 Bouton also founded the Lake Roland Elevated Railway, a streetcar line for commuters, and three years later built a small Tudor-style **shopping center** between Elmhurst and Upland Rds.—perhaps the first instance of intentionally grouping retail stores for the sake of a new development in the United States.

Near the turn of the century, the company hired the Boston firm of Olmsted and Eliot to plan for additional development. Olmsted Jr. and his brother John laid out five more plats, which followed the hilly landscape and linked the winding streets with interior pedestrian pathways. By the time Bouton retired in 1935, Roland Park had become a favorite neighborhood for the city's elite. Incorporated into the city in 1918, it has retained its wooded, secluded character. The old restrictions against the ethnicity of homeowners have long been declared illegal, and the neighborhood now prides itself on its openness and tolerance. Many of novelist Anne Tyler's characters reputedly draw on Roland Park residents. Tyler lives nearby, as do other literary figures and critics. The neighborhood has found its way onto the National Register of Historic Places.

A drive on Roland Ave. will prove pleasant. To continue the tour, drive northwest up Roland Ave. between a small shopping area on the right and the Roland Park branch of the Enoch Pratt Free Library on the left. Roland Ave. then immediately passes **Roland Park School** on the right (coeducational public, elementary and middle grades) and **Roland Park Country School (RPCS)** on the left (girls' private, pre-elementary through high). Roland Park public offers an example, all too rare given the racial make up of Baltimore City, of blacks and whites learning together. RPCS dates from 1901; its graduates include the renowned poets Josephine Jacobsen and Adrienne Rich. On the right, the campus—for such it is—of **Gilman School** (boys' private, pre-elementary through high) lies at the corner of Roland Ave. and Northern Pkwy. Founded in 1897, the first country day school in the United States, Gilman has prepared young men for leadership in Baltimore and the nation ever since. Prominent alums include the late diplomat David K. E. Bruce, the author Walter Lord, and CBS international correspondent Tom Fenton.

North of RPCS and opposite Gilman School notice the imposing main building of the Roman Catholic **St. Mary's Seminary and University School of Theology and Ecumenical Institute,** where diocesan priests prepare for their ministries. Diagonally across the busy Roland Ave.–Northern Pkwy. intersection from St. Mary's, down Melrose Ave., one finds the grounds of another well-regarded private academy for girls, **Bryn Mawr School** (pre-elementary through high). M. Carey Thomas, a member of the Society of Friends, who helped to ensure that the Johns Hopkins School of Medicine admitted women and who went on to found Bryn Mawr College outside of Philadelphia, was among five pioneering women who established this school in 1885. Its graduates include the actresses Mildred Natwick and Bess Armstrong and a former president of Barnard College, Millicent Carey McIntosh.

Farther north of this intersection (continuing up Roland, left on Lake Ave.) lies the **Boys Latin School of Maryland** (private, pre-elementary through high), the oldest nonsectarian school in the state. Founded in 1844 by an erstwhile classics professor at Princeton, Evert Marsh Topping, the school has adopted a Latin motto that translates into English as, "To be, rather than to seem." The school moved to this site from downtown in 1960. Among its graduates are the writer and critic Murray Kempton and historian Curtis Carroll Davis. Along with the Park School, Boys Latin, RPCS, Gilman, and Bryn Mawr epitomize the nonsectarian, academically challenging private-school tradition in Baltimore.

To explore some of the attractions of the western bank of the Jones Falls Valley, proceed west on Northern Pkwy. across Falls Rd. and up the long hill on the other side.

Cylburn Park

After driving over the Jones Falls Expressway, make the first left from Northern Pkwy. onto Cylburn Pkwy. Follow it through a wooded area to Greenspring Ave. and there turn left. The main entrance to **Cylburn Park** lies immediately off Greenspring to the left. Enter and follow the road to **Cylburn Mansion.** In 1889 George A. Frederick designed this Victorian stone residence, with elaborately parqueted floors, for Jesse Tyson's country estate Cylburn. It once stood in formal gardens with a commanding view of Baltimore across the Jones Falls Valley. The city bought the estate in 1942 for $42,300 and created the surrounding 180-acre park. Until 1959, Cylburn Mansion housed a city orphanage; it now houses office and meeting areas, a horticultural library, and nature museum. The Cylburn Wild Flower Preserve and Garden Center Organization, a volunteer group, has helped turn the grounds into a public nature preserve and arboretum, where more than 150 species of birds have been identified.

Coldspring, a "new town" project designed by Moshe Safdie, the architect of Montreal's "Habitat," lies off Greenspring Ave. just south of Cylburn Park (turn left at either Springgarden Dr. or Ruscombe Ln.). The hilly, heavily wooded terrain long had been considered unsuitable for housing, but in 1977 Safdie proposed a terraced, landscaped plan that eventually would contain 3,800 units on 140 acres with lakes and parks.

Only a few hundred dwellings have emerged from this imaginative scheme, and it may never develop as planned—though more than 100 new units were completed in 1997. The project demonstrates Baltimore's efforts during the 1970s to make the city attractive to people who might otherwise choose the suburbs. During warm months, nonresidents may enroll in the community swimming pool and sports club.

Returning to Greenspring Ave., turn right to Northern Pkwy. **Hebrew Medical Center and Sinai Hospital,** one of the city's distinguished medical institutions, stands to the left at the intersection. Sinai was founded in 1866 and in 1996 merged with Levindale Hebrew Geriatric Center to form the Sinai Health System. The largest community hospital in Maryland, Sinai Hospital ranks third in size among the city's teaching hospitals. Its nine special-care units include coronary-progressive and pediatric-intensive care.

Pimlico Race Course

Once better known as "Old Hilltop," Pimlico, America's second-oldest Thoroughbred race track still operating, each year serves as the venue for the second jewel of the Triple Crown, the Preakness Stakes.

The Maryland Jockey Club, which operates both Pimlico and the track in Laurel, Maryland, dates to 1743, when it was founded by a group of Annapolis sportsmen. After almost a century of intermittent races, interrupted by the Revolution and the War of 1812, the club in 1830 obtained a congressional charter and moved to Baltimore. In 1870, with the aid of former Maryland governor Oden Bowie, it bought property known as Pimlico and built a race course here. On the first day of racing, October 26, 1870, Milton H. Sanford's horse "Preakness" won the Dinner Party Stakes. Almost three years later, on May 23, 1873, Bowie helped organize the first Preakness race. The race moved to the Gravesend Course in Brooklyn, New York, from 1894 to 1908 but returned to Pimlico in 1909, where it has been run every May since. Since 1917 the winner has been awarded the Woodlawn Cup, a carved silver trophy that Tiffany and Company created in 1860. Valued (in 1983) at $1 million, the cup—the most valuable trophy in American sports—remains on permanent display at the Baltimore Museum of Art. A smaller replica, crafted by the Kirk-Stieff Company, Baltimore silversmiths, goes annually to the winner. Each year, nearly 100,000 spectators crowd the stands and infield to witness the running of the Preakness, which has spawned a week-long spring festival in Baltimore.

A Trip up Park Heights Ave. to Some Jewish Cultural Sites

For a concentrated view of Jewish cultural and religious life in Baltimore, continue west on Northern Pkwy. from Pimlico to Park Heights Ave., there turning right. Park Heights Ave. has been a central corridor for Baltimore Jewish life since World War II. The **Baltimore Hebrew College,** 5800 Park Heights Ave., was founded in 1919 as a center for "higher Hebrew and Semitic learning," by Dr. Israel Efros, who became a well-known Hebrew poet. The college's present quarters, built in 1958, house the **Joseph Meyerhoff Library,** with more than 25,000 volumes of Judaica, an auditorium, reading room, and a small museum that features art objects as well as historic Jewish ceremonial objects. Just south of the college at 5700 Park Heights Ave. one finds the **Jewish Community Center,** which has offered a wide range of cultural and social activities since 1960. The facility expanded to a second building, in Owings Mills, in 1978. With approximately 14,000 members, the center serves a Jewish population estimated at 92,000 in northwest Baltimore and the surrounding Baltimore County neighborhoods.

Among the synagogues that line the avenue is **Temple Oheb Shalom** at 7310 Park Heights Ave., designed in 1960 by Sheldon I. Leavitt with consultation from Walter Gropius. The temple of the **Baltimore Hebrew Congregation** (1951, Percival Goodman, New York) at 7401 Park Heights Ave. features a great triple stone arch over the entrance. Highly stylized, sculpted panels of symbols and scenes from the Hebrew Bible decorate each doorway. This congregation, incorporated by the General Assembly in 1830, is the oldest in the city. Established by 13 poor immigrant families, mostly from Bavaria, with the Hebrew name Nidhei Israel (The Dispersed of Israel), the congregation's current prosperity reflects the rise of Baltimore's most successful ethnic group since the 19th century.

To return to the exploration of the Jones Falls Valley, return south on Park Heights Ave. to Falstaff Rd., there turning left. After a short distance, bear right and proceed on Cross Country Blvd., which becomes Kelly Ave. and follows Western Run to Mount Washington.

Mount Washington

From the heights of Pimlico, return east on Northern Pkwy. toward the Jones Falls and at Falls Rd. turn left. One soon approaches a small collection of traditional-looking service shops—bicycles, flowers, foreign cars—at the spot where the Kelly Ave. Bridge intersects Falls Rd. Turn left and explore a sheltered neighborhood that began in about 1810 as Washingtonville, a mill village that owed its existence to the Washington Cotton Manufacturing Company. This firm built up at the confluence of Western Run and the Jones Falls. Later, a railroad station provided easy access to Baltimore, then more than five miles away; in 1854, George Gelbach Jr. began promoting a "Mount Washington Rural Retreat" to prospective buyers. Country homes of various sizes and shapes sprouted along the wooded hillsides, gradually developing into a melange of styles on steep, winding streets. Today, many residents make their living in the professions and the arts. A boutique shopping complex has developed in the area around Newberry St. and Smith Ave. The community can point proudly to its elementary school, one of the most successful in the city, by any standard.

From Mount Washington, the visitor may continue on Falls Rd. to more specialty shopping, the city line, and the Baltimore County tour along this axis. To return to the harbor, travel up Falls Rd. to Lake Ave. on the right, follow Lake to Roland Ave., a right-hand turn on which will head one back downtown, via Roland, University Pkwy., and St. Paul St.; or return to Northern Pkwy., turn right, and follow signs to the Jones Falls Expressway south to the St. Paul St. exit.

To explore north central Baltimore from the Inner Harbor, drive north on Charles St. past North Ave. At 23rd St., go one block right. At 22nd and St. Paul sits **Lovely Lane Methodist Church.** The church building one sees dates from 1884—a "centennial monument" to mark the founding of the Methodist Episcopal Church at the Lovely Lane Meeting House in Baltimore. Three colleges—including Morgan State University and Goucher College—and 46 other congregations have sprung from this historic congregation. The first recorded instance in American Methodism of a woman preaching also occurred within its folds.

Fresh from a study of little-known medieval buildings, New York architect Stanford White created a monumental Romanesque church with a Port Deposit granite exterior and a remarkable domed interior. The corner bell tower, tapered in nine tiers of stone to a height of 186 feet, is modeled after the tower of the 12th-century Church of Santa Maria in Pomposa, near Ravenna, Italy. The only openings in the massive walls of the church are those from the deep arcaded portico on either side of the tower and the small windows in the apse and clerestory. The windows under the elliptical interior dome reproduce in Tiffany stained glass the mosaics from the fifth century Church of San Piaceta, which are now on display in Rome's Lateran Museum. The stained-glass windows encircling the first floor of the sanctuary contain the names of every pastor assigned to Lovely Lane, beginning with Francis Asbury in 1773. Deceptively intimate for a space that seats a thousand people, the circular sanctuary with its theater-type seats has outstanding acoustics—well suited to a denomination that has placed such a strong emphasis on preaching. On the advice of Dr. John F. Goucher, the pastor who spurred the fund raising efforts for the centennial church, the ceiling dome was painted to represent the appearance of the sky over Baltimore at 3 a.m. on November 6, 1887, the day the church was dedicated. Originally, 340 gas jets lit the church; they formed a circle of fire just below the frieze, causing the painted stars to twinkle.

Since 1980, the United Methodist Church has committed itself to a massive $5 million restoration effort to refurbish this nationally significant structure, which now serves a congregation of about 500, considerably diminished in numbers from its earlier years.

The **Lovely Lane Museum,** located in the church basement, was established in 1955 to house the records and historical artifacts of the Baltimore Conference Methodist Historical Society. The library contains papers, letters, and books associated with the history of American Methodism. A simple oak pulpit, believed to have been made by Robert Strawbridge, is probably the first pulpit ever used by a Methodist preacher in America. A restored portrait of Francis Asbury painted by Charles Peale Polk in 1794 hangs in an adjacent meeting room. For further information, call 410-889-1512.

Goucher Hall (1886–88, Charles L. Carson) is located immediately adjacent to the church, at St. Paul and 23rd Sts. While Lovely Lane was under construction, Dr. Goucher was also organizing the Woman's College of Baltimore, a Methodist-supported school. This active pastor, who lived at 2313 St. Paul St., donated the land and instructed the architect to

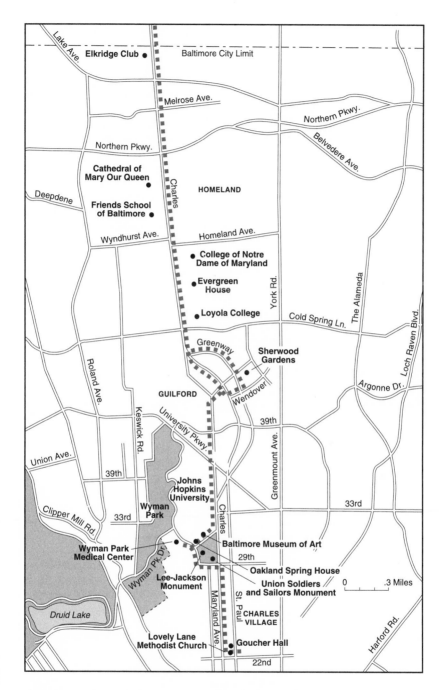

design this granite, Romanesque hall to blend with the church. Goucher served as the college's first president, from 1890 to 1907, and the school was renamed after him in 1910. Goucher College completed its move to Towson in 1952. The Baltimore Regional Chapter of the Red Cross occupied Goucher Hall until the state bought the property and turned it into the headquarters for the Maryland Geological Survey.

Wyman Park

Return to Charles St. and travel north to 29th St., passing through the western side of a neighborhood area once called Peabody Heights and now known as **Charles Village.** It dates to the late Victorian period (1880–1900). In 1816 the city expanded its northern limit to North Ave., in 1888 to an east-west line just above the Homewood campus of Johns Hopkins University, and in 1918 to its current location. As Baltimore's population grew between 1870 and 1891, the city and developers extended the north-south arteries—Howard, Maryland, Charles, St. Paul, Calvert, and Guilford—north to 33rd St., lining them mostly with row houses. The great suburban estates north of Homewood gradually gave way to garden suburbs with large, freestanding houses. Then developers expanded the row houses into this countryside. Twenty-ninth St. marks the beginning of property formerly owned by the Wyman family, which in 1902 became in part a public park and in part the new site of the Johns Hopkins University. Turn left (west) on 29th from Charles St. and shortly curve to the right along Wyman Park Dr., around the southern end of the Wyman Dell. On the right is the **Lee-Jackson Monument** (1948), a rare example of double-equestrian statuary. Across the dell stands the **Union Soldiers and Sailors Monument.**

Bearing right at the Lee-Jackson Monument takes one along Art Museum Dr., past the Baltimore Museum of Art, and back onto Charles St.

The Baltimore Museum of Art

The Baltimore Museum of Art (10 Art Museum Dr.), Maryland's largest and best-attended art museum, preserves a permanent collection of more than 100,000 objects, ranging from ancient mosaics to contemporary art. The BMA exhibits its works to a growing regional audience.

Founded in 1914, the museum had no home until 1922, when Mary Garrett persuaded M. Carey Thomas, then president of Bryn Mawr College, to provide her mansion at 101 West Monument St. as an exhibition space for an original collection of oil paintings, watercolors, sculpture, silverware, engravings, furniture, and metalwork. The museum held its first public show in February 1923 and drew 6,775 visitors the first week. Such public response stimulated a 1924 referendum for $1 million to build a permanent museum, which trustees planned for a six-acre plot in Wyman Park (Johns Hopkins University donated the land). Despite controversy, voters approved the expenditure. John Russell Pope designed the neoclassical building of Indiana limestone, and it opened on April 18, 1929. In the intervening years, the museum has made nine major additions, including the **Antioch Court** (1937) and the **West Wing for Contemporary Art** (1994).

Known as a "collection of collections," the BMA has benefited over the years from extraordinary donations. One of them came indirectly from George Lucas, a Baltimore civil engineer, who traveled to France in 1857 and never returned. Instead, he became a painter in Paris, befriended many artists, and then left his extensive collection—18,000 prints and more than 400 other items—to Henry Walters, who gave it to the Maryland Institute College of Art, which placed it on indefinite loan at the BMA. (In 1995, when the institute threatened to sell the collection to increase its endowment, public outcry eventually kept the collection intact in Maryland.) Other loans followed and turned into bequests: the collections of Mary Frick Jacobs (1938), Jacob Epstein (1946), and Saidie A. May (1951) among them.

The most famous collection, the one that placed the BMA on the international map, came from

Dr. Claribel Cone and her sister Etta. The Cone sisters had become friends of literata Gertrude Stein (1874–1946) during the latter's residence in Baltimore as a commuting college student and then as a medical student at Johns Hopkins (1897–1902). Stein, who considered herself a Baltimorean ("where we were born longer"), moved to Paris in 1903 to join her brother Leo and within two years had introduced the Cone sisters to the Parisian art world. Guided by Stein and her friends Picasso and Matisse, the Cones bought a monumental assemblage of modern art, including the largest Matisse collection in the Western Hemisphere. Their rooms at the Marlborough Apartments—partly duplicated in the renovated **Cone Wing** of the museum—overflowed with approximately 3,000 objets d'art ranging from Coptic textile fragments to Cezannes. Dr. Cone died in 1929, and for the next 20 years museum directors from elsewhere pursued her sister Etta on the presumption that their collection was "far too good for Baltimore." When Miss Cone died in 1949 and bequeathed the collection to the BMA, the museum—hitherto a rather conservative institution dedicated to Old Masters—suddenly became one of the world's significant centers of 20th-century art.

The BMA's original building, which reopened with a new gallery design in the spring of 1997, exhibits an outstanding collection of American painting and sculpture from before 1900, decorative arts of the 18th through 20th centuries, and period rooms from six Maryland historic houses. The West Wing for Contemporary Art houses 16 galleries of post-1945 art. The **Wurtzburger and Levi Sculpture Gardens** showcase modern and contemporary sculpture; the gardens cover nearly three acres at the museum's northeast end and compose one of the nation's largest sculpture gardens in an urban setting. The museum also draws strength from its exceptional collection of the arts of Africa, the Americas, and Oceania; a distinguished selection of Chinese ceramics; notable textile holdings, including several important Baltimore album quilts; eight galleries devoted to European Old Master painting and sculpture; and one of the finest collections of prints, drawings, and photographs in the country.

Each year, besides its exhibitions, the BMA plans diverse performing arts programs, lectures, films, and special events. The museum's education department—one of the first in the United States—offers exciting programs for children and families, adults, and educators.

Open Wednesday through Friday, 11 a.m. to 5 p.m.; Saturday and Sunday, 11 a.m. to 6 p.m.; closed Monday, Tuesday, July 4, Thanksgiving Day, and Christmas Day. Admission: free for BMA members and visitors ages 18 and under; $4.00 for seniors and full-time students; $6.00 for ages 19 and older. Admission is free to all visitors every Thursday. On the first Thursday evening of each month (except major holidays) from 5 p.m. to 9 p.m., FREESTYLE (no admission fee) offers visitors music, film screenings, workshops, guided tours, and cash bars. Parking on- and off-street. Museum shop. Café. For further information, call 410-396-7100.

The **Oakland Spring House,** a miniature Greek temple with four Ionic columns, stands outside the museum at the west end of Art Museum Dr., adjacent to the BMA building and the new West Wing. Benjamin H. Latrobe, a remarkable genius who became America's first trained architect and engineer, designed it in 1827 for the Oakland estate, now part of Roland Park.

Homewood Campus,
The Johns Hopkins University

The Homewood Campus of the Johns Hopkins University covers more than 100 acres of land bordered on the west by Wyman Park Dr. and San Martin Dr., on the north by University Pkwy., and on the east by Charles St. Each border contains an entrance to the campus; the entrance off Wyman Park Dr. near the Baltimore Museum of Art offers the most practical avenue to the main campus buildings, along with parking possibilities. The entrance at Charles and 34th Sts. offers the most sweeping view of Homewood and the best pedestrian approach.

When Johns Hopkins died, on Christmas Eve 1873, bequeathing almost $7 million for the founding of a university with a medical school and hospital, he left few instructions for the university. The trustees surveyed leading American educators and in 1874 selected Daniel Coit Gilman (1831–1901), then president of the University of California, as the first university president. Both parties agreed that what the country needed was not another college but a true research university, modeled after the best European institutions. Dr. Gilman took a year to survey the field and recruit faculty for a postgraduate institution, which emphasized original scholarship, academic freedom, and the seminar method of teaching. This combination transformed American higher education and served as a subsequent model for American graduate training. The new university purchased two houses on N. Howard St. near Centre St. and opened its first classes on October 3, 1876. The new faculty included James Joseph Sylvester (mathematics), Ira Remsen (chemistry), Henry Augustus Rowland (physics), Henry Newell Martin (biology), Basil L. Gildersleeve (Greek), and Charles D. Morris (Latin). The poet and musician Sidney Lanier lectured in English literature from 1879 until shortly before his death in 1881. Among the early denizens were Herbert B. Adams, Frederick Jackson Turner, Josiah Royce, Charles S. Peirce, John Dewey, and Woodrow Wilson, the only U.S. president to have earned the Ph.D. degree (1886).

From these early beginnings, the Johns Hopkins University has grown into an international institution with more than 8,000 graduate and almost 5,000 undergraduate students scattered across a variety of schools and campuses: School of Arts and Sciences (1876), with affiliates that include the Space Telescope Science Institute and Zanvyl Krieger Mind/Brain Institute, G.W.C. Whiting School of Engineering (1913, reestablished 1979), Peabody Institute (1857), School of Medicine (1893), School of Nursing (1889, 1983 as a division), School of Hygiene and Public Health (1916), Applied Physics Laboratory (1942), School of Continuing Studies (1909, renamed 1984), and the Paul H. Nitze School of Advanced International Studies (1943). Beyond these shores the university maintains the Charles S. Singleton Center for Italian Studies, Florence, and the Bologna Center in Italy, and the Hopkins-Nanjing Center for Chinese and American Studies in China. Also operating under the umbrella of the university are the Institute for Policy Studies and the Johns Hopkins University Press (1878), oldest university press in the country. After the state and city governments, the university and hospital together constitute the largest employer in the Baltimore area.

At its start, the university set up shop on N. Howard St., to take advantage of the proximity of the research library at the Peabody Institute, but this location soon proved too small and too noisy. Dr. Gilman eventually managed to combine property owned by Samuel and William Wyman with acreage donated to the university in 1902. The university moved here in 1916.

The property included **Homewood,** an estate given by Charles Carroll of Carrollton to his son Charles in 1800 on the occasion of his marriage to Harriet Chew of Philadelphia. (The name Homewood apparently derives from a tract surveyed in 1670 for John Homewood.) The son, much to the consternation of his conservative father, spent a small fortune to build the Georgian mansion (1801–3) that still stands on an elevation above Charles and 34th Sts.

Homewood House
drawing room as
pictured by the WPA

This five-part brick structure with its four-columned, Doric portico reflects the studied elegance cultivated by the aristocrats of the era. The outer walls are trimmed with white-painted wood and brick and decorated with plaster panels and facings. The interior of the square, central section has high ceilings; a wide central passage is crossed by a narrow corridor that leads to the wings, which are slightly lower in elevation. Despite the luxuriousness of his surroundings, an attractive and fashionable wife, and six children, the younger Carroll apparently was not happy. His wife and children returned to Philadelphia, and he died an alcoholic in 1825. His son Charles inherited the property but sold it to Samuel Wyman in 1840. Wyman lived here for some years, until he built a nearby Italianate villa, after which Homewood stood empty for a while. The Country School for Boys, later known as the Gilman School, occupied the property for 13 years, until 1902, when the university acquired the old estate. The Carroll mansion served as a faculty club, then was renovated in 1932 and used as an administration building. Hopkins alumnus and Baltimore banker Robert G. Merrick Sr. supported another restoration, completed in 1980. The structure now attracts visitors, provides a site for special events, and houses a museum shop. For information call 410-516-5589.

The Georgian architecture of Homewood dictated the style for the buildings that gradually occupied the new Hopkins property. The first to be constructed, **Gilman Hall,** was dedicated in 1915. The **Gilman Memorial Room** at the main entrance (on the second floor) contains manuscripts, books, and other personal possessions of Dr. Gilman, who served as the university's president until 1901. Opposite Gilman Hall, dominating the 34th St. entrance, is the **Milton S. Eisenhower Library,** named for the university's eighth president (1957–67). This largely subterranean building (1964) has a capacity of 1.5 million volumes. On the University Pkwy. side of the campus are the **Newton H. White Jr. Athletic Center** and the **Lacrosse Hall of Fame**—appropriate for a school that has excelled in this intercollegiate sport, winning more national championships than any other school in the country. (Lacrosse has such a long, successful history in Maryland that periodically a state legislator will create a stir among the equestrians by proposing that it supplant jousting as the state sport.)

The **Alfred Jenkins Shriver Hall** (1957), located just north of the Baltimore Museum of Art, contains a series of unusual murals executed under the bequest that made this auditorium facility possible. Shriver (1867–1939), a bachelor lawyer, bon vivant, and Hopkins alumnus, stipulated that the portraits of ten of the most beautiful women from the Baltimore of his youth, each "at the height of her beauty," be displayed in the lobby. He also named 110 other persons who were to appear on the walls, including the original Hopkins faculties, boards of trustees of the schools of philosophy and medicine, various local philanthropists, and the entire class of 1891. In addition to the portraits, his will also named famous Baltimore clipper ships for the murals. James Owen Mahoney painted the ships, and Leon Kroll did the people. Their work covers 90 feet of wall space; 63 of the human figures are life-size.

Several monuments give personality to the Charles St. boundary of the campus. The quaintly Victorian home of the student newspaper, the Johns Hopkins *Newsletter*, stands not far from the BMA sculpture garden on the southeast corner of the Homewood campus. Hans Schuler, a Baltimore artist, created the **Johns Hopkins Memorial Monument** at Charles and 34th Sts., designed by William Gordon Beecher and erected in 1934 by the Municipal Art Society. Schuler also did the bronze relief of Sidney Lanier a few hundred yards farther to the north, next to the tennis courts.

Guilford

Follow Charles St. north from the Homewood Campus. This route passes the **University Baptist Church** (1926, John Russell Pope), a neoclassical structure on the east, and then intersects University Pkwy., where a statue honoring sacrifices of the women of the Confederacy faces southeast. A left turn (northwest) onto University Pkwy. leads to Roland Park. To the right, one sees the **Episcopal Cathedral of the Incarnation** (1909–47), which stands at University Pkwy. and St. Paul St. Originally conceived as a massive edifice, this English Gothic church represents only a segment of what planners envisioned.

Continue on Charles St. to **Guilford,** a community of almost 700 large single-family homes developed by the Roland Park Company in 1913. Named after the A. S. Abell estate that once occupied this landscape, Guilford is known for its small interior parks and stately houses. In many cases, three generations of the same family have lived in this fashionable neighborhood.

Off to the northwest, in a section devoted to comfortable town houses, many of English Tudor design, one finds the **Calvert School,** at 105 Tuscany Rd. Concerned parents founded the school (downtown) in 1896, and since then it has become a champion of academically rigorous elementary and middle schooling; its first headmaster, Virgil Mores Hillyer, voiced the goal of opening a child's eyes "to the world without and the world within." Well-known graduates include the film maker John Waters.

The **Scottish Rite Temple of Freemasonry** (1930–33) at Charles and 39th Sts. was designed by Clyde N. Fritz and John Russell Pope in the form of a Greek cross with an imposing Corinthian entrance portico. **Highfield House** (1964), at 4000 N. Charles St., is the second building in Baltimore designed by Mies van der Rohe (One Charles Center being the first).

Proceed past the handsome colonial Second Presbyterian Church on the right to the light at St. Paul St. and bear left. At the top of the hill, turn right onto Greenway and follow it as it bears to the right until it crosses Stratford Rd. Park on Greenway to admire **Sherwood Gardens,** the nine-acre Guilford hallmark bordered on the northwest by Stratford and Greenway. John W. Sherwood originally owned the private estate at 204 E. Highfield Rd., which included about six acres of private gardens. After his death, when the property seemed threatened by subdivision, the Guilford Association raised money to buy the land and maintain a public garden in cooperation with the city. The annual spring bloom of tulips (150,000 bulbs), dogwood, and azaleas (10,000) draws thousands of visitors. The gardens feature a great variety of trees as well as old boxwood from various Southern Maryland estates. The evergreen rock gardens contain plants from almost every country in the world.

Continue south on Greenway past Highfield and Lambeth Rds. to Wendover Rd., turning right for a short block to return to St. Paul, a right on which leads up the hill past mini-manors in the English style, past the entrance to Greenway, to the northern portion of Charles St.

After crossing Cold Spring Ln., the visitor passes through the campus of **Loyola College** (the apartment buildings on the western side of the street having been converted to student dormitories). The Society of Jesus established this Baltimore academy in 1852; it moved to this pastoral location in 1922. With more than 6,000 students, almost half of them nonresident graduate students, the college has grown considerably during the past two decades, particularly in business education.

Evergreen House (4545 N. Charles St.) stands back from the street on a wooded knoll. In 1878 T. Harrison Garrett bought this classical-style mansion with a dominant Corinthian portico, built around 1855. The Garrett family made extensive changes and additions to the property, which Mr. and Mrs. John Work Garrett bequeathed to the Johns Hopkins University in 1942. Through the Evergreen House Foundation, Hopkins now maintains the estate as a research library, museum, ensemble concert hall, and meeting place for university and private groups. For information call 410-516-0341.

The College of Notre Dame of Maryland, north of Loyola, occupies a parklike setting to the north of Evergreen House. The School Sisters of Notre Dame founded an academy in Baltimore in 1847 and began offering college courses in 1895, making this institution the first Catholic college for women established in the United States. The college now has an enrollment of some 2,600 students (more than 200 of them men), including about 1,700 part-time students who take advantage of its innovative programs for adults.

As Charles St. continues north beyond Homeland Ave., it runs between notable institutions on the west and the residential area of **Homeland** on the east. A private developer carved the latter from the 391-acre Perine family estate known as Homeland. The city considered buying the property in 1922 for conversion to a public park but declined for lack of funds. The Roland Park–Homeland Company bought the estate in 1924 and created a neighborhood known for its traditional architecture, wide variety of trees, and ornamental median complete with pond.

The **Stony Run Friends Meeting,** 5116 N. Charles St., takes its name from a nearby stream. The traditional, story-and-a-half stone meeting house (1949–50) stands on the grounds of the **Friends School of Baltimore** (coeducational, pre-elementary through high). Founded in 1784 and Baltimore's oldest school, it moved to this site in 1942. It maintains historic and philosophic ties to the Stony Run Friends Meeting; its nearly 1,000 students in all grades receive rigorous preparation for college. Accomplished graduates include Howard Jones, M.D. (1927), director of the Jones Institute for Reproductive Medicine in Norfolk, Virginia; journalist and poet Rose Burgunder Styron (1946); and David A. (now Sara Davis) Buechner (1976), internationally known concert pianist.

Just before Charles St. crosses Northern Pkwy., it passes the **Cathedral of Mary Our Queen,** a massive, 373- by-239-foot stone structure with two 128-foot towers, designed by Maginnis and Walsh. Thomas J. O'Neill (1849–1919), an Irish-born, Baltimore dry-goods merchant, left a fortune to the Catholic archdiocese on the condition that it be used to build a second cathedral in Baltimore; it was completed 40 years after his death. Two side chapels serve as abbreviated transepts in a deliberate effort to combine contemporary and Gothic styles. The exterior has been criticized for its eclecticism, but the interior contains beautiful details: coffered ceilings, elaborate stained-glass windows, and stations of the cross carved into the stone arches. The windows in the Lady Chapel, in the apse, depict defining moments and leading figures in the history of Christianity, including the election of John Carroll as the first Catholic bishop in America and the Council of Baltimore (May 1789).

Beyond the cathedral, Charles St. crosses Northern Pkwy. and passes the **Church of the Redeemer** at Charles St. and Melrose Ave. The newer structure built for this Episcopal parish was completed in 1958 and represents the efforts of Massachusetts architect Pietro Belluschi and Baltimore engineering firm RTKL Associates to create a modern church without overpowering the original—the little Gothic Revival stone building next to it (ca. 1856), still used as a chapel.

Just before Charles St. leaves the city, it passes the **Elkridge Club** (formerly the Elkridge Hunt Club, 1878), a country club that stands on the site of an estate once the property of Augustus W. Bradford, Maryland governor between 1862 and 1866. A Unionist, Bradford suffered the wrath of Maryland Confederates in August 1864, when troops under fellow Baltimore Countian Harry Gilmor burned the Bradford house, supposedly to retaliate against Union troops' destruction of Virginia governor John Letcher's dwelling in the Shenandoah Valley. Much later, in 1955, Baltimore corporate and civic leaders met at the clubhouse and formed the Greater Baltimore Committee, a group that tried with much success to revitalize the downtown.

North of the club and west, down Woodbrook Ln., splendid houses dot the landscape dropping down to Lake Roland and Robert E. Lee Park. The Baltimore modernist architect Alexander Smith Cochran grew up in one of these homes. Robert G. Merrick, generous benefactor of the Johns Hopkins University and Maryland Historical Society, later lived on the same site.

On its path to the Baltimore Beltway, Charles St. passes the **Motherhouse of the School Sisters of Notre Dame,** a Roman Catholic teaching order that pioneered in the education of girls and women in Baltimore. Farther along, also on the east side of the winding roadway, one sees the charming gatehouse of **Sheppard and Enoch Pratt Hospital,** a private institution for the treatment of mental and nervous disorders. Moses Sheppard, a wealthy Quaker merchant, endowed the Sheppard Asylum at his death in 1857. The following year, trustees bought Mt. Airy farm here and began building; the asylum did not admit its first patients until 1891. In 1898 the institution received additional funding from the estate of Enoch Pratt, and its name changed. The main buildings, designed by New York architect Calvert Vaux, who worked with Frederick Law Olmsted and helped lay out Central Park in New York, have been designated National Historic Landmarks. Now a leading state provider of psychiatric care, the Sheppard and Enoch Pratt Health System has centers in Anne Arundel, Baltimore, Frederick, Harford, and Howard Counties.

Greater Baltimore Medical Center, at the next entrance on the right, formed in 1965 with the merger of the Hospital for the Women of Maryland and Presbyterian Eye, Ear, and Throat Charity Hospital. Now one of the largest health care centers in metropolitan Baltimore, GBMC (with 372 beds) admits about 22,000 patients and conducts 25,000 surgical procedures a year; its specialties, besides surgery, include gynecology, neonatal care, fertility, and orthopedics. GBMC has continued to operate an outpatient center at the site of the Presbyterian Charity Hospital on E. Baltimore St. in the heart of the city; in 1998, that clinic will become part of the new GBMC Weinberg Community Health Center at E. Pratt and Central Ave.

On high ground just past Towsontown Blvd. stands **Loyola Blakefield,** a Jesuit school for grades 6–12. The television sportscaster Jim McKay and techno-adventure writer Tom Clancy are numbered among its best-known graduates.

The Baltimore Beltway (I-695) rings the city. Going west on the Beltway will lead one to the Jones Falls Expressway (I-83), the southern end of which is in eastern downtown.

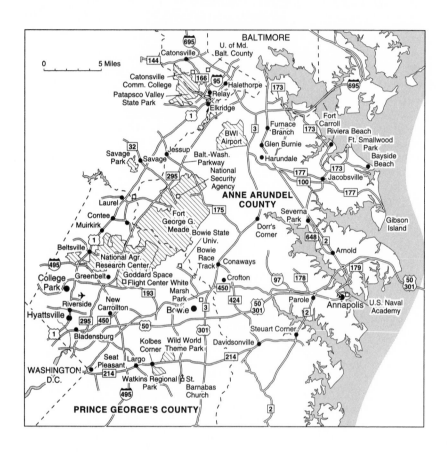

Along the Baltimore-Washington-Annapolis Triangle

U.S. 1, Baltimore-Washington Pkwy., Md. 450, Md. 2

A spider's web of expressways, highways, and secondary roads links Baltimore, Washington, and Annapolis. The Baltimore-Washington Pkwy. (Md. 295), opened in 1954, and Interstate 95 (1971), offer the fastest connections between the first two cities. Interstate 97 (1987–92) speeds traffic between Baltimore and Annapolis. U.S. 50 connects Annapolis and Washington. Described below are two routes to the D.C. area and two routes from there to Annapolis that will give the traveler a more leisurely look at the sights within the Baltimore-Washington-Annapolis triangle. The wise visitor expects traffic, particularly near Washington, and avoids morning and evening rush hours.

When driving to Washington—or anywhere else—from Baltimore City one will likely need to contend with the Baltimore Beltway. Dedicated in 1954 and built in stages until the Francis Scott Key Bridge closed the circle in 1977, Baltimore's beltway was among the first in the United States. When the major portion was completed in 1962, officials called the $68 million job the largest peacetime public works project undertaken to that date. Conceived as a by-pass, the beltway soon became a suburban shortcut, a quick way to move among the shopping centers, businesses, and residences that developed along its 52-mile course. In 1970 more than 800,000 people lived outside the beltway and 1.2 million inside. Twenty years later, the population beyond the beltway had increased by 58 percent while the the number living inside it had declined by 17 percent. In the 1890s, when the first suburbs arose outside Baltimore, the majority of commuters used streetcars and then automobiles to work and shop in the city. Since completion of the beltway, more than half of all Baltimore County commuters travel to other suburban locations instead of into the city, a pattern now common throughout the United States.

BALTIMORE TO BLADENSBURG VIA U.S. 1

Until completion of the Baltimore-Washington Pkwy., U.S. 1 was notorious as one of the nation's busiest and most dangerous roads. Commercial signage—including billboards and neon sculptures—overwhelmed the driver's vision; traffic to and from roadside motels, restaurants, fast-food stands, service stations, and shopping centers created constant road hazards. Area residents believed that fellow Marylander

Ogden Nash (1902–71) must have had this stretch of road in mind when he wrote:

I think that I shall never see
A billboard lovely as a tree;
Perhaps unless the billboards fall,
I'll never see a tree at all.

U.S. 1 runs a parallel course between I-95 and the Baltimore-Washington Pkwy. (off limits to trucks); both expressways have exits to U.S. 1 and the points described below.

Halethorpe

U.S. 1 branches from Wilkens Ave. and leaves Baltimore as Southwestern Blvd.; Alt. U.S. 1 branches south from Caton Ave. and leaves the city as Washington Blvd., briefly paralleling the original route of the Baltimore and Ohio Railroad. After crossing under or over the Baltimore Beltway, they pass by Halethorpe, where they merge.

At the turn of the century, this area between the city limits and the river consisted primarily of farmland and small estates. Then land developers, encouraged by extension of streetcar lines in 1908, began to sell residential lots in commuter communities with such fanciful names as Arbutus (the ornamental strawberry tree) and Halethorpe ("hale" for "healthy, safe" plus "thorp," an Old English word for "village"). An airfield at this site was one of Baltimore's first; here Hubert Latham took off and landed in 1910, completing the first successful flight over a large American city.

Relay and Thomas Viaduct

Immediately after U.S. 1 and Alt. 1 merge, turn right on Selford Rd. to the old railroad community of Relay. Cedar Ave. branches southwest from Selford, becomes Rolling Rd. as it passes through Relay, and takes one to the railroad tracks as Railroad Ave. This isolated community is named for Relay House, where the first B&O passengers rested while horses were changed for the pull to Ellicott City. The railroad began using steam locomotives in 1831, but Relay retained its significance as a stopover. When a Washington branch of the B&O was completed in 1835, the railroad created a "mealing house" here, the first in the country.

Construction on the Thomas Viaduct, a great stone bridge across the Patapsco, began in 1832. Scoffers laughed at Benjamin H. Latrobe Jr.'s design, claiming that it would never carry the weight of a moving train. No one had ever built a railroad viaduct more than 600 feet long. Latrobe used 8 elliptical arches to support a curving, 26-foot-wide railbed 60 feet above the river. "Latrobe's Folly" opened in 1835 and has never closed since, handling heavy modern freight trains with ease. Named for Philip Thomas, first president of the B&O, the viaduct is the oldest, multiple-arch stone bridge in the world and has been declared a National Historic Landmark.

Relay occupied a strategic point during the Civil War. Union troops under the command of Gen. Benjamin F. Butler seized Relay House on May 4, 1861, and fortified the heights above Thomas Viaduct. Nine days later, troops of the 6th Massachusetts (which had fought Southern sympathizers along Pratt St. on April 19th) and the 8th New York regiments

The Thomas Viaduct,
Relay

here boarded a train for Baltimore, occupied Federal Hill during the night, and proceeded to suppress the city's considerable pro-Confederate sentiment. Abraham Lincoln came through Relay in late February 1861, his inauguration speech in his pocket; again in 1862, en route to Sharpsburg; and in 1863 on the way to Gettysburg, with another speech in mind. On April 21, 1865, Relay figured in that president's history once more, when his seven-car funeral train passed here on its journey to Springfield, Illinois. In 1872 the B&O built the Viaduct Hotel in the juncture formed by the original tracks, heading west along the river, and the Washington branch, which crossed the river here.

Virtually nothing remains from Relay's past. The small Relay Hotel sits at the intersection of Viaduct and Railroad Aves. One can walk carefully along the railroad tracks to the point where they pass over the (still active) Thomas Viaduct. There a memorial obelisk commemorates the viaduct's dedication; the area where the Viaduct Hotel stood is overgrown with vegetation.

Selford Rd. travels northwest from Relay across an interchange with I-95 to an intersection with Sulphur Spring Rd., named for a nearby 19th-century spa, which flourished as a fashionable resort before its decline in the 1890s. The road then passes an old portion of Rolling Rd. and becomes Rolling Rd. (Md. 166) at the intersection with Wilkens Ave. (Md. 372).

Side Trip on Rolling Rd.

During the colonial period, great hogsheads of tobacco were rolled along this route from local farms to the shipping point at Elkridge Landing. The road once connected the Patapsco River with points in the surrounding countryside as far north as Randallstown. Its southern course has been interrupted by the I-95 interchange above Relay. Selford Rd. north from U.S. 1 becomes Rolling Rd., as does Metropolitan Blvd. north of I-95. In this highly built-up space between Ellicott City and Baltimore City, one finds the remnants of many old institutions and enterprises.

A portion of the old road branches off Selford Rd. to the river, just beyond its interchange with Metropolitan Blvd., and intersects Gun Rd. Gun Rd. passes the **Motherhouse of the Oblate Sisters of Providence** on its way to the **Avalon–Orange Grove Area** of the Patapsco State Park. The Oblates were founded in Baltimore in 1829 by Father James Joubert and Mother Mary Elizabeth Lang, a French-speaking refugee from Saint Domingue who opened a school for African American children. In 1831 Mother Lang and her three sisters became the first Catholic religious order for black women in the world. Still a teaching order with an international outreach, the Oblates moved their motherhouse, **Our Lady of Mount Providence Convent,** to this location from Baltimore in 1962.

The southern half of Rolling Rd. passes between the **University of Maryland, Baltimore County (UMBC),** to the east and **Catonsville Community College** to the west. UMBC opened in 1966 as a doctoral research university for the Baltimore region and now has more than 10,000 students, almost 9,000 of them undergraduates. The community college was established in 1957 on the grounds of **Hilton.** Hilton Mansion is a Georgian Revival summer home designed by Baltimore architect Edward Palmer for industrialist George Knapp and completed in 1919. Palmer transformed an existing structure, the origins of which can be traced to the first third of the 19th century. The owners of the earlier house included John Glenn, a prosperous lawyer who was appointed to the federal bench in 1852 by Millard Fillmore, and William Wilkins Glenn, the publisher of a pro-Southern newspaper, *The Baltimore Daily Exchange,* who used the house as a sort of underground railroad in reverse—a refuge for those on their way to join the Southern cause—until July 1863, when it was surrounded by Union troops. Glenn escaped, supposedly by crawling between two sentries, and fled to sanctuary in England, where he remained until the close of the war. The mansion still stands and can be toured. The school has 10,700 students registered for credit as well as 2,700 at a campus in Westminster. In addition, another 22,000 students enroll in noncredit courses.

Catonsville High School and the **Rolling Road Country Club** are located opposite the community college. Bloomsbury Ave. angles north from Rolling Rd. at the high school to the **Spring Grove Hospital Center,** the oldest hospital for the mentally ill in Maryland and the third oldest in the United States. Established in 1797 in Baltimore, the hospital moved to Catonsville in 1872. With an average of 485 patients, the center admits patients from Baltimore, Harford, and Prince George's Counties. The **Children's Home,** known for many years as the German Orphan Home, occupies a tract on nearby Bloomsbury Ave. This institution, an example of a Baltimore ethnic community's taking care of its own, originally stood in Old Town, on Aisquith St. near Orleans St. By 1920 it had moved to this site, then a bucolic setting.

From Rolling Rd.near the intersection with Frederick Rd., Hilton Ave. takes one south, back to Patapsco Valley State Park and the site, since 1916, of **All Saints Convent.** The All Saints Sisters of the Poor, an Anglican order, established their first American mission on Baltimore's Eutaw St. in 1872. The sisters are still involved in that neighborhood, where they help operate the **Joseph Ritchie Hospice;** at the convent they maintain a retreat house and scriptorium that produces religious cards that are sold around the world. The Hilton area of the park includes a camping and picnic site. A swinging bridge here connects to the Orange Grove site on the south bank of the river.

Catonsville

Rolling Rd. intersects the oldest pathway from Baltimore to the west, Frederick Rd. (Md. 144). Approaching Frederick Rd. from the south, turn right to pass through the heart of Catonsville (500' alt., 35,233 pop.), a suburban area known for comfortable homes and numerous churches and schools. In 1810, Richard Caton laid out the town, then surrounded by farms and estates. Caton, a son-in-law of Charles Carroll of Carrollton, was an owner of the Baltimore Iron Works Company, the first locally owned and operated iron company in Maryland. Carroll's father had joined with other investors in 1733 to form the company, which prospered and acquired thousands of acres in southern Baltimore County around the Gwynns Falls and along the north bank of the Patapsco River. The company divided its holdings in 1810, and the Catons began to subdivide Carroll's share. The Glenn family developed the south acreage along the river; Caton's village developed at the intersection of Md. 144 and Ingleside Ave. In 1859 the town had four taverns, six stores, two blacksmiths, two wheelwrights, and four shoe shops; by the turn of the century, Catonsville had become the most populous "streetcar suburb" in Baltimore County.

St. Timothy's Episcopal Church, a stone building of Gothic design built in 1844, stands on Ingleside Ave. just north of the Frederick Rd. intersection. On this site in 1847 the Rev. Dr. Libertus Van Bokkelen, rector, opened St. Timothy's Hall, perhaps the first religiously affiliated military school in the United States. Although the rector was a Unionist sympathetic to African Americans, many of the school's cadets left to join the Confederacy in the Civil War; John Wilkes Booth studied here in 1850–51. The academy burned in 1872. Van Bokkelen became Maryland's first superintendent of public instruction, in 1864.

To reach **Mount De Sales Academy,** another historically important school, follow Frederick Rd. east to Edmondson Ave., turn left, and then left again on Academy Rd. Established in 1852, this Roman Catholic school for girls (grades 9–12) once was a boarding school that attracted young women from all over the country. Its graduates included members of the Carroll family and Mary Hardy MacArthur, Gen. Douglas MacArthur's influential mother. The library contains 142 rare plates of Audubon's *Quadrupeds of North America;* a special "bird room" is devoted to plates of Rex Brasher's *Birds and Trees of North America.*

A short distance farther east on Frederick Rd., south on Maiden Choice Ln., lies the **site of St. Charles College,** on whose grounds an Italian marble chapel went up over a 10-year period beginning in 1913. The Roman Catholic school, which educated numerous bishops, including James Cardinal Gibbons (1834–1921), closed after World War II, but in 1983 **Charlestown,** a 110-acre "life-care retirement community," opened on the parcel and made use of some of the buildings. With 1,614 apartments, it claims to be the second largest such establishment in the United States. The chapel is now nondenominational.

Back at the intersection of the southern branch of Rolling Rd. and Frederick Rd., one may turn left and proceed west for a few blocks to Hilltop Rd., which descends to the river bank and forms a loop with Thistle Rd. A fiberboard company still operates a factory at **Thistle,** where George and William Morris built a mill for the manufacture of printed cotton in 1821. The stone portion of the present mill is part of the original Thistle Factory, operated by Welsh workers, whose abandoned stone houses still perch on cliff ledges across the road. Thistle Rd. intersects another River Rd., which runs from a bridge near the railroad tunnel north to Md. 144. The current automobile bridge is near the site of the arched, stone Patterson Viaduct, destroyed by the flood of 1868. The railroad replaced the viaduct with a Bollman Truss bridge—designed by Wendel Bollman, the B&O engineer who pioneered its distinctive use along the railroad route—and later straightened the track for a new tunnel-bridge connection. Farther south on River Rd., the remains of the Patapsco Factory, built by Edward Gray in 1820, are visible.

To return to Rolling Rd., drive a very short distance east of the point where Frederick Rd. crosses Hilltop Rd. and take the northern branch of Rolling Rd., which continues to Liberty Rd. (Md. 26).

Lower Patapsco River Valley

Below Relay and south of Halethorpe, stretches the lower Patapsco River. During the 18th and early 19th centuries, this wooded, picturesque area contained cotton mills and residences on elevated sites on which visitor Washington Irving once envisioned chateaus. The river originates at Parr's Spring, a pond south of Mount Airy, and flows 52 miles east to the Chesapeake Bay. In its last 15 miles, between Woodstock and the bay, the Patapsco falls 300 feet, creating water power once extensively used for mills and forges. Despite the danger of periodic floods, the B&O Railroad selected the river valley for its route west from the city. People of wealth built summer estates above the river during the 19th century, but a disastrous flood in 1868 permanently ended that practice. Another flood in 1972, precipitated by Hurricane Agnes, caused similar damage to the river valley. During the past 20 years, the lower river valley has become a battleground between conservationists and polluters. Where the main river enters the harbor, it once stank from raw sewage, offended the eyes with assorted trash, and endangered the public health with various industrial pollutants. The sewage problem has been addressed; the river is marginally cleaner, and some of the spawning fish have returned. More than 13,000 acres along the river are now included in the Patapsco Valley State Park, which encompasses riverfront land in Baltimore, Howard, Carroll, and Anne Arundel Counties. Dammed and monitored, the Patapsco will never return to its pristine state, but it is no longer an environmental disgrace.

Patapsco Valley State Park

Just before U.S. 1 crosses the river, South Rd. turns off to the main entrance of Patapsco Valley State Park (admission fee required). The park originated in 1907, when John Glenn donated 43 acres along the lower river to the state. By 1912, his gift had become the Patapsco State Forest Reserve, the first truly recreational land reserve in Maryland. The Civilian

Conservation Corps made many improvements during the 1930s, a process that continues today: the park is currently building fish passages to encourage what once was a thriving fishery.

The road goes to a ranger station and then passes near the Thomas Viaduct, giving the observer an opportunity to examine the stone design that impressed 19th-century Baltimoreans. Just around the bend; the modern, high, twin concrete bridges that carry I-95 across the Patapsco provide a vivid architectural contrast between the two centuries. South Rd. has become River Rd. by this point and leads to a park area known as **Avalon Field.** An 18th-century forge operated along the river at this location and by 1822 had evolved into an iron company named Avalon, which later became the Avalon Nail and Iron Works. The company and town surrounding it were destroyed in the flood of 1868. The **Orange Grove** flour mill was established above Avalon on the same side of the river in the 1850s; its products were marketed throughout the United States as well as in the West Indies, South America, and Europe. The mill, which escaped the 1868 flood, was acquired by the Charles A. Gambrill Manufacturing Company and burned to the ground in 1905. A recent automobile bridge crosses the Patapsco at this location; parking lots on both sides of the river provide the visitor an opportunity to walk the many trails crisscrossing the riverbank, particularly on the south, the Howard County side. A swinging bridge at the Orange Grove site about one and one-half miles upriver makes it possible to walk a round trip on both sides of the river between Avalon and Orange Grove.

The shallow, placid river one sees now gives no hint of the power that once made the Lower Patapsco Valley an industrial center. The mills have disappeared, but the wooded, rolling terrain is ideal for biking and hiking. This portion of the park is only the southern tip of an extensive state reserve.

Elkridge

U.S. 1 crosses the Patapsco into Howard County, named for John Eager Howard and created from Anne Arundel County in 1851. The first town one reaches along Rte. 1 is Elkridge (12,953 pop.), originally a tobacco shipping point known as Elkridge Landing. In the 1760s, when the river was still deep enough for ocean-going vessels, more than half the tobacco grown in Anne Arundel County was brought here for inspection, warehousing, and shipping. The Elkridge iron furnace and forge produced arms for the Continental Army. For two days in 1781 Lafayette's troops encamped here on their way to Yorktown. By 1800 the river had silted, and the town lost its maritime significance. Now Elkridge is a small commercial center surrounded by suburbia.

Levering Ave. briefly ascends the river valley off U.S. 1 from Elkridge, then stops at an access road limited to use by the park service. River flooding has closed much of this route to automobile traffic, but the walking trails remain. The Ellicott brothers landed here in 1772 and arduously constructed a wagon road upriver along an Indian trail to their new mill site six miles to the north, where Ellicott City now thrives.

Montgomery Rd. slants northwest from U.S. 1 beyond Elkridge to locations along the river's south bank. After crossing beneath I-95, the road intersects Elibank Dr., which leads to the **Belmont Conference Center** (private). This 80-acre site above the Patapsco is all that remains of

Belmont, the large estate established by Caleb Dorsey, the pioneer iron-maker and landowner who in 1738 built the long, narrow mansion that now houses the conference center. The Dorsey family held the property until 1918, when Howard Bruce bought it. The Smithsonian later acquired the site and operated it as a meeting center before selling it to the American Chemical Society in 1983. The mansion serves a wide variety of organizations for meetings and conferences.

Montgomery Rd. continues to Landing Rd., which passes between Belmont and the Catholic **Trinity Preparatory School,** before ending at Ilchester Rd. Follow Ilchester Rd. north to the river, where the Bonnie Branch rushes into the Patapsco at a narrow river canyon. **Ilchester**—a 19th-century mill town named after Joseph Holland, Earl of Ilchester—stood here. On the high bluff opposite Thistle lies the **site of St. Mary's College,** which the Redemptorist Fathers established in 1867. They built a five-story brick novitiate for young candidates but, after a century, moved the operation to Wisconsin. Despite plans for alternative uses, the property remains abandoned.

Jessup

East of U.S. 1 on Md. 175, one may visit a complex of state institutions at Jessup (1,213 pop.). The **Maryland Wholesale Food Center** opened in 1975 and continues to develop a 398-acre site for warehousing a variety of food operations in one location. The center includes a **Wholesale Produce Market and Seafood Market** open to consumers. The **Patuxent Institution,** an experimental detention center opened in 1959, provides psychiatric treatment for "defective delinquents" and people judged to have unstable, criminal personalities. The **Maryland House of Correction,** a medium-security prison created in 1874, is farther down Md. 175, flanked by the **Maryland Correctional Institution for Women** on the south and the **Clifton T. Perkins State Hospital** on the west. Perkins Hospital opened in 1960 as a maximum-security mental hospital for people who are found not guilty of crimes by reason of insanity or who become mentally ill while imprisoned elsewhere.

Savage Mill

U.S. 1 crosses the Little Patuxent River at **Savage-Guilford** (9,699 pop.), centered around the intersection of I-95 and Md. 32 just to the west. Turn on Gorman Rd. to **Savage Park,** where an old mill site (1810) has been restored and developed as a commercial art and antique attraction. John Savage acquired the property in 1822 and built on it a textile plant specializing in cotton duck. During World War II, the mill employed 400 people who produced about 400,000 pounds of cloth a month in 16 mill buildings. The working textile mill closed in 1947. Warehousing and other enterprises occupied the site until 1984, when listing in the National Register of Historic Places spurred a $12 million renovation by a limited partnership. Eight mill buildings have since been restored and house 200 antique dealers, 50 art and craft studios, 25 specialty shops, and a banquet facility and eatery. Here see another Bollman Truss bridge (1869), which the railroad moved to this location in the 1880s.

Laurel

U.S. I crosses the Patuxent River into Prince George's County and enters Laurel (150' alt., 19,438 pop.), which was the county's first industrial center. The town occupies land patented in the 17th century to Richard Snowden, whose Quaker family played a prominent role in developing the upper Patuxent valley with iron mines and furnaces. Nicholas Snowden built a gristmill here that operated until 1824, when it was converted into a factory for spinning yarn. A stage road passed through the Laurel area in the early 19th century, connecting the new capital at Washington with Baltimore. The B&O followed nearly the same route in 1835, the same year Snowden's son-in-law, Horace Capron (1804–85), founded the Patuxent Company, a cotton mill that employed 400 people at the end of the 19th century. Laurel then had a population of about 3,000 and promised to become a metropolitan center. After 1879, the town even contained an academy of music, the only one in Prince George's. The county created its first high school here in 1898. However, by 1911 the textile mills had all closed, the music academy burned down in 1917, and Laurel became one of Washington's many growing suburbs. Activity around nearby Fort Meade sustained the Laurel economy for many years; then in 1956 Melvin and Wolford Berman opened the Laurel Shopping Center, a testament to the suburban expansion around the old industrial town.

U.S. I crosses Main St., which may be the best preserved "Main Street" of any small town in the county. **Old Frost's Store,** at the corner of U.S. I and Main, dates to 1810, when it housed a blacksmith's shop. The **Laurel Railroad Station** (1884), one block east of Main, was designed by E. Francis Baldwin; the one-story brick Queen Anne–style structure entered the National Register in 1973.

Montgomery Ave., two blocks south of Main, runs west from Laurel via Brooklyn Bridge Rd. to an intersection with West Bond Mill Rd., which terminates at the **Rocky Gorge Dam.** Constructed in 1954, the dam created the T. Howard Duckett Reservoir, a wooded lake that stretches nine miles up the Patuxent River. Along with the **Triadelphia Reservoir,** set even farther up the river, between **Brighton Dam** and Md. 97, the Duckett Reservoir forms part of the Washington area's water supply system. The Washington Suburban Sanitary Commission owns the reservoirs and cooperates with the state and federal governments to maintain a series of parks and wildlife refuges along the river's 110-mile run from Parr's Ridge to the bay.

The **Laurel Race Track,** one of two one-mile Thoroughbred tracks in Maryland, is located east of town in Anne Arundel County between the railroad tracks and Md. 198 (Fort Meade Rd.). Racing started at Laurel in 1911. One of the track's best-known events, the Washington D.C. International, originated in 1952 and features celebrated horses from around the world. Queen Elizabeth sent her three-year-old Landau to Laurel in 1954, the first time a royal British entry had ever raced outside the United Kingdom. The track alternates its racing dates with Pimlico, home of the Preakness. In 1994, the owner of the Washington Redskins proposed to build a new football stadium near here, setting off an intense debate about land usage in this strategic location half-way between Washington and Baltimore.

Montpelier

Md. 197 (Laurel-Bowie Rd.) branches southeast from U.S. 1 in Laurel to Montpelier mansion, one of the most famous five-part brick houses in Maryland. Just before the road intersects the Baltimore-Washington Pkwy., Montpelier Dr. climbs a hill to the historic mansion and the nearby cultural center named for it. The Snowden family built this 18th-century estate along the Patuxent River and provided the entrepreneurship that led to the later formation of Laurel. The first Richard Snowden, a Welshman believed to be a veteran of service with Oliver Cromwell, immigrated to the Annapolis area and built an estate there. In 1669, his properties included a large iron mine at the head of the South River. Snowden's son Richard, "the Iron Master," established the Patuxent Furnace before 1734 at the site of an older Snowden ironworks on the Little Patuxent River, now in the center of Fort Meade. The family owned thousands of acres from the South River north to Sandy Spring, near the upper Patuxent in Montgomery County.

Maj. Thomas Snowden (1751–1803), the Iron Master's grandson, built the Montpelier mansion during the 1780s. Dendrochronology confirms the construction date, suggested by two initialed firebacks, dated 1783. Many distinguished guests, including Abigail Adams and George Washington, visited Montpelier and enjoyed the major's hospitality.

Opened in 1979, the **Montpelier Cultural Arts Center** sits adjacent to the mansion, on property once occupied by outbuildings that included the estate's barn. It provides exhibit areas and studios for the 20 to 30 artists, who work and teach here. The center also produces musical concerts and sponsors traveling exhibits of the visual arts. The **Maryland–National Capital Park and Planning Commission** owns and operates both the mansion and the arts center.

Montpelier, Prince George's County, in the 1930s

Muirkirk and Rossville

U.S. I continues toward Washington, passing through **Contee** and **Muirkirk,** named by homesick Scottish settlers. A left turn onto Muirkirk Rd. leads to the **Mineral Pigments Corporation,** a historic industry that originated with an iron furnace that William and Elias Ellicott, then owners of the Patuxent Iron Works, built in 1847. Muirkirk iron had great tensile strength, so the plant outlasted most others using Maryland ore. The ironworks advertised in 1892 that it produced cannon for the government, as well as plowshares, car wheels, etc. The factory subsequently converted to the production of ocher from local ores but since 1924 has produced dry pigments from higher-grade foreign ores. Continuing east on Muirkirk Rd., the traveler passes **Rossville,** a small African American community established in the 1880s, largely by freedmen who worked at the Muirkirk Furnace.

Beltsville

Beyond Muirkirk, U.S. I crosses Indian Creek and enters Beltsville (14,476 pop.), a town that grew up around a B&O Railroad depot named for local landowner Trueman Belt. Beltsville is best known for the **National Agricultural Research Center,** which extends over a rural area nine miles long and four miles wide in the heart of suburban Washington. The U.S. Department of Agriculture operates this internationally famous center—popularly known as BARC (the B is for Beltsville)—divided into BARC West, 1,000 acres between I-95 and Md. 201 dedicated to food plants, and BARC East, 6,200 acres devoted to animal programs and feed production. U.S. I passes through the middle of BARC West; the Baltimore-Washington Parkway bisects BARC East.

More than 2,500 USDA employees, including 450 scientists, work in about 800 buildings scattered across 36 square miles of pastures, orchards, cultivated fields, gardens, vineyards, experimental soil plots, and wetlands. BARC East has almost 700 Holstein dairy cows, 300 beef cattle, 400 sheep, 1,000 swine, and 3,000 turkeys. The popular Beltsville turkey, known for its compact body and ample breast meat, was developed here. The Department of Agriculture calls its research service here "the principal scientific agency of the USDA and the foremost agricultural research organization in the world."

Powder Mill Rd. (Md. 212) exits east from U.S. I to the research center's **National Visitor Center,** a log lodge modeled after those in Yellowstone National Park built by the Civilian Conservation Corps in 1936–37. Between 1942 and 1985, the lodge served as a government cafeteria and hosted a range of dignitaries from Dwight Eisenhower to Nikita Khrushchev. The renovated center opened in 1988; it provides maps and guides to this sprawling complex, where a thousand experiments may be under way on a given day. The Administration Building to the west houses the National Fungus Collection and the U.S. National Parasite Collection. The 17-story **National Agricultural Library,** to the east of U.S. I, contains more than two million volumes. To arrange 90-minute tours of the center for groups of eight or more, write Tour Coordinator, USDA, ARS National Visitor Center, Bldg. 302, Log Lodge, BARC-East, Beltsville, Md. 20705.

Adelphi Mill

U.S. I crosses the Capital Beltway (completed in 1964) and heads down a commercialized strip toward College Park. Md. 193 (University Blvd.) branches west through a portion of the campus of the University of Maryland and crosses the Northwest Branch of the Anacostia River. Follow the boulevard to Md. 212 (Old Riggs Rd.) and turn right to the large stone Adelphi Mill, perhaps the oldest surviving mill in the greater Washington area. Two brothers, Issachar and Mahlon Scholfield, built the gristmill around 1796 on a tract of land they named Adelphi (Greek for "brothers"). The mill and storehouse have been restored and are owned by the Maryland–National Capital Park and Planning Commission, which uses the mill for meetings.

College Park

Below University Blvd., U.S. I enters College Park (21,927 pop.), home to the flagship campus of the **University of Maryland** (34,623 enrollment). The university traces its origins to Charles Benedict Calvert (1808–64), great-grandson of the fifth Lord Baltimore, who at his peak served as president of the Maryland Agricultural Society, sat on the executive board of the United States Agricultural Society, and, as a Maryland congressman, led the fight to establish the U.S. Department of Agriculture. He also led efforts, which succeeded in 1856, to establish a Maryland agricultural college. The state built it here, on part of Calvert's land holdings. It was only the second agricultural school established in the New World. Later, in 1920, the college combined with the older (and private) University of Maryland in Baltimore to become the University of Maryland. In 1988 the University of Maryland at College Park (UMCP) became part of a statewide "system" that includes nine other Maryland campuses, has programs in other countries, and is governed by a 17-member board of regents. In 1991, enrollment in the University of Maryland System numbered 132,161 students, including 22,513 at the graduate level.

The UMCP offers programs in arts and sciences, agriculture, business and management, engineering, education, human ecology, journalism, physical education, recreation and health, architecture, and library and information services. The university's College of Agriculture, together with the National Agricultural Research Center and the nearby Patuxent Wildlife Research Center, make up one of the world's foremost centers for agricultural and natural-science research. The Schools of Medicine, Nursing, Law, Dentistry, Pharmacy, and Social Work and Community Planning are located in downtown Baltimore.

Look for either of two entrances to the university campus (via Regents Dr.) on the west side of U.S. I. Aside from agricultural-research acreage, the UMCP campus encompasses some 500 acres and contains 70 or so Georgian Revival structures. The **chapel,** on high ground overlooking U.S. I, commemorates alumni and students who died in 20th-century American wars. The **administration building** and **Symons Hall** form one end of a large grassy open space, at the western end of which stands **McKeldin Library,** a major research library that also houses important collections in Maryland history. The university's basketball team plays in **Cole Field House. Byrd Stadium,** home of the

football, lacrosse, and soccer teams, is named for Harry Clifton ("Curley") Byrd, university president from 1936 to 1954.

A flight out of historically important College Park Airport looks down on the University of Maryland campus in the 1930s.

The **Rossborough Inn,** a brick tavern built about 1800, faces U.S. 1 between the university entrances. Travelers on stage coaches once stopped here on the way between Baltimore and Washington; Lafayette was a guest during his triumphant return trip to the United States in 1824. The inn became part of the Maryland Agricultural College in 1858. During Jubal Early's raid in July 1864, Gen. Bradley T. Johnson, a Frederick native, commandeered the building for a Southern ball. Extensively renovated just before World War II, the building now serves as a faculty club. The keystone above the door contains a stone head of Silenus, the satyr who advised Dionysus in matters of wisdom and wine.

Opposite the main entrance to the university campus, a new road branches east from U.S. 1, crosses the railroad tracks, and passes the entrance to the **College Park Airport,** billed as the "world's oldest continuously operating airport." Orville and Wilbur Wright brought their new "aeroplane" here to teach the first two Army pilots to fly. The U.S. Army Flying School opened here in 1911, and the airport became associated with a number of firsts in military and civilian aviation. The first testing of aerial bombardment and of an airplane-mounted machine gun occurred here in 1911–12. Gen. Henry Harley ("Hap") Arnold made the first mile-high flight from here in 1912. The first female airplane passenger flew from here in 1909, and the first scheduled U.S. airmail service connected Washington, Philadelphia, and New York from this terminus in 1918. The first pilot-controlled helicopter flight was made from College Park in 1924. Listed in the National Register of Historic Places, the airport is owned by the Maryland–National Capital Park and Planning Commission, which operates the site as both a working airport and a museum.

Riverdale

South of the airport and Berwyn Heights, U.S. 1 crosses East-West Hwy. (Md. 410), which divides Hyattsville (13,864 pop.) and Riverdale (5,185 pop.). All of these early-20th-century suburban communities grew

The combined post office, general store, and real estate and insurance office at the suburban village of Berwyn, an automobile and rail link to Washington, as it appeared during the Depression

up along the Baltimore-Washington Turnpike (forerunner of U.S. 1) and at the railroad stations outside the District. Hyattsville lies largely south of East-West Hwy. and Riverdale largely north. Follow the highway east from Rte. 1 to Riverdale, on the west bank of the Northeast Branch of the Anacostia River. In 1887 the Riverdale Park Company purchased hundreds of acres from the **Riversdale** plantation and planned a residential community. The resulting small town was incorporated in 1920 and now features a range of housing styles from Queen Anne–style of the 1890s and bungalows of the 1920s to modern apartment buildings.

Riversdale in the New Republic

Turn right from the East-West Hwy. onto 48th Ave. and drive a short distance to **Riversdale,** a five-part brick mansion near the river, now hidden by highways and streets. Henri Joseph Stier, whose ancestors included the painter Peter Paul Rubens, fled the French Revolution in 1794, bringing with him an extensive art collection. He built this large plantation home, partly modeled after his Belgian chateau, between 1801 and 1803. Stier returned to Belgium in 1803, but his daughter Rosalie, who in 1799 had married George Calvert, remained with her husband to complete the work and manage the estate. Calvert was a grandson of Charles Calvert (fifth Lord Baltimore) and son of Benedict Calvert, who lived at Mount Airy in lower Prince George's County.

George and Rosalie Calvert had nine children. Their son Charles Benedict Calvert, the agricultural reformer, inherited Riversdale and expanded its acreage. He also supported the efforts of Samuel F. B. Morse (1791–1872) to obtain federal funds for the first telegraph. On April 9, 1844, Morse made the first successful test of a telegraph line he had run from the capital to Riversdale, just a few weeks before the official world premiere of the technology with his message sent from Washington to Baltimore.

Henry Clay, a friend of both George and Charles Calvert, visited Riversdale frequently and had a bedroom there reserved for his use. Tradition relates that Clay wrote much of his famous 1850 sectional-compromise speech here. Later, three senators (Hiram Johnson of California and Thaddeus and Hattie Caraway of Arkansas) and a representative (Abraham Lafferty of Oregon) lived at Riversdale.

The interior of Riversdale contains elaborate friezes, cornices, and wall panels, reflecting its European prototype; plainer features in the later wings reveal the sturdy Federal style of the young American republic.

The Maryland–National Capital Park and Planning Commission bought the property in 1949 and works with the Riversdale Historical Society to protect the house. Caretakers undertook extensive renovations in the late 1980s, and the mansion opened to public visits in 1993.

Hyattsville

U.S. 1 continues south beyond the East-West Hwy. to Hyattsville. Christopher Clark Hyatt (1799–1884) started a store in the 1840s at the crossroads of the Baltimore-Washington Turnpike and B&O Railroad. He and others subdivided adjacent land in the 1870s and '80s, and Hyattsville incorporated in 1886. The town contributed a number of business and civic leaders for the new suburbs, including William Pinkney Magruder (1857–1939), a member of an old Prince George's County family who moved to Hyattsville in 1882 and invested heavily in suburban real estate.

Rte. 1 forks in Hyattsville, just north of the point where two streams merge as the Anacostia River and flow along parklands, through Washington, and into the Potomac River. The Anacostia, known by several other names during early settlement, including Eastern Branch (of the Potomac), received its current name, after an Indian tribe, in 1927. Heavily polluted by industrial and development sites along its drainage basin in Montgomery and Prince George's Counties, the Anacostia has become a focus for environmental cleanup efforts. U.S. 1 bends southwest through **North Brentwood, Cottage City,** and **Mt. Rainier** before crossing the District line as Rhode Island Ave.

Follow signs for Alt. U.S. 1, which continues south across the Northwest Branch, and at Bladensburg intersects Md. 450, which wanders across Anne Arundel County into Annapolis.

BALTIMORE TO BLADENSBURG VIA THE BALTIMORE-WASHINGTON PKWY.

The Baltimore-Washington Pkwy. (Md. 295), a landscaped, limited-access highway, replaced U.S. 1 as a primary route between the two cities in the mid-1950s. Faster and in some instances closer to attractions in central Maryland, the parkway offers an attractive alternate route south from Baltimore to Washington. The B-W Pkwy. is accessible from the Baltimore Beltway (I-695) and from downtown as the extension of Russell St.

BWI Airport

The B-W Pkwy. parallels U.S. 1 out of Baltimore through the Lansdowne–Baltimore Highlands area (15,509 pop.), crosses the Harbor Tunnel Throughway (I-895), and intersects the Baltimore Beltway (I-695) beyond the Patapsco River. A new access road, I-195, leads to the **Baltimore-Washington International Airport.** In June 1950, on what had been 3,200 acres of farmland, the city of Baltimore opened

Friendship Airport (the name changed when the state acquired the airport in 1973). In 1997 BWI served almost 14 million commercial passengers with 600 daily flights on 19 airlines. The airport underwent modernization and expansion in 1979; additional enhancements, completed in 1995, include the two-level **Observation Gallery** between Piers B and C which gives travelers sweeping views of the runways and displays cut-away exhibits of modern jet aircraft. The $140 million **William Donald Schaefer International Pier** opened in 1997.

Fort Meade

After passing Dorsey Rd. (another way to get to BWI Airport), the parkway intersects Md. 175, which connects Jessup and **Fort George G. Meade.** Exit southeast from Md. 175 to Mapes Rd., the major entrance to the fort. Named for Maj. Gen. George G. Meade (1815–72) of Pennsylvania, the fort first served as a training installation in 1917, when the United States entered World War I; it expanded dramatically during World War II as a center for military orientation, replacement, training, and separation from the service. In 1945 almost 70,000 soldiers were quartered on its 13,000 acres. The 1st U.S. Army headquarters departed Ft. Meade in 1995 and now maintains only a satellite command here. With 20,000 employees and a multibillion-dollar budget, the **National Security Agency,** guarded and hidden from public access, now occupies most of the installation. Signs at the Mapes Rd. entrance indicate major points of interest at the fort, including a military museum on Leonard Wood Ave.

The next exit off the parkway, Md. 32, leads southeast to the National Security Agency and the **National Cryptologic Museum** on Colony 7 Rd. Opened in 1994, the museum exhibits a wide range of code devices and documents, particularly from the World War II era. An plaque in the museum reads: "To commemorate the Men and Women of American Cryptology, uniformed and civilian, who, unknown to the public, and oftentimes their families, served their country and the free world, constituting what was truly America's silent service."

Md. 32 northwesterly leads to Savage Station.

Patuxent Wildlife Research Center

From the parkway, Md. 198 east leads to the **Visitor Contact Station** of the **Patuxent Wildlife Research Center** on Bald Eagle Rd. The center opened in 1936 on 4,700 marshy acres along the Patuxent River. The transfer of 8,100 acres from Fort Meade to the U.S. Fish and Wildlife Service in 1991 made this center for experimental wildlife research the largest in the world. The more than 100 staffpersons study environmental contaminants, endangered species, and migratory birds. Ten field stations around the country report to the center, which has limited biking and hiking, and fishing and hunting in season. At the next parkway exit, Md. 197 east passes the original, southern portion of the refuge along the river. Md. 197 west takes one to the Montpelier mansion and Montpelier Cultural Arts Center.

The parkway cuts through the middle of **BARC East,** the larger portion of the **Beltsville Agricultural Research Center;** follow Powder Mill Rd. (Md. 212) west for a mile and a half to stop at BARC's visitors center.

Goddard Space Flight Center

Just before the parkway intersects the Capital Beltway (I-495), Md. 193 exits west to Greenbelt and east to the Goddard Space Flight Center. The National Aeronautics and Space Administration opened this 550-acre installation in 1959. It commemorates Robert Hutchings Goddard (1882–1945), a Massachusetts native and pioneer American rocket scientist. Goddard worked briefly at the U.S. Naval Ordnance Station at Indian Head, in Charles County, during the 1920s and near Annapolis during World War II. Goddard Space Flight Center is one of NASA's largest research and development facilities. It is primarily responsible for the nation's near-Earth satellites: for managing the design, development, and construction of spacecraft and for operating the worldwide tracking and communications network of manned and unmanned spacecraft. Much of the work necessary for the Apollo Lunar-Landing project took place here. Goddard scientists and engineers also control systems for the space shuttle program and the Hubble Space Telescope. To visit the small visitors center and gift shop featuring satellite and other exhibits, take Soil Conservation Rd. two miles east of the intersection of Md. 193 and the parkway.

Greenbelt

Greenbelt (21,096 pop.), one of the first planned communities in the United States, lies west of the parkway's interchange with Md. 193, also known as Greenbelt Rd. During the most experimental phase of President Franklin D. Roosevelt's New Deal, between 1935 and 1938, the Resettlement Administration, under Rexford Guy Tugwell, designed and built

Children happily helping with grocery shopping at the Greenbelt commissary in 1938, when the community was brand new

Greenbelt as one of three pilot "green towns" in the United States (the others were Greenhills, Ohio, and Greendale, Wisconsin). The concept had evolved in the 1890s from the "garden city" idea that Sir Ebenezer Howard championed in Great Britain. The design of Radburn, New Jersey, built in 1929, also influenced the Greenbelt planners, who in turn had considerable impact on the "new town" movement that helped to produce Columbia, Maryland.

On 3,300 acres in rural Prince George's County, Greenbelt's planners allowed for about 885 houses and apartments. The houses went up around open spaces that were closed to vehicles; pedestrian walkways crossed above roads between green "super blocks." In 1937, when the development was incorporated, Greenbelt had about 3,000 residents, all of whom met the family income ceiling of not more than $1,250 a year. Tugwell had the entire town fashioned in the Art Deco mode. The inclusion of parks, schools, swimming pool, a recreation center, and even a small shopping center gave Greenbelt a self-contained and futuristic style. The focal point, now named Roosevelt Center, was originally known as the Utopia Center.

Washington's World War II housing shortage forced alteration of Greenbelt's original plan. The Public Works Administration added 1,000 more units, for which there was no income restriction or time for the careful planning that distinguished the first houses. The federal government sold Greenbelt in 1953 to the residents, who now own the houses individually. Various nonprofit groups have purchased much of the original community open spaces and developed them for additional housing; private development in northern Prince George's has surrounded this "green" community with dense pockets of offices, shopping areas, and more housing.

Nonetheless Greenbelt retains certain "garden" characteristics and avoids heavy automobile congestion. The **Greenbelt Regional Park,** a 1,100-acre wildlife sanctuary opened in 1964, helps preserve the atmosphere. The entire original community has been listed in the National Register of Historic Places.

The gap between the parkway and U.S. 1 narrows as the two highways approach Washington through one of the earliest portions of Prince George's County to become suburban. The county's estimated population (773,810) now exceeds that of Baltimore County (675,401). African Americans, many originally District residents, now make up more than 50 percent of the county's populace and constitute the largest, best-educated, and wealthiest concentration of black Americans in the United States. About 25 percent of Prince George's residents have college degrees; 30 percent classify themselves as executives or professionals.

Before ending at U.S. 50, the Baltimore-Washington Pkwy. crosses over the Capital Beltway, which opened in 1964 with two lanes each in the outer and inner loops and a grassy strip separating them. From the American Legion (originally Cabin John) Bridge at the northern end to the Woodrow Wilson Memorial Bridge on the southern, the highway runs slightly longer than 40 miles. Suburban growth and traffic between suburbs has increased markedly since the mid-1960s, and the state has expanded the number of lanes to three and in places four, eliminating the grassy divider and making lanes of what were shoulders. The first HOV (high occupancy [two or more passengers] vehicle) lanes opened in Montgomery County in 1996. Two years later, between 165,000 and 180,000 vehicles used the beltway each day. As the number continues to rise, state transportation officials seek alternatives to adding more traffic lanes.

After the exit to Riverdale Rd., take the Md. 450 exit east to reach Bladensburg.

BLADENSBURG TO ANNAPOLIS VIA MD. 450

The quickest way to get from Washington to Annapolis is by U.S. 50 (New York Avenue in the District). The stretch of Rte. 50 between the Anacostia River and the Severn River is called the John Hanson Hwy., named after a Marylander who was president of the United States under the Articles of Confederation. This highway, opened in 1955, is a limited-access road that avoids all towns. Md. 450, which originates in Bladensburg, travels the old stage route, giving the traveler a better sense of the historic countryside.

Bladensburg

Md. 450 and Alt. U.S. 1 intersect at Bladensburg (8,064 pop.), where the Northeast and Northwest Branches converge to form the Anacostia River, which flows to the Potomac. A hamlet known as Garrison's Landing appeared at this location in 1742 and later was renamed after Thomas Bladen, governor of Maryland from 1742 to 1747. In the 18th century, ocean-going ships could sail up the Anacostia to this point, and Bladensburg became one of the most active tobacco ports in Maryland. As elsewhere, however, silting from surrounding farms took its toll, and by the end of the century the Anacostia this far north had grown impassable to shipping. Periodic floods (not arrested until 1959) also prevented the town from becoming a major city. Even so, roads from all directions crossed at Bladensburg, and in the 19th century stagecoaches naturally used the crossroads as a stop.

The British paid the town a monumental visit on August 24, 1814. About 4,500 veteran troops had embarked from their ships on the Patuxent River at Benedict and advanced down Lowndes Hill to cross the river to Washington. Some 6,000 American militia faced them from entrenched positions on the other side of the Anacostia. The unseasoned troops quickly fled the deafening sound of Congreve rockets and terrifying sight of gleaming bayonets. Only Commo. Joshua Barney and his flotillamen offered any resistance. The British, who referred to the encounter as the "Bladensburg Races," marched that evening into Washington and burned the public buildings.

Thereafter the river port slowly declined. The B&O, completed to Washington in 1835, effectively bypassed Bladensburg. Modern highways, fast-food stops, and scattered industry overlay its 18th-century origins. The **Peace Cross,** erected between 1919 and 1925 to commemorate those from Prince George's County who died in World War I, stands at the intersection of Alt. U.S. 1 and Md. 450. The **Prince George's**

Boat Marina occupies the riverbank immediately to the south. Prince George's established the second county high school here in 1930. Now a 3A institution, it supplied state champions in girls' basketball in 1993.

George Washington House, a narrow, two-story brick building constructed between 1755 and 1765, stands just north of the Peace Cross on Alt. U.S. 1 (Baltimore Ave.). Jacob Wirt probably built this structure, which over the years has served as a residence, tavern, store, and hotel. Wirt operated the Indian Queen Tavern at this site, where his son William spent his boyhood. William Wirt (1772–1834) grew up to become a famous lawyer, politician, biographer (of Patrick Henry), and essayist. He led the prosecution in the famous Aaron Burr treason trial in 1807 and later served longer as U.S. attorney general (1817–29) than anyone before or since. Wirt ran for president of the United States in 1832 as an anti-Masonic candidate, carrying only the state of Vermont.

In downtown Bladensburg, see the **Market Master's House** (private), a small stone cottage near the corner of 48th St. and Md. 450 (4006 48th St.). Christopher Lowndes, Bladensburg's leading colonial merchant, built the cottage in about 1760. Earlier, in 1746, Lowndes had built **Bostwick** (private), a large brick house with single end chimneys, on terraced grounds farther south on 48th St. Lowndes imported slaves and indentured servants in addition to merchandise; Bostwick features a buttressed gable wall with two cells for unruly slaves.

From the crossroads, Bladensburg Rd. (Alt. U.S. 1) runs southwest across the river to Washington, passing the entrance to **Fort Lincoln Cemetery** on the Prince George's County–District of Columbia line. Named after a Civil War fort that stood here, the cemetery repays a visit; one can see remnants of fortifications, an old springhouse, an architect-designed chapel-mausoleum, and a bronze statue of Abraham Lincoln. The nearby **Bladensburg Dueling Grounds** were used by antagonists even after the state outlawed the practice in 1816. Three years after passage of the law, Armistead T. Mason, a senator from Virginia, challenged his brother-in-law, Col. John M. McCarty, to a duel. Opposed to the practice, McCarty tried to laugh off the challenge. He first suggested the contestants leap from the Capitol dome, then proposed a fight with lighted matches on a barrel of gunpowder. Mason persisted. The weapons chosen were muskets at 12 paces, and after shots rang out Mason lay dead. In the most famous, or infamous, Bladensburg duel, Commo. James Barron here shot and killed naval hero Stephen Decatur on March 22, 1820.

Follow Md. 202 (Landover Rd.) east from the center of Bladensburg and proceed on Md. 450 where the two roads split (the Publick Playhouse Cultural Arts Center stands near the south side of the junction). Md. 202 thereafter follows the route the British followed on their return march from Washington to their ships at Benedict, passing through Upper Marlboro. The road intersects U.S. 50 and then passes **Beall's Pleasure** (private), a two-story brick house that Benjamin Stoddert (1751–1813) built in 1795. Stoddert, appointed first secretary of the navy by John Adams, married Christopher Lowndes's daughter Rebecca, and the two inherited Bostwick. They built Beall's Pleasure as a country home.

Md. 450 passes **Bladensburg High School,** dating from 1899 and the oldest in the county. The school has produced state championships in wrestling (1972 and 1973), boys' basketball (1980), cross country

(1985), track (1988), and football (1987). Bladensburg graduates of note include the political figure Robert J. DiPietro, the college track star and coach Myrtle C. Ferguson, and Tico Wells, a television and film actor.

Md. 450 crosses the Baltimore-Washington Pkwy. and passes through the southern section of Prince George's County's largest single development project of the 1950s, **New Carrollton** (12,002 pop.). The road then intersects the Capital Beltway (Exit 20), crosses the railroad at Lanham, and cuts east across a mixture of rural and suburban countryside to an intersection with Md. 193, known here as Glenn Dale Blvd. The brick house visible in the distance on a high hill is **Prospect Hill** (private), a 19th-century building that now serves as the clubhouse for the Glenn Dale Golf and Country Club.

The longtime residence of Justice Gabriel Duvall (1752–1844) and today the home of the Prince George's County Historical Society, **Marietta** lies left and north of Md. 450 on Bell Station Rd. Duvall's civic service of more than 60 years included terms as state legislator and congressman. President Thomas Jefferson appointed Duvall comptroller of the treasury in 1802, and nine years later James Madison appointed him an associate justice of the Supreme Court. He served on the court until 1835, then retired to Marietta. Duvall began construction of this brick, Federal-style plantation mansion around 1812; he added a wing in 1832 when, at the age of 80, he became guardian of three minor grandchildren. The justice's small brick law office stands on the grounds.

Md. 450 crosses Hillmeade Rd. and passes **Holy Trinity Church,** visible on the north side of the road. The ivy-covered brick building was erected in 1836; the nearby brick rectory dates to 1829. The highway continues eastward past High Bridge Rd. and Church Rd., which cuts to the south through a former rural landscape rapidly filling with houses. About a mile down Church Rd., a narrow lane leads to **Fairview** (private), built about 1800 by Baruch Duckett. Duckett bequeathed the house to his son-in-law, William Bowie, with the proviso that he not "suffer to be cut down the enclosed woods below my dwelling house for cultivation." Oden Bowie (1826–94), governor of Maryland from 1869 to 1872, here maintained a famous stable that produced such winning horses as Compensation, Belle D'Or, Oriole, and Crickmore.

Bowie

Md. 450 crosses the Conrail railroad tracks east of Church Rd. and enters the city of Bowie (37,589 pop.), Maryland's fifth largest municipality and the largest in Prince George's County. The town originated as a 19th-century railroad junction named for Oden Bowie. Then, between 1961 and 1968 it mushroomed, as a "Levittown." During this period, the late William J. Levitt's housing corporation constructed 9,000 units over 11 square miles in a development the company called "Belair at Bowie." The subdivision was named for Belair, the 18th-century plantation originally located here, but it soon became known simply as Bowie. A city map reveals the town's dual origins: the original town at the railroad junction is connected by a narrow corridor to the sprawling bedroom suburb built by Levitt.

Beyond the intersection with Md. 197 in Bowie, Belair Dr. turns south from Md. 450 to Tulip Dr. Turn right from Tulip Dr. to **Belair.** A long double avenue of tulip poplars leads to this Georgian house, built in the 1740s by Benjamin Tasker for his son-in-law, Gov. Samuel Ogle (1694–1752). The hyphens and two-story wings were built after 1900. Samuel Ogle was Maryland's governor on three separate occasions: 1731–32, 1733–42, and 1747–52. Like many Maryland gentlemen-farmers, Ogle enthusiastically supported horse racing, and in 1747 he imported from England two expensive Thoroughbreds, Spark and Queen Mab. The bloodlines of many winning Maryland-bred horses can be traced to this famous pair. Benjamin Tasker Jr., Ogle's brother-in-law and the next owner of Belair, added the mare Selima to **Belair Stables'** hall of fame. William Woodward Sr., a later owner, contributed Triple Crown winners Gallant Fox (1930) and Omaha (1935) as well as Nashua to the stables' list of winners. The Woodward family maintained the Belair estate and its famous stables until 1955, when the land was subdivided. Within eight years, the horse farm had disappeared, supplanted by multiples of the five basic house models that the Levitt Corporation sold to eager suburbanites. The 1907 stables building remains, however, as the **Belair Stables Museum,** located on Belair Dr. east of the mansion, which also is open to the public.

Beyond Belair Dr., Race Track Rd. angles north from Md. 450 to the **Bowie Race Track,** which opened in 1914 and closed in 1985. The site has been acquired by the Southern Maryland Agricultural Association. The old track and stables are used to train and exercise horses.

Race Track Rd. parallels the Patuxent River northward to a junction with Jericho Park Rd. and the campus of **Bowie State University.** This institution originated in Baltimore in 1865, when the Baltimore Association for the Moral and Educational Improvement of Colored People established a school to train African American teachers in a segregated age. The state of Maryland purchased the private school in 1908 and moved it

Demonstration classroom at the Maryland Teachers College at Bowie, ca. 1938

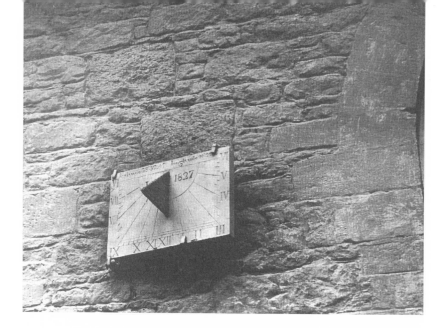

Sun dial, Sacred Heart Church, Prince George's County

to Bowie, where it was known as the Maryland Normal and Industrial School; it became the Maryland Teachers College in 1935 and Bowie State College in 1963. Now a fully accredited liberal arts institution with more than 4,400 students, the college was made part of the state university system in 1988.

Md. 450 leaves Bowie in an area known as White Marsh, named for the small creek that flows from Bowie into the nearby Patuxent River. **White Marsh Park,** a large wooded area along the stream, lies just south of the highway, opposite Race Track Rd.

The **site of Sacred Heart Church,** one of the earliest Catholic churches in Maryland, is off the highway about half a mile east of the park. Follow the marked paved road up a steep hill to the small stone sanctuary. In 1728 James Carroll bequeathed 2,000 acres and 100 slaves to the Jesuits at St. Thomas Manor House in Port Tobacco, and they created a settlement here. Because Roman Catholics were forbidden at the time to conduct public services, the priests in 1741–42 built a chapel and called it a private residence. The Declaration of Rights (1776) provided for freedom of worship, and in 1783 a delegation of Roman Catholic clergy met at White Marsh to plan a government for the Catholic Church in the newly created United States. Father John Carroll was nominated to be first bishop of the Roman Catholic Church in North America at this site on May 18, 1789. The main structure of the nave was constructed in the early 1800s, and together with the original chapel, burned in 1853. The church was rebuilt and enlarged later in the 19th century.

Md. 450 intersects Md. 3 and crosses the Patuxent River into Anne Arundel County at **Priest Bridge,** named for the early Jesuits at White Marsh. In 1927 Gov. Albert C. Ritchie led a motorcade from Priest Bridge south to Upper Marlboro to commemorate the opening of the Robert Crain Hwy., named for the Charles County legislator who championed its design and construction. The highway provided the first concrete link between Baltimore and Southern Maryland. The stretch of Md. 3 (U.S. 301) between I-97 and Upper Marlboro retains the name Crain Hwy.

From its intersection with Md. 450, Md. 3 north parallels the Little Patuxent River on the west, passing Crofton on the east. At Conaways the road branches northeast toward I-97 and passes Johns Hopkins Rd. Nearby lies **Whites Hall** (private), formerly known as Whitehall. The brick central portion was probably built in the 1760s and certainly was standing in 1784, when Samuel Hopkins inherited the house from his father. Johns Hopkins, founder of the hospital and university, was born here in 1795, the second son in a family of eleven children. The Hopkins family raised tobacco on their 500-acre farm and used a number of slaves. This latter fact disturbed their Quaker sensibilities, particularly after the Baltimore Yearly Meeting condemned slavery in 1777. A year later, Hopkins's grandfather freed his 42 slaves, and the family struggled thereafter to run the plantation on a different basis. Johns left the farm in 1812 at the age of 17 to work in his uncle Gerard's wholesale grocery business in Baltimore.

Along Defense Hwy.

In Anne Arundel County, Md. 450 is known as Defense Hwy. As it proceeds across the county, it passes clusters of residential developments that have mushroomed in size and number since World War II. **Crofton** was built between 1964 and 1975 within the triangle formed by Md. 3, Md. 450, and Md. 424 (Davidsonville Rd.). Like the "crofts" (small pieces of enclosed pasture) of the English highlands, Crofton is ringed by a circular drive enclosing residences built around a golf course. Each resident in this community pays additional tax for police and groundskeeping forces. Crofton's original 500 homes are now surrounded by "Greater Crofton," a residential area that houses more than 15,000 people. Additional housing construction is under way, and Md. 3 is now lined with shopping centers, fast-food outlets, and service stations.

In dramatic contrast to its surroundings, **Bright Seat,** a frame house dating at least to the early 18th century, stands opposite Crofton on Md. 424 near Crofton Park. The shorter wing may have been a tavern; the 2½-story main house with its great double chimneys was built 100 years later.

Md. 450 continues through farmland, angling closer to U.S. 50 on the south and crossing Bell Branch, North River, and Bacon Ridge Branch, small streams that form the headwaters of South River. The many inlets, creeks, and bays along South River are filled with marinas, condominiums, and small beach towns that demonstrate the expansion of Annapolis. Defense Hwy. passes under I-97, which connects the Baltimore Beltway and U.S. 50, and crosses Broad Creek, dammed to the north to provide a water supply for Annapolis.

Side Trip on Generals Hwy. (Md. 178)

Md. 450 intersects Md. 178 at the site where Generals Horatio Gates and William Smallwood, accompanied by a welcoming committee of Annapolitans, met George Washington under an oak tree on December 19, 1783. **Three Mile Oak,** now a blackened tree stump set in concrete, rests on the south side of the crossroads. The generals escorted Washington to the State House, where he resigned his commission before the Continental Congress. After this event, and because in 1781 French General Rochambeau also had traveled the road, while marching from Annapolis to take part in the siege of Yorktown, Md. 178 became known as Generals Hwy.

Secondary roads branch from the highway to assorted "necks" along the Severn River. Two miles along the way, Generals Hwy. passes **Iglehart** (private), a two-story, gable-roofed frame house built before 1809. The recessed porch and the brick pent (closet projecting from a wall) adjacent to the single chimney form part of the original house and represent distinctive Southern Maryland design elements.

Slightly more than three miles along Generals Hwy., a narrow road leads east to **Belvoir** (private), a house built about 1730 by John Ross, great-grandfather of Francis Scott Key. The brick house overlooks Little Round Bay, which shelters a number of small waterfront communities. The oldest section of the house is a gambrel-roofed brick wing in the back; the main house is a six-bay building with unusually thick walls laid in English bond; the frame wing is modern. Ann Arnold Key, Francis Scott Key's grandmother, is buried on the property.

Crownsville State Hospital Center, west of Generals Hwy. at Crownsville, was established in 1910 as the Hospital for the Negro Insane of Maryland; it was renamed Crownsville State Hospital in 1912. Desegregated in 1949, the hospital now cares for an average of 253 mentally ill patients from Southern Maryland counties as well as Baltimore City. The state of Maryland has built a large state office complex—including the Maryland Historical Trust and its library—on the expansive hospital grounds.

Generals Hwy. intersects Md. 32 beyond Crownsville and veers to the northeast toward Dorrs Corner and the **Severn Run Natural Environmental Area,** a wildlife refuge along the headwaters of the Severn River. The highway passes **Part of Providence** (private), a small house built about 1800 on the west side of the road. Another half mile to the north, **The Rising Sun Inn** (private), a 1½-story frame building, is visible from the west side of the road. Half of this building has a steep gable roof; the other half has a gambrel roof.

As it approaches Annapolis, Md. 450 crosses under U.S. 50 (which one may take to bypass Annapolis) and intersects Riva Rd. at Parole Plaza.

Riva Rd. angles to the southwest and, just before crossing South River on Riva Bridge, passes **Old Bloomfield** (private). This striking, two-story brick Georgian house, overlooking the river, is only one room deep.

Md. 450 crosses Md. 2 at Parole (see Tour 4). Just before entering Annapolis as West St. the road passes the **National Cemetery,** established in 1862. The tree-shaded cemetery contains about 2,800 graves of Civil War veterans, including those of 24 Confederate soldiers and 206 unknowns.

FROM THE WASHINGTON AREA TO ANNAPOLIS VIA MD. 214

Md. 214 connects the eastern corner of Washington with the Annapolis area, passing through rural and residential sections of Prince George's and Anne Arundel Counties. The road branches from East Capitol St. in the District of Columbia and enters Maryland as Central Ave. in

Capitol Heights (125' alt., 3,633 pop.), a suburban community straddling the Maryland-District line. The road then angles slightly north to Addison Rd.

Seat Pleasant

Addison Rd. is the main thoroughfare of Seat Pleasant (5,359 pop.). Named for a colonial estate, the town has served as a suburban rail terminus since the 1890s, when Otto Mears constructed the Chesapeake Beach Railway from here to a bay resort town by that name in Calvert County. A streetcar line connected Washington to the railway in 1900; Seat Pleasant and Capitol Heights developed as "streetcar suburbs," following a pattern similar to the one that spawned new villages around metropolitan Baltimore. The town also became the Washington link of a suburban railroad, built in 1908, which linked Baltimore and Annapolis. The railroads and streetcars disappeared, but when the blue line of Washington's subway system arrived here in 1980, Seat Pleasant resumed its familiar role as station stop.

Turn right on N. Addison Rd. to Martin Luther King Hwy. (Md. 704). Turn left onto Md. 704 and follow it briefly to the resumption of N. Addison Rd., which turns right to **St. Matthew's Episcopal Church.** Also known as **Addison's Chapel,** this simple brick church stands on a hill above the road, overlooking the bustling traffic. At this site almost 300 years ago, Col. John Addison erected a log chapel for his tenants. No one knows definitively when the brick chapel, laid in Flemish bond with a steep gable roof, was constructed. Dates ranging from 1746 to 1816 have been suggested, creating an appropriate enigma for this quiet refuge of the past.

Raljon and Largo

Central Ave. continues east, crossing Summerfield Blvd., which leads north (left) to the **Jack Kent Cooke Stadium,** opened in 1997 as the playing field of the Washington Redskins (National Football League) in the suburban area of Raljon. The new stadium, named for the team's late owner, seats more than 80,000 fans and was built with private funds. Beyond the stadium, Central Ave. crosses the Capital Beltway at Largo (9,475 pop.), a suburban area clustered around the **USAir Arena,** formerly known as the Capital Centre. Mary Truman Dr. intersects the road beyond the beltway and leads to the arena, built in 1973 as a center for sports and entertainment events. The Washington Wizards (formerly the Bullets, National Basketball Association) and the Washington Capitals (National Hockey League) once played here. Sugar Ray Leonard, a native of nearby **Palmer Park,** defended his middleweight boxing title at the arena in 1980; former President Reagan held his first inaugural gala here a year later.

Md. 214 intersects Landover Rd. (Md. 202) in the center of Largo. Turn south (right) on Md. 202 to **Prince George's Community College** (3,263 full-time and 10,044 part-time students) and the 18th-century house known as **Mount Lubentia** (private), located just beyond the college. Ninean Beall patented this property in 1696, naming it for his birthplace in Fifeshire, Scotland. He had been captured by the English at the Battle of Dunbar in 1650 and shipped to America as an indentured servant. As soon as his servitude ended, he began to patent land and take an active part in local affairs. Eventually Beall became commander in chief of the Maryland rangers, who patroled the colony's northern and western frontiers. The Magruder family purchased his estate and built the present house around 1760; additions and alterations, including a widow's walk and porch, were made by subsequent generations.

Mount Lubentia was rented from 1770 to 1774 to Jonathan Boucher (1737-1804), rector of St. Barnabas Church, noted tutor and ardent Tory. Among his pupils were John Custis, George Washington's stepson; Charles Calvert, eldest son of Benedict Calvert; and Overton Carr of Virginia, who named their school Castle Magruder. While a student here, Custis met his future wife, his classmate Eleanor Calvert of Mt. Airy, Charles's sister. Boucher returned to England with his family on September 10, 1775, during the British siege of Boston. He had met Washington several times during his tutoring of Custis and considered him a friend, but an ordinary man. He later expressed astonishment at the general's military and political achievements.

Watkins Regional Park

Central Ave. crosses the Western Branch, which rises near Bowie and flows through the **Robert M. Watkins Regional Park** immediately to the south on its way to the Patuxent River. Take Watson Park Dr. (Md. 193) south from the crossroads at **Kolbes Corner** to the entrance of the park, which features playing fields, picnic and camping facilities, a nature center, antique carousel, miniature train, and farm.

SixFlags America, which bills itself as "a family entertainment park," lies off Md. 214 just beyond Kolbes Corner. The 98-foot-high, wooden roller coaster, built more than 70 years ago, was imported from Paragon Park in Massachusetts and has been rated by enthusiasts as one of the 10 best in the United States.

St. Barnabas Church

Beyond the amusement park, Central Ave. intersects Church Rd., which leads to St. Barnabas Church. Turn right (south) and follow the road to its end at Oak Grove Rd. near **Leeland.** The church serves Queen Anne's Parish, formed in 1704 in what was then one of the richest tobacco growing areas in Maryland. Eighteenth-century Anglican rectors regarded the parish, supported by aristocratic plantation families, as a prize. The first brick church replaced a wooden chapel in 1710, and the present church was built in 1774. The two-story structure with its steep, double-hipped roof was restored in 1974, when the 19th-century stained-glass windows were replaced by the clear glass that characterized the earlier century.

Gustavus Hesselius (1682–1755), a Swedish artist who came to America in 1711, was commissioned by the vestry in 1721–22 to paint an altarpiece of the Last Supper for the first brick church. The painting disappeared when the present church was built and did not reappear until 1848. For many years, Hesselius's work had been on loan to and displayed at the American Swedish Historical Museum and the Philadelphia Museum of Art, where authorities touted it as the first major departure by an American artist from the portraiture that had dominated American painting during the colonial era. The painting's owner willed it to the parish, and the Last Supper now hangs on the choir gallery.

Davidsonville

After intersecting U.S. 301, Md. 214 crosses the Patuxent River and enters Anne Arundel County and an area that has managed to escape extensive development. Eighteenth-century houses sit back from country lanes; the fields reflect traditions of cattle and horse breeding. People still ride to the hunt over these gentle, wooded hillsides. Hunters shoot for dove during season. Md. 214 passes through Davidsonville, intersects Solomons Island Rd. (Md. 2), then continues into the peninsula defined by the South River and the Rhode River, ending at **Beverley Beach.** A left onto Solomons Island Rd. will lead one to the edge of Annapolis and junctions with Md. 450 and U.S. 50.

Severn River Bridges

The Severn River, named for the longest river in Britain, forms the northeastern boundary of Annapolis. U.S. 50/301 skirts the northern edge of Annapolis, crosses the river upstream of the city, and continues east toward Sandy Point State Park, the Bay Bridge, and the Eastern Shore. Md. 450 travels through the center of Annapolis, follows King George St. across College Creek, and then crosses the Severn River as Old Annapolis Blvd. on the newer of the two bridges. This bridge replaced a drawbridge that had stood since the Governor Ritchie era and that delayed both boat and automobile traffic, but was also a very popular fishing spot. The new, much higher, bridge, built in 1994, offers uninterrupted passage to cars and boats and includes a fishing pier that extends from the eastern shore. It also affords the traveler a sweeping view of the river's confluence with the bay.

Side Trip to Sandy Point State Park on Md. 648 and 179

To reach Md. 648 from U.S. 50, follow signs to Md. 450 south and the U.S. Naval Academy and make a left turn at the foot of the bridge. Coming from Annapolis on Md. 450, turn right on Md. 648 immediately upon crossing the bridge. Md. 648 passes **the U.S. Naval Research and Development Center.** The radio station here is one of the most powerful on the East Coast, capable of reaching any naval vessel in the world. Its towers are visible from the bay and low-lying points on the Eastern Shore almost 30 miles away. Locals call the facility, on Greenbury Point, the "Experiment Station."

Md. 179 (St. Margaret's Rd.) branches northeast from Md. 648 and crosses the headwaters of Mill Creek.

St. Margaret's and Whitehall

A white frame building with a shingled tower built in 1895, **St. Margaret's Church** stands at the junction of Md. 179 and Pleasant Plains Rd. The congregation of the Westminster Parish (formerly Broad Neck Parish) has maintained a church here or near here since 1696. Sir Robert Eden, last colonial governor of Maryland, was buried below the chancel of the second Westminster Parish Church, which stood on the banks of the Severn several miles away.

After the Revolution, Eden returned from Britain with Henry Harford—illegitimate son of Frederick Calvert, the sixth and last Lord Baltimore—to press proprietary claims to estates that the state had confiscated during the war. The assembly denied Harford's petition, thus ending the last formal connection between the Calvert family and its province. Eden remained in Maryland and died at the home of Dr. Upton Scott on September 2, 1784. On his deathbed, he asked to be buried in the churchyard at St. Anne's, in Annapolis. The vestry at St. Anne's had closed its small churchyard to further burials and refused to make an exception for Eden, so he was buried at Westminster Parish. The church burned in 1803, and when Eden's relatives later came to Annapolis to seek his grave, they could not locate it. In 1923 Daniel Randall excavated the Westminster Church site and, with the aid of the Society of Colonial Wars in 1925, uncovered a skeleton under the spot where the pulpit had been. Those remains—tentatively identified as Eden's—were moved in 1926 to the churchyard at St. Anne's. Eden finally received his deathbed wish.

St. Margaret's Rd. continues to U.S. 50. Stay right and enter Access Rd., which parallels the highway and intersects Whitehall Rd., a narrow lane down the short neck formed by Whitehall Creek on the west and Meredith Creek on the east. **Whitehall** (private), a landmark of American architecture, overlooks the Chesapeake. This private estate is not visible from the lane, but one may catch a discreet glimpse of its famous portico from the water. Whitehall was the home of Horatio Sharpe (1718–90) governor of Maryland from 1753 to 1769. Sharpe had the central block of this five-part brick mansion built in 1764–65. Tradition has it that he built Whitehall in hopes of marrying Mary Ogle, daughter of his gubernatorial predecessor. She chose instead to marry John Ridout, Sharpe's secretary and close friend. Interestingly, Sharpe at his death bequeathed Whitehall to Ridout.

Approached from the road, Whitehall has the formal, somewhat austere look of a baronial English residence. Sharpe added hyphens to the center portion shortly after its construction and connected them to square, hip-roofed wings via porticoes. Additional hyphens, since removed, led from each wing to a springhouse on the east and a water closet—unusual in the colonies—on the west. Excavation has revealed semi-octagonal fortifications that ran the 200-foot length of the house on the land side and had a bastion for cannon at each corner. Other accoutrements, such as petard gates and chevaux-de-frise fences, gave this side of Whitehall the appearance of a fortified castle.

Bay side of Whitehall, Anne Arundel County, in the 1930s

The surprising, evocative side of the mansion faces the Chesapeake. Sharpe constructed a classical temple, which he called his "elegant lodge," a garden tribute to an antiquity then being rediscovered in Europe. From the water, an observer can see the great portico supported by four fluted Corinthian columns with an entablature that includes a sculpted Maryland coat of arms on the pediment. Joseph Horatio Anderson, who may have been the first architect for the Maryland State House, is believed to have created the design for Whitehall. William Buckland may have been responsible for all the neoclassical woodwork and plasterwork. This temple on the Chesapeake was built 30 years before Thomas Jefferson popularized the neoclassical style as appropriate to a federal republic independent of Europe. Whitehall is known as the first true Classic Revival dwelling in America. It became a National Historic Landmark in 1960.

In 1769, unexpectedly relieved of his office by the sixth Lord Baltimore, Sharpe retired to Whitehall to live in respectable bachelorhood. In his letters he revealed unhappiness in his difficult role as governor, torn between loyalties to king and proprietor and sympathies for the colonists. Family business required his presence in England in 1773, and the American Revolution prevented his return. The state of Maryland spared his properties from confiscation in the hope that he would return after the conflict, but he never did. Sharpe died in England in 1790 at the age of 72.

Sandy Point State Park

Md. 179 continues briefly beyond Whitehall Rd. over Meredith Creek and crosses U.S. 50 to Sandy Point State Park. The state acquired this shoreland near the Bay Bridge in 1949 and imported sand to create a beach, which opened to the public in 1952. Stone jetties protect this 786-acre park and provide spots for fishing. Some of the original marshland has been preserved for hiking and nature study. A great expanse of sand stretches around the point for almost two miles. Each fall the park supplies the setting for Chesapeake Appreciation Days, a long weekend of exhibits, educational events, and sailboat races.

From the park return on U.S. 50 west to its intersection with Ritchie Hwy. (Md. 2) and continue the tour north to Baltimore.

ANNAPOLIS to BALTIMORE VIA GOVERNOR RITCHIE HWY. (MD. 2)

Ritchie Hwy., completed with great fanfare in 1939, commemorates the long service of Albert C. Ritchie (1876–1936), Baltimore attorney, two-time presidential candidate, and governor of Maryland from 1920 to 1935. The new highway (Md. 2) represented a modern marvel, connecting Baltimore and Annapolis and following in a perfectly straight line through Anne Arundel County forest between Glen Burnie and the turn onto the bridge over the Severn. South of U.S. 50, the lower stretch of the highway now carries the designation Md. 450.

On its northward trek, Md. 2 passes **Arnold** (20,261 pop.) and **Anne Arundel Community College** on its way to **Severna Park** (25,879 pop.), located near the narrowest portion of the neck formed by the Severn and Magothy Rivers. Neither Arnold nor Severna Park is an incorporated town but rather a suburban cluster populated by commuters and the retailers who serve them. With the exception of Annapolis, the 16 localities in Anne Arundel County that have populations above 10,000 fit this description. A few, like **Glen Burnie,** contain significant industries, but most are bedroom suburbs. In 1990 these unincorporated areas greatly outnumbered Annapolis in population (260,100 vs. 33,187).

After the new portion of I-97 between the Baltimore Beltway and U.S. 50 opened in 1987, Ritchie Hwy. gradually lost its status as the primary connection between Baltimore and Annapolis. This highway, now less congested, and an even older, snake-like road, Baltimore-Annapolis Blvd. (Md. 648), have now become the best ways to see and appreciate this part of Anne Arundel County. The two roads travel north across unnamed, wooded peninsulas cluttered with commercial and residential developments that mask the presence of nearby creeks, bays, and coves.

Ritchie and World War II Memorials

Up the hill from the eastern end of the newer Severn River bridge sits a modest monument to Governor Ritchie. From this point the traveler has a spectacular view of Annapolis across the river. The massive gray buildings of the Naval Academy rise from the opposite shore with the chimneys of Annapolis and the white dome of the State House in the background. When illuminated at night, the State House dome is visible for miles. On good sailing days, the expansive water below is filled with private sailboats, navy yawls, and knockabouts.

Just in front of the Ritchie Monument, another memorial, dedicated by the state in 1998, honors all those Marylanders—285,000 of them—who served in uniform during World War II.

The Baltimore and Annapolis Trail Park

Opened in 1990, this 13.3-mile paved biking and hiking trail parallels Ritchie Hwy. along the old route of the Baltimore and Annapolis Railroad.

The popular trail begins at Boulters Way, just north of the interchange of U.S. 50 and Ritchie Hwy., and travels north to Dorsey Rd. (Md. 176) in Glen Burnie. The trail was selected in 1996 by the East Coast Greenway Alliance as one of the first sections of a planned, 2,500-mile recreational path from Maine to Florida. Signs along Md. 2 and Md. 648 direct the visitor to the trail and accompanying parking.

Patapsco-Magothy Neck and Return to Baltimore via Side Roads

For a leisurely drive back to Baltimore while exploring a scenic and long-settled part of Anne Arundel County, depart Md. 2 and just north of Arnold turn onto Md. 648, Old Annapolis Rd., following it through Severna Park and back across Md. 2 until 648 reaches Magothy Bridge Rd. (The traveler may choose instead to turn right off Ritchie Hwy. and onto Md. 648 just north of Hahn Dr. and Macy's Corner.) Turn right on Magothy Bridge Rd. and follow it to Md. 607 and Jacobsville.

At Jacobsville, Md. 607 intersects Md. 177, Mountain Rd., a right on which leads to **Downs Memorial Park,** a public picnic site facing Chesapeake Bay. Mountain Rd. ends at a long causeway connecting the mainland to **Gibson Island** (private). A guard checks visitors, who must have permission from a resident to enter the community. Its secluded residences line the wooded coves and bays along the island. The **Gibson Island Club** dates from 1921.

North of Jacobsville, Md. 607 makes a wide Y with Fort Smallwood Rd. (Md. 173), a right on which leads to Bayside Beach Rd. and **Hancock's Resolution,** a fieldstone house located more than two miles down a small peninsula formed by Back Creek on the south and the wide Patapsco River. Hancock family tradition tells that the stone wing may have been a fort built in the 1670s for protection against the Susquehannocks, but the interior woodwork dates to about 1720, when Anne Arundel County was no longer an exposed frontier. A frame wing was added to the house between 1830 and 1850. The Hancock family has donated the house to Historic Annapolis.

Fort Smallwood Rd. continues to **Rock Point** and **Fort Smallwood Park.** Fort, road, and park are named in honor of Gen. William Smallwood. The U.S. government acquired 100 acres here in 1896 and erected the fort at the mouth of Rock Creek. The fortifications remain, but the government sold the property to Baltimore City in 1926 for use as a park. Picnickers can view maritime traffic at the confluence of the bay and the Patapsco River, including the dramatic procession of freighters leaving the river on an ebb tide. Fort Howard Park occupies North Point, directly across the river, and the smokestacks at Sparrows Point are visible upriver of the fort.

Backtrack on Md. 173 from Fort Smallwood past Md. 607. This leg of Fort Smallwood Rd. takes one across Rock Creek to **Riviera Beach** (11,376 pop.) and across Stony Creek to Marley Neck. Across Marley Creek and one mile north of Forman's Corner, a secondary road on the right leads to another element in 19th-century Baltimore's defense network, **Fort Armistead,** named for the man who commanded Fort McHenry in September 1814. The site now belongs to the city parks department. From Fort Armistead, **Fort Carroll** is visible in the middle of the Patapsco, left of Sparrows Point and below the Francis Scott Key Bridge. Construction of this man-made island began in 1847 on a shoal called Sollers Flats. Between 1849 and 1852, Robert E. Lee, then a brevet colonel of engineers in the U.S. Army, supervised building of the fort, originally intended as a full military post. Named after Charles Carroll of Carrollton, the fort was never completed. Two batteries from Fort McHenry occupied the island in 1898, but it was subsequently used solely as a lighthouse and fog-bell station. Various plans for development of the abandoned, privately owned property have been proposed in recent years, but none has come to fruition.

_____

From Pasadena, Ritchie Hwy. continues north, crosses Marley Creek, and passes **Harundale,** a community typical of the post–World War II housing developments built around Baltimore between 1945 and 1950. The Servicemen's Readjustment Act (the G.I. Bill), with its provisions for subsidized mortgages, spurred a boom of suburban housing construction after the war. Builders rushed to meet the demands of young couples drawn to the dream of a detached, single-family house in the suburbs. By 1948 more than 1,000 prefabricated houses had been built on concrete slabs in Harundale, which offered two styles for under $7,000. The **Harundale Mall**—the Baltimore region's first suburban, enclosed shopping center—opened 10 years later. Now outdated and partially vacant, it may soon be partially or totally demolished.

Glen Burnie

As Md. 2 enters Glen Burnie (37,305 pop.), the suburban landscape changes to a dense mixture of residences, businesses, and industries. John Glenn acquired an estate here in the 1880s, hence the name. At Glen Burnie the highway curves to the north and crosses the head of Furnace Creek, which flows into Curtis Creek to the east. The adjacent town of **Furnace Branch** and the creek take their name from an iron furnace built here in 1759 by Caleb and Edward Dorsey. The furnace operated for almost a century, closing in 1851.

Md. 2 then passes the headquarters for the state Motor Vehicle Administration and under the Baltimore Beltway. It traverses the suburb **Brooklyn Park** before entering the industrial Brooklyn–Curtis Bay neighborhood and proceeding to central Baltimore.

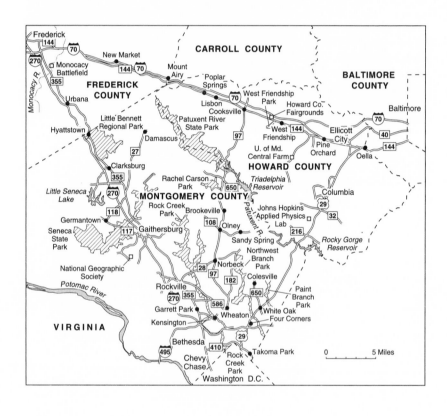

Along the Washington-Baltimore-Frederick Triangle

East-West Hwy. (Md. 410), U.S. 29, Md. 144, and Md. 355

For colonists in tidewater Maryland, building a serviceable road to Frederick represented one step in their eager search for a pathway through the mountains to the Ohio country. Georgetown (before Washington) and Baltimore each laid out its own Frederick Rd., two sides of a triangle within which approximately 850,000 people now live—more than in either metropolis.

BETHESDA to ELLICOTT CITY VIA EAST-WEST HWY. AND U.S. 29

East-West Hwy. (Md. 410), a proto-beltway for two counties, travels around the northern corner of the District of Columbia, linking Wisconsin Ave. (Md. 355) in Montgomery County to Kenilworth Ave. (Md. 201) in Prince George's County. Traveling east on the highway from Bethesda, and then turning north on U.S. 29 toward Baltimore, one can quickly grasp the enormous changes suburban development has brought to this part of Maryland. East-West Hwy. passes through many of the older suburbs and villages that began to cluster around Washington with the expansion of train and streetcar lines within 20 years after the Civil War. Rte. 29 carries one through the rings of housing and commercial development that emerged during and especially after World War II.

Chevy Chase

Winding gracefully eastward from Bethesda, Md. 410 soon reaches Connecticut Ave. (Md. 185). About a mile and a half south lies Chevy Chase, developed in 1890 by the Chevy Chase Company on 1,700 acres of farmland outside Washington. Sen. Francis G. Newlands, made wealthy from Nevada's silver mines, established the company, which still exists. The name derives from a Scottish ballad that celebrates the scene of a famous border skirmish. A "chevy chase" could refer to any noisy, running pursuit and seems particularly appropriate during the area's notorious "rush" hours.

The highway continues to a portion of **Rock Creek Regional Park,** where Jones Mill Rd. branches north and Beach Dr. follows Rock Creek south into the park. The **Audubon Naturalist Society,** established in 1897 as an independent regional conservation organization, occupies **Woodland,** a Georgian mansion at 8940 Jones Mill Rd. John Russell Pope, architect of the Jefferson Memorial and a number of other Washington landmarks, designed this house, built by Capt. and Mrs. Chester Wells on a 40-acre estate in 1928. Mrs. Wells bequeathed the property to the society, which has created a wildlife sanctuary and an education center that includes a bookshop. Here also are the offices of the **Rachel Carson Council,** which commemorates and carries on the extraordinary work of the longtime Silver Spring resident and crusader against pesticides.

Rachel Carson

Rachel Carson (1907–64) grew up near Pittsburgh but spent most of her adult life in central Maryland. She obtained a master's degree in genetics from Johns Hopkins University, saw the sea for the first time at Woods Hole, Massachusetts, and decided upon a career as a naturalist and writer after discovering Howard Beston's *The Outermost House* in Baltimore's Pratt Library. She taught at the University of Maryland and then worked for the U.S. Fish and Wildlife Service before publishing *The Sea Around Us* in 1951. With this book she achieved financial independence, and in the mid-1950s she moved to a house near Northwest Branch Regional Park. Throughout this period, she and her friends explored Maryland's seashore, went birding along the C&O Canal and Rock Creek, and became alert observers of the natural world.

Like Harriet Beecher Stowe, Carson wrote a book that galvanized public opinion around a social issue, generated powerful opposition, and inspired reforms that still provoke debate. *Silent Spring* (1962) announced that "the most alarming of all man's assaults upon the environment is the contamination of air, earth, rivers and sea with dangerous and even lethal materials." The book became an immediate best seller, and 30 years later was selling as many copies as it had in its first year.

A room in the White Oak branch of the Montgomery County Library and a regional park along Hawlings River near Laytonsville have been named in Carson's memory. Pursuing the same concerns, the Rachel Carson Council in 1993 published the comprehensive *Basic Guide to Pesticides.*

Silver Spring and Takoma Park

After crossing Rock Creek, the East-West Hwy. touches the northern corner of the District of Columbia, intersects 16th St. (Md. 390), and angles south to intersect U.S. 29 (Colesville Rd.), along which this tour will continue.

Near this spot in 1842, Francis Preston Blair—member of an influential Montgomery County family—built an estate he named Silver Spring, for the clear waters that flowed from the ground there. The urban area that developed around the spring now has a population of more than 76,000 people. After crossing Georgia Ave., Md. 410 continues to the lively community of **Takoma Park** (11,544 pop.), where it becomes Philadelphia Ave. and then Ethan Allen Ave. A local developer, Benjamin Franklin Gilbert, laid out this village in 1883. After the turn of the century, the Seventh-Day Adventist Church moved its national headquarters here from Battle Creek, Michigan, and established a complex of institutions that includes **Columbia Union College** and the **Washington Adventist Hospital** (1907). Both border Sligo Creek off Maple Ave. The **Takoma Park Campus of Montgomery College** lies between

Chicago and Takoma Aves., near **Jessup-Blair Park** and the District of Columbia line. Established after World War II, the campus is Maryland's oldest community college, with a current enrollment of 1,052 full-time and 3,892 part-time students.

Beyond Takoma Park, Rte. 410, then in Prince George's County, again becomes East-West Hwy., crosses Sligo Creek, named after the Irish county, town, and bay, and continues into the suburban Washington communities discussed in Tour 12.

U.S. 29 leaves Washington as Georgia Ave. and becomes Colesville Rd. as it heads northeast through portions of Silver Spring. It then crosses Sligo Creek and intersects the Capital Beltway. Roughly paralleling I-95 to the Patapsco River, U.S. 29 takes the traveler closer to the countryside.

Beyond the beltway, U.S. 29 passes **Four Corners,** crosses the Northwest Branch, and then intersects New Hampshire Ave. (Md. 650) at **White Oak.** The **White Oak Library** and **Quaint Acres,** where Rachel Carson built her house, lie immediately to the north off Md. 650, which continues north to **Colesville** (18,819 pop.). The **U.S. Naval Surface Weapons Center** is located on New Hampshire Ave., immediately south of the intersection.

The **George Meany Memorial Archives** are farther south, just above the Capital Beltway. Exhibits here include Robert Berks's bronze sculpture of the labor leader, as well as photographs, posters, and other memorabilia related to the labor movement in America. Meany (1894–1980) forged the 1955 merger of the American Federation of Labor, a crafts union, and the Congress of Industrial Organizations, which organized unions by industry. The tough-talking organizer served 12 terms as president of the AFL-CIO before retiring in 1979.

After the intersection with Md. 650, U.S. 29 continues as Columbia Pike and crosses Paint Branch, where the **Martin Luther King Recreational Park** has been created as part of the Paint Branch Valley Park. The road parallels the Montgomery–Prince George's county line, which runs less than two miles to the east, and crosses the **T. Howard Duckett Reservoir** of the Patuxent River into Howard County. Duckett was a prominent Prince George's County land developer in the early part of the 20th century.

Johns Hopkins Applied Physics Laboratory

Beyond the intersection with Md. 216, Columbia Pike intersects Johns Hopkins Rd. and the entrance to the Johns Hopkins University Applied Physics Laboratory. This major research facility originated in 1942, when the U.S. government asked Johns Hopkins scientists to develop a proximity, or variable-time, fuse. The university set up a secret laboratory in Silver Spring and in the same year produced the fuse, used successfully in both the Pacific and Atlantic fronts. Under contract with the Navy, the laboratory continued its work after the war and in 1954 moved to a new setting, in Howard County. Because of its ongoing secret military contracts with the federal government, the Applied Physics Laboratory came under fire from university students and faculty during the tumultuous years of the Vietnam War; but it weathered these storms and continues to work in a variety of areas, including signal and data processing, navigation satellite systems, and heart pacemakers.

Columbia

After crossing Md. 32, U.S. 29 enters the most densely populated area of Howard County—the "new town" of Columbia (75,883 pop.). It represents the vision of James W. Rouse, an Eastern Shore native and successful mortgage banker, who started out in the 1950s as a developer of shopping malls: Mondawmin (1955) in Baltimore and Harundale (1957) in Anne Arundel County. Working through paper corporations and second parties to keep prices down, Rouse acquired more than 14,000 acres of land between Baltimore and Washington. In 1963 he announced plans to build Columbia, a new town consisting of ten "villages" clustered around a town center. Rouse set out to employ private capital to create a humane, comfortable community open to all income levels. The land would be respected and commercial development controlled. Each village would have its own character and a mixture of housing styles; houses would be built around a village center. Two more years of persuasion were necessary before the Rouse Company received the required government approvals; the first residents arrived in 1967. The **Merriweather Post Pavilion,** an outdoor concert center off the 10400 block of Little Patuxent Parkway, opened on July 4, 1967. Architect Frank Gehry contributed to the design of this and several other Columbia structures, including the Rouse Company general offices at 10275 Little Patuxent Parkway. In 1971 the **Columbia Mall** opened. By 1972, in a county that in 1940 had had a population of 17,000, the town of Columbia had 25,000 residents. Columbia has attracted offices and industries that challenge—some critics charge have defeated—Rouse's idea of carefully managed development.

Owen Brown Rd. branches left from U.S. 29 to the original portion of Columbia. A right on Cedar Ln. leads to Little Patuxent Parkway and the **Howard County General Hospital,** which the Columbia health maintenance organization founded in 1973 as a short-stay hospital. In 1997 the 230-bed hospital had on staff nearly 600 physicians in 30 some specialties and subspecialties. A right onto the parkway takes one past **Howard Community College,** the Merriweather Post Pavilion, Columbia Mall, and **Town Center** on **Lake Kittamaqundi.** The parkway then loops back to another intersection with U.S. 29.

Follow U.S. 29 north then take Old Columbia Pike to Ellicott City.

Ellicott City

Ellicott City (144' alt., 41,396 pop.), the Howard County seat, looks down upon the Patapsco River, which once ran strong and fast. The town developed because on the opposite bank the Ellicott brothers, remarkable early entrepreneurs, built their first mill.

The Ellicotts and Benjamin Banneker

Andrew Ellicott (1683–1766), a wool manufacturer and Quaker from Devonshire, arrived in Bucks County, Pennsylvania, with his son named Andrew (1708–41) in 1730. The younger Andrew eventually fell in love with a local belle, whom he married. The couple had five sons, each endowed with mechanical ability, scientific curiosity, and adventuresome spirit. Three of the brothers—Joseph

(1732–80), Andrew (1734–1809), and John (1739–95)—changed the Maryland landscape. Armed with family resources and a patrimony, they explored the Maryland and Pennsylvania hinterlands for a place to build a commercial flour mill. They recognized the enormous growth potential in Baltimore, already an expanding port, and soon settled here on the Patapsco River. Over the next couple of years, the brothers transported necessary mechanical equipment, wagons, draft horses, and other supplies by land and sea from Philadelphia. By 1774 they had constructed their first mill and were producing flour. To acquire wheat and to market their flour, the Ellicotts had to construct or help finance the necessary roads—to Elkridge, to Baltimore, to Charles Carroll's Doughoregan Manor, even to Frederick. Such enterprise brought considerable ridicule from local tobacco growers. However, when the roads were provided, Carroll converted 10,000 acres of land to wheat, and grain from German farmers in the west poured in. Ellicotts' Mills became the largest flour milling operation in the American colonies. It also put the area on the leading edge of water-power technology.

Joseph constructed Ellicotts' Upper Mill three miles upriver. The other brothers built homes and established a store. In his spare time, Joseph dabbled in clockmaking; Andrew and John also tinkered with mechanical and scientific inventions. Meanwhile a town of traders and mill workers grew up on the south bank of the river. Ellicotts' Mills became a major stopping point on the Baltimore-Frederick turnpike. When the B&O Railroad reached Ellicotts' Mills in 1830, the Ellicotts became even wealthier. Two of Joseph's sons grew up in Maryland and became noted surveyors. The commissioners of the new city of Washington hired one of his sons (another Andrew [1754–1820]) to complete L'Enfant's plan and survey for the federal district. He also surveyed the boundary line between Virginia and Pennsylvania, the western boundary of New York, and the frontier boundary between the United States and Florida. His brother Joseph (1760–1826), an agent of the Holland Land Company, laid out the city of Buffalo, New York, in 1803 and advocated construction of the Erie Canal, for which he later made corrective surveys.

The Ellicott dynasty lasted 60 years on the Patapsco, but it could not compete with the big new mills on the western prairies; the Ellicott Company went bankrupt during the Panic of 1837. Little remains of the once-flourishing mill industry along the river. The **George Ellicott residence,** a three-story stone building erected before 1790, still stands, near the river, a much altered and isolated testament to the mutability of family fortunes.

The Ellicotts are respected for their business acumen and technological daring, but many remember them best for befriending Benjamin Banneker (1731–1806), a self-educated, African American farmer who lived nearby. Sometime around 1683, Molly Welsh, an indentured servant, arrived from Wessex, in south England. After serving her indenture and acquiring her freedom, around 1690, she rented or bought some land near Cooper Branch and farmed it alone. Family tradition relates that she then bought two African slaves, including one called "Banneky," whom she freed and married around 1696. This union, proscribed by law, produced four daughters. Banneky died young, and Molly raised the children to adulthood. The oldest daughter, Mary, who would become Benjamin's mother, married his father, Robert, a freed slave from Guinea, around 1730. The family acquired more acreage.

Benjamin Banneker became known as a careful farmer, skillful at calculating, who played violin and flute. The mill-founding Ellicotts and their children became friendly with this dignified, well-dressed man and lent him books and instruments. Banneker visited Joseph Ellicott at his Upper Mill home to inspect the latter's elaborate, four-faced clock. Banneker attended the local Quaker meeting, and in 1791 he assisted Andrew Ellicott in his survey work for the new federal city of Washington.

Shortly thereafter, eager to publish an almanac he had written, Banneker sent Thomas Jefferson a manuscript copy with the suggestion that Jefferson wean himself "from the narrow prejudices" imbibed from slavery. "No body wishes more than I do," Jefferson quickly and ambiguously replied, "to see such proofs as you exhibit, that nature has given to our black brethren, talents equal to those of the other colors of men, and that the appearance of a want of them is owing merely to the degraded condition of their existence, both in Africa & America." Banneker published his almanac, and other almanacs, containing careful astronomical calculations. He continued to live alone in his one-room cabin, observe the skies at night and bees during the day, play his music, and record some of his dreams in a commonplace book.

For more information about one of the most accomplished African Americans in the early republic, visit the Benjamin Banneker Historical Park (see below).

On Main St., where Ellicott Mills Dr. meets it from the north, the Howard County Tourism Council occupies a transplanted stone building. It sits next to an 18th-century log cabin that once stood on Merryman St. and is surrounded by a free parking lot for visitors. Here one may obtain maps and directions; from this point Main St. beckons to the pedestrian.

Ellicott City, usually busy with traffic, lends itself to walking. From the tourism office, Main St. descends a steep incline, bordered by buildings of dark local granite carved from the rocky hillsides. Some structures on the south side of Main St. straddle Tiber Creek, which rushes steeply down to the Patapsco. Water power built the town but also brought it suffering. The flood of 1868, in which 42 people drowned, washed the mill, bridge, dam, and several houses away. Hurricanes Agnes (1972) and Eloise (1975) caused damage to the remaining structures. The town also experienced hard times after World War II and a major fire in 1984. After each setback, it emerged with new vitality. No longer a mill town, Ellicott City has become known for its specialty stores, restaurants, and historical attractions.

The following short walking tour begins at the foot of Main St.

The **Baltimore and Ohio Railroad Depot,** on the southwest corner, has not changed much since May 24, 1830, when the first horsecars arrived here from Baltimore over strap-iron rails. This stone building, a National Historic Landmark, contains a railroad museum with a scale model of the B&O's route to Baltimore as well as a reconstruction of the freight agent's quarters. The rounded stone wall south of the station, now part of the platform, is the foundation of a turntable. The Tom Thumb, Peter Cooper's diminutive steam locomotive, made its debut the summer of 1830 over the 13-mile distance between Baltimore and this station.

According to John H. B. Latrobe (in what may be an apocryphal tale), during the inaugural test run of the Tom Thumb, "some excited gentlemen of the party pulled out memorandum books, and when at the highest speed, which was eighteen miles an hour, wrote their names and even some connected sentences, to prove that even at that great velocity it was possible to do so." On the return to Baltimore, according to Latrobe's account, promoters staged a race between the engine and a horse at Relay. When a belt slipped on the engine, the Tom Thumb lost. Whether the race ever took place or not, the accelerated age of steam clearly had dawned.

The former **Patapsco Hotel,** constructed from local granite, stands opposite the depot. Local tradition indicates that Henry Clay appeared on the balcony one Sunday morning during a presidential campaign. A crowd gathered for a speech by the famed orator, but before he could begin a church bell sounded. "My friends and fellow citizens, the notes of yonder church bell remind me that this is a day for prayer and not for public speaking," he told them. Then he raised his hands in benediction and retired. Two doors west of the hotel is the building that housed the **Old Colonial Inn and Opera House.** This five-story structure contains a series of cellars dug from the hillside behind each of the first four stories. John Wilkes Booth is reputed to have made his theatrical debut here.

Old Columbia Pike (Md. 987) angles southwest from Main St. past **Tongue Row,** stone rowhouses built for mill workers by Mrs. Ann Tongue in the 1840s, now specialty stores. The **Ellicott Burial Ground,** site of the graves of Andrew and John Ellicott and their descendants, is also located nearby on this pike. Beyond the cemetery a private lane leads to the **Friends Meeting House,** a plain rectangular building with low gables built in 1800. Used as a hospital for wounded Union soldiers after the Battle of the Monocacy, it later became a school before conversion to a private residence.

Church Rd. makes a sharp angle to the east off Main St. to a ridge above the river. The **Old Manse** on Church Rd. served as the parsonage for the Presbyterian church. William Ellicott built **Mount Ida,** a neo-classic mansion farther up the road, in 1828. In 1831, Samuel Vaughn, a French artist, conceived and built the **Angelo Cottage** (private), a Gothic Revival castle with octagonal turrets. At the top of the hill lie the ruins of the **Patapsco Female Institute,** a large granite Greek Revival structure built on seven acres of land that the Ellicotts donated in 1829. This premier antebellum finishing school for Southern ladies opened its doors in 1837. For the 15 years prior to the war, Mrs. Almira Hart Lincoln Phelps served as headmistress, offering courses in math and science for the first time to American women. Winnie Davis, daughter of Jefferson Davis, and Robert E. Lee's daughter were pupils. The school closed in 1890, and the building subsequently became a summer retreat, a hospital, and a summer stock theater before being abandoned to ruin. In 1995, through the efforts of private volunteers, supported by Howard County and foundation funds, the remodeled building was opened again to the public. A garden park now surrounds the old institute.

Court Ave. makes a gentler turn off Main St. opposite Merryman St. to the **Howard County Courthouse,** a Greek Revival structure of local granite. Completed in 1843, it stands on "Capitoline Hill." The battered old cannon on the courthouse lawn were allegedly captured from the British by "Bachelor" John Dorsey after the Battle of Bladensburg in 1814. The **First Presbyterian Church,** located next to the courthouse, was built in 1844 and now houses the Howard County Historical Society.

To visit the opposite bank of the Patapsco and the Benjamin Banneker Historical Park, drive down Main St. and cross the river, the boundary between Howard and Baltimore Counties.

Oella

Just across the river, Oella Ave. leads north to a restored mill town founded in 1809 by the Union Manufacturing Company. A year later, the textile company christened its 865 acres Oella, allegedly after one of the first women in America to spin cotton. Two mills, a blacksmith's shop, and stone row houses for mill workers gradually emerged along the forested river bank to form a village. Despite occasional floods and fires, the company operated thousands of water-powered, mechanical spindles and produced hundreds of thousands of cotton textiles from raw cotton during the early and mid-19th century. A paper mill operated here in the 1880s. Local industry gradually declined, and Oella became an isolated, poor enclave. This situation changed in the 1980s, when the village finally was connected to municipal sewage lines and the houses restored. The **Oella Methodist Episcopal Church** at 803 Oella Ave., a wooden frame structure built in 1904, has been restored and serves as a centerpiece for the historic district.

Benjamin Banneker Historical Park

Continue on Oella Ave., which curves away from the Patapsco toward Old Frederick Rd. Turn left on Westchester Ave. to see **Mount Gilboa Chapel.** It once was the home of a historic African American congregation that erected an obelisk to honor Banneker. Remain on Oella Ave. to the **Benjamin Banneker Historical Park,** on a site adjacent to Cooper Branch. Beginning in 1985, the state, Baltimore County, and volunteers worked to develop this 130-acre field as a monument to Banneker. The site includes a reconstruction of his cabin and exhibits of more than 100 artifacts discovered in two archaeological digs on his farmsite. Although his grave has not yet been discovered, historians have documented the site's authenticity and hope to re-create its appearance in 1800. Some personal belongings, including the primitive table on which Banneker did his calculations, have been preserved and will also be exhibited.

Oella Ave. terminates at Frederick Rd. (Md. 144). Some of Banneker's descendants live in Catonsville's historic African American community, centered around Winter's Ln., which intersects Md. 144 about two miles to the east.

ELLICOTT CITY TO FREDERICK
VIA MD. 144, U.S. 40 WEST, I-70

Before 1765 only a primitive road connected the Patapsco basin and Frederick Town. Then the Ellicotts and others built the links that became the Frederick Turnpike. The railroad chose the same route—Baltimore to Ellicott City to Frederick. The turnpike, eventually macadam-surfaced, served horsedrawn wagons and coaches well, and people willingly paid the tolls (as late as the turn of the century, 25 percent of Maryland's main roads were toll roads). The turnpike later provided much of the bed for U.S. 40, which after 1926 formed part of the national roads system. Straightened for the sake of the automobile and truck, U.S. 40 bypassed Catonsville and Ellicott City. Today the limited-access expressway I-70, completed to Frederick in 1956, has cut a new path, north of the old pike, which the state designates as Md. 144.

To follow this old route, simply go west on Main St., which becomes Frederick Rd., crosses beneath U.S. 29, and continues west through a mixture of suburban development and rural countryside. The assembly created Howard County, named for John Eager Howard, from Anne Arundel County in 1851, and in so doing recognized growth at the time around Ellicott City and westward. In 1940, the county had a total population of 17,175 people, only 14.2 percent of them "urban." Fifty years later, the county was 84 percent urban and had a population of 187,328. In the decade between 1980 and 1990 the county grew 58 percent, more than four times the rate for Maryland as a whole (13.4 percent). About 110,000 of the county residents commute to work, and 81 percent of these drive without passengers. Almost 72 percent of the county's house-holds have two or more cars. The median household income in 1990 was more than $54,000, with 47 percent claiming jobs in executive, manage-rial, or professional fields (a quarter of these residents worked for gov-ernment). More than half the people living in the county in 1990 had moved to their current residence within the last five years.

Such statistics illuminate what the traveler sees: an automobile cul-ture of commuters living in suburban housing on disappearing rural farm-land. Much of this growth can be attributed to the town of Columbia, but it has its counterparts throughout Central Maryland.

St. John's Episcopal Church, beyond the intersection with U.S. 29, emerges from this expansive development as a reminder of the rural past. Originally a chapel belonging to Queen Caroline Parish, created in 1728, St. John's dates from 1822.

Md. 144 crosses the Little Patuxent River and intersects Centennial Ln. About a mile south and a short distance west on Burnside Rd. stands **Burleigh Manor** (private), a yellow brick house built around 1805 by Col. Rezin Hammond. Hammond, a Revolutionary War leader, partici-pated in the burning of the *Peggy Stewart* at Annapolis in 1774. He and his neighbor, Charles Carroll of Carrollton were frequent political oppo-nents during the revolutionary period. Carroll's father, Charles Carroll of Annapolis, considered Hammond "a noisy, obstinate fool" whose family could not be trusted. The historical record does not indicate what Ham-mond thought of the Carrolls. The house remained in the Hammond family for almost 150 years.

At Pine Orchard Md. 144 briefly joins then branches away from U.S. 40. At Manor Ln. an old Gothic Revival house, formerly a gatehouse, marks the entrance to **Doughoregan Manor** (private). This property remains a working farm in the possession of Carroll descendants, who discourage visits and request that tourists view the manor from a vantage point on Folly Quarter Rd.—on the left of Md. 144 about two-fifths of a mile beyond Manor Ln.

Charles Carroll of Carrollton

Charles Carroll of Carrollton (1737–1832), Maryland patriot and signer of the Declaration of In-dependence, made his home at Doughoregan Manor. Carroll was the only Catholic to sign the Dec-laration, one of the richest men to do so, and the longest-lived of them all.

Carrollton's grandfather, Charles Carroll the Settler, began this branch of the famous Maryland family when he arrived in Maryland from Ireland in 1688 to serve as land agent and attorney general for Lord Baltimore. In that capacity, he acquired thousands of desirable acres, a holding that his son, Charles Carroll of Annapolis, expanded and used as the basis for investments in early industry (*Doughoregan* is Gaelic for "king's gift"). The third Carroll in this line, Charles Carroll of Carrollton, his father's only son, was raised to manage the family's fortunes in a shifting, sometimes hostile, Protestant world. In 1748, when he was only 12 years old, the lad was sent, along with his 14-year-old cousin John, to St. Omer's, an English Catholic refugee college in French Flanders. There he began extensive studies of law, theology, philosophy (Rousseau, Montesquieu, Voltaire), and accounting which helped him become the most successful businessman-politician in the new United States. His cousin John became a priest and the first Catholic bishop and archbishop in the United States.

Charles lived in France and later in England throughout his early manhood, exchanging letters with his father on economic and political affairs. (America would not see such a shrewd example of practical intellect shared within a family until another rich, Irish-Catholic family named Kennedy in the 20th century.) Charles established a political base in the colony in 1773 in a series of letters signed "First Citizen," in which he debated with Daniel Dulany, "Antilon," in the pages of the *Maryland Gazette.* Carroll, defending a popular view, spoke against taxes and fees by prerogative, which he compared to "an act of tyranny which in a land of freedom cannot, must not, be endured." At first apprehensive about the colonies' abilities to sustain any united opposition to Great Britain, Carroll later helped lead Maryland's effort to support a vote for independence. Although not present when the Continental Congress took the vote on July 4, he was among the Marylanders who later signed the parchment copy now on display at the National Archives in Washington. After the Revolution, Carroll served in the first Congress as a senator from Maryland.

Physically timid but intellectually strong and calculating, Charles Carroll of Carrollton supported the Ellicotts with their mills and was a member of the C&O Canal Company and a director of the B&O Railroad. When he turned the first spade of earth at the dedication of the new B&O Railroad at Mount Clare, on July 4, 1828, Carroll allegedly remarked that this act ranked second only to his 1776 signing and perhaps was even more important. When he died in 1832, he was reputedly the wealthiest man in the United States. Carroll spent the last years of his life in a Baltimore town house instead of this rural manor, but he was buried in the chapel here. A subsequent occupant of the manor, John Lee Carroll, was governor of Maryland from 1876 to 1880.

The two-story manor house, built between 1735 and 1745, extends 300 feet with its two ell-shaped wings. The south ell contains servants' quarters, and the north is a richly furnished Catholic chapel named for St. Mary, reflective of the era in Maryland history (1689–1776) when Catholics were prohibited from worshiping in public. The original estate consisted of more than 13,000 acres and housed almost 1,000 slaves to work its fields.

Charles Carroll of Carrollton's home at Doughoregan Manor, chapel to the right, 1930s

North of Md. 144, a short distance east of Folly Quarter Rd. (named for an early tract), Turf Valley Rd. leads to a 1,080-acre resort and conference center that dates from 1988 and has its origins in a country club of 1959 vintage. South and east of the center one finds a county park that

A storehouse at
Waverly which the
WPA identified as
having served as a
slave jail

preserves both banks of the Little Patuxent River for a length of about one and one-half miles.

South of Md. 144, Folly Quarter Rd. travels through the **University of Maryland Central Farm** and runs into Sheppard Ln., which leads to **Walnut Grove** (private). This 2½-story stone house, visible on a knoll some distance away from the road, was built about 1740. Folly Quarter Rd. branches west at Sheppard Ln. to a road on the right leading to the **Novitiate of the Franciscan Fathers,** a large marble structure built in 1930 and patterned after the Convent of St. Francis, at Assisi, Italy. The **Folly Quarter Mansion,** built in 1832 with matching front and rear porticoes, now serves as a recreation hall. Charles Carroll of Carrollton planned this house for his granddaughter. Long neglected, it was bought by Van Lear Black (1875–1930), who in 1914 became chairman of the board of the A. S. Abell Company, publishers of the *Sunpapers*, and proceeded to reorganize that enterprise. Black, an avid aviator and energetic businessman, staged rodeos and elaborate entertainments here for prominent guests. He disappeared from his yacht off the New Jersey coast, and—despite special efforts on the part of his friend Franklin D. Roosevelt, then governor of New York—his body was never recovered. The entrance to **Glenelg Manor,** location of the **Glenelg Country School,** is less than two miles farther down Folly Quarter Rd.

About half a mile west of its intersection with Folly Quarter Rd., Md. 144 meets Marriottsville Rd., a right turn on which takes the traveler over I-70 to **Waverly Historic Site** (on the right). This property first belonged to Daniel Carroll of Upper Marlboro, then to Dorseys of local prominence, then, after 1786, to John Eager Howard of revolutionary fame. Howard gave the house (1756–64) to his son George in 1811, on the occasion of George's marriage to Prudence Gough Ridgely, who had grown up at Hampton in Baltimore County. The couple named the site Waverly because of their fondness for Sir Walter Scott's historical romance of that title (1814). George Howard served as state governor between 1831 and 1833. After his death the property passed out of family hands. A local real estate firm donated the mansion and 3.4 acres to the Society for the

Preservation of Maryland Antiquities in 1975. Restoration began in 1979, and ten years later Howard County acquired the site for its historical importance and for use as a place for meetings and receptions.

Despite rapid urbanization, Howard County along Md. 144 retains some rural character. Here one ascends rolling hills to Parr's Ridge—an elevation that stretches along a northeast-southwest axis from southern Pennsylvania and northern Carroll County across Howard and into Montgomery County to the Potomac River. The ridge has an average height of 800–900 feet and forms a divide for streams, which to the east flow directly into Chesapeake Bay and to the west empty into the Potomac. Parr's Ridge also divides the geologic province known as the Piedmont into eastern and western divisions. The former includes most of Central Maryland, from the ridge to the fall line, and is marked by a diverse typography with swift-flowing streams. The western division consists primarily of the Great Frederick Valley, drained by the Monocacy River and its tributaries. Md. 144 ascends a route between the Patapsco and Patuxent Rivers, which rise along Parr's Ridge near Mt. Airy.

Md. 144 passes Triadelphia Rd., **West Friendship, West Friendship Park** (on the left), and the **Howard County Fairgrounds** (to the right) on its way to **Cooksville** and **Lisbon**. In June 1863, Gen. J.E.B. Stuart and 5,000 of his troopers passed through this area on a ride across Maryland in advance of Lee's infantry. They crossed the Potomac on the 28th and reached Rockville the same day, capturing 125 wagons on the road between Washington and Frederick. On the 29th, they scattered Maryland militia at Cooksville and destroyed the railroad tracks at nearby **Hood's Mill** before continuing to Westminster.

Side Trip down Md. 97

From Cooksville, Md. 97 south passes through pleasant rural countryside and a large expanse of the **Patuxent River State Park.** To reach the park turn right on Jennings Chapel Rd. at Roxbury Mills and then left on Howard Chapel Rd. Cattail Creek feeds into the **Triadelphia Reservoir** to the east, a water source for the Washington area. Three brothers who had married daughters from the same family founded a mill town on the Patuxent River here in 1809, naming it Triadelphia (city of three). The town grew into a commercial center of 300–400 people during the 19th century. In 1943, when the Washington Suburban Sanitary Commission constructed **Brighton Dam** to form the reservoir, the town, condemned and evacuated, was submerged. To reach an overlook, turn left on Triadelphia Lake Rd. after crossing the river.

After intersecting Md. 650, Md. 97 crosses Hawlings River, which flows through **Rachel Carson Park** to the west and **Hawlings River Park** to the east.

Farther south, Md. 97 passes through **Brookeville** (120 pop.), one of the county's oldest settlements. Richard Thomas established the town here in 1794 on land inherited by his wife Deborah Brooke. President James Madison stayed overnight in this Quaker community on August 26, 1814, after fleeing the British invaders of Washington. Caleb Bentley and his wife entertained the president and other refugees in their home, built in 1779. The next day, Madison and James Monroe, his secretary of state, rode back to Washington, which lay smoldering from fires the British had set the night of August 24.

Just south of Brookeville, Md. 97 intersects Md. 108 at **Olney,** site of the official "State Summer Theater of Maryland." Olney Theater, east on Md. 108 (Sandy Spring Rd.), was founded in 1954 by the Rev. Gilbert V. Hartke, head of the drama department at the Catholic University of America in Washington. By presenting professional actors in serious drama and comedies from the international repertoire, the theater immediately distinguished itself. Many staff members and performers have graduated from the Olney program to become active in New York and elsewhere. Under the direction of James D. Waring, all the plays by Irishman Hugh Leonard, including "Da," made their American premiers at the Olney Theater.

Montgomery General Hospital also lies off Md. 108 to the east, and less than three miles farther one reaches **Sandy Spring,** a community settled by Quakers from Maryland, Pennsylvania, and Virginia in the 18th century. A log meeting house was constructed here in 1817, and Friends have gathered in Sandy Spring ever since.

Md. 97 continues to Norbeck and Wheaton.

Mount Airy

Most of the small towns along Md. 144 developed along the turnpike that linked Baltimore to Frederick and Cumberland, where the National Road began. The B&O Railroad followed the stage route as far as Mount Airy (850' alt.) on Parr's Ridge, then began a gradual descent just east of New Market through the Monocacy Valley to the Potomac River at Point of Rocks. The stage road continued west to Frederick.

Located at the intersection of Md. 144 and I-70, Mount Airy occupies the convergence of four counties—Howard, Frederick, Montgomery, and Carroll; about 1,500 of its 3,700 residents live in Carroll County, the others in Frederick County. The town lies near the headwaters of two major rivers, the Patapsco at **Parr's Spring** (a farm pond south of nearby **Ridgeville**) and the Patuxent near the same area in Frederick County.

Housing development, Frederick County, 1997

When the B&O Railroad reached Frederick from Ellicott City in the early 1830s, Mount Airy developed as a station-stop business center. An Irish railroad worker supposedly remarked that the weather at this location on the summit of Parr's Ridge was "airish," so the place acquired a name. Company K of a New Jersey regiment guarded the small railroad town during the Civil War, and in the 1890s Mount Airy briefly became a roaring boomtown while construction workers built a tunnel for the railroad, to avoid the climb up the ridge. After the tunnel's completion, the saloons closed and the temporary jail shut down. An era quietly ended on December 31, 1949, when the B&O made its last passenger run between Baltimore and Point of Rocks via Mount Airy.

New Market

From Mount Airy the traveler continues westward on Md. 144, here called the Old National Pike, to New Market (328 pop.), which bills itself as "the antiques capital of Maryland." New Market was established as a stage stop in 1793 and now consists of a long Main Street lined by more than 35 antique shops, restaurants, and inns. The town has restricted commercial development to antique stores and has achieved listing on the National Register of Historic Places. Traffic on nearby I-70 moves at high speeds, but the village retains the pace and flavor of the 19th century.

Md. 144 continues west and then merges briefly with I-70, which crosses the Monocacy River outside Frederick. As the expressway crosses the river, the traveler can catch a glimpse, on the right, of the **Jug Bridge,** a Frederick County landmark. The stone bridge was constructed in 1807 for the turnpike company that built the Frederick road. The bridge received its name from the 40-ton stone jug placed at the eastern end by a trowel master who is alleged to have sealed a demijohn of whiskey inside it. When U.S. 40 was rerouted over a new bridge in 1942, the jug remained at its location for 22 years, then was moved to its present site at the exit of Patrick St. from U.S. 40.

Md. 144 enters Frederick as E. Patrick St. and intersects Md. 355, the old road to Washington.

FREDERICK TO BETHESDA VIA MD. 355 AND I-270

Md. 355, known in Frederick County as the Urbana Pike and in Montgomery County as Frederick Rd., roughly follows an Indian path, later a colonial road, which General Braddock used in 1755. This ancient route parallels I-270, a high-speed limited-access highway dedicated in 1957. The two roads form a corridor between Frederick and Washington, D.C., for residential and business commuters. Aerospace, computer, health, nuclear, and other high-tech industries—many of them allied to the federal government—have located along this path. So have suburban developments.

At the time Montgomery County was created from Frederick County in 1776, no one could have imagined that a federal district along the Potomac would expand to fill the 37-mile distance between the cities of Frederick and Washington. For about 175 years, both Frederick and Montgomery Counties remained rural, places of small towns, sturdy family farms, and gentlemen-farmers. After World War II, Montgomery's population quickly increased as affluent families moved northwest of Washington. In subsequent years, despite moratoriums on further extension of sewer lines and other local-government efforts to control growth, the expansion has continued. Frederick County changed from 38.6 percent urban in 1980 to 57.7 percent urban in 1990, with most of the transformation occurring along this corridor. Ninety percent of the county's 80,850 workers commute to work in their cars, most of them alone.

As the traveler moves into Montgomery County and closer to Washington, traffic becomes denser. The commercial stores, shopping centers, and residences reflect the county's high per capita income. Thanks to the foresight of the Maryland–National Capital Park and Planning Commission (established in 1927), the effects of suburban expansion have been mitigated by the presence of more than 28,000 acres of county parks built along stream valleys, one of the largest local systems in the United States.

Montgomery County in the early 1990s had the largest population (816,999) of any political subdivision in Maryland, followed by Prince George's (773,810) and Baltimore (717,859) Counties, then Baltimore City (675,401). Almost 50 percent of the residents had college degrees and classify themselves as executives, managers, or professionals. Asians and Hispanics outnumber African Americans in the county; more than 20 percent of the entire population spoke a language other than English, reflecting a growing, Spanish-speaking minority from throughout Latin America.

Md. 355 leaves the city of Frederick as S. Market St. and within a mile crosses the Monocacy River at the site of the **Monocacy National Battlefield,** which opened to the public as a national park in 1991. The **Visitor's Center** has been created in **Gambrill's Mill,** one of two Araby Flour Mills established at this location in 1830. Monuments along Md. 355 commemorate the units that fought here. The National Park Service, supported by nonprofit community organizations, plans to add trails and interpretive facilities to the site.

The Battle of the Monocacy

This relatively unknown but strategically important battle in 1864 represented the last serious Confederate advance north of the Potomac and probably saved Washington from an embarrassing and diplomatically damaging capture. In June of that year, Gen. Robert E. Lee ordered Gen. Jubal Early and 25,000 Confederates to defeat Union forces in the Great Valley of Virginia and then to cross the Potomac and threaten Washington. Lee hoped this maneuver would ease pressure on his own army, pinned down at Petersburg, Virginia. Early succeeded in the Shenandoah Valley and seized the moment. His troops crossed the Potomac near Sharpsburg and moved with force into the Maryland countryside for the third time in the war.

Maj. Gen. Lew Wallace, commander of the Middle Military District headquartered in Baltimore, uneasily pondered the meaning of the Confederate military movements. Like Early, he was a lawyer and veteran of the Mexican War who would later write books. Wallace became famous as the author of *Ben Hur: A Tale of the Christ* (1880); Early wrote memoirs of the war and historical essays. Wallace commanded fewer than 3,000 green troops, "100-day men" who had never seen combat. He did not know whether the Confederates were headed toward Baltimore or Washington; his superiors knew even less. So on his own initiative, Wallace notified Grant of the danger, hastily assembled a force of about 5,800 men (veteran troops under Gen. James B. Ricketts joined him at the last minute), and took up a position at Frederick Junction, where the B&O Railroad tracks crossed the Monocacy River outside Frederick.

General Early's forces entered Frederick on Saturday, July 9 and extracted ransom money. Cavalry units under Maryland Confederates Bradley T. Johnson and Harry C. Gilmor set off to raid the countryside and free the 14,000 prisoners at Point Lookout, in St. Mary's County. That same day the two armies clashed at the Monocacy River. Union forces, outnumbered three to one, put up stiff resistance and then retreated to Baltimore, leaving over 1,600 dead, wounded, and captured. Although the Confederates were victorious, 1,300 of them were killed or wounded and they lost a day's march. By the time Early came within sight of Fort Stevens in Washington on Monday, July 11, his own troops were exhausted and reinforcements had arrived to strengthen Union defenses. Early and his men probed Fort Stevens the next day, taking pot shots at the tall figure of Abraham Lincoln—the only U.S. president to expose himself to such fire—and then retreated to Virginia across White's Ferry.

A few months later, General Early was decisively defeated in Virginia by Gen. Philip Sheridan, relieved of duty by Robert E. Lee, and fled to Mexico. He later returned to Virginia and practiced law in Lynchburg. Lew Wallace resigned from the army in 1865, served as governor of New Mexico from 1878 to 1881, then minister to Turkey 1881–85. He died a rich and successful novelist in his native Indiana.

Just beyond the bridge, Araby Rd. turns off Md. 355 to Baker Valley Rd., where the **Thomas House** (private) is visible from the road. This 2¹/₂-story brick residence was constructed about 1760 by James Marshall. The Thomas family and their neighbors took refuge in the cellar during exchanges of cannon fire at the nearby battle along the Monocacy. Less than a month later, on August 5, 1864, Generals Grant, Hunter, and Sheridan met here to plan the Virginia campaign against Jubal Early.

Md. 355 goes through the village of **Urbana,** paralleling I-270 on the west. Also to the west, the Monocacy River flows south toward the Potomac, passing near **Lily Pons** and Sugar Loaf Mountain. The road crosses into Montgomery County near **Hyattstown** (450' alt.), founded in 1809 by Jesse Hyatt. Nearby quarries supplied roofing slate for the first Capitol in Washington.

At Hyattstown, the road crosses **Little Bennett Creek,** which flows through a regional park named for it. The road then ascends the park's western boundary to an intersection with Md. 121 at **Clarksburg** (700' alt.), thought to be the site of an early Indian trading post. A stone marks the **site of Dowden's Ordinary,** a 17-room log tavern built by Michael Dowden in 1754. Maryland troops sent to assist General Braddock camped here in 1755. The tavern was razed in 1920.

Frederick Rd. diverges slightly from its parallel route with I-270 and crosses Little Seneca Creek, a Potomac tributary that rises near **Cedar Grove** to the north and flows through **Black Hill Regional Park** and Little Seneca Lake before joining Great Seneca Creek near **Dawsonville.** The Seneca name probably derives from the Iroquoian tribe in New York and upper Pennsylvania, which occasionally fought the Susquehannocks in this Piedmont hunting territory during the 17th century.

Md. 355 intersects Md. 27, which travels north to **Damascus.** Md. 118 crosses the road further south and travels southwest past the Germantown branch of **Montgomery College** (756 full-time and 3,233 part-time students) to a major interchange with I-270. Md. 118 continues through the old and new communities of **Germantown** and a portion of the Seneca Creek State Park. Germantown has developed into a significant scientific research center with the presence of the U.S. Department of Energy and Fairchild Space and Defense, which produces spacecraft and communications equipment.

Just before it enters the city of Gaithersburg, Md. 355 crosses Great Seneca Creek, which rises near Damascus and flows the width of Montgomery County to the Potomac River. The state first acquired land along the creek in 1951 and has since expanded **Seneca Creek State Park** along the creekbank to 6,102 acres, including a 90-acre lake. Most of the park lies west of I-270 and includes a portion of the Potomac River bank. In the expanded city of Gaithersburg, the highway passes the **Forest Oak Cemetery** and Montgomery Village Ave., which turns northeast to a planned community of the same name. Kettler Brothers, a Washington development company, started this satellite city—similar to Columbia, Maryland, and Reston, Virginia—in 1967.

Quince Orchard Rd. branches south to I-270 and the **National Institute of Standards and Technology,** located in Gaithersburg since 1960. Earlier the National Bureau of Standards, this internationally known agency was renamed in 1988 with the added mission of assisting industry in the development of technology and the commercialization of products based on new scientific discoveries. The institute also insures a consistent system of physical measurements for national and international use. A public museum in its library features instruments from the past as well as exhibits on current research. Industrial parks with businesses specializing in computers, communications, and engineering have developed around this federal complex.

Clopper Rd. (Md. 117) branches west from Quince Orchard Rd. at this location and crosses Seneca Creek State Park to Old Germantown. Thousands of peonies bloom along this road in late May. The large publishing operation of the National Geographic Society is located farther south on Quince Orchard Rd. at the intersection of Darnestown Rd. (Md. 28).

Md. 355 then intersects Chestnut Ave., which leads to the **Montgomery County Fairgrounds.** The fair, an annual event, has been held in Gaithersburg every August since 1949.

Gaithersburg

Gaithersburg (512' alt., 39,524 pop.) is now Maryland's fourth largest incorporated place. As late as 1957, the town was a rural milling and trading center with about 2,000 people. By the early 1970s Washington's suburban expansion had reached this rural crossroads and transformed it into an urban service and business center. The city celebrated its centennial in 1978, and local officials have used federal community development block grants to create parks and restore old structures in a visual celebration of the city's past.

In 1802, Benjamin Gaither built a house near the junction of what are now Md. 355 and Md. 124, on farmland that was part of the Deer Park tract surveyed in 1722. The settlement that grew around Gaither's house was known briefly as "Forest Oak," because of the enormous oak trees in the vicinity; but after the B&O Railroad arrived in 1873, the locale became known as Gaithersburg.

Md. 355, called Frederick Ave. at this point, bridges the railroad tracks and intersects DeSellum Ave., which leads to the **Gaithersburg Latitude Observatory.** In 1900, Gaithersburg was selected, along with locations in Ohio, California, Japan, Turkey, and Italy that were also at 39°8' north latitude, as sites for observatories from which to study the wobble of the earth on its axis, which can be measured by the changes in the relationship between points of latitude on the earth and fixed stars. International navigators and mapmakers needed such information to keep their measurements consistent. The Gaithersburg and Ohio locations were temporarily discontinued in 1914 and 1915, and a Russian station replaced the one in Turkey. The Gaithersburg Station and Observatory reopened in 1932 in a small, turn-of-the-century building on this narrow avenue. Every night—despite world wars, natural disasters, and other calamities—the five stations, spaced evenly throughout the Northern Hemisphere, used the same equipment to measure 18 pairs of stars. More sophisticated instruments replaced the observatory in 1982, and it was named a National Historic Landmark. In 1987 the federal government deeded it to the city, which hopes one day to develop a science center around the historic structure.

Summit Ave., located off Md. 355 just beyond DeSellum Ave., leads through "Olde Towne," the city's turn-of-the-century center. Turn left to **City Hall,** at 31 S. Summit Ave., formerly a private residence, purchased by the city in 1958. Built in 1895, the mansion house once stood amid the "world's largest peony gardens." Edward P. Schwartz, a Washington real estate broker, acquired the property in 1913 and began a garden that eventually included 410 varieties of peonies from throughout the world. He shipped buds throughout the East Coast from this location, and his annual display attracted national attention, including regular visits from President Woodrow Wilson. Mr. Schwartz's family sold the house in 1941 and moved approximately 40,000 peonies to the property that was later acquired for Seneca State Park. The peony became the official city flower in 1989, and peonies are sold during Old Town Days, an annual September festival.

Continue on Summit Ave. to the former B&O railroad station and freight house at 5 S. Summit Ave., restored in 1988. Commuters still use the station, and the National Historic Railway Society uses the freight office for meeting and exhibit space. A static display of rolling stock includes a steam locomotive and tender, kitchen car, post office car, and caboose.

Beyond its intersection with Summit Ave., Md. 355 passes the **Summit Hill Farm Park,** at 502 Frederick Ave. The city acquired the last 57 acres of this farm in 1982 and has developed the property as a park and recreation center. James and Catherine (Fulks) DeSellum built their estate at this location, beginning in 1806 with the purchase of one acre in Log Town, an 18th-century settlement along the road which predated Gaither's arrival in the area. By 1857, their children had created Summit Hill, a 251-acre property with a mansion. The log storehouse next to it, a remnant of Log Town, is the oldest structure in Gaithersburg. Portions of the farm were gradually sold, leased, or donated as the city became less rural. During the late 1940s and early 1950s, Summit Hill sold Zoysia grass and became one of the first scientific turf farms in the United States.

As the highway leaves Gaithersburg, it passes the **Casey Community Center,** located at 810 S. Frederick Ave. in a former dairy barn

(1936). Eugene B. Casey donated the barn and six acres to the city in 1970; it has been transformed into a multipurpose center and visible reminder of Gaithersburg's agricultural heritage.

Md. 355 continues through a metropolitan area that merges almost indistinguishably into the community of Rockville.

Rockville

Rockville (421' alt., 44,835 pop.) has been the Montgomery County seat since 1777. In the 18th century, Charles Hungerford operated a tavern somewhere near the intersection of Washington St. and Montgomery Ave. in downtown Rockville. When a group of citizens met here on June 11, 1774, to protest the British presence in Boston, they resolved to end trade with the mother country. This spirit led to the formation of Montgomery County in 1776, and the following year, local patriots selected "Hungerford's" as their temporary county meeting place. County officers met at the tavern and later in a house donated by Thomas O. Williams that was later improved to function as a courthouse. Williams laid out lots in 1784 for a town around the courthouse, to be called Williamsburg. Boundary disputes led to a new survey in 1803, at which time the town was named Rockville, after nearby Rock Creek.

Only a few structures testify to Rockville's antebellum period. During the Civil War, in search of horses, Confederate raiders frequently came through, and in 1864 Jubal Early's army marched up and down Frederick Rd. through Rockville during an unsuccessful attack on Washington. Postwar farmers came to Rockville for their supplies, to attend court sessions, and later to retire.

The town was the logical place for the county's first high school, now called **Richard Montgomery High School,** in 1892. Pupils from Silver Spring and Dickerson journeyed to the crowded school on the railroad. Reflecting the county's commitment to public education (and its considerable resources), other high schools rapidly followed after the turn of the century, among them Gaithersburg (1904), Darnestown (1907), Brookeville (1909), Poolesville/Damascus (1911), Chevy Chase (1913), Germantown (1917), Takoma/Silver Spring (1924), Bethesda/Chevy Chase (1925), Montgomery Blair (1935), and Kensington (1938).

In 1940 a village of 2,000, Rockville in 1998 was the second largest municipality in Maryland. Comparable to Towson, outside Baltimore, Rockville has expanded on an even richer, larger scale into a commercial office and business center for metropolitan Washington. These suburban centers have generated suburbs and commuters of their own. The federal Food and Drug Administration and Health Services Center are both located here. The Metro, Washington's subway system, reached Rockville during the 1980s, tying the city even more firmly to the District of Columbia.

As Md. 355 enters Rockville, the road passes the Rockville campus of **Montgomery College,** established here in 1965. With 4,776 full-time and 10,222 part-time students, this branch is three times larger than the original campus in Takoma Park, which was founded in 1945 as the first junior college in the nation.

Known at this point as Hungerford Dr., Md. 355 passes through the center of Rockville. N. Washington St. angles right from the highway to Montgomery Ave. The limestone **Montgomery County Courthouse,** built in 1931, is located at the intersection. The nearby **Old Courthouse** (1891)—with its bronze monument to the Confederate soldier—has been preserved and is used by the county.

The **Beall-Dawson House,** 103 W. Montgomery Ave., was built around 1815 by Upton Beall, one of the county court's first clerks and a member of a prominent local family. Only the front and street sides of the two-story, brick Federal-style house are laid in Flemish bond, seemingly giving substance to the Beall family legend that building materials were stolen by American militia fleeing through Rockville after the British burned Washington in 1814. (Actually, houses commonly sported more extravagant brick bonds on walls that were in public view and a cheaper surface for unseen sides.) After the Civil War, Margaret Beall, one of three unmarried daughters, invited her cousin Amelia to live with her. Amelia married John Dawson, and the house remained in their family until 1946. The **Montgomery County Historical Society** has its headquarters in the restored mansion and maintains a library here. **Doctor's Museum,** once the office of Dr. Edward E. Stonestreet, is located on the grounds. Photographs, medical instruments, and other paraphernalia illustrate the practice of a country doctor in the Rockville area from 1852 to 1903.

The **West Montgomery Avenue Historic District** features more than 100 buildings that reflect Rockville's Victorian heritage. Retired farmers, business proprietors, and professional land developers built residences along the street from 1880 to 1900.

Vinson St. intersects S. Montgomery and leads to **City Hall,** where William Woodward created a mural depicting Rockville's traditional Memorial Day parade. On the southern exterior wall of 232 N. Washington St., a 3,600-square-foot mural designed by Gerardo Gomez Morena depicts the modern city from an abstract perspective. A panoramic 15' x 115' mural illustrating a polo match decorates the **Rockville Metro Center** at 250 Hungerford Dr.

Side Trip on Norbeck, Layhill, and Veirs Mill Rds.

Md. 355 (from here south known as Rockville Pike) meets Md. 586 (Veirs Mill Rd.) close to the heart of Rockville. **St. Mary's Roman Catholic Church,** a modern (1967) structure with eight stained-glass windows set into dramatic arches, stands here. The old brick parish church, now **Our Lady's Chapel,** built in 1817, stands next to it. The remains of **F. Scott Fitzgerald** and his wife Zelda were moved to the adjacent cemetery in 1975, joining his father Edward and other forebears in the family plot. The **B&O Railroad Station,** built in 1873 for commuters, is located behind the cemetery on Stonestreet Ave.

Veirs Mill Rd. angles southeast and soon crosses Norbeck Rd. (Md. 28), which branches northeast through several stream valleys. On its way out of the city, Norbeck Rd. passes the **Rockville Civic Center** (turn onto Baltimore Rd. from Norbeck Rd. and enter this complex at Edmonston Dr.). This 100-acre municipal park contains formal gardens, the **Municipal Art Gallery, F. Scott Fitzgerald Theatre,** and **The Mansion,** a 30-room residence (built around 1812) that serves as a community meeting place.

Norbeck Rd. continues to **Rock Creek Regional Park,** part of an extensive stream-valley park that begins near the creek's headwaters at

Laytonsville and extends the length of Montgomery County into Washington.

Continue east on Norbeck Rd. across Georgia Ave. to Layhill Rd. (Md. 182). Turn south (right) and look for Bonifant Rd., where the visitor will find the **National Capital Trolley Museum** (No. 1313). The last electric streetcar ran in Washington on January 28, 1962. A. E. Savage, then a Washington Transit Company vice president, hid a few cars in the Navy Yard Car House to prevent their destruction for scrap. His six rescued cars created the nucleus for this museum, which also features cars from Pennsylvania, New York, Germany, and Austria. The **Visitor's Center** features exhibits and educational materials; rides are offered on a few of the cars on weekends.

Bonifant Rd. travels east from Layhill Rd. to the **Northwest Branch Regional Park,** a park that follows this branch of the upper Anacostia all the way to its intersection with the Northeast Branch near Bladensburg.

Follow Layhill Rd. south to Georgia Ave., a left on which soon leads to Randolph Rd. East of Randolph Rd., Glenallen Ave. branches off to **Brookside Gardens,** 50 acres within **Wheaton Regional Park,** an offshoot of the park system following the Northwest Branch. The gardens include a variety of native and tropical plants in conservatories and outdoor gardens. The nearby **Nature Center** contains guides to the park's numerous trails, many of them accessible by wheelchair. The park also features a wide variety of recreational options for all ages, including an equestrian center, ice skating rink, amphitheater, miniature railroad, carousel, and athletic fields.

Follow Georgia Ave. south to **Wheaton** (53,720 pop.). Formerly known as Mitchell's Crossroads, this community lay on Jubal Early's line of march to Washington in 1864. After the repulse of the Confederates at nearby Fort Stevens (inside the District), Unionist citizens renamed the town after the fort's commander, Gen. Frank Wheaton.

From downtown Wheaton, Veirs Mill Rd. returns one to Rockville and Md. 355, cutting across a densely populated suburban landscape that dates to the end of World War II. Samuel Veir operated a gristmill along the creek in this vicinity. As in Baltimore County, many of the streams in Montgomery County rise above the fall line. In the 18th and 19th centuries, they flowed with enough strength to power a number of mills, now remembered only in place names. With the exception of the Rock Creek Valley southwest of the road, the only undeveloped land along Veirs Mill Rd. now is a strip along Turkey Branch, recently acquired by the state for development as the **Matthew Henson State Park.**

Veirs Mill Village lies west of the intersection of Veirs Mill Rd. and Randolph Rd. A developer constructed more than 1,100 identical Cape Cod bungalows here in 1947–48, to meet the strong postwar demand for affordable, single-family housing. A prototype of smaller developments to come, the "village" is now surrounded by a wide assortment of variously named "forests," "estates," "heights," "knolls," "manors," "woods," "hills," and "groves."

For a shortcut back to Md. 355, take Randolph Rd. west to the Rockville Pike and turn left.

Garrett Park

South of Rockville, Md. 355 passes Garrett Park (884 pop.), planned in 1866 as an English-style village to sit along the B&O railroad tracks. The developer, Henry W. Copp, named the town after John Work Garrett, president of the railroad, and the streets after places in Sir Walter Scott's novels. In the 1920s, another developer advertised three styles of bungalows for sale here, complete with Atwater Kent radios. For an additional sum, the buyer could get a garage with a new Chevrolet. About 50 of these "Chevy Houses" were sold. Since that time, the town—with its mixture of Victorian houses and Flapper Age cottages—has attracted writers, scientists, and other individualistic souls. Garrett Park has successfully registered as a historic district, declared itself a nuclear-free zone, and developed its own arboretum.

At the junction of Md. 547 (Strathmore Ave.), the Rockville Pike passes **Georgetown Preparatory School,** which Bishop John Carroll established in Georgetown in 1789. Still employing the Jesuits' system of core studies, known as the *ratio studiorum,* the school opened at this suburban site in September 1919. Among its graduates are the actor John Barrymore and U.S. senator Christopher Dodd.

To view the graveyard of John Carroll's family, take Strathmore Rd. from Md. 355, follow it through Garrett Park and across Rock Creek. (Beach Dr., once accessible by automobile, is now primarily a walker's and biker's trail, winding along the stream valley as it loops to the east.) Continue past Beach Dr. on Md. 547 into **Kensington** (1,713 pop.), a subdivision created from farmland in 1890 and named after the London suburb. Make a left on Connecticut Ave. (Md. 185) and a right onto Metropolitan Ave. (Md. 192), which makes an immediate sharp right as Capitol View Ave. The narrow street travels across a hilly, heavily wooded stream valley. Continue on Md. 192, turn left onto Forest Glen Rd., and make another left on Rosensteel Ave. to the cemetery. When John Carroll created the parish near his mother's manor house in 1774, it became the first secular Catholic parish in the United States. Previously, there had only been Jesuit missions. In 1963, the parish built a church in nearby Silver Spring, but it still uses this red stone church, which dates to 1893. Many Carrolls are buried here, including the matriarch, Eleanor Darnall Carroll.

The Carrolls of Rock Creek

The Upper Marlboro branch of the Carroll family settled in Montgomery County after the death of Daniel Carroll I, in 1751. His remarkable widow, Eleanor Darnall Carroll, moved to her estate at **Rock Creek,** now **Forest Glen,** which became a refuge for her two sons, Daniel Carroll II and John.

Daniel Carroll II, friend of James Madison and in 1787 an active participant in the Philadelphia Convention that produced the federal constitution, came here to live with his mother after his wife died in 1763. His brother John, a Jesuit priest, returned to the United States from Europe in 1774 to lay the foundation for what would become the Catholic church in America. Their cousin, Charles Carroll of Carrollton, was a friend and ally. Well educated, aristocratic, and rich in land and slaves, the Catholic Carrolls supported the American Revolution and actively engaged in state and national politics. Daniel II served in the Maryland legislature for 15 years, promoted Maryland's ratification of the Constitution, won election to the first U.S. House of Representatives, and was one of the three commissioners George Washington appointed to survey the new capital in Washington.

Although Daniel's brother John had taken vows of poverty, he demonstrated his family's political acumen by skillfully structuring a church organization that fit the new republic. While acknowledging Rome's spiritual authority, he argued throughout his career that American Catholics owed political allegiance only to their own government. In 1776, he had accompanied Benjamin Franklin, Samuel Chase, and his cousin Charles on a mission to Canada to explain the American cause and perhaps enlist Canadian participation against Great Britain. The mission failed, but his friendship with Franklin probably helped his later appointment by Pope Pius VI in 1784 as head of missions in the young United States. In 1789, his fellow American priests elected Carroll the first U.S. Catholic bishop. In 1811 he became archbishop of Baltimore with suffragans in Boston, New York, Philadelphia, and Bardstown, Kentucky.

John Carroll's mother and brother died within a few months of each other in 1796. Her body was placed in the Carroll family churchyard at St. John's; no one knows exactly where Daniel II was buried. When the Society of Jesus was reactivated in the United States in 1814, Archbishop Carroll wished to return to Georgetown as a simple teaching priest, but he died in office in 1815 and was interred in the Baltimore Cathedral. Ann Carroll, or "Miss Nancy," the archbishop's great niece, lived on the family property at Rock Creek, surrounded by slaves descended from those who had served the family for generations. She freed them at her death in 1862. The Carroll Cottage became Carroll Springs Sanitarium and later served as a guest house on the Walter Reed Hospital Annex until it was torn down during the construction of the Capital Beltway.

While in the Kensington neighborhood, note that Stoneybrook Ave. angles south from Capitol View Ave. to the **Mormon Washington Temple** (No. 9900). The Carrolls could never have imagined that a temple of the Church of Jesus Christ of Latter-Day Saints would sit on part of their Montgomery County plantation. Built in 1974, the temple has become a landmark, particularly from the outer loop of the Capital Beltway, which at this point descends into the Rock Creek Valley. This nine-level marble structure with its six towers seems like an apparition. A gleaming gold figure with a trumpet, representing the angel Moroni, stands 288 feet above the ground on top of the east spire. Joseph Smith, founder of the faith, related that this angel appeared to him near Palmyra, New York, and directed him to buried golden plates from which, with the aid of magic stones, he translated the Book of Mormon. The **Visitor's Center** tells the story, but public access to the temple itself is limited.

Just before the Grosvenor Metro stop, Md. 355 passes the **Strathmore Hall Arts Center** (No. 10701), a turn-of-the-century Georgian-style mansion that serves as a Montgomery County center for the literary, visual, and performing arts. Capt. and Mrs. James Oyster built this mansion in 1902 as a country retreat; it later served as a residence of the Sisters of the Holy Cross and then headquarters for the American Speech-Language-Hearing Association before the county acquired the property in 1979.

Bethesda

The Rockville Pike passes under I-495 and eventually becomes Wisconsin Ave., the main thoroughfare through the unincorporated suburb

Bethesda (340' alt., 62,936 pop.), which takes its name from the small white frame church sitting atop a hill on the west side of Wisconsin Ave. south of the National Institutes of Health. The church's name comes from the New Testament (John 5:1–9) and, appropriately, refers to healing. The road soon passes, on the west, the main entrance to NIH, which moved to this then-rural location during World War II. The **Visitors Center,** in Building 10, illustrates the NIH mission with audio-video materials and a working lab. The nearby **National Library of Medicine,** the largest medical library in the world, features a reading room and a collection of historic and rare books.

The **Naval Medical Center** stands directly opposite the NIH complex on the eastern side of the Rockville Pike. The navy built it as a research and training hospital during World War II, when many hundreds of wounded sailors and marines received treatment here. The first secretary of defense, James Forrestal, committed suicide by jumping from one of the tower rooms in 1949.

Just west of the NIH complex, on Old Georgetown Rd. (an older roadbed that connects with the Rockville Pike in Bethesda and below Rockville and may follow Braddock's original path westward), one finds **Suburban Hospital,** a 397-bed community-owned institution dating from 1943. Besides supplying the regional shock trauma and emergency services, Suburban Hospital specializes in geriatrics, orthopedics, neuroscience, cardiology, and oncology.

Farther to the south and west, on Wilson Ln., lie the grounds of a well-known independent college preparatory academy for boys, the **Landon School.** A local educator, Paul Landon Banfield, founded the school in 1929; its famed graduates include Knight Kiplinger, of Kiplinger Publications, historian Alan Brinkley, and Washington-area television personality Maury Povich.

The destination for thousands of Washington office workers at 4:30 p.m., Bethesda has also recently become home to a number of small, biotechnology businesses. The Topographic Center of the Defense Mapping Agency is also located here. In the heart of Bethesda, the Rockville Pike meets Md. 410 (East-West Hwy.) from the east and Md. 187 (Old Georgetown Rd.) from the northwest, and becomes Wisconsin Ave., which continues south to the District of Columbia line at Wohlshire and the Chevy Chase Shopping Center.

No trace remains at the intersection of Wisconsin Ave. and Old Georgetown Rd. of the plantation where Josiah Henson (1789–1883) grew to manhood. Henson was born a slave in Southern Maryland and was separated from his family at the age of five or six as part of an estate sale. In adulthood Henson supervised his master's farm at this location and even sold the farm's produce in nearby markets. In 1830, when he learned that he might be sold in the New Orleans slave markets, he escaped to Canada. From his Canadian base, Henson became an active Methodist preacher, abolitionist, and conductor on the underground railroad in Kentucky. He also served in the Canadian army, founded a Canadian settlement for African American youths, and visited England to raise money for the abolition cause. Henson's life and experiences became the model for Harriet Beecher Stowe's monumental *Uncle Tom's Cabin; or Life Among the Lowly* (1852). In his own book, *Truth Is Stranger than Fic-*

tion (1879), Henson described the people and the life he had known in Montgomery County. One of his Maryland descendants, Matthew Henson, accompanied Adm. Robert E. Peary on his expedition to the North Pole in 1909. The state named an undeveloped Montgomery County park site for Henson in 1991.

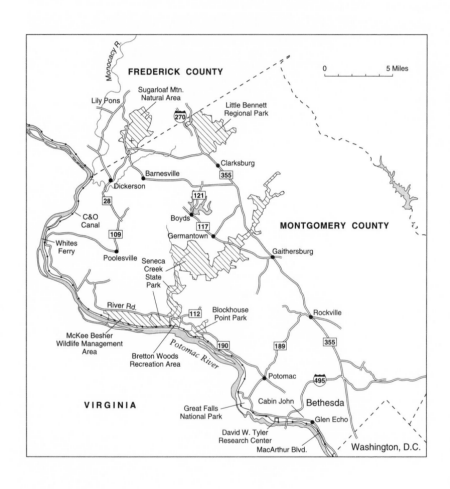

FREDERICK COUNTY

Monocacy R.

Sugarloaf Mtn.
Natural Area

Lily Pons

Little Bennett
Regional Park

270

0   5 Miles

Clarksburg

Barnesville

355

Dickerson

28

121

Boyds

117

MONTGOMERY COUNTY

C&O
Canal

109

Germantown

Whites
Ferry

Poolesville

Gaithersburg

Seneca
Creek
State
Park

River Rd.

112

Blockhouse
Point Park

Rockville

McKee Besher
Wildlife Management
Area

190

189

355

Bretton Woods
Recreation Area

Potomac River

VIRGINIA

Potomac

495

Great Falls
National Park

Cabin John

Bethesda

Glen Echo

David W. Tyler
Research Center

MacArthur Blvd.

Washington, D.C.

The Lovely Potomac Valley: Montgomery County into Frederick County

MacArthur Blvd., Md. 189, Md. 190, Whites Ferry Rd., Md. 28, Park Mills Rd., and Mt. Ephraim Rd.

From Point of Rocks at the foot of the Catoctin Mountain to Great Falls, the Potomac River flows through rolling Piedmont countryside. State and federal parklands, small towns, open fields, and spacious residences give the river valley above metropolitan Washington a distinctive quality, reflective of its rural past.

Within the District of Columbia, MacArthur Blvd. (the old Conduit Rd.) travels northwest from Georgetown, following the river and paralleling both the C&O Canal and George Washington Memorial Pkwy. The boulevard crosses into Montgomery County at **Little Falls Branch Park** near **Dalecarlia Reservoir,** which straddles the District line. The reservoir, named for a former estate, acts as a storage and settling area for some of Washington's unfiltered water supply. Beyond the city, the route passes the Defense Mapping Agency and continues north along the Potomac past **Little Falls Dam** and **Snake Island.** The Central Intelligence Agency complex is located across the river in Langley, Virginia.

Glen Echo

MacArthur Blvd. continues north through the community of Glen Echo and a park area that has been associated with amusement and recreation for a century. In 1891, two brothers, Edwin and Edward Baltzley, established the Glen Echo Chautauqua "to promote liberal and practical education, especially among the masses of the people." That same year they also donated land to Clara Barton, as part of their effort to lure prominent Washingtonians to their "Rhineland on the Potomac." The chautauqua lasted only one summer, hindered by a rumor that one of the residents had died from malaria. However, the Baltzleys continued to rent the property for public shows and entertainment until 1899, when the Glen Echo Company leased the land for a full-scale amusement park. With its rides, large swimming pool, and ballroom, Glen Echo—then for whites only—became one of Washington's most popular attractions, with special trains carrying customers from throughout the region.

The park closed in 1968, but a citizens' group raised money to preserve the **1921 Dentzel Carousel,** and the federal government acquired the land in 1971. Glen Echo is now a cultural arts park operated by the National Park Service. Professionals in the visual and performing arts occupy the existing structures as well as government surplus "yurts" that have been recycled as studio spaces. Arts groups give classes and performances at Glen Echo in an effort to revive the chautauqua ideal in a modern context.

The national park grounds also contain the **Clara Barton House,** a National Historic Site. This unusual 2½-story frame house is modeled after the relief hotel used by the Red Cross for victims of the Johnstown Flood of 1889. The building contains 10 bedrooms built around a center hall with a library in front, sitting room in back, and one bathroom. Clara Barton, founder of the American Red Cross, came here to live in 1897, and the house served as headquarters for the American Red Cross until her resignation as president in 1904. She died in her bedroom here, and the building became a boarding house. The National Park Service acquired the property in 1976.

Clara Barton (1821–1912), born in Massachusetts, came to Washington in 1856 to work as a clerk in the U.S. Patent Office. When the Civil War began, she assisted the troops by providing medical supplies, nursing help, and comfort to wounded soldiers. After the Battle of Antietam, she earned the nickname "The Angel of the Battlefield." Following the war, she searched for missing prisoners from an office in Annapolis. She sailed to Europe in 1869 to recuperate from her war experiences but soon became involved with the international Red Cross movement, after reading Henri Dunant's book, *A Memory of Solferino.* She aided victims in the Franco-Prussian War of 1870, returned to the United States, lobbied for adoption of the Treaty of Geneva, and in 1881 became president of the American Red Cross. She also supported the growing feminist movement in the United States.

Cabin John

Beyond Glen Echo, MacArthur Blvd. passes the **Old Cabin John Bridge,** a single masonry arch built in 1857–63 over the Cabin John Creek Valley. The bridge carried a water conduit that supplied Washington from the Potomac River at Great Falls. The sandstone and granite bridge has a 220-foot span and a rise of more than 57 feet. Jefferson Davis, secretary of war under President Franklin Pierce, directed the Army Engineers at the start of the construction, but feeling against him was so intense during the Civil War that his name was chiseled off the commemorative inscription at the bridge entrance. President Theodore Roosevelt ordered Davis's name restored in 1908.

The name Cabin John—affixed to creek, park, post office, and other landmarks—dates to 1750, when the creek was called Captain John's Branch. Legend relates that a mysterious hermit, perhaps an Indian or a pirate, lived in a log cabin near this location. Residents apparently believed the pirate story, because land buyers in the vicinity as late as the 1930s had to sign an agreement to share any buried treasure discovered on their property.

Still paralleling the river and the canal, MacArthur Blvd. passes under the Capital Beltway, crosses Rock Run, and passes the **David W. Taylor Research Center,** formerly the Naval Ship Research and Development Center. As the road leaves the riverbed and curves north, it passes the **site of the Maryland Gold Mine.** John Clear, stationed with other California soldiers on the Potomac during the war, helped discover the precious metal around 1864. He returned after the war and organized a mining company that retrieved small quantities of gold between 1869 and

1880. The mines were briefly reopened in 1935, when the price of gold increased after revaluation of U.S. currency.

Great Falls

MacArthur Blvd. ends at the intersection with Falls Rd. (Md. 189), where a secondary road leads to the entrance of **Great Falls National Park.** Here the great Potomac begins its descent to tidal waters in a spectacular series of cataracts, rapids, and short whitewater falls over great granite boulders. The water falls about 90 feet in three miles along the rocky riverbed, creating a visual spectacle that has attracted tourists since the 18th century. The deep **Mather Gorge,** located just below the falls, was carved over the centuries by this rushing water.

One of the three major visitor centers for the **Chesapeake and Ohio Canal Park** is located within Great Falls National Park. The **C&O Canal National Historic Park** includes the **Great Falls Tavern,** built as a lockhouse and now a museum, as well as five restored locks of the C&O Canal. Trails—some of them rugged—provide scenic views, and one leads to John Clear's old mine. Biking and hiking along the towpath between Georgetown and Great Falls has become a popular pastime during warm weather.

From the park, take Falls Rd. (Md. 189) north until it crosses River Rd. (Md. 190).

Potomac

The intersection marks the center of a residential area with more than 45,000 residents. The **Potomac Polo Club,** the only polo club in Maryland, is located on Glen Rd., which roughly parallels River Rd. to the north. The club regularly plays teams from throughout the United States and sometimes other countries during the summer months. North of the Potomac town center, opposite the public Falls Road Golf Club, one finds the **Bullis School,** an independent, coeducational academy that retired navy commander William Bullis and his wife Lois founded in 1930. Its best-known graduate may be the rock musician, actor, and poet Henry Rollins, who finished in 1979 as Henry Garfield.

A Chesapeake and Ohio Canal lock in the summer

Turn left on River Rd. and follow it northwest through wooded countryside, crossing a number of small streams that empty into the nearby river on the south. Beyond the suburban developments around Potomac, the road passes agricultural fields and country lanes; secondary roads lead to sites along the nearby C&O Canal. River Rd. crosses Muddy Creek in **Blockhouse Point Park** and intersects Seneca Rd. (Md. 112) at **Bretton Woods Recreation Center.**

Continue on River Rd. to Rileys Lock Rd., which descends to the canal along Seneca Creek. The creek is fed by the watersheds of both the Little Seneca and Great Seneca Creeks, which flow through a network of river valley parks in Montgomery County. Several gristmills existed along Seneca Creek at this point; the Tschiffely Mill operated until 1931 and burned in 1956. A short hike leads to the remains of the aqueduct that opened in 1833 and carried the canal over the creek during its years of operation. The abandoned **Seneca Stone Cutting Mill** and small stone quarries are also located near the canal. The red sandstone milled here can still be observed in a number of canal structures and Washington buildings, including the Smithsonian "Castle."

The **Seneca Schoolhouse Museum** stands on River Rd. (No. 6800), just beyond Partnership Rd. This one-room structure built of Seneca sandstone dates to 1865–66. Upton Darby, one of the millers along Seneca Creek, donated money for the school, where classes in grades one through seven were taught from 1866 to 1910. The interior of this nationally registered Historic Place has been restored.

River Rd. continues past Seneca Creek State Park and **McKee Beshers Wildlife Management Area,** havens for the many varieties of bird, animal, and reptile life that flourish along the Potomac River. Beaver have returned to the Montgomery County portion of the river, where the Potomac runs swiftly, dotted with more than 100 small islands. Moonshiners used **Tenfoot** and **Van Deventer Islands,** visible from the canal towpath, during Prohibition. The river bends to the west, creating an undeveloped pocket that retains an element of wildness. Indian tribes occupied both sides of the river and the islands in this region for at least a millennium.

River Rd. angles briefly away from the river and becomes Mt. Nebo Rd. Follow it to the intersection with W. Offut Rd., bear left, and make another left at the intersection with Edwards Ferry Rd., which cuts back to a continuation of River Rd. A ferry and later a bridge used this river site during the 19th century; **Lock 25** of the C&O Canal was also built here. Jubal Early's cavalry used the ford here to return to Virginia after its 1864 raid on Washington; the infantry used Conrad's Ferry, now Whites Ferry.

Whites Ferry

River Rd. terminates at **Whites Ferry,** the only commercial ferry still operating on the Potomac River. Elijah White, erstwhile Confederate colonel, bought the business after the Civil War from the family of Ernest Conrad, who started poling a barge here around 1828. Ferry service was interrupted when a flood destroyed the barge during World War II. Edwin Brown and his Virginia partners acquired a surplus army barge in 1946 and renewed a commuter service between Loudoun County on the Virginia side and the growing upper Montgomery County. Brown ac-

quired a new steel ferry, named the *Gen. Jubal A. Early,* in 1953. A steel
barge of the same name now carries 15–18 cars across the river 75–90
times a day in a crossing that lasts about three minutes.

Poolesville

Whites Ferry Rd. leaves the river and travels directly east to Poolesville
(3,796 pop.), in the Medley Historic District of Montgomery County.
John Poole II built a **one-room log store** at the intersection of two
country roads here in 1793, and a small crossroads town gradually developed. The store, at 19923 Fisher Ave., is now a National Historic Landmark. Frame additions were built in 1810 and 1866, but the log structure,
with its sleeping loft and stone chimneys, has survived. The upstairs has
been turned into a museum that includes a general store and Civil War
memorabilia.

Union soldiers stationed in Poolesville guarded the Maryland side of
the Potomac and its nearby river crossing throughout the war. More than
15,000 troops camped in the fields around the town at the beginning of
the war, when federal officials feared an imminent attack on Washington. Despite gun emplacements and a permanent garrison, the Confederates forded the nearby Potomac frequently during the war.

From Poolesville take the Beallsville Rd. (Md. 109) to Darnestown Rd.
(Md. 28). Make a left and follow Md. 28 across the Little Monocacy River.
At **Dickerson** the road goes under a railroad overpass and intersects
Mouth of the Monocacy Rd., which, if one turns left, leads to the C&O
Canal and the **Monocacy Aqueduct.** This stone aqueduct, the largest
of 11 that carried the canal across Potomac tributaries, extends 516 feet
over seven arches 54 feet above the Monocacy River. Canal aficionados
rank it among the chief physical features of canals in the United States.

The Monocacy River enters the Potomac at the Frederick-Mont-
gomery county line within the C&O Canal National Historic Park. Louis
Michel, a Swiss prospector, created a camp at this spot in 1707. A small
settlement of French traders and their Indian wives briefly existed here.
Christoph de Graffenried, a Swiss baron authorized by Queen Anne to
establish a colony above the falls of the Potomac in Virginia, visited the
settlement in 1711 and rhapsodized about "those enchanted islands in the
Potomac." The baron even climbed nearby Sugar Loaf Mountain, but his
colony never materialized, and the settlement disappeared.

Md. 28 crosses the Monocacy River into Frederick County east of the
canal. Turn right on Park Mills Rd.

Lily Pons

Park Mills Rd. travels up the river valley to Lily Pons Rd. Make a left
to the **Lily Pons Water Gardens,** a 300-acre tract along the Monocacy
River and Bennett's Creek. In 1917 G. Leicester Thomas Sr. decided to turn
his goldfish hobby into a business, which has since expanded into a national enterprise specializing in all aspects of water gardening. A wide variety of lilies, lotus, and other aquatic plants fill the numerous ponds scattered throughout the property. To meet the demand of the mail orders
generated from this rural location, the U.S. Post Office created a station
here in 1934. Thomas, an opera buff, decided to name the watery complex for diva Lily Pons, who attended an official dedication of the site on

June 20, 1936. Every year, the business commemorates the event with a weekend festival of music, art, and water gardening lectures. Thomas's grandsons now operate the enterprise, which has branches in Texas and California.

Sugar Loaf Mountain

Park Mills Rd. continues beyond Lily Pons to Mt. Ephraim Rd., which makes a sharp right to Sugar Loaf Mountain (1,282'), a tree-covered geologic monument that rises 800 feet above the surrounding farmland. Like Mt. Monadnock in New Hampshire, this quartzite formation resisted the elements for more than 14 million years while the surrounding land eroded. Sugar Loaf provides a haven for more than 500 species of plants, forest birds, and woodland mammals; its overlooks, used by lookouts during the Civil War, provide scenic views of the entire region.

Gordon Strong came here in 1902 and eventually bought the entire mountain. In 1912, he built **Stronghold,** a colonial mansion on the mountain, where he entertained prominent friends, including President Franklin D. Roosevelt. When Roosevelt expressed a desire to acquire the property, Strong steered him to federal land on Catoctin Mountain, near Thurmont, which subsequently became Camp David, the presidential retreat. Stronghold, Inc., owns and manages the property, but it has been named a National Natural Landmark and is open free to the public every day of the year from sunrise to sunset for hiking, horseback riding, and picnicking. No camping, cooking fires, or alcoholic beverages are permitted; and visitors must be off the mountain by dark.

From Sugar Loaf, the traveler has several options for the return trip to lower Montgomery County. Picturesque Comus Rd. leaves Stronghold at the base of the mountain and crosses to a junction with Md. 355 at **Little Bennett Regional Park.**

Mt. Ephraim Rd. cuts back into Montgomery County and intersects W. Harris Rd., which ends at **Barnesville** (170 pop.). An Arabian Horse museum, associated with a nearby farm, is located southeast of Barnesville. From Barnesville, Old Baltimore Rd. east leads to Md. 355 and Gaithersburg. After a short distance on Old Baltimore Rd., a right onto Barnesville Rd. takes one to **Boyds** and Little Seneca Lake. Md. 117 angles southeast from Boyds to Germantown, Seneca Creek State Park, and Gaithersburg.

The Spokes That Made Baltimore a Hub

Md. 26, 140, 25, 45, 146, 147, U.S.I., Md. 150, and U.S. 40 East

The wagon roads that carried wheat to Baltimore and enriched its port connected the city with the hinterlands like spokes on a wheel. Many of them have since grown into wide concrete courses; others retain something of their horse-drawn charm. Visitors to Baltimore frequently are surprised to discover how close to the edge of the city one finds green, wooded landscapes. The following tours travel the major historic turnpike routes and extend into the marshy necks of southeastern Baltimore County.

A. LIBERTY RD. (MD. 26)

An old turnpike route, Liberty Rd. leaves Baltimore as Liberty Heights Ave. and passes through a corridor of housing and commercial establishments that has grown up mostly in the 20th century; the area was predominantly rural even 50 years ago. In 1877, when a turnpike traveler crossed Gwynns Falls, Powhattan Mills, a busy textile center during most of the 19th century, dominated the valley immediately to the south. **Woodlawn Cemetery** opened in the early 1900s. The community of **Woodlawn,** located south of the cemetery, adjacent to I-70, has a population of 32,907 people. Much of the development owes its origins to the national headquarters of the Social Security Administration, based here since 1960. Next to the Baltimore County government, this federal agency is Baltimore County's largest single employer (more than 13,000 employees and an annual payroll of $500 million).

Randallstown

Liberty Rd. crosses the Baltimore Beltway at the suburban community of **Milford** and enters Randallstown (26,277 pop.), an unincorporated area with shopping centers and residences on both sides of the highway. John and Christopher Randall established a tavern in the 1770s on the road somewhere near its intersection with Church Ln. The town had a population of 100 in 1880, including two doctors, a postmaster, three blacksmiths, a hotel-tavern proprietor, three storekeepers, and a tollgate operator.

Soldiers Delight

Beyond Randallstown, the urban congestion begins to thin, and Liberty Rd. passes through wooded landscapes to Wards Chapel Rd., which turns right to the **Soldiers Delight Natural Environment Area,** known for its unusual serpentine rock formations and forested meadows. The state first acquired acreage here in 1970 and has since developed more than 2,000 acres for walking and skiing. The name comes from the Soldiers Delight Hundred, created in 1773 from the Upper Patapsco Hundred (hundreds in the colonial era were subcounty administrative and election districts). In about 1817 Isaac Tyson Jr. established a chrome mine along the North Branch of the Patapsco River. The mine became part of a mining business that spanned parts of both Maryland and Pennsylvania and between 1828 and 1850 made Tyson the world's chief producer of chrome. He also formed the Baltimore Chrome Works, which pioneered in the synthesis of chromium compounds. The **site of Choate Mine,** operated for chromium ore from about 1839 to 1886 and again briefly during World War I, lies within Soldiers Delight.

Liberty Rd. continues past the state preserve and crosses **Liberty Reservoir,** created in 1954 to increase Baltimore City's water supply.

On the other side of the Patapsco's North Branch, Liberty Rd. enters Carroll County and soon reaches Md. 32 and the residential community of **Eldersburg** (9,720 pop.). Turn south (left) on Md. 32, known as the Sykesville Rd., to the entrance of the **Springfield Hospital Center.** William Patterson, a wealthy Baltimore merchant, owned a summer estate here, named Springfield, and was responsible for bringing the railroad through the property. The state purchased 728 acres of the estate and in 1896 opened the Second Hospital for the Insane of the State of Maryland (the first was Spring Grove Hospital in Catonsville, 1872). Springfield Hospital admits mentally ill patients from Baltimore City and Carroll, Frederick, Garrett, Howard, and Montgomery Counties. With facilities for more than 800 patients, Springfield is one of the county's largest employers.

Sykesville (2,303 pop.), just below the Springfield Center, traces its origins to James Sykes, son of a Baltimore merchant who bought land here in 1825 and rebuilt a mill on the South Branch of the Patapsco River. The railroad arrived in 1831, and Sykes built both a hotel and a tavern; a cotton mill followed in 1845. Legend relates that the town may also have been a stop on the Underground Railroad for escaped slaves fleeing north to Pennsylvania and beyond. The town thrived for more than a century, until the end of passenger train service in 1949. The **Town House** on Main St. contains a second-floor museum.

Just beyond the junction with Md. 32, Liberty Rd. passes **Piney Run Park,** accessible by Martz Rd. and White Rock Rd., both of which branch south from the main highway. The park contains a 300-acre lake stocked for fishing and offers a wide variety of other recreational opportunities ranging from nature walking to cross-country skiing and ice skating.

Liberty Rd. crosses over Parr's Ridge to Frederick County and the village of **Libertytown,** which may have given the road its name. The arrival of liberty was well celebrated in this neighborhood. In April 1783, 200 people living along nearby Israel Creek and Cabbage Run assembled at **Woodsboro** (now 513 pop.) to mark the end of the Revolutionary War. They heard a sermon and then gathered at the home of Col. Joseph Wood Jr., founder of Woodsboro. The celebrants toasted the United States of America and many toasts later closed with a prayer that "the peace now concluded be perpetuated."

Liberty Rd. crosses the Monocacy River and ends on the northern side of Frederick.

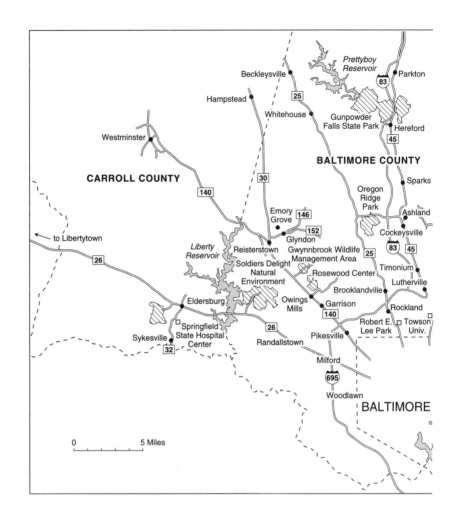

B. REISTERSTOWN RD. (MD. 140)

Reisterstown Rd. leaves the northwestern corner of Baltimore and traces a 35-mile diagonal line to the Pennsylvania border. The road's southern end follows the valley of the Gwynns Falls, a stream that rises near Glyndon and flows southeast to the Middle Branch of the Patapsco River. By 1741 a frontier trail had appeared beside the stream. In 1802 it became a year-round wagon road operated by a private toll company. Before construction of railroads and development of farmland beyond the Appalachians, much of the produce of central Maryland and central Pennsylvania followed this path to the port of Baltimore. Since the end of World War II, the 10-mile distance between Baltimore and Reisterstown has become dense with housing developments, shopping centers, country clubs, and institutional properties. Many of the country estates that lined the road before World War I have disappeared. The largest cluster of horse farms in Maryland lies east of the road, in the Green Spring and Worthington Valleys.

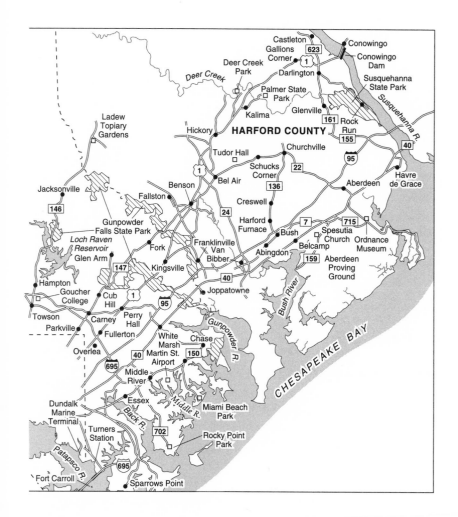

Pikesville

Reisterstown Rd. passes the grounds of the **Suburban Country Club** (on the right) and the **Maryland National Guard Armory** (on the left) as it leaves Baltimore and then enters the old Baltimore County town of Pikesville (516′ alt., 24,815 pop.). Seven of Baltimore's major Jewish congregations are clustered along nearby Park Heights Ave., which parallels Md. 140 out of the city. Pikesville was settled before the Revolution but not named until after the War of 1812. Dr. James Smith, who had purchased land along the pike, named the village after his friend Gen. Zebulon Pike, killed in 1813 during the burning and siege of York (now Toronto), Canada.

Sudbrook Park, one of the earliest planned suburban communities in the United States, is located off Sudbrook Ln., which angles south (left) from Reisterstown Rd. Frederick Law Olmsted designed this as a summer community, near the banks of the Gwynns Falls on Sudbrook, an estate once owned by James McHenry. Olmsted's design followed the typography, creating curving streets and irregular lots. Such suburban communities became fashionable in the early 1890s when electric railways linked city and countryside.

Continue on Reisterstown Rd. to the old United States Arsenal, completed in 1819, in the center of Pikesville. This complex of red brick buildings, once painted yellow, served as a military post and weapons repository until 1879, when it was conveyed to the state. In 1888 the General Assembly turned the property over to the Association of the Maryland Line, which soon opened it as a Confederate Soldiers Home. It is not known exactly how many Marylanders served the Confederacy during the Civil War, but about 130 of them originally occupied the home, raising much of their own food and donning old uniforms every June 10 on Confederate Decoration Day. The veterans also kept local saloons busy for a while. By 1932 most had died, and the remaining two moved to private homes. At mid-century, after renovation and upgrading, the venerable buildings became the headquarters of the **Maryland State Police.** Today the complex houses police administrative offices, other state offices, and a training school for state police recruits. A state police museum has been created in the Commandant's House.

Lined with shops and restaurants, Reisterstown Rd. narrows in the congested center of Pikesville, crosses Old Court Rd. (Md. 133), and then passes a section of **Druid Ridge Cemetery.** The cemetery contains a monument to Queen Victoria, erected in 1903 by the St. George's Society of Baltimore and may be the only commemoration to that monarch in the United States.

The road then intersects the Baltimore Beltway at Exit 20. Exit 19 to the west takes one to the Northwest Expressway (I-795), which roughly parallels Md. 140 until it returns to the older road at Reisterstown.

Beyond the beltway, Reisterstown Rd. passes near a cluster of educational, recreational, and religious institutions. On the left Woodholme Ave. leads to a country club of the same name. Gray Rock Rd. (on the right) travels a short distance to what was once the country estate of John Eager Howard. Between 1946 and 1990 it housed the monastery of the Order of the Most Holy Trinity. The Trinitarians sold the property to a private developer, who is building houses on the grounds and using the rebuilt mansion house for meetings. (The monks relocated to the former **Kiesler Mansion** at 8400 Park Heights Ave.)

Mt. Wilson Ln. (left) travels by the campus of the **Ner Israel Rabbinical College,** founded in Baltimore in 1933 by Rabbi Jacob I. Ruderman. The yeshiva, which has an enrollment of 466 students from all over the world, moved to this suburban location in 1969. The lane crosses Gwynns Falls and ends at the **site of the Mount Wilson Sanitarium.** Thomas Wilson, a wealthy Quaker merchant, opened this property in 1884 as a summer resort for poor children from Baltimore. The state established a tuberculosis sanitarium here in 1925.

Stone Chapel Rd. (right) leads to an abandoned white stuccoed church. Built in 1862, it made use of stones from an earlier chapel constructed in 1785. Robert Strawbridge, one of the founders of American Methodism, preached at the first church on this site.

Reisterstown Rd. then intersects McDonogh Rd. (west) and Craddock Ln. (east). McDonogh Rd. takes one to **McDonogh School,** endowed in 1850 by John McDonogh, a wealthy Baltimore-born New Orleans businessman. After litigation over his will, the school was established in 1873 to give a free education to "poor boys of good character." The pupils were also required to work the extensive farm here. McDonogh has since developed into a nondenominational, coeducational day school for grades K–12 and boarding school for grades 9–12. Distinguished graduates include tennis champion Pam Shriver (1979), Todd Kiplinger (1964), vice chairman of Kiplinger Publications, and ABC News correspondent Jack Smith (1963).

Craddock Ln. leads past **Trentham** (private), a square, 2½-story stuccoed house erected in 1860. Trentham stands on the site of a house the Rev. Thomas Cradock (1718–70) built in 1746. He named it for the Free School of Trentham in Staffordshire, England, where he had taught before coming to America. Cradock was born on the estate of the Duke of Bedford, who sent him to Oxford and sponsored his career in the Anglican Church. Under the duke's patronage in England, he was destined to become a bishop, but after he developed a liaison with the duchess's sister, he was quickly induced to emigrate to Maryland. Cradock became the first rector of nearby St. Thomas Church (see below). In 1747 he opened a school at Trentham, which was attended by boys of such prominent Maryland families as the Dulanys of Annapolis and the Cresaps of Western Maryland. An octagonal bathhouse, built about 1750 and equipped with two mahogany bathtubs, still stands between the house and the road.

Beyond the McDonogh-Craddock intersection, Reisterstown Rd. passes **Ten-Mile House** (on the left), a 2½-story stone tavern built around 1810 with wide windows and a low gable roof. The tavern catered to wagon drivers and less affluent travelers during the antebellum heyday of the Reisterstown Pike. The Green Spring Valley Hunt Club had its first clubhouse here. Jake Kilrain, defeated in 1889 by John L. Sullivan after 75 rounds in the last American bareknuckle heavyweight fight, had several training workouts here before the fight in Mississippi.

On the right, the road next intersects Greenspring Valley Rd. (Md. 130) in **Garrison** (5,045 pop.). The **Green Spring Valley Hunt Club** (private) lies a short distance east on Greenspring Valley Rd. (east of Garrison Forest Rd.), a site it has occupied since the 1920s, when one of its members was Gen. Douglas MacArthur. He had married a Baltimore woman, a divorcée whose property settlement included a luxurious Green Spring Valley estate (the home had nine bedrooms, the garage space for 10 cars), which MacArthur named Rainbow Hill, to mark his World War I experience as commander of the 42nd, or "Rainbow," Division. Farther along Reisterstown Rd., the visitor passes the **Garrison Forest School** (right), a private day school for girls. Called to the Green Spring Valley by a brother-in-law who then presided at St. Thomas Church, Mary Livingston, a New York native, founded the school in 1910. At the end of the 20th century the school enrolled more than 620 students, 80 of them boarders, in a pre-kindergarten to 12th grade program. Garrison Forest shares the motto of Boys Latin, "*Esse quam videri*"—"To be rather than to seem."

St. Thomas Ln. turns right from Reisterstown Rd. to the **Garrison Forest (now St. Thomas) Episcopal Church,** a red brick cruciform building with a steeply pitched roof and cupola belfry. Built in 1743 and greatly altered over the years, the church was established by St. Paul's Parish in Baltimore as a "chapel of ease for the forest inhabitants." Two years later, under the spiritual guidance of Thomas Cradock, the congregation became a separate parish and took the name of St. Thomas. The lane ends at Garrison Forest Rd. To the right a short distance, on Caves Rd., Charles Carroll, Barrister, framer of Maryland's Declaration of Rights, built **The Caves** (private) in 1730 on a tract patented in 1710 as Bear Run. Carroll lived here until 1754, when Mount Clare was completed in Baltimore; part of his original manor house has been incorporated into the present mansion.

Owings Mills

Beyond St. Thomas Ln., Reisterstown Rd. passes through Owings Mills (9,474 pop.), an unincorporated area of residences and light industries named after Samuel Owings Jr. (1733–1803). Owings, who had extensive land holdings in Baltimore County, built four mills along the Gwynns Falls in this area. The flour produced here was named "ULM," after his upper, lower, and middle mills. Painters Mill Rd.—named for William Painter, who bought Owings's home and mills in 1844— branches south (left) through an industrial park along the Gwynns Falls flood plain. **Ulm House,** the two-story brick home that Owings built in 1765, occupied the adjacent hill until it was bulldozed in 1996 to make way for an office tower.

Beyond Painters Mill Rd., Rosewood Ln. branches north (right) from Md. 140 to the **Rosewood Center,** established in 1888 as the "Asylum and Training School for the Feeble Minded of the State of Maryland." The institution admitted children in 1889 and from 1912 to 1961 was known as the Rosewood State Training School. It became the Rosewood State Hospital in 1961 and then the Rosewood Center, when the state departments of health and mental hygiene merged in 1969. The 536-bed facility treats, educates, and trains patients from all over the state.

A short left on Owings Mills Blvd. leads to the Owings Mills Mall and Town Center, also served by I-795. This planned development opened in 1986 on 13,300 acres to provide commercial services for area housing and industrial developments. **Owings Mills New Town** a "planned unit development," is located on 430 acres north and west of the mall.

Take a right on Owings Mills Blvd. and follow the Western Maryland Railroad tracks into countryside now dotted with new residences. A right at Gwynnbrook Ave. leads one to the **Gwynnbrook Wildlife Management Area,** the oldest of 37 such areas now scattered throughout the state. Established in 1917 as a game farm, this 74-acre facility features a self-guided, 1.5-mile nature trail and a stocked public fish pond. The earliest state research on Maryland's white-tailed deer, quail, and rabbit was conducted here.

The offices and production studios of the **Maryland Center for Public Broadcasting** are located off Owings Mills Blvd. just north of the wildlife management area. Maryland Public Television began broadcasting from these studios in 1969 and now maintains additional transmitters in Oakland, Hagerstown, Frederick, Annapolis, and Salisbury. The center produces a wide variety of educational and cultural programming for regional, national, and international audiences.

Reisterstown

Md. 140 passes under the tracks of the Western Maryland Railroad and then crosses the Gwynns Falls. The road passes through rapidly growing suburban development clustered around the unincorporated villages of Reisterstown and Glyndon (735' alt., combined 19,314 pop.). After crossing Franklin Blvd., the road passes **Hannah More Park** (right), site of the Hannah More Academy, a Protestant Episcopal school for girls that was open from 1832 to 1974.

The highway bends sharply at the intersection with Cockey's Mill Rd., because Jacob Medairy built a house in its path, around 1804, to prevent the road from coming through town. The roadbuilders simply went around the house, creating a deflection that has survived numerous road alterations over the years. **Beckley's Blacksmith Shop / Polly Reister House** is located on the west side of the bend (left). This 2½-story brick building with its single-story wing was erected in 1779; the lane that originally separated the house and shop has disappeared. John Reister (see below) gave the land to his son-in-law, John Beckley, the village blacksmith.

Cockey's Mill Rd. follows an old Indian trail to nearby Patapsco Falls, the North Branch of the Patapsco River. The road passes the old **Lutheran Cemetery,** surrounded by a low brick wall, which developed around a log cabin used for Lutheran services as early as 1765. Next to the cemetery is the former **Franklin Academy,** which now houses a branch of the Baltimore County Library. Founded in 1820 as a private liberal arts school, the Franklin Academy became a public high school in 1849. Edgar Allan Poe, struggling to make a living in Baltimore, applied for the advertised position of academy principal but was rejected.

Just north of Cockey's Mill Rd., the traveler enters the section of Reisterstown Rd. where John Reister, a German immigrant, settled in 1758. After the completion of the road that connected Baltimore with Gettysburg and Hanover, Pennsylvania, his settlement became a regular stage stop. The village stretched about a mile on either side of the road and was lined with taverns, inns, and other establishments dedicated to wagon, stage, and buggy customers. Hitshue's Hotel became a summer resort after the Civil War, and Forney's Tavern, noted for the excellence of its food and liquors, catered to "persons of wealth and fashion." Other establishments served the rowdy farmers, teamsters, and traveling salesmen. With the rise of the automobile, the road changed its character but kept its energy, as shopping centers, gas stations, and fast-food stops replaced their predecessors. Some of Reisterstown's earlier rural quality remains in the quiet, shaded streets behind the commercial development.

Side Trip into the Worthington Valley

Before leaving Reisterstown, one may visit **Glyndon** and **Emory Grove,** each a short distance east on Md. 128 (Butler Rd.). Glyndon developed as a 19th-century commuters' village around a local railroad station; Emory Grove, a Methodist meeting ground located off Butler Rd. on Waugh Ave., dates to the end of the 18th century. After 1870, when a Victorian hotel and cottages replaced the original tents, thousands of two-week pilgrims came here every summer for physical and spiritual recreation. The site takes the name of Bishop John Emory, who died in 1835. The presence of Emory Grove and the Western Maryland Railroad station, then called Reisterstown Station, probably stimulated Dr. Charles Leas to lay out, in 1871, the maple-lined residential streets that still dis-

tinguish Glyndon. As the hamlet grew in size, the residents determined
that it should have a name. They placed their choices of names in a hat,
and a representative of the railroad drew out the name Glyn (Welsh for
"mountain valley"). Thus, in 1879, both the town and the railroad station took the name Glyndon.

From Glyndon, drive east, departing Md. 128, and follow Worthington Ave. to the Worthington Valley, an area of famous equestrian landmarks and old estates. About 40 farms lie within an area bounded by Mt.
Carmel on the north, I-83 on the east, and the Carroll County line and
Reisterstown Rd. on the west.

Montmorenci (private), located off Worthington Ave. about a mile
from Glyndon, was one of the original estates of the Worthington family.
The earliest part of the 2½-story fieldstone house may have been built in
1742. From Worthington Ave., a left on Tufton Ave. and another left on
Belmont Rd. will lead one to **Sagamore Farm** (private), once the home
of such noted horses as Discovery and Native Dancer. The extensive
physical plant, now leased to training and breeding operations, includes
90 stalls and a quarter-mile track. Since their sale in 1987, Sagamore's 575
acres have come under intense development pressure and have been the
subject of more than one zoning dispute. **Worthington Farms** (3203
Tufton Ave.) is home of the Maryland Hunt Cup, one of the world's best-
known and most demanding steeplechases. The first running of this four-
mile, cross-country event took place in 1894 in the nearby Green Spring
Valley. Since 1922 the course has been fixed at Worthington Farms and
is run on the last Saturday in April. Maryland, along with Virginia and
Pennsylvania, is a major steeplechasing center in the United States. Instead of gambling, the sport promotes family-oriented crowds and outdoor gaiety.

From Reisterstown, Md. 30 (Hanover Pike) branches north from Md. 140, following another old wagon route, once heavily traveled, to Hanover, Pennsylvania. Slightly more than a mile north of the intersection with Butler Rd., Montrose Rd. leads west (left) to the former Montrose School for Girls, closed by the state in 1988 in a reform effort to avoid institutionalization of delinquent juveniles.

William Patterson, a Baltimore shipping magnate and father of Elizabeth ("Betsy") Patterson Bonaparte, built the **Montrose Mansion** on this estate in the early 1800s after his daughter married Jerome Bonaparte, youngest brother of the Emperor Napoleon. Patterson named the French-style, 2½-story, 24-room granite mansion after the Marquis of Montrose, a Scottish nobleman and royalist military leader hanged during Oliver Cromwell's Protectorate in 17th-century England. Napoleon annulled the marriage in 1812, and Betsy lived here with her son, Jerome Napoleon Bonaparte, until 1840, when they moved to Baltimore. During Patterson's occupancy, the estate became locally famous for a royal style of entertainment. Col. Franklin Anderson continued this tradition during his ownership of the house, but its fame slowly declined, and the property was sold to the state in 1920. The Female House of Refuge was transferred here in 1922; it subsequently became known as the Maryland Industrial Training School for Girls and then simply the Montrose School.

Anderson Chapel—a small, rectangular stone structure with a square tower, surrounded by a wall—is located along Montrose Rd. Colonel Anderson erected the chapel in 1854.

Beyond Montrose, Md. 30 parallels the railroad tracks through the crossroad villages of **Woodensburg** and **Fowblesburg** and crosses into Carroll County. The large manufacturing plant of the Black and Decker Company, one of the county's largest employers, is visible from the road as it enters **Hampstead** (913' alt., 2,608 pop.), a townsite since the 18th century.

West of Reisterstown, Md. 140 crosses Liberty Reservoir and then becomes a divided highway known as Baltimore Blvd. At Green Hill Rd., one may turn left onto the more pastoral Old Westminster Pike. Follow either road through rolling Piedmont countryside that has filled with suburban housing developments and shopping strips. Old Westminster Pike enters Westminster from the southeast and becomes Main St.; from Md. 140, take the first turnoff, at Washington Rd., and then turn right onto the pike, heading toward downtown Westminster (see Tour 16).

C. FALLS RD. (MD. 25)

Falls Rd. follows the Jones Falls Valley out of Baltimore into green countryside that has supplied the scene for attractive homes for more than two centuries. The road crosses the Jones Falls four times during a 22-mile, northwestward ascent through Baltimore County. Named for an early downstream settler, David Jones, the stream rises in Green Spring Valley near Garrison and flows into Baltimore's inner harbor.

Just beyond the city limits, the road crosses the renovated Northern

Central Railroad bed, which now carries the Light Rail between Timonium and downtown Baltimore.

Robert E. Lee Memorial Park and Lake Roland

This old recreation spot lies between Falls Rd., on the west, and Baltimore City's first city-water reservoir, on the east. In 1854 Baltimore City acquired the Baltimore Water Company, and in 1858 municipal authorities began construction of a dam on the Jones Falls. The stone dam and Greek Revival valve house were completed in 1862, creating the city's main reservoir.

Originally named for Thomas Swann, Baltimore mayor from 1856 to 1860, the reservoir later became Lake Roland, after Roland Run, which empties into the lake from the north and in turn derives its name from Roland Thornberry, a 17th-century settler. The railroad bridge that passes over the lake (now part of the Light Rail system) was a key entry point into Baltimore during the Civil War and closely guarded by Union troops. Lakeside Park, a recreational and amusement area, flourished along the reservoir at the turn of the century, when trolley car excursions from the city became popular in the summer. The lake was abandoned in 1915, apparently due to silting problems. The city decided in the midst of World War II to make this area a park named after the Confederate general, employing funds originally bequeathed to the city for a statue honoring Lee. The park has become a favorite dog-running and bike-riding area for a large number of citizens as well as a good place for observing birds and other wildlife and searching for examples of native plants.

Along the Jones Falls near the entrance to the park, one still can see the **site of the Bellona Powder Mills.** The Bellona Mills began making gunpowder in 1800, and in the early 19th century, despite accidental blasts in 1817 and 1820, rivaled E. I. du Pont's more famous plant near Wilmington, Delaware, as a national producer of gunpowder.

Rockland

Falls Rd. passes under the Jones Falls Expressway (I-83) and enters Rockland, near the confluence of Slaughterhouse Branch and the Jones Falls at the intersection of Old Court Rd. (Md. 133) and Ruxton Rd.

Three English brothers established the Rockland Bleach and Dye Works here in 1831; their mills, surviving financial panics, floods, and fires, lasted into the 20th century. A restored gristmill now stands here, a reminder of a time when grist-, flour, textile, gunpowder, rolling, and other water-supported mills lined the Jones Falls and Gwynns Falls valleys.

Old Court Rd. travels west of Rockland and passes the entrance (on the left) to **Park School** (pre-elementary through high). A Goucher College professor, Hans Froelicher, established this progressive school in 1912, believing that children should enjoy learning, act rationally, and grow in tolerance. The school moved to this campus from Baltimore City in 1959. It flourishes as an independent, nonsectarian preparatory school with a high academic reputation. Among its many accomplished graduates, Park School can count business and civic leader Walter Sondheim Jr. (1925) and Princeton University theoretical physicist Edward Witten (1968). Ruxton Rd. proceeds east over the expressway to the old suburban community of **Ruxton,** just north of Lake Roland. Col. Nicholas Ruxton Moore, a Maryland congressman and veteran of the Revolution and the

War of 1812, lived and farmed in this area until he died in 1816. In 1885 the Northern Central Railroad used the name Ruxton for one of its local station stops. Developers subdivided the farmlands on either side of Bellona Ave. in the 1890s, and a summer resort community soon developed. It emerged in the early 20th century as a suburban haven for Baltimore's business and professional elite and still retains that identity.

After passing Rockland and the Baltimore Beltway, Falls Rd. reaches an old stagecoach stop, the **Valley Inn,** which dates from 1832. Across the road lies the entrance to a fanciful estate that Sumner Parker, an engineer and president of a local steel firm, built for his wife in 1930. The 27-room, Tudor Revival structure is modeled after medieval European castles; it has its own small chapel and cloister. In 1972 Mrs. Parker willed the house and the 53-acre estate to the city of Baltimore, which opened it in 1977 as the **Cloisters Children's Museum.** The city auctioned off its contents in 1995 and plans to reopen a children's museum at the Brokerage complex in downtown Baltimore at 34 Market Place. The city retains and rents the Cloisters as a site for special events. Just beyond the Cloisters, Hillside Rd. turns west (left) and leads to an intersection with Greenspring Ave., just south of which, on the right, one finds the 234-acre campus of **St. Timothy's School.** This independent boarding and day school for girls, grades 9–12, dates from 1882. The school's notable alumnae include Jean Harvey Baker (1951), a Goucher College history professor and the author of studies of Mary Todd Lincoln and the Stevenson political family in Illinois; fashion designer Liz Claiborne (1948); Laird Grant Groody (1963), president of Rockefeller and Company; and Elizabeth Valk Long (1968), a high-ranking female executive at Time, Inc. The **Irvine Natural Science Center** on campus welcomes visitors and offers nature trails for educational walks.

North of Hillside Rd., Falls Rd. intersects Joppa Rd. and a short extension of the Jones Falls Expressway at the community of **Brooklandville.** Here are specialty shops, professional offices, and offices of the state highway administration. Greenspring Valley Rd. (Md. 130), an attractive country lane, branches west from Brooklandville and passes **Villa Julie College,** a Catholic school that specializes in preparing women for careers in private business. Barely visible on a hilltop opposite the college is **Villa Pace** (private), the home of opera diva Rosa Ponselle (1897–1981), who lived in Maryland for more than 40 years after her retirement in 1937 from 19 seasons as principal soprano with the Metropolitan Opera Company in New York. The Rosa Ponselle Foundation, based in Stevenson, Maryland, still sponsors symposia and an annual all-Maryland vocal competition named for the singer, whom many critics rank as the greatest operatic soprano of all time.

Farther north, Falls Rd. intersects Seminary Rd. On the west, one sees **St. Paul's School,** a private preparatory academy for boys, later joined by the **St. Paul's School for Girls.** Founded in 1849 at Old St. Paul's Church downtown, it moved in 1952 to the Brooklandwood estate that Charles Carroll of Carrollton bought as a gift for this daughter Mary and son-in-law Richard Caton in the early 1800s. The nearby **Maryvale School for Girls** adjoins **Chestnut Ridge Country Club.** Winding through rural countryside, Falls Rd. then crosses Padonia Rd. and drops down to Beaverdam Run. In season, corn and soybean fields share the landscape with horse pastures and new housing developments.

Oregon Ridge Park

From Falls Rd. follow Shawan Rd. east (right) to Oregon Ridge Park, a county recreational and cultural area that rises above pastoral valleys formed by Oregon Branch and Western Run, tributaries of the Gunpowder Falls. Iron ores were mined here for Oregon Furnace and nearby Ashland. The park features a swimming pond, nature trails, a ski run, and a concert shell that serves as a summer home for the Baltimore Symphony Orchestra.

Merryman's Ln., east of the park, recalls John Merryman, who owned **Hayfields** (private), a 474-acre farm north of Shawan Rd. just west of I-83. Nicholas Bosley first transformed this countryside into an agricultural showcase in the early 1800s. While Lafayette was touring America in 1824, he presented to Colonel Bosley a silver cup from the Maryland Agricultural Society for building the best farm in the state. Merryman, who inherited the estate, imported Hereford cattle from England and added to the farm's reputation. A Confederate sympathizer and officer in the local militia, he helped destroy Baltimore's northern rail links after the April 19, 1861, riot in Baltimore. Later arrested and held without charge at Fort McHenry, Merryman became the focus of a famous court opinion. Military authorities ignored a writ of habeas corpus that likely would have led to his release, and Chief Justice Roger B. Taney in *Ex parte Merryman* wrote forcefully in favor of individual protections under the Constitution, even in wartime. Merryman was later released and must have felt some satisfaction when, in the summer of 1864, he entertained Gen. Bradley T. Johnson and Maj. Harry Gilmor at Hayfields during their raid through Maryland. The Merryman family sold Hayfields in 1975, and subsequent owners have sought to develop the land for upscale housing and a golf course. Area residents and other farmers have fought such rezoning efforts, hoping to preserve the rural qualities of the surrounding countryside.

Falls Rd. continues above Shawan Rd. through horse-breeding and -training country to **White House** and Mount Carmel Rd. (Md. 137). At **Beckleysville,** the road loses its paved surface and begins to resemble its 19th-century appearance. Today it terminates in Carroll County at Schalk No. 1 Rd. At that point, turn right to travel through a remarkable "Old West" village at the River Valley Ranch on the way to the Pennsylvania line. A secondary road (right) leads back to I-83.

In its heyday Falls Rd., originating still farther north and fed by numerous back country roads, formed a river for the movement of farm products to Baltimore.

D. YORK RD. (MD. 45)

Md. 45, known as York Rd., runs the length of Baltimore County, from the Pennsylvania line into Baltimore City, roughly paralleling the new interstate highway I-83 (completed in 1959), which connects Baltimore to York and Harrisburg, Pennsylvania. York Rd. first appeared on maps in 1743 as the Susquehanna Rd. and became an improved turnpike in about 1807. The road opened the fertile Pennsylvania and Maryland hinterlands to the Chesapeake and contributed greatly to the growth of

Baltimore. Commuters, interstate travelers, and truckers with farm and factory products now use I-83; York Rd. serves local residents, farmers, and visitors who wish to escape the interstate.

The transition from city to county occurs seamlessly, as York Rd. follows a commercial strip from the city into the pleasant residential areas of **Stoneleigh** (on the east), named for a country estate, and **Rodgers Forge** (west), named for a blacksmith's shop. Much of the land that the Rodgers Forge townhouses stand upon once provided the setting for an antebellum great house named **Dumbarton,** which the merchant Robert A. Taylor built on 190 acres in 1840–41. Architectural historians attribute the design to Robert Cary Long Jr. The building, which today houses the Baltimore Actors' Theater Conservatory, stands on the grounds of Rodgers Forge Elementary School and Dumbarton Middle School (take a left off York Rd. just above the Regester Ave. traffic light). A quarter of a mile away, at Bellona Ave. and the western end of a county playground for young children, one can see the pillars that once belonged to Dumbarton's formal entrance.

Farther north on York Rd., on the left, St. Joseph Hospital Rd. leads to the **St. Joseph Medical Center,** a Catholic institution of 434 acute-care beds, more than 2,000 nurses, and a medical staff in excess of 1,000 physicians. The Sisters of St. Francis of Philadelphia founded the hospital downtown in 1864; it moved to this suburban setting in 1965. St. Joseph's offers a Family Childbirth Center, a holistic Center for Health Enhancement, a Center for Eating Disorders, and a program that treats spinal diseases and irregularities. Its Heart Institute has made the hospital especially well known as a cardiac care center. More open-heart surgery takes place at St. Joseph's than at any other Maryland hospital. The grounds of Sheppard and Enoch Pratt Hospital lie directly west of St. Joseph's.

Towson

York Rd. passes **Towson University,** founded in 1866 as the first state institution devoted exclusively to preparing teachers for the public schools. The school moved to its current site from Baltimore in 1915, when the older, red brick buildings were constructed in the Tudor-Gothic style. Expanded arts and sciences offerings and graduate programs enabled the college to become a university in 1976. With a current total enrollment of 15,403 students, Towson now ranks second only to the University of Maryland at College Park (34,623) in numbers of students at one campus. In 1997 the university, formerly known as Towson State, changed its name, evidently believing that "State" lacked cachet.

Bosley Ave. and Towsontown Blvd. by-pass the busy center of the town of Towson (465' alt., 49,455 pop.), the Baltimore County seat since 1854. York Rd. continues through a narrow, shop-lined area to an intersection with Joppa Rd. and Dulaney Valley Rd. (Md. 146), the crossroads area where Towson originated as a tavern stop on the way to Baltimore. Ezekiel Towson established an "ordinary" here in 1768, the year that the county seat moved from Joppa to Baltimore. As traffic increased to the growing port city to the south, Ezekiel Towson prospered, and he persuaded the General Assembly to route the York turnpike by his tavern. Nathan Towson (1784–1854), Ezekiel's 12th and last child, distinguished himself as an artillery officer, serving near Lake Erie during the War of 1812. After the war, Baltimoreans wanted to make him sheriff, but he preferred and accepted a ceremonial sword instead. He later served as paymaster general of the army, became a major general during the Mexican War, and retired in Washington.

When agitation for county separation from the city peaked in 1853, an election fixed Towson as the county seat. "Towsontown" briefly incorporated in 1870 but reverted to unincorporated status two years later. At the turn of the century, about 2,000 people lived here, a place of farmlands and a few satellite villages, such as Ruxton, that had developed along railroad lines. This population remained largely unchanged until World War II.

Postwar Towson reflected postwar America, when suburban development overwhelmed local government. The PTA and the zoning board, both of which contributed to the election of Spiro T. Agnew as Baltimore County executive in 1962, became battlegrounds between oldtime Democratic politicos, novice suburbanites, and developers. Towson attracted a small army of polyester-clad "carpetbaggers" who vied with old Baltimore Countians, earnest government planners, and new homebuyers to give form to the suburban chaos. Towson is now a small city, consisting of towers of offices and condominiums, parking garages, government agencies, high-tech industrial plants, gleaming shopping centers, and bustling small businesses.

From the central Towson intersection, Joppa Rd., the 18th-century route to the original county seat, continues eastward on its trek across Baltimore County to the Philadelphia Rd. (Md. 7). Dulaney Valley Rd. (Md. 146) branches northeast, eventually becoming Jarrettsville Pike. York Rd. angles northwest and crosses the Baltimore Beltway.

Lutherville

Beyond the Beltway, York Rd. passes suburban shopping centers and crosses Seminary Ave. (Md. 131) to Lutherville. A charming community by this name was planned in the 1850s and then founded in 1854 by three Lutheran ministers. One of them, a man of science and an early librarian at the Peabody Institute, John Gottlieb Morris, started the Lutherville Female Seminary here. It closed in 1925, but its main building still does service as a retirement home. Throughout the 19th and early 20th centuries, the town and academy attracted summer residents, including prominent professionals who commuted to Baltimore on the Northern Central Railroad. The town briefly incorporated in 1868, the first in the county to do so, then joined the pattern of other Baltimore County communities by repealing incorporation in 1874.

The **Fire Museum of Maryland** (1301 York Rd.), founded in 1971 by Stephen G. Heaver, displays antique firefighting apparatus and alarm equipment. With more than 60 vehicles dating from 1822, the museum is one of the largest in the United States.

Timonium

Lutherville folds into **Timonium,** forming a suburban area with a population of 16,422. This locale was little more than a railroad stop, a tollgate, and tavern in 1878, when the Baltimore County Grange held a one-day fair here. The event expanded to the current 10-day annual **Maryland State Fair,** which every September attracts hundreds of thousands to the **Fairgrounds.** The grounds include the **Timonium**

Race Track, a half-mile track on which Thoroughbred races are run during the course of the state fair. The first airmail delivery in the United States occurred here in 1918, when the postmistress at Timonium received a letter on the racetrack's infield.

A young shepherd and one of his charges in the show ring during the 1933 Maryland State Fair, then as now held in Timonium

Cockeysville

York Rd. continues through extensive commercial and residential development to Cockeysville (264' alt., 18,668 pop.), named after an old county family. The locality originally grew around the Beaver Dam marble quarries and the railroad that followed the York turnpike north. (The Baltimore and Susquehanna Railroad reached York, Pennsylvania, in 1838 and became part of the Northern Central system in 1854.) High-grade marble from Cockeysville helped build the Washington Monument in the District of Columbia, the City Hall in Baltimore, and St. Patrick's Cathedral in New York. The stone **Sherwood Episcopal Church** at the corner of York and Sherwood Rds. was erected in 1830. A member of the Cockey family donated the land and money, naming the church after the family's English home. The building was enlarged and the belfry added in 1876.

Three-quarters of a mile north, Ashland Rd. turns right (east) off York Rd. and crosses Western Run, which empties into the upper portion of the Loch Raven Reservoir. The town of **Ashland** was a thriving iron manufacturing center after 1837; the Ashland Iron Furnace operated until 1893, using local ore banks. Rows of stone houses clustering near a Presbyterian church evoke a 19th-century era when small mill and furnace owners created company towns throughout rural Maryland. Once an isolated, poor hamlet, Ashland Village has become a fashionable development in recent years. The **Gunpowder Falls State Park–Northern Central Railroad Trail** begins here.

Shawan Rd., a left turn from York, passes the Hunt Valley Mall and a business-industrial park before intersecting I-83. This complex of stores, businesses, and industrial and recreational facilities occupies the middle of a valley that was famous for fox hunting in the 19th century.

Office parks, industrial centers, and housing developments continue to expand along I-83, but much of the original countryside remains, often beautifully cultivated and maintained. York Rd. bends briefly to the east, and as it straightens to the north an entrance lane bordered by tall Norway spruce marks the way to the gray stone **Jessop Church** on a high hill. The main part of this Methodist church was built in 1811. The Gothic-type vestibule, steeply pitched dormered roof, and belfry were added in 1887.

In **Sparks** the **site of the Milton Academy** has been a county landmark along the road since John E. and Eli M. Lamb established the school here in 1847. Lambs' School remained here until 1877; it moved to Baltimore in 1885 and continued there until 1899. For many years the 2½-story stone building with dormers has housed a well-known restaurant, the Milton Inn.

Horse farms flank the road in this section of Baltimore County. Two miles north of the Milton Inn, the **Old Gorsuch Tavern** (private) is visible from the road (right). Around 1810, Capt. Joshua Gorsuch constructed the north wing of this 2½-story, T-shaped brick house. The captain allegedly stored valuable silks, spices, and other goods from Far Eastern voyages in arched chambers underneath the tavern. Edward Gorsuch, his son and a slave trader, used the 3½-story stone barn across the road to house his human "merchandise." Two African slaves escaped in September 1851 and, with the aid of the local Underground Railroad, made their way north to Lancaster County, Pennsylvania. Gorsuch, leading a posse after the runaways, was killed by their protectors as he attempted to reclaim them. His son Dickerson and several other members of their party were wounded in what came to be known as the "Christiana Massacre."

York Rd. passes through **Hereford,** crosses **Gunpowder Falls State Park** and continues north through **Parkton,** once the northernmost station of the commuter line that ran to Baltimore. New suburban housing developments dot the farmland in a slow but steady march north from Towson. York Rd. crosses over I-83 and then closely parallels the interstate highway before both cross into Pennsylvania at **Maryland Line.**

E. DULANEY VALLEY RD. / JARRETTSVILLE PIKE (MD. 146)

Md. 146 follows another route used by wagoners between Pennsylvania and Baltimore. It begins as Dulaney Valley Rd. in downtown Towson—at a traffic circle that in 1998 replaced an awkward intersection—and strikes off to the northeast.

From the traffic circle, follow the road past Towson Town Center, a major regional mall, on the right and a postwar shopping center on the left, and turn right on Goucher Blvd. for a visit to the **Richard and Annette Bloch Cancer Survivors' Park,** an acre of land at Goucher Blvd. and Fairmount Ave. dedicated in 1997. One of 12 such parks in the nation, it features lifelike bronze figures, a waterfall and reflecting pool, and plaques along a "positive mental attitude walk."

Goucher College

Dulaney Valley Rd. takes one past Goucher College, located on more than 300 acres purchased in 1935. In 1888 the school opened as the Woman's College of Baltimore, a Methodist institution at St. Paul and 23rd Streets. A liberal arts college, it became nonsectarian in 1914 and changed its name, to honor John F. Goucher, president from 1890 to 1907. In 1986 the college voted to become coeducational. It now has an enrollment of 932 students, three out of four of them women.

Hampton

Just beyond the road's cloverleaf intersection with the Baltimore Beltway, Hampton Estate Ln. turns right to the 60-acre **Hampton National Historic Site.**

The Ridgelys of Hampton

Six generations of the Ridgely family lived in this large colonial mansion for more than 150 years, until its presentation to the federal government in 1948. The large, stuccoed stone house—with a huge central hall, four square rooms on either side and dormered roof crowned by an octagonal cupola—has been consistently ranked among the most significant Georgian mansions still intact in the United States. At the time of its construction, wolves still roamed the countryside at night and some called the elaborate house in the middle of semiwilderness "Ridgely's Folly." Now surrounded by commercial traffic, visitors admire the bygone elegance of its handiwork.

Col. Charles Ridgely (1702–72), whose English forebears came to Maryland within 40 years after the first settlers, purchased the 1,500-acre Northhampton tract here in 1745. Taking advantage of the plentiful supply of local iron ore, he established a furnace around 1760 on land now covered by the Loch Raven Reservoir. The property became the basis of an agricultural and industrial complex that made the Ridgelys rich and influential. His son, Capt. Charles Ridgely (the mansion's builder), continued to expand the family estates, supported by a small battalion of slaves, indentured servants, convict servants, and free laborers. The Northhampton Iron Works, later known as the Hampton Estate and Iron Works, provided cannon and other utensils for the Continental Army during the Revolution. After the war, Captain Ridgely began construction of the house, assisted by John Howell, a master builder and amateur architect. It was completed in 1790, the year Ridgely died, childless.

Charles Ridgely Carnan, son of Captain Ridgely's sister Rebecca, inherited the 33-room mansion on condition that he reverse the order of his name and "become" a Ridgely. He did so. This Ridgely, later a governor of Maryland (1815–18), landscaped the property in a grand manner. The iron works ceased production in the 1820s, but the Ridgelys continued their position in the county as influential, landed gentry. Interior furnishings and objets d'art from around the world added to the grandeur of the family mansion.

In 1945, David E. Finley, former director of the National Gallery of Art, visited Hampton to buy two Thomas Sully portraits from John Ridgely. When he learned that the owner wanted to sell the house as a historic site, Finley began putting together the pieces of an unusual, pioneering deal. The Avalon Foundation, controlled by Mrs. Ailsa Mellon Bruce, was persuaded to buy and repair the house for the National Park Service, which at the time had no funding for maintaining and managing the site. The Society for the Preservation of Maryland Antiquities (SPMA) signed an agreement to take responsibility for the house and gardens and open the estate to the public. When the National Park Service finally did acquire the mansion in 1948, Hampton became the first historic site accepted on architectural merit rather than historical significance. This cooperation between public and private organizations led to discussions which eventually resulted in formation of the National Trust for Historic Preservation in 1949. The SPMA ended its agreement with the Park Service in 1979 but recently sponsored a study to reexamine the archival, physical, and historical-interpretive possibilities at Hampton—one of the most richly documented dwellings in the United States. In 1997, faced with deficits and the need for basic repairs, the Park Service began charging admission to the house. The public still has free access to the 63-acre grounds.

Glen Ellen

Beyond Hampton, Dulaney Valley Rd. skirts the watershed of the **Loch Raven Reservoir** (see below), a peaceful wooded site that conceals a colorful episode in the region's history. In about 1830, Robert and William Gilmor, descendants of the Scottish immigrant and highly successful Baltimore merchant Robert Gilmor, bought 2,000 acres along the Gunpowder River Valley from the Ridgelys. Returned from diplomatic service in Europe, Robert set out to build in Baltimore County something as gothic and romantic as Sir Walter Scott's home, Abbotsford, a castle he named **Glen Ellen,** after his wife. The full extent of his vision was never realized, but in the large structure that was completed the couple raised 11 children, including six sons who joined the Confederacy. One, Harry Gilmor (1838–83), seemed right out of Scott's novels. He rose to the rank of major in the Confederate cavalry, serving for a time under Gen. Bradley T. Johnson. It was Harry Gilmor who in 1864 led a small group of raiders through Baltimore and Harford Counties during Jubal Early's invasion of Maryland. Major Gilmor occupied Cockeysville on July 10 and rode to Glen Ellen to visit his family. The Confederate cavalrymen later partially burned a bridge across the Little Gunpowder at Magnolia in Harford County, burned two trains, and captured a Union general. He and his raiders then returned to Towson and chased Union cavalrymen down York Rd. Later that year, Gilmor was wounded and captured. After the war he returned to Glen Ellen. By his own account a ladies man, marksman, and reckless romantic (whose war experiences included being tried by a Confederate military tribunal for robbing passengers on a B&O train), Gilmor set forth his exploits in a memoir entitled *Four Years in the Saddle* (1866). He served as a Baltimore City police commissioner from 1874 to 1879. The estate was sold just before his death in 1883. By 1920, the city had acquired the entire property to create the Loch Raven Reservoir watershed. The Gilmor castle gradually deteriorated and was finally razed.

Loch Raven Reservoir

In 1881, a dam and water tunnel were constructed at Raven's Rock, an outcrop on the Gunpowder Falls near Robert Gilmor's home, to channel water from the Gunpowder River to Lake Montebello and Lake Clifton in the city. In 1914, to increase its municipal water supply, the city of Baltimore created the Loch Raven Reservoir. A new dam was constructed near the Cromwell Bridge, east of Hampton; its reservoir submerged much of the old agricultural-industrial complex to the north, including the mill village of Warren. In 1923 the height of the dam was increased from 52 feet to 240 feet. The Scottish "Loch" recalls the romantic Gilmors.

Md. 146 crosses the reservoir and becomes Jarrettsville Pike, which passes through a section of the **Gunpowder Falls State Park,** intersects Md. 145 at the crossroads community of **Jacksonville** and crosses the Little Gunpowder Falls into Harford County.

Ladew Topiary Gardens

Off Jarrettsville Pike, just south of its intersection with Md. 152 (Fallston Rd.), one discovers a fanciful world carved of greenery, the Ladew Topiary Gardens. Harvey Smith Ladew (1886–1976), avid traveler, bachelor bon vivant, and fox hunter extraordinaire, bought Pleasant Valley Farm here in 1929 and created an idiosyncratic, personalized world in the midst of rural, horsey countryside. In 1971, when he was 85 years old, the Garden Club of America presented Ladew its Distinguished Service Medal for "great interest in developing and maintaining the most outstanding topiary garden in America, without professional help." After his death, a nonprofit foundation took over his manor and its 15 gardens, laid out in a great variety of ornamental shapes and styles over 22 acres. Ladew's gardens, now on the National Register of Historic Places, have become a tourist attraction, offering a café, gift shop, and warm weather festivities.

F. HARFORD RD. (MD. 147)

Harford Rd. follows a former turnpike route northeast from Baltimore through a landscape that remained rural longer than did comparable areas north and northwest of the city. Streetcar service did not reach the small towns of **Parkville** and **Carney** until 1918. Developers began to fill the land gaps between the towns after World War I, but suburban expansion proceeded slowly until the industrial boom around East Baltimore during World War II. Now Parkville (31,617 pop.) and Carney (25,578 pop.) supply more than 8 percent of Baltimore County's population, Parkville being the most densely populated area in the county.

Beyond the Baltimore Beltway, Cub Hill Rd. branches west from the highway to Old Harford Rd., which terminates at the **Charles H. Hickey Jr. School,** formerly the Maryland Training School for Boys. Renamed in 1985 for a Baltimore County sheriff, the institution was first established for delinquent boys in 1850 on a farm along the Gunpowder Falls. The state acquired the facility in 1918; it now serves as a training and detention center for youths between the ages of 15 and 17.

Harford Rd. continues past **Graham Memorial Park,** on the east, a good spot for fishing and hiking, and crosses Gunpowder Falls through a portion of the **Gunpowder Falls State Park,** which lines the streambed along its course to the Gunpowder River near Joppatowne.

Just beyond Gunpowder Falls, a marker near Factory Rd. indicates the **site of the Gunpowder Copper Works,** established in 1804 by Levi Hollingsworth, who was also manager of the Harford Turnpike. Hollingsworth imported foreign ores and local ore from Frederick County and in 1815 spent $100,000 on a copper rolling mill modeled on those he had studied in England. His manufacturing company, one of the earliest in the United States, became a forerunner of the copper smelting, rolling, and refining industries that later developed around the port of Baltimore. The dome of the U.S. Capitol contains copper sheeting from Hollingsworth's mill.

Turn left onto Factory Rd. and follow this country lane north along a portion of the park. It becomes Long Green Pike and continues north through the crossroads hamlet of **Glen Arm** to Boordy Vineyards, Maryland's oldest and largest winery.

Boordy, now owned by the Deford family, became nationally famous as the experimental brainchild of Philip M. Wagner, a Baltimore *Sun* editor who introduced French-American hybrid grapes to the East Coast. Wagner promoted the hybrids as successful alternatives to American and European grape varieties, which often succumbed to winter in the northeastern states. He and his wife, Jocelyn, built a winery on their Riderwood estate near Ruxton and began selling Boordy wine (the name's origin remains private) in 1945. He sold his winery in 1980 to Rob Deford, whom he had persuaded to grow grapes on his farm near **Hydes.** Boordy's success stimulated a small Maryland wine industry that has created a viable market niche for its products. Ten commercial vineyards, most in central Maryland, produce more than 300,000 bottles annually.

Maryland has a long tradition of experimentation in the cultivation of vineyards. Lord Baltimore sent European vines to his colony in the 17th century, but they did not survive the journey. Planters experimented with native grapes with limited success, complaining about their "foxy" taste. Col. Benjamin Tasker made a "burgundy" from the Alexander grape at his Belair estate around 1756. Maj. John Adlum, owner of The Vineyard, a 200-acre estate once located within the Rock Creek Park valley in modern Washington, experimented unsuccessfully with foreign vines in the early 19th century. Then he discovered the native Catawba grape and created a distinctive American wine. Thomas Jefferson, a connoisseur, tasted the wine in 1823 with knowledgeable friends and pronounced it "truly fine . . . of high flavor . . . of good body of its own." That same year Adlum completed *A Memoir on the Cultivation of the Vine in America and the Best Mode of Making Wine,* the first book on winegrowing published in the United States. Philip M. Wagner continued this literary tradition with an American classic, *American Wines and Wine-Making,* now known as *Grapes into Wine.*

Harford Rd. continues its northeasterly course to **Fork,** a village built around a rural Quaker meeting house. Sunshine Ave., which connects Fork with nearby Kingsville, follows the route taken by Harry Gilmor's 135-man cavalry force on July 28, 1864, when it encountered Ishmael Day, who was flying the American flag from his farmhouse. Day later said he shot and killed Confederate sergeant William Fields (of Baltimore) when the Rebel called the flag a "damned old rag." Day fled; Gilmor's troops burned his property and stole valuable possessions, while Mrs. Day berated Gilmor as "a highway robber." On August 23, 1864, Gen. Lew Wallace ordered that all disloyal and disaffected persons within five miles of Day's farm be assessed for his loss. Ishmael, then a folk hero, received contributions from points far beyond Fork; he later moved to Baltimore and became an inspector at the Customs House.

Beyond Fork, Harford Rd. crosses Little Gunpowder Falls and enters Harford County, where it intersects Fallston Rd. (Md. 152). Turn left and make another left on Connelly Rd. to Old Fallston Rd., which runs through **Fallston** (442′ alt., 5,730 pop.), another village built around a Quaker meeting house and now a prosperous residential center.

Laurel Brook Rd. turns left off Old Fallston Rd. to **Bonair** (private), a dwelling built in 1794 by Francis de la Porte, an officer under General Rochambeau, who landed in Rhode Island in 1780 with 6,000 French troops to aid the American Revolution. Like some other European officers and soldiers, de la Porte decided to stay in the new country after Cornwallis's defeat at Yorktown in 1781. He, his mother, and his wife are buried near the house, which resembles a small chateau on the Loire.

Old Fallston Rd. continues past the **Little Falls Meeting House,** a 1¹/₂-story stone structure built in 1843 with a door at each end of the front and an interior partition that separated men from women. Local Friends established a meeting place in a log cabin on a farm along the Little Gunpowder Falls in 1738 and moved the meeting to this location in 1749. The current stone building, constructed in 1843, is the fourth meeting house for the Quakers in this part of the county. Before the Civil War, the Friends operated a station on the Underground Railroad here.

The original turnpike may have led to Bel Air; today Harford Rd. ends where it meets U.S. 1 near Fallston.

G. BELAIR AND CONOWINGO RDS. (U.S. 1)

When the new State Roads Commission announced its intention to eliminate private turnpikes in 1908, the Belair Turnpike was selected to form part of the new national road between New York and Washington, later to become U.S. 1. Electric streetcars had already reached **Overlea** (12,137 pop.) and **Fullerton** in 1904, so the path was set for the residential development that later mushroomed in this area. Bohemians, Poles, Ukrainians, and Italians moved from cramped neighborhoods in East Baltimore into single-family cottages. The small farms and family estates that once characterized the area gradually disappeared.

Perry Hall

Northeast of Overlea and Fullerton, U.S. 1 (Belair Rd.), crosses White Marsh Run and continues east to Perry Hall (22,723 pop.). Just before the Gunpowder Falls, Perry Hall Rd. branches northwest (left) from the highway to **Perry Hall Mansion** (private, but visible from the road).

Perry Hall Mansion, Baltimore County, as it looked in the late 1930s

Before a fire in 1824 reduced the structure to its present size, this stuccoed stone house had two wings and hyphens that led to square pavilions at each end. One pavilion contained a bath, and the other a Methodist chapel. The main block of the house was built about 1773 and sold to Harry Dorsey Gough (1745–1808) in 1774. Gough added the wings and pavilions after the Revolution.

After the Goughs were converted to Methodism in 1775, Perry Hall became a center of hospitality for itinerant Methodist preachers, especially Thomas Coke and Francis Asbury, who came here to rest and recuperate from extensive preaching trips on horseback into the hinterlands. "Black Harry" Hosier, an ex-slave who was illiterate but a powerful preacher, accompanied these Methodist divines on their journeys and also stayed at Perry Hall. In December 1784, a number of Methodist preachers and their followers assembled at this house and then rode to Baltimore for the conference at the Lovely Lane Church which resulted in the organization of the Methodist Church in America.

Gough was elected in 1786 as the first president of the Society for Improvement of Agriculture in Maryland. The following year, his daughter Sophia married James Carroll of Mount Clare. These and other connections with the Carroll and Ridgely families created an interlocked gentry that exerted great influence in county politics and business ventures. The mansions at Mount Clare, Hampton, and Perry Hall symbolized a political economy and social order now long disappeared, along with slavery and the farmlands that sustained them.

Belair Rd. crosses Gunpowder Falls and passes through one of the many sections of **Gunpowder Falls State Park** which line the valleys of both the Gunpowder and Little Gunpowder Falls.

At **Kingsville** one may admire the three-story **Kingsville Inn,** a small house believed to date from 1740 or earlier. The Rev. Hugh Dean of St. John's Parish occupied the house, which was subsequently owned by his son-in-law, John Paul, a Quaker who during the Revolution was suspected of being a Tory. Paul was arrested in April 1781 for supplying flour to the British, but he later escaped.

Beyond Kingsville, Belair Rd. crosses the Little Gunpowder Falls and converges with Harford Rd. (Md. 147) at **Benson.** Business U.S. 1 continues into Bel Air, while U.S. 1 swerves west and north as the Bel Air Bypass.

Alternate Route: From Kingsville to Bel Air on Jerusalem Rd.

From Belair Rd. in Kingsville, Jerusalem Rd. angles northeast and crosses the Little Gunpowder at **Jerusalem Mill.** David Lee, a Pennsylvania Quaker, constructed at least part of this mill in 1772. The first story is made of stone and the second of log and frame topped by two half-stories under a steep gabled roof. Two tiers of alternating dormer windows light the third story and loft.

Just beyond the mill, turn right on Jericho Rd., which crosses the Little Gunpowder on the **Jericho Covered Bridge,** believed to have been constructed around 1800, using the bowstring method of bending single timbers to form arches that stretch from bank to bank. Follow the road along the falls, through the park, to Franklinville Rd. Turn left and cross

the falls again, on Franklinville Rd., which terminates at Old Joppa Rd. During the early 19th century, when virtually every main road across a major stream passed a mill of some type, cotton mills flourished at Jericho and Franklinville near these two bridges. Although still indicated on an 1877 Baltimore County atlas, the mill towns here had already declined by then and soon succumbed to competitors located closer to Baltimore City.

Jericho Covered Bridge, Harford County, on the country road so named

Turn north (left) on Old Joppa Rd., which crosses Jerusalem Rd., and continue to a junction with Mountain Rd. Harry Gilmor and his Confederate raiders camped overnight here on July 10, 1864, in a stone building that had served as an old stagecoach headquarters; the next day they moved south to Magnolia Station to burn the Pennsylvania Railroad bridge across the Gunpowder River. Continue on Old Joppa Rd., passing through horse country. Just before the intersection with Hollingsworth Rd., the highway passes a gate to **Olney** (private), a brick house built in 1810 by John Saurin Norris and enlarged about 1850.

Whitaker Mill Rd. slopes southeast (right) from Old Jericho Rd. to Winter's Run, where a mill has existed since the late 18th century. Named first Gibbon's or Gibson's Mill, then Mitchell's, and then Duncale Mill, the site was leased in 1846 to Franklin and Rachel Whitaker, who built the present stone structure in 1851. The gristmill operated until the early 1900s and was later remodeled as a private residence.

Country Life Farm, known for breeding prize-winning race horses, is located off Old Joppa Rd. just before its intersection with Business U.S. 1, which leads northeast (right) and crosses Winter's Run and Toll Gate Rd. into Bel Air.

Bel Air

The seat of Harford County, Bel Air (396' alt., 8,860 pop.) dates to 1780, when land near Bynum's and Winter's Runs was subdivided as Scott's Old Fields. In 1784, the choice for the seat of Harford County (es-

The motor speedway at Bel Air in the 1930s, when speeds of a mile a minute defied death

tablished in 1773) was between Havre de Grace and "Belle Air." The latter won a public election, and by 1786, the spelling "Bel Air" had become firmly established in government records. The town, which consisted of a few hotels, taverns, lawyers' offices, residences, and stores clustered around the courthouse, grew slowly. The courthouse burned in 1858 and was immediately rebuilt, but the town did not incorporate until 1874. No longer a trading and banking center for farmers, Bel Air has become a commercial center for the 41,000 people who live in surrounding suburban developments. The number of housing units in Harford County almost doubled between 1970 and 1990, from 33,483 to 66,446. Most of the new housing constructed in the 1980s consisted of single-family houses whose mean value mushroomed during the decade, from $65,161 to $126,315.

The **Hays-Jacobs House,** on Kenmore Ave. off the Baltimore Pike (Business U.S. 1) in the middle of Bel Air, stood on Main St. until 1960, when it was removed to make way for a supermarket. Restored and converted to a small museum, this gambrel-roofed, 18th-century frame house provides a home to the **Harford County Historical Society.**

Dr. Howard A. Kelly, a surgeon from New Jersey who became one of the famous "Four Doctors" of the new Johns Hopkins Medical School, built **Liriodendron** (private), 502 W. Gordon St., as a summer home in 1898. The house appears on the National Register of Historic Places.

Business U.S. 1 leaves Main St. at Broadway, which crosses Bynum's Run and unites with U.S. 1 just north of Bel Air.

Side Trip on Churchville Rd. (Md. 22)

To travel east toward Churchville and visit the homestead of the Booths, America's most celebrated 19th-century family of actors, take Churchville Rd. (Md. 22) out of Bel Air and turn left on Tudor Ln. beyond the road's junction with Md. 543. The lane passes through a housing development and then arrives at an old brick house with casement windows and other details of English design.

Tudor Hall, completed in 1846, belonged to Junius Brutus Booth (1796–1852). A popular English actor, Booth deserted his wife and emigrated to America with a flower girl in 1821. He purchased this farm property and started a large family. Edwin Thomas (1833–93) and his brother John Wilkes (1839–65) were born in a house that stood earlier on this site. Mental instability haunted this brilliant acting family. Edwin accompanied his eccentric and erratic father on traveling productions of Shakespeare's plays and even as a youth in 1850 performed readings at the Bel Air courthouse. Following his father's death, the young actor continued the family's barnstorming tradition, touring as far away as Australia. He withdrew briefly from the theater, following the assassination of Abraham Lincoln by his younger brother, a less successful actor who had inherited the family's nervous histrionics. Edwin soon returned to the stage, however, and by the time of his death, this native Harford Countian was recognized as one of America's greatest tragedians, particularly known for the role of Hamlet. A museum in the house, now operated as a bed-and-breakfast, contains artifacts from the family's colorful history.

At Schucks Corner, Churchville Rd. arrives at the 214-acre campus of **Harford Community College,** which started in Bel Air High School in 1957 with an enrollment of 100. Now 5,348 full- and part-time students attend the college, which also features the **Edwin Booth Theater.**

Near this intersection, on Medical Hall Rd., stands **Medical Hall** (private), a 2½-story stuccoed brick house with delicate reeding and other doorway details typical of woodwork popular around 1800. Dr. John Archer (1741–1810), who was born nearby, built this dwelling around 1799. He had obtained his diploma, the first medical degree granted by an American school, from the Philadelphia Medical College in 1768. In 1775, Archer signed the Bush Declaration of Independence, a document committing the men of Harford County to fight for their rights as English citizens. He later raised a militia company to fight during the Revolution. John Archer fathered five physicians and also founded the Medical and Chirurgical Faculty of Maryland in 1799 with his son, Dr. Thomas Archer. Then the patriot physician served two terms in Congress (1800–1804), after which he conducted a medical school at his home. His will stipulated that those of his debtors unable to pay at the time of his death should be released from their obligations, and that his slaves above certain ages should be set free, the males at the age of 30 and the females at 25. Another son, Stevenson Archer (1786–1848), served in Congress (1811–17, 1819–21), sat as chief judge of the Circuit Court (1823–44), and then as chief judge of the Court of Appeals (1844–48). He was born and died at Medical Hall.

Follow Md. 22 farther east to **Churchville.** In the 18th century, this community was known as Lower Cross Roads and then Herbert's Crossroads. Tradition indicates that the Rev. George Whitefield, an English evangelist, passed through this region in 1739 and left an inspired Presbyterian congregation, which moved here in 1759. One of the earliest Presbyterian centers in the state, the town became known as Churchville. A church building was here constructed in 1820 and subsequently destroyed. When its successor was remodeled in 1870, the Italian Gothic bell tower was added and the interior greatly changed. Additional reconstructions and redecorations have occurred in this century.

South from Churchville, Md. 136 leads to Md. 543 at **Creswell.** Md. 543 (Creswell Rd.) passes **Eastern Christian College** and then takes one to the **site of Harford Furnace.** Pennsylvania investors established Harford Furnace on James Run in 1830, using local iron ore deposits. The enterprise flourished and developed into an industrial complex that included an iron and rolling mill, post office, general store, warehouses, and residences spread over more than 5,000 acres owned by the company. The furnace closed in 1864, and by 1878 the settlement around it had declined to a small village.

North of Bel Air, U.S. 1 (now Conowingo Rd.) leads to **Hickory.** Here Ady Rd. (Md. 543) branches north to **Walter's Mill** on Deer Creek. John and Samuel Forwood, from Delaware, erected a gristmill here around 1774. The mill later passed through various owners until it was purchased by Charles S. Walter in 1911. The original mill burned around 1900, and the present frame building rests on its stone foundations. Walter's Mill Rd. travels east along the creek to **Sandy Hook** and the entrance to **Deer Creek Park.** One may also reach the park by traveling north from Hickory, taking a left on Gibson Rd. and an immediate right on Sandy Hook Rd.

About two and one-half miles above Hickory on Conowingo Rd., a right turn on Forge Hill Rd. leads one to **Palmer State Park,** 463 undeveloped acres adjacent to Deer Creek. Gerald and Ruth Palmer donated the land to the state in 1965.

Just after Gallions Corner, on its way toward the Susquehanna River, Conowingo Rd. passes **Wildsfell** (private, but visible on the right), an octagonal, white frame house believed to have been built in the 1840s by a ship's carpenter who used beams from an old clipper ship in its construction.

Side Trip to Susquehanna State Park on Darlington Rd. (Md. 161)

About two miles before the river, Md. 161 (Darlington Rd.), curves south from Conowingo Rd. and passes **Deer Creek Friends Meeting,** a traditional 18th-century 1½-story stone meeting house with a partition creating separate sections for men and women.

The village of **Darlington** dates to 18th-century settlers who established farms in the area. Darlington became a stagecoach and wagon stop as well as a local center for traffic from the Susquehanna and Tidewater Canal. Churches and local industries added substance to the community; the school system traces its origins to the 19th-century Darlington Academy.

Md. 161 descends to Deer Creek and the **site of Wilson's Mill** (private), one of the oldest gristmills still standing in Harford County. The stone mill is located on land deeded to Nathan Rigbie in 1743. Beyond the creek, turn left on Wilkinson Rd. and follow it to Susquehanna State Park. A short distance farther on Md. 161, the road crosses (on the right) Green Spring Rd., which passes the **Prospect Schoolhouse.** Joshua Stephen, a local stonemason, built this small, hexagonal stone building in about 1850—according to legend, to disprove scoffers who claimed he did not have the skill.

Susquehanna State Park

The state started land acquisition along this riverfront in 1958; development of the Susquehanna State Park began in 1965. With addition of land across the river in Cecil County, the park now contains 2,646 acres, which include boating and fishing areas, campgrounds, and nature trails. Deer Creek and its tributaries and also Rock Run flow through park land down to the wide Susquehanna River, at this point filled with boulders, small islands, and rapids. The **Steppingstone Farm Museum** features a small stone farmhouse furnished in turn-of-the-century styles. In adjacent outbuildings, exhibits of rural crafts and antique tools illustrate rural life around 1900. During warm weather months, volunteers and local craftspeople display their skills in live demonstrations.

The restored **Rock Run Mill** occupies a site near that stream's confluence with the river, a short distance south of Wilkinson Rd. John Stump Jr. built this stone and frame structure near an earlier mill site around 1794. John Carter, his partner for a while, erected a 13-room stone residence near the mill in 1804. Stump, a rich man, later bought the entire property and left it to his heirs. The state restored both mill and mansion in 1965. A renovated toll house nearby recalls the Rock Run Bridge, the first structure to span the lower Susquehanna, previously crossed only at fords or by ferries. Completed in 1818, the toll bridge lasted until 1856, when winter ice demolished it.

To the south of the park, Stafford Rd. takes one beyond Rock Run and to a few abandoned locks that recall the **Susquehanna and Tidewater Canal.** Completed in 1839, the canal connected Wrightsville, Pennsylvania, and Havre de Grace. Canal boats with coal, timber, wheat, and other farm products descended almost 1,000 feet over 29 locks, as the canal paralleled the river, which was basically unnavigable. From Havre de Grace, the cargo moved down the bay to Baltimore, the region's biggest marketplace, and to New York and Philadelphia. Traffic peaked around 1870; the Johnstown flood of 1889 destroyed much of the upper canal, but the nine locks in Harford County remained active until the early 1900s. A railroad spur continues down the old towpath to Havre de Grace after the road curves away from the river.

The Lower Deer Creek Valley

The Lower Deer Creek Valley Historic District, in north central Harford County, entered the National Register of Historic Places in 1993, one of more than 1,100 such places in Maryland (the state ranks 14th in the number of sites on that list). The district consists of about 12,000 acres of rolling countryside along Deer Creek between the Susquehanna River on the east and Md. 543 (Ady Rd.) on the west. About 350 separate sites within this area also appear in the Maryland Inventory of Historic Properties, maintained by the Maryland Historical Trust. Of 37 buildings described more than a century ago in a newspaper series entitled "Homes on Deer Creek," 36 still stand. With good reason we may view the valley—protected by hilly terrain and the stability of local families—as a museum of cultural development in this part of the state.

The Susquehannocks were the first known people to roam the Deer Creek Valley, although pre-historic petroglyphs, under water since completion of the Conowingo Dam in 1927, demonstrate a longstanding human presence in this part of the lower Susquehanna River Valley. Capt. John Smith encountered a Susquehannock hunting party on his second expedition up the Chesapeake Bay in 1608, perhaps along Deer Creek, and described them as "the strangest people of all these countries; both in language and attire; for their language, it may well become their proportions, sounding from them as a voyce in a vault." The Susquehannocks were an Iroquoian people related to tribes of the Five Nations to the north, their traditional enemies. Captain Smith, a military man, estimated that the tribe could muster 700 warriors. After a smallpox epidemic in the 1660s, this number shrank to 300. In 1674 the Senecas drove the diminished Susquehannocks from their towns and hunting grounds, and only after the tribe submitted to the Five Nations did a few remnants return to their homes along the river.

By the late 17th century, Lord Baltimore had granted a few settlers large tracts of land in north-ern Baltimore and Harford Counties. In 1684 the Rev. John Yeo, Anglican rector of St. George's Parish, patented 400 acres just south of Deer Creek as Mt. Yeo. (No great friend of the Catholic Calverts, Yeo earlier had written to the archbishop of Canterbury that in Maryland, where there was then no established church, "the Lord's Day is profaned, religion is despised, and all notorious vices are com-mitted, so that it is becoming a Sodom of uncleanness and a pesthouse of iniquity.")

Attracted by its swift flowing streams, wooded hillsides, and fertile meadows, Europeans settled the Deer Creek area in the early 18th century, protected by a string of small forts and garrisons of special rangers. The newcomers were farmers, English colonists, and native-born Marylanders, who joined Germans from Pennsylvania. The few remaining Susquehannocks, distrusted and hemmed in by the settlers' fences, gradually departed their ancestral lands and by 1750 had disappeared. The new residents had names like Stump, Silver, Hopkins, Worthington, Rigbie, Husband, Wilson, and Coole. They and their laborers cleared large fields, built mills, fished the Susquehanna River and Deer Creek, and established small, interlocking rural networks that sent wheat, flour, lumber, flint, iron, and herring and shad to the metropolitan markets of Baltimore and Philadelphia. The established, landed families created a complicated genealogical web of kinsmen that dominated the Deer Creek Valley economy for more than a century. Henry Stump (1731–1814) first exploited the fisheries from the shipping center of Lapidum; his nephew John Stump (1752–1816) became one of the richest merchants in Maryland, creating company towns at Rock Run and Stafford.

Priest Neale's Mass House, located at 2618 Cool Spring Ln. (near Priestford Bridge and the U.S. Army Tank Proving Center), dates to 1743, when the Anglican Church, by then the established church in Maryland, forbade Roman Catholic priests to say mass in public. John Digges, a Jesuit who rode circuit, constructed the house (a story-and-a-half stuccoed-stone structure) and said masses in it. Father Digges died in 1746, and Bennett Neale took his place until his own death in 1773. Around 1750, Neale built a mill on the north bank of Deer Creek (now an archaeological site), perhaps the first in the valley.

By the time of the Revolution, the countryside was dotted with small manor houses, a few churches, and mills along Deer Creek, many constructed from local granite. **Deer Park,** a two-story frame house on Ady Rd. near Dublin Rd. (Md. 440), dates to the late colonial period; its main sec-tion was probably constructed around 1740 by Benjamin Wheeler (d. 1741), who migrated to the valley from Southern Maryland in the late 17th century. Ignatius Wheeler II (d. 1793) served as a colonel during the Revolution and doubled the size of his family farm from confiscated Tory prop-erty; he also helped establish **St. Ignatius Church** (1793) in Hickory.

During the Revolution, French and American troops under the command of the Marquis de Lafayette crossed the Susquehanna at nearby Bald Friar, and a number of the French officers were struck by the natural beauty of the countryside. Angus Greme, a captain, and his friend, Col. Jean Joseph de Gimat, returned after the war and bought 800 acres west of Priest Neale's Mass House. Gi-mat was killed in Saint-Domingue during the French struggle with Toussaint L'Ouverture, but Greme settled here with his family and farmed the land until his death in 1800. His simple tombstone still sits in the churchyard at **Trappe Church** (Trappe Church and Priest Ford Rds.), once a chapel of ease for St. George's Parish.

After the Revolution, as family fortunes rose and fell in a new economy, the large farms were increasingly subdivided. Successful Quaker businessmen-farmers built the Deer Creek Meeting House in Darlington in 1784, and that village became a market center for the surrounding farms. The **Massey-Ely Tavern and Store**, a two-part, two-story frame structure located at 2101 Shuresville Rd., was built around 1820 and may be the oldest house in Darlington. Four stone houses built between 1853 and 1859 by three sons and a nephew of Benjamin Silver II (above the south bank of Deer Creek off Harmony Church Rd.) further demonstrated Darlington's new prosperity. Outside the town, Elisha Cook constructed a dam and mills along Deer Creek after 1816; Noble's Mill went up in 1854.

Around 1800, Joshua Hubbard Sr. (1764–1837) built a flint milling complex on Deer Creek. There he employed free African Americans, who established a community in **Kalmia** (just east of U.S. 1 before it crosses Deer Creek). The mill's surviving foundations, quarry pits, and kilns remain the best preserved site of Maryland's extinct flint industry. The Kalmia community has endured, symbolized by **Clark's Chapel AME Church** (2001 Kalmia Rd.), which in 1883 replaced an earlier structure. Five rubblestone houses in Kalmia may be the work of a free African American stonemason named Rumsey.

Probably encouraged by the tolerance of local Quakers, free African Americans settled in the valley as early as 1813. They and the local Friends later supported a section of the Underground Railroad that helped escaping slaves to cross the Susquehanna River. The Worthington family operated a river landing just below the current Conowingo Dam at the end of Shuresville Rd. Fugitives would hide in the cornfields on William Worthington's farm until nightfall, when they would be escorted across the river. The foundations of Worthington's house are one of the few tangible Maryland remnants of the Underground Railroad.

The abundance of local granite and other stone fostered the development of a distinctive architecture in the Deer Creek Valley during the 19th century. Millers had no trouble finding millstones, and skilled local craftsmen created such rare stone structures as the **D.H. Springhouse,** located on the north side of Sandy Hook Rd. about half a mile north of Allibone Rd. The finished granite facade features a pyramidal, ball-topped finial, an unusual ornamentation for an isolated rural building. The initials "D.H." and the date "1816" are carved in an oval on a recessed stone tablet. The initials are those of the builder, David Hopkins, who was hired by William Smithson. The room in the upper level of the springhouse was used as a schoolroom.

Later in the 19th century the lower Deer Creek Valley attracted a number of wealthy outsiders who found its rolling, rural beauty an attractive respite from hectic urban life. Hugh Judge Jewett (1817–98) established a social pattern when he returned in 1884 to Lansdowne, his family's estate south of Deer Creek near Glenville. Jewett, a former Ohio congressman and president of the Erie Railroad, hired Philadelphia architect Walter Cope to expand his family's house. Cope then designed a number of country houses and outbuildings for clients who had bought a few acres in the creek valley between Darlington and Indian Spring Farm.

Although the Great Depression stemmed this influx of "high society" residents, a Victorian tradition of private philanthropy and preservation has continued in the valley. Francis and Lelia Stokes acquired **Wilson's Mill** in 1931 and hired Philadelphia architects to remodel and restore the old buildings. Located near the intersection of Darlington and Harmony Church Rd. (where Deer Creek Harmony Presbyterian Church was founded in 1837), the old mill dates to the 18th century and has been owned by a succession of well-known families, including Parkers, Rigbies, Brintons, Stumps, Prices, and Wilsons. J. Gilman D'Arcy Paul, a retired diplomat, moved to the valley in 1936 and championed preservation efforts that led to the formation of Susquehanna State Park.

The rapid suburbanization of central Maryland in the 1950s and 1960s did not overwhelm the lower Deer Creek Valley with highways, shopping centers, and housing developments. The historic district has remained rural, crisscrossed with small streams and country roads. The architecture, characterized by old mills, unusual stone buildings, and early modern country houses, has remained unchanged for almost a century.

Just beyond its intersection with Md. 161 at Darlington, Conowingo Rd. crosses Md. 623, which travels north along the Susquehanna River less than a mile before reaching the **Nathan Rigbie House** (private, but visible from the road). Col. Nathan Rigbie was willed a 2,000-acre tract in this area by his grandfather in 1708 and built this 1½-story stone house around 1732. One of the stones in the Deer Creek Friends Meeting cemetery marks the grave of Sarah Rumsey Rigbie, Colonel Rigbie's wife. The couple's son, Col. James Rigbie, made additions to the house in 1750. During the Yorktown campaign in 1781, General Lafayette and his 1,200-man force, with French and American officers, left Elkton on April 11 and crossed the Susquehanna at Bald Friar ford; they stopped here to visit Col. James Rigbie, sheriff of Harford County, on the 13th. Ill equipped, poorly fed, and without pay for months, the disgruntled soldiers were deserting and threatening mutiny. Their officers met in council at Rigbie's house and decided to try Walter Pigot—a miller caught selling flour to the British at Joppa—for treason. Pigot was found guilty and hanged, setting an example that quieted the troops. They dutifully marched to Virginia, where in October they helped force the surrender of Cornwallis.

Beyond the Rigbie House, Berkley Rd., to the right, leads to **Glen Cove,** site of a canal lock and a 19th-century paper mill that once employed 300 people. About a mile north of Glen Cove at **Castleton,** the old Conowingo Bridge crossed the Susquehanna. Built around 1820, the bridge was destroyed by a spring flood in 1846. It was rebuilt in 1859, defended by Union troops during the Civil War, and finally deliberately destroyed by dynamite in 1928 as part of the construction of the Conowingo Dam.

<hr>

Conowingo

U.S. 1 crosses the Susquehanna River over the **Conowingo Dam,** begun in 1926 and completed in 1928. The name Conowingo is thought to come from the word for "at the rapids" in the language of the Susquehannocks, who roamed both sides of the river from a village on Octoraro Creek in Cecil County. Most evidence of the Susquehannock presence disappeared underneath the lake—one mile wide and 14 miles long—formed by the dam. The lake covers the site of **Mile's Island,** where Native American pictographs of fish, crabs, and other animals were discovered. (Some are preserved at the Maryland Science Center in Baltimore.) During the dam's construction, the Philadelphia Electric System relocated 16 miles of Pennsylvania Railroad tracks, destroyed the village of Conowingo, rerouted U.S. 1 over the dam, and built a 58-mile transmission line to Philadelphia. Almost 4,000 workers helped build what was then one of the largest hydroelectric projects ever completed.

H. EASTERN AVE. (MD. 150) AND PULASKI HWY. (U.S. 40 EAST)

Most of the industrial development around Baltimore during the 19th century centered around the city's harbor and the streams that flowed into the Patapsco River from the north and northwest. The areas east of Baltimore, where rivers formed indented peninsulas jutting into the upper Chesapeake Bay, remained rural and marshy until the early 20th century. Small truck farms, recreational estates, and hunting and fishing villages dotted these "necks," where no towns took root, and the country roads ended at the water. Private clubs carved special hunting territories out of the wetlands, and public amusement parks attracted enthusiastic patrons from the nearby city.

A few small communities grew along the tracks of the Philadelphia, Wilmington and Baltimore Railroad (later incorporated into the Pennsylvania Railroad system and now part of Amtrak), skirting the top of the necks. Most of the early commercial development occurred along the Philadelphia Turnpike (now Md. 7, the Philadelphia Rd.), which followed the northeast line of the bay's shore from Baltimore County to the Susquehanna River and on to Wilmington and Philadelphia. The B&O Railroad (now part of the CSX system) completed tracks from Baltimore's harbor to Philadelphia in 1880, along a route just south of the old turnpike.

Industrial transformation of this traditional Chesapeake neck country began in 1887, when the Pennsylvania Steel Company bought Patapsco River Neck farmland and developed the steel town of Sparrows Point. World Wars I and II and the Korean War stimulated steel, aircraft, weapons, and shipbuilding activities throughout the small peninsulas. As the area became increasingly industrialized and as automobile traffic mushroomed along the Eastern Seaboard, new highways followed the old connecting routes. U.S. 40—named Pulaski Hwy., after Casimir Pulaski, the Polish hero of the American Revolution—was constructed in 1941 parallel to the railroad route just south of the old turnpike. I-95, the John F. Kennedy Memorial Hwy., was constructed parallel to U.S. 40 in 1963.

Connecting these highways to the Harbor Tunnel Thruway (1957) and the Baltimore Beltway (1962) led to a snarl of interchanges that made the old necks of eastern Baltimore County difficult to see. However, secondary roads descend into the necks from Eastern Ave. (Md. 150), which runs to the south of and roughly parallel to U.S. 40. Artful maneuvering along these side roads reveals unusual ethnic and social heritage.

Side Trip on Dundalk Ave.

The Patapsco River Neck is a deeply indented peninsula bordered by the Patapsco River on the west, Back River on the east, and the Chesapeake Bay. Bear Creek almost cuts the peninsula in two near North Point. Most of the neck lies within Baltimore County, although the city annexation of 1918 claimed a northwest section around Highlandtown and Canton.

Dundalk Ave. branches south from Eastern Ave. just east of the **Francis Scott Key Medical Center** in Highlandtown. Holabird Ave. angles to the left and continues to Delvale Ave., which turns right to **Dundalk Community College,** opened in 1971. The college has a current enrollment of 596 full-time and 2,983 part-time students.

Beyond its intersection with Holabird Ave., Dundalk Ave. passes the **site of Fort Holabird** (now Holabird Industrial Park), and crosses the city line into Baltimore County and Dundalk. During World War I the army built Fort Holabird, naming it for Brig. Gen. Samuel Beckley Holabird, of the Army Quartermaster Department during the Civil War. It became the largest U.S. Army Signal Corps depot in the world during

World War II and later served as headquarters for the U.S. Army Intelligence School. Army security and counterespionage investigators trained at this site, which also served as a records center for more than 7.5 million people who received security clearances from the army after World War II. Generations of inductees from the Baltimore-Washington area bound for basic training camps in the South were processed here. The army abandoned the facility during the 1970s, the buildings were razed, and the property was transferred to the city for use as an industrial park.

Dundalk

In 1894 Henry McShane, owner of a bell foundry, named the Baltimore and Sparrows Point Railroad station Dundalk after his birthplace in Ireland. When Bethlehem Steel bought the nearby Sparrows Point facility in 1916, the Dundalk Company was formed to provide housing for workers. U.S. entry into World War I spurred housing construction, and by 1930 Dundalk had a population of about 8,000 people. Dundalk Ave. passes the original planned town center, which contains shops, a theater, and a fire station, all back from the road, next to a public park (left). The name Dundalk now refers to a metropolitan community of more than 66,000 people spread over numerous residential developments on the peninsula.

The **Dundalk Marine Terminal,** opened in 1959 and operated by the Maryland Port Authority, occupies much of the Patapsco River waterfront southwest of the residential heart of Dundalk. The 570-acre, general-cargo facility is the port's largest; more than 20 steamship lines call here regularly. Eleven cranes handle containers and "break bulk" cargoes; the automobile storage areas cover 152 acres.

From Dundalk Ave., Main St. bears right (southeast) toward Sollers Point and **Turner's Station,** at the tip of the point. Originally named Steelton, this historic African American community began as a segregated housing area for the overflow of black workers at Sparrows Point at the turn of the century. The area was later named after another station on the railroad and by the end of World War II had grown to 9,000 people, making it the largest African American community in Baltimore County.

Side Trip on North Point Rd. (Md. 20)

From Eastern Ave., North Point Rd. (Md. 20) winds down the eastern side of Patapsco River Neck. Just to the north, Md. 151 passes the Back River Sewage Treatment Plant, opened in 1911 to serve the city. A short distance past Trappe Rd. (on the right), look for Kimberly Rd. to the left. Not far off the road, on Kimberly, stands the **Aquila Randall Monument,** raised in 1817 to commemorate a member of the Mechanical Volunteers, 5th Regiment of Maryland Militia, who died in the Battle of North Point.

Near this place—between Bread and Cheese Creek and the head of Bear Creek, where the peninsula is little more than half a mile wide—British and American forces met on September 12, 1814, in a brief but spirited battle for Baltimore. A British expeditionary force under the general command of Sir Alexander Cochrane had routed militia at Bladensburg and burned Washington. The British next turned on Baltimore, which they considered a "nest of pirates" because of its successful privateers. About 4,700 British troops, veterans of the Napoleonic Wars, landed at the tip of the peninsula early in the morning. As part of a defensive effort organized by Gen. Samuel Smith, John Stricker and about 3,185 Americans had taken positions the night before at the head of Bear Creek. Maj. Gen. Robert Ross, commander of the land troops, had unwisely led a small British advance party and was killed near this location by American sharpshooters. When the main British force attacked, about 900 of the militia troops fled; but the remaining 1,500 stood firm for about half an hour before retreating in some disorder to a rear line held by about 600 reserves. The British believed they had won a "second version of the Bladensburg races" but decided not to pursue. Each side had taken casualties. Of the Americans, 163 had been killed or wounded and another 50 taken prisoner. The British had lost their commander and taken 300 casualties. Stricker regrouped his tired men and withdrew to Worthington's Mill, near the well-fortified American position at Hampstead Hill, now Patterson Park. That night a British fleet bombarded Fort McHenry, to no avail, and the disappointed British land forces marched back to their ships.

North Point Rd. continues south and again joins North Point Blvd. (Md. 151) just before an intersection with Wise Ave., which angles west (right) across Bear Creek. To the right of the intersection is the **site of the Gorsuch Farmhouse,** where General Ross breakfasted the morning he died. Legend relates that he had told his staff that on that day he would "eat dinner in Baltimore or in Hell."

Return to Md. 20 after navigating through connections to the Beltway. Md. 151 (now Sparrows Point Blvd.) heads south to the remnants of Maryland's largest industrial complex.

Sparrows Point

When the Pennsylvania Steel Company bought farmland on the neck in 1887, the lowlands and marshes were drained to make room for furnaces, mills, shipyards, and Bessemer converters. The slag-filled marshland became a regional employment magnet. The labor was hard and dangerous, polluting air and water; but the economic rewards attracted workers of all ethnic backgrounds, who made Sparrows Point the "cleanest and greenest steel town in the United States." Steel was first made here by 1891. A company town segregated by occupation and race developed in the 1890s, providing residences, a company store, an elementary school (1888), and a high school (1908). The streetcar reached Sparrows Point in 1903, and the farmlands on the peninsula began to disappear with the growing demand for housing. Bethlehem Steel bought the plant in 1916, adding acreage, buildings, and workers. The plant had 12,000 employees in 1934, a number that more than doubled during World War II, when the shipyards churned out Liberty and Victory ships. At the height of its production—after a $200 million expansion in 1957— Bethlehem employed 29,000 people and claimed to be the largest steel mill in the free world, with an annual production of 9 million tons.

Around 1970, when the Soviet Union and Japan began to challenge U.S. preeminence in steel production, "The Point" started a decline. Now most of the furnaces, the coke ovens, and the rod mill are closed. The shipyards have shut down, and the huge gray complex with its towering smokestacks employs fewer than 6,000 people. Residents worry about a deteriorated environment, and retired employees are dying from asbestos poisoning incurred before 1974. No longer do generations of the same family look to The Point as a source of secure incomes for a house, car, children's education, and perhaps a boat (small marinas line the coves and inlets of the tidewater rivers).

North Point and North Point State Park

North Point Rd. continues down the peninsula through flat, marshy countryside. Shore Rd. branches east to the new 1,310-acre **North Point State Park,** which includes the **site of Bay Shore Park** and the **Black Marsh Wildlife Refuge.** Bay Shore Park opened in 1906 and flourished as an amusement area for white Baltimoreans until 1947, when Bethlehem Steel bought the property for an expansion that never occurred. The old trolley station here has been renovated, the concrete paths repaired, and underbrush removed from the park's few remaining structures. Future plans call for construction of a multipurpose building and stabilization of a 1,000-foot pier that juts into the bay.

Md. 20 ends at **North Point,** where a marker indicates the British embarkation point in 1814. **Fort Howard,** named for Colonel, and later Governor, John Eager Howard, has occupied the point since the 19th century. The Coast Guard operated an artillery station here from 1896 to 1924, to protect Baltimore; the gun emplacements are still visible. The U.S. Army used the fort as a training area for intelligence students from its school at Fort Holabird. Now, half the fort area has been turned into a public park. The other half still belongs to the Veterans Administration, which has maintained a medical center here since 1944.

Essex

Continuing out Md. 150 (now Eastern Blvd.) one encounters Essex. The heart of this old community lies at the intersection of Mace Ave. and Eastern Blvd., just northeast of the bridge over the Back River. Essex emerged in 1909 as a Taylor Land Company garden suburb. It originally consisted of a 10-block strip of building lots that attracted many Germans from Baltimore's Canton neighborhood. A stainless steel plant at the head of Back River spurred employment, and business boomed during World War II, when Essex was known as a "hot bed area": shifts in the local industries operated 24 hours a day, and no one's bed had an opportunity to get cold. Essex is now home to more than 41,000 people. Nearby **Essex Community College** opened in 1957 at a local high school. The college has since expanded to 3,242 full-time and 8,233 part-time students, the fifth largest enrollment among the state's 19 community college campuses.

The **Heritage Society of Essex and Middle River** (516 Eastern Blvd.) occupies a fire station built in 1921. The museum features memorabilia from the Essex Vigilant Volunteers, who established the first Essex fire station, in 1915.

Southeast Blvd. (Md. 702) and Back River Neck Rd.

From Eastern Blvd., the Southeast Blvd. (Md. 702) takes one south, into Back River Neck. A left at Old Eastern Ave. and immediate right onto Back River Neck Rd. places one on the more scenic parallel path. Back River Neck Rd. travels down the peninsula, gradually leaving the dense residential developments around Essex and descending into flat, wooded countryside that supports a wide variety of wildlife. Private homes and summer vacation enclaves turned year-round communities line the coves and creeks that indent the rural wetlands here. The road passes the **Essex Skypark,** a public airport along Back River, and ends at **Rocky Point Park,** site of a public golf course and an 18th-century plantation.

Ballestone Mansion

Cecil Calvert, second Lord Baltimore, granted William Ball, a Virginia ancestor of George Washington, 450 acres on the neck in 1659. The manor remained vacant until about 1780, when the Stansbury family built Ballestone Mansion, a 2½-story brick house near the river. The Leakin family expanded the house in 1819, and the Miller family added a two-story, eight-columned portico after the Civil War. As the neck's fortunes fell with the decline of industry after 1960, the mansion also fell to neglect and vandals until the Heritage Society of Essex and Middle River stepped in and restored it. The mansion contains period furnishings reflective of Maryland during the past two centuries.

Hart-Miller Island State Park, 244 acres on three small islands off the end of Back River Neck, is visible from the Ballestone property. Acquired in 1975, the park remains undeveloped.

Continuing north and east on Eastern Blvd., the traveler next reaches **Middle River** (24,616 pop.), at the head of Middle River Neck, which is formed by Middle River on the south, Saltpeter Creek on the north, and the bay on the east.

Glenn L. Martin (1886–1955) moved his airplane manufacturing operations from Cleveland, Ohio, to Middle River in 1929. The waterfront provided room for the flying boats pioneered by this barnstorming inventor, and the labor force he needed to build them already existed in the surrounding steel industries. Within 10 years, Martin's aircraft plant employed 4,100 workers. In 1942 some 53,000 employees turned out military aircraft like the Baltimore and the Marauder for the Allies. The plant work force had declined to 7,000 by 1950, then jumped to 27,000 during the Korean War period. The numbers steadily declined in the 1960s. The company became a division of Martin Marietta and now employs about 1,000 people, who work on aerospace projects and aircraft modifications. The Vanguard satellite was made here. In 1975 the state of Maryland acquired the extensive Martin airfields and modified them to create the **Martin State Airport.** The field handles corporate and other private jets as well as commuter flights. **The Glenn L. Martin Aviation Museum,** opened in 1993, is located in Hangar 5, near the old control tower, off Wilson Point Rd.

Shortly past the airport, Carroll Island Rd. and Bowley's Quarters Rd. lead down to the water, crossing each other shortly after they leave Eastern Blvd. The first extends onto Carroll Island, owned by the federal government as part of the Aberdeen Proving Ground. Bowley's Quarters Rd. takes one past lush farms that sell produce at roadside stands and to the entrances of the numerous marinas that flourish along the nearby inlets formed around Frog Mortar, Galloway, and Seneca Creeks. At the end of the peninsula, Baltimore County has established a family-style picnic and swimming area whimsically named Miami Beach.

Md. 150 ends at Ebenezer Rd., near the village of **Chase** and **Dundee Saltpeter Creek Natural Environment Area** and another section of the **Gunpowder Falls State Park** system. Secondary roads lead to beach, marina, and other recreational sites near the mouth of the Gunpowder River.

Ebenezer Rd. angles to the left and returns the traveler to U.S. 40, Pulaski Hwy., at White Marsh. The first right off Ebenezer Rd., Harewood Rd., leads to the **site of Harewood Park,** a 160-acre park that the Philadelphia, Wilmington, and Baltimore Railroad opened for family recreation on the Gunpowder River in 1878. The Pennsylvania Railroad (now Amtrak) Bridge across the Gunpowder River is visible from the road. On July 11, 1864, Harry Gilmor's Confederate cavalry arrived at the Magnolia station, across the river. They captured a train from Baltimore and arrested Gen. William Franklin, who happened to be on board. Then they waited for another train, set it afire, and backed it onto the bridge, where it burned through the draw span and fell into the river. A Federal gunboat, which was supposed to protect the bridge, failed to get up steam, but Gilmor allowed it to rescue the passengers and most of the captured Union soldiers, but not their general. Gilmor later claimed that with a few more men (the raiders numbered only about 135), he could have taken Baltimore with ease, for he met almost no resistance.

White Marsh

The area south of the Gunpowder Falls on either side of Pulaski Hwy. has been labeled White Marsh since the 1750s, when the Nottingham Company, the Maryland colony's leading prerevolutionary iron producer, had a plantation of that name in this region. The Harry T. Campbell Sons' Corporation built a large concrete plant at White Marsh in the 1930s and in the 1980s the area became the location for a planned community with a shopping mall, businesses, and satellite residential developments. Pulaski Hwy. passes through this growing area (8,183 pop.) and crosses the Gunpowder Falls and the Little Gunpowder Falls into Harford County.

Joppa Town

Just over the Gunpowder River, Pulaski Hwy. passes **Joppatowne** (11,084 pop.), a modern planned community named after the seat of Baltimore County from 1712 to 1768. Turn right on Joppa Farm Rd. to Townewood Dr., then right on Townewood Rd., left on Town Center Dr. and right on Bridge Dr. to the **site of Joppa Town** on the Gunpowder River.

First known as Taylor's Choice, this river site received its biblical name around 1712, when the Baltimore County court was moved here from a nearby location at the fork of the Gunpowder River and Little Gunpowder Falls. The town laid out here in 1724 became a major tobacco exporting port during a brief heyday. But the river silted, and nearby Baltimore—with a more favorable harbor—grew in importance as a commercial center. Joppa quickly declined after the county seat was moved to Baltimore in 1768. In April 1781, John Paul, Walter Pigot, and two others were arrested in the town for furnishing the British with flour. Pigot had somehow mistaken Lafayette's men for Englishmen, as the French were returning by ship from Annapolis to Elkton. He offered them flour, hidden on a boat in the Gunpowder River, and was arrested. John Paul escaped, allegedly by hiding under the hoop skirts of a Joppa lady, but poor Pigot was quickly tried and executed.

The **Rumsey House** (private), a 2¹/₂-story brick structure with gambrel roof on Bridge Dr., is the only remaining structure from old Joppa Town. James Maxwell, one of the county's early justices, probably built the house in 1720. Col. Benjamin Rumsey, a member of the Continental Congress, enlarged the house around 1771. Rumsey died here in 1808, by which time the town had fallen into decay and held only four houses and a crumbling church.

Edgewood

Pulaski Hwy. continues past Magnolia Rd., which leads to the scene of Major Gilmor's train robbery, and intersects Md. 24, the main road to **Edgewood Arsenal.** In 1917, when the United States entered World War I, the federal government appropriated 35,000 acres on large necks jutting into the upper Chesapeake Bay, to create a center for chemical warfare and a weapons proving ground. The Edgewood Arsenal became a U.S. Army chemical warfare station and manufactured both gas masks and poisonous chemicals during both world wars. The facility was merged with Aberdeen Proving Ground in 1971. The entire section of land at Gunpowder Neck between the Gunpowder and Bush Rivers is referred to as the Edgewood Area of the Proving Ground.

Side Trip on Philadelphia Rd. (Md. 7)

Near Edgewood, Md. 24 north takes one from Pulaski Hwy. to the Old Philadelphia Rd. (Md. 7), on which a right turn leads to the **site of Chilberry Hall** (marker on the right side of the road), birthplace of Gov. William Paca (1740–99). The Paca homestead may actually have stood closer to the water, south of what is now Pulaski Hwy. The road crosses Ha or Haha branch, a tributary of Otter Point Creek, which empties into the Bush River. The small stream's unusual name comes from nearby land tracts named "Ah Ah, Indeed," "Ah Ah, the Cow Pasture" and others. The name also gave rise to old legends of a laughing ghost.

Abingdon, named for an English town in the Berkshires, is one of the oldest towns in Harford County. John Paca, father of William, laid out the town in 1779. A number of its citizens were active in business and politics during the revolutionary period, and the place supported several working silversmiths. At this location in June 1785, Bishops Thomas Coke and Francis Asbury established Cokesbury College, the first Methodist college in the Western Hemisphere. The curriculum included seven hours of daily study, gardening, and a manual training course. One of the school's rules stated: "Students shall be indulged with nothing which the world calls play. Let this rule be observed with the strictest nicety: for those who play when they are young will play when they are old." The college building burned in 1795 and was not replaced.

Md. 7 continues to **Bush,** which, as Harford Town, served as the first Harford County seat. The assembly carved the new county from Baltimore County in 1773 and named it, interestingly, for the illegitimate son of Frederick Calvert (last Lord Baltimore), Henry Harford, whose awkward legal position left him no claim on the peerage. In 1782 the county seat moved to Bel Air, and Harford Town's name soon reverted to Bush, after the river on which it sat. Its location on a post road kept the town viable; its taverns and hostelries attracted notable visitors, including the patriots who traveled between south and north while they stitched together a revolution and a country. On March 22, 1775, the 34 members of the Committee of Observation for Harford County met at the local tavern and signed the Bush Declaration. This document approved resolves of the Continental Congress and concluded: "we do most solemnly pledge ourselves to each other, and to our Country, and engage ourselves by every tie held sacred among mankind to perform the same at the risque of our lives and fortunes." A marker in Bush claims that the document—signed more than a year before Jefferson's historic Declaration of Independence—was the "first declaration of independence ever adopted by an organized body of men duly elected by the people."

Md. 7 returns to and crosses over U.S. 40, taking one to Perryman Rd. A right turn on Perryman and another sharp right after a mile and a half leads to the **Old Spesutie Church** (1851). Bricks from the 1760 church structure were used to build the current church on the old foundations. At one corner, the architects added a pentagonal apse and a bell tower, which tapers from a square base to an octagonal spire. The church serves St. George's Parish, laid out in 1693 as one of Maryland's original Anglican parishes. The small brick vestry house (1766), which doubled as a schoolhouse, still stands in the churchyard. Among those buried under the old trees is Col. Thomas White (1704–79), father of William White (1748–1836), first presiding bishop of the Protestant Episcopal Church.

Pulaski Hwy. crosses Winter's Run and passes Otter Point Creek enroute to **Belcamp** on the Bush River. This small town houses the Bata Shoe Company, part of an international business that left its home in Zlin, Czechoslovakia, just before Nazi occupation in 1939. In the 1970s the Maryland branch plant turned out 170,000 pairs of shoes weekly. The factory operation included a hotel, community center, and nearly 100 houses occupied by employees at low rentals. Increased competition from the Far East forced the company in 1985 to scale back its operations. It now specializes in industrial, safety protective footwear. The houses have been sold, and the property is being developed as an industrial park.

Just beyond the Bata property, a small lane crosses the railroad tracks to the left to **Sophia's Dairy** (private), a large, 2$\frac{1}{2}$-story brick house built in 1768 by Aquila Hall, sheriff, county justice, and signer of the Bush Declaration.

Aberdeen Proving Ground

Md. 715, a main access road to the Aberdeen Proving Ground, angles southeast from Pulaski Hwy., just beyond its intersection with Md. 7. The proving ground was created in 1917 to develop and test ordnance on almost 80,000 acres of land and water. Follow signs to the **U.S. Army Ordnance Museum,** which bills itself as the world's most complete collection of military weapons. More than 300 pieces—tanks, artillery, armored cars, and other assorted large items—are arrayed outside. Inside the museum displays military equipage and weapons of every type: Gatling guns, modern machine guns and rifles, combat helmets and uniforms, even German V-1 and V-2 rockets.

Spesutie Island

Proving Ground Rd. leads southeast across the large peninsula occupied by the Aberdeen facility to Spesutie Island, a pioneer outpost in the 17th century, occupied by one of the Maryland colony's most adventurous souls. Nathaniel Utie, a Virginia explorer and Indian trader, was granted an entire 2,300-acre island in the upper Chesapeake in 1658. He built a manor house and renamed his property Spesutie, Latin for "Utie's hope" (spes Utie). Utie traded with the Susquehannocks, supervised all the Maryland forces in the upper bay, and represented the area in the Maryland Assembly. He also argued for Maryland's territorial interests with the Dutch in New Amstel (New Castle, Delaware) and helped negotiate the fledgling colony's treaties with the native tribes. Nothing now remains on the island of Utie's hopes. After his death, the island passed through a number of hands until 1800, when William Smith bought the entire property and constructed a low brick manor house. The land remained in the Smith family's possession until the island became part of the Aberdeen Proving Ground. Now virtually abandoned, it has become part of the **Susquehanna National Wildlife Refuge.**

Aberdeen

U.S. 40 continues into the town of Aberdeen (80' alt., 13,087 pop.), known in the 18th century as a stagecoach stop called Hall's Cross Roads. The Philadelphia, Wilmington and Baltimore Railroad came through the area in 1835, and the first stationmaster requested that his stop be named for his native town in Scotland. By 1890, Aberdeen had developed into a railroad shipping and canning center with a population of about 700. The Aberdeen Proving Ground attracted many civilian employees in World War I, and the region boomed during World War II. In City Hall, located at the intersection of U.S. 40 and Bel Air Ave., the citizens have established the **Ripken Museum,** honoring the baseball achievements of the Ripken family, particularly native son Cal Ripken Jr., Baltimore Oriole shortstop/third baseman, who on September 6, 1995, surpassed Lou Gehrig's major league record of 2130 consecutive games played.

Just outside the town, U.S. 40 crosses Md. 132. Turn right and follow Oakington Rd. to the 555-acre estate known as **Oakington** (private), home of Millard D. Tydings (1890–1961), U.S. senator from Maryland from 1927 to 1951, and his son Joseph, who served in the Senate from 1966 to 1971. The buildings and grounds now belong to a substance-abuse rehabilitation center. The central section of the great stone house reputedly dates to 1810. Two frame wings were added in 1900; one was subsequently replaced by a large stone addition.

The Pulaski Hwy. by-passes the center of Havre de Grace and crosses the Susquehanna River over the **Thomas Hatem Memorial Bridge,** a toll facility constructed in 1939.

Havre de Grace

Md. 7 (known here as the Old Post Rd.), branches off U.S. 40, taking one to Havre de Grace (pron. Hav'-er dee Grace) (35' alt., 8,952 pop.), a charming town at the mouth of the Susquehanna River. This point has inspired admiration since the 17th century. Edward Palmer, a trader and visionary, briefly occupied the island in the river at this site around 1622, 12 years or so before Calvert's colonists arrived in Maryland. William Claiborne's men traded with the Susquehannocks here during the early 1630s. Capt. Thomas Stockett, one of the first permanent settlers, built a house along the river near here around 1660. The post road that connected Philadelphia and points north to the southern coastal colonies naturally ran through this location, which around 1700 became known as the Susquehanna Lower Ferry. Just before the Revolution, the town had a population of about 200, and the taverns on both sides of the river had reputations as the best between Philadelphia and Edenton. Col. John Rodgers, father of Commo. John Rodgers of Sion Hill, reportedly built a tavern here in the 18th century and later moved his enterprise to Perryville on the other side of the river.

Local legend claims that the Marquis de Lafayette gave the town its latest name. In 1782 he was traveling as a guest of the Congress from Mount Vernon to Philadelphia along the Old Post Rd. Impressed by the view of the river, the bay, and the village at their confluence, he supposedly exclaimed "C'est Le Havre" in fond memory of the French port. In 1786, although a well-established town with about 50 brick houses, Havre de Grace failed in its bid to become the county seat. On May 3, 1813, British forces under Adm. George Cockburn shelled and burned the town, damaging or destroying nearly every building. Lt. John O'Neill fired a single cannon at the British and was later captured and held prisoner for three days. Whether his cannon shot slowed the British attack or not, O'Neill became a local hero.

Havre de Grace survived the British and prospered during the 19th century as a transportation and retail center and a fishing port. A local fisherman, Asabel Bailey, devised an anchored floating platform from which huge seine nets were set and hauled. Before the advent of industrial pollution and the construction of the Conowingo Dam upstream, thousands of barrels of herring and shad were packed here each spring. Canning and packing factories added to the town's industries. The **Harford Memorial Hospital,** established in 1911, attracted physicians, whose presence added a dimension of culture and sophistication to the town. Despite its physical attractions and refinements, Havre de Grace has declined in population over the past 20 years. Industrial and commercial development has centered around Bel Air and Aberdeen, where some citizens of Havre de Grace hope it will stay.

As Md. 7 leaves U.S. 40 and crosses the railroad track on the outskirts of Havre de Grace, a paved road branches to the right. A historic marker records that the Comte de Rochambeau camped at this location with his French troops on September 9, 1781, on their way to Yorktown. The road once led to the Havre de Grace Race Track, a one-mile course that opened in 1912 (patrons referred to it as "the Graw"). Until the track closed in 1950, special trains arrived here from Philadelphia, Baltimore, and Washington for the brief racing season every year.

Md. 7 enters Havre de Grace as Revolution St. and intersects Union St. from which a pedestrian can begin a stroll through the town. Start at the north end of Union St., where the entrance lock and lockhouse of the former **Susquehanna and Tidewater Canal** have been restored. The **Susquehanna Museum,** which illustrates the canal's history, is located inside a stone office building, which also functioned as the locktender's residence.

The **Rodgers House,** the town's only tangible reminder of its 18th-century legacy, is two blocks to the east (226 N. Washington St.). Also called the "Ferry House," this 2½-story, stuccoed brick structure occupies a site near the former ferry and current railroad bridge. The original building at this location was burned by the British in 1814. The current structure on its foundations serves as headquarters for the Joseph L. Davis American Legion post.

St. John's Episcopal Church, at the corner of Union St. and Congress Ave., was built in 1809. The British wrecked the interior in 1813, but the walls survived. The building has been expanded twice but remains a simple brick structure with narrow roundheaded windows.

Continue south along Union St. Where Lafayette Ave. branches to Concord Point on the river, the **Concord Point Lighthouse** stands as a civic landmark and guidepost for visitors. The town erected this stone beacon in 1829 on the site of Lt. John O'Neill's battery and named him the lighthouse keeper. In honor of his resistance to the British attack, O'Neill's descendants continued to hold the post from the time of his death, in 1838, until the 1920s, when the light was automated. The **Havre de Grace Decoy Museum** lies just north of the lighthouse.

Union St. passes the Harford Memorial Hospital and ends at the **Millard Tydings Memorial Park,** which provides boat anchorages and superb views of the bay.

Outside of Havre de Grace, Md. 155 passes **Sion Hill** (private). The Rev. John Ireland, rector of St. George's Parish, owned this estate from 1789 to 1795, during which time he operated Sion Hill Seminary. Gabriel Dennison, of Philadelphia, bought the property in 1795. His daughter married Commo. John Rodgers (1771–1838), hero during the War of 1812, who also led naval forces defending Baltimore from British attack in 1814. The Sion Hill family produced four additional generations that included a son bearing the name John Rodgers, and all became senior officers in the U.S. military, together serving the country almost continuously until 1926.

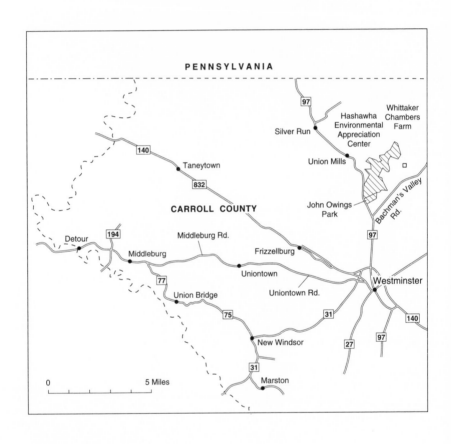

PENNSYLVANIA

97

Silver Run

Hashawha
Environmental
Appreciation
Center

Whittaker
Chambers
Farm

140

Taneytown

Union Mills

832

CARROLL COUNTY

John Owings
Park

Bachman's Valley
Rd.

194

Middleburg Rd.

97

Detour

Middleburg

Frizzellburg

Westminster

77

Uniontown

Union Bridge

Uniontown Rd.

75

31

140

New Windsor

27

97

0   5 Miles

31

Marston

Westminster and Its Byways

Westminster (744' alt., 13,068 pop.) originated in 1764, when William Winchester laid out a town on land bought from Capt. John White, a pioneer who in 1733 built a cabin near the present corner of Manchester Rd. and Main St. Winchester, an Englishman, named the town Westminster, although it seems to have been known as Winchester during its early years. The new town sat on Parr's Ridge, at the border between Baltimore and Frederick Counties in a wooded, fertile landscape near the headwaters of numerous creeks. The village grew slowly at first, but its central location made Westminster a logical choice for the seat of Carroll County, created in 1837 from sections of Baltimore and Frederick Counties. As transportation improved, the town became a busy stopover on the road linking Baltimore to Gettysburg and other points as far off as Pittsburgh.

In 1861, when the Western Maryland Railroad arrived, Westminster had 2,500 citizens, 40 stores, three banks, numerous hostelries, stables, tanneries, and several factories. Other factories, including a cannery first established by the Shriver family at Union Mills, soon moved to Westminster to take advantage of the railroad's presence. Local wheat farmers kept five cooper shops busy making barrels for shipping and storage during the mid-19th century.

A scouting party of Virginia cavalry camped overnight here on September 11, 1862, as part of Lee's northern advance prior to the Battle of Antietam. Southern sympathizers entertained the officers at special parties, while Unionists kept out of sight. Gen. J.E.B. Stuart and his cavalry troopers arrived in Westminster on June 29, 1863, during the campaign that led to the Battle of Gettysburg. The Confederates repulsed a brave but foolhardy charge by a small group of 1st Delaware cavalrymen, then spent the night before moving on. Expecting Lee's army to advance into the Pipe Creek Valley to threaten Washington and Baltimore, Gen. George G. Meade used Westminster as a major Union supply depot, here quartering an estimated 5,000 wagons, 30,000 mules, and 10,000 men. A Confederate force again visited Westminster on July 9, 1864, when cavalry under Harry Gilmor dashed into town to cut telegraph lines.

After the Civil War, Westminster became a peaceful commercial and industrial center for a rural county. The great midwestern wheat belts supplanted Baltimore's hinterlands as major grain centers, and local farmers turned to dairy and poultry production. Westminster developed a coterie of businessmen, professionals, and educators who made it the most important town in north-central Maryland. The county established a high school in Westminster in 1899, and since then Westminster High School has won awards for excellence in English, served as a national demonstration center for physical education, won a presidential award for math-

A late-1930s display of patriotism in Westminster

ematics, and supplied state champions in wrestling, track and field, field hockey, and cross country. Maryland has named faculty at the school Teachers of the Year in English, science, biology, and psychology.

For 15 or so years after 1975 the population of Carroll County about doubled, and in the last years of the century political leaders and civic groups have wrestled with all the issues that growth brings with it. Meantime, Westminster has spawned its own suburban sprawl, with shopping centers and residential developments extending in nearly all directions.

Turning onto Church St. from Main St., the traveler will reach **Westminster Cemetery** and the **site of the Union Meeting House.** An urn at the cemetery entrance marks the knoll where the meeting house was erected in 1755 to replace a log structure. The grave of William Winchester lies near the urn.

The **Shellman House** (206 E. Main St.), contains the meeting space and library of the **Carroll County Historical Society,** as well as exhibits that include early household implements. The 2½-story brick town house, furnished with authentic period pieces, was built in 1807. One of the former residents, Miss Mary Shellman, allegedly gave J.E.B. Stuart a "piece of her mind" when his Rebel soldiers occupied the town. Later, as the town's first telephone operator, she entertained Alexander Graham Bell when he visited Westminster. A garden behind the Shellman House contains a replica of **God's Well,** which received its name during a protracted drought in 1806. Lydia and Betsy Winchester, the aged daughters of the town's founder, were the only ones to open their gates to thirsty travelers and neighbors whose wells had gone dry. The sisters placed a sign on their well which read: "Free Admittance to All. Water belongs to God." Legend relates that eventually all the wells in town went dry except for "God's Well."

The **Kimmey House** (210 E. Main St.), also maintained by the historical society, contains a museum of 19th-century dolls and toys in Miss Carroll's Children's Shop.

The **Carroll County Courthouse,** on N. Court St. one block from Main St., dates to 1838. The columned portico, steps, cupola, and wings were added to the Classic Revival original. The **Church of the Ascension,** located diagonally across from the courthouse, was erected in 1844. The **Westminster Post Office,** at Main St. and Longwell Ave., evokes the area's historic role in the development of rural postal service. A marker notes that in 1899 Carroll County was selected by the U.S. Post Office as one of 44 sites in the United States to begin rural free delivery (RFD). Countywide postal service was achieved here before it reached any other location in America.

The campus of **Western Maryland College,** a private liberal arts institution (1,128 full-time, 98 part-time students), lies farther west on Main St. and occupies land once called The Commons. Before the college was founded in 1867, local horse races and political meetings occurred on the site. Fayette Buell, a practiced teacher at the Male and Female Collegiate School in Westminster, conceived the idea for the college, which became the first coeducational college south of the Mason-Dixon line. Not until well into the 20th century, however, did students of both sexes actually attend the same classes together. Now, more than 60 percent of the students are women. The college was the first school in Maryland to employ trained athletic instructors and to build a gymnasium.

Established in 1965 to illustrate the life of a typical 19th-century farmer, the **Carroll County Farm Museum** sits in a 140-acre park just south of Westminster at 500 S. Center St., between Md. 32 and Md. 27. The Victorian farmhouse, built in 1852 as the county almshouse, or poorhouse, has been furnished in period style; its kitchen displays old-fashioned utensils. Craft barns on the property illustrate such skills as tinning and blacksmithing; other outbuildings include a springhouse, barn, and animal pens. Costumed guides complete the evocation. The park also includes nature trails, picnic areas, and a community pond.

The **William Winchester house,** which Winchester built in the 1760s, stands diagonally across from the farm museum.

A future farmer of Maryland grooms a calf, early 1930s

Friendship Valley Farm (private), a two-story brick house standing beyond the museum property on Gist Rd., was built in 1795 by Col. Joshua Gist, brother of Gen. Mordecai Gist, both heroes of the Revolutionary War. During the Whiskey Rebellion of 1794, a mob of "Whiskey Boys" marched into Westminster and erected a "liberty pole," a symbol of resistance to the federal government's excise tax on whiskey. According to legend, Colonel Gist rode into town with drawn sword and had it cut down. A colorful character in other respects as well, Colonel Gist was affected deeply by an incident regarding his brother, who was revived three days after he had apparently died, when a friend, Gen. Nathaniel Greene, noticed an eyelid twitching on the supposed corpse. During the waning portion of Colonel Gist's 90-year lifetime, he frequently had his manservant lay him out in a custom-built coffin, properly attired and arranged. He would then summon his family and admonish them not to bury him until three days had passed after his death.

Time permitting, the traveler may wish to explore further in this attractive region. The western portion of Carroll County still reflects the influence of pioneer preachers who spread the Christian gospel in both English and German. Church steeples rise from small villages as visible reminders of the Methodist circuit riders, Quaker leaders, and strict German Protestants who advocated a simple religion built on the model of Jesus' life. Both the Brethren and the Friends found sanctuary in this peaceful countryside and pursued their nonviolent ways in concert with their Mennonite counterparts in Pennsylvania and scattered portions of Maryland.

New Windsor and Union Bridge
via Md. 31 and Md. 75

New Windsor

New Windsor Rd. (Md. 31) leaves southwest Westminster and travels about three miles to the community of New Windsor (450' alt., 757 pop.), laid out in 1797. At first called Sulphur Springs, the town was renamed in the early 19th century, possibly after its English namesake. Since 1942, New Windsor has been headquarters for the international missionary efforts of the **Church of the Brethren.** Through the Church World Service of the National Council of Churches of Christ in the U.S.A. and the World Council of Churches, the Brethren have trained young social workers to serve without pay in a variety of tasks in poor countries. Their efforts at New Windsor and other centers served as a forerunner of the Peace Corps, whose first director, appointed in 1961, was a Marylander with roots in central Maryland, Sargent Shriver. The international gift shop at New Windsor features crafts, handwork, arts, and other products sold under the sponsorship of the church's World Ministries Commission.

South of New Windsor, Wakefield Valley Rd. branches from Md. 31 to the **Strawbridge House,** located on Strawbridge Ln. This replica of a 1764 meeting house and the adjacent cabin constitute one of 12 designated National Methodist Shrines. Robert Strawbridge, who had been converted to Methodism by one of John Wesley's preachers in his native Ireland, came to Maryland sometime after 1759. Strawbridge converted

John Evan, who lived in the cabin from 1764 to 1827, and built a homestead here for himself. Under Strawbridge's leadership, at least 10 Methodist chapels had been built in Maryland before the American Revolution; and the state had more Methodists than any other colony. After Francis Asbury arrived in 1771, Baltimore became the center of American Methodism.

A marker on Marston Rd., which branches from Md. 31 immediately south of Wakefield Valley Rd., indicates the **site of the Sam's Creek Meeting House,** Strawbridge's original log chapel and probably the first Methodist meeting house in America. Like Strawbridge House, in 1764, the square log building was razed in 1844. The congregation has since used the present **Bethel Chapel,** built in 1821 and remodeled in 1860. Strawbridge preached throughout Maryland and died in 1781 at Towson. He is buried in Mount Olivet Cemetery in Baltimore.

Md. 31 follows the route of the Western Maryland Railway, first founded by Carroll County entrepreneurs in 1852 as the Baltimore, Carroll and Frederick Rail Road Company. At New Windsor, Md. 75 continues to follow the railroad route west.

Hard Lodging, an 18th-century house named by Solomon Shepherd after a nearby land grant, lies just north of New Windsor on Md. 75. Now listed on the National Register of Historic Places and owned by the **Carroll County Historical Society,** the brick structure stands on a solid rock ledge. Like many country houses that have sheltered generations of residents, the house reflects a variety of styles. The main portion was constructed in the 1790s; wings have been added in subsequent centuries. The interior furnishings are eclectic.

Union Bridge

Md. 75 continues to Union Bridge (402′ alt., 910 pop.), on Little Pipe Creek. William Farquhar, a Pennsylvania Quaker, settled here with his wife Ann in the 1730s and became prosperous by selling buckskin breeches. The village received its name when the settlers built a bridge over the creek, uniting the scattered Quaker settlements in the Pipe Creek area. The residents soon established a reputation for unusual industry and conviction. A linseed oil mill and the first nail factory in the state operated here around 1800. Jacob R. Thomas invented a mechanical reaper that failed a trial run in 1811 but was later perfected by his cousin, Obed Hussey. The villagers prided themselves that no slave ever lived in the town.

William H. Rinehart (1825–74), one of Maryland's foremost sculptors, was born on a farm near Union Bridge. He demonstrated an early ability to carve on stone at a marble quarry on the family property. When he moved to Baltimore to study, he was befriended and supported by William T. Walters, who financed his studies in Italy. Rinehart's sculptures can be seen in Baltimore and the U.S. Capitol building. The Carroll County country boy died in Rome.

Now Union Bridge serves as a terminus for scenic rail excursions offered by the Maryland Midlands Railway. Travelers can depart from the brick, turn-of-the-century railroad station for an 18-mile Sunday round trip to Rocky Ridge or the 50-mile journey along the old Western Maryland route to Blue Ridge Summit on Catoctin Mountain. Special trains travel the latter route in autumn, when the mountain foliage becomes spectacular. The **Western Maryland Railway Historical Society** has assembled exhibits and artifacts from the railroad in the Victorian station, located on N. Main St.

Uniontown and Middleburg Rds.

Uniontown Rd. travels west from the center of Westminster across rural countryside and over Meadow Branch toward **Uniontown,** a picturesque village, developed in 1809–11 along the Baltimore-Hagerstown Turnpike. The houses and churches cluster along the modern highway in much the same way they did during wagon days. Only the horse troughs, hitching posts, and dirt roads are missing. A **German Reformed Church** was built here in 1814 as well as an academy to teach English to the new immigrants. Beyond Uniontown, the road becomes Middleburg Rd. and continues westward, crossing Bark Hill Rd.

Middleburg stands near the point where the east-west Maryland Midland Railway tracks intersect those connecting Taneytown and Frederick. Turn north on Francis Scott Key Hwy. (Md. 194) and left on Keysville-Bruceville Rd. to **Terra Rubra** (private), birthplace of Francis Scott Key (1779–1843), author of "The Star-Spangled Banner." In 1850 a storm destroyed the first house, completed in 1770; it was replaced by the present brick building.

Philip Key, Francis's English grandfather, patented this tract before the Revolution and named it after the reddish color of the soil. Half the land was confiscated from Francis's Tory uncle (he joined the British army during the Revolution); the other half, including the mansion, was inherited by his father, John Ross Key, an officer in the Continental Army.

Francis Scott Key graduated from St. John's College in Annapolis in 1796. While studying law in Annapolis under Judge J. T. Chase, he became acquainted with Roger B. Taney. The two set up law practice in Frederick, and Taney married Key's sister Anne. Key, an acknowledged leader of the Maryland aristocracy, moved to Georgetown, where he practiced law with his uncle, Philip Barton Key, and became a political arbiter, becoming close to presidents. He was employed in 1814 by President Madison to secure the release of Dr. William Beanes, of Upper Marlboro, from the invading British. On that mission Key composed the words that in 1931 became the national anthem.

When Middleburg Rd. crosses Md. 194, it becomes Md. 77 and continues west toward **Detour** (from Terra Rubra, travel north to Keysville Rd. and make a sharp left toward the town). Detour was first known as Double Pipe Creek, after the nearby stream. Here in 1794 Joshua Delaplane, a French settler, built a sawmill and a woolen mill. A village developed around the mills, which operated until 1849. When the Western Maryland Railway arrived after the Civil War, the name Double Pipe Creek, too long for timetables, was changed.

As Rocky Ridge Rd., Md. 77 crosses the Monocacy River at **Millers Bridge,** following the railroad route to **Thurmont.** The road intersects Md. 76 at **Rocky Ridge** and crosses Beaver Branch and Owens Creek en route to **Graceham,** a village of tree-lined streets and old houses with gardens in the rear. The **Moravian Congregation of Monocacy** purchased 30 acres here in 1782. Twelve half-acre lots were leased to church members for an average of 88 cents a year. Ten years later, a man named

Moeller received permission to bake gingerbread and brew small beer dispensed "under strict regulation." The log church was replaced in 1822 by the present stuccoed brick church.

Graceham Rd. leads north from the village to the intersection with Apple's Church Rd. and the **site of Apple's Church,** mother church to both the Lutheran and Reformed congregations in the area. German services were held for the two groups in a log church on this site from about 1770. A stone building replaced the log structure in 1826; shortly thereafter, some services were conducted in English. The Lutherans moved to a separate church in Thurmont in 1857, and the Reformed congregation continued to meet here until 1879.

Taneytown via Md. 832

Follow W. Main St. out of Westminster. Md. 140 leads to Md. 832, Old Taneytown Rd., on the left. The older road, less traveled, crosses Big Pipe Creek, leads through places like Fountain Valley and Frizzellburg, and takes one past weathered graveyards to Taneytown (493' alt., 3,695 pop.), the oldest town in Carroll County. This fine old town bears the name of Raphael Taney (pron. taw'nee), a member of the Southern Maryland family that produced Roger Brooke Taney, a chief justice of the U.S. Supreme Court. In 1754, along with Edward Diggs, Raphael acquired a land patent for almost 8,000 acres of this countryside, then regarded as a wilderness. In 1762 Taney divided the town into lots. Taneytown grew slowly, as a stage stop on a north-south road between Maryland and Pennsylvania and a supply center for the surrounding farms. Gen. George G. Meade located his headquarters outside Taneytown prior to the Battle of Gettysburg. Townspeople observed the ebb and flow of Union troops throughout the Civil War. When a railroad spur arrived in 1872, the town had a population of about 500; the population grew so slowly that it was 1930 before that number had doubled. As suburban developments have encroached on Carroll County farmland during the past 50 years, Taneytown has remained a viable country town, known for its good food and hospitality.

Washington Rd. / Littlestown Pike (Md. 97)

Md. 97 bisects central Maryland along a roughly north-south line from Pennsylvania to the District of Columbia. It offers appealing scenery and historical places that range from famous to infamous.

As Washington Rd., Md. 97 south leaves the east side of Westminster and passes the **Westminster Campus** of **Catonsville Community College** (2,700 full-time, 4,300 part-time students), established in 1976. Make a left (east) at Nicodemus Rd. to the **Greenway Gardens and Arboretum,** a 27-acre complex featuring a wide variety of trees and flowering plants in season. The road continues to the **Morgan Run Natural Environment Area.**

Whittaker Chambers Farm

Just north of Westminster, as Littlestown Pike, Md. 97 intersects Bachman's Valley Rd., which angles northeast past the farm (private) once owned by Whittaker Chambers (1901–61). As a pivotal figure in the 1950

Alger Hiss trial, Chambers participated in a landmark event, influencing American public life for decades. In 1948 Richard Nixon, then an obscure California congressman and member of a House of Representatives investigating committee, visited this farm at Chambers' invitation. Here the former senior editor of *Time* magazine showed Congressman Nixon microfilmed copies of classified State Department files that Chambers claimed Hiss had passed to him while both men were serving as communist spies in the 1930s. Chambers had hidden the incriminating microfilm in a hollowed-out pumpkin in his garden. The "Pumpkin Papers" proved the undoing of Hiss—a member of a prominent Baltimore family, a Johns Hopkins and Harvard Law graduate, and formerly a high-ranking State Department official. Although he denied any knowledge of Chambers, Hiss later was convicted of perjury.

The case had widespread and powerful impact. Nixon gained fame as a tough opponent of communism. Refusing to repudiate Hiss, Secretary of State Dean Acheson offered to resign his post (Hiss's brother Donald was a member of Acheson's law firm). President Harry Truman labeled the trial a Republican attempt to discredit his administration. Joseph McCarthy, a senator from Wisconsin, used the Hiss affair in part to launch his own attacks on subversives within the government. The investigation and trial of Alger Hiss polarized opinion and infected public discourse throughout the Cold War. Chambers died without changing his story. Hiss served 44 months in jail, returned to private life, and consistently maintained his innocence until his death in 1996. President Ronald Reagan awarded Chambers a posthumous Medal of Freedom and declared the farm a National Historic Site. People still debate and write books about the "great case."

Md. 97 next takes one to two family-outing sites, **Hashawha Environmental Appreciation Center** and **John Owings Park.**

Union Mills

Littlestown Pike passes through the village of Union Mills, on Big Pipe Creek, location of the **Shriver Homestead.** Andrew and David Shriver, brothers, arrived here in 1797, built two two-room log cabins connected by a "dog walk," constructed a sawmill and gristmill, and built shops for a smithy, tannery, and cooperage. David moved on to Westminster and then Cumberland, but Andrew remained to father 11 children and build a family dynasty. The original log houses eventually expanded into a 23-room structure that reflects its various functions as residence, inn, store, post office, magistrate's office, and school. The family saved documents, furniture, and other domestic and business accoutrements, so the present homestead mirrors the lives of six generations of Shrivers. When the house functioned as an inn on the stage line between Baltimore and Pittsburgh, the fireplace warmed the feet of such distinguished travelers as Washington Irving and James Audubon.

The restored, water-powered mill opposite the house operated from 1798 to 1942. Visitors may buy samples of flour produced by its machinery, which is based on the designs of Oliver Evans, a self-taught mechanical wizard from Delaware who in the 18th century revolutionized milling. Evans, who often talked with the Ellicott brothers (see Tour 15), successfully sued them in 1813 for infringing on his patents.

Like many Maryland families, the Shrivers were deeply divided during

The Shriver Mill sun dial, Union Mills, Carroll County

the Civil War. Andrew Jr., a Protestant and Republican, owned the homestead and tannery and sent two sons to fight for the Union. His brother William, a Catholic and Democrat, owned the gristmill and contributed four sons to the Confederacy. When Confederate, then Union, troops passed through Union Mills en route to Gettysburg, the remaining family members fed and entertained both sides.

Silver Run Valley

Silver Run Valley Rd. turns northeast just after the crossroads community of **Silver Run** and leads to **Montbray Vineyards** (now inactive), a landmark in Maryland viticulture. In 1966 Dr. G. Hamilton Mowbray, a retired research physiologist at the Johns Hopkins Applied Physics Laboratory, established a winery on a 100-acre farm here, with the aim of growing French hybrid and European-style Vinifera grapes. He and William Klul first successfully cloned a grapevine from a single cell, and his Seyve-Villard grapes grew into the world's first vineyard of cloned vines. Dr. Mowbray also successfully demonstrated that such famous grape varietals as Cabernet Sauvignon and Chardonnay could be commercially grown in Maryland.

Littlestown Pike leads to the Mason-Dixon line, near the 68th marker, and, as Pennsylvania 97, continues to Gettysburg.

Manchester Rd. / Ridge Rd. / Cedar Grove Rd. (Md. 27)

North of Westminster, Md. 27, here known as Manchester Rd., angles northeast past an industrial park named for Bennett Cerf (the warehouses belong to Random House Publishers) and **Cranberry Park.** The road ends at Manchester, but the leisurely traveler should there turn left, and then right on Md. 86 for a delightful drive through unspoiled Maryland countryside to Lineboro, a village that has kept its late-19th-century charm.

South from Westminster, Md. 27, as Ridge Rd., follows Parr's Ridge the length of Carroll County into Montgomery County. English, Scots-Irish, and German settlers populated this part of Central Maryland in the 1740s and thereafter. At the beginning of the 19th century, more than 30 mills operated along the many creeks and rivers that rise from springs along the ridge. Quakers, Brethren, Lutherans, and Methodists built cross-roads churches, and villages grew around them, like islands in the undulating farmland.

Both the Patapsco and the Patuxent Rivers begin in the vicinity of **Mount Airy** (see Tour 13), south of which Md. 27 crosses into Montgomery County to **Damascus** (815' alt., 9,817 pop.), once a quiet rural village and now a thriving suburban community. Three state highways—Md. 27, 124, and 108—radiate south from it toward the megalopolis of Washington. Occupying part of a land grant originally called Pleasant Plains at Damascus, the town sits on the ridge, at 875 feet above sea level. From here Magruder Branch flows south to Great Seneca Creek.

As Cedar Grove Rd., Md. 27 leaves Damascus, paralleling **Damascus Regional Park** on the east and intersecting Md. 355 near the German-town campus of Montgomery College north of Gaithersburg.

Just a Little South of the Mason-Dixon Line: Northern Carroll, Baltimore, and Harford Counties

Scenic Back Roads between Westminster and the Susquehanna River

For another perspective on the countryside along the Maryland-Pennsylvania border, try following this 60-mile route over secondary roads and through some of the most peaceful rural farmland left in Maryland. Take Littlestown Pike (Md. 97) north from Westminster and angle to the northeast on the New Bachman Valley Rd. (Md. 496) to **Bachman Mills** on Big Pipe Creek. (The name *Pipe* reportedly derives from the red clay found along area streams and used by local Indians for making pipes.) The road continues beyond Bachman Mills to an intersection with Md. 30. Turn right (south) on Md. 30.

Manchester

The first settlers of this area were English, followed by Germans in the mid-18th century. The hilly land escaped widespread tobacco cultivation. As with Pennsylvania farmlands to the north, agriculture in this region concentrated on grains and vegetables for the Baltimore market. A tract of land, now part of the town of Manchester, was patented in 1758 to the "German churche," a combined Lutheran and Evangelical Reformed congregation that by 1760 had built a church on the site. Capt. Richard Richards established the town (975′ alt., pop. 2,810) after the Civil War, naming it for the English city where his family had lived. Railroad development by-passed Manchester, but it remained a trade center for local farmers. The Pennsylvania line lies less than five miles to the north. Much of the architecture and agriculture along this border reflects more the Pennsylvania Dutch influence than the English tidewater culture. The **site of Cepowig,** a Susquehannock town at the headwaters of the Gunpowder River, is located near Manchester.

From Manchester follow Water Tank Rd. northeast to Millers Station Rd. Relatively isolated and obscure, the road crosses the CSX tracks to the village of **Millers.** Follow Alesia Rd. along the tracks north from Millers to Alesia and then make a right on Hoffmanville Rd. to Falls Rd. Falls Rd. angles south into Baltimore County and becomes Md. 25 at **Beckleysville.**

Prettyboy Reservoir and Gunpowder Falls State Park

Beckleysville, located west of Prettyboy Reservoir, occupies fertile countryside where paper mills flourished in the 19th century. By 1850, 10

mills existed in this northwest portion of Baltimore County. William Hoffman, a German immigrant from Frankfurt, started the paper industry in Maryland after 1775, when he constructed **Clipper Mill** on the West Branch of the Great Gunpowder Falls. Hoffman may have supplied some of the paper for the continental dollars used during the Revolution. The area at the northwest corner of the reservoir is still known as **Hoffmanville.**

Jacob Beckley built a paper mill in the early 1800s on George's Run south of the town named after his family. His son Daniel inherited the mill and served as postmaster for the village that grew up around the operation. The two general stores and hotel that it possessed at the time made Beckleysville an important rural center after the Civil War. The mill was closed in the early 1900s, after Daniel's children sold the business. Fires, floods, and competition from western states took their tolls, and by 1900 paper production had virtually ceased in this area.

Beckleysville Rd. travels east from the village across **Prettyboy Reservoir,** one of three supplying water to Baltimore. The reservoir was completed in 1933 by damming Gunpowder Falls; its name comes from Prettyboy Creek, a tributary stream that in turn got its name from a farmer's favorite horse. Local tradition relates that the owner often returned to the miry creekbank where the animal had disappeared and called the horse's name.

Continue south from Beckleysville on Md. 25 to **White House** and then follow Mt. Carmel Rd. (Md. 137) east to Prettyboy Dam Rd. and **Mount Carmel.** Prettyboy Dam Rd. leads north to the dam and intersects another Falls Rd., which passes through **Gunpowder Falls State Park.** The park currently consists of more than 14,000 acres spread along the valleys of the Great Gunpowder and Little Gunpowder Rivers as they descend from Baltimore and Harford Counties to the bay. First acquisitions for the park were made in 1960, and it has been expanding ever since. This portion of the park lies adjacent to the Prettyboy Reservoir and straddles the Harrisburg Expressway (I-83) and York Rd. (Md. 45). Beyond Mount Carmel, Md. 137 continues east, crosses I-83, and ends at the intersection with York Rd. in Hereford.

Hereford and Monkton

Hereford is surrounded by horse farms and cross-country race courses that rank among the oldest and most challenging in the United States. More than 25 percent of Maryland's 336 horse farms cluster southwest and southeast of Hereford; the majority lie in the rolling valleys between I-83 and Md. 140. Fourteen are located in the Monkton area. The Charles Fenwick farm, also located here, maintains a Grand National Steeplechase Course. **My Lady's Manor Course,** located outside Monkton, features such annual races as My Lady's Manor Point-to-Point, a four-mile test for hunters; the Right Royal Cup, three miles over timber; and the John Rush Street Memorial, a two-mile steeplechase over brush jumps.

Make a right (south) on Md. 45 at Hereford, then quickly a left turn (east) on Monkton Rd. (Md. 138) to the village of the same name. Thomas Brerewood in the early 18th century inherited My Lady's Manor, a 10,000-acre grant made in 1713 by Charles Calvert, the third Lord Baltimore, to his fourth wife, the former Margaret Charlton. Most of the grant lay south of a line between Monkton and **Shepperd.** Brerewood laid out

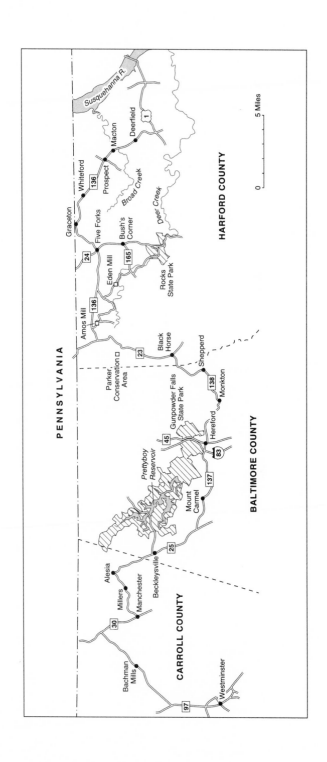

A scene truly deserving of the word traditional: fox hunters and their hounds, Baltimore County, as they looked in the 1930s and still do

Charlotte Town on the present site of Monkton, which later changed its name and developed into a thriving mill and railroad village on the Great Gunpowder Falls. The Baltimore and Susquehanna Railroad, founded in 1828, came through Monkton on its route between Baltimore and Harrisburg, Pennsylvania. The railroad line merged in 1854 with other lines to become the Northern Central, which later became an important access line for the Pennsylvania Railroad to Baltimore's port. The railroad also carried commuters from Parkton south to Baltimore until local passenger service was terminated on June 27, 1959. Tropical Storm Agnes severely damaged the rails north of Cockeysville in 1972, and the railroad then abandoned the line. The state acquired the roadbed in 1980 and has turned the 20-mile route between **Ashland** and the Pennsylvania line into a well-maintained walker's and biker's trail managed by the Maryland Park Service. Hikers can park in a lot for the **Gunpowder Falls State Park–Northern Central Railroad Trail** at Monkton. Other park visitors enjoy floating down the Gunpowder on an inner tube, a warm weather pastime that has become increasingly popular.

Md. 138 continues east of Monkton as Shepperd Rd., branches north at Shepperd, crosses Little Gunpowder Falls, and enters Harford County. Turn left (north) on Norrisville Rd. (Md. 23) at **Black Horse,** site of a crossroads tavern, general store, and blacksmith's shop in the 19th century. In 1849 the tavern was remodeled into a private residence that still stands.

Follow Md. 23 north toward the Mason-Dixon line, the boundary between Pennsylvania and Maryland, surveyed by Charles Mason and Jeremiah Dixon between 1763 and 1768. The road crosses Deer Creek near the **Jolly Acres Summer Camp,** which adjoins the **Parker Conservation Area.** At each of those sites there is a mill along Deer Creek. The mill at the camp was rebuilt around 1800 by Matthew Wiley Sr., a member of an Irish family that began operating mills in Pennsylvania during the early 18th century. **Wilson's Mill,** in the conservation area, may date to the 1780s.

Ivory Mills, on Deer Creek about two miles south of Norrisville, was acquired by Wiley around 1790 and rebuilt in stone. Five generations of Wileys owned the building. At one time, more than 100 gristmills operated in Harford County, grinding grain for export from the port of Baltimore.

Md. 23 intersects Harkins Rd. (Md. 136) at **Norrisville,** a rural hamlet on the road to Stewartstown, Pennsylvania. In 1770 Edward Norris erected a house, known as Long Corner, near the head of Deer Creek. The town named for his family became a rural trading center for the larger towns of York and Lancaster in Pennsylvania. A public school has existed here since 1850. Follow Harkins Rd. as it continues east from Norrisville, roughly paralleling the Mason-Dixon line to the north. About a mile down the road, Amos Mill Rd. branches south to **Amos Mill,** on a small stream named Island Branch. Matthew Wiley Sr., who came to Harford County as a young man, probably built this 200-year-old three-story log and stone structure. The mill was sold to Isaac Amos in 1891, and his son John worked the mill for almost 70 years.

Continue to the end of Amos Mill Rd. and make a right (south) on Carea Rd. to **Deer Creek Park,** a county park adjacent to the **Hidden Valley Girls Camp.** Follow Telegraph Rd. north from the creekbank to Eden Mill Rd., which angles south to **Eden Mill Park,** a 56-acre county park created in 1965 around **Stansbury's Mill.** Local tradition relates that a Father Eden, a relative of Sir Robert Eden, one of Maryland's royal governors, may have established a Catholic mission in this area. The name Eden has been associated with the area from an early period and was retained even after Elijah Stansbury bought the site and built the mill and the adjoining brick house around 1805.

Deer Creek winds its way across the width of Harford County, from Long Corner to the Susquehanna River. From Eden Mill Park, the traveler can follow a portion of its twisting path by following the bank to Grove Rd. and crossing the creek south to Hill Rd. Make a right and then the first left onto St. Clair Bridge Rd., which crosses the creek twice again on the way to **Rocks State Park.** The creek has cut a gorge at this location, creating unusual rock formations. Written and physical evidence indicates that American Indian tribes, perhaps Susquehannocks and Mingoes, had villages in this vicinity.

The road ends at Spring Rd. (Md. 24). Turn left (north), cross the creek again, and pass the **site of the La Grange Iron Works,** which operated from 1836 to 1874. Continue on Md. 24 beyond **Bush's Corner** to a reunion with Md. 136 at **Five Forks.** Make a right (east) on Md. 136, which loops to the north, passing near Marker 32 of the Mason-Dixon line at **Constitution.** At the crossroads community of **Graceton,** the highway changes its name to Whiteford Rd. and continues slightly southeast toward the Susquehanna River as Md. 136.

Slate Ridge

Md. 136 ascends to **Whiteford,** located on an arching 10-mile ridge extending north to Peach Bottom, Pennsylvania. William and James Reese, Welshmen, settled on the ridge in 1725 on land known as the York Barrens, where they discovered easily worked slate rock. Quarries were later dug on what became known as Slate Ridge, and the first commercial slate was exported in 1785. Imported Welsh workers, familiar with the industry in their home country, worked the quarries, and Peach Bottom slate became internationally famous for its quality. The Welsh settled in the Maryland communities of Whiteford and Cardiff, as well as the towns of Delta and West Bangor across the Pennsylvania line. Roofing and flagstone slates were shipped throughout the country from these locations. Local slate has been put to many uses in this corner of the state, from roofing materials to burial vaults and tombstones. Active for almost 150 years, the quarries declined as new building materials supplied market demand. By 1930 most local quarries were no longer being worked; they still exist, filled with water.

Susquehanna River

Md. 136 slopes southeast from Whiteford, intersects Md. 646 at **Prospect,** passes through **Macton,** and then crosses Broad Creek near the Boy Scout camp of the same name. Broad Creek rises close to the Pennsylvania line near Constitution and flows through the northeast corner of the county to the Susquehanna River. A few of the numerous mills constructed along Broad Creek still exist in various stages of repair. A group of Quakers led by David McCoy built a meeting house near Broad Creek in 1828. The frame **Broad Creek Meeting House** is located in a grove of oaks off Scarborough Rd., which angles southwest from Md. 136 beyond the creek.

The highway passes through **Deerfield** and **Dublin** before intersecting U.S. 1 at **Poplar Grove.** U.S. 1, known here as Conowingo Rd., continues east to the Conowingo Dam, which spans the Susquehanna River.

Western Maryland wheels, past and present

PART IV

WESTERN MARYLAND

Western Maryland extends from the foot of Catoctin Mountain (part of the Blue Ridge geologic province) westward to the Allegheny Plateau. For almost two centuries, travelers found the ridges and valleys of the Appalachian chain a formidable barrier; their efforts to reach the Ohio River provide a colorful chapter in the history of American transportation.

George Washington, living on the lower Potomac, saw the river as a possible link between the Chesapeake Bay (and the European markets it opened onto) and the rich Ohio-country interior. But the Potomac was navigable only as far as Great Falls, where the river fell from the rolling Piedmont to the coastal plain. Above the fall line were mountains, which early white explorers, hunters, and surveyors crossed—with the assistance of American Indian guides—on foot or on horseback. German-born farmers later followed the paths of buffalo herds along stream and river valleys. Professional wagoners eventually urged their horses over macadamized turnpikes. Mules towed boatmen on the Chesapeake and Ohio Canal from Georgetown to Cumberland and back. Engineers urged steam locomotives up steep grades. Each traveler battled up, around, and through the Western Maryland mountains at costs difficult to imagine as today we drive along smooth superhighways. Modern engineers have blasted huge gaps in the old adversaries.

The original National Road led from Cumberland, Maryland, to Wheeling, Virginia, on the Ohio River. Congress authorized the road—the first nonmilitary federal internal improvements project—in 1806, despite the objections of constitutional purists. The road ultimately led on to Indiana and Illinois. Thanks to semiprivate Maryland turnpikes that connected Cumberland, Hagerstown, and Frederick to Baltimore, the National Road effectively made the produce and markets of western Pennsylvania and the Ohio River Valley Baltimore's own. For many years, the road echoed with the sounds of stages, wagons, mules, and horses in motion. Many travelers rode in Pennsylvania-built Conestoga wagons, which to some eyes resembled schooners on wheels—the inland equivalent of the graceful Baltimore Clipper. The National Road spawned towns and a wide assortment of industries across Western Maryland. Incorporated into the federal highway system as U.S. 40, the old route now lies not far from the parallel Interstates 70 and 68.

The C&O Canal and the B&O Railroad also have left their marks on the region. Both canal and railroad followed the Potomac River Valley westward and upward into the Alleghenies. Irish immigrants signed up to dig the canal; stonecutters from England and Wales came to Maryland to construct the 74 lift locks that the canal required between Georgetown and Cumberland. Canal developers had surveyed a route as far as Pittsburgh, but in 1850, when the canal reached Cumberland, the railroad had been there for eight years, and further canal building stopped. The C&O hauled freight between Cumberland and Washington for 73 years. In 1875 alone a million tons of coal went down the canal. Yet floods and other troubles took their toll; the canal closed, more or less in ruins, in 1924.

The federal government took over the canal property in the 1930s, and in 1954, Supreme Court Justice William O. Douglas led a symbolic walk along the towpath to protest proposed plans to build a new highway along the route. The C&O became a national monument in 1961 and a national historical park in 1971. The National Park Service operates information centers at Georgetown, Great Falls Tavern, Hancock, and Cumberland. Most of the canal's length, about 185 miles, follows the northern side of the Potomac.

The B&O, America's first railroad, proved the steam locomotive to be the best way westward. Beyond Cumberland, the railroad opened Maryland's Allegheny plateau to logging and tourism. Historic railroad depots grace many Western Maryland towns, and more than a few original bridges and tunnels, constructed at great cost, remain in use. Garrett County is named for John W. Garrett, the energetic B&O railroad executive who kept the trains moving during the Civil War.

Out of this long transportation history, which required skilled laborers and machinists, Western Maryland developed an industrial tradition. Western Maryland coal miners, who established a distinctive culture during the 19th century, have lived in this area since the 1830s. The houses of workingmen sprawl across the hills and narrow valleys of the region in clusters that set this area apart in the western part of the state as much as tidy farms and rolling fields do in the east.

During the Civil War, Western Maryland three times lay in the path of Confederate forces as they struck out for the north. Robert E. Lee's early autumn expedition across the Potomac in 1862 resulted in the Battle of Antietam (or Sharpsburg), which stemmed the tide of early Southern victories, indefinitely postponed European intervention on behalf of the Confederacy, and prompted President Lincoln's Emancipation Proclamation. In late June 1863, the second venture of the Army of Northern Virginia drew it into Pennsylvania and the Battle of Gettysburg. A third incursion, this one in the summer of 1864, briefly threatened Washington. Western Marylanders referred to the hostilities as "the war amongst us." Towns were ransomed. Skirmishes were fought in the countryside throughout the war. In several places the bodies of Confederate and Union soldiers lie together in mass graves.

The automobile and the improved roads that followed it helped to diminish Western Maryland's isolation and to promote economic growth. Coal mining south of Frostburg, rubber manufacturing in Cumberland, production of aircraft and trucks in Hagerstown, truck farming throughout the region, and both the B&O and Western Maryland railroads all drove the regional economy during the middle decades of this century. More recently, as larger economic trends have overtaken and depressed American industry generally, Western Marylanders—and tourists—have taken a new tack, rediscovering the area's many charms.

Shocks of corn on a Frederick County farm, 1930s

Following the Road to the West

Alt. U.S. 40, U.S. 40, I-70, I-68

This tour begins in Frederick and follows the pikes that proceeded westward to Cumberland and connected to the National Road, which led settlers on to the Ohio country. Tour 19 takes the traveler on a series of side trips off of Route 40 or its older alternates. Using the two tours creatively on an east-to-west course, one can explore both the much-traveled and the less-traveled roads of Maryland's mountainous west.

FREDERICK

Maryland's third largest city, Frederick (296' alt., 40,148 pop.) grew slowly in the rolling countryside at the foot of Catoctin Mountain, as a center of retail and wholesale trade for prosperous dairy and other farmers. As the farms have disappeared and the land has filled with modern developments, this historic town has also become a tourist attraction and residential center for the growing expansion around Washington, which is only 45 minutes to the south by car via I-270.

Many of the first settlers in this area were German immigrants who moved down from Pennsylvania along an old Indian trail that followed the Monocacy River valley into the Shenandoah Valley and then down into the Carolina backlands. The Germans were welcomed by Chesapeake aristocrats who had speculated in the western lands and were joined by English settlers who had found the Tidewater lands exhausted after a century of tobacco cultivation. A new Maryland culture developed along the "green walls" of the mountains: bilingual, based on grain rather than tobacco, Lutheran rather than Anglican, and neutral on the question of slavery.

Frederick Town was laid out in 1745 on Beaver Creek for Daniel Dulany, the Elder, an astute Annapolis lawyer and proprietary official who had bought about 20,000 acres from Benjamin Tasker the previous year to sell at a profit to the Germans. (The name presumably honored Frederick Calvert, the sixth Lord Baltimore.) John Thomas Schley, a German immigrant born in 1712, is credited with building the first house in Frederick, on the northeast corner of Patrick St. and Middle Alley. His daughter Mary, the first child born in the town, was reportedly nursed by an Indian woman, perhaps a survivor from one of the Delaware, Shawnee, or Iroquois tribes that occasionally camped nearby. In 1748, the assembly created Frederick County from parts of Baltimore and Prince George's Counties, and Frederick Town was named the county seat.

The first houses, shops, taverns, and churches were log structures;

local stone was sometimes used when conveniently available. The use of brick—first for the churches—spread quickly. The extent of brick construction was regarded as a measure of civilization, and in 1791 a French traveler remarked that in "Fredericktown . . . nearly all the houses are brick." Increasing numbers of travelers passed through Frederick on the route between Pennsylvania and Virginia, consuming large quantities of "Monocacy ale" at the ubiquitous colonial taverns. A market was soon established for the local farmers, who raised cereal grains and basic food crops. The wheat from these western hinterlands helped Baltimore become an international flour port and surpass other maritime towns along the Chesapeake by the end of the 18th century.

By the time of the French and Indian War (1754–63), Frederick was well behind the western edge of settlement, and it served as a supply point for the British regulars sent under Gen. Edward Braddock to secure the Ohio Valley for King George II. Braddock stopped in Frederick in 1755 on his way to Cumberland, where he was to join the main body of his troops and march with colonial militia to Fort Duquesne (Pittsburgh). Angry over delays and ignorant of frontier conditions, he showered "curses upon the colonies and especially upon Maryland." Benjamin Franklin, ever the diplomat, hurried down to Frederick to assist Braddock in procuring horses and wagons for his troops, gently explaining to the general that the Appalachian wilderness posed different military problems from those of the plains of Europe. Braddock stubbornly insisted that ignorant savages, who might pose problems for untrained colonials, were no match for his disciplined British soldiers. The general marched from Frederick to his death on July 13, 1755, four days after a French and Indian force routed his expedition and exposed the Maryland-Virginia frontiers to attack from warring tribes.

The Braddock expedition deeply influenced the life of young George Washington and graphically highlighted the growing differences between the colonists and the mother country. When the British Parliament imposed the Stamp Act upon the colonies in 1765, the 12 judges of the Frederick County Court were the first to repudiate it. After the Battle of Bunker Hill, two companies of riflemen assembled in Frederick and marched to help relieve the siege of Boston.

Throughout the Revolution, Frederick remained a patriotic source of supplies and soldiers. When seven of the few Tories in the county were caught and convicted for trying to recruit soldiers for Great Britain, the court sentenced them to be "drawn to the Gallows of Frederick Town, and be hanged thereon; that they be cut down to the earth alive, that their Entrails be taken out and burned while they are yet alive, that their Heads be cut off and their Bodies divided into four Parts, and that their heads and quarters shall be placed where his excellency the Governor shall appoint." The sentence was later commuted to death by hanging.

After the war, Frederick continued to grow and prosper as a supply point along the new national road to the west and as the principal town in a flourishing agricultural county that also claimed more than 400 whiskey stills, 80 busy gristmills, and some industry—glassworks, iron furnaces and forges, and paper mills. At the beginning of the 19th century, the town had about 3,000 inhabitants, including 300 African Americans. Lawyers, like Francis Scott Key and Roger Brooke Taney, found the place good for their practices. Wealthy farmers and merchants

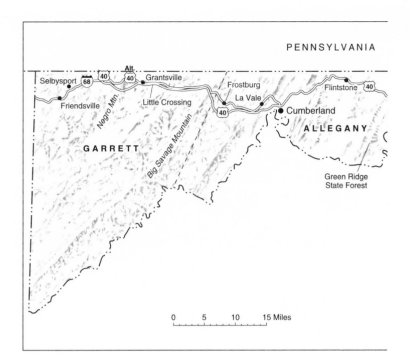

PENNSYLVANIA

Selbysport · Grantsville · Frostburg · Flintstone
Friendsville · Little Crossing · La Vale · Cumberland
GARRETT · Big Savage Mountain · Negro Mtn. · ALLEGANY
Green Ridge State Forest

0   5   10   15 Miles

helped give Frederick a veneer of city life. The thriving little town had seven churches, about 450 houses, a courthouse, a jail, and an academy.

During the Civil War, the town lay in the path of both armies as they advanced and retreated across the Western Maryland countryside. Confederate cavalrymen danced part of the night away at the Frederick Female Seminary in early September 1862. The ragged Confederates seemed like lean, shoeless wolves to Unionist (or wavering) Frederick citizens, though they had what one observer called "dash." Soon afterward Union troops used Frederick extensively to stage supplies and care for wounded. In the fall of 1862 Dr. Oliver Wendell Holmes, of Boston, came to Frederick to search for his son, who had been wounded at the Battle of Antietam. In that year's December issue of the *Atlantic Monthly*, Holmes wrote of the "singular beauty" of Frederick; "the town has a poetical look from a distance," he said, "as if seers and dreamers might dwell there." Townspeople saw many of the war's major characters parade through their streets in the early months of the war: Robert E. Lee, "Stonewall" Jackson, J.E.B. Stuart, George B. McClellan, and Abraham Lincoln.

Almost two years after Antietam, in July 1864, an invading Confederate force under Gen. Jubal Early crossed into this part of Maryland to ease the pressure on Lee in Virginia and to threaten Washington. As Gen. Lew Wallace gathered a hasty defense at the Monocacy River, he was astonished to see townspeople climbing fences and housetops to watch the fight. Even battle, Wallace later wrote, had apparently ceased to have horrors for the people of Frederick.

On July 9, the morning before the battle, General Early rode into Frederick and demanded a $200,000 ransom, threatening to burn the town if not paid in cash or "stores at current prices." Fighting for time, the mayor

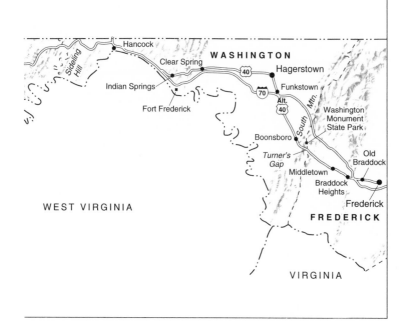

and other leading citizens sent the Confederates a written petition arguing that the city only had 8,000 residents "and as the assessment made in other places in Maryland is relatively much less than that imposed upon our City, we respectfully request you to reconsider and abate the said assessment." The request was denied, and five city banks were persuaded to advance the money. Over the next 87 years, the town paid hundreds of thousands of dollars in interest before making the last payment on this debt in 1951. Marylanders serving in Congress have sought reimbursement from the U.S. Treasury, thus far unsuccessfully.

After the Civil War, Frederick acquired a few small industries (canning, fertilizer, clothing, lime, crushed rock) but remained an active little city in a sea of prosperous farms. As late as 1990, the surrounding county led the state in production of silage corn, hay, milk, and number of milk cows. The Frederick County Fair on a site at E. Patrick St. still draws large crowds every September.

The development of the federal government in Washington, spurred by crash programs during World War II, has changed the character of Frederick more than any other factor in the past 50 years. In 1943 the U.S. Army Chemical Corps established the Biological Warfare Laboratory at Fort Detrick, which adjoins the north end of town. From 1953 to 1973 this facility was the largest single employer in Frederick County, drawing college-trained engineers, chemists, and technicians from around the country. Despite occasional public outcrys about possible dangers from the secret work conducted there, the research continued until canceled in 1972–73. A branch of the National Institutes of Health now operates the site for cancer research, although it remains a U.S. military installation.

When I-270 connected Frederick to Washington in 1957, the town became more attractive as a residential community for employees of the high-tech companies that have located along this corridor. Indeed, Frederick has become an ex-urban neighborhood in the new Washington-Baltimore metropolis, almost as much a part of Central Maryland as of the west. Like Georgetown and Fells Point, Frederick has developed gentrified residences and specialty shops; its population has increased by 70 percent since 1970. Among the costs one must count the beautiful Piedmont countryside celebrated by John Greenleaf Whittier:

> Up from the meadows rich with corn
> Clear in the cool September morn
> The clustered spires of Frederick stand
> Green-walled by the hills of Maryland.

Walking Tour

Downtown Frederick contains a 33-block historic district that is accessible via Patrick St. (Md. 144), along the old route of U.S. 40 through the town.

Follow signs to the **Visitor Center** at 19 E. Church St. The nonprofit Tourism Council of Frederick County manages the center year-round and offers a wide range of general information, including walking tours. The walk around the historic district described below assumes that the visitor has parked downtown and found the corner of Church and Market Sts.

East Church St., East and West Second St.

Church and Market Sts. mark the heart of old Frederick. **Kemp Hall,** a three-story brick structure built in 1860 at the southeast corner of E. Church and N. Market Sts., became a significant place on the eve of the Civil War. Gov. Thomas Holliday Hicks had ordered the Maryland General Assembly to meet in Frederick April 26, 1861, "in view of the extraordinary condition of affairs" (Federal troops had occupied Annapolis; strong sentiments were being expressed in favor of the Southern states; the governor had legitimate fears for "the safety and comfort" of both the legislators and his own person). Because the Frederick courthouse proved inadequate, the assembly moved to Kemp Hall to ponder Maryland's precarious position on the North-South border. If the question had ever come to a vote, this body, which some called a "Rebel Legislature," might have voted for secession. But moderate voices prevented a vote by employing adroit parliamentary maneuvers, including the argument that the legislature had no authority to make such a decision. In May, after weeks of rhetoric and posturing and the use of local militia to protect lawmakers from a rumored Southern threat, the assembly adjourned, just as Federal troops occupied Baltimore. By this time, pro-secession fervor had diminished, particularly in Western and Central Maryland. Military authorities soon arrested and detained secessionist leaders. Legislators more favorable to the Northern side won election in November, and Maryland remained in the Union.

From Kemp Hall, walk east on Church St. **Winchester Hall,** at 14 E. Church St.—two brick Greek Revival buildings connected by a corridor—was erected in 1843–44 as the Frederick Female Seminary and named for its president, Hiram Winchester. Like many other large buildings in Frederick, it was used as a hospital during the Civil War. Hood College later

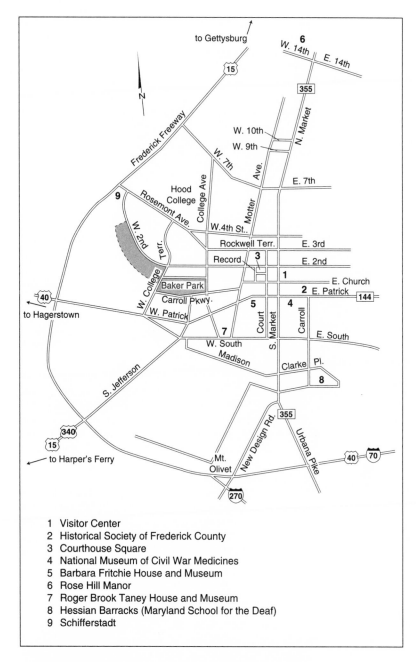

to Gettysburg

6
W. 14th   E. 14th

15

355

N

W. 10th
W. 9th

N. Market

W. 7th

Ave.

E. 7th

9

Hood
College

Rosemont Ave.

College Ave

Motter

W. 2nd

W.4th St..

Terr.

Rockwell Terr.

E. 3rd

Record

3

E. 2nd

1

W. College

Baker Park

E. Church

2 E. Patrick

144

40

to Hagerstown

Carroll Pkwy.

W. Patrick

5

4

Court

S. Market

Carroll

E. South

7

W. South

Madison

Clarke Pl.

8

S. Jefferson

355

340

15

New Design Rd.

to Harper's Ferry

Mt.
Olivet

Urbana Pike

40 70

270

1 Visitor Center
2 Historical Society of Frederick County
3 Courthouse Square
4 National Museum of Civil War Medicines
5 Barbara Fritchie House and Museum
6 Rose Hill Manor
7 Roger Brook Taney House and Museum
8 Hessian Barracks (Maryland School for the Deaf)
9 Schifferstadt

occupied the structure, which now houses offices of the Frederick County government.

The **Historical Society of Frederick County** occupies a four-story brick residence at 24 E. Church St. constructed in the 1820s by the family of a Dr. Baltzell. The annex was probably added after 1854; it does not appear on a map of that date in the society's extensive research library. By terms of the will of the last private owner, who died in 1879, the house became the Loat's Orphanage for young girls. In 1958 the orphanage closed and the Historical Society acquired the property. The museum contains collections of early Frederick printing, decorative items such as furniture and silver, and other artifacts of historical interest.

A large, green-glass goblet in the museum evokes the memory of John Frederick Amelung (1742–98), a German glassmaker who established a pioneering business on Bennett Creek at Park Mills, south of Frederick near Lily Pons. Amelung brought 68 workmen and their families with him from Bremen in 1784, arrived in Baltimore, and immediately set forth to Frederick. By 1785 the "New Bremen Glassmanufactory" was producing engraved, multicolored glassware that has since attracted the attention of international collectors and museums. Amelung's factory burned in 1790, and he appealed to the U.S. Congress to secure an $8,000 loan; it was the first time a private business had brought such a request to the new body. In the ensuing debate on the floor of the House of Representatives on June 3, 1790, despite support from the Maryland delegation, Congress decided that the loan would create bad precedent. Amelung's request was denied, and although he continued to make outstanding pieces of engraved glassware, his financial situation never stabilized. He died at his daughter's home in Baltimore, shortly before his property at New Bremen was sold in bankruptcy.

The **Evangelical Lutheran Church** at 35 E. Church St. dates from 1762. It replaced another church, built of logs in 1746. The German Gothic front with twin spires was added in 1854. The church's west tower contains a bell cast in England and shipped to Frederick in 1771. During the Civil War, a false floor was built over the pews so that sick and wounded soldiers could be hospitalized here.

The **Trail Mansion,** an Italian Renaissance house at 106 E. Church, was constructed in 1852 by Col. Charles Trail.

Farther along, at 115 E. Church St., the county board of education occupies a building that housed **Frederick High School,** which Dr. Henry Knox established (on another site) in 1797 as the Fredericktown Academy. Recently renovated and expanded, this structure dates from 1939. Frederick High graduates include former school newspaper editor and U.S. senator Charles McC. Mathias, whom Queen Elizabeth II knighted on his retirement from Senate service.

Turn left (north) from Church St. into Chapel Alley. The **Frederick Academy of the Visitation Convent** fronts 200 E. Second St. and hides behind the walls that line the east side of Chapel Alley. In 1824, the Sisters of Charity from Emmitsburg established a school here. The cloistered order of the Sisters of the Visitation replaced them in 1846, adding the south wing for classrooms in 1847. An east wing for the chapel and convent was built in 1851. The order still operates an elementary school for girls that has both resident and day students.

Turn left (west) from Chapel Alley onto Second St. **St. John the Evangelist Church** stands on the left corner. Irish Catholic workmen on the C&O Canal built the church in 1837. The residence at 100 E. Second St. once belonged to Enoch Louis Lowe, a former governor of Maryland.

Continue west to the intersection of N. Market St. and note local artist William M. Cochran's mural on the northeast corner building. **Old City Hall,** where city officials struggled to meet General Early's ransom demand, is located just to the south at 124 N. Market St.

"The clustered spires of Frederick," as viewed from Baker Park

On Second St., cross N. Market and N. Court Sts. The buildings at 106–114 W. Second St. were the **carriage house and slave quarters** for the Ross and Mathias Mansions behind them.

Frederick Presbyterian Church, 115 W. Second St., was built in 1825 by a congregation tracing its formation to the Rev. Stephen Balch, who rode horseback from Georgetown to conduct monthly services in 1780. This church, too, served as a hospital during the Civil War.

Turn left (south) from Second St. to Record St., a small connector to Church St.

Courthouse Square

Record and Council Sts., both only a block long, together with W. Church St. on the south and N. Court St. on the east, form a square around the **Frederick County Courthouse.** A number of distinguished homes from the Federal period cluster near the square, which has served Frederick as a center of government for almost 240 years. The following walk takes one around the square in a counterclockwise direction.

President Lincoln stayed at the **Ramsey Home,** at 119 Record St., the night of October 4, 1862, when he came here to visit the wounded Brig. Gen. George L. Hartsuff. Lincoln spoke impromptu to a gathering outside the house and later in the day to a crowd assembled at what was then the **B&O Railroad Station,** at the corner of Market and All Saints Sts.

The house at 111 Record St. is the birthplace of William Tyler Page, author of *The American's Creed* (1918). An administrative official of the U.S. House of Representatives, Page also wrote *Page's Congressional Handbook* (1913). An elementary school in Silver Spring commemorates him.

The **Spite House,** 112 W. Church St., now an inn, was built in 1814 by Dr. John Tyler, one of the first eye specialists in America. A third story and two-story wing were added to this brick Georgian home in 1857. The house received its name because the good doctor built it to spite city officials who had planned to extend Record St. across Church to W. Patrick St. Dr. Tyler actually lived at 108 W. Church St. From this address, a cast-iron dog, modeled after Tyler's own dog, named Guess, was stolen before the Battle of Antietam, presumably to melt down for bullets. The figure was later found on the battlefield and returned to stand guard at its intended location. The house next to Spite House, 114 W. Church St., belonged to John Nelson, born in Frederick in 1794. Nelson served as a congressman and as minister to Naples during the Jackson administration; in 1843 President John Tyler appointed him attorney general.

All Saints Episcopal Church (Richard Upjohn, 1855) occupies the corner of W. Church and N. Court Sts. In the colonial period, All Saints Parish included all of Western Maryland. Since the population of the parish determined the income of the rector, All Saints was also the richest parochial appointment in the state and consequently a political prize. Never popular among the Lutherans populating this area, the established church at least was made palatable through the good work of Thomas Bacon, rector of All Saints from 1758 until his death in 1768. Bacon helped compile Maryland laws and establish charity schools for poor children. He was succeeded by Bennet Allen, a favorite of the proprietor who had already made himself unpopular in Annapolis. Allen, by all accounts a reprobate and sometimes rumored to be a bastard son of Lord Baltimore, legally installed himself at the (padlocked) church with the aid of a pistol. Then he hired a rector and retreated to Pennsylvania, where he continued to collect income from the parish until the Revolution, which ended the state-supported church. The Rev. William Pendleton was rector of All Saints Parish from 1847 to 1853. A Virginian and graduate of West Point, he later became a brigadier general in the Confederate Army as Lee's chief of artillery.

Continue around the square, making a left (north) on Court St. The three-story brick house at 100 N. Court St. was designed by Robert Mills. The law offices of Roger Brooke Taney and Francis Scott Key were probably located at 104 N. Court St.

Turn left (west) on Council St. Col. John MacPherson and his son-in-law John Brien built the virtually identical **Ross and Mathias Houses** at 103 and 105 Council St. in 1817, on the site of the old jail. In 1824, in the Ross House, MacPherson hosted Lafayette at a gala reception during his visit to the United States. Charles McC. Mathias Jr., U.S. senator from Maryland (1969–87), grew up in the house named for his family. Both houses had extensive outbuildings—smokehouse, slave quarters, icehouse, and stables; some are still visible from Second St.

The one-story, red brick building at Council and Record Sts., erected in 1936, stands on the **site of the Frederick Academy** building, constructed in 1796. During Roger Brooke Taney's service on the governing board of the academy, a teaching post was denied to the eloquent and outspoken opponent of slavery Salmon P. Chase, who eventually succeeded Taney as Supreme Court chief justice.

This building also housed the **C. Burr Artz Free Library** until 1982, when the library moved to its current location at 100 E. Patrick St. C. Burr Artz, a Frederick County farmer, died in 1874 and his wife, Catherine Thomas Artz, died in 1887. Her will stipulated that if their daughter died without issue, her estate was to be placed in the hands of three trustees. The money was to be used for a library named after her husband.

The building that now houses **City Hall** used to be the Frederick County Courthouse. It was constructed during the Civil War on the site of a predecessor built in the 1750s. The second courthouse, erected in 1787, served as the first meeting place for the "Rebel Legislature" (which later moved to Kemp Hall). Shortly after that notorious meeting, in 1861, that courthouse burned, and this two-story red brick building replaced it. The city acquired the structure in 1983 and soon renovated it.

In 1765 citizens assembled in Courthouse Square to cheer the decision of Frederick County judges to defy the Stamp Act. Ten years later, frontiersmen from throughout the region gathered in the square on July 18, 1775, before setting off to aid the rebels in Boston. Busts of Roger Brooke Taney and Gov. Thomas Johnson by local sculptor Joseph Urner stand in the courtyard.

West Church St.

From the Courthouse Square walk east on Church St. to the **Evangelical Reformed Church,** 15 W. Church St., built in 1848 when the congregation outgrew the stone chapel across the street. This red brick structure, trimmed with granite, has an Ionic portico in the Greek Revival style and two open towers. While in Frederick in September 1862, Gen. Thomas J. "Stonewall" Jackson attended a Sunday evening service here. The minister had announced his intention to pray for the success of the Union forces, and Jackson may have wished to prevent any reaction by his own soldiers. Whatever the case, the general reportedly slept through the entire service.

Trinity Chapel at 10 W. Church St. is a two-story building with a square stone tower that supports a high octagonal spire. Daniel Dulany reserved this site for the Reformed congregation in 1745, although the legal transfer was not completed until 1764. A schoolhouse was first built on the lot and then a log church in 1747–48. The first steeple appeared in the valley in 1764, when a stone church was built. The current clock tower was installed in 1807 and the old steeple replaced by the present spire. Part of the original 18th-century building is visible in the stonework beneath the spire. The venerable town clock still marks the passage of time in downtown Frederick with the chimes of 10 bells.

Patrick St.

Patrick St. runs parallel to Church St. a block to the south. The **National Museum of Civil War Medicine,** 48 E. Patrick St., is on the south side of the street between N. Market and Maxwell Sts., in a three-story red brick building that served as a funeral home during the Civil War. Established at this location in 1994, the museum's holdings center around the 3,000 artifacts of the Gordon E. Dammann Medical Collection, which includes the only known surviving tent, instruments, chests, uniforms, and documents of a Civil War surgeon. Virtually the entire town of Frederick was turned into a hospital during the war, particularly after nearby battles at South Mountain and Antietam. Almost 6,000 wounded from both sides were treated in more than 20 separate buildings scattered throughout the town. The museum documents the struggles by doctors and nurses, who had limited tools, to keep alive men with horrible wounds—a "real war" that Walt Whitman predicted would never "get in the books."

West of N. Market St., the **Weinberg Center for the Performing Arts,** 20 W. Patrick St., was created in 1978 from the restored Tivoli Theater, an Art Deco movie theater that first opened in 1926. The Weinberg Center offers year-round programming in the performing and visual arts. The Maryland Lyric Opera, a professional company founded in 1989 and based at Hood College, sometimes performs here.

The **John Hanson House,** a three-story brick house at 108 W. Patrick St., has been greatly altered since John Hanson (1721–83) lived here from 1773 until his death. Hanson, a Southern Maryland–born lawyer attracted to opportunities in Frederick, represented Maryland in the Continental Congress from 1780 to 1782. In 1781, under the Articles of Confederation, he was elected "President of the United States in Congress Assembled." Although he had none of the powers granted the president in the later Constitution, Hanson is sometimes referred to as the first president of the United States.

The **Barbara Fritchie House,** at 154 W. Patrick St., stands near Carroll Creek (once Beaver Creek), which rises in the foothills and flows through Frederick on its way to the Monocacy River. The $1\frac{1}{2}$-story brick structure, with dormers on a steep gable roof is a reconstruction of the original house, severely damaged during a flood in 1868. The house has been a Frederick tourist attraction ever since 1863, when John Greenleaf Whittier immortalized Mrs. Fritchie in his famous ballad, "Barbara Frietchie." Whittier, who polemicized for the Union during this period, described an old woman who flew the American flag from her attic window in defiance of Stonewall Jackson. "Shoot, if you must, this old gray head," she says in the poem, "But spare your country's flag." The poet has Jackson pause at her patriotic gesture and gallantly respond: " 'Who touches a hair on yon gray head / Dies like a dog! March on.' he said."

No one knows if this incident ever occurred. Whittier once wrote: "There has been a great deal of dispute about my poem, but if there is any mistake in the details, there was none in my estimate of her noble character, her loyalty and her patriotism." Barbara Fritchie was an actual resident of Frederick; she died here in 1862 and is buried in Mt. Olivet Cemetery. She belonged to the Evangelical Reformed Church; her husband John worked as a glovemaker. The house has become a private museum. During World War II, Sir Winston Churchill accompanied President Roosevelt on a drive to the presidential retreat of Shangri-la (now Camp David) north of Frederick. In response to Churchill's questions about the Barbara Fritchie signs along the road, Roosevelt sang out "Shoot, if you must . . . ," whereupon Churchill, with some assistance, proceeded to recite the entire poem. He said afterward that he had not thought of it for at least 30 years.

Driving Tour

To visit one of Frederick's major attractions, drive out N. Market St. past 14th St. to **Rose Hill Manor** (on the left). This 43-acre historical park features early American gardens and an orchard, a log cabin, blacksmith shop, summer kitchen, icehouse, smokehouse, carriage museum, and farm museum. Rose Hill itself, a rural Georgian mansion with a stately two-story portico, was built in 1790 by John Graham and his wife, Anne Johnson Graham. A children's museum occupies the first floors with hands-on exhibits that demonstrate such activities as quilt making and preparation of beaten biscuits. The second floor contains historic furnishings, including a fully appointed study to illustrate how Gov. Thomas Johnson, who was Anne Graham's father, might have lived and worked during his retirement.

Thomas Johnson (1732–1819) lived with his daughter and son-in-law at Rose Hill Manor from 1794 until his death. A reticent man who never aggressively sought office or power, Johnson was nevertheless active as lawyer, politician, general, and judge during the formation and early years of the republic. He served as a member of the Continental Congress (1774–76), first governor of Maryland (1777–79), and associate justice of the U.S. Supreme Court (1791–93). Johnson especially cherished his friendship with George Washington, whom he had nominated for commander in chief of the Continental Army.

To continue the driving tour to points of interest on the south and west sides of town, follow Market St. south (turning right at 9th or 10th St.—Market becomes one-way north) to Motter Ave. Turn left on Motter, which crosses W. Patrick St. and becomes Bentz St. Find parking to visit the **Roger Brooke Taney House and Museum** (121 S. Bentz St.). A Calvert County native, Taney moved to Frederick in 1801 to practice law with Francis Scott Key, whom he had met while studying for the bar in Annapolis. Five years later, he married Key's sister Anne. Although physically frail and not an inspiring orator, Taney was a highly successful lawyer and became influential in local and state politics, winning election to the Maryland senate in 1816 and, after his move to Baltimore in

Rose Hill, Frederick

1823, serving as Maryland attorney general, between 1827 and 1831. (On Taney's career in federal government see Tour 4.)

Taney lived in this two-story brick structure from 1815 until he left Frederick. The house contains articles and portraits that belonged to the Taneys, including the robe he wore as Supreme Court chief justice and the table on which he wrote the Dred Scott decision. One room contains belongings of Francis Scott Key, a Frederick County native. Taney died in 1864 and is buried next to his mother in St. John's Roman Catholic Cemetery at East and Third Sts.

From the Taney House, turn left (east) on South St. The **site of the Free Colored Men's Library** is located to the left at 111–113 Ice St. This small duplex now provides affordable housing for two families. In the early 1900s, when the town was strictly segregated, the structure housed a library and reading club for black men. Continue on South St. to S. Market St., and there make a right (south).

One block down S. Market St. turn left on Clarke Place and proceed one block to the **Maryland School for the Deaf,** which the state established in 1868 as a free public school for resident deaf and hearing-impaired children. At that time classes met in barracks that had been used for Hessian prisoners during the Revolution.

The **Hessian Barracks,** a stone building erected in 1777–78, was commandeered during the Revolution for prisoners, including Hessian mercenaries captured at Bennington, Saratoga, and Yorktown. Many of the Hessians shared a common German background with Frederick's inhabitants, and a number of the prisoners settled here after the war. After the Revolution, Daniel Dulany, the original landowner, reclaimed the property, which his family in 1799 deeded to the state. Maryland used the barracks as an arsenal during the first half of the 19th century. It served as a staging area for the Lewis and Clark expedition in 1803. U.S. troops were quartered here in 1812. The barracks became a hospital during the Civil War. Then the students at the School for the Deaf used the old barracks until a four-story red brick building was constructed for them in 1870. The restored Hessian Barracks is now open only by appointment with the school.

A block south of Clarke Place, S. Market St. leads to **Mt. Olivet Cemetery** (on the right), where the remains of more than 32,000 people lie buried in a green, wooded Victorian setting. A private corporation chartered the cemetery in 1852. The **Francis Scott Key Monument,** designed by Alexander Doyle in 1898, sits just beyond the entrance. This nine-foot, bronze figure of Key, author of "The Star-Spangled Banner," stands on a pedestal above smaller figures representing Patriotism, War, and Music. Key (1779–1843) was born at Terra Rubra, then in Frederick County but now a part of Carroll County, and, after practicing law in Frederick, moved to the District of Columbia in 1805. Citizens organized as the Key Monument Association had the bodies of Key and his wife brought here from Baltimore for burial. The monument is one of the few places in the United States where without violating protocol the flag is never lowered.

The **Barbara Fritchie Monument** stands in the southern part of the cemetery. Her remains and those of her husband were removed from the Evangelical Reformed graveyard in 1913 and placed here, and this

Maryland granite monument was unveiled the following year. A bronze tablet bears the complete text of Whittier's famous poem.

Nearby is the grave of Thomas Johnson, first governor of the state of Maryland, moved here in 1913 from the cemetery of All Saints Episcopal Church. The graves of Union and Confederate soldiers killed in the battles of the Monocacy and Antietam lie in separate sections of the cemetery.

Return north via Market St. to Patrick St., there turning left (west) and soon passing the Barbara Fritchie House. The **Steiner House** (368 W. Patrick St.) stands on the left just before Patrick St. crosses S. Jefferson St. Col. Stephen Steiner, architect and prominent citizen (some of the earliest settlers in the county were Steiners) built this two-story brick building in 1807. Well proportioned, it has a particularly wide—and striking—front doorway. A later member of the family, Lewis H. Steiner, was an outspoken Unionist during the Civil War and afterward was first director of the Enoch Pratt Free Library in Baltimore.

From the Steiner House, turn right on N. Jefferson St. and then right on Carroll Pkwy., which skirts the southern edge of **Baker Park.** This 44-acre green space along Carroll Creek opened in 1927 and was named for Joseph D. Baker, a banker and civic leader who died in 1938. The park's band shell and memorial carillon are visible to the east.

Turn left on College Ave. and continue to Rosemont Ave. and the entrance to **Hood College,** now a coeducational, liberal arts college with a total enrollment of about 2,000 students, including 450 men. The Potomac Synod of the Reformed Church in the United States founded the college in 1893 as the Women's College of Frederick. It opened with 80 students and eight faculty members on the site of the Frederick Female Seminary. The college changed its name in 1913 to recognize the benefactions of Mrs. Margaret E. S. Hood. Two years later, it moved to this 100-acre campus, a wooded site with Georgian Colonial brick buildings. The college's first president, Henry Joseph Apple, served until 1934, creating a reputation for academic excellence that continues to the present.

Next to the Hood College grounds on the north lies **Frederick Memorial Hospital,** the site for which is owed to a donation Emma J. Smith made to the newly formed Frederick City Hospital Association in 1897. (At the time, some residents complained that the land lay too far out in the country.) In 1952 the institution changed its name to Frederick Memorial and rededicated itself to "longer life, better health, and increased happiness for all the people in the wide area it serves." At the end of the 20th century, FMH has six satellites, provides 248 beds, employs 1,600 staff persons and 250 physicians, and enjoys the support of about 1,200 volunteers.

West of the college, at 1110 Rosemont Ave. and adjacent to its junction with U.S. 15, stands **Schifferstadt,** the oldest surviving house in Frederick. Joseph Brunner and his son Elias completed the sandstone and wood structure in 1756 on a 303-acre farm Brunner had bought 10 years earlier from Daniel Dulany. The family, which had immigrated from Germany to Philadelphia around 1729, named the house near Carroll Creek after their birthplace, a river town southeast of Mannheim in the Rheinland-Pfalz palatinate of Germany. Many of the house's features—including a five-plate German-inscribed stove, hand-hewn beams, and vaulted chimney and cellar—are original. A two-story brick wing was added in the 19th century to replace a log structure that probably served as a kitchen. The Frederick County Landmarks Foundation has maintained the 18th-century farmhouse as an architectural museum since 1974, proclaiming the structure "probably America's finest example of German colonial architecture." During warm weather months, the foundation operates a museum shop, sponsors festivals and handcraft exhibits, and conducts tours. From Schifferstadt, take U.S. 15 south to U.S. 40 west.

ALTERNATE ("OLD") U.S. 40

The Blue Ridge Mountains first loom in the distance when the westbound traveler reaches the Monocacy Valley, a transition area between the western and central parts of the state. Just west of Frederick, one faces a choice of routes. While the interstates serve Western Maryland's historic communities, they do not take the traveler into the towns. The most interesting and instructive route through Western Maryland begins on "Old National Pike," or Alternate U.S. 40, signs for which appear just west of Frederick on both U.S. 40 and I-70.

Braddock Heights

Old Route 40 evokes memories of Edward Braddock, the British general who left Frederick in the spring of 1755 on an expedition to expel the French from the Ohio Valley. He departed in a governor's coach and on July 13 died in the wilderness near Fort Duquesne (now Pittsburgh). Braddock's death and the rout of his British and American army by a much smaller force of French and Indians reverberated throughout the Western world. In Maryland, the debacle forced settlers to flee their frontier homes and seek protection in places like Fort Frederick. George Washington, who accompanied Braddock, wrote a friend that "when this story comes to be related in future Annals, it will meet with ridicule or indignation; for had I not been witness to the fact on that fatal Day, I sh'd scarce give credit to it now."

Braddock's fate has ceased to generate much emotion, but his name still appears in local place-names. **Old Braddock** at the intersection of U.S. 40 and Alt. U.S. 40, was a stop on the eastern extension of the National Road. Teamsters stopped here for rest and uproarious drinking bouts. In 1830, according to neighborhood legend, a guest buried a chest of jewels on a nearby mountainside. Two years later he returned and was fatally injured during a mountain storm while attempting to recover his cache. As he was dying, the stranger confessed that the jewels had been stolen from a grand duchess in France. The landlord dug fruitlessly, and residents of the vicinity insist the treasure awaits the lucky prospector. Similar undocumented tales of buried treasure date to the 18th century. Early-20th-century accounts of the mythical "snallygaster," a rare winged beast with horrible appetites, indicate that Catoctin moonshine had special potency.

Locals call the section of the **Catoctin Mountain** crossed by Alt. 40 **Braddock Mountain,** and the small community at the crest is named **Braddock Heights** (950' alt.). The highway does not follow Braddock's exact route (an old Indian path located about a mile south), but a stone marker dedicated by the Daughters of the American Revolution in 1921 and moved to its current site in 1957 indicates the location of **Braddock Springs,** where some of the general's redcoats may have sought relief from the heat, humidity, and chiggers.

Braddock Heights dates to 1901, when local entrepreneurs took advantage of the new trolley line from Frederick to establish a summer resort on the ridge. The resort hotel burned in 1929, but several Victorian houses reflect their former roles as boarding establishments for rich and famous visitors, particularly from Washington (Franklin D. Roosevelt came in the 1930s). The town still offers swimming in the summer and skiing in the winter.

Middletown

Alt. U.S. 40 descends the ridge to Middletown (575' alt., 1,834 pop.), where it becomes Main St. A farming village of 18th-century vintage, Middletown has experienced much change since mid-century. Only 30 years ago, when viewed from Braddock Mountain, the village could appear to be floating on a sea of grain or green pasture. Although still home to scattered dairy farms, the Middletown Valley, between Catoctin and South Mountains, is now rapidly filling with suburban housing.

Some of the heritage of old Middletown survives in two Lutheran churches, whose spires dominate the town. **Christ Reformed Church** on S. Church St. was built in 1818 and remodeled in 1889. Tombstones behind the church carry such old German names as Remsburg, Kefauver, and Coblentz. **Zion Lutheran Church** on W. Main St. was built in 1859, but the graves in its churchyard date to the 1750s. A 12-foot marble shaft marks the grave of a Sergeant Everhart, whom legend credits with saving the lives of the Marquis de Lafayette and Lt. Col. William Augustine Washington during the Revolution. Sergeant Everhart carried the wounded Lafayette to safety at the Battle of Brandywine, September 11, 1777, and came to the aid of William Washington at the Battle of Cowpens, January 17, 1781. After the war, as a Methodist minister, the Rev. Mr. Everhart preached at this site, then called Martenbox Church.

An era ended in 1991 when the *Valley Register,* a Middletown weekly established in 1844, shut down. Four generations of the Rhoderick family had published the paper. Its records now reside in the town's historical society, whose offices are housed in the oldest stone building on Main St.

Turner's Gap

Departing Middletown, Alt. 40 heads toward **South Mountain,** an extension of Virginia's Blue Ridge, and beyond it into the Great Valley, an extension of the Shenandoah Valley. An inn has stood at Turner's Gap, where Alt. 40 crosses South Mountain, since the early 18th century. In 1876 Madeline Dahlgren, widow of the Union admiral and ordnance expert John A. B. Dahlgren, bought the Mountain House Tavern and renamed it the **South Mountain Inn.** So it was known for more than a century. Across from the inn, Mrs. Dahlgren ordered the building of the Gothic Revival Chapel of St. Joseph of the Sacred Heart of Jesus, as a family mausoleum, in about 1881. The **Dahlgren Chapel** is now closed and the bodies reburied.

The mountain has inspired more than a few tall tales. Locals believe that as late as 1859 bands of Indians secretly used South Mountain paths. Another local story tells of mysterious lights moving along the mountainside and referred to as "the Saxon's fire." According to folk tale, a young Saxon soldier on his way to the Seminole War fell in love with the daughter of the innkeeper at Mountain House Tavern, deserted, and hid in the woods until his unit departed and he could marry his sweetheart. The region's folklore captured the imagination of Madeline Dahlgren, who collected enough of it to publish *South Mountain Magic* (1882).

The Battle of South Mountain

On September 14, 1862, during Gen. Robert E. Lee's first foray north of the Potomac, slightly fewer than 5,000 Confederates under the command of D. H. Hill stood in and around Turner's Gap and watched nearly 24,000 Union soldiers, banners flying and muskets gleaming, march up toward their positions from the east. Having divided his army, Lee quickly ordered Gen. James Longstreet's forces in Hagerstown to Hill's aid. Longstreet's corps began arriving in the afternoon, just in time to keep the thin defenses from crumbling. Men fought from behind rocks and trees, Indian style, and from shallow trenches all over the thickly wooded mountain.

Maj. Gen. Jesse Lee Reno, commander of the Union Ninth Corps, was killed in the Battle of South Mountain; to reach a marker placed on the site of his death, backtrack about a mile to the east on Alt. 40, turn right on Reno School Rd. and right again on Reno Monument Rd. A few yards from the monument lie foundation stones of a cabin once belonging to a local eccentric known in legend as "Old Wise." After the Battle of South Mountain, the federal government supposedly paid Wise $5 per body to bury the scattered dead. To save time and effort, according to lore, he threw 50 or so corpses down a nearby well, whereupon their ghosts haunted him until the old man gave the bodies a decent burial. Ghosts of dead soldiers still supposedly wander South Mountain at night.

Two future presidents, both soldiers in the 23rd Ohio Infantry, fought at South Mountain: Lt. Col. Rutherford B. Hayes was wounded; Sgt. William McKinley escaped injury. Confederate forces retreated in darkness on the night of September 14–15 and headed toward Sharpsburg, leaving behind about 500 dead or wounded and 440 missing. Union losses on the mountain exceeded 1,800 killed or wounded. The North claimed a brilliant victory. General Hill later noted that the reports of front-rank Union commanders were far more modest.

Washington Monument State Park

From Turner's Gap, less than a mile away, Washington Monument Rd. leads to a state park of the same name. Residents of nearby Boonsboro marched up the mountain on July 4, 1827, to the music of fife and drum, and constructed a rough stone monument to George Washington. At the end of the day, they read the Declaration of Independence, sent three veterans to the top of the 20-foot-high tower to fire their muskets, and went home. This simple structure and ceremony may have been the first such tributes to Washington. At the time of the Battle of South Mountain, when Union troops used this site as a signal station, the monument had fallen to ruin. The Odd Fellows of Boonsboro rebuilt it (to a height of 40 feet, with a roofed observatory on top) in 1882. The Washington County Historical Society donated the again-crumbling monument to the state in 1934, and the Civilian Conservation Corps soon rebuilt it from local stone. On a clear day the view from the top includes valley vistas to east and west alike. From here the traveler can return to

Civilian Conservation Corpsmen in 1936, completing restoration of the nation's oldest monument to George Washington

the summit or take Zittlestown Rd. down the mountain to rejoin Alt. 40 outside a hamlet named for the large Zittle family.

Boonsboro

Alt. 40 continues west through Boonsboro, founded in 1792 by George and William Boone, who may have been related to the famous Daniel. By 1803, the town had two dozen houses and was growing as a rural crossroads. Boonsboro grew prosperous in the 1830s with traffic from the National Pike. A wide variety of 19th-century celebrities passed through its streets. David Belasco, the pioneering American impresario, used several of its neat, porched houses close to the street in his Civil War melodrama, *The Heart of Maryland; A Drama in Four Acts* (1895).

The **Bowman House** at 343 Main St., constructed ca. 1826–40, is typical of the log dwellings built in Western Maryland villages of the period. John Bowman, a Civil War veteran whose family had moved to the area from Pennsylvania, ran a pottery business from this house from 1868 until his death in 1906. Now listed on the National Register, the Bowman House shelters the town's historical society.

The **site of Salem Union Church,** on Potomac St. near Main St., illustrated an early religious controversy that often caused trouble in communities in this part of Maryland. Between 1810 and 1870, this church building housed both Lutheran and Reformed congregations. The Lutherans favored roundheaded windows for the church, while the Reformed faithful advocated square windows, contending that the other type was sinfully ostentatious. These German-Americans compromised by placing round windows on one side of the building and square windows on the other. A dispute arose again when some of the brethren felt that a stove for winter comfort would represent "sacrilege and gross impiety." So the elders installed a stove on one side of the church, presumably the one with the round windows. In 1935, the people of Boonsboro erected a monument to William Boone in the graveyard adjoining the church, replacing the simple stone that had marked his grave for 137 years.

Because the local soil is unusually sandy, Boonsboro melons, particularly cantaloupe, have become justly famous for their taste.

Funkstown

Alt. 40 continues northwestward from Boonsboro to Funkstown (1,136 pop.), named for Jacob Funk, to whom Frederick Calvert granted the land tract in 1754. First called Jerusalem, the town lost an opportunity for growth when Jonathan Hager successfully petitioned to have his settlement named the county seat. Although overshadowed by adjacent Hagerstown, Funkstown has remained an independent municipality and boasts a small historic center. A war memorial recalls local participation in conflicts since the Civil War; and the **site of South's Hotel,** built when the turnpike passed through the town, recalls an 1859 visit by John Brown on his way to arm slaves for his planned uprising at Harpers Ferry.

Alt. 40 crosses Antietam Creek on a three-arched **limestone bridge** (1823) that both sides used during the Civil War and enters Hagerstown via Frederick St. Turn right on N. Locust St. and then left a few blocks later onto Franklin St. (U.S. 40 West). Cross Potomac and Jonathan Sts. to Prospect Street Park and proceed left and south to Washington St.

To reach the **Washington County Convention and Visitors Bureau** at 1826-C Dual Hwy. (U.S. 40's eastern approach to Hagerstown), follow Edgewood Dr. north from Funkstown and turn west on U.S. 40. Open throughout the year, the visitors bureau offers general information about Hagerstown's and Washington County's historical, cultural, and recreational attractions.

HAGERSTOWN

This old crossroads community (560′ alt., 35,445 pop.) lies in the Great Valley, a wide swath between Appalachian ridges that extend from the Cumberland Valley of Pennsylvania to the Shenandoah Valley of Virginia. The Great Valley has served as a north-south pathway for centuries. American Indian tribes used it long before European settlers arrived. Conestoga wagons followed it in the 18th century as whites moved from Pennsylvania to Virginia and farther south. The old wagon road became U.S. 11 in the federal system; modern travelers now follow the same path on I-81 between Harrisburg, Pennsylvania, and Knoxville, Tennessee.

Conococheague and Antietam Creeks flow from Pennsylvania across the Maryland portion of the valley to the Potomac River, creating a fertile, well-watered countryside that appealed strongly to the immigrant German farmers who entered the uncultivated land before the Revolution. They arrived speaking little English and carrying Lutheran Bibles. Jonathan Hager (1714–75), a Westphalian German, arrived in the valley in 1739 and patented 200 acres which he named Hager's Fancy. He built a stone house over two adjacent springs and a year later married Elizabeth Kershner, one of his neighbors. The young German prospered and his estate grew. In 1745, he sold his original house—which still stands—and

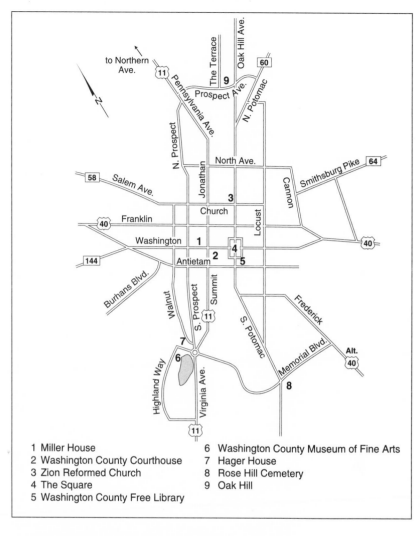

1 Miller House
2 Washington County Courthouse
3 Zion Reformed Church
4 The Square
5 Washington County Free Library
6 Washington County Museum of Fine Arts
7 Hager House
8 Rose Hill Cemetery
9 Oak Hill

moved to Hager's Delight, a 1,780-acre tract about two miles west of Hager's Fancy. He survived the French and Indian War, achieving the rank of captain, and in 1762 began laying out Elizabeth Town in 520 half-acre lots. The town was variously known as Elizabeth Town or Hager's Town or Elizabeth Hager's Town until 1829, when the current name and spelling were finally standardized.

Within a decade of its founding, Hager's town had 100 dwellings and had developed into an important trading point for the surrounding region. In 1776, a year after the founder's accidental death, Hagerstown became the county seat of Washington County, created from part of Frederick County. Population continued to increase in the region, and the town developed into a stage stop and important location on the road network linking Baltimore to the West.

As a county seat in a frontier setting, Hagerstown attracted boisterous crowds from the countryside for horse racing, cockfighting, bullbaiting, and other roisterous amusements. Long Bullet, a popular game that involved players' hurling a five-pound iron shot, eventually had to be declared illegal. The shots, wielded by men who had sampled too heavily from the plentiful whiskey, caused serious injury to hurlers and bystanders. During the 18th century, public hangings were also popular amusements. Bands played the condemned men to the gallows, where impassioned preachers delivered rousing sermons in fire-and-brimstone fashion. Then the victim was given a chance to talk to the crowd, usually to warn them and presumably improve public morality.

As early as 1814, however, Hagerstown was losing its rough edges and developing into a thriving, civilized community. The town had about 2,500 inhabitants and had become a small manufacturing center (brushes, shoes, hats, nails, rope, linseed oil, guns, flour, whiskey distilling equipment) as well as a commercial hub for the surrounding farms. Unlike Frederick, which produced an unusual number of prominent lawyers, Hagerstown nurtured bankers, merchants, millers, manufacturers, and entrepreneurs.

For example, John Gruber, a young printer from Pennsylvania came to Hagerstown in 1795 and established a German-language newspaper to rival the *Washington Spy*, an English-language paper that had started printing in 1790. In 1797, Gruber published the first issue of the *Hagers-Town Town and Country Almanack* in German. The Almanack has been published annually ever since and currently claims a circulation of 225,000 copies. An English version was added in 1822; the German edition lasted until 1918.

Hagerstown also generated another founder of towns. Col. Nathaniel Rochester—the first president of the Hagerstown bank, owner of an iron and nail factory, sheriff, politician, judge—left the town in 1810 with a band of settlers and headed to the Genesee Valley in New York. Rochester had served as the deputy commissary general of military stores for the Continental Army and had moved to Hagerstown after the Revolution. Apparently, Rochester felt uncomfortable raising his family in a slave state and decided to move north. He laid out the village of Rochesterville in 1811, and it grew to become the city of Rochester, where Marylander Frederick Douglass lived from 1847 to 1872, published his antislavery paper, and is buried.

Hagerstown was appealing enough in the 1820s to attract the attention of Anne Royall (1769–1854), a Maryland woman who wrote ten travel books and edited two newspapers in Washington, where she was a fearless, often caustic critic of Congress. "Hagerstown is principally settled by Germans and their descendants, and, of course, retains many of their customs," she wrote in 1827. "The women are short and ill-shaped and have a vacancy of countenance which too evidently shows the want of proper schools." Such remarks were typical of her and probably did not disturb the burghers too much. (Royall once called Baltimore "the most illiterate, proud and ignorant city, excepting Richmond, in the Union.") In 1829, Mrs. Royall's waspish commentaries led to her trial and conviction in Washington City for being a "common scold."

The massive German immigration to America in the 1840s did not change Hagerstown, which was rapidly becoming "Americanized," as the German language slowly faded from publications, church pulpits, and social events. (This process culminated during World War I, when anti-German sentiment swept the country.) The German-Americans in Hagerstown retained their antislavery, pro-Union sentiments during the years leading to the Civil War. Local citizens wondered about a tall, arresting figure who appeared in 1859 as "I. Smith" to order supplies for a farm he had rented near the Potomac River. He had a strange stare, concluded his transactions with a prayer, and people rumored he had a strange power over animals. Hundreds of Hagerstown citizens later crossed the Potomac to Charles Town to watch the same man, John Brown, walk to the scaffold on December 2, 1859, after his failed raid on Harpers Ferry.

Its location in the Great Valley put Hagerstown in the path of Robert E. Lee's two expeditions north of the Potomac. Confederate troops occupied the town before "Bloody Antietam," which filled local churches and homes with the wounded from both sides. One of them—Oliver Wendell Holmes Jr., then a young captain in the 20th Massachusetts Infantry and later a U.S. Supreme Court justice—recuperated at Colonel Rochester's old house.

Just as valley residents had finished healing the wounded, burying the dead, and repairing the countryside, Lee's army returned, nine months after Antietam, in another effort to claim victory in the North. When the first columns crossed the Potomac on June 15, 1863, thoughts of "liberating" their "sister state" had disappeared. Lee hoped to capture Harrisburg, Pennsylvania, and force arbitration to end the war before the wealthier, more populous Union overcame the Confederacy.

As the Confederates marched through Hagerstown, even Union sympathizers craned their necks for a glimpse of Lee, who was already assuming mythic proportions. A Union column crossed at Shepherdstown and Williamsport to guard the mountain gaps. J.E.B. Stuart's cavalry rode through Rockville, Eldersburg, and Westminster to create a diversion. Lee met his advance force in Chambersburg, Pennsylvania (18 miles north of Hagerstown and about 13 miles north of the Mason-Dixon line) on June 27. Neither army quite knew the location or intention of the other. When Lee finally discovered the proximity of Union forces, he concentrated his columns east of South Mountain, leaving an escape route down the Great Valley through Hagerstown. Following the climactic Battle of Gettysburg, Confederates retreated through Hagerstown. The procession lacked any allure it may have had before the battle. The ragged soldiers had lost their dash, and commanders were unable to prevent incidents of looting. The wounded cried from their wagons, the train of which stretched for 17 miles.

In 1864, Gen. John McCausland rode into the town with 1,500 Confederate cavalrymen and demanded a ransom of $20,000 in cash and a large amount of clothing. The citizens hurriedly met the terms of his "assessment," and McCausland then rejoined Gen. Jubal Early's force marching on Washington. (Early, who levied $200,000 from Frederick, later claimed that McCausland was supposed to have done the same in Hagerstown.)

It is difficult to imagine now the legacy of bitterness that the Civil War left in Maryland. Not until 1994 did Marylanders at long last dedicate a monument honoring Old Line State soldiers who fought on *both* sides at Gettysburg.

After the war industrial growth turned Hagerstown into a regional urban center. A spur of the B&O Railroad connected the town to the main line in 1867, and the Western Maryland Railroad reached Hagerstown from Baltimore in 1872 and established a division office here. In 1880 the Shenandoah Valley Railroad connected the town to Virginia. That year Mathias Peter Möller (1855–1937) opened a factory here for the manufacture of pipe organs. He had emigrated from Denmark in 1872 and constructed an organ for the Philadelphia Centennial Exposition of 1876. Like many others, he was attracted by the quality of the work force in Hagerstown, where he developed new manufacturing methods that won his factory international recognition. Möller was made a Knight of the Ancient Order of Danneborg by Denmark in 1926, and his organ factory became one of the world's largest.

As early as 1905, town officials were offering tax concessions to industries willing to build plants in the area, and by 1914, Hagerstown was the second largest manufacturing city in Maryland, edging out Cumberland in a category dominated by Baltimore. Although Cumberland remained the state's second largest city, Hagerstown more than doubled its population between 1880 and 1914, from 6,627 to 16,507, making it the third largest.

In the early 1920s two young Hagerstownians, Lewis and Henry Reisner, experimented with aircraft designs in an old shack in back of their house on Salem Ave. With financial assistance from their father and Ammon Kreider, they expanded their work in 1926 and soon had a shop for building and servicing airplanes. Their first plane, a low-winged racer, won the air meet at the Philadelphia Sesquicentennial celebration. The firm organized as the Kreider-Reisner Airplane Company and opened a larger plant in 1928. After Kreider was killed in 1929 at the Detroit Air Meet, the company sold out to Sherman Fairchild, a New York aviation entrepreneur and inventor who expanded the plant for large-scale production. The Fairchild Aircraft Division of the Fairchild Corporation in

A Hagerstown street scene from the 1930s

Hagerstown built the famous "Flying Boxcars" during World War II and branched into space technology during the 1950s and 1960s.

Such industrial activity, combined with the town's role as county seat, provided a financial base for cultural development. The city's library pioneered the concept of the bookmobile in 1904, and the arts have flourished here, supported by a wide range of churches and civic clubs. Hagerstown has maintained a pleasant residential character, displaying Victorian and early-20th-century architecture that reflects its solid, conservative past. The large, well-patronized farmers' market, established in 1791, ties city and county together every Saturday. Beginning in 1956, with Ford Foundation funding, Hagerstown and Washington County led the nation in experimenting with closed-circuit television in the public schools. Washington County Hospital, which began in 1904 in a single-family house on the east side of town, has grown to a 300-bed institution on E. Antietam St. It serves as the regional shock trauma center and the designated emergency hospital for nearby Camp David.

The emergence of a new international economy has disrupted Hagerstown almost as seriously as did the Civil War. The Möller factory closed in 1992 after making almost 12,000 pipe organs during its 117-year history. Rohr, Inc., which bought the Fairchild aircraft assembly plant in 1987, announced in 1993 that it was closing down its Hagerstown operations.

The town's emblem, **Little Heiskell,** remains an enduring symbol for Hagerstown's demonstrated ability to weather such storms. A German tinsmith named Heiskell designed this weathervane in the shape of a Hessian soldier in 1769, when it was placed on top of City Hall. During the Civil War, a sharpshooter used the flattened tin figure for target practice, but it remained on its perch until 1935, when city leaders retired it. The original now rests in the Hager House Museum in City Park; a duplicate stands atop City Hall.

Walking Tour

On Washington St., walk east from its intersection with Prospect St. to downtown Hagerstown.

W. Washington St. and N. Potomac St.

The **Miller House and Garden,** 135 W. Washington St., houses the **Washington County Historical Society,** from which downtown walking maps and related guide materials are available. The society's library contains valuable historical and genealogical documents, including a fine collection of Gruber's almanacs.

This property was part of Lot 91 in Jonathan Hager's original plat of Elizabeth Town. The earliest record, in 1804, indicates that a potter lived with his large family in a house at this location. The present Federal-style town house dates to 1824, although the rear of the house may be part of an earlier structure. Several lawyers lived here and were followed in 1912 by Dr. Victor Davis Miller Jr. The Miller family occupied the house for more than 50 years before the historical society bought it and opened it to the public in 1967. The society maintains the somewhat altered building as a museum featuring period furnishings, more than 200 clocks, 250 dolls, and assorted memorabilia from the county's past.

Continue down W. Washington St. to the **Washington County Courthouse** (1873) at the corner of Summit Ave. Walk another block and then turn left (northeast) into the small alley that crosses W. Franklin St. The alley passes the **Farmer's Market Building** and ends at Church St. The churchyard of the Zion Reformed Church lies behind a short wall to the right.

The limestone **Zion Reformed Church,** at N. Potomac and Church Sts., the oldest surviving religious structure in Hagerstown, underwent modification in the late 19th century, but the square tower and its two bells, cast in Rotterdam in 1785, are original. In 1770, German and Swiss refugees established the Zion and Evangelical Reformed Church in Elizabeth Town, "Fridrich County, Province of Mereland"; they laid the cornerstone for this building in 1774. Jonathan Hager died here when a large piece of timber fell during the church's construction. During the Revolution, grain, blankets, guns, powder, and tomahawks were assembled at this location for shipment by wagon to Washington's troops. Eleven veterans of the Revolution are buried in the churchyard, including Peter Humrichhouse, who supplied Washington's troops with much-needed ammunition for the siege of Yorktown. Jonathan Hager is also buried here, as is John Gruber. The old church now houses the Zion United Church of Christ.

From this corner, walk south on Potomac St. **City Hall,** at the southeast corner of N. Potomac and W. Franklin Sts., dates from 1941. The first seat of city government stood just to the south, on arches that sheltered a market space in the town square. A second city hall went up on this spot in 1818, and it served its purpose until World War II.

The Square (or Public Square) enlarges the intersection of N. Potomac and W. Washington Sts., and it has been here since the town's earliest days. A local jeweler, R. Bruce Carson, bought the eight-day clock—**Carson's Clock**—at the southeast corner in 1908. Until 1929 it stood in front of his store in the Baldwin Building, on W. Washington St. Now a municipal landmark, the clock became city property in 1974.

S. Potomac St. and W. Antietam St.

Continue walking south on Potomac St. to the **Maryland Theatre,** in the next block. It opened in 1915, described as a "high-class vaudeville" and "feature picture" house with 2,500 seats. Local investors hired famed architect Thomas Lamb to design a "palace of the average man" and spare no expense on the neoclassical interior. The theater cost a total of $200,000; a four-story apartment building was built over its ornate, embossed, and mosaicked lobby. "The Maryland" became a county landmark, the second theater in the state to feature "talkies" and the scene of many high school commencements. Audiences dressed up to attend the "A" pictures shown here and applaud the stars who occasionally visited to plug their latest movie.

Like similar movie palaces around the country, the Maryland gradually lost its luster, particularly after television brought the stars to the living room. The deteriorating downtown landmark closed in 1973. When a five-alarm fire destroyed the lobby and the overhead apartments in 1974, most people thought this memory-filled playhouse would never be rebuilt. Fortunately, however, Citizens to Save the Maryland Theater raised money, renovated the facility, and opened it again in 1978. A nonprofit organization with a full-time staff of five now runs a theatrical season that includes pop and classical music, pageants, comedy acts, and musical shows. The Colonial Theatre, a smaller venue built in 1914, sits across the street.

The **Washington County Free Library,** a modern structure at the corner of S. Potomac and W. Antietam Sts., offers patrons various media and students of the region the **Western Maryland Room.** The library was founded in 1901 by a clergyman, a banker, a papermaker, two lawyers, a farmer, and a storekeeper. At that time, only one small, private high school existed in Hagerstown; there were no bookstores, and reading was regarded as a pastime of the idle rich. On opening day, a country woman left with a book in her apron and remarked: "It's a great day when poor folks like us can take home such handsome books." One farm boy, who stumbled onto a Shakespeare play, returned it with this request: "Give me another by that same man; I think he's a right good writer."

Mary L. Titcomb, the first librarian, devoted half a lifetime to the development of this institution, one of the first county libraries in the United States. Miss Titcomb reached out to the countryside by placing books in country stores, schools, and private homes. In 1904 she equipped a two-horse Concord wagon with bookshelves and delivered books to 22 deposit stations throughout Washington County. The only interruption occurred in 1912, when the truck that had succeeded the wagon stalled on a railroad track and was struck by a train. Avoiding railroad crossings, the library's bookmobiles still travel to the remotest parts of the county.

Turn right onto W. Antietam St. and return to S. Prospect St. The **Herald-Mail Company,** which publishes two newspapers, occupies a modern facility (1980) to the right of the intersection with Summit Ave. The **original library building,** designed by Bruce Pierce, stands to the right on the western side of Summit Ave. Continue on W. Antietam St. Steps lead to the **Dry Bridge,** which carries Prospect St. over Antietam. In 1832 this iron bridge replaced the original stone bridge across the ravine.

S. Prospect St.

Running (one way) from W. Washington St. to the City Park, this old avenue offers vistas that one may take in while driving or, for at least part of the way, walking. Now listed on the National Register of Historic Places, the street was laid out in 1832. The residences and churches along this tree-lined, three-block street reflect a time when a Prospect St. address was the most fashionable in town. **Mount Prospect,** built in 1789 by Nathaniel Rochester (who later founded Rochester, New York), once stood on the hill overlooking the town from the place where Prospect St. crosses W. Washington; a parking lot, which visitors may find useful, occupies the site.

The **Women's Club** building, a Federal-style structure at 31 S. Prospect St., was built as a residence in 1838. The club purchased and renovated the house in 1923, adding an auditorium. The Potomac Playmakers, who claim, like the Vagabonds in Baltimore, to be the oldest (1926) continuously operating community theater in America, make their home here.

The street is home to impressive churches also—the spireless, limestone **Presbyterian Church** (1873) and the Gothic stone **St. John's Episcopal Church** (1872), the former by Edmund G. Lind, a Baltimore architect, and the latter by Emlyn T. Littel, from New York.

The now-closed **Hagerstown Academy,** begun in 1813, originally stood in the middle of what is now S. Prospect St., just south of the intersection with W. Baltimore St. The school closed when public education came to Hagerstown in 1867, and the academy was torn down. The property at **213 S. Prospect St.** dates from about 1890; it stood on the academy grounds. The two-story Queen Anne house was the boyhood home of William Preston Lane Jr., Maryland governor from 1947 to 1951.

Driving Tour

Follow Prospect St. south to a traffic circle where Virginia Ave. (U.S. 11), S. Prospect St., Summit Ave. and Memorial Blvd. converge at Millstone Circle. Bear right for public parking. Hagerstown created 50-acre **City Park** in 1915.

The **Washington County Museum of Fine Arts,** a simple brick building with limestone facing designed by New York architect William E. Shepherd overlooks a large man-made lily pond. Anna Hyatt Huntington's bronze "Diana of the Chase" (1922) stands on the front portico. William Henry Singer Jr. (1868–1943), an American landscape painter raised in a wealthy Pittsburgh family, gave the museum to Hagerstown in honor of his wife, Anna Brugh, who was born here. Married in 1895, the two spent most of their time in Europe, particularly in Holland and in Olden, Norway, where they built a home, collected art, and entertained fellow artists while Singer painted Norwegian landscapes. The couple donated part of their collection to the museum, which opened in 1931. (There is also a Singer museum in Laren, Holland, where Mrs. Singer died in 1962 at the age of 86.) In 1949, Mrs. Singer added a memorial gallery for her husband's work and a small concert gallery for the performance of chamber music.

Mr. Singer apparently never saw the results of his gift to Hagerstown, but he surely would have been delighted at its growth. A staff of five supervises a permanent collection of about 5,000 paintings, sculptures, and specimens of the decorative arts. Items in the collection range from Old Masters to works of 20th-century artists, with a major emphasis on American art. Shows change every month, in order to display diverse portions of the collection and to make room for traveling exhibits. In 1995, the museum opened a new wing, more than doubling its total space, refurbished its original building, and acquired the permanent gift of 130 complementary paintings, drawings, watercolors, prints, and drawings from the collection of Dr. and Mrs. Albert R. Miller Jr.

The **Hager House,** at the north end of the park, is the original structure built by Jonathan Hager in 1739–40 after he bought Hager's Fancy. Built with 22-inch walls over two adjacent springs, the stone house seems impregnable and must have provided good security during the French and Indian War. The Hagers lived here for several years, farming and operating a trading post, until they sold the house to Jacob Rohrer in 1745. The property remained in the Rohrer family until 1944, when the Washington County Historical Society acquired the house and began a restoration effort. The society presented Hager House to Hagerstown in

1954; it was opened to the public in 1962 during the city's bicentennial. *The Washington County Museum of Fine Arts, Hagerstown, 1998*
The interior has been furnished with authentic items of the period in which it was built.

Besides the original Little Heiskell, the symbol of Hagerstown, the adjacent **Hager Museum** contains artifacts uncovered beneath the stone porch in 1953 during restoration of the Hager House.

The **Mansion House,** located on a hill in the middle of the park, was originally part of **Cedar Lawn,** an estate the city acquired in 1915. William Heyser II, son of one of the first settlers, bought the property from Jacob Rohrer in 1806. Included in the purchase was a gristmill that is located near the Virginia Avenue entrance to the present park. When Heyser deeded 50 acres to his son John in 1842, the younger man began construction of this Georgian-style mansion. The bricks were handmade from marl found in a swampy area that is now part of the lake. John Heyser, reputedly a winemaker as well as amateur painter, also built a vaulted wine cellar in the hill just north of his residence. During the 1850s the Hagerstown Fair Association held harness races on the property, and it was occupied by both armies during the Civil War. Heyser moved in 1882 to Florida, where he was murdered; his family sold the property in 1884, and it had a number of owners until being bought by the city. The Valley Art Association moved into the building in 1991; members from Maryland, Pennsylvania, and West Virginia use it for meetings, workshops, and displays of their works.

Additional city attractions are accessible by driving from City Park. Follow Walnut St. north along the park to Antietam St. and turn left across the railroad tracks to S. Burhans Blvd. The **Hagerstown Roundhouse Museum,** at 300 S. Burhans Blvd., illustrates the history of the Western Maryland Railroad.

Follow Memorial Blvd. from the park to **Rose Hill Cemetery** on S. Potomac St. Adjoining it, one finds the entrance to **Washington Cemetery,** where 2,468 Confederate soldiers killed in the battles of Antietam and South Mountain—more than 2,000 of which are unidentified—are buried. The bodies were reinterred here after removal from shallow battlefield graves. Soon after the war, Confederate general

Firzhugh Lee spoke at dedication ceremonies; in 1961, when the town rededicated the ground as part of its Civil War centennial observances, the speaker was former President Dwight D. Eisenhower, a Gettysburg resident. Standing among the graves is a marble figure representing Hope leaning on an anchor.

The **Kennedy Monument,** a gray granite shaft honoring Thomas Kennedy (1776–1832), stands in the southeastern part of the Rose Hill Cemetery. Kennedy, a Scottish-born lawyer, merchant, and poet, championed the cause of Jewish voting rights when he was a Washington County delegate in the Maryland General Assembly. Beginning in 1819, he persistently introduced the issue into the assembly for seven unsuccessful years. "There are no Jews in the county from which I come, nor have I the slightest acquaintance with any Jew in the world," he explained to his fellow legislators in 1824, and went on to point out, "Maryland is the only state in the union where Jews are excluded from all office. . . . I demand it [passage of his bill] as an act of justice, sheer justice." After much controversy, Mr. Kennedy's "Jew Bill" was passed in 1826, and immediately thereafter two Jewish gentlemen were elected to the Baltimore City Council. The Brith Shalom, an Jewish fraternal society, erected this monument near Kennedy's grave in 1918.

South of Rose Hill, S. Potomac St. crosses Wilson Blvd. and leads to **South Hagerstown High School** and the original site of Hagerstown Junior College (both on the right). The **E. Russell Hicks Middle School** on these grounds honors a local historian and teacher who in the late 1950s helped form the Hagerstown Civil War Round Table.

From City Park the visitor may also drive north on Summit Ave., continue on as it changes to Jonathan, and then bear left onto Pennsylvania Ave. (U.S. 11 north). This straight old thoroughfare leads to North **Hagerstown High School** and **Western Maryland State Hospital** (both on the right). Founded in 1958, the hospital specializes in the treatment of the chronically ill—including patients with respiratory illnesses and those requiring dialysis—and in rehabilitative care. A Veterans Administration outpatient facility occupies one floor. Pennsylvania Ave. passes Northern Ave. and proceeds to the **Hagerstown Municipal Airport,** which occupies the site of the Fairchild Aircraft plant.

Turn right on Northern Ave. On the left, **Fountain Head,** an established neighborhood in a sylvan setting, stretches north between Pennsylvania Ave. on the west and the old Western Maryland Railroad tracks on the east. Most of the houses near Northern Ave. went up in the prosperous 1920s; the **Fountain Head Country Club** dates from 1924. Northern Ave. continues eastward across N. Potomac St. to the village of Fiddlersburg, but for a pleasant wander turn right onto Oak Hill Ave. North and west of this intersection stands **St. Maria Goretti Catholic High School** (earlier St. Mary's and located on W. Washington St.), which opened at this suburban site in 1956. The Pangborn family contributed heavily toward construction of the neocolonial main building. Following Oak Hill Ave. south returns one to the Square (Oak Hill joins N. Potomac just south of a railroad crossing above Maple Ave.). Lined with dozens of linden trees, Oak Hill in the spring becomes a boulevard almost worthy of Vienna. The names of parallel streets in this quiet residential quarter echo the blossomy theme: Apple, Currant, Peach, Quince, and Rose. Oak Hill Ave., takes its name from the home of William T. Hamilton, Maryland governor between 1880 and 1884, which lies just to the west via Prospect Ave., at 921 The Terrace. Oak Hill (private) offers a superb example of late-19th-century Victorian-Gothic architecture—white, wooden, and rambling. When Hamilton sat in the governor's chair, Marylanders told the story that he consulted the famous Hagerstown "almanack" before scheduling public executions, preferring fair weather for such events.

Conococheague Creek and Clear Spring

West from Hagerstown, U.S. 40 follows the route first known as the Bank Rd., a turnpike built between 1816 and 1821 to connect Baltimore to Cumberland and the National Road. As the price of charter or recharter, the General Assembly required Maryland banks to finance the turnpike. It replaced a wagon road that forded the Potomac and passed through Virginia, avoiding the steep mountain grades. The Bank Rd., shorter and relatively well built, avoided the sometimes dangerous river crossings and kept profits from the traffic within Maryland. The road generated substantial toll revenue and stimulated trade along its route.

The highway crosses Conococheague Creek west of Huyett's Crossroads near the **Hagerstown Speedway.** To the right of the highway is the old **Conococheague Bridge,** a limestone masonry span built in 1819. It served as a model for similar stone bridges scattered throughout Washington County. Conococheague Creek (the meaning of the Algonquian name is uncertain) winds its way from Pennsylvania south to the Potomac. During the third quarter of the 18th century, the river's seven-mile valley in Maryland marked the westernmost settlement in the state. Only hunters and trappers ventured into the mountains beyond. Apple and peach orchards, stately barns, and limestone and "worm" fencing in this part of Washington County testify to its long history of fertility and prosperity.

Clear Spring (566' alt., 415 pop.), by-passed by Interstate 70, was a thriving commercial town along Bank Rd. in the 19th century. The town, which originated as a trading post, is named for a large spring that once turned a mill wheel. John Thomson Mason, a Virginia native, married the sister of Richard Barnes, the wealthy St. Mary's County planter who built **Montpelier,** an 18th-century Georgian mansion that sits on a bluff off Broadfording Rd. two and a half miles northeast of here. Thomas Jefferson visited Montpelier in 1800 to ask Mason to be his attorney general, an offer that Mason's chronic ill health forced him to decline. Not long afterward Mason's brother-in-law, Barnes, died. By terms of his will, all of his slaves were freed upon reaching the age of 21. Many of those not yet of age worked at Montpelier.

Among those slaves was a young man who refused to take the name of his former master and later became well known as Thomas W. Henry, an itinerant preacher in the African Methodist Episcopal Church. Henry suddenly fled the state in 1859 when a slip of paper with his name on it turned up in John Brown's pocket after his capture at Harpers Ferry. The minister's son, Thomas W. Henry Jr., served during the Civil War in an African American recruiting band. He later settled in Hagerstown and won renown as a trumpet player.

Meanwhile, John Thomson Mason II built **Stafford Hall,** an early, two-story brick, 19th-century mansion almost one and a half miles east of

In what may have been a staged photo (to emphasize the need for federal roadbuilding assistance), a trucker pays a farmer for pulling his rig out of the mud in Washington County, 1935.

Clear Spring just north of Cohill Rd. He served on the Maryland Court of Appeals in the 1850s. He and his family, like many in Clear Spring, leaned toward the Confederacy during the Civil War. Judge Mason was imprisoned with other Southern sympathizers in Fort McHenry. After his release, he resumed law practice; he died in 1873 while arguing a case in court.

Indian Springs

U.S. 40 continues west to the village of Indian Springs; a wildlife management area of the same name lies to the north along the Pennsylvania line. **Park Head Evangelical Church,** a 1½-story brick structure built in 1833, stands about two and a half miles west of Indian Springs on U.S. 40. In 1756, at an unknown site north of the highway, pioneers erected a small log outpost named Fort Mills, one of several wooden forts built during the French and Indian War (1754–63) to protect settlers and support Fort Frederick. In the late 1950s and early 1960s an Indian Springs resident and antique gun collector, Reuben U. Darby III, assembled one of the first Civil War reenactment groups, a body of Union "artillery men" who fired a Napoleon field gun at local civic events as part of a large campaign to preserve Antietam Battlefield from commercial development. Darby could not afford a team of horses to pull limber and cannon; though garbed in authentic woolen uniforms, his men drove mules.

Fort Frederick

From high above the Potomac's north bank, Fort Frederick testifies to the deadly seriousness of the three-way struggle to control the American backcountry during the first half of the 18th century. By constructing a string of forts from Quebec to New Orleans, the French and their allied Indian tribes aimed to prevent British expansion into the Ohio Valley. George Washington's failure to seize Fort Duquesne in 1754 and Braddock's defeat the following year forced Maryland to build a cantonment that would protect settlers in the Conococheague Creek country from Indian marauders and possible French invasion. For a few years, the frontier atmosphere was tense: farms were raided, Catholics were suspected of aiding the French, rumors flew, letters from the hinterland to the *Maryland Gazette* warned that the French and Indians were only 100 miles from Annapolis.

Horatio Sharpe, governor of Maryland, personally supervised the construction of this stone fort in 1756. He named it after Frederick Calvert, the sixth Lord Baltimore and Maryland's last Lord Proprietor. A square-shaped structure with pointed bastions at each corner, the fort encloses 1½ acres with a perimeter wall 1,660 feet long, 17½ feet high, and 4½ feet at the base, tapering to 3 feet at the top. This may be the largest American fort of the time still standing. Fort Frederick served as a supply and training center until the British captured Fort Duquesne in 1758. Although the fort was never attacked, more than 700 settlers took refuge here during Pontiac's war in 1763. During the Revolution, the fort served as a prisoner of war camp for British and Hessian soldiers captured at Saratoga. It then fell into disrepair and disuse, except for a minor military role during the Civil War. After the Civil War a former slave, Nathan Williams, bought the property and farmed within its crumbling walls. When in 1922 the state acquired the 190-acre site, it became Maryland's first state park. The Civilian Conservation Corps mounted a reconstruction effort in 1934, and in 1975 the state rebuilt two of the barracks. No one has ever found the original plans, so the current restoration represents an educated guess.

Fort Frederick State Park is open year-round from 8 a.m. to dusk. The barracks and Visitor Center are open from May to October. Special military musters, battle demonstrations, and shooting competitions are held during summer months. The 561-acre park around the fort offers opportunities for camping, picnicking, and hiking, and for boating along the nearby river and canal.

From the fort, backtrack to Indian Springs and follow Alt. 40 west to I-70 (U.S. 40 merges into I-70 just west of Park Head Church), or simply take I-70 where Md. 56 crosses it, not far from the park.

Hancock

I-70 and U.S. 40 follow the Potomac River from Indian Springs about 11 miles west to Hancock (450' alt., 1,926 pop.), a river town that contains one of several visitors centers for the **Chesapeake and Ohio Canal National Historic Park.** Hancock, apparently named for a colonial settler, Joseph Hancock, arose on land formerly called Maryland's Neck. (The state is less than two miles wide at this location, its narrowest point.) Follow the exit sign from the main highway to reach the town's center, which lies along the old canal. Hancock now serves as a local shopping and packing center for surrounding fruit growers. **St. Thomas Episcopal Church,** at Church and High Sts., dates from 1835. During the Civil War, like many churches and schools in this region, it served from time to time as a hospital. Union artillery guarded the town from Rebel soldiers, who were so close that they could shout at the Yankees from across the river.

Canal Rd. runs along the C&O Canal from Hancock to **Fort Tonoloway State Park,** the site of a wooden, stockaded blockhouse built in 1755 after Braddock's defeat. The fort took its name from Tonoloway (Algonquian for "long tail") Creek, which flows into the Potomac at Hancock. Settlers abandoned the blockhouse after completion of Fort Frederick.

Sorting apples for market in Allegany County during the Depression

Sideling Hill

At Hancock I-70 strikes northward toward Breezewood, Pennsylvania, and the interstate that continues west is numbered I-68 and named the National Freeway, completed in 1991 and dedicated to the state's Vietnam veterans. Between Hancock and Cumberland, I-68 and U.S. 40 coincide. Four miles west of Hancock I-68 cuts through Sideling Hill, one of the most revealing rock exposures in the entire northeastern United States. A visitors center offers travel information and houses a geological museum.

The original wagon road twisted up the side of this elevation for four tortuous miles, the longest ascent during the entire journey west to Cumberland. More than one wagoner lost his team and wagon; even modern truckers had a difficult time until this section of the interstate opened in 1986. Motorists now whisk through a cut in the top of the mountain that exposes almost 850 feet of strata on either side and is visible for miles from either side of the ridge.

The various strata of sandstone, siltstone, shale, coal, and conglomerate curve downward in the shape of a bowl, forming a tightly folded syncline. Four hundred million years ago, this part of Maryland and adjoining Pennsylvania lay under a shallow inland sea. The water receded, and the low, dry land was riven by a series of undulating rivers (345–330 million years ago). Then the entire landscape was transformed violently when the tectonic plate that we know as the African continent collided with the East Coast. This event, known as the Applachian Revolution, or the Allegheny Orogeny, occurred over a long period of time (240–230 million years ago) and folded the relatively flat land into mountains. Since that time, water, weather, and chemical change have worn the rock. The erosion-resistant sandstones remained as ridges, while more soluble limestones and shales sank into valleys. The Applachians, once as high as the

Rockies or perhaps even the Himalayas, now resemble worn, decayed teeth. At Sideling Hill the cavities are visible at close range.

Interstate 68 making its deep cut in Sideling Hill

"SCENIC 40"

I-68 curves down Sideling Hill, crosses Sideling Hill Creek, and cuts a clear path to Cumberland. More interestingly, the old road, "Scenic 40," departs the expressway at Exit 72, takes one through a part of the **Bellegrove Game Refuge,** passes through Piney Grove, and ascends, the old-fashioned way, to the summit of **Town Hill,** site of a hotel and scenic overview. Scenic 40 then descends past the **Billmeyer Wildlife Management Area** (renamed for Frank Billmeyer, once owner of a lumber company in these parts), passes over Green Ridge, and rejoins I-68. In the mid-20th century Bellegrove was one of several state game farms on which rangers attempted to breed turkey, pheasant, quail, and other wild animals for later release in public forests. Eventually it became clear that these creatures seldom survived—or did so only with great difficulty— and the state adopted instead a strategy of capturing wild game in areas where it was overabundant and transplanting the animals to less crowded preserves. By the late 20th century wild fowl, deer, and even black bears had made strong recoveries in Western Maryland.

The **Green Ridge State Forest** straddles I-68, with most of its acreage south of the highway, extending toward the Potomac River. The forest has an instructive history. Various timber and mining interests— notably the Town Hill Mining, Manufacturing, and Timber Company— originally bought up this area of some 40,000 acres, beginning in 1820. Between 1880 and 1912 (corresponding to the building boom in Baltimore) the forest lost its last stands of virgin timber. In 1917 speculators using absentee capital advertised Green Ridge as the world's largest apple orchard in the making and sold the land to mail order investors in 10-acre lots. When this firm went bankrupt in 1932, Maryland acquired the

A bend in the Potomac as seen from Green Ridge State Forest

ravaged land to create a state park. The Civilian Conservation Corps worked at forest replanting and fire control in the later 1930s, also building roads, trails, and recreational sites. Today, Green Ridge—the second largest forest in Maryland—includes three designated wildlands (Potomac Bends, Deep Run, Maple Run), 32 special wildlife habitats, two fishing ponds, scenic overlooks, and 100 primitive campsites.

I-68 crosses **Polish Mountain** (1,340′ alt.) and then descends 500 feet, passing **Flintstone,** a small town nestled in the valley formed by Polish and Martin Mountains with Warrior Mountain to the south. The brick **Flintstone Hotel,** also called the Piper Hotel, has stood here since about 1807, when it operated as an inn on the road to Cumberland.

Beyond Flintstone and just east of Cumberland lies **Rocky Gap State Park,** developed in 1962 and afterward. It covers almost 3,000 acres and includes a 243-acre artificial lake named for the late Edward Habeeb, who once owned the land that makes up the park and sold it to the state for about one-third its market value. A multimillion-dollar golf course and conference center, opened in 1997, enhances the regional tourist industry.

CUMBERLAND

One of the rare Maryland towns that owes its origins to military necessity, Cumberland (641′ alt., 23,706 pop.) occupies the most dramatic physical space in Western Maryland—the convergence of Will's Creek and the North Branch of the Potomac River in a bowl-shaped valley sur-

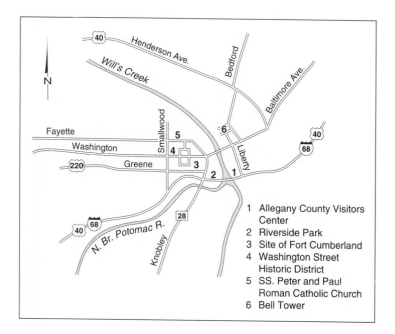

1 Allegany County Visitors
   Center
2 Riverside Park
3 Site of Fort Cumberland
4 Washington Street
   Historic District
5 SS. Peter and Paul
   Roman Catholic Church
6 Bell Tower

rounded on all sides by mountains more than 1,000 feet high. The Potomac at this point makes a great bend to the north, passing within six miles of the Pennsylvania border. Cumberland began at the top of the loop, where the creek meets the river. A small hill now topped by the Gothic spire of Emmanuel Episcopal Church marks the **site of Fort Cumberland,** the frontier outpost around which the town developed. From its beginnings, it served as a staging area for passage to the West.

The Shawnee (Shawanese) tribe inhabited a village on the lowlands along the Potomac west of Will's Creek and had long used the Narrows along the creek as a passage north to the Ohio River. The 18th-century European traders and explorers who first witnessed the site quickly perceived its strategic importance as a pathway through the Appalachians to the Ohio Valley, which had been claimed by the French since the 17th century explorations of La Salle. All but a few of the Shawnee abandoned the village in the early 18th century. One who remained was "Indian Will," for whom the creek and nearby mountain were named. After the British government negotiated a treaty with the tribes in 1744 to establish a rival claim to the Ohio Valley, English speculators joined Virginian and Maryland colonists to establish the Ohio Company in 1749. In the winter of 1749–50, the company built a storehouse on the south bank of the Potomac across from Will's Creek in what is now Ridgely, West Virginia. Christopher Gist, a Maryland frontiersman and surveyor, was hired in 1750 to explore and map the Ohio country, a task that lasted seven months. Trade with outlying native tribes flourished at the Will's Creek post, and the Ohio Company added a larger building there in 1752.

For the next ten years, this location played a key role in the French and British struggle for possession of the great Ohio River Valley. Disturbed by British intrusions into their Indian trade, the French sent troops from Canada and New Orleans in 1753 to build forts at strategic points on the Allegheny River, which flows south to join the Monongahela River at the Forks of the Ohio, site of modern Pittsburgh. Late the same year, Gov. Robert Dinwiddie, the lieutenant governor of Virginia and a stockholder in the Ohio Company, ordered 21-year-old Maj. George Washington to find the French commandant and give him a letter of warning. Washington traveled to the Will's Creek trading post and hired Christopher Gist as his primary guide for a 54-day journey by horse, canoe, and foot in the middle of winter. Washington delivered the letter, made notes about the French forces, engaged in talks with the tribes, and on his return to Virginia easily convinced authorities that the French intended to drive the British colonials from the Ohio territories.

In the spring of 1754, Washington became second-in-command (eventually commander) of a Virginia regiment organized to secure the Forks of the Ohio, where a volunteer company was already constructing a fort. Washington arrived at Will's Creek in April with about 160 men and discovered that a much larger French force had kicked the English out of their flimsy stockade, occupied the forks, and built Fort Duquesne. Expecting reinforcements, the Virginians marched from Will's Creek into southwestern Pennsylvania. Their first encounter with the enemy left 10 Frenchmen dead and scalped by Indians allied with the British. The French claimed that a diplomatic party had been assassinated. Horace Walpole later wrote: "The volley fired by a young Virginian in the backwoods of America set the world on fire." Washington's troops built a circular stockade, "Fort Necessity," in the Pennsylvania area called the Great Meadows and worked on cutting a road to Christopher Gist's settlement on Red Stone Creek. When 600 French and 100 Indians descended from Fort Duquesne, Washington's Indian allies disappeared into the forest. After a day of shooting, the young colonel surrendered and led his defeated troops back to Will's Creek. Later criticized for signing surrender terms that seemed to admit he had assassinated a French emissary, Washington resigned his commission and returned to Mt. Vernon. Col. James Innes, leader of some North Carolina troops sent too late to aid the expedition, began fortifications on the Maryland side of the Potomac, calling them Fort Mt. Pleasant. Governor Sharpe visited the site and ordered that a stonger fort be built to provide a staging point for operations against the French.

The following year, in February 1755, Maj. Gen. Edward Braddock arrived in Virginia with two full regiments of regular British troops, more than 1,400 men. Braddock had been sent to eliminate the French challenge, following plans drafted in England, chiefly by the Duke of Cumberland, third son of King George II. The strategy included strengthening the Will's Creek fort, which Braddock renamed in honor of the duke. Confident and arrogant, the veteran British general rode through Western Maryland, complaining all the way of colonial inefficiency. A combined force of almost 2,400 men—British, colonials, and Indians—marched out of Fort Cumberland on June 10, the largest army ever seen in North America. Unable to resist the excitement, Washington enlisted as an unpaid, unranked aide on the general's staff.

The forward element of the Braddock expedition was routed by a French and Indian force on July 9 after crossing the Monongahela River about seven miles from Fort Duquesne. Braddock was mortally wounded. His men secretly buried him on the march back to Fort Cumberland. Washington, who acquitted himself bravely under fire, later wrote: "It's true, we have been beaten, most shamefully beaten, by a handful of Men! who only intended to molest and disturb our March; Victory was their smallest expectation, but see the wondrous works of Providence! the uncertainty of Human things!" Another British and colonial army, marching to Fort Duquesne in 1758, arrived the day after the retreating French had burned it.

Fort Duquesne became Fort Pitt, named to honor William Pitt the Elder, and developed into Pittsburgh, the largest inland river port in the United States. Fort Cumberland evolved into Cumberland, "Queen City of the Alleghenies," once the second largest and now the eighth largest city in Maryland. The two locales would share several characteristics: origins as Appalachian forts at the junction of two streams and proximity to major coal seams. Each served as a terminus for canals and roads. They were linked by railroad to a major eastern city around the same time (Cumberland to Baltimore in 1842, Pittsburgh to Philadelphia in 1854). Before federal flood control, both suffered disastrous floods. In the mid-20th century both would become old industrial centers with declining populations. But Pittsburgh was on the navigable Ohio River in a geographic location that allowed for expansion. Cumberland was on the unnavigable Potomac and enclosed by high ridges. After the Civil War, Pittsburgh would benefit from an influx of Northern and European industrial capital. Outside investment in Cumberland and environs, while heavy, would never match that made in Pittsburgh.

During the Revolution, the population around Fort Cumberland slowly grew, and in 1785 a town was laid out. "Washington Town" in the original survey, it officially became Cumberland in 1786. Never agricultural, Cumberland owed its growth to transportation and industry. For a time, the Potomac Company, headed by George Washington, tried to create a navigable waterway to Cumberland. The company dug canals around the falls at Harpers Ferry and Seneca Falls and even constructed locks around the Great Falls, which enabled small-keeled boats to be hauled upstream against the current as far as Cumberland. Flatboats carrying coal rode spring floods downstream. A commercial waterway never resulted, but with improved wagon roads Cumberland became an overland gateway to the Ohio, Indiana, and Illinois country. In 1811 work began on the National Road. It reached Wheeling, in the Ohio Valley, in 1818.

To take advantage of the road and to counter Virginia's control of feeder routes to Cumberland, Maryland constructed a turnpike entirely within the state to connect Baltimore to the National Road. The state stipulated that in order to do business in Baltimore and Western Maryland, banks had to subscribe to turnpike stock. The strategy worked, as heavy traffic quickly developed between Baltimore and Cumberland, stimulating both cities and deepening Baltimore's hinterland farther into the Ohio Valley. The road was extended year by year until in 1837 it reached Vandalia, Illinois. By 1830, Cumberland had 1,162 residents, including 129 slaves and 36 "free colored."

Both the Chesapeake and Ohio Canal and the Baltimore and Ohio Railroad ceremonially began construction on July 4, 1828, starting a race along the Potomac Valley to Cumberland. The railroad reached Cumberland in 1842, the canal in 1850. Ambitious early plans had called for the canal's extension to the Great Lakes, but the railroad had already proved cheaper, faster, and more competitive. Within 10 years after the arrival of the first train, Cumberland's population increased six times; the town thrived as the junction of highway, railroad, and canal—one of the few commercial hubs of its kind in the young United States. New hotels and warehouses developed along Baltimore and Mechanic Sts. The railroad crossed the mountains to the Ohio in 1851 and thus eclipsed the National Road. Plagued by spring floods and summer drought, the canal never developed beyond the role of a supplementary carrier for bulk cargo, especially coal. Cumberland quickly became a B&O town.

As a railroad center, Cumberland also became a target during the Civil War. A regiment of Zouaves under Gen. Lew Wallace arrived in June 1861. Gen. Benjamin F. Kelley was assigned the task of protecting the railroad from Confederate attack and made Cumberland his headquarters. Although raiders frequently interrupted railroad service along the tracks and snipers slowed traffic on the C&O Canal, Cumberland, unlike Frederick and Hagerstown, never experienced Confederate occupation and assessment. The most embarrassing moment for the Union in Cumberland occurred during the icy night of February 22, 1865. While more than 6,000 Union troops camped here, about 60 of McNeill's Rangers entered Cumberland secretly (several of the raiders were Cumberland natives and knew the town intimately). Small groups found Generals Kelley and George Crook in the hotels where they were sleeping, kidnapped them, and rode out of town posing as Union cavalry. The Union generals were sent to Richmond and later exchanged for captured Confederate officers. Military censorship kept the news out of the newspapers during the war, but it became a great tale after the war ended.

The decade after the war brought great prosperity to Cumberland. The B&O built a rolling mill in 1867 to manufacture steel rails, and in 1872 constructed the Queen City Hotel, a four-story Victorian symbol of the city's new wealth. Stately homes of merchants and stockholders began to appear on Washington St. This burst of industrial energy after the Civil War was soon marred by economic depressions and protests from employees about unfair working conditions. A depression followed the Panic of 1873, and the coal miners began to strike. In July 1877 the B&O announced a systemwide, 10 percent wage cut, while stockholder dividends increased by the same percentage. The pay cut sparked the simmering discontent over lack of safety and other company practices that made the worker's life hard. (When working at distant points on the line, many had to stay over at their own expense and then pay for the train to take them home.) On July 16 railroad workers in Martinsburg, West Virginia, blocked the trains, and within a few days, railroad strikers, miners, and unemployed workers stopped the trains in Cumberland. At almost the same time, Pennsylvania Railroad workers in Pittsburgh also went on strike. Newspapers prated about a labor revolution; Allan Pinkerton reported to the B&O headquarters in Baltimore that the Cumberland strikers had broken into boxcars loaded with perishable foods. Gov. John Carroll called up the Maryland National Guard in Baltimore to quell the strike in Cumberland. The resulting riots at Camden Station on July 20–21 killed nine people and injured scores of others. President Rutherford B. Hayes sent federal troops into Maryland for the first time since the Civil War. The trains began running again within two weeks of the first walkouts.

The B&O rolling mill, closed in 1876 because of worker discontent,

Downtown
Cumberland in the late
1930s, from the site of
Fort Cumberland

reopened in 1878. The town became a major division point along the railroad line, and by the first decade of the 20th century, the B&O employed
2,000 people here. Twenty trains a day stopped at the B&O station alone.
By the start of World War I, Cumberland had a population of about
25,000 people and was the second largest city in the state. The Celanese
Corporation, which manufactured synthetic fibers, opened here at this
time. The Kelly-Springfield Tire plant, established in 1920, contributed to
the industrial activity that kept the town alive during the Depression. By
1940, Cumberland had a population of almost 38,000 people, more than
twice that of Frederick and three times that of Annapolis.

In the nearly six decades since then, the city has lost more than one-
third of its 1940 population. Federal assistance to the Appalachian region
may have helped slow Cumberland's decline. Concrete levees and flood-
ways enclose the North Fork of the Potomac River and Will's Creek as
they pass through the city. This extensive system largely controls the
spring floods that periodically devastated the town (as late as 1936, flood-
waters covered nearly five square miles of the city). In 1991, I-68 linked
Cumberland to the interstate expressway system to the west. It runs
through the Will's Creek Valley like a metaphorical freight train.

The Celanese rubber and tire plant, once touted as the best equipped
in the world, closed in the 1980s. Since then, the CSX Corporation,
which in 1987 finally dropped the old B&O name altogether, has maintained an active railroad presence in Cumberland. In the 1980s, the railroad accounted for 800 jobs beyond those attached to its locomotive repair shop and school for engineers. Today the town still supports
industries, such as Allegany Ballistics Laboratory and Westvaco Corporation. An attractive pedestrian mall, completed in 1980, has revitalized
downtown Cumberland. The city has two hospitals which, since the
spring of 1996, have shared some staff and facilities but developed separate specialties under the rubric Western Maryland Health System.

Memorial Hospital of Cumberland, founded in 1888 as Western Maryland Hospital, sits on the east bank of Will's Creek; it provides shock trauma services to the far-western part of the state. Sacred Heart Hospital emerged on the west bank in 1905 as Allegany Hospital and six years later became associated with the Daughters of Charity.

Despite demolition of the Queen City Hotel in 1971 (one critic called it "an act of corporate and municipal vandalism that ranks proportionately with New York's destruction of Pennsylvania Station"), tourism increases in this visually stimulating city. A passenger train again stops in Cumberland, and the site of the old fort has been carefully marked and preserved.

Walking Tour

The best place to begin a walking tour of Cumberland may be the **Western Maryland Station Center,** a complex of museums and tourist offices located in the restored 1916 terminal of the Western Maryland Railroad. Follow the "Visitor Center" signs from the major highways to the old depot, on the east bank of Will's Creek at the end of Canal St., just west of the intersection of Mechanic and Harrison Sts. Here the visitor will find adequate parking and the offices of the **Allegany County Visitor's Information Center,** open year-round and filled with printed information about Cumberland, including maps and walking-tour guides.

Although the B&O dominated Cumberland's history and the CSX Corporation remains the city's largest employer, the Western Maryland Railroad, chartered in 1852, also made an impact in the region. The line reached Williamsport in 1873, enabling the railroad to move cargo sent by canal from Cumberland. Under the leadership of John Mifflin Hood and George W. Gould, the Western Maryland expanded to the George's Creek coal fields and to Pittsburgh (in 1912), then acquired Port Covington on the Baltimore waterfront. The railroad disappeared as an independent line in the 1950s, but its Cumberland depot has survived as a tourist attraction.

The Scenic Railroad Development Corporation organized in 1986 and began running excursion trains from the depot in 1988. This organization acquired the tracks to nearby Frostburg in 1991 and now owns a 1916 Baldwin 280 steam locomotive and coal tender, which operates during warm weather months. The Scenic Western Maryland Railroad takes passengers on a 45-minute trip through the Narrows and up the mountains to the Old Depot in Frostburg, once a Cumberland and Pennsylvania Railroad freight station, restored in 1989. With soldout trains to Baltimore's Camden Station for Oriole baseball games, this recreational version of passenger railroading has become one of the region's most popular attractions. Since 1992, the corporation has also sponsored an annual, week-long Rail Fest in Cumberland.

The Western Maryland Station Center also houses a visitor's center for the **C&O Canal National Park,** a transportation and industrial museum, and the Allegany Arts Council. The old Cumberland terminus of the C&O Canal, located near the depot, has been completely altered by flood control construction and other development since the canal closed in 1924. At the turn of the century, the basin in Cumberland was alive with activity—ranging from respectable hotels, railroad offices, carpentry shops, and boat repair yards to Shantytown, a collection of wooden shacks where hustlers of all types catered to the boat crews. In 1993, a quasi-public group broke ground for **C&O Canal Place,** a recreational and commercial complex that celebrates the city's unique transportation heritage. The Cumberland group was modeled after the Maryland Stadium Authority in Baltimore, with the purpose of reconstructing the canal basin west of the depot as a major tourist attraction.

West of Will's Creek

From the railroad station walk up Canal St. to Baltimore St., where a small "heritage parklet" marks the beginning of the **Fort Cumberland Trail,** a walking trail created and maintained by the Cumberland Parks and Recreation Department. Twenty-eight narrative plaques and markers along the route describe the role of Fort Cumberland during the French and Indian War as well as its impact on the history of the city.

The walk crosses Will's Creek and goes south to **Riverside Park,** a small, grassy point on the creek's west bank at the point where it flows into the Potomac River. A restored log cabin, the only building remaining from the original fort, was moved here in 1921. The cabin was originally built within the walls of Fort Cumberland and according to legend served as George Washington's headquarters.

Near the cabin a granite monument honors the memory of Thomas Cresap, who assisted by Nemacolin, an Indian guide, laid out the course of a road from Will's Creek to the Forks of the Ohio. Christopher Gist does not yet have his own memorial. From this Cumberland base, Gist explored the Ohio Country as far away as modern St. Louis, guided Washington on his expeditions, and played a major diplomatic role with the Indian tribes.

Greene St. follows General Braddock's road from the fort and curves to the west. The first buildings in Cumberland were clustered along this street, but none survived the floods and fires that have periodically swept through the city. The Fort Cumberland Trail returns to the Will's Creek bridge and turns left (west) onto Washington St. to make a loop around the original site of the fort.

Site of Fort Cumberland

Fort Cumberland, a log structure strengthened by mud and stone, stood on the hill that rises to the northeast of Riverside Park between Washington and Greene Sts., now occupied by Emmanuel Episcopal Church (see below). The square fort, with star bastions at the corners for cannon, faced the confluence of the creek and the river. The fort proper contained storehouses for provisions, a command headquarters, and the powder magazine. A log stockade, running from the east wall of the fort almost down to Will's Creek enclosed a small parade ground, barracks, and officers' quarters. The grand parade ground west of the fort, now Prospect Square, was not enclosed.

When the fort was built in 1754, it guarded the westernmost position under the British flag in North America. One British officer noted its isolation in the mountains and commented: "It covers no country, nor has it the communication behind it by land or water." The nearest Maryland settlements were more than 40 miles to the east on the Conococheague, connected only by rough mountain paths. Winchester, a substantial Virginia town, was more than twice as far away on a road that became virtually impassable during bad weather. Fort Cumberland nonetheless defended against French intrusion and supported British advances into the Ohio Valley.

After the French threat ended by treaty in 1763, the fort's role changed. During the Whiskey Rebellion, in 1794, American troops were sent to Fort Cumberland to control unruly Americans. Whiskey was an important commodity in Western Maryland, Pennsylvania, and Virginia; farmers found it easier and more profitable to distill spirits from their corn and rye than to transport the bulk grain by wagon over rough roads. When in 1791 Congress imposed a tax on whiskey and revenue collectors entered the hills, the mountain men revolted. Negotiation failed, and when armed men gathered in the mountains between Cumberland and Pittsburgh, President Washington ordered militia units to Fort Cumberland and other points in the area. The insurgents soon disbanded. Washington, who in a sense had launched his military career at Fort Cumberland, donned his old uniform to review the troops as commander in chief in 1794. After the Whiskey Rebellion the fort served no military purpose.

Washington St.

The **Washington Street Historic District,** named to the National Register of Historic Places in 1973, begins at the western property line of 630 Washington St. and extends east to Will's Creek. This tree-shaded area with its large houses reflects the prosperity of Cumberland bankers, industrialists, and other affluent citizens in what Mark Twain called "the Gilded Age," the 20-year period after the Civil War when American cities, including Cumberland, reached new economic summits. The architectural styles on Washington St. range from Federal to Georgian Revival.

Emmanuel Episcopal Church (1849–50, John Notman of Philadelphia), at Washington and Greene Sts., was modeled after St. Paul's Church in Brighton, England. The cruciform structure made of local yellow sandstone has a buttressed bell tower with a graceful spire. The church stands on the site of Fort Cumberland, whose stone-lined tunnels and trenches are still intact among the church's foundations. The adjacent parish house (1903) was designed by Bruce Price, who grew up in Cumberland and was father to Emily Post (1872–1960), the famous Baltimore-born arbiter of etiquette.

A marker at **27 Washington St.** indicates the homesite of Lloyd G. Lowndes, the only Maryland governor to date from Allegany County.

The **Allegany County Courthouse** (1893–94, Wright Butler) and the **Allegany County Public Library** (1849–50) look out onto **Prospect Square,** once the formal parade grounds of Fort Cumberland. The library building originally housed the Allegany County Academy, chartered in 1798, the first school in Maryland west of Sideling Hill.

The **Gephart House,** 104 Washington St., a 2½-story brick house with gable roof, brick cornice and recessed Doric portico, was built in 1841–43 for Thomas Perry. A prominent lawyer, judge, and politician of the mid-19th century, Perry served one term in the U.S. House of Representatives, from 1845 to 1847. John Gephart, organizer of the First Methodist Protestant Church, later lived here.

The **Board of Education Building,** 108 Washington St., was constructed in the 1860s and served as the residence of William Walsh (1828–92), a two-term U.S. congressman who served from 1875 to 1879.

History House, 218 Washington St., houses the museum and offices of the **Allegany County Historical Society.** Josiah H. Gordon, a lawyer, judge, and politician, built this 18-room, 3-story, Second Empire brick house in 1867. He became president of the C&O Canal in 1869. The museum here contains original furnishings from Gordon's occupancy and a number of specialized rooms that illustrate life in Victorian Cumberland. A landscaped garden, enclosed by a brick wall, adjoins the property.

The house at **400 Washington St.** was built in 1890 for Bayse Roberts, a construction engineer on the first railroad in South America. In the Italianate house at **527 Washington St.,** built around 1860, lived Will Lowdermilk, who founded the *Daily Transcript*, the first daily newspaper published in Cumberland, and served as postmaster for eight years during the Grant administration. His *History of Cumberland*, published in 1878, was the first book-length history of the city.

Washington St. was home to those who owned the industries and controlled local politics. Most Cumberland citizens did not live in this elegant district. The workers and employees lived in far simpler neighborhoods, in small houses clustered around the canal and the railroad tracks and in the company coal towns of the George's Creek Valley west of Cumberland. On the walk back to Will's Creek, turn left (north) on Smallwood St. and then right on Fayette St. to the **SS. Peter and Paul Roman Catholic Church,** connected by a two-story passageway to a monastery built in 1848 by the German Redemptorist Fathers. The order was established here in response to the demand for a separate parish for Catholics of German origin.

The monastery has indirect associations with John Neumann, the first American male to be made a Catholic saint. Neumann selected the site, may have contributed to its simple design, and visited there on two occasions. Later occupied by Carmelites and Capuchin friars, the six-story building was abandoned in 1986 and later became a source of controversy between the parish, which wanted to tear it down, and preservation officials, who wanted to restore the deteriorating brick-and-stone building as a civic landmark.

East of Will's Creek

Cross Will's Creek and follow Baltimore St. to the **Cumberland Mall,** a three-block–long pedestrian mall with two blocks of side streets. City officials and merchants combined resources to refurbish this business district in 1980, thereby enhancing a federal urban renewal project that had already created four downtown parks (Hospitality, Heritage, Gateway, and The Maze) and other public works improvements. The mall has also provided a viable commercial response to competition from suburban shopping malls. Most of the buildings date from between 1860 and 1930. Fountains, "parklets," and other landscaping have made this once-drab area a pleasant place.

Turn left on S. Centre St. to a plaza facing **City Hall,** located at this street's intersection with Bedford and Frederick Sts. The **Bell Tower** opposite City Hall was built in the last quarter of the 19th century and used as a police station until 1936. The two-story brick building with a square wooden belfry now houses the Western Maryland Chamber of Commerce.

Alternate U.S. 40 continues, following the east bank of Will's Creek in downtown Cumberland then crossing the stream to **The Narrows.** (Travelers on I-68 must use Exit 40 to join Alt. 40.) This narrow passage in the rock developed over eons as Will's Creek rushed between Will's Mountain and Haystack Mountain. American Indians made the gap a part of their war path between what became Pennsylvania and Virginia. In 1755 Braddock's army tried to move wagons across the rugged mountains surrounding Cumberland and lost at least three before a Lieutenant Spendelowe discovered the gap. Here the National Road and then the railroad had to squeeze through an opening no more than 25 feet wide.

The municipal **Narrows Scenic Park** lies on the west bank, within the city limits. **Will's Mountain State Park** sits high above the stream on the west bank; Judge George Henderson of Cumberland donated its 100 acres to the state in 1966.

West of The Narrows, Alt. 40 leads to two remnants of the days when the National Road consisted of a 20-foot-wide crushed gravel pathway linking Baltimore to the West. **Six-Mile House,** a toll house from that era, stands at **La Vale.** Original signs display the toll rates; gateposts still stand on either side of the road. Maryland authorities completed this unusual two-story brick structure—seven-sided with single-story rooms added on two sides—in 1836, after Congress turned over control of the road to the states it lay within. The house is open to the public.

The **Eight-Mile House,** or **Clarysville Inn,** is located two miles farther west. Little changed since its construction in 1807, this brick and stone structure recalls a time when the pike earned a colorful reputation. "The National Road had its contingent of quaint characters, eccentric men, philosophers in one sense, and loafers in another," wrote Thomas B. Searight in 1894, when the best days of the road had dimmed in living memory. "The lodestone that attracted them and attached them to the road, probably above all other influences, was the pure whiskey."

Eckhart

Alt. 40 ascends Piney Mountain to **Eckhart Mines,** a center of Maryland's early coal mining activity. Eighteenth-century visitors had observed easily accessible coal beds west of Cumberland. Local families never wanted for fuel; some accounts claim that coal was mined at Eckhart as early as 1804. Construction of the National Road may have revealed the first large coal deposits. In any event, the advent of the road and then the railroad made mining the high-grade, bituminous coal the business of large companies that made large profits. Wagons hauled the coal down to the banks of the Potomac in Cumberland. Before the B&O and C&O reached Cumberland, coal wagons accumulated at the river until flatboats could move on spring floods. On the way to tidewater, wrecks were frequent. Surviving boatmen returned on foot or horseback.

Frostburg

This rugged but charming town (1,929' alt., 8,075 pop.), 12 miles west of Cumberland, was a major stage stop on the National Road as well as a retail center for the surrounding coal towns. Meshach Frost founded the town in 1812, placing Main St. on a ridge that climbs toward **Big Savage Mountain** to the west. Townspeople and English and Welsh miners created clean, attractive residences along the rolling plateau that descends south to the Potomac between **Dans Mountain** and Big Savage. During the period when it served as a coal miners' center, Frostburg held an annual Welsh festival, called an Eisteddfod. In 1873, the Frostburg mining journal announced the featured performer at that year's celebration to be Mr. Crwdgimpas Ap Thomas, a native of Moclgwynstrwnstrell, who would appear in ancient Druid costume to play the Llanrhauadrmochant and other selections on the Brownwrw-Cymrongldrwstcwmdathugwestly (Welsh harp).

More recently, Frostburg has developed into a cultural center, a transformation due largely to the presence of **Frostburg State University,** which draws its 4,500 students from a five-state area. Founded in 1898 as Maryland Normal School No. 2, this teacher's college became a regional state university in 1987. In 1988 the university opened a center at Hagerstown for upper-division coursework; its accommodations have been a major factor in attracting international white-water competitions, summer theater events, and academic conferences.

Big Savage and Little Savage Mountains

At the crest of the Big Savage (2,850' alt.), Alternate 40 enters Garrett County, created in 1872 from adjacent Allegany County and named for B&O president John W. Garrett (1820–84). This westernmost of Maryland's counties lies in what geologists call the Appalachian Plateau Province, a tableland that extends from Somerset County, Pennsylvania, through Maryland to northeastern West Virginia and beyond. Northeast-southwest ridges, rolling valleys, timber stands, and occasional "glades" mark the landscape. The areas locally referred to as glades are mountain bogs, remnants of prehistoric marshes and seldom found this far south.

The Little Savage River drains the eastern slopes of the county south through the state forest of the same name and empties into the Potomac River near Bloomington. The river's rapids have made it a mecca for white-water enthusiasts and the site of international competition. An eastern continental divide runs through Garrett County. Streams that rise west of the Big Savage Mountain–Backbone Mountain chain in Garrett County flow northward into the Youghiogheny Valley to the Ohio River, then to the Mississippi and the Gulf of Mexico. Because the river seems to flow in the wrong direction, the Youghiogheny (pron. "yock-a-gay'-nee") was given the Algonquian name for "contrary stream."

Alt. 40 takes one over and across **Little Savage Mountain** on a route wagoners called the "Shades of Death." Here tall pine trees loomed over the National Road and provided cover for highwaymen, who robbed and murdered travelers.

Those same pines produced many a useful product, including axle grease for the wagons that made the difficult mountain climbs. After the Civil War, settlers cut their share of timber for shelter and fuel. Loggers altered the landscape, methodically taking down large stands of trees, sliding the logs into ponds behind "splash dams" created in creeks, then, breaching the dams, sending the wood downstream to sawmills. Programs to replant a mixed evergreen-hardwood forest have been under way since the 1930s, when the Civilian Conservation Corps established camps here. Now more than 70 percent of the county is forested, mostly with second- and third-growth hardwoods. State conservation programs control lumbering and create habitats for wildlife. The panther and buffalo, once abundant, have not returned, but the woods are full of deer, grouse, and wild turkeys. Occasionally someone will spot a black bear or a wildcat roaming these woodlands. Hunting and fishing in season have become favorite recreations in the state forests.

Alt. 40 continues past the **Savage River State Forest,** which is accessible by the Lower New Germany Road. Two state parks in this 52,770-acre forest, **New Germany**—455 acres, established in 1964—and **Big Run**—300 acres, also dating from 1964—provide campsites, boating, and hiking over miles of unpaved roads and trails.

After crossing **Meadow Mountain** (2,900' alt.), Alt. 40 descends to **Little Meadows,** a pleasant glade where Braddock's expedition camped in 1755. In deep forest, such glades, with their lush grasses and rich soil, beckoned like oases in the desert, and they attracted the first settlers. **Stone House Inn,** built in 1818, is located near the **site of the Red House Tavern,** built in 1760 to serve the earliest travelers.

Penn Alps and Casselman River Bridge

The Casselman River used to be called the Little Youghiogheny, and the point where Alt. 40 crosses it was called Little Crossings. (Big Crossing was farther down the road, where the road crosses the Youghiogheny itself at Friendsville.) Jesse Tomlinson built a gristmill and store here in 1797. The mill was rebuilt in 1856 and deeded in 1862 to William Stanton, a member of one of the earliest families in this area.

The Little Crossings community, centered around the mill and an inn, grew with the development of the National Road and became an impor-

An Amish wheelwright, Garrett County, 1997

tant stage and wagon stop. Important travelers ranging from presidents (Andrew Jackson and Zachary Taylor) to foreign dignitaries (General Santa Ana and Chief Black Hawk) stopped here. Part of the original log inn, built about 1818, survives in **Penn Alps,** a nonprofit center for the study and promotion of Allegheny life. Dr. Alta Schrock, an educator with deep Appalachian roots, opened Penn Alps in 1958. Local Amish and Mennonite families soon added a craft shop and restaurant, both open year round. The center now includes an "artisan village" built from restored plank structures relocated from the nearby mountains. During warm-weather months, the traveler can find craftspersons at work in the village.

Casselman River Bridge, a National Historic Landmark, lies next to Penn Alps in a small state park with picnicking facilities. When built for the National Road in 1813, the bridge was the longest single-span stone arch bridge in the United States, 80 feet long and slightly peaked at the top of the arch. Skeptics who watched its construction were convinced that it would collapse when the supports were removed, but the bridge, restored in 1955, has weathered all tests of stress and time. One can stand on its now-unused surface and watch traffic flow over two more modern parallel bridges, the iron structure built for Alt. 40 in 1933 and the sleeker span that carries I-68, built more than 50 years later.

Grantsville

Grantsville (2,351′ alt., 505 pop.), a mile west of the Casselman River, began as a small settlement, called Tomlinson's or Little Crossings, along the Braddock Rd., which wound westward from Cumberland over Negro Mountain. Later, a new village flourished as a stop along the nearby National Road. It took its name from Daniel Grant, whom a local historian described as "of the noted Fountain Inn of Baltimore." Grant had acquired land here after the Revolution; he called the tract Cornucopia. The town remains a rural retail center. Maple syrup and sugar have been produced in the area since it was first settled; country-smoked hams and other fresh farm products are also available here.

The Casselman, one of the few remaining Federal-style buildings in this area, has stood near the road since 1824. First named Drover's Inn, this 2½-story brick building still serves as a hotel.

Negro Mountain

Alt. 40 climbs from Grantsville to the summit of Negro Mountain (3,075′), the highest altitude the National Road reaches in Maryland. The mountain supposedly received its name in the 18th century from Nemesis, an African American member of an expedition headed by Capt. Michael Cresap. Attacking Indians killed Nemesis, reportedly a giant of a man, and his compatriots buried him on the mountain.

Earlier, in 1774, Michael Cresap had been among the whites who wandered into the Ohio Valley, marking out valuable plots of land and avenging Indian "outrages" on traders and settlers. In the process, many innocent Indians, including women and children, lost their lives—among them the entire family of Chief Logan, a Mingo married to a Shawnee and a notable friend of the settlers. The chief in turn blamed Cresap, who probably was not personally responsible. After the ensuing struggle—known as Lord Dunmore's War, after the Virginia governor who defeated

Mingoes, Shawnees, and Delawares—Logan sent a messenger to Dunmore, saying that his vengeance had been satisfied but lamenting that "there runs not a drop of my blood in the veins of any living creature. . . . Who is there to mourn for Logan?—not one." Thomas Jefferson cited Logan's lament as an example of the American Indian's natural eloquence.

Friendsville

Alt. 40 crosses U.S. 219 at the summit of Keyser's Ridge and then angles northwest along the approximate route of the National Road to the Pennsylvania line three and a half miles away. Interstate-68 continues west to the West Virginia line, passing a Maryland highway information center and a turnoff to Friendsville (1,500' alt., 577 pop.), a historic town at the confluence of the Youghiogheny River and Bear Creek.

The Youghiogheny, a designated and protected Wild and Scenic River, is unpolluted for its first 25 miles in Maryland; its drainage area provides the visitor glimpses of countryside relatively unchanged over the past two centuries. Most residents call it simply "the Yock." Bears once populated caves and dens along the stream named for them. Fattened for hibernation on acorns and chestnuts, they were highly prized by the Indians and early settlers. Now Bear Creek is known for native trout, stocked by the **Bear Creek Fish Rearing Station,** located east of the Alt. 40–U.S. 219 intersection on the Accident–Bear Creek Rd.

Before the arrival of John Friend and his family in the 1760s, this part of Maryland was sparsely populated by Algonquian tribes and Shawnee bands. As settlers began cultivating the land, the natives abandoned their Maryland hunting grounds and moved farther west. Friend, an immigrant from the Tidewater, bought an empty Shawnee town, which soon became "Friendsville." An iron furnace operated here between 1828 and 1839, using local coal and ore from the river basin. After 1890, when the railroad reached Friendsville, the town enjoyed a lumber boom. The larger timber went down. Today second and third growths still sustain a small industry that supplements recreational fishing and boating on the **Youghiogheny River Reservoir,** which extends into Pennsylvania. "River rats"—recreational white-water rafters and kayakers—enliven the

Looking west from Friendsville, the traveler even today can feel the lure of America's West.

town from April through October. Archaeological digs have unearthed Indian artifacts that one can see in the town museum. A small reconstituted band of the Shawnee tribe has turned four donated acres of farmland above I-68 into a ceremonial retreat.

Northeast of Friendsville on County Rte. 53 lie the remains of what once was a flourishing river port at the head of navigation on the Youghiogheny. The town was named for Evan Shelby, captain of a company of rangers in the French and Indian War and father of Gen. Isaac Shelby, first governor of Kentucky (1792). Evan Shelby laid out lots here in 1798. During the War of 1812, the locally legendary hunter Meshach Browning, commissioned a captain, ordered his company to muster in "Shelby's Port." Politics intruded on the military when Democrats among the troops refused to serve under a Federalist officer. A fracas started on the banks of the river and spilled into a millrace. Browning won the engagement, but he was so badly injured that his military career came to an end. For more on Browning see Tour 19-1.

West of Friendsville, Md. 42 passes Friends graveyard, where members of the pioneer clan are buried, and then goes through **Blooming Rose,** where in the 1790s about 40 white families first made homes west of Savage Mountain. Their church and school were the first in Garrett County.

Side trips north and south of the pikes that linked the Chesapeake and Potomac to the West follow. They enable the traveler to explore the hinterlands, appreciate the region's history, and come to terms with the changes Western Maryland has experienced in the 20th century.

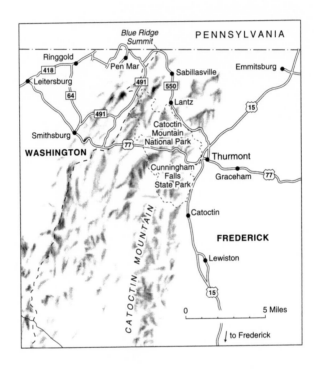

PENNSYLVANIA

Blue Ridge
Summit

Ringgold

418

Pen Mar

491

Sabillasville

550

Emmitsburg

Leitersburg

64

491

Lantz

15

Catoctin
Mountain
National Park

Smithsburg

77

WASHINGTON

Thurmont

Cunningham
Falls
State Park

Graceham

77

Catoctin

FREDERICK

CATOCTIN MOUNTAIN

Lewiston

15

0   5 Miles

↓ to Frederick

Exploring Western Maryland

North and South of U.S. 40, I-70, and I-68

A. NORTH FROM FREDERICK ALONG CATOCTIN MOUNTAIN VIA U.S. 15 AND SIDE ROADS

Northbound U.S. 15 leaves historic Frederick and travels along the eastern slope of Catoctin Mountain, part of the Blue Ridge range. The Blue Ridge Mountains reach the Pennsylvania border at a point nine miles southwest of Gettysburg; a Maryland tourist information and rest center is located just inside the state line there.

Side roads west of U.S. 15 ascend into the mountain forests, frequently along tumbling streams that have been stocked with trout. To the east lie the farms of the Monocacy River basin, where farmers raise grain, apples, vegetables, and livestock along patterns of husbandry that English, Scots-Irish, and German settlers first established in the mid-18th century. Some of the less productive land has reverted to forest, in which native wildlife flourishes once more. Festivals in the spring and fall attract visitors to the spectacular change-of-season displays of color—delicate white apple blossoms set against the pale greens of new crops in the spring; the brilliant yellows, reds, and oranges of autumnal mountain foliage.

Lewistown, about five miles north of the Frederick city limits, was first settled around 1745. After the Revolution it became the home of several Hessian soldiers captured during the war. The **Lewistown State Fish Hatchery** is west of town near the **Frederick Municipal Forest** and **Gambrill State Park** (Frederick gave the state more than a thousand acres for Gambrill in 1934).

Three miles north, the traveler passes the ruins of **Catoctin Furnace** and its settlement. Local histories claim that the old Catoctin Furnace Iron Works, built in 1774, supplied cannonballs for the siege of Yorktown during the Revolution and plates for the Union ironclad *Monitor* during the Civil War.

Thurmont

Hunting Creek flows down the Catoctin Mountain through Thurmont (519' alt., 3,398 pop.) on its winding way to the Monocacy River. Jacob Weller and his family settled here around 1751, dropping out of a group of German immigrants from Pennsylvania. According to legend, one of the Weller children had fallen ill, and the family stopped at a large spring here to nurse him. The Wellers stayed, and a village grew slowly from their settlement. In 1800 a hotel was built; a store opened in 1806.

*Harvesting corn in
Frederick County, 1997*

A tannery began curing cattle hides in 1810, using acids from the bark of nearby oaks. Tanneries later became numerous in Western Maryland.

In 1811, another Jacob Weller, son of the original settlers, opened a forge and manufactured edged tools with power from the creek waters. The plant was the first of its kind south of New York. It supplied iron augers, chisels, axes, and other tools to a large market in the southern states and in the West Indies. Jacob's son, Joseph, took credit for manufacturing the first friction matches, or lucifers, in the United States. In 1825, he purchased some French matches and successfully duplicated their chemistry. In a stone building still standing on W. Main St. and now called the **Old Match House,** he produced wooden matches dipped into a mixture of his secret formula. The town came to be known as Mechanicstown, perhaps because of the residents' talent in mechanical crafts.

The Western Maryland Railroad reached Mechanicstown in 1871 and brought significant changes, including a change of name. "Mechanicstown" was too long for railway timetables, so the townspeople voted to accept a newspaper editor's suggestion of Thurmont. Everyone agrees that it means "gateway to the mountains," but no one knows its exact derivation.

While accessible by rail, Thurmont became a popular mountain resort as well as small manufacturing center. Today the town has a diverse industrial base and attracts hunters and fishermen in season. Occasionally, a distinguished visitor from nearby Camp David will be seen in a local store. The friendly townspeople take it all in stride. In the words of one native, "We don't make no beans about it."

Side Trip to Smithsburg and Early Catoctin Resorts via Md. 550, 491, and 77

Two routes from Thurmont lead west into the Catoctin hills. Md. 550 hugs the northern edge of the **Catoctin Mountain National Park** to Blue Ridge Summit; Md. 491 then takes one to Pen Mar and Smithsburg. Md. 77 follows **Hunting Creek** directly west, through the national park and adjacent state parks, to Smithsburg. Both paths lead through lovely Western Maryland forest and farmland; combining the routes enables one to drive a loop and return to Thurmont.

Blue Ridge Summit and Pen Mar

Md. 550 follows the path of the old Gap Rd. over the Blue Ridge, built to connect the Catoctin Furnace with the forges of Franklin County, Pennsylvania. The road passes through the villages of Lantz and Sabillasville on its northwesterly course to Blue Ridge Summit, an old resort area that occupies small parts of two Maryland and two Pennsylvania counties at the states' border. Look for **Marker 89 of the Mason-Dixon line.**

The Western Maryland Railway arrived here in the 1870s, pushed several hundred yards into Pennsylvania to avoid a difficult passage through copper rock formations, and doubled back into Maryland. The railroad connection stimulated construction of Blue Ridge Summit's Victorian summer homes and hotels, built to take every advantage of the cool mountain air. The Western Maryland's "Blue Mountain Express" enjoyed particular popularity among foreign diplomats in Washington, D.C. Blue Ridge Summit liked to be called the "ambassadorial summer resort of the United States." The old railroad depot has been converted into a library at Blue Ridge Summit, Pennsylvania.

From the state line, Md. 550 loops south, following the railroad route, and intersects Md. 491 at **Cascade.** Turn right at the entrance to **Ft. Ritchie,** then left under the railroad trestle to **Pen Mar** and the **Pen Mar County Park.** The Western Maryland Railway developed Pen Mar as a mountain resort and amusement park in 1877, but by 1929 virtually no one traveled here by train. An independent company operated the park until 1943. Washington County later acquired the scenic area and made it a public park. **High Rock** (1,822' alt.), offers an excellent view to the west. Period prints show vacationers happily mounted on it to watch the sun set. It now supplies a take-off point for hang gliding. Reach **Quirauk Mountain** (1,445' alt.) from High Rock Rd. The **Appalachian Trail** crosses the road here.

From Cascade follow Md. 491 south and then west over South Mountain to **Smithsburg** (833 pop.). Founded around 1806 at the base of South Mountain, Smithsburg developed as a banking and trading center for fruit growers. Like many small communities in this part of Maryland, the town was visited by both Union and Confederate troops before and after the Battle of Gettysburg. After that engagement—and clearly in ill humor—J.E.B. Stuart's mounted artillery fired a few rounds into the town on their return trip to Virginia.

Sculptor Emily Clayton Bishop (1883-1912) was born and lived all her life in a 2½-story brick house that her father, Dr. Elijah Bishop, built here in 1813. Many of her works belong to the Pennsylvania Academy of Fine Arts in Philadelphia.

Loop to Leitersburg and Ringgold via Smithsburg-Leitersburg Rd., Md. 418, Md. 64

To reach Leitersburg (596' alt.), travel northwest of Smithsburg on the Leitersburg-Smithsburg Rd. Leitersburg took its name from Jacob Leiter, a German immigrant who purchased land here in 1762; his grandson, Andrew Leiter, laid out the town site in 1815. Leitersburg State Line Rd. leads north from the town to the **Leiter Burying Ground** and **Strite's Mill,** erected in 1792. Christian Strite purchased the mill in 1843. He and his descendants ground wheat and corn at the site for more than a century.

Taking Md. 418 eastward, just south of the Pennsylvania line the motorist reaches Ringgold, settled in 1825 as Ridgeville and renamed in 1850 for Maj. Samuel Ringgold. Major Ringgold, who suffered fatal wounds at the Battle of Palo Alto in 1846, early in the Mexican War, made significant innovations in the use of field artillery. He also invented the McClellan saddle, which remained the standard in the army until World War I; highly durable, unpadded, the McClellan design featured a long opening down the center, ventilating the rider's seat and removing pressure on the horse's backbone. Md. 64 south returns the traveler to Smithsburg.

Leading east, Md. 77 leaves Smithsburg as the Foxville Rd. and ascends South Mountain on its way east.

Catoctin Mountain National Park

At the summit of South Mountain, Md. 77 crosses from Washington into Frederick County and leads through Foxville to the Catoctin Mountain National Park. The federal government acquired this marginal farmland in 1936 as part of the New Deal's Rural Demonstration Program. Over the generations, many trees had been cut down to fire the furnaces of local industry, which included distilling moonshine whiskey (on Saturday nights in bygone times bootleggers would descend on Thurmont to buy 500-pound bags of sugar for their hidden stills). Tanners killed many of the remaining oaks and chestnuts by stripping their bark for use in the tanning process. On this steeply contoured land, the timber losses, combined with unscientific farming practices, had produced severe soil erosion. Of the 50 families that were relocated in the federal purchase, only eight had been able to make a living entirely from their land.

Since creation of the park, almost 6,000 acres have been permitted to develop into an Eastern hardwood climax forest, populated by numerous deer, a few foxes, many raccoons, squirrels, and other small animals, including a wide variety of birds. Campgrounds, hiking trails, and marked nature trails have been constructed for park visitors.

The presidential retreat, **Camp David,** site of numerous historic meetings, lies in the middle of the park. Closed to the public, its entrance and some of the maximum security fencing can be seen off Park Central Rd., north of the **National Park Service Visitor Center** on Md. 77.

Cunningham Falls State Park, located along the south side of

Md. 77, dates from 1954, when the federal government gave Maryland 4,446 acres from the Catoctin demonstration area. The state park includes the upper reaches of Big Hunting Creek; **Cunningham Falls** lies on one of its tributaries. To reach the falls from the visitor center, ask directions to nearby Catoctin Hollow Rd. Follow it about one mile, heeding directions to the **West Picnic Area.** Marked trails from the picnic area lead to the falls. Or continue past the Catoctin Hollow Rd. turnoff to a parking area off Md. 77. The falls are a short walk from this point.

The state park offers picnicking, camping, and other recreational facilities at the West Picnic Area and at the **Manor House Day Area,** just off U.S. 15 in the southeast quadrant of the park.

Md. 77 descends along the Hunting Creek valley into Thurmont, completing this excursion from the main tour on U.S. 15.

Emmitsburg

Continuing north on U.S. 15 past Thurmont brings one to Emmitsburg (400' alt., 1,688 pop.). Previously known as Poplar Fields and Silver Fancy, the town was renamed in 1786 in honor of William Emmit (or Emmitt), a prominent local landholder. Emmitsburg has experienced a modern residential building boom and faces the challenge of accommodating a population that is expected to double within the next few years. The town attracts increasing numbers of religious pilgrims, drawn by the reputation of Elizabeth Ann Seton (Mother Seton), the first American-born Catholic saint, canonized here in 1975.

Mrs. Seton, mother of five and a devout Episcopalian, had started a charitable organization in New York. After her husband died, in 1803, she converted to Catholicism, in 1805. She moved to Baltimore, then the center of the Catholic Church in this country, where in 1808 she started a girls' school. In 1809, she and several followers moved to just outside of Emmitsburg and established the Sisters of Charity in a simple, stone farmhouse. Catholic families from St. Mary's City had been settling in this valley since 1728, so the sisters had a community to serve; they started a school for local children. The school became St. Joseph's College, and the religious order spawned generations of sisters active in schools, orphanages, and hospitals. The college closed in 1973, but the original houses where the sisters lived and worked, as well as a mortuary chapel and cemetery, now make up the **National Shrine of Saint Elizabeth Ann Seton.** Mother Seton died in 1821, was beatified in 1963, and canonized 12 years later. Her tomb stands next to that of her nephew, James Roosevelt Bayley, archbishop of Baltimore from 1872 to 1877.

The **Main Chapel,** which is attached to the **St. Joseph's Provincial House,** now serves as the religious focus for the shrine. Construction of the chapel began in 1962; adorned with murals, stained-glass windows, and carved altars, the structure was dedicated as a basilica in 1991. The sound of its bells over the valley evokes Elizabeth Seton's joy in the natural setting and her admonition to "walk meditatively."

Beyond the Seton shrine, U.S. 15 passes **Mount St. Mary's College,** a four-year Roman Catholic college and seminary, founded in 1808 by Father John Dubois, later bishop of New York. The first American cardinal, John McCloskey (1810–85), studied here, as did Edward Douglass White (1845–1921), who in 1910 became the first southerner after the Civil War to serve as chief justice of the U.S. Supreme Court.

A natural grotto, formed by a stream flowing down a wooded ravine, rewards a walk up the side of the mountain above the college. For generations, this area—favored by Mother Seton and her sisters—has been a favorite spot for students and teachers seeking a moment's quiet. Nearby, in 1879, a seminarian built a replica of the original Lourdes grotto. Extensively improved over the years and now known as the **National Shrine of Our Lady of Lourdes,** it may be the oldest shrine to Mary in continuous existence in the United States. The pilgrim reaches it through a wide, wooded path bordered by stations of the cross. The **Pangborn Memorial Campanile** marks the entrance, its 95-foot tower surmounted by a 25-foot gilded statue of the Virgin Mary. A gift of Hagerstown industrialists, the campanile has 14 cast bronze bells.

B. SOUTH FROM FREDERICK TO POINT OF ROCKS VIA U.S. 15

U.S. 15 joins U.S. 340 in Frederick, and the two highways coincide for about four miles. Follow the U.S. 15 fork south along the foot of Catoctin Mountain to the Potomac River, which at this point is dotted with numerous small islands.

The largest, **Heater's Island,** is a wildlife management area visible from shore and the bridge crossing into Virginia. Numerous fish, reptiles, song birds, waterfowl, occasional otters and beavers and other fur-bearing animals still inhabit these woodlands. Around 1713, the island provided shelter for a group of Tuscarora Indians, members of an Algonquian tribe from North Carolina, who had fought the English and, after several defeats, accepted land from the Iroquois in the Five Nations country. The Tuscarora lived on the island for several years during the long migration to the north, thus imparting their name to a nearby creek and town.

Point of Rocks

Md. 28 cuts east from U.S. 15 along the river to Point of Rocks, a small town and river site well known to fishermen. The southern foot of Catoctin Mountain creates a narrow strip of land at the river, a piece of land not large enough to handle both the B&O Railroad and C&O Canal. The two companies fought over the right of way, and the courts eventually ruled in favor of the canal, which held the earlier charter. The B&O tunneled through the ridge in 1867; a century later the railroad constructed a track around the tunnel and over the moribund canal.

At the west end of Point of Rocks, canal enthusiasts can examine the remains of a pivot bridge. The mechanism no longer exists, but the central pillar upon which it turned, built in the 1830s, still stands. The distinctive **B&O Railroad Station** in the tiny village of Point of Rocks is on the National Register of Historic Places. Like other ford and bridge locations, Point of Rocks was a strategic location during the Civil War and the site of much skirmishing and raiding. While here, Gen. Joseph Hooker received telegraphed orders to turn over the Army of the Potomac to Gen. George G. Meade just before the Battle of Gettysburg.

Near Point of Rocks lies a quarry that contributed building materials to the Capitol in Washington, in the form of unusual, highly prized calico marble, which was used for columns.

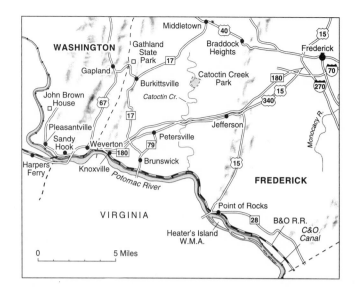

U.S. 15 crosses the Potomac into Loudoun County, Virginia, and continues to Leesburg, nine miles away.

C. FROM FREDERICK TO HARPERS FERRY VIA U.S. 340, MD. 180, MD. 17

U.S. 340, a limited access expressway, offers the most direct route to Harpers Ferry. But take the slower, more scenic route, Md. 180 (Jefferson Pike), which branches from U.S. 340 in southwest Frederick at a cloverleaf located on a tract originally patented as Dickson's Struggle. **Prospect Hall** (now Prospect Hall School), the country home of Benjamin Tasker Dulany, also stands on this tract. Unlike his father Daniel, this Dulany took up the patriot cause. In the Continental Army, he became one of Washington's aides. Washington's favorite horse, Blueskin, was a present from Benjamin Dulany; according to legend, the mount was returned here after the war and lies buried somewhere on the grounds.

The road descends into lower Middletown Valley and passes through the small town of **Jefferson,** first settled in 1779 and nicknamed "The Trap" or "Traptown," presumably because a group of highwaymen secreted themselves nearby. In 1832, six years after Thomas Jefferson's death, the town washed clean that stain by assuming the name of the third president. Md. 180 parallels U.S. 340 as both cross Catoctin Mountain and descend to the Potomac River. A right turn on Old Middletown Rd. and then left on Sumantown Rd. lead one to **Catoctin Creek Park,** a small picnicking area along a creek that rises about eight miles to the north, near Meyersville, and flows to the Potomac. Md. 180 bridges Catoctin Creek and then passes over the 340 expressway to Petersville, where it joins Md. 79.

A steam passenger train enters the B&O yard at Brunswick in the 1930s

Side Trip to Brunswick via Md. 79

From Petersville Md. 79 heads south to the village of Rosemont, where it joins Md. 17 into Brunswick (248' alt., 5,117 pop.), the second largest town in Frederick County. Brunswick developed on a large land tract that John Hawkins patented in 1753 as Hawkins' Merry Peep o'Day. The town, then known as Berlin, emerged in 1787; in 1890 townspeople changed the name, to avoid confusion with the Berlin in Worcester County on the Eastern Shore. That year the B&O Railroad established repair shops here, and Brunswick quickly expanded along the river bank and up the adjoining hills. Since the 1950s, diesel power and railroad automation have left Brunswick a shell of its former self. Remnants of the old, brick shop buildings stand near the tracks, however, and the site still functions as a commuter stop and CSX transportation facility. The **Brunswick Railroad Museum,** a small storefront facility at 40 W. Potomac St., houses railroad memorabilia and pieces relating to the town's history.

The **Potomac River Bridge,** at least the third at this location, was built in the 1950s. The preceding one went up in 1894, on the piers of a covered bridge that the Confederates had destroyed in 1861. Before burning this bridge behind them, Confederate cavalrymen had frequently dashed across it into Maryland to disrupt the railroad, damage the canal, and break telegraph lines.

Return to Petersville and turn left to rejoin the Jefferson Pike.

Less than half a mile beyond Petersville on Md. 180, on the right, Catholic Church Rd. branches north to **St. Mary's Catholic Church.** Thomas Sim Lee, an Anglican who converted to Catholicism after his marriage to Mary Digges, of Prince George's County, lived in a house north of here after the Revolution. A member of the Continental Congress and the Maryland Convention that ratified the Constitution of the United States in 1788, Lee served as governor of Maryland from 1779 to 1782 and again from 1792 to 1794. Elected state senator in 1794 and governor of Maryland for a third time in 1798, he declined both posts. When he died in 1819, he left $1,000 toward the building of the church that became St. Mary's.

From Petersville Md. 180 continues to the Potomac River and **Knoxville.** Laid out in 1772, this town prospered with the canal and later depended on the railroad's maintenance shops. Iron smelting for the railroad and other purposes continued here until about 1890. During the 1930s, Knoxville's environs harbored a large "hobo jungle." Now the railroad and local citizens are making an effort to clean up the industrial debris around the tracks.

Weverton

Just west of Knoxville, in Washington County, lie the ruins of Weverton, the creation of Casper W. Wever, the civil engineer who built the first bridge to Harpers Ferry. In 1835 Wever set about building a model manufacturing town. He purchased land, chartered Weverton Manufacturing Company, and started work on a dam, mills, and factory buildings. Wever ran into territorial conflicts with the C&O, however, and his dreams collapsed with his death. A utopian group later tried a communal-living experiment there. During the Civil War the Union army took over the buildings for barracks. Now only a few crumbling stone walls remain of Wever's town.

Sandy Hook

Md. 180 joins U.S. 340 from Frederick. Before the highway crosses the Potomac, leave it by following signs to Sandy Hook. Sandy Hook emerged in the early 1830s to serve traffic on the C&O Canal; it also became a busy railroad center before the rise of nearby Brunswick. **Lock No. 32** and the **Shenandoah River Lock** are located nearby. Hikers along the towpath buy provisions in stores that retain the village's old-time character.

Side Trip to John Brown House
via Harpers Ferry Rd. and Chestnut Grove Rd.

Departing Sandy Hook on Sandy Hook Rd., follow it to Pleasantville, then drive straight ahead on Harpers Ferry Rd. for about two and a half miles, to the intersection of Chestnut Grove and Hoffmaster Rds. Turn left, then immediately right onto Chestnut Grove Rd. and within a mile's distance look for signs to the John Brown House, which stands on the Kennedy farm (private). Visitors can tour the sparsely furnished landmark, which has remained virtually unchanged since Brown's occupancy.

John Brown's Raid

A native of Connecticut, John Brown had, by the late 1850s, fully earned his reputation for militance in the war against slavery. He and members of his family had taken conspicuous parts in the murderous confusion popularly called "Bleeding Kansas." For turning words into action, Brown had won widespread support among militant abolitionists, including native Marylander Frederick Douglass. For years Brown had dreamed of fomenting guerrilla warfare against "the slave power" from strongholds in the Appalachian Mountains. In early 1858, while a guest in Douglass's home in Rochester, New York, and with the encouragement of wealthy New Englanders, Brown wrote a constitution for a new revolutionary government. To set his fluctuating plan in motion, he determined to capture the Federal arsenal at Harpers Ferry.

In July 1859, Brown used the alias "Isaac Smith" when renting this Maryland farmhouse and an adjoining 160 acres. Two of his sons, his daughter, daughter-in-law, and a follower named Jerry Anderson joined him. For about three months, the group received packages of arms and ammunition from supporters in the North. In the attic of the house, Brown hid about a thousand pikes, sent from Connecticut. At a secret meeting in Chambersburg, Pennsylvania, in the fall of 1859, Brown pleaded with Douglass to join the expedition. Douglass warned that the conspirators were headed "into a perfect steel trap."

Convinced of divine support, Brown nonetheless followed his risky plan. After attending church services on the night of October 16, he and fewer than 20 followers surprised the small garrison at Harpers Ferry, captured the town's firehouse, and greatly alarmed the citizenry. Brown's anticipated uprising of slaves failed to materialize, and three days later U.S. Marines under the command of an army officer, Robert E. Lee, captured Brown, after killing or wounding most of his company. Another detachment, under J.E.B. Stuart, seized the house in which Brown had been living, confiscated the weapons, and found his papers, including letters from Douglass. During the outcry that followed, many of Brown's supporters went into hiding. Douglass escaped to Canada and then traveled to Great Britain for a lecture tour.

Brown was tried, sentenced, and on December 2, 1859, hanged at Charles Town, Virginia (now West Virginia). Though many abolitionists had disapproved of Brown's act, his dignified conduct both during his trial and at his execution made him an antislavery martyr. The incident widened the breach between the North and South and made the course of moderation difficult to trace. The song "John Brown's Body," set to an African American folk hymn, became popular almost immediately after his death. Julia Ward Howe used the melody in writing the "Battle Hymn of the Republic," which first appeared in early 1862.

Maryland Heights and Harpers Ferry

Back in Sandy Hook, Tryst Rd. leads to the Maryland side of the **Harpers Ferry National Historical Park.** Maryland Heights (1,448' alt.), with its trails and a spectacular overlook, gives the walker a panoramic view. Harpers Ferry, West Virginia, sits at the spot where the Shenandoah River drains into the Potomac, which may be the most picturesque point along the entire Potomac River. Loudoun Heights (Virginia) looms above the Shenandoah on its southern bank, Bolivar Heights (West Virginia) above the town, on the northern side. American Indian tribes assembled here to fish for yellow sucker and other varieties, particularly during the spawning season. The first European settler, trader Peter

Stephens, arrived in 1733. Fourteen years later, Robert Harper, miller and merchant, took over Stephens's ferry operation and advertised his gristmill to nearby farmers. Many early ferry operators were African Americans. Thomas Jefferson, who visited the site in 1783, thought the view from the rocky heights above the Shenandoah "worth a voyage across the Atlantic."

George Washington chose Harpers Ferry in 1797 as the site for a U.S. armory. Lewis and Clark used rifles produced here on their famous, 1804–6 westward expedition. By 1850 the town was a successful industrial center with a diverse population of skilled workers. During the Civil War, Union and Confederate troops alternately occupied the cliffs on both sides of the river, each side struggling to control the strategic railroad crossing. Confederate forces seized the arsenal in September 1862, just before the Battle of Antietam, and captured most of the 12,500-man garrison, the largest single surrender by Union troops during the war.

With the arsenal destroyed and other buildings in ruins, Harpers Ferry languished after the war. Fires, floods, and epidemics also took their toll. Storer College, a normal school for freed slaves, opened here (and closed in 1955). In 1944 Congress created the Harpers Ferry National Historical Monument and in 1955 began acquiring nearby land. The monument became a National Historical Park in 1963. Since that time, the park has continued to grow, with further land acquisitions being made on both sides of the river in Maryland and West Virginia.

Appalachian Trail

The Appalachian Trail crosses the Potomac at Harpers Ferry, and the trail's supervisory agency, the Appalachian Trail Conference, makes its headquarters here. In 1921 Benton MacKaye first proposed the idea of a trail along the length of the Appalachians. By 1937, as a result of a mammoth New Deal civil works project, workers had completed a trail that stretched from Springer Mountain in northern Georgia to Mount Katahdin in central Maine—a length of 2,015 miles. In Maryland, the trail leads upward from the C&O Canal to the crest of South Mountain and continues north to Pen Mar, where it enters Pennsylvania, after covering a distance of 40.67 miles within the state. With the assistance of the Mountain Club of Maryland (Baltimore) and the Maryland Appalachian Trail Club of Hagerstown, the Potomac Appalachian Trail Club (Washington, D.C.) maintains 235 miles of the trail in Maryland and northern Virginia.

Return to Alt. 40 via Md. 17

From Maryland Heights or Harpers Ferry, return four or five miles northeast on U.S. 340 to Md. 17 for a pleasant trip back to Alt. 40, which it joins at Middletown.

Md. 17 angles northwest along the Middletown Valley at the foot of Catoctin Mountain and carries the name **Horsey Distillery Rd.** The name derives from a local rye whiskey firm that dated from 1850 and flourished until Prohibition. Owner of one of many small companies that produced the once-popular Maryland rye, O. Horsey proudly claimed the distinction of sending his freshly filled bottles of rye by slow-moving ships around Cape Horn to California and returning them overland to the plant.

Hauling milk on a secondary road in Frederick County during the Depression

Constant rolling and pitching was said to age the whiskey more rapidly and give it special smoothness.

The road soon reaches **Burkittsville** (550' alt., 194 pop.), a hamlet that was called Harley's Post Office until laid out as a town in 1829 and named for a settler, Henry Burkitt. It has two active religious congregations—Church of the Resurrection (1829) and St. Paul's Church (1859), one Reformed, the other Lutheran—which reflect its divided Lutheran heritage. The cemetery here offers a magnificent view of the lower valley. From this location, a visitor can easily imagine how the valley might have looked in September 1862, when wounded soldiers from nearby Crampton's Gap sought refuge here after the Battle of South Mountain.

Gathland State Park

Gapland Rd. ascends the mountain from Burkittsville to **Gathland,** the unusual mountain complex created by George Alfred Townsend, Civil War correspondent and novelist, whose pen name was Gath.

Born in Delaware in 1841, Townsend spent most of his life in Maryland. He began his career as a correspondent for New York papers and later served as a foreign reporter and syndicated columnist in Washington. He became the epitome of a successful 19th-century journalist: wealthy, sophisticated, individualistic to the point of eccentricity. After royalties from *The Entailed Hat; or, Patty Cannon's Times* (1884) began to pour in and *Katy of Catoctin; or, The Chainbreakers, a National Romance* appeared in 1886, he bought this mountain property and began building a barony in stone.

Townsend spent a total of half a million dollars on the establishment. He put up at least five houses—one for his own use, one for his wife, and the others for his children, their nurses, and servants. Like an American Count of Monte Cristo, he entertained extravagantly on his mountain top; invitations to parties at Gathland were welcomed by notables of the period. Each of the houses reflected a fantastic architectural conceit, with entrances and exits placed at the whim of the owner. Numerous spires, arches, and turrets jutted from the roofs. The marble walls bore inscribed quotations from the classics. **Gath Hall** has been restored.

In honor of fellow newspapermen who covered the Civil War, Townsend in 1896 dedicated the **War Correspondents' Arch,** another prominent feature in today's park. It combined intentional and whimsical elements of a Moorish arch, a firehouse tower, a European castle, and a Roman aqueduct. Forty feet wide and 50 feet high, the arch is made of local stone trimmed with brown sandstone, blue limestone, and brick. A niche near the top of the arch encloses a six-foot figure of Orpheus, the mythical ancient Greek musician with magical powers. With sword sheathed, he plays a pipe. Tablets on one side of the arch bear the names of 147 correspondents and artists of the war; other panels list the engagements that occurred on South Mountain. Townsend gave the arch to the state of Maryland in 1904.

When Gath's fortunes declined, he moved to simpler quarters in Washington, D.C., where he died in 1914. In 1922 his heirs sold Gathland for $9,500. The purchaser made an effort to convert the complex into a summer hotel, but abandoned the plan, leaving this remarkable place to the mercy of vandals, wild animals, and the elements. At its nadir, in 1938, it fetched a mere $750 at auction. The state acquired the property in 1949. The Appalachian Trail passes by Townsend's mausoleum, a crumbling stone structure with the handwritten inscription, "Good Night, Gath."

Follow Md. 17 north to rejoin Alt. 40 at Middletown. Or, from

Slaughtering hogs, Boonsboro

Burkittsville, follow the secondary road over South Mountain to Gapland, and take Md. 67 north via Rohrersville and rejoin Alt. 40 just before Boonsboro.

D. FROM BOONSBORO TO BLOODY SHARPSBURG VIA MD. 34 AND 65

Md. 34 angles southwest from Alt. 40 at Boonsboro and leads to the Potomac River. The abundant limestone in this part of Washington County accounts for the many bluish-gray stone fences, bridges, and farmhouses. Limestone caverns also abound here. **Crystal Grottoes,** the state's only commercial cave and a geologic landmark, is located about two miles outside the Boonsboro town limits.

There has been a settlement at **Keedysville** (350' alt., 464 pop.) since at least 1770, the year when a church of the United Brethren was formed here as an offshoot of the Reformed Church congregation in Frederick. The town first carried the name Centerville, but residents petitioned for a name change, in the mid-19th century, because of the confusion between their home and an older town on the Eastern Shore (as in the case of Berlin/Brunswick). So many members of the Keedy family were among the petitioners that "Keedysville" was chosen.

Beyond Keedysville, the road crosses **Antietam Creek,** which rises in Pennsylvania and flows the length of eastern Washington County into the Potomac. The name has Algonquian origins; the Delaware, an Algonquian people, and the Catawba, a Siouan people, hunted and lived in this area.

Sharpsburg

The founder of this town (425' alt, 659 pop.), Joseph Chapline, named the place in 1763 for his friend Horatio Sharpe, governor of Maryland. Chapline, an English-educated lawyer, helped organize the defense of the region during the French and Indian War. His Mount Pleasant estate covered more than 15,000 acres in the Antietam Valley and south toward Harpers Ferry.

C&O Canal construction reached Sharpsburg in 1832, soon followed by an outbreak of cholera in the shanty camps housing the Irish construction workers. Fear of contagion left many of the afflicted unattended. Hundreds died and were hastily buried in a mass grave. To reach the **C&O Canal National Park Headquarters,** located at Ferry Hill Place, take Snyder's Landing Rd. from the town.

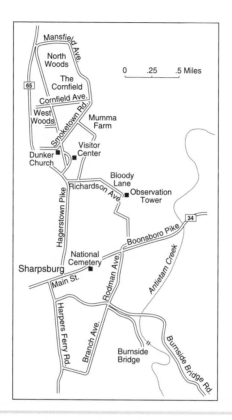

The Battle of Antietam or Sharpsburg

Sharpsburg gave its name to one of the Civil War's pivotal engagements. By late summer in 1862, it appeared that the Confederate States of America might succeed in their "second revolution." Lee's army of about 40,000 men had recently defeated Federal troops at the second Battle of Manassas. As the Confederacy withstood attempts to subdue it, the prospects of European intervention on its behalf improved. A negotiated peace appeared a distinct possibility. Confederate leaders decided to cross the Potomac and carry the war into Union territory. If Lee pushed far enough north, he could successfully flank Washington, perhaps gain Baltimore (believed to be ripe for Southern picking), and threaten Philadelphia—all the while relieving his native Virginia. Maryland itself, a sister slave state with citizens already in the Rebel armies, might join the cause. The stakes were high, and the world watched.

On September 5, 1862, advance Confederate troops crossed the Potomac south of Frederick between White's Ferry and Point of Rocks. Regimental bands played the popular Southern ballad "Maryland, My Maryland." Their objective was Harrisburg, on the Susquehanna, a strategic site from which Lee could resupply his tattered army with essentials like food, clothing, shoes, and horses.

There he could sue the North for peace. On September 6, the Confederates reached Frederick, where Lee's Maryland-bred adjutant issued a call inviting residents to throw off the "foreign yoke." The local response to the bivouacked Rebels, a great many of them barefoot, was mixed. Some townspeople welcomed the men in "butternut" (a reference to their home-dyed uniforms), inviting officers to dinner, passing refreshments to the troops. Others, like the staunchly pro-Union physician Lewis Steiner, were quietly resistant, closing their shutters in disapproval. Many Frederick citizens simply kept their sympathies to themselves.

Before Lee could safely advance into Pennsylvania, he needed to subdue the 12,000 Union troops who occupied Harpers Ferry, located directly on his line of supply and communications to the Shenandoah Valley. He divided his army, sending Stonewall Jackson to seize Harpers Ferry, moving another force to Hagerstown in search of supplies, and ordering a third to hold the gaps in South Mountain in the event that the Army of the Potomac gave chase. In a few days the units were to converge at Boonsboro and prepare to invade Pennsylvania. Lee outlined these plans in a special order numbered 191. Headquarters clerks wrote and rewrote the orders for various commanders.

As Confederate cavalry moved west, they galloped into Middletown, where 17-year-old Nancy Crouse stood before her house on Main St., wrapped in a Union flag. Rebel troopers wrested the banner from her and destroyed it. Near Boonsboro, on September 11, a detachment of Federal cavalrymen came close to capturing Jackson when they happened upon and gave chase to Col. Henry Kyd Douglas (whose home was in nearby Shepherdstown, Virginia) and a few other of Jackson's staff officers. Douglas and his men were racing back to camp when they encountered General Jackson, walking his horse and far ahead of his troops on their way to Harpers Ferry. With quick presence of mind, Douglas and his men wheeled about, called to imaginary reinforcements, and charged their pursuers. The Union cavalry fell for the ruse and withdrew, and Jackson continued on his way.

Such chance events made this campaign especially dramatic; it developed as no one had planned. The Army of the Potomac, again under the command of Gen. George B. McClellan, groped for Lee's forces in a northwesterly direction from Washington. Union soldiers received a warm welcome as they marched through Frederick, flags waving and citizens cheering. On September 13, in a field near Frederick, two soldiers from Indiana discovered a copy of Lee's order 191 wrapped around three cigars, carelessly left behind. Both McClellan and Lincoln, whom the general wired that day, knew they had it within their grasp not only to defeat, but to destroy Lee's divided forces and crush the rebellion.

McClellan planned to pass through Turner's Gap and defeat whatever force he found near Boonsboro and to send another column through Crampton's Gap, six miles to the south, to relieve Harpers Ferry. On September 14, Union troops forced Confederates holding Turner's Gap to withdraw toward Lee's chosen strongpoint, the low ridges west of Antietam Creek near Sharpsburg. There Confederate troops took up defensive positions and waited for McClellan. A ford over the Potomac at Shepherdstown, the closest avenue of escape to Virginia, lay to the south.

McClellan advanced with the great caution that marked his tenure as army commander. His 87,000 men, he knew, represented the only viable Federal force east of the Alleghenies; a defeat would be catastrophic for the Union cause. He studied the Confederate positions and ordered an attack at dawn on September 17.

In Washington, President Lincoln—following the logic that the conduct of war had imposed upon him—realized that the blot of slavery, not merely the advantages of union, lay at the heart of the conflict. In July he had drafted a proclamation that he believed would address this issue while shortening the war; his advisors warned him that without a victory it would amount to a desperate and empty gesture.

In London the British prime minister, Lord Palmerston, watched the telegraph wires closely. "A great conflict is taking place to the northwest of Washington," he wrote, "and its issue may have a great effect on the state of affairs."

In three separate offensives on September 17, Union forces drove at the outnumbered Confederates. The earliest offensive proceeded south, along the Hagerstown-Sharpsburg Turnpike, and produced vicious fighting, in a cornfield whose stalks soon were shot to pieces, and around the small white **Dunker Church,** which the pacifist Society of Brethren, or Dunkers, had built a few years before. The second attack, in the middle of the day and in the center of the lines, forced some of Lee's men into a sunken road that was afterward dubbed **Bloody Lane,** so deeply were the mangled bodies piled within it. Each time the Federals seemed on the verge of breaking through, Lee's men plugged a gap or mounted a counterattack. Late in the afternoon, troops on McClellan's left, under the command of Ambrose P. Burnside, finally forced their way over an Antietam bridge known thereafter as **Burnside Bridge.** Just when they had gained the creek's western shore in large numbers and were threatening to sweep up Lee's weakened right flank, the last of the Confederates who had captured Harpers Ferry ran up the road and blunted the Union attack. By the end of September 17, 1862—the bloodiest single day in American history (5,000 killed)—Union and Confederate troops had fought to a draw. Robert T. Coles of the 4th Alabama Infantry described Sharpsburg as "a perfect homespun Waterloo."

The next day the exhausted armies faced each other in the heat, smelling the slaughter and listening to cries from the wounded as physicians went about the gruesome work of amputating limbs. That night, two weeks after jauntily crossing the Potomac, Lee's soldiers retreated quietly across the Shepherdstown ford to Virginia. Their famous general sat atop Traveler and watched silently.

Lincoln faulted McClellan for not aggressively pursuing Lee, but five days after the battle, on September 22, the president issued the preliminary Emancipation Proclamation.

One of the decisive documents in American history, Lincoln's presidential order, effective January 1, 1863, declared that, "all persons held as slaves within any State or designated part of a State the people whereof shall be in rebellion against the United States, shall be then, thenceforward, and forever free." With this proclamation, the war assumed new meaning. More than a contest between sections, it became a war for freedom. Coupled with Lee's retreat to Virginia, the Union cause against slavery insured that Europe would remain aloof from the conflict. "Bloody Antietam," the Battle of Sharpsburg (as Confederates called it), had changed the character of the war.

Photographs of the casualties at Antietam also changed the public perception of warfare. No longer did anxious civilians rely totally on the printed word. Alexander Gardner's stark photos of dead young men—mouths gaping, body parts scattered on the peaceful farmland, corpses lying in rows as the men fell—contrasted strongly with martial music, clean uniforms, and bright banners snapping in the wind.

The dead men and horses had to be buried. More than 1,800 of the fallen Federals remained unidentified. They, along with 4,776 more Union soldiers, lie in the **National Cemetery** on the south side of Md. 34 at the entry to Sharpsburg. Most of the Confederate dead are buried in Hagerstown and Frederick, as well as in church and family cemeteries in the region. Some 18,000 men had been wounded; caring for them took weeks and required the aid of scores of civilians and the loan of their barns, houses, and churches. Virtually the entire towns of Hagerstown and Frederick became hospitals. Clara Barton, founder of the Red Cross, helped to tend the wounded. Lee's own wounded son was treated at **Ferry Hill,** a large, early-19th-century brick house about three miles off Md. 34 east of Sharpsburg.

Lincoln visited the field a few weeks later to observe the site of the carnage and goad McClellan into further action. The president, and the public, knew that an event of great significance had occurred at Sharpsburg. The National Battlefield was established in 1890 and transferred to the National Park Service in 1933.

Antietam National Battlefield Park includes more than 800 acres and encompasses a **Visitor Center** (north of Sharpsburg and just east of Md. 65; open daily throughout the year except Thanksgiving, Christmas, and New Year's Day), an observation tower, and roadside descriptions of the battle. Monuments to various military units stand scattered around the peaceful countryside, which remains remarkably similar to its pre-battle appearance in 1862.

The guns of Antietam Battlefield

Soldiers of the 5th Maryland (USA), under the command of a prominent Jewish citizen-soldier of Baltimore, Leopold Blumenberg, took part in the assault at Bloody Lane. Near there, the Baltimore-born West Point graduate and division commander Gen. William H. French died in the fighting. Troops of the 2nd Maryland (USA) took part in the struggle to cross Burnside's Bridge. The Maryland state monument, commemorating troops on both sides, stands near the Visitor Center, almost directly across the old Hagerstown-Sharpsburg Turnpike from the Dunker Church.

Site of Lee's Headquarters and Rumsey Bridge

Follow Md. 34 (Main St.) through Sharpsburg. A marker indicates the site from which General Lee directed his troops during the battle. Continue driving on Md. 34 to see the place where Lee's men returned to Virginia.

The bridge that now crosses the Potomac River commemorates James Rumsey, a Cecil County native who moved to Sharpsburg as a young man, then moved across the river to Shepherdstown to experiment with his new invention, the steamboat. Rumsey had tried smaller models, but on March 14, 1787, he publicly demonstrated an 80-foot vessel with machine parts largely made in the furnace at Antietam. Residents of both towns lined the Potomac and cheered as the vessel struggled against the current. Rumsey traveled upriver a short distance and returned to Shepherdstown, having proved that steam could propel boats. He never received the financial backing he needed, however, and, after Robert Fulton in 1807 launched a commercial steamboat on the Hudson River, most of his contemporaries forgot him.

Town of Antietam

Antietam, about two miles south of Sharpsburg on the road to Harpers Ferry, once flourished as an industrial center. An iron forge produced cannon and cannonballs from 1765 to 1880. Pig iron went down the C&O Canal to Harpers Ferry for further fabrication at the Federal armory. A number of water-powered mills created the energy necessary for the Antietam operations, which in the 1840s employed more than 200 ironworkers. All that remains of these factories are three lime-kiln chimneys.

Harpers Ferry Rd. continues south through pleasant, rolling countryside between the river and Elk Ridge, passes Pleasantville, and ends at Sandy Hook Rd., which continues to that village and on to Harpers Ferry.

From Sharpsburg to Hagerstown via Md. 65 (Hagerstown Pike)

From Sharpsburg, the traveler can return north to U.S. 40 or I-70 via Md. 65 (the old Hagerstown-Sharpsburg Turnpike), which passes through the Antietam National Battlefield and leads to the intersection of Md. 68 at a crossroads named **Lappans.** A left turn on Md. 68 leads to an Episcopal preparatory school located to the right on College Rd., two miles northwest of the junction. **Fountain Rock,** a home built here in 1792, was the center of Gen. Samuel Ringgold's 17,000-acre estate. Henry Clay and Presidents Madison and Monroe were among the famous guests at the house. St. James School began here in 1842 as the diocesan school of the Episcopal Church of Maryland. During the Civil War most of its students joined the Southern army. After the Battle of Antietam, the faculty gave food, water, and medical attention to soldiers from both sides. Fire destroyed the house in the early 1900s.

A right turn from Lappans on Md. 68 takes the traveler to **Devil's Backbone County Park,** a recreational area on Antietam Creek. A waterfall, grassy banks, peaceful expanses of shaded water, and unusual waterfowl make the park a haven for picnicking and relaxing. From the junction at Lappans, Md. 65 proceeds north past the Maryland Correctional Institution-Hagerstown (east of the road), which houses and attempts to rehabilitate more than 6,000 inmates. Md. 65 continues to the southern limits of Hagerstown.

Lunchtime at a typical one-room schoolhouse in Western Maryland in the 1930s

For a tour of the upper Potomac, follow U.S. 11 southwest from Hagerstown through residential developments and the village of Halfway, a quiet, unassuming spot midway between Hagerstown and the river, and continue for five miles.

Williamsport

Otho Holland Williams, a Revolutionary War general and entrepreneur, founded this town (380' alt., 2,103 pop.) in 1787. Williams was born in 1749 in Prince George's County and orphaned at age 13. After working as a clerk in Frederick and Baltimore Counties until 1776, he secured a commission as a lieutenant in an infantry battalion under the command of William Smallwood. Williams joined the Continental Army outside Boston and later served with distinction during Washington's campaigns in New York. The British captured him late in 1776 at Washington Heights, where he and his company, protecting the Continentals as they retreated across the Hudson River to New Jersey, fought a furious rear-guard action. Williams spent 15 months as a prisoner of war, much of it sequestered in a damp prison hulk in New York Harbor. Returned to the Continental Army in a prisoner exchange in 1778, he continued his military career and rose to brigadier general, serving with the Maryland Line in the southern campaigns that led to the British surrender at Yorktown.

After the war, Williams moved here and purchased property on the high ground around the confluence of Conococheague Creek and the Potomac River. **Springfield,** his stone and brick mansion, now covered with clapboard, represents a transplanting to the western regions of an architectural style popular among the mid-18th-century Tidewater gentry. General Williams laid out lots for a town on this site, where there was ample water for mills and where wagons following the Great Valley Rd. from Pennsylvania to Virginia (roughly the course of U.S. 11) could normally ford the Potomac. The Great Falls to the south limited river navigation, but Williams and others anticipated improvements. His health damaged by his imprisonment, Williams died in 1794 at the age of 45. He lies buried at Williamsport.

In 1791 George Washington, then president, had visited the town to look it over as a possible site of the proposed federal city. Officials cited the barrier at Great Falls as one reason for denying the Williamsport petition (Congress selected the site of present-day Washington, well below the falls, the same year). In the 19th century the town, by then served by a B&O line that ran just to the north, made a bid to become the site of a national foundry, but in 1858 it again missed a chance at greater prominence. Nevertheless, Williamsport flourished in a modest way as a busy point on the C&O Canal, which had reached the town in 1834.

During the Civil War, the town provided a setting for high drama, as Lee's army returned to Virginia from the Battle of Gettysburg in a column that stretched for 17 miles from through Hagerstown, back into Pennsylvania. Rains fell mercilessly on the retreating Confederates, whose lead elements, wagons of wounded and remaining supplies, reached Wil-

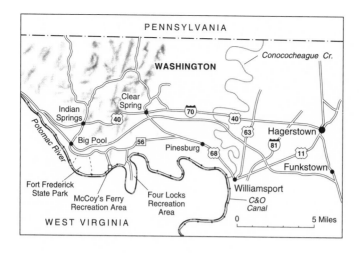

PENNSYLVANIA

WASHINGTON

Conococheague Cr.

Indian Springs

Clear Spring

40

70

40

63

Hagerstown

81

Big Pool

56

Pinesburg

68

11

Funkstown

Potomac River

Fort Frederick State Park

McCoy's Ferry Recreation Area

Four Locks Recreation Area

Williamsport

C&O Canal

WEST VIRGINIA

0   5 Miles

liamsport on July 7. A pontoon bridge that had crossed the river had been destroyed and the river was running five feet above normal level. Lee's engineers constructed a line of defense three miles in either direction from Williamsport and waited—either for the Federals to arrive or for the river to subside. Spurred on by Lincoln, Gen. George G. Meade set his army on the heels of Lee's infantry column as it wound its way through Emmitsburg, down the Catoctin Mountain, and past Frederick along the east side of South Mountain. At a site near **Benevola** near Beaver Creek (on Alt. 40 just north of Boonsboro), Meade and his corps commanders planned an attack. They delayed too long, however, and by the time the Union army moved, on July 14, the Confederate trenches were empty. During the previous night most of Lee's troops had crossed the Potomac on an improvised pontoon bridge and others had waded across the receding river. Lee had escaped again, and the war continued.

To cross the C&O Canal to **River Front Park** along the Potomac, one may choose either of two historic structures: a Bollman truss bridge built in 1879—quite an innovative use of iron in its day—or an unusual railroad lift-bridge, built in 1923.

The C&O Canal from Williamsport to Big Pool

The **Conococheague Aqueduct** lies within easy walking distance of River Front Park. Completed in 1834, this masonry structure was the fifth of 11 aqueducts that carried C&O Canal boats over the Potomac's feeder streams. In 1920 part of this aqueduct collapsed into Conococheague Creek, taking a canal boat with it. The boat remained where it had fallen until 1936, when flood waters carried it downstream. Potomac floods have submerged portions of the canal at least ten times, notably in January 1996.

The aqueduct offers but one of many visual delights one finds in the **C&O Canal National Historic Park.** The canal towpath, an elevated trail 184½ miles long, gives hikers and bikers probably their best means of exploring and enjoying the Potomac Valley. Picnicking, camping, boating, and horseback riding are also available along the canal route. For general information, including Park Service regulations, write Superintendent,

C&O Canal National Historic Park, Sharpsburg, Maryland 21782. Maps and books about the canal are also available at information centers in Georgetown, Great Falls, Hancock, and Cumberland.

If you cannot walk or bike to canal sites upriver, drive along Md. 68 (Clearspring Rd.) for about four and a half miles through Pinesburg and bear left onto Md. 56, which branches southwestward to the canal.

At the first intersection, Dam No. 5 Rd., turn left to view the C&O's **Dam No. 5.** This dam enabled the C&O to feed Potomac River water into the canal itself. During the Civil War, Confederate forces tried several times, with only limited success, to destroy it. Numerous small skirmishes occurred along this section of the Potomac during that war. Locks 45 and 46, collectively known as **Two Locks,** are nearby.

A well-marked road from Md. 56 leads south to the **Four Locks Recreation Area,** which includes a public boat ramp. The river bends dramatically here, creating a neck that the canal crossed in a series of locks. The grassy canal bed, stone locks (numbers 47, 48, 49, 50), and brick locktender's house offer a reasonably clear picture of the C&O during its operation. Union troops used this area as a headquarters for the canal's defense.

McCoy's Ferry Recreation Area lies just upriver from Four Locks and is reachable by a road branching south from Md. 56. One of the early Civil War actions in Maryland occurred here in May 1861. A party of Confederates seized the ferry boat and headed for Virginia. Home Guards fired at them in midstream, and they fled by skiff to the other side.

Md. 56 crosses Green Spring Run just past McCoy's Ferry Rd. Upstream, note the ruins of the **Green Spring Furnace.** Lancelot Jacques and Thomas Johnson obtained this site in 1768 for a forge mill and "Iron Work for running of Pigg Iron." Johnson became state governor in 1776; Jacques manufactured cannon for the Continental Army.

Md. 56 then passes **Fort Frederick State Park** and, before intersecting I-70, goes by **Big Pool,** a small lake built for the C&O Canal and now a popular fishing spot. For years it was also the terminus of the Western Maryland Railroad. At the turn of this century, a syndicate headed by Jay Gould acquired the railroad in its efforts to compete with roads that already had east-west connections. Gould and his friends successfully petitioned Maryland for permission to follow the canal route, crossing and recrossing it, on the way to Cumberland, thus opening the road to more western markets.

F. THROUGH THE GREEN RIDGE FOREST TO OLDTOWN AND CUMBERLAND VIA MD. 51

A drive through the **Green Ridge State Forest** cannot help but remind us of Maryland's frontier past. Its roads, although unpaved, are reasonably passable, and the more hazardous side routes are marked for four-wheel-drive vehicles only. This route should be explored only during warm weather months, however.

Turn south from Alt. 40 on M. V. Smith Rd. just beyond the **Billmeyer Game Refuge.** Cross I-68 and continue until the road turns into Oldtown Rd. Follow it south along Town Hill, then angle southwest at Thomas Rd. and continue to Md. 51. Or take Fifteen Mile Creek Rd. south from I-68 to Green Ridge Rd. and follow it to Md. 51.

These routes pass hunting cabins in thick, lush woods that offer occasional glimpses of rugged, ridged hollows and small valleys. Small streams drain the ridges on their way to the Potomac below. Civilization seems far away; the Appalachian wilderness becomes tangible. Because the terrain is so rough, the nine-mile journey through the forest requires at least 45 minutes. At the end of the descent to the Potomac River, the traveler can appreciate the engineering achievement at Paw Paw Tunnel.

Paw Paw Tunnel

Turn east on Md. 51 and follow the road to the C&O Canal. Just before the Potomac River Bridge, park and walk along the towpath about one-half mile, beyond milestone #156, to the **Paw Paw Canal Tunnel,** the canal company's most ambitious and expensive achievement. The C&O dug this 3,117-foot passage through Anthony Ridge to avoid two loops in the river and thus save five miles over the river-bank route alternative. Cutting such a tunnel typified the engineering feats that the C&O—as compared to the Erie Canal—called for. Construction adhered to the highest quality attainable at that time; precise and expensive masonry work minimized later repairs. Many tales were told about the Irish, Welsh, English, and local "Dutch" workers who labored during the 14 years of the tunnel's construction. The time required to complete the stonework and arrange financing to cover escalating costs delayed opening of the canal. Final arching of the tunnel with an 18-inch brick lining was deferred until after the formal opening of the canal to Cumberland in 1850.

Despite its status as an enormous engineering feat, the one-way tunnel proved a bottleneck during the most prosperous years of the canal between 1870 and 1875. The traffic jam at Paw Paw and delays at the locks handicapped the canal in its competition with the railroad. On one memorable occasion, two boat captains met in the middle of the tunnel and refused to yield, blocking the tunnel for days.

Return to Md. 51 and travel west. Two miles before Oldtown, the road passes **Potomac Forks,** where the South Branch of the Potomac joins the North Branch. To see the forks, one may have to descend to the C&O towpath. Their importance stems from the terms of Lord Baltimore's original charter, which established the Potomac River as Maryland's southern boundary and the river's western "fountain" as Maryland's western boundary. A squabble ensued between Maryland and Virginia, and the crown sided with the larger colony (see Tour 19-I).

Oldtown

Improvements to Md. 51 have bypassed historic **Oldtown,** the first European settlement in what is now Allegany County. To reach the town, proceed cautiously through a one-lane railroad underpass and then onto the old road.

At this low spot on the river plain, a branch of the *Athiamiowee* (literally "path of the armed ones"), known to the English as the Warrior Path, crossed the North Branch of the Potomac. The path connected the Six Nations of the Iroquois Confederation with the Catawbas, Cherokees, and other southern tribes. Both hunting and war parties used the crossing, at which, in the last decade of the 17th century, Shawnees built a village known as King Opessa's Town. Sometime before 1732, they abandoned the village, and the site became known as Shawnee Old Town or, more simply, Oldtown.

Thomas and Michael Cresap

In 1741 Thomas Cresap (ca. 1700–1790), a legendary character in Maryland's frontier history, built a fortified dwelling at Oldtown and engaged in fur trading with the Indians.

Born in Yorkshire, Cresap arrived in Maryland about 1717 and by 1729 had established a farm in the considerable strip of land that both the Calverts and Penns claimed on Maryland's northern border. A Maryland magistrate and captain of militia, Cresap so stubbornly asserted Calvert sovereignty in the area that he caused the controversy with Pennsylvania to escalate into armed conflict, the Conojacular War. Maryland officials lionized Cresap. Pennsylvanians called him the "Maryland Monster." In 1736, a Pennsylvania sheriff and two dozen armed men surrounded his house before dawn and for 14 hours besieged the rebel. The sheriff captured Cresap only after setting the house afire and wounding its owner. He was put in irons and taken to Philadelphia, which he promptly declared to be the prettiest city in Maryland. (The courts decided the border dispute in favor of Pennsylvania in 1750.)

Cresap's confinement lasted about a year. After his release, the monster took his family farther west, building a home on Antietam Creek near Hagerstown. When a French ship captured a cargo of furs he had sent to England, Cresap deeded his Antietam landholdings to his principal creditor, Daniel Dulany Sr., and again moved westward, this time beyond the edge of settlement to Oldtown.

At Oldtown Cresap soon established extensive trading relationships with the tribes using the Warrior Path. In the Treaty of Lancaster (1744) between the British and the Six Nations, his cabin served as a marker. The treaty required the colonists, who had decimated the supply of game, to furnish food and supplies to Indian parties passing along the great western path. As Maryland agent, Cresap handed out food so generously that the Indians called him Big Spoon. He extended hospitality to others traveling in the west—missionaries, traders, explorers, and surveyors. Besides offering rest and refreshment, Cresap sold supplies and recommended Indian scouts. In 1748 George Washington, then on his first surveying trip into the west, commented on the well-stocked trading post and described a "Daunce" performed by some 30 Indians whom Big Spoon had cheered on with offerings.

Thomas Cresap also assisted Virginia's Ohio Company in settling lands beyond the Appalachians and diverting Indian trade from the French and the Pennsylvanians. His travels established regular trade routes westward from the Potomac. He served as a magistrate and colonel of militia; it was Cresap who surveyed both forks of the Potomac in 1754. At about this time the French moved into the Ohio country in force and warned Cresap to retire from his settlement, which they placed in French territory. They evidently had not heard of Cresap's earlier career in territorial disputes. He refused "like a man of Spirit" and proceeded to assist Washington and Braddock as a commissary in the fighting that led to the French and Indian War. Some complained that the "Rattlesnake Colonel" and his son Daniel profiteered in the exchange.

After Braddock's defeat, Indian raids seriously menaced the settlers at Oldtown, and in 1756 Cresap removed some members of his family to Williamsport and relative safety. He and his sons maintained the outpost, counterattacking Indian raiders. One of his sons, Thomas, died in the fighting. As late as 1763, Indians drove settlers around Oldtown to the stockade surrounding Cresap's post.

After the French and Indian War, the aging colonel and his son Michael pursued interests in the Ohio lands—despite British policy forbidding settlement beyond the crest of the Appalachians. They laid out and sold lots at Oldtown. When he was at least 70 years old (Cresap himself was unsure of his age), Cresap undertook the long voyage back to England, where he visited friends and family and pressed his western land claims. Michael took a group of settlers into the Ohio Valley and later distinguished himself in the conflict that broke out with the Indians in 1774 (Lord Dunmore's War). That affair also became known as Cresap's War, because Chief Logan blamed Michael for the massacre of his family. Daniel, the other surviving son, prospered as a frontier trader in the Potomac Valley west of Cumberland.

The Cresap family strongly supported the patriot cause during the Revolutionary War. In 1775, when Washington had assumed command of the American forces besieging the British at Boston, Michael marched a company of Western Maryland riflemen to join the Continentals—the first unit from the south to arrive in response to Washington's call. (Before departing, Michael had been briefly delayed. At more than 70 years of age, the old colonel had seized the moment "and determined to join the army at their head, if his son should not arrive in season.") At Boston the frontiersmen, in their fringed leather jackets, astounded the other troops with their feats of marksmanship. Michael's health failed, and in October, on his way home, he died in New York. He is buried in the graveyard at Trinity Church, Wall Street.

The **Michael Cresap House,** a battered stone building in the center of Oldtown, has been altered extensively since completion of its original section in 1765. Skipton, the fortified dwelling and trading post that Thomas Cresap built in 1741, stood overlooking the river about one-half mile south of his son's home.

The turnpike that connected to the National Road at Cumberland passed 10 miles north of Oldtown and diverted the wagon commerce that formerly had cut through the village. The B&O also bypassed Oldtown, running along the south side of the river, from Harpers Ferry to Cumberland. By contrast, the C&O Canal passed right through Oldtown, bringing first the trade of construction work and then water traffic linking the village to Cumberland and Georgetown. For the **Oldtown–Battie Mixon Area** of the C&O Canal Historical Park, visit the canal at the Oldtown lock.

Digging the canal was rude work accompanied by recurrent violence. Most of the men who did the work had come from Ireland, and antagonism among natives of different Irish counties caused frequent fights. When the C&O's recurring financial crises forced postponement of paydays, the workers revolted, and the help of the local militia was sometimes required to restore order. Conflict also marked relations between crews working at different tasks; tunnel workers formed a particularly cohesive group. When contractors hired Germans or native-born local residents, the Irish violently objected, for such measures frequently meant cuts in pay and fewer jobs.

One incident took place at Oldtown on New Year's Day 1838, when tunnel workers, settling some obscure score, set out to demolish a tavern in the village. Before a sheriff's posse and the Cumberland militia arrived to challenge them, the rioters dispersed.

Early in the Civil War, in the spring of 1861, Confederates firing from the Virginia side of the river wounded three members of the 2nd Regiment of the Potomac Home Guard. They may have been the first Marylanders to shed blood for the Union. The town remained in Union control throughout the war, but on several occasions Rebels seized horses and supplies. By the summer of 1864, Union forces in the Shenandoah Valley had embarked on a war of attrition, which meant wholesale burning of crops and destruction of anything of possible military value. To retaliate, a Confederate raiding party under Gen. John C. McCausland crossed the Potomac in July and visited Chambersburg, Pennsylvania. Citizens failed to raise the $500,000 McCausland demanded in ransom, so he burned most of the town. Union troops along the Potomac prepared to frustrate McCausland's return to Virginia long enough for Federal cavalry to catch up with him. At Oldtown, men in blue positioned themselves in the woods between the canal and river to protect the ford.

On the morning of August 1, Confederate cavalrymen, including Baltimore County's Maj. Harry Gilmor and his Maryland battalion, approached Oldtown to ford the river. Union forces surprised them but the Confederates pressed on their flanks and forced the Union troops to beat a retreat across the river. Now on the West Virginia side of the Potomac, the Northerners took refuge in ironclad railroad cars on the B&O tracks. Confederate gunners hit the engine's boiler and it exploded, sending the Union men running to a nearby blockhouse. Confederates soon crossed the river, destroyed the train, and took as prisoners the 80 or so men in the blockhouse. By noon, all of McCausland's force had crossed the Potomac and escaped their pursuers.

In the years after the Civil War, Oldtown remained a rural village. Traffic on the canal was minor and erratic compared to that of the thriving B&O. For years the post office serving Oldtown's residents was located in the West Virginia town of Green Spring. Construction of the Hancock-to-Cumberland section of the Western Maryland Railroad in 1905–6 and of the Potomac River Bridge, begun in 1910, improved access to Oldtown, but the village itself withered. With the arrival of the automobile and decline of the canal, the isolation of Oldtown deepened. With the exception of the Cresap house and three canal locks, nothing tangible remains of the town's colorful, vibrant history.

Chesapeake and Ohio Canal Sites

Beyond Oldtown, Md. 51 swerves north from the river and the canal for several miles. After the bridge over Mill Run, the state highway passes Cresap Mill Rd., which climbs up the hollow between Martin Mountain and Warrior Mountain to the **Warrior Mountain Wildlife Management Area,** which encircles the mountain's crest just south of its high-

Consolidated Coal boatyard, Cumberland

est point (2,133' alt.). Cresap Mill Rd. follows the route of one of the branches of the Warrior Path.

Md. 51 angles back to the canal park's **Spring Gap Recreation Area** and then heads northward to Cumberland. At the base of **Irons Mountain,** the C&O Canal Historical Park has restored **Lock 72** and the two-story, board and batten, locktender's house. Locktenders could be responsible for up to three locks, and each was given a house, an acre of land for a garden, and a salary. In return, he or she—several women served as locktenders—was on duty 24 hours a day, ready to operate the cumbersome lock gates upon the calls of passing boatmen.

Beyond Lock 72, Md. 51 follows a roadbed incised into steep slopes that drop down to the Potomac River, which skirts the jutting ends of Irons and Collier Mountains. The road crosses **Evitts Creek,** named for the first European known to have settled in the mountains of Allegany County. By the creek about seven miles north, James Evitt, or Evart, built a solitary cabin on the mountain. He lived as a hermit until his death sometime before 1749.

Near the highway is the place where in 1755, Jane Frazier, an early settler, was captured by Indians. According to a narrative thought to have been written by Jane Frazier herself, she was taken to her captors' village in the Ohio Territory, where she was adopted into the tribe. Nearly a year later she escaped with two fellow captives. They faced a perilous journey of more than 300 miles through territory controlled by tribes allied with the French. After her male companions collapsed, Jane went on alone, living on bark and herbs and sleeping in trees or hollows to conceal herself at night. Eighteen days after her escape she found a trail that she followed to Oldtown, where she was rejoicingly greeted by friends.

Escorted by about 50 neighbors, who were singing, blowing horns, and carrying flags, Jane Frazier rode home to Evitts Creek, where her husband lived with his new wife. "Nearing the house my husband came out very frightened at the parade," she wrote. "Then coming nearer he saw me and grabbed me off the horse shouting with all his power 'The lost is found, the dead alive,' and so would not let me go for some time fearing it was all an apparition. We went into the house and I met his second wife. She seemed a very nice woman but he told her he could not give me up again, that as I was living their marriage had been illegal, but he would support her as he had promised. . . . And she being a woman of good sense took it all in good part, wishing me luck and said she would come some time and hear me tell about my captivity."

Md. 51 continues past railroad yards through the narrow, wooded Potomac Valley into Cumberland.

G. ALONG THE RAILROAD ROUTE FROM CUMBERLAND TO OAKLAND VIA U.S. 220 AND MD. 135

U.S. 220 was developed as Maryland's link in the Appalachian Thruway, which runs from Cumberland north across Pennsylvania to New York, where it joins U.S. 81 just south of Syracuse. South of Cumberland, U.S. 220—named the McMullen Highway in memory of John J. McMullen, an Allegany Countian who served on the State Roads Commission in the 1950s and early '60s—follows the original B&O Railroad

route along an agricultural valley cut by the North Branch of the Potomac River. The road passes across one of the few relatively broad plains in Allegany County and is bordered by Haystack Mountain and Dan's Mountain immediately to the west and the ragged ridges of Knobly Mountain across the river in West Virginia on the east.

Although the B&O reached Cumberland in 1842, it required 10 more years to make the 100-mile distance to Wheeling, then in Virginia. As it follows the river valley and then ascends almost 2,000 feet to the Allegheny Plateau, this drive conjures up the difficulties encountered by those railroad crews.

Potomac Park, a residential area just outside Cumberland, is the site of the **Cumberland Fairgrounds,** where Allegany County stages its fair each summer. The highway passes **Cresaptown,** named for Joseph Cresap, a son of Daniel Cresap, who settled here after the Revolution.

Rawlings was named for Col. Moses Rawlings, of Oldtown, who commanded a rifle regiment under George Washington during the Revolution. He and his unit were highly commended for their bravery when they covered Washington's withdrawal from Fort Washington to New Jersey in 1776. Colonel Rawlings later commanded Fort Frederick when it sheltered Hessian prisoners of war.

McCoole, a suburb of Keyser (formerly New Creek), West Virginia, lies directly across the river. Keyser grew as an important point on the B&O Railroad, which crossed the Potomac here, ran north up the valley about six miles to Bloomington, then recrossed to the Maryland side to ascend Seventeen-Mile Grade over the Eastern Continental Divide.

Westernport via Md. 135

From McCoole follow Md. 135 through the narrow gorge to Westernport (922' alt., 2,454 pop.), where George's Creek empties into the Potomac River. Westernport received its name in the 18th century, when it was located at the limit of navigation on the North Branch of the Potomac. Traders and explorers with horses and pack wagons left the river here to strike out on Indian and buffalo paths to the Ohio country. Logs were boomed downstream when timber companies stripped the slopes of the upper Potomac and Savage River watersheds in the post–Civil War period. Flatbeds of coal were also shipped from this river port during flood seasons. George's Creek Valley, the heart of Maryland's coal mining country, lies immediately to the north between Westernport and Frostburg.

This river town bears strong resemblances to Frostburg and Cumberland. Standardized frame housing clings to the steep hillsides; main streets are studded with church steeples. As in so many other small industrial communities once dominated by the railroads and coal companies, Westernport appears almost out of place in this forest setting. Many of the older houses have been swept away in floods or cleared during highway construction. Of those remaining, **Mullins House,** 69–75 Main St., has solid, reinforced beams (it once was a bank). Perhaps the oldest surviving structure is the **Welsh Theater,** located on the west side of the first block of Main St. Constructed of logs, now sheathed, the building sports an unusually slanted roof.

West on Md. 135, at **Luke,** one encounters a large upriver paper and pulp plant that has been a major economic influence in this isolated valley since its establishment in 1888. The factory, employing about 2,000 people, once filled the area with a noxious odor, but recently it has adopted improved antipollution measures.

Savage River

For a visit to rugged-river country, leave Luke on Savage River Rd., which climbs north along the original B&O route up a steep river valley. **Bloomington** was originally a company town, named for the Langollen Coal Company. Railroad workers struggling to lay track up Backbone Mountain called it a "blooming town"—perhaps for its many early spring flowers, perhaps for other reasons. Such slopes, draining into both sides of the Potomac River Valley, are rich in coal seams. Although most of the mining now done involves strip mining, much larger reserves lie below the surface. Water drainage from the unused underground mines remains a problem. Runoff pollutes almost one-third of the surface water of Garrett County.

The **Savage River Reservoir,** five miles up the Savage River Rd. from Bloomington, provides unspoiled mountain water for boating, fishing, and swimming at **Big Run State Park,** which the assembly authorized in 1964. White-water canoe racing has become popular on the wild river, and enthusiasts from around the world consider the Savage

River course highly challenging. Olympic tryouts are held here and draw large crowds.

A rural home in Garrett County during the Depression

Francis Thomas, governor of Maryland between 1842 and 1845, had a farm near the remains of the old town of **Bond,** south of the Savage River Reservoir. He raised alpacas there after his return from an ambassadorship to Peru in 1875. Following his gubernatorial term and a divorce scandal that ended his bid for the presidency, Thomas lived almost as a recluse. He remained a Garrett County resident, intermittently active in state and national politics, until the Civil War, when he resumed his public career. He died in 1876 after being struck by a train while walking along the tracks near his home on the Seventeen-Mile Grade.

Seventeen-Mile Grade and the Eastern Continental Divide

From Westernport, Md. 135 parallels the railroad route up Backbone Mountain, a ridge that becomes Big Savage Mountain when it reaches I-68 to the north. The road narrows to cross the Savage River at the base of the mountain and then ascends steeply. Railroaders called this climb the **Seventeen-Mile Grade,** a steep slope rising 116 feet every mile. Although many of the coal and lumber spur tracks from mountain ravines had even steeper sections, this grade is close to the limit for long and heavy mainline trains. Brakemen on the descent rode outside the cars even on the coldest winter days to control the dangerous momentum built up on the long grade. Cars and trucks must also respect this grade, whether climbing it or going down.

Md. 135 crosses the B&O Railroad tracks at the top of the grade, near **Altamont,** the highest point on the railway (2,628') in Maryland. This point also marks the Eastern Continental Divide, a geographer's line along mountain summits from which streams flow either west to the Mississippi River or east to the Chesapeake Bay. From here, the road rambles across a wooded, relatively flat plateau toward Oakland.

Deer Park

Md. 135 passes through the village of **Deer Park,** home of nationally famous resort hotels during the Victorian era. Deer Park Hotel Rd. leads to the **site of Deer Park Hotel,** which the B&O built in 1873. Heavily promoted by the railroad, the hotel became a favorite resort for wealthy and prominent citizens of Baltimore and Washington. Presidents Grant, Harrison, and Cleveland were among its guests; William McKinley visited the establishment before he became president. The **Deer Park Spring,** which still produces pure mountain water that is sold commercially, supplied the hotel, its swimming pool, and Turkish baths. Deer Park's popularity declined after 1900, and the resort finally closed after the onset of the Depression in 1929. The grand hotel itself was razed in 1944, although a few of the opulent cottages remain as reminders of the park's faded majesty.

A lawn marker in front of the **Grover Cleveland Cottage** (private) describes polite details of the honeymoon that President Cleveland and his wife spent at Deer Park after their White House wedding in 1886. The gray-shingled frame building is two and one-half stories tall and contains room sufficient for a considerable entourage.

At Deer Park, Boiling Spring Rd. turns off Md. 135 and intersects the dirt-surfaced Eagle Rock Rd., which branches left to **Eagle Rock.** Carriages once drove from Deer Park Hotel to the wooden observation tower, now in ruins, that stood on top of this enormous outcropping. The view offers vistas of the surrounding valleys as well as the Potomac State Forest on Backbone Mountain.

John Garrett's B&O created Deer Park as a mountain sanctuary for the well-to-do, but Garrett's grandsons Robert and John share credit for helping to establish the Maryland system of public parks. In 1906 they gave the state about 2,000 acres of virgin timberland between the Youghiogheny and the West Virginia border, on the condition that Maryland adopt a scientific approach to forest management. State senator William McCulloch Brown, of Garrett County, drafted legislation that led to acceptance of the Garretts' offer. Brown had trained as an engineer at Yale and knew Gifford Pinchot, also of Yale and an early champion of wilderness preservation. Maryland established a board of forestry. Today Garrett State Forest remains a haven for wildlife and ordinary citizens.

Mountain Lake Park

Ahead on Md. 135 the village of Mountain Lake Park (1,938 pop.) is all that remains of the hotels, auditorium, and tabernacle that made this annual summer "Mountain Chautauqua" popular at the turn of the century. Founded in 1881, Mountain Lake Park drew visitors for its summer religious revivals and cultural activities alike. Professors from universities in Baltimore, New York, Philadelphia, and Boston provided college-level instruction in languages, literature, and the sciences. William Jennings Bryan, Samuel Gompers, and President William Howard Taft all at one time or another gave addresses in the amphitheater, which seated 3,500 people. The recreational schedule featured magicians, jugglers, bell ringers, and decorous sports. In its publicity brochures, Mountain Lake proudly distinguished itself from the "social frivolities" and "meaningless idling" at nearby Deer Park. Although no longer boasting the same attractions, the crossroads town has grown into the largest municipality in Garrett County.

After intersecting U.S. 219, the state highway ends in Oakland.

H. FROM CUMBERLAND TO WESTERNPORT, VIA MD. 36

West from Cumberland, follow Md. 36 north and west through an area that experienced sudden industrialization in the 19th century. The road passes through rough-and-tumble Kriegbaum, Corriganville, and Barrellville before reaching a historic district devoted to an early "iron city."

Mount Savage

Mount Savage (1,206' alt.) became an industrial center after English investors financed blast furnaces and a rolling mill here in 1839–40. Within a few years, the complex was producing around 200 tons of iron a week; the furnaces burned 150 tons of coal a day. In 1844, the rolling mill produced the first solid iron rails made in the United States, and they were used on the new railroad link to Cumberland.

The iron works failed in the late 1840s, but a firebrick plant that was established during the town's boom period prospered for decades longer. During the 1880s, James Roosevelt (President Franklin D. Roosevelt's father) headed the company that owned the firebrick factory (most of the

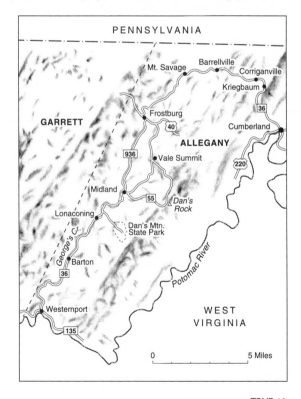

enterprises in Maryland's coal basin were controlled by New York investors). The railroad machine shops constructed here also prospered, and skilled workers from Mount Savage achieved a national reputation.

Some of the Mount Savage street names—Old Row, New Row, Brickyard Row, Foundry Row, Low Row, Jealous Row—reflect its past as a company town. Although most units were rented, some of the company-built houses on these streets were sold outright to workers, unlike the true company towns of Pennsylvania and West Virginia. As landlord, the companies could and did use the threat of eviction to keep workers subservient during labor controversies. On the other hand, rents in company housing were generally lower than those charged by private landlords. In a typical early industrial combination of the profit motive and paternalism, residents in company housing tended to be the last laid off and the first rehired. The more enlightened employers reduced rents during hard times, a practice which made pay cuts somewhat more tolerable.

Company owners and bosses built estates and large houses in the English style favored by many wealthy Americans. During the 1890s young FDR spent part of his summers at the **Bruce House,** owned by his uncle Warren Delano, an officer of the Union Mining Company.

This little town, which has never had a population higher than 5,000, can claim an unusual number of famous visitors and residents, particularly Irish Catholics, whose presence earned Mount Savage the nickname, "Limerick of Allegany." Father Stephen Theodore Badin, the first Roman Catholic priest ordained in the United States, who later donated the land for the University of Notre Dame, celebrated mass here in 1793. William Cullen Bryant visited in 1860 and described the town and adjacent coal mines to New York readers in the *Evening Post.* Edward Cardinal Mooney, the first American Apostolic Delegate to India and later Japan, was born here in 1882. John Charles Thomas, an operatic baritone who achieved national prominence in the 1920s and '30s, was once a choir boy in the **Mount Savage Methodist Church.**

Follow Md. 36 uphill through Frostburg and continue south into the George's Creek Valley, choosing either Md. 936 or Md. 36 (the roads merge in Midland as Md. 36). You will trace a route that J. Thomas Scharf, a 19th-century Maryland historian, described as "one continuous street and town, 24 miles in length, inhabited by miners and their families." Here immigrant miners from Ireland, Germany, Wales, and Scotland created a culture distinctive from their counterparts in Pennsylvania, Ohio, West Virginia, and Kentucky.

The Maryland Coal Rush

Until the second quarter of the 19th century, the George's Creek Valley remained a lush, near-primeval woodland high in the Western Maryland mountains. A narrow forest path followed the creek on its descent from Frostburg to Westernport, where George's Creek met the North Branch of the Potomac River. The region had provided hunting and fishing for sustenance, but only outcroppings along the mountainsides and a few small, 18th-century mines hinted at the valley's other vast resources. Then the rise of steam in America, the cheap labor in the form of new immigrants, and improved access to the valley swiftly transformed it from a hunter's haven to the site of bustling communities dominated by extractive industry.

In 1833 John Alexander, an Annapolis merchant, and Philip T. Tyson bought 3,817 acres in the creek basin, and soon thereafter they petitioned the General Assemby to charter the George's Creek Coal and Iron Company. Investors, mostly from Baltimore and London, bought 3,000 shares at $100 each. Alexander, Tyson, and other entrepreneurs knew that steam engines were changing the face of western Europe and soon also would make their mark in the United States. Steam power called for coal, and the George's Creek fields contained some of the richest bituminous fields in the country.

The B&O Railroad reached Cumberland in 1842, as did the C&O Canal in 1853. Both linked Maryland's mountain coal to international markets. By 1850 almost 30 coal companies were mining the valley. The "Big Vein," a 14-foot-thick seam of coal that gained fame for being clean-burning, produced over 60 million tons between 1854 and 1891. George's Creek coal powered ocean steamers, river boats, locomotives, steam mills, and machine shops; after tests in 1844 confirmed its even-burning qualities, it became the U.S. Navy's preferred fuel. By 1900, thanks to interlocking directorates and complicated stock connections, the Consolidation Coal Company, established in 1864 and headquartered in Cumberland, had become the largest bituminous coal company in the eastern United States. Cumberland had financial connections that reached beyond Washington and Baltimore to New York and London; mine owners and their lawyers announced their importance by building large houses on Cumberland's highest ground. A few miles to the west, miners clustered in company towns that lined the valley and spread into adjoining ravines.

A prototypical miners' town was Lonaconing, constructed about 1835 where Koontz Creek and Jackson Run joined George's Creek (a spot reportedly once occupied by the Indian chief Lonacona). Workers cut a road along George's Creek, turning the felled trees into lumber for a store, sawmill, church, dwellings, and mine buildings. A Baltimore brickmaker practiced his trade using local clay; limestone was quarried and burned to provide mortar. In two years the "Lonaconing Residency" had grown into a company town of about 700 people. Main St. (the town's only street) passed the company headquarters, stores, and miners' houses. George's Creek Coal and Iron's coke-fired blast furnace opened on May 9, 1839, and may have been the first such furnace in the United States.

The company superintendent and some of his managers had come from Wales. Other workers arrived from England, Scotland, Ireland, and parts of Germany. The mining company provided log housing that ranged from simple cabins without chimneys to double cabins called "shantees" and framed double houses called "blocks." Town rules included the provision that "every person in the Employment of the Company will be required to be present at work on every day of the year excepting Sundays and Christmas Day: And the hours of Employment (excepting in special cases, which the Superintendant allows in his discretion) shall be from Sunrise to Sunset, with such intermission for meals as shall from time to time be appointed." Wages were paid monthly after deductions for accounts at the company store, mills, and post office and after each worker's contribution toward the town doctor and school. Distilled liquor was prohibited within town limits as was "all brawling, quarreling, fighting and gaming"; no dog was permitted on company grounds without special permission of the superintendent.

The miners used a standard set of tools—two picks, two wedges, one shovel, one sledge—to pry loose slabs of coal from tunnels dug deep into the surrounding mountainsides. Most worked in pairs, in a tiny, dark room lit only by the oil lamps on their heads, judging the quality and stability of the coal by the sound of their picks. Huge lumps were carefully chiseled and sheared from the seam, then broken into smaller lumps, placed in small cars and hand pushed to a "heading" (main tunnel, 9 or 10 feet wide), where they were hauled by horses or mules to the main entrance. The mine cars were sent down the slopes and their contents emptied into waiting railroad coal cars for shipment to Cumberland and Baltimore. Mining was dark and dirty work; like factory and other heavy labor in this period before safety regulations it was dangerous. Masses of coal could collapse without warning, ventilation sometimes failed, and the cool mines (60 degrees summer and winter) occasionally filled with water. "Shut out from air and daylight, engaged in arduous toil, exposed to damp and danger," reported a Maryland inspector in 1885, "the miner who lives to 45 or 50 years of age is decrepit and broken down."

Despite the rigors of the work, George's Creek attracted skilled miners (about 5,500 in the early 20th century) who hoped eventually to own land and a house. The Maryland mines, with their easy access and horizontal cuts, established safety records far superior to those of Pennsylvania and West Virginia, which employed deep vertical shafts. No major disasters occurred in the Maryland coal fields, and labor disputes seldom reached the intensity of those in surrounding states. While general strikes in 1882, 1886, 1894, and 1900 called attention to the workers' pleas for better pay and working conditions, the mining towns along the valley nonetheless developed a stability and cohesiveness that led some observers to label the workers along George's Creek "gentlemen miners." Maryland miners did not universally participate in the United Mine Workers union until after World War I.

Peak Maryland coal production occurred in 1907 and thereafter hovered at about 4 million tons annually until 1920. Afterward, competition from oil and anthracite coal, rising labor and production costs, and financial fluctuations all contributed to the decline of the Western Maryland coal industry. Underground coal reserves remain in George's Creek, but Consolidation Coal disposed of its Maryland assets in 1944; the original George's Creek Coal and Iron Company went out of business in 1952. Although it was the third state to produce coal and one of the nation's primary producers from 1850 to 1910, Maryland no longer plays a significant role in the industry (coal moving through the port of Baltimore these days comes from Pennsylvania and West Virginia). The villages remain—still neat, industrious, and conservative—but the miners have turned to other occupations.

The easily accessible coal from the Big Vein fueled the steam engines and private fortunes of the Victorian era. In our own age, thoughts naturally turn to the environmental costs of that success story—the coal industry permanently altered the George's Creek landscape and polluted its waters—and to the matter of historic preservation.

While we may never recover the original beauty of the valley, its residents have preserved its social heritage. Today the George's Creek Coal and Iron Company's brick office building, constructed in 1840, remains in Lonaconing, as does the Klots silk-throwing mill, a long, two-story brick building constructed in 1906 for the miners' wives, who worked there. Workers' houses in Mount Savage, Frostburg, and Lonaconing are listed on the National Register of Historic Places. In Cumberland, Washington St. still exhibits the prosperity and influence of 19th-century mine owners, bankers, and railroad executives.

These four historic districts, all within 15 miles of each other, testify to the quality of Maryland life during that vibrant period when coal-powered steam engines helped to turn the United States into a world power.

Md. 936 stays on the valley floor, close to George's Creek, and passes by the site of **Ocean,** which in 1907 was a community of more than 1,200 residents. The name derived from the nearby Ocean mine and from the nautical demand for George's Creek coal. Md. 36 takes a jaunt into the uplands.

To view the valley from above, follow Md. 36 to Md. 55 and take Dan's Rock Rd. to Vale Summit, formerly known as Pompey's Smash. This little village, once a stop on the George's Creek and Cumberland Railroad, was built by miners in 1851. The road ascends to Dan's Rock (2,895' alt.), a peak with vistas of the George's Creek Valley to the west with Big Savage Mountain in the background. To the east lies the agricultural plain along the Potomac with West Virginia ridges visible beyond the river. From here the traveler can descend to the valley on Old Dan's Rock Rd., which rejoins Md. 36 at Midland.

Md. 36 south of the intersection with Md. 55 takes one past strip-mining residue and then to **Midland** (1,715′ alt., 574 pop.), named for the Midland Coal and Iron Company. The company built many of the houses here in 1856 and sold them for about $400 each.

Lonaconing

Farther along Md. 36, one reaches the old company town of Lonaconing (1,560′ alt., 1,122 pop.) (see "The Maryland Coal Rush," above). During the economic expansion following the Civil War, Lonaconing's population increased from about 880 in 1865 to more than 3,000 in 1870, when it was reported that "houses [were] being built on the steep hills and far back into the ravines." The population reached 5,000 in 1881 but leveled off during the depression of 1877. Lonaconing miners were among the first in the United States to establish cooperative stores. Mining sustained the community until about 1950.

An attractive town park, opened in 1980, has been created around the ruins of an early blast furnace, which once stood behind the local high school. The park also commemorates Philadelphia Athletics pitcher and Lonaconing native Lefty Grove, most valuable player in the American League in 1931, and Arthur F. Smith, long-time principal of the high school.

From the northern end of Lonaconing, one may follow Water Station Rd. east to **Dan's Mountain State Park,** a small picnicking area. From the southern end of the town, Jackson Mountain Rd. ascends to **Dan's Mountain Wildlife Management Area.**

Barton

Md. 36 continues its descent down the valley to Barton (1,320′ alt., 530 pop.), laid out in 1853 along the railroad that connected Lonaconing with the main line of the B&O Railroad at Westernport. Barton grew quickly, as mines were dug into the Big Vein several hundred feet above the village. Mined coal went down the steep slopes in cars operating on the inclined plane principle. At the bottom, it was loaded on railroad cars. Below Barton, Md. 36 follows George's Creek to the Potomac River. The slopes of the narrow valley show evidence of strip mining above the road; George's Creek, no longer diverted to power mill wheels, runs red with oxidized pyrites from the exposed ridges.

The highway ends at Md. 135 just west of Westernport. From here the traveler may go west on Md. 135 to Oakland or east on Md. 135 and northeast on U.S. 220 (McMullen Hwy.) along the Potomac Valley back to Cumberland.

I. FROM GRANTSVILLE TO THE FAIRFAX BOUNDARY STONE VIA U.S. 219

U.S. 219 follows the Casselman River valley in Pennsylvania, enters Maryland just east of Grantsville, then joins I-68 and U.S. 40 west to **Keysers Ridge,** where it turns south and crosses the rolling ridges, glades, valleys, and marshlands of the central plateau. Large herds of buffalo once grazed on these grasslands, where now in summer domestic cattle pasture contentedly. In warm weather months, the days are pleasant and the nights refreshingly cool. For more than a century, this sec-

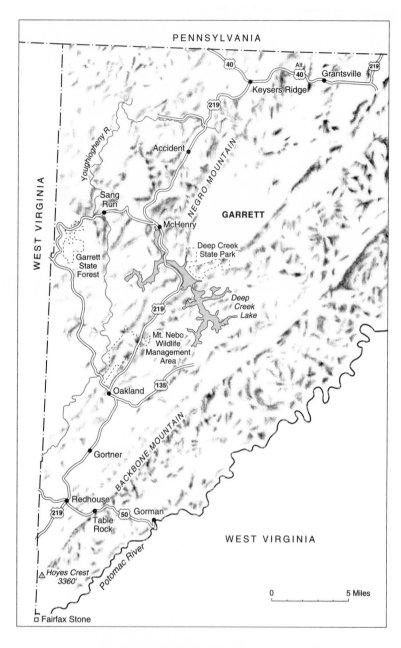

tion of Garrett County has been known for its camping, boating, and swimming. In the fall, the mountainsides glow with multicolored leaves; and in the winter, heavy snows and subzero temperatures drive off all but the natives and winter sports enthusiasts. In the past 20 years, skiing has become popular around Deep Creek Lake.

Many of the original land tracts here date to the revolutionary period. The proprietary government opened this region for settlement in 1774, but after opting for independence, Maryland employed grants as an inducement to military service. In a 1778 survey, the state created 4,165 50-

acre lots to be awarded to military veterans. The extent of state park and forest lands today owes in part to the fact that veterans failed to claim the hilliest, most heavily timbered tracts, those it would have been impossible or too difficult to farm.

Civilian Conservation Corps workers building a park road in Garrett County

Accident

This high-altitude village (2,400' alt., 349 pop.) acquired its name when two separate surveying parties accidentally claimed the same land in the rush of 1774. The conflict was resolved amiably. The site of Accident is reported to have been a summer camping site of Indians. Pennsylvania Germans later settled here, clustering around a Lutheran church. From 1875 to 1915, somewhat to the consternation of the conservative congregations in the area, Accident also was the home of Melky Miller's Maryland Rye Whiskey. The distillery eventually succumbed to fire and neglect. Now wood products and peat moss supplement the incomes of local farmers. **Northern Garrett High School,** at 86 Pride Pkwy., dates from 1952, when the county consolidated Friendsville High (1907), Grantsville High (1908), and Accident High (1915). Since the mid-1990s, Northern has been in the forefront of the movement to incorporate the Internet into education. In 1997 Northern was one of ten high schools in the nation to use "virtual reality" exploration as a teaching tool.

U.S. 219 passes by McHenry, a small village named for James McHenry, aide to General Washington during the Revolution and secretary of war from 1796 to 1800. The **Wisp Resort** here pioneered downhill skiing in Maryland more than 20 years ago.

Alternate Route: Oakland via Sang Run Rd. and Garrett State Forest

Sang Run Rd. angles west from U.S. 219 about three miles south of Accident, passes a ski area at **Marsh Mountain** (3,080' alt.), and meanders along a creek through a heavily wooded area rich with mountain lore. Members of John Friend's family stumbled upon this clear creek while following a high stand of timber. They also discovered a herd of buffalo and a mountainside of the medicinal "seng" or "sang," a local term for *Panax quinquefolium*, the North American cousin of Chinese ginseng. The discovery attracted many diggers of this human-shaped root to the creek valley and gave the run its name. Before roads and logging activities intruded on this wild area, farmers and hunters supplemented their incomes by selling the sang for markets in Shanghai and Hong Kong, where the plant had been valued for its medicinal qualities for thousands of years.

Meshach Browning (1781–1859), the best-known early-Maryland hunter and mountain man, lived on Sang Run. He estimated his total kill at "1,800 to 2,000 deer, 300 to 400 bears, about 50 panthers and catamounts, with scores of wolves and wildcats." Famed throughout the region for his exploits and encouraged by his friends to write his memoirs, he produced *Forty-four Years of the Life of a Hunter; Being Reminiscences of a Maryland Hunter, Roughly Written Down by Himself* (1859). In the early 1800s a system of bounties on wolves, foxes, hawks, wildcats, and owls attracted and supported such hunters; but Browning expressed regret at the gradual extinction of wildlife, particularly when they were being shot for sport. By the time the railroad reached Garrett County, in 1851, small farms and towns had largely replaced the wilderness, and such animals had largely disappeared. State forests would later be created to control wasteful hunting, logging, and agriculture.

The bears and cats have begun to return to these new wilderness areas. The ginseng remains in hidden spots along the mountainsides, both here and in other wooded areas of Maryland. Children and old people still sneak out to hidden, shaded spots to dig the "sang," which allegedly promotes long life and is an aphrodisiac.

Cranesville Swamp

Sang Run Rd. divides at the village of **Sang Run** on the Youghiogheny River. The Oakland–Sang Run Rd. proceeds south along the river to Oakland. For a view of the **Cranesville Sub-Arctic Swamp,** cross the river to the Sang Run–Cranesville Rd. and follow it west for nearly four miles to a junction with White Rock–Cranesville Rd. (from the north) and there turn south, still on Cranesville Rd. Follow it to the Maryland–West Virginia border and the National Natural History Landmark at the head of Muddy Creek, visible from the road on the right. Beneath an insulating layer of soaked sphagnum moss, the water of the swamp stays very cold, acting as a refrigerant and creating a habitat for plants and animals seldom seen this far south. A number of the plants, including the tamarack family of trees, are relics of an earlier era before climate changes pushed their range toward the Arctic Circle. Birdwatchers are likely to see rare varieties of thrushes, warblers, and finches here.

Swallow Falls and Herrington Manor State Parks

Cranesville Rd. continues south into **Garrett State Forest,** where it forks. The road to the east enters **Swallow Falls State Park,** where hiking trails lead to **Muddy Creek Falls,** a 51-foot watery cascade over rock ledges. Henry Ford, Thomas Edison, and Harvey Firestone camped here in 1918 and 1921. They were not young men (Edison was in his 70s, the other two in their 50s), but they did enjoy camping. A photograph at the Ford Museum in Dearborn, Michigan, shows the founder of the auto company happily washing his laundry in the creek. No one knows exactly what these self-taught businessmen, soothed by the sound of running water, discussed in the Maryland woods. One topic may have been rubber. Firestone supplied the pneumatic tires for Ford's cars and later looked to other continents to break the monopoly of Southeast Asia on the substance. Edison would spend his later years attempting to develop latex from native plants. The Civilian Conservation Corps developed this recreational site in the 1930s; Maryland designated it a state park in 1964.

Downstream from the falls—which still attract dreamers—Muddy Creek empties into the Youghiogheny River. The swallows that nest in the rock crevices here give the park its name. Below **Swallow Falls** a trail leads from the river bank to a virgin stand of pines and hemlocks, largest in Maryland.

The southern fork of Cranesville Rd. continues through the Garrett State Forest as Herrington Manor Rd., passing the entrance to **Herrington Manor State Park,** which takes its name from a land grant a

Swallow Falls State Park, Garrett County

Revolutionary War veteran, Alijah Herrington, claimed after 1783. A Baltimore land investor later constructed the manor house. Here visitors may swim, boat, and fish in Herrington Lake, or picnic on the shore. One of the many trails in the park follows the Indians' Great Warrior Path. The state acquired 656 acres at this site in 1917, and later the Civilian Conservation Corps built roads, trails, cabins, and the lake, and also repaired the original house. Herrington Manor Rd. leads to the northwestern side of Oakland.

Deep Creek Lake

Beyond McHenry, U.S. 219 crosses Deep Creek Lake, the largest body of freshwater in Maryland (3,900 acres). The road passes a scenic overlook on the right before reaching the main part of the lake. Dammed in 1923–25, Deep Creek had been well known as a trout stream. Now its lake has a fine reputation among fishermen, who look for bass and bluegill in the summer and northern pike in the winter. **Deep Creek Lake State Park,** located across the lake to the east, offers a wide range of outdoor activities, including foot and snowmobile trails. One trail up the southern slope of Meadow Mountain offers a panoramic view from a summit almost 600 feet above lake level. Deep Creek offers the most spectacular of many examples of the benefits that have followed Maryland's adoption in 1969 of the Outdoor Recreation Land Loan, or Program Open Space. The law provides for a .5 percent transfer tax on all real estate transactions, the funds going toward the acquiring, maintaining, and developing of outdoor recreational sites across the state. The farsighted program aims to protect natural habitats from the march of urbanization and suburbanization. Besides Deep Creek, the plan has enabled state forestry and parks officials to implement master plans for Point Lookout, Cunningham Falls, Greenbrier, and Elk Neck state parks.

U.S. 219 leaves the lake at the village of **Thayerville** and angles southwest to Oakland, passing the **Mount Nebo Wildlife Management Area.**

Oakland

At the southern foot of Hoop Pole Ridge, a small community known as Yough Glades long ago grew up where Glades Path, a packhorse trail from Virginia, crossed the nearby Little Youghiogheny River. In 1849, when the B&O finally decided on its path through the state's western mountains, entrepreneurs at this site laid out the town of Oakland (2,650' alt., 1,741 pop.). Then, in 1872, Garrett Countians selected Oakland to be the county seat (Grantsville and McHenry's Glades lost out by only a few votes), and for many years Oakland was Garrett's largest population center.

Once the B&O Railroad established double track to Oakland in 1873, the town turned its attention to tourism. In 1881, "to make the town more charming as a summer resort," the council passed an ordinance making it unlawful for cows to have bells on from 8 p.m. to 7 a.m. The B&O invested in resort hotels and advertised its holdings in Garrett County as "The Switzerland of America." Summer visitors from Washington and elsewhere made Oakland a fashionable retreat. Gen. George Crook, celebrated for his success against the Apaches in Arizona, built a rambling frame house in Oakland just before he died in 1890. His funeral, held in Oakland, attracted old friends and army acquaintances from around the country. Among them was Buffalo Bill Cody, whose fame permitted him to cash a $100 check in an Oakland store. Gen. Lew Wallace, earlier the Union commander at the Battle of Monocacy, stayed at a local hotel one summer while writing *Ben Hur.*

Despite the decline of the railroad and the disappearance of the grand hotels, tourism has remained important to Oakland and environs. The **Garrett County Historical Museum** at Center and Second Sts. has a collection of early equipment and tools, household furnishings, Indian artifacts, and other historical objects. The **B&O Railroad Station** on Liberty St., a distinctive, two-story brick building in the Queen Anne style, was built in 1884 and remains a regional landmark. **Southern Garrett County High School,** like Northern established in 1952, produced the state cross-country champions in 1996; its band has marched in the Macy's Thanksgiving Day Parade (1975) and taken part in festivities surrounding the Indianapolis 500 auto race (1973), the Preakness Stakes (1974), and the Kentucky Derby (1977). Distinguished graduates include stage artist Rita Shrout Mosley, professional singer Kathryn Sincell, and artist Laura Stutzman.

South of Oakland, U.S. 219 crosses what used to be **McCulloch's Path,** itself part of the Great Warrior Path, by which early traders and pioneers traveled between Virginia and the Ohio River. George Washington, exploring the possibilities of a water route from the Potomac over the Alleghenies in 1784, wrote in his diary that McCulloch's Path owed "its origin to buffaloes, being none other than their tracks from one lick to another."

The countryside to the east of **Gortner,** known as **Pleasant Valley,** harbors a considerable Amish community. It also is the site of a large farm that Gen. Benjamin F. Kelley bought from the Pendleton family in 1864. The Pendletons were Union sympathizers from Virginia who had temporarily moved to Maryland; General Kelley, a cavalry officer from New Hampshire, commanded the Union troops assigned to protect the strategic and extremely vulnerable railroad tracks through Maryland west of Harpers Ferry. After purchasing the farm, Kelley was able to ship ill and injured army horses there, where the chance of their recovery was considered good if they survived the railroad trip to Oakland and the walk to the farm from the depot. He lived on the farm after the war and died there in 1891. His military saddle, found in a box of unclaimed freight at the Oakland railroad station in 1910, is now on display at the Garrett County Historical Museum in Oakland.

At **Redhouse,** U.S. 219 intersects U.S. 50, known here as the Northwestern Turnpike (or George Washington Hwy.). **The Red House Tavern** was built here when the turnpike came through about 1840. The turnpike, intended as Virginia's route to the west, stretched across northwestern Virginia for its entire length except for a nine-mile stretch at the tip of Maryland. Like the National Road, which it was built to rival, Virginia's pike lost much of its traffic when the railroad crossed the mountains in the early 1850s.

Table Rock and Gorman

To the east of Redhouse, U.S. 50 ascends Backbone Mountain. To visit Table Rock, an outcropping that was a favorite picnic spot at the turn of the century, turn right at the crest, at Table Rock Rd. A footpath on the left not far from the intersection leads to the site. U.S. 50 follows the route of the Northwestern Turnpike to Gorman, where the old road crossed the Potomac on a covered bridge. During the Civil War, **Fort Pendleton** was built on the Maryland hillside overlooking the bridge, to protect the crossing. Rarely garrisoned, the wooden fort burned in 1888, but the marks of its trenches—best seen from the West Virginia hillside across the river—can be discerned in the pasture (private) where it stood.

U.S. 219 continues south of Redhouse, crosses into West Virginia, and takes one to the Monongahela National Forest. About two miles beyond **Silver Lake,** a footpath from U.S. 219 leads up Backbone Mountain to **Hoyes Crest,** the highest point in Maryland (3,360').

A gravel road turns left from U.S. 219 to the **Fairfax Stone,** which marks Maryland's western boundary. The current stone, a replica of the original, is located by a spring in a small park at the end of the gravel road, surrounded by abandoned coal mines and gas wells.

Fixing Maryland's Western Boundary

Lord Baltimore's original royal charter, written in 1632 in Latin, identified "the first fountain of the River Pattowmack" as the western boundary of his land and "that part of the Bay of Delaware on the North which lieth under the fortieth degree of north latitude" as the northern boundary. Unfortunately, the boundaries conflicted with those in the charters of Virginia and, later, Pennsylvania. The resulting border disputes were not fully resolved until the 20th century.

Maryland's boundaries result from official surveys, compromises—and defeats. The northern border, which Mason and Dixon surveyed during 1763–67, is probably the most famous boundary in the United States (see Tour 10 for a discussion of the Chesapeake-border struggle). Maryland's border with Virginia (and after 1863 West Virginia) followed the curves of the Potomac, but in the 17th century no one knew where the river began—where its "first fountain" was. In the 18th century, Lord Fairfax acquired land in Virginia running as far west as the headsprings of the Potomac. He petitioned the crown in 1733 to create a commission to determine just where those headsprings were. The commissioners investigated, realized that two forks, north and south, converged on their way to the Chesapeake, and determined the North Branch to carry more water and therefore be the chief stream. In 1746 they placed the Fairfax Stone to mark the headspring of the Potomac. But was this location the "first fountain" of the Potomac River? In 1754 a survey determined that the South Branch had the westernmost origin. Virginia defended its boundaries and prevailed. We now also know that the South Branch splits again into two forks near Petersburg, West Virginia, and that the headwaters of both rise deep in the Monongahela National Forest. If the South Branch had been determined to be the Potomac's origin, Western Maryland would include a chunk of what is now West Virginia. Moreover, the North Branch rises more than a mile to the west of the Fairfax Stone—a discovery made during a late-19th-century survey as Maryland and Virginia took their most recent boundary dispute to the U.S. Supreme Court. In 1897 Maryland erected the Potomac Stone to mark the North Branch's "first fountain." Maryland lost the Supreme Court case, just as it had lost disputes over boundaries on the north, south, and east. The western boundary now runs due north to the Mason-Dixon Line on a line with the Fairfax Stone, beginning at a point about a mile north of the stone, which sits on the south bank of the Potomac on West Virginia soil.

Further Reading and Research

Since 1976, when the first edition of *Maryland, A New Guide to the Old Line State* appeared, the information available to students of Maryland history and culture has grown considerably. The following short list offers portals—published volumes, reference collections, and electronic sources—through which one may pass to find additional materials of interest.

Books

Anderson, Elizabeth B. *Annapolis, A Walk through History.* Centreville, Md.: Tidewater Publishers, 1991.

Brugger, Robert J. *Maryland, A Middle Temperament, 1634-1980.* Baltimore: Johns Hopkins University Press, 1988.

Dorsey, John, and James D. Dilts. *A Guide to Baltimore Architecture.* 3rd ed. Centreville, Md.: Tidewater Publishers, 1997.

Kenny, Hamill. *The Placenames of Maryland, Their Origin and Meaning.* Baltimore: Maryland Historical Society, 1984.

Olson, Sherry H. *Baltimore: The Building of an American City.* Baltimore: Johns Hopkins University Press, 1997.

Shivers, Frank R. *Walking in Baltimore, An Intimate Guide to the Old City.* Baltimore: Johns Hopkins University Press, 1995.

Libraries

Maryland Department, Enoch Pratt Free Library (http://www.pratt. lib.md.us/slrc/md), 400 Cathedral St., Baltimore, Md. 21201. Responsible for a collection of materials relating to the history, economics, social conditions, literature, arts, and all aspects of the development and status of Maryland and its citizens. In its role as part of the State Library Resource Center, the department builds resources to provide statewide access to a comprehensive collection that fill the needs of library users across the state. The department serves patrons at all age levels and depths of need.

Maryland Historical Society (http://www.mdhs.org), 201 West Monument St., Baltimore, Md. 21201. See description of holdings at the Society's entry in this volume. Reference library hours are Tuesday through Saturday, 10 a.m. to 4:30 p.m.; the manuscripts, prints, and photographs departments are open Tuesday through Friday, 10:00 a.m. to 4:30 p.m. and the third Saturday of each month. The staffs of these departments accept telephone queries Tuesday through Friday, 10:00 a.m. to 4:00 p.m. Telephone research queries for the reference library are accepted Tuesday through Friday, 10:00 a.m. to 11:30 a.m.

Maryland Historical Trust (http://www.ari.net/mdshpo), 100 Community Place, Crownsville, Md. 21032. Principal repository for information about Maryland's architectural, archaeological, and cultural resources. The archival collection includes survey documentation for archaeological sites and historic properties listed in the Maryland Inventory of Historic Properties and the National Register of Historic Places. Documentation files are maintained for more than 8,000 prehistoric and historic archaeological sites and for approximately 80,000 historic structures and sites. Open to the public on Tuesdays, Wednesdays, and Thursdays by appointment only.

Maryland Room, University of Maryland Libraries (http://www.lib.umd.edu/UMCP/PUB/collections.html), Theodore R. McKeldin Library, University of Maryland, College Park, Md. 20742. Service point for three special collections departments of the University of Maryland Libraries. The room is open to researchers from the general public as well as those from the University of Maryland community. Collections available in the Maryland Room are Marylandia and rare books (printed material relating to all aspects of Maryland, including maps, photographs, books, pamphlets, newspapers, and ephemera); archives and manuscripts (manuscripts relating to diverse subjects, including Maryland political leaders and organizations and the history of the university); and the National Trust Library (books and manuscripts concerning the preservation of historic structures in the United States).

Maryland State Archives (http://www.mdarchives.state.md.us), 350 Rowe Blvd., Annapolis, Md. 21401. Central depository for government records of permanent value dating from 1634, including colonial and state records, business and church records, state publications and reports, special collections of private papers, maps, photographs, and newspapers. Requests for information may be telephoned between 8:00 a.m. and 5:00 p.m., Monday through Friday. Orders for specific items may be placed via a 24-hour fax service (410-974-2525). For further information call 410-260-6400 or 800-235-4045 (toll free in Maryland). The archives' search room is open Tuesday through Friday, 8:00 a.m. to 4:30 p.m., and Saturday, 8:30 a.m. to noon and 1:00 p.m. to 4:30 p.m. On weekdays the search room remains open at lunchtime, but no records are retrieved from the stacks. Closed on Mondays and state holidays.

Other Websites

Maryland Electronic Capital (http://www.mec.state.md.us). The homepage for the state of Maryland. It is the place on the Internet for Maryland state, county, city, and community information, an official source of Maryland government information, linking to all government agencies through their websites. The other official source of Maryland government information is the *Maryland Manual On-Line,* accessible from the Maryland State Archives' homepage (see above). The *Maryland Manual On-Line* furnishes information on the organization, budget, functions, historical evolution, origins, and reports of each government agency.

Sailor (http://www.sailor.lib.md.us). Maryland's Online Public Information Network. From this site, in addition to the libraries listed above, the searcher can reach virtually all sites related to Maryland.

H-Maryland (http://www.h-net.msu.edu/lists). A refereed, interdisciplinary discussion and information site. H-Maryland provides a means of communication for those persons who research, write, read, teach, and preserve Maryland history and culture. H-Maryland posts reviews of exhibits, books, audio-visual materials, and electronic presentations. It serves as a forum for serious discussion; a bulletin board for news of newly opened collections, upcoming conferences, exhibits, public programs, etc.; and provides storage and retrieval of materials (syllabi, reading lists, helpful hints) useful in classroom teaching at every level.

Photo Sources

All the photographs printed in black are the work of Edwin H. Remsberg and are copyrighted by him.

The photographs printed in brown were provided by the Maryland State Archives (see Preface), with these additional acknowledgments: photographs on pages 5 and 30 courtesy of Historic St. Mary's City and Ruth A. Birch; 27, 66, 67, 409, and 523 by E. H. Pickering; 204 and 279 by Arthur Rothstein; 229 courtesy of Graham Wood; 365 by Cronhardt and Son, courtesy of the Baltimore Museum of Industry; 394 by John Vachon; 397 by Marion Post Wolcott; 463 by Klemm; 493 courtesy of McKeldin Library, University of Maryland, College Park; 570 courtesy of Raymond Hicks; 575 by C. D. Young, courtesy of Doug Bast; and 601 by F. W. Besley.

The photographs owned by the Maryland State Archives come from several special collections: the Maryland Writer's Project Collection, MSA SC 908; the Hayman Collection, MSA SC 1406; the Robert G. Merrick Collection, MSA SC 1477; the E. H. Pickering Collection, MSA SC 1754; and the Baltimore News American Collection, MSA SC 2117. The accession number of each photograph is shown below opposite the number of the page on which the photo appears. (Copies of these photographs may be obtained from the Maryland State Archives for a fee.)

Page	Accession Number	Page	Accession Number
8	MSA SC 908-19-535	68	MSA SC 908-02-16
11	MSA SC 908-19-528	78	MSA SC 908-02-63
20	MSA SC 908-19-526	80	MSA SC 908-02-70
27	MSA SC 1754-78	84	MSA SC 908-02-80
32	MSA SC 908-19-541	85	MSA SC 908-02-783
35	MSA SC 1477-6611	86	MSA SC 908-02-787
37	MSA SC 908-17-483	88	MSA SC 1477-6726
44	MSA SC 908-09-509	98	MSA SC 1477-6724
51	MSA SC 908-02-65	99	MSA SC 908-05-499
54	MSA SC 908-02-779	105	MSA SC 1477-6751
58	MSA SC 908-02-41	109	MSA SC 908-17-459
59	MSA SC 908-02-7	113	MSA SC 908-17-486
60	MSA SC 908-02-67	120	MSA SC 908-25-782
62	MSA SC 908-02-39	126	MSA SC 908-25-673
63	MSA SC 908-02-37	128	MSA SC 908-25-676
66	MSA SC 1406-97	139	MSA SC 908-08-591
67	MSA SC 1406-102	145	MSA SC 908-08-558

Page	Accession Number	Page	Accession Number
150	MSA SC 2117-483	365	MSA SC 1477-6180
155	MSA SC 908-15-234	375	MSA SC 908-03-345
156	MSA SC 908-15-238	383	MSA SC 908-04-147
163	MSA SC 908-21-722	390	MSA SC 1406-218
167	MSA SC 908-06-631	393	MSA SC 1477-6196
175	MSA SC 908-21-645	394	MSA SC 1477-6565
179	MSA SC 908-21-634	397	MSA SC 1477-6577
183	MSA SC 908-20-679	402	MSA SC 1477-6129
198	MSA SC 908-10-408	403	MSA SC 908-17-464
202	MSA SC 908-10-260	409	MSA SC 1406-311
204	MSA SC 1477-6564	410	MSA SC 908-02-89
208	MSA SC 908-23-666	424	MSA SC 908-14-439
210	MSA SC 908-23-669	425	MSA SC 908-14-432
215	MSA SC 908-23-788	443	MSA SC 908-16-295
217	MSA SC 908-25-684	446	MSA SC 908-16-294
222	MSA SC 908-20-625	456	MSA SC 1477-5687
224	MSA SC 908-25-680	463	MSA SC 1477-5692
229	MSA SC 1477-6258	469	MSA SC 908-13-514
230	MSA SC 908-24-651	471	MSA SC 908-13-441
235	MSA SC 908-23-668	472	MSA SC 1477-6752
239	MSA SC 908-24-708	492	MSA SC 1477-6332
262	MSA SC 1477-6276	493	MSA SC 1477-6514
272	MSA SC 908-03-131	499	MSA SC 908-07-450
279	MSA SC 1477-6561	504	MSA SC 908-27-791
286	MSA SC 908-03-333	505	MSA SC 908-21-447
286	MSA SC 908-03-364	511	MSA SC 908-11-421
290	MSA SC 908-03-325	523	MSA SC 1754-55
298	MSA SC 908-03-755	529	MSA SC 908-22-751
313	MSA SC 908-03-339	534	MSA SC 908-22-404
318	MSA SC 908-03-832	542	MSA SC 1477-6575
319	MSA SC 908-03-850	544	MSA SC 908-01-208
330	MSA SC 908-13-835	551	MSA SC 908-01-219
338	MSA SC 908-03-135	570	MSA SC 1477-6059
339	MSA SC 908-03-838	574	MSA SC 908-11-698
343	MSA SC 908-03-833	575	MSA SC 1477-5351
344	MSA SC 1477-6185	581	MSA SC 908-27-800
349	MSA SC 908-03-332	584	MSA SC 1477-6058
350	MSA SC 908-03-330	589	MSA SC 1477-5701
356	MSA SC 908-03-166	593	MSA SC 908-12-707
357	MSA SC 908-03-129	601	MSA SC 1477-6066
361	MSA SC 908-03-861		

Name and Place Index

In addition to individual entries for names and places, the reader will find subentries under the following selected subjects: battles, bridges, cemeteries, city halls and municipal buildings, colleges, courthouses, dams, fairgrounds, forts, high schools (public), historical societies, hospitals and medical centers, libraries, museums, schools (private), state forests, state parks, universities, and wildlife management areas and refuges. The table of contents provides, essentially, a geographical index to the book.

Godefroy, Maximilien, 287, 297, 298, 314
Godiah Spray Tobacco Plantation, 21, 28
Godolphin Arabian (racehorse), 104
God's Well, 492
Golden Quarter, 237
Golder House, 74
Goldsboro, 165
Goldsborough, Gov. Charles, house of, 196
Goldsborough, Dr. G. W., 165
Goldsborough, Gov. Phillips Lee, 196
Goldsborough, Richard Tilghman, 184
Goldsborough, Robert, 174
Goldsborough, Robert, IV, 174
Goldsborough family, 175
Goldstein, Louis L., 90–91
Gompers, Samuel, 594
Goodman, Percival, 369
Gordon, Douglas H., 299
Gordon, Rev. John, 182
Gordon, Josiah H., 555
Gorsuch, Dickerson, 464
Gorsuch, Edward, 464
Gorsuch Farmhouse, site of, 481
Gorsuch, Capt. Joshua, 464
Gortner, 605
Gott, Jackson C., 326
Goucher, Dr. John F., 370–71, 465
Goucher Hall, 370
Gough, Harry Dorsey, 470
Gould, George W., 552
Gould, Jay, 585
Government House (Annapolis), 65
Grace and St. Peter's Episcopal Church
   (Baltimore), 306
Grace Episcopal Church (Dorchester Co.), 200
Graceham, 496
Graceton, 506
Graffenried, Baron Christoph de, 445
Graham, Anne Johnson, 523
Graham House, 90
Graham, John, 523, 532, 536
Graham, Malcolm, 90
Graham Memorial Park, 467
Grant, Daniel, 559
Grant, Felix, 251
Grant, Ulysses S., 81, 114, 430, 594
Grantsville, 559
Grapevine House, 187
Gray, Edward, 386
Grazer, Laura Gardin, 372
Great Falls National Park, 443
Great Falls Tavern, 443

Great Mills, 16
Great Pocomoke Swamp, 235
Greek Orthodox Cathedral of the Annunciation
   (Baltimore), 335
Green Hill Episcopal Church, 207
Green, Jonas, 76–77; house of, 76
Green Spring Furnace, 584
Green Spring Valley Hunt Club, 453
Greenbelt, 397
Greene, Gen. Nathaniel, 494
Greenfields, 142
Greensboro, 166
Greenway Gardens and Arboretum, 497
Greme, Angus, 476
Grieves, James R., 289
Groen, Theo de, 274
Groody, Laird Grant, 459
Gropius, Walter, 369
Gross, Roger, 174
Gross's Coate, 174
Grove, Lefty, 599
Guilford (Baltimore), 376–77
Gunpowder Copper Works, site of, 467
Gutenberg, Johannes, 296
Gwynn, Richard, 358
Gwynns Falls Valley, 358

Hackerman House, 298
Hackett, Charles, 159
Hadzi, Dimitri, 292
Hager, Elizabeth Kershner, 530–31
Hager House, 538
Hager, Jonathan, 530–31, 535, 536, 538
Hagerstown, 530–41
Hagerstown Municipal Airport, 540
Halethorpe, 382
Haleugua, Alfredo, 212
Haley, Alex, 62
Hall, Aquila, 486
Hall, Marcellus, 61
Halsted, Dr. William, 324
Hambleton, 189
Hamerik, Asger, 301
Hamilton, Edith, 340
Hamilton, Gov. William T., 540
Hammann, Ens. Charles H. , 340
Hammond, Matthias, 58, 59, 74
Hammond, Philip, 74
Hammond, Col. Rezin, 423
Hammond-Harwood House, 58
Hampden, 362
Hampstead, 457

Library of Congress Cataloging-in-Publication Data

Arnett, Earl.
  Maryland : a new guide to the Old Line State / Earl Arnett, Robert J. Brugger, Edward C. Papenfuse. —
2nd ed.
    p.   cm.
  Includes bibliographical references and index.
  ISBN 0-8018-5979-4 (alk. paper). — ISBN 0-8018-5980-8 (pbk. : alk. paper)
   I. Maryland—Tours.   I. Brugger, Robert J.   II. Papenfuse, Edward C.   III. Title.
F179.3A66 1999
917.5204'43—dc21   98-46982
                                                                                      CIP